THE STATE, THE LAW, AND THE PEOPLE IN THE ROMAN EMPIRE

The intimidating volumes of the *Digest* and *Codex Justinianus* are underused by students and teachers of Roman history, yet they contain a treasure trove of evidence for the administrative, social, and economic history of Rome. What happened when people encountered the government exercising legal jurisdiction through governors, magistrates, and officials within the legal framework and laws sponsored by the state? How were the urban environment of Rome and Italy, the state's assets, and human relations managed? How did the mechanisms of control in the provinces affect local life and legal processes? How were contracts devised and enforced? How did banks operate? What was the experience of going to court like, and how did you deal with assault or insult or recover loss? How did you rent a farm or an apartment and protect ownership? The emperor loomed over everything, being the last resort in moderating relations between state and subject.

BRIAN CAMPBELL is Professor Emeritus of Ancient History at the Queen's University of Belfast, and was a Visiting Fellow at All Souls College, Oxford (2005). He has published on Roman military history (1984, 1994, 2002), land survey (2000), and *Rivers and the Power of Ancient Rome* (2012), and has contributed extensively to the *Oxford Classical Dictionary* and *Der Neue Pauly*.

THE STATE, THE LAW, AND THE PEOPLE IN THE ROMAN EMPIRE

A Sourcebook

BRIAN CAMPBELL

Professor Emeritus, the Queen's University of Belfast

CAMBRIDGE
UNIVERSITY PRESS

CAMBRIDGE
UNIVERSITY PRESS

Shaftesbury Road, Cambridge CB2 8EA, United Kingdom

One Liberty Plaza, 20th Floor, New York, NY 10006, USA

477 Williamstown Road, Port Melbourne, VIC 3207, Australia

314–321, 3rd Floor, Plot 3, Splendor Forum, Jasola District Centre, New Delhi – 110025, India

103 Penang Road, #05–06/07, Visioncrest Commercial, Singapore 238467

Cambridge University Press is part of Cambridge University Press & Assessment, a department of the University of Cambridge.

We share the University's mission to contribute to society through the pursuit of education, learning and research at the highest international levels of excellence.

www.cambridge.org
Information on this title: www.cambridge.org/9781107163164

DOI: 10.1017/9781316678688

When citing this work, please include a reference to the DOI 10.1017/9781316678688

First published 2025

A catalogue record for this publication is available from the British Library

Library of Congress Cataloging-in-Publication Data
NAMES: Campbell, John, author.
TITLE: The state, the law, and the people in the ancient Rome / John Campbell, Professor Emeritus, the Queen's University of Belfast.
DESCRIPTION: Cambridge, United Kingdom ; New York, NY : Cambridge University Press, 2025. | Includes bibliographical references and index.
IDENTIFIERS: LCCN 2024040191 | ISBN 9781107163164 (hardback)
SUBJECTS: LCSH: Status (Roman law) | Persons (Roman law) | Slavery (Roman law) | Civil rights – Rome. | Citizenship – Rome. | Crime – Rome. | Punishment (Roman law)
CLASSIFICATION: LCC KJA2192.C36 2025 | DDC 340.5/4–dc23/eng/20240830
LC record available at https://lccn.loc.gov/2024040191

ISBN 978-1-107-16316-4 Hardback

For
Ken, Vi, Billy, and Mina

Contents

Illustrations and Maps

Cover Illustration: Mosaic (late second/early third century AD) from the Piazzale delle Corporazioni in Ostia, where many trade and artisan associations had their offices, often with a mosaic depicting their business activities. The Karalitani are shippers and businessmen from Caralis in Sardinia who specialized in transporting corn, as illustrated in their mosaic by the image of corn measures with a ship. Photo courtesy of the Bridgeman Art Library.

Preface

Latin legal texts are potentially a valuable historical resource, yet they are often underused, as available translations and commentaries are widely scattered in a variety of books which are sometimes difficult for students to consult. This volume collects texts related to the study of the administrative, economic, and social history of the empire, in those circumstances where citizens encountered in a legal context magistrates, governors, and officials empowered by the state, in the management and conduct of facilities and services, and in response to those facing or proposing litigation.

I present material not only from the *Digest* and *Codex Justinianus*, but also from ancient writers, inscriptions, and papyri that contain legal or quasi-legal material. Some of the passages will be familiar to students of the Roman empire, but my emphasis on legal texts gives a new dimension to the topics covered, and offers a compendium of additional source material not usually available in a single volume, which will supplement traditional sourcebooks. The chronological period is c. 31 BC – c. AD 235, embracing what is conventionally described as the classical period of Roman law. A glossary of legal terms and a who's who of jurists and principal authors cited in the text are appended. The book, which is presented in a way that can be understood by students with no previous knowledge of Roman legal practice, should enable a wider use of legal texts in the study of Roman imperial history.

The book has a long history, starting with discussions with Richard Stoneman at Routledge years ago. Then other projects and duties supervened. The final completion of the text was much delayed by unforeseen circumstances including a pandemic. Over the years since the inception of the project I have incurred many debts from friends and colleagues. It is impossible to name all of them, but I must particularly thank Professor David Buck, steadfast in support and friendship since our first meeting as graduate students in 1970s Oxford. I have been assisted by wise and helpful guidance from several readers of Cambridge University Press. My thanks are also due to Michael Sharp for his patience and guidance over a long process.

Finally, during my university career and over the long period when I was trying to complete this book, I owe more than I can adequately express to the love and support of my wife Karen.

Abbreviations

AE	*L'Année épigraphique*, Cagnat, R. et al. (eds.), (1893–). Paris
AJP	*American Journal of Philology*
BGU	*Ägyptische Urkunden aus den königlichen Museen zu Berlin* I–IX (1895–1937). Berlin
BIDR	*Bullettino dell'Instituto di diritto romano*
CA	*Classical Antiquity*
CIL	*Corpus Inscriptionum Latinarum*, Mommsen, Th. et al. (eds.), (1863–). Berlin
CJ	*Codex Justinianus*, Krueger, P. (ed.), (1877). Berlin
CQ	*Classical Quarterly*
CRAI	*Comptes rendus de l'académie des inscriptions et des belles-lettres*
D	*Digest*, Mommsen, Th. (ed.), (1870–3). Berlin
EHR	*Economic History Review*
EJ	Ehrenberg, V. and Jones, A. H. M., *Documents illustrating the Reigns of Augustus and Tiberius*, edited by Stockton, D. L. (1976). Oxford
FIRA	*Fontes Iuris Romani Anteiustiniani*, Riccobono, S. et al. (eds.), (3 vols, 2nd ed. of vol. 1; 1940–3; repr. 1968). Florence
GRBS	*Greek, Roman, and Byzantine Studies*
HSCP	*Harvard Studies in Classical Philology*
IGR	*Inscriptiones Graecae ad Res Romanas Pertinentes*, Cagnat, R. et al. (eds.), (vols. 1, 3, 4, 1906–27). Paris
IJ	*Irish Jurist*
ILLRP	*Inscriptiones Latinae Liberae Rei Publicae*, Degrassi, A. (ed.), (2 vols. 1957–63; vol. 1 2nd ed., 1965). Florence
ILS	*Inscriptiones Latinae Selectae*, Dessau, H. (ed.), (1892–1916). Berlin

JLH	*Journal of Library History, Philosophy and Comparative Librarianship*
JRA	*Journal of Roman Archaeology*
JRS	*Journal of Roman Studies*
OGIS	*Orientis Graecae Inscriptiones Selectae*, Dittenberger, W. (ed.), (2 vols. 1903–5). Leipzig
P. Fayum	*Fayûm Towns and their Papyri*, Grenfell, B. P., Hunt, A. S., and Hogarth, D. G. (1900). London
P. Fouad	*Papyrus Fouad* I, Bataille, A., Guéraud, O., and Jouguet, P. (eds.), (nos. 1–89) (1939). Cairo
P. Hamb.	*Griechische Papyrusurkunden der Hamburger Stadtbibliothek*, Meyer, P. (ed.), (1911–24). Leipzig and Berlin
P. Lond.	*Greek Papyri in the British Museum*, Kenyon, F. G. and Bell, H. I. (eds.), (vols. I–V, 1893–1917). London
P. Mich.	*Papyri in the University of Michigan. Miscellaneous Papyri*, Winter, J. G. (ed.), (1936). Ann Arbor
P. Oxy.	*The Oxyrhynchus Papyri*, Grenfell, S. P., Hunt, A. S. et al. (eds.), (1898–). London
P. Ryl.	*Catalogue of the Greek Papyri in the John Rylands Library at Manchester*, Hunt, A. S., Johnson, J. de M., Martin, V., Roberts, C. H., and Turner, E. G. (eds.), I–IV (1911–52). Manchester
P. Strassb.	*Griechische Papyrus der kaiserlichen Universitäts und Landesbibliothek zu Strassburg*, Preisigke, F. (ed.), 2 vols. (1906–20). Leipzig
P. Tebt.	*The Tebtunis Papyri*, Grenfell, B. P., Hunt, A. S., Smyly, J. G. et al. (eds.), (1902–). London
RIDA	*Revue Internationale des Droits de l'Antiquité*
SB	*Sammelbuch griechischer Urkunden aus Ägypten*, Preisigke, F. and Bilabel, F. (eds.), vols. I–V (1915–50). Strassburg
SEG	*Supplementum Epigraphicum Graecum*, Hondius, J. J. E. et al. (eds.), (1923–). Leiden
SP	*Select Papyri: Non-Literary Papyri*, Hunt, A. S. and Edgar, C. C. (eds.), (2 vols., 1932–4). Cambridge, Mass.
Sylloge^3	*Sylloge Inscriptionum Graecarum*, Dittenberger, W. (ed.), (4 vols., 3rd ed., 1915–24). Leipzig
T	Thulin, C., *Corpus Agrimensorum Romanorum* I.1 (1913), Leipzig; repr. 1971. Stuttgart

TAPA	*Transactions of the American Philological Association*
TJ	*Tijdschrift voor Rechtsgeschiedenis*
TPSulp	*Tabulae Pompeianae Sulpiciorum (TPSulp.): edizione critica dell'archivio puteolano dei Sulpicii* (*Vetera* 12), Camodeca, G. (ed.), (1999). Rome
ZPE	*Zeitschrift für Papyrologie und Epigraphik*

1 Map of the empire in the time of Marcus Aurelius: *CAH* (2nd ed.) vol. XI, p. xvi

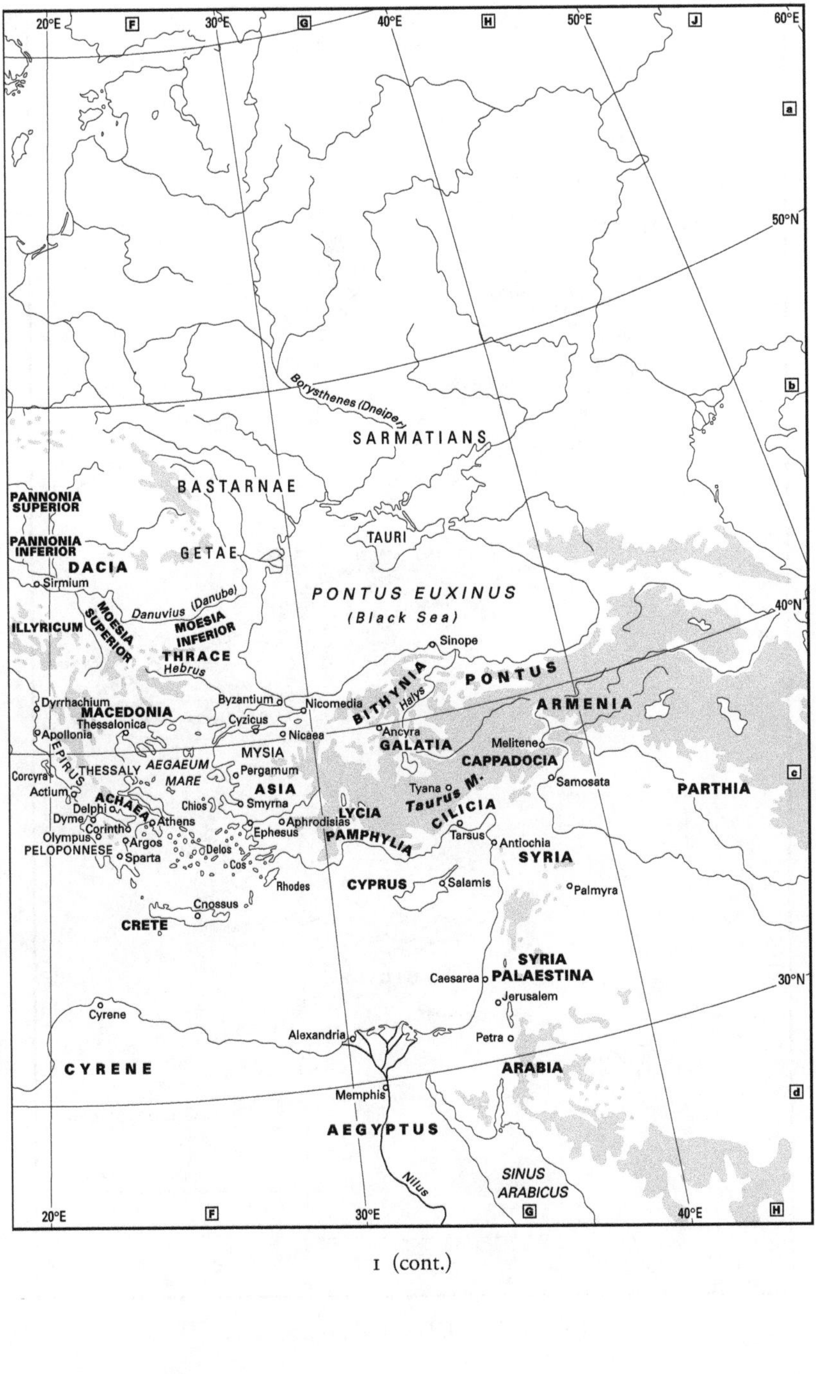
20°E
F
30°E
G
40°E
H
50°E
J
60°E
a
50°N
b
Borysthenes (Dneiper)
SARMATIANS
BASTARNAE
PANNONIA SUPERIOR
PANNONIA INFERIOR
GETAE
TAURI
DACIA
Sirmium
PONTUS EUXINUS
(Black Sea)
40°N
Danuvius (Danube)
MOESIA SUPERIOR
MOESIA INFERIOR
ILLYRICUM
THRACE
Hebrus
Sinope
PONTUS
BITHYNIA
Halys
ARMENIA
Dyrrhachium
MACEDONIA
Thessalonica
Byzantium
Nicomedia
Cyzicus
Nicaea
Ancyra
GALATIA
Apollonia
EPIRUS
MYSIA
Melitene
CAPPADOCIA
c
Corcyra
THESSALY
AEGAEUM MARE
Pergamum
ASIA
Samosata
PARTHIA
Actium
Tyana
Taurus M.
ACHAEA
Delphi
Chios
Smyrna
CILICIA
Dyme
Corinth
Athens
Aphrodisias
LYCIA
Olympus
Argos
Ephesus
PAMPHYLIA
Tarsus
Antiochia
PELOPONNESE
Sparta
Delos
Cos
SYRIA
Rhodes
CYPRUS
Salamis
Palmyra
Cnossus
CRETE
SYRIA PALAESTINA
Caesarea
30°N
Jerusalem
Cyrene
Alexandria
Petra
CYRENE
ARABIA
Memphis
d
AEGYPTUS
Nilus
SINUS ARABICUS
20°E
F
30°E
G
40°E
H

1 (cont.)

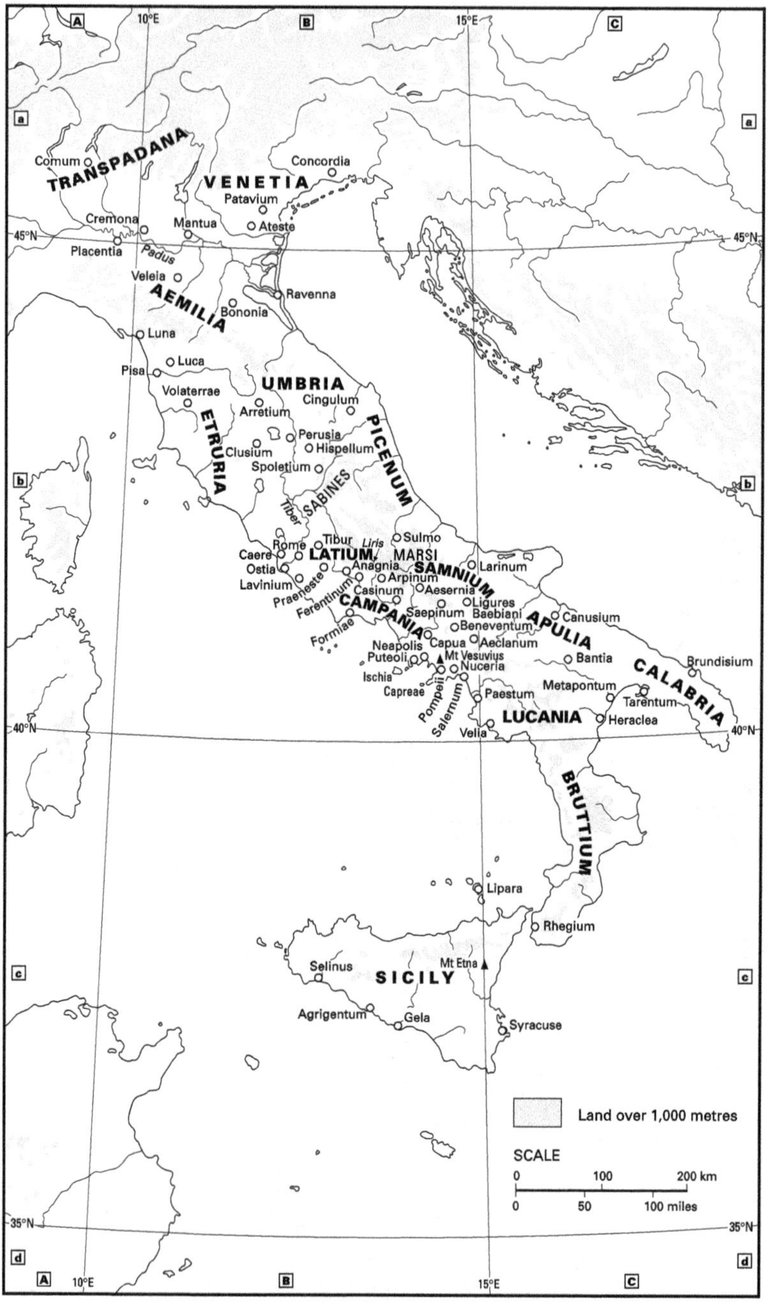

2 Map of Italy: *CAH* (2nd ed.) vol. XI, p. 404

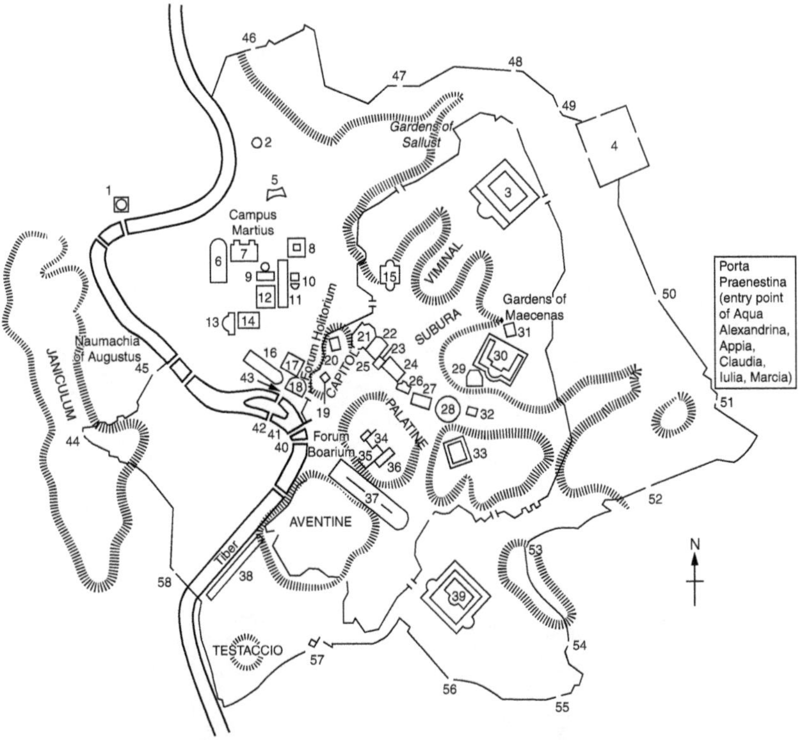

3 Map of the centre of Rome: M. Le Glay, J-L. Voisin, and Y. Le Bohec, *A History of Rome* (4th ed. Wiley-Blackwell, 2009), p. 353 Fig. 11.1

1 Mausoleum of Hadrian
2 Mausoleum of Augustus
3 Baths of Diocletian
4 Praetorian camp
5 Horologium of Augustus
6 Stadium of Domitian
7 Baths of Nero
8 Temple of the divine Hadrian
9 Pantheon
10 Temple of Isis
11 Saepta Iulia
12 Baths of Agrippa
13 Theatre of Pompey
14 Portico of Pompey
15 Baths of Constantine
16 Circus Flaminius
17 Portico of Octavia
18 Theatre of Marcellus
19 Temple of Jupiter Optimus Maximus
20 Arx
21 Forum of Trajan
22 Forum of Augustus
23 Forum of Nerva
24 Forum of Peace
25 Forum of Caesar
23 Forum of Nerva
26 Basilica of Constantine
27 Temple of Venus and Rome
28 Colosseum
29 Baths of Titus
30 Baths of Trajan
31 Portico of Livia
32 Ludus Magnus
33 Temple of the divine Claudius
34 Palace of the Flavians
35 Palace of Augustus
36 Stadium
37 Circus Maximus
38 Portico of Aemilia
39 Baths of Caracalla
40 Sublician bridge
41 Aemilian bridge
42 Cestian bridge
43 Fabrician bridge
44 Porta Aurelia
45 Porta Septimiana
46 Porta Flaminia
47 Porta Pinciana
48 Porta Salaria
49 Porta Nomentana
50 Porta Tiburtina
51 Porta Praenestina
52 Porta Asinaria
53 Porta Metronia
54 Porta Latina
55 Porta Appia
56 Porta Ardeatina
57 Porta Ostiensis
58 Porta Portuensis

Introduction

The Sources of Law in Rome

Roman legal texts open a view onto the life and society of the empire at its height, its management, its peoples, their activities, interrelations, and problems, and their experiences when facing the juristic power of the state and its officials. Now, the first step in the study of these texts is the identification of the sources of the law. Sources are defined first as the mechanisms by which the law was introduced and regarded as authoritative by the Romans, and second the legal works transmitted to us by writers and compilers in the ancient world, which have been translated and analysed by modern scholars. This introduction offers a brief overview of these topics and some of the issues associated with the use of legal texts in the study of Roman social, economic, and political history. For helpful discussions see Crook (1994b), Robinson (1997), especially 1–78; Johnston (1999), 2–29; law after AD 235 Ibbetson (2005); Matthews (2006); Riggsby (2010).

The earliest statement of Roman legal procedure was the Twelve Tables, dating to c. 450 BC, a collection of rules of customary law, which became obsolete but were never formally abrogated. In the third century AD the distinguished jurist Papinian summed up the basis of the law's authority as follows: 'The civil law is what issues from laws, plebiscites, decrees of the senate, imperial decisions, and the authority of jurists' (*D* 1.1.7). In the republic, the assembly of the plebs (*concilium plebis*) was the principal source of law, in that it accepted or rejected the formal proposals put to it by the appropriate magistrates. We know of more than 900 statutes or proposals for statutes, which indicate the developing interests and sophistication of government as the republic expanded its horizons. This legislation mainly relates to public activities and the interests of the state and the people (*ius publicum*).

The senate as the most prestigious assembly in Rome expected to be consulted by magistrates, most importantly the consuls, before any initiatives were taken or proposals for statutes put before the people. The senate then offered its advice in the form of a decree (*senatus consultum*). Therefore, throughout the republic, despite its enormous influence, the senate did not itself make law. However, early in the imperial period the *senatus consultum* came to have the force of law, as the vote of the people's assembly was increasingly merely a formality (see Talbert (1984), 431–59). This suited the emperor because his influence could be more direct in a shorter path to legislation. Eventually, the senatorial decree also declined in importance, and the basis for new law became the emperor's speech to the senators (*oratio principis*) proposing a measure (Ibbetson (2005), 193).

Magistrates, particularly the praetors, were an important source of civil or private law (*ius civile*). They were mainly responsible for responding to plaintiffs in civil jurisdiction, the praetor *urbanus* dealing with suits between citizens, and the praetor *peregrinus* with suits between citizens and non-citizens. The praetor had to decide if there was a case to answer, and if so, what statute or procedure was appropriate. In a sense therefore the praetor could interpret and develop the law, and on entering office issued an edict setting out how he intended to conduct his legal duties, the nature of suits he would receive, and legal defences. He could offer remedies for situations not currently protected under the civil law; he could even grant a legal fiction to permit a suit to be brought where previously no legal process was possible. The praetor's intentions were expressed in the first person, for example, 'I shall grant an action ...'. This could serve to modify or reform the civil law without repealing it; the importance of the praetor's role should be set against the relatively limited number of statutes dealing with private law (Matthews (2006), 485–6).

The praetor's edict was handed down to his successor but was also flexible in that subsequent praetors could bring fresh interpretations and add material. This work of the praetors made up a substantial part of the *ius honorarium*, or the law introduced by magistrates through the issuing of edicts for the public good. This source of law continued in the imperial period until the revision of the praetorian edicts (also the edicts of the aediles relating to the sale of goods in marketplaces) by the jurist Salvius Iulianus on the instructions of Hadrian (for Iulianus' career see *ILS* 8973 from Hadrumetum in Africa). This consolidation of the praetorian edict 'marked the end of the independent legislative power of praetors' (see Ibbetson (2005), 193–4). This consolidation shows imperial determination to maintain control of the law, as Hadrian laid down that imperial authority would establish any new legal rules. The reconstruction of the praetor's edict in modern times was the outstanding work of Lenel (1927).

The emperor became a major source of law, the pattern for which had been set by Augustus. Having achieved control of the Roman world he did not destroy the mechanism of the law but inserted himself into it and gradually became the central figure in jurisdiction, intervening anywhere if he chose, and exercising both original and appellate jurisdiction in both civil and criminal cases. Thereafter, emperors loomed over the judicial process, acting as judge, sometimes with the help of their *consilium* of advisers, and answering legal queries from citizens. An imperial decision was a *constitutio* and it could take several forms (see p. 415). Such was the burden of legal activity for conscientious emperors that they often delegated jurisdiction to senior officials, notably the praetorian prefects, so that over time the role of these officers changed from commanding the imperial bodyguard to exercising administrative and judicial responsibilities (see p. 91). The leading jurists Ulpian, Papinian, and Paul all served as praetorian prefect during the Severan dynasty.

Jurists constituted another important influence on the development of law at Rome. In Roman legal practice there was limited professional expertise. The praetors and judges were not lawyers, and other senior magistrates, such as the consuls, did not necessarily have legal experience. Therefore, magistrates with legal responsibilities turned to jurists, men who in the imperial period studied the law and expressed opinions on jurisprudence. In the republic Cicero defined a jurist as someone who was skilled in the statutes and the procedures which private people made use of in the state, and in giving opinions, helping in litigation, and preparing documents (*De Oratore* 1.212 with Robinson (1997), 44). Indeed, in the republic some of the upper classes had been learned in the law, but under the emperors jurists came from varied backgrounds, were often of equestrian rank, and sometimes served in administrative posts. They were the closest Rome came to having professional lawyers, increasingly important as the administration became more complex, citizenship spread, and the burden of litigation became ever greater. When approached they offered guidance to magistrates and judges, gave advice to litigants, answered legal questions, and assisted emperors in various aspects of their jurisdiction. Consequently, in the imperial period jurists were much more involved in public law, and by offering advice at the highest level could influence how the law was interpreted in individual cases, and hence the development of the law. It is a striking aspect of Roman culture that juristic opinion was important in administration and law, though jurists were in general men who were outside the court circle and had no official position of legal leadership (see Watson (1995), 57). But the Romans had long respected an ability to pronounce on legal matters and held that it conferred distinction. For the juristic *ius publice respondendi* see p. 418.

We do not know how many jurists there were at any time or what communication they had with one another. There are few details of their education and legal training, but many probably attended on established lawyers, absorbing their methods, listening to lectures, and reading textbooks or commentaries (see Harries (2016)). Aulus Gellius, writing in the second century AD, comments on his attempts to learn about the law: 'When I emerged from the nooks and crannies of books and teachers into the company of men and the light of the forum, I remember that I asked of men teaching the law or giving opinions in public in various parts of Rome, whether a quaestor of the Roman people could be summoned to law before the praetor' (*Noctes Atticae* 13.13). By a statute of 204 BC lawyers were unable to accept a fee. Augustus maintained this practice, but after a bad-tempered debate in the senate Claudius compromised by laying down a maximum fee of ten thousand sesterces (no. 651). Evidence for payment does indicate increasing professionalism (see p. 366). Furthermore, in the first century AD two traditions within legal scholarship had emerged in which jurists came to be described as Proculians or Sabinians after the leading exponents Proculus and Sabinus (de Zulueta (1953), vol. II, 9–10; Buckland (1975), 25–7). The differences between the two are unclear, but it was perhaps mainly a matter of detail, in that they disagreed on how the law could be applied in individual cases.

Ancient Writers and the Law

The second to early third century AD saw great juristic activity, with the publication of treatises, commentaries, and responses to legal questions. Juristic literature tended to fall into two categories: in one, material was systematically arranged with the purpose of offering education in the law. The only surviving legal textbook is the *Institutes* of Gaius, published in the second half of the second century AD (see Gordon and Robinson (1988)). Gaius also wrote over thirty other books, and was interested in the history of legal developments and in establishing proper classification of the law. His textbook was very influential in the time of Justinian, whose own *Institutes* were modelled on it.

The other category aimed to analyse the law: commentaries provided detailed examination of legal institutions, of particular importance being the commentaries on the praetor's edict, and would have served to guide a practising lawyer. Other literature discussed individual legal cases and might have assisted a lawyer looking for parallels or precedents (Ibbetson (2005), 187–9). The jurists aimed to explain the law through their examination of imperial decisions and other available evidence. Although each jurist tended to follow an individual approach, which often led to contradictions, sometimes a significant consensus emerged (see Robinson (1997), 45).

Much of the surviving legal writing is about private law, the *ius civile*, and much less about public law or constitutional matters. However, that may be partly a result of the remit of the excerptors (see p. 11), and there are indications of substantial works on aspects of public life. For example, Callistratus wrote on law relating to the treasury (*fiscus*), Ulpian studied the duties of a proconsul and other officials, Marcian wrote on procedure in public courts, Papinian on the laws relating to adultery, and Macer on military law. On private law, Ulpian, Paul, and Pomponius analysed the edict of the praetor, and wrote commentaries on the works of earlier jurists. These works took the form of quotations from the work of the subject and then a detailed line-by-line commentary. There were also many casuistic studies including collections of replies, opinions, and disputes which dealt with cases involving seemingly fact-based situations. For a useful survey see Robinson (1997), 42–8; Ibbetson (2005), 184–90; Sirks (2015b), 349–50.

The main publicly sponsored collections of legal writings in the ancient world which are used in this volume are firstly the *Codex Justinianus*, published in 529, a collection (on the emperor Justinian's instructions) of imperial laws and rescripts from the three existing collections – *Gregorianus*, *Hermogenianus*, and *Theodosianus*; it consists of twelve books divided according to legal topic with subdivisions dealing with different aspects of the main topic; the rulings are set out in chronological order, from Hadrian to Theodosius, citing the emperor, the date given by consular year, and the name of the petitioner. New material required a fresh edition, published in 534, which constitutes the surviving text (see most recently, Frier (2016)).

In 530 Justinian ordered that the old works of Roman jurists (about 1,500) should be studied, abbreviated, and collected in one book, the *Digest*. The project was conducted under the guidance of the distinguished jurist Tribonian (Honoré (1978), 139–86), and published in 533. The *Digest* extends to fifty books, each dealing with a particular legal topic, divided into sub-headings of related material, though some topics such as testaments took up more space. In each section the names and works of the relevant jurists are cited (see most recently, Watson (1998)). For our collections of Roman legal works we are therefore reliant on the editorial decisions of others, and the existing text resembles a scrapbook, often lacking context because of this process of excerpting by the compilers. Furthermore, in the three centuries between the composition of classical juristic texts and the sixth century, changes will have occurred, and there will certainly have been some omissions and mistakes in the copying, possibly most seriously in heavily consulted works, as they were copied more often (see Robinson (1997), 56–62; Johnston (1999), 14–17; 21–4; Matthews (2006), 481–9).

In addition to these texts, we have the *Fragmenta Vaticana* (*FIRA* 2, pp. 461–540), compiled in the fourth century AD, an assortment of material including extracts from jurists both named and unnamed, and imperial letters and rescripts, some of which do not appear in other legal sources. The *Mosaicarum et Romanorum Legum Collatio* (*FIRA* 2, pp. 541–89) is a modern title for a work compiled in the fourth century; its method is to quote in Latin a law of Moses and then provide extracts from Roman law on a similar theme, including imperial letters and rescripts. The *Tituli ex corpore Ulpiani* or *Epitome Ulpiani* is possibly a collection of Ulpian's *Regulae*, though some have argued that it is an epitome of a post-classical jurist (*FIRA* 2, pp. 261–314). The *Pauli Sententiae* is a collection assembled probably at the end of the third century of genuine opinions of Paul (*FIRA* 2, pp. 319–417).

Finally, it is important to emphasize that ancient writers, historians, commentators, and scholars can be a useful source for the legal process. For example, Quintilian, tutor to the emperor Domitian's great-nephews, published his textbook for advocates, *Training in Oratory*, probably before AD 96; it has much to offer about the role of advocates in using or shaping legal procedure (pp. 369–72). Pliny the Younger recounts in his letters how he appeared (both for the prosecution and the defence) in several important cases before the senate involving alleged corruption and malpractice by provincial governors. He also served as assessor for Trajan at a hearing before the emperor (p. 440). The writings of the Roman land surveyors are valuable because surveyors often dealt with legal problems of land ownership and boundaries, were well-experienced in the law, and consulted jurists, such as Cassius Longinus, 'a very learned man and legal expert' (Campbell (2000), p. 91.31). Surveyors therefore offer valuable evidence on the management of property, responsibilities to neighbours, and the wider question of inter-community jurisdiction (see further p. 10).

Furthermore, collections of inscriptions, papyri, and wax tablets provide crucial evidence for dealings that involved individuals or communities, such as boundary disputes, financial records, contracts, sales documents, birth declarations, and private litigation. This evidence provides a direct record of ancient legal procedure with no extraneous problems related to possible interpolation or lawyerly interpretation. For the value of epigraphy in Roman legal history, see Beggio (2016), for papyrology, Alonso Rodríguez (2016).

Law and the Roman World

'The entire law employed by us relates either to persons or to things or to actions' (Gaius, *Institutes* 1.8). In this fundamental threefold division, the law of persons established an individual's gender, status, and place in society based on free birth, and Roman citizenship, to which there were various avenues. Within this definition, wealth and status produced distinct social groups of which senators and *equites* were the most important; rank brought enhanced social responsibilities. Outside the upper classes was the social milieu of the plebs and ex-slaves, who were status-conscious in their own way. Within the sphere of the law of persons, the family or household (*familia*) was of great significance; the *pater familias* was head of the household and all its members were under his power, which was extensive, though limited by tradition and social convention. Private law issues relating to the household, such as marriage, children, the management of the family, inheritance, and issues of testamentary provision, form an important part of the law of persons, but are not the central topic of this book, except in so far as the state became involved in mandating benefits and penalties in respect of marriage, and in giving soldiers testamentary privileges, both of which gave rise to controversy and debate.

I am therefore principally concerned with the law of things and actions since this study emphasizes life in the public domain overseen by the state, the issues, problems, and outcomes when citizens and subjects encountered at law the agents of the government, as it attempted to manage the huge territory and assets of the empire, and its disparate peoples. The evidence reveals the whole of Roman society at many different levels, not just the usual view from the level of wealth and privilege. We can examine the regulation of the built environment in Rome, and the management of relations between citizens in a crowded urban area; the mechanisms for feeding the population, providing water, entertainment, and other amenities; it was also the state's responsibility to preserve law and order. Within Italy, the government and individuals were responsible for the legal management of Italian communities and the rural infrastructure, the exercise of jurisdiction, and the extension of social interventions through the authorization of *collegia* and the *alimenta* scheme. In the provinces, the evidence shows the crucial role of governors in preserving the delicate relationship with the urban elite on whom Romans relied for administration and tax-collection; Rome's assets had to be managed and the city infrastructure supervised; municipal regulations had to be devised and enforced; the response to complaints about corrupt or abusive administration helps to show the theory and practice of effective and equitable provincial administration. Throughout the provinces Roman governors and officials encountered local legal systems, laws, traditions, and customs. Since the Romans deployed a limited number of administrators and officials in each province, they did not have the resources to impose the process of Roman law autocratically even if they had so wished. Therefore, in the provinces the government worked with local law and customary practice. Although the governor's court would normally hear cases involving Roman citizens, the non-citizen population had access to their own courts following traditional practices (see p. 148). The Romans adopted a flexible approach, though of course operating in their best interests. How the Romans adapted and worked with local legal process is a good illustration of how Roman administration functioned with ad hoc solutions rather than strict bureaucratic procedures.

Away from the debate over the nature of the Roman pre-modern economy, legal texts illustrate everyday business dealings, the making of contracts, buying, selling, hiring, and setting up partnerships; how banks functioned, how security was obtained, and how business could be conducted through agents. Even the poorer citizens might aim to own or exploit some property, and legal texts show how possession was acquired and protected, the nature of landholding, how disputes arose and were settled, and the opportunities and problems of tenancy in both the rural and urban environments.

It was important for citizens at all levels of society to feel that they could obtain redress for injury or insult, and we see how this process worked in practice with the development of the concept of fault and negligence. Theft was not normally a criminal offence, and it was up to the wronged citizen to pursue the perpetrator through channels which had various legal consequences. Meanwhile, the permanent jury courts dealt with a series of crimes such as corruption and adultery that mainly were the concern of the upper classes. Confronting the legal system was a challenge for those marginalized by their behaviour, profession, or religion, such as Jews and Christians.

Those who attempted or managed to plead their case in court before a magistrate or judge probably found it a daunting experience; they would need to get to court, find an affordable lawyer, and perhaps face postponements and bias in favour of the wealthy and socially advantaged. Evidence from papyri is particularly useful in assessing how ordinary people fared in court. Central to the entire legal process was the emperor. This went back to Augustus, whose formal legal authority was by no means clear but who operated within the civil and criminal law and offered advice when approached. In a way the emperor could act as a last resort for those seeking justice.

Using Legal Texts

The use of legal texts to illustrate Roman society and economic life is complicated by the question of how far the law influenced developments in society, or merely reflected changes brought about by other factors. On one view, Roman private law may have developed within the juristic tradition without reference to everyday society with which it had little connection (Watson (1995), especially 64–8; (2007)). There may be a discrepancy between theory and practice in the law, in that lawyers were interested in discussing technical aspects of the law that were legally interesting or challenging, but not necessarily relevant to wider popular concerns. Furthermore, it is difficult to link legislation to specific social or economic conditions or policies, and the law tends to have a bias towards elite Roman interests, which makes it difficult to connect to society. The relationship of law and society and the delicate balance of reciprocal influences remain areas of vigorous current debate, and it is true that legal texts cannot necessarily show how frequently issues arose, or how many people they affected, or how they developed over time.

It is also uncertain how many of the legal cases cited in the *Digest* are purely imaginary. However, it is unlikely that jurists collected material and assembled arguments that were entirely hypothetical and remote from reality. It is more plausible to suppose that such descriptions will at least represent what was thought likely to happen or what was known to have happened, and that even hypothetical problems were based on legal experience. Although jurists did not present cases in court and were not necessarily interested in the issues that would concern a practising courtroom advocate, they had to prepare material for those who represented real people. Treatises dealing with issues of substantive law, or works of instructions for students, were perhaps not regularly based on real legal queries. However, books dealing with responses or imperial *decreta* were more likely to be collections of material based on genuine incidents. Sometimes we find that apparently the real names of litigants have been used. And even when stock names are used, they might have been inserted into a real case (Johnston (1999), 24–6). Ulpian describes an actual case in which he sat with the praetor as legal assessor when the magistrate dealt with an issue involving people from Campania who had extracted a promise under duress (*D* 4.2.9.3). Naturally, the historian must look for other evidence outside the legal texts, in inscriptions or papyri, to see the methods, procedure, and legal issues in real life and the courtroom (see Crook (1967), 9–12; (1995)). Overall, Matthews' comment (2006, 483) on the value of legal texts is apposite: 'Whether real, or imagined in order to illustrate points of law, such situations are part of the thought-world of the writers, and so part of the history of their society'.

Many scholars now emphasize the interconnections between legal practice and the history of Roman society and culture. Johnston (1988, viii) argues that there is good reason for thinking that the institutions of Roman law are important for social history, and that is particularly important in respect of the law of commerce, where, arguably, legal sources have an enormous amount to tell us. Lawyers presumably developed such careful and sophisticated rules only if there was somewhere to use them. The wax tablets from Puteoli demonstrate that businessmen assumed that the whole range of law applied to their activities (see Crook (1994a), 261). In commerce the provision of certain types of contracts in law might encourage business transactions; on the other hand, perhaps extensive business activity created pressure for legal measures, in a kind of circular process. The law of course did protect, at least originally, the political and economic interests of the elite. But even if the law was elite dominated, that itself is relevant as the elite were at the heart of so many activities. All conduct of economic business benefitted from the secure framework of Roman law, with defined process and clear penalties. Frier (2000) cogently argues that that Roman law should not be isolated from its social and economic context.

The writings of the Roman land surveyors allow us to set the theoretical legal resolution of land disputes against what is known of real disputes based on the evidence of inscriptions. For example, in a dispute between the communities of Lamia and Hypata in Macedonia, the governor, instructed by the emperor, arranged for a measurement of boundaries:

> Quintus Gellius Sentius Augurinus … since I myself have been constantly present on the spot day after day and have heard the case in the presence of the representatives of both communities, after summoning Iulius Victor, imperial veteran and surveyor, I decided that the start of the boundary should be from that place where I understood Sides to have been, which is situated below the enclosure sacred to Neptune, from which as you go down, a straight line boundary is maintained right up to the fountain Dercynna, which is situated across the river Sperchion, so that the boundary of the people of Lamia and the people of Hypata runs through the Amphispora lands to the fountain Dercynna mentioned above, and from there to the tomb Pelion along the downward slope called Sir [. …] to the monument of Eurytus, which lies within the territory of the people of Lamia [… .] (*CIL* 3.586 = *ILS* 5947a).

This methodology of boundary scrutiny closely resembles the hypothetical principles of boundary designation described by the surveyor Hyginus, which follow natural phenomena, hills, rivers, man-made roads, mountain ridges, watersheds, and monuments (Campbell (2000), p. 79.32). This inspires confidence that surveyors in dealing with legal issues were not setting out mere theories but discussing real problems and procedures for their resolution (see further Campbell (2005)).

Even if it is accepted that legal texts are potentially very valuable in understanding government and society in the imperial period, historians using the *Digest* and the *Codex* face a long-standing problem of interpretation. In the editing of legal texts dating from several hundred years earlier great change has obviously taken place, since the *Digest* preserves only about 5 per cent of the original material, and scholars have argued that such texts were updated and made to conform to the law as it was in Justinian's time. There has been a significant and unresolved debate about the extent of such interpolations (for a useful summary see Robinson (1997), 105–13; Johnston (1999), 17–21). However, Watson (1994) gave a fresh slant to the defence of the integrity of classical law in the *Codex* and *Digest*, emphasizing the importance of the nature of the instructions that Justinian gave to the compilers. The *Codex* was to replace earlier collections and include any subsequent constitutions. This action was partly a response to the need for those working in the law to discover and have access to the material in imperial rescripts. In section 2 of the instructions to the compilers, Justinian states:

> We specifically extend permission to them to cut out prefaces that are redundant to the substance of the law, as well as repetitions and contradictions … and also those that have become obsolete; and to compose from the

> same three *Codes* and new constitutions certain laws presented in a brief format, to put them under appropriate titles, adding and subtracting, indeed even further, changing their wording when the usefulness of the material required it, even collecting in one law material scattered in several constitutions, clarifying their meaning.

It appears from this that Justinian did not extend permission for the compilers to make extensive change or reform the law as expressed in existing constitutions. As Watson notes, it was Justinian's subsequent undertaking, the *Fifty Decisions*, that was intended to produce reform of substantive law (Watson (1994), 116). This is confirmed by the Preface of the new *Code* published on 7 April 529.

In the Preface of the second edition of the *Codex* in 534 Justinian refers to the production of the *Digest*: 'and we presented all the old law, free from superfluous prolixity and also condensed, in our *Institutes* and *Digest*' (section 1). He implies that the *Digest* contains old (classical law) and not new material. In the instructions for its compilation the emperor states:

> There is another point which we wish you to observe carefully. If you find anything in the old books that is not well-expressed, or anything that is redundant, or lacking polish, you should remove superfluous verbosity, supplement what is deficient, and present the whole work within proper bounds and in the most elegant way possible. Furthermore, you should also follow up this point, namely, that if you discover anything incorrectly expressed in the old statutes or constitutions, which ancient authors cited in their books, you should correct this and present it in proper form, so that what you have chosen and presented there should be considered to be the correct and best version, and be accepted as if it were the original text. And no one is to dare to claim that your version is defective through comparison with the old text (De Deo auctore 7).

What is envisaged here is an exercise to tidy up the texts of the jurists and remove repetition within texts, and to avoid putting in the *Digest* what was already in the *Codex*. There is no authority to change the content of the texts beyond editorial work. Therefore, the *Digest* should contain the bulk of classical law, and this is confirmed by the care taken by the compilers to quote the name of the jurist responsible for each text and the work in which it was written, indicating the importance of maintaining the connections with classical law. Arguably there would be little point in embarking on the *Digest* if Justinian did not want to preserve the work of the classical jurists. Indeed, since the compilers had to work their way through three million lines of text in a few years, there was limited opportunity for substantial rewriting. The fact that contradictions exist within the texts does not necessarily show interpolation, but might reflect the state of classical law itself, which was not static but had been through a continuous process of development in the post-classical period.

On the other hand, it must be admitted that Justinian did grant permission to the compilers to make changes, presumably on their initiative. Abbreviation was to be an important element in this; they also had to make texts as accessible as possible while not adding confusion by rewriting. In addition, there was a significant difference in legal procedure; by Justinian's day the formulary system had been entirely replaced by *cognitio* (see pp. 336–7), though this change had been ongoing from the classical period. Watson (pp. 120–2) suggests that while interpolations do appear in the *Digest*, they can mainly be explained on the grounds that they were of a particular and limited type, firstly in circumstances where an imperial decision had altered substantive law, and the most helpful texts of the jurists to explicate the law therefore needed some qualification; secondly in cases where, of classical legal institutions related by purpose, one had lapsed or been abolished by Justinian, but a juristic text dealing with that institution was retained to help explain the other remaining institution. For example, Justinian abolished the formal method for the conveyance of property (*mancipatio*) with the result that the informal *traditio* was now used on all occasions. This meant that in editing the words of classical jurists *mancipatio* was replaced by *traditio* (for these legal terms, see p. 246).

In this volume I accept the premise that the *Digest* and other legal sources represent, in the words of Fergus Millar, 'an almost inexhaustible treasure house of economic and social history, and of ideologies, conceptions and attitudes' (1986, 272). I have selected texts from the period c. 31 BC – AD 235 to illustrate not just the responsibilities of emperors and magistrates in the application of the law, but the plans, activities, and troubles of a wide range of people in various social, business, and legal contexts, and how, against the dynamic of ruler and subjects, the local population and Rome often found a way of co-operating. In this unfolding story the empire changed and developed, but with an underlying stability that encouraged the consistent engagement of individuals with the law and the government.

CHAPTER 1

Status and Responsibility
Freedom, Slavery, Citizenship

Introduction

The Romans recognized under the law of nations (*ius gentium*) a fundamental distinction between free and non-free. The non-free were legally the chattels of their owners, and their participation in society was limited. Even here there was a hierarchy; household salves and slaves who worked in their master's business were in a much better position than farm workers, or worst of all those who worked in the state-run mines. Slaves of the emperor were at the top of the enslaved social tree with opportunities for advancement in the emperor's service. Servile status came about through capture in war, or the activities of slave-dealers, or by birth, in that children born to a slave mother would be slaves (*vernae*). There were also cases of self-enslavement for particular motives, often involving fraud (no. 3).

The free were either citizens or non-citizens, and by the civil law (*ius civilis*) and political convention, citizens (*quirites*) had rights and duties. According to Gaius, within the citizen body some were independent with full rights (*sui iuris*) while others were to some extent in the authority of another (*alieni iuris*), notably those children who were in the power of their father (*Institutes* 1.48).

The activity of citizens was partly determined by their tribe (the four city tribes had, at least during the republic, a better opportunity to participate in electoral and political assemblies), and by their wealth category, which influenced their voting rights, the assemblies they could attend, and their voting century in the *Comitia Centuriata*, which under Augustus still elected senior magistrates. Roman society was status-conscious. Three distinct groups (senators, *equites*, and plebs) had their place and role, though within each group there were gradations depending partly on wealth or social connections or family traditions or type of employment. The most formal division was the rank of patrician, which by the mid third century BC was an inner group of the senatorial order restricted to certain clans. Furthermore, the term 'noble' (*nobilis*) had come to refer to members of families whose ancestors had held the consulship. The working of the constitution of the Roman republic is conveniently discussed in detail by Lintott (1999). In the early imperial period Augustus and Tiberius were keen to preserve the ethos of the upper classes and used legislation to ensure family status and appropriate standards of behaviour (pp. 50–5).

The Roman practice by which slaves, if properly set free by their masters, acquired the rights of a Roman citizen as a freedman (*libertus*) or freedwoman (*liberta*) encouraged the emergence of ex-slaves as an important social group. Because of their slave background they were often looked down upon as socially inferior, and they faced certain restrictions, but they could be very useful in business management, and for many the way was open to social and economic advancement (pp. 60–3). Moreover, any descendants were freeborn. Freedmen of the emperor increasingly had an important role in the imperial administration. This ad hoc use of talented people was a typical aspect of Roman government and society.

Citizenship was jealously protected, and in the case of a liaison between a Roman citizen and a foreign woman the status of any child depended on the status of the woman. But by the end of the republic and in the imperial period citizenship became a gift to bestow on individuals or entire communities, often as a reward for services rendered on the battlefield or elsewhere. This encouraged a long process of assimilation by which more and more people were absorbed into the Roman way of life. Finally, in the early third century the emperor Caracalla granted citizenship to virtually all people under his rule, though by this stage citizenship was less important than membership of the elite (p. 398). In the first and second centuries AD there was a further variation in status, in that some people were granted Latin rights. This status had originally been granted to the Latin peoples of Italy, but later was extended to communities elsewhere in the empire, and conferred rights possibly relating to business and marriage; most importantly, some members of communities with Latin rights could acquire full citizenship (pp. 34–5).

It is not possible in this book to offer a detailed study of Roman slavery. For detailed examination of the legal aspects of slavery see Buckland (1908), Watson (1987); for a useful collection of source material relating to slavery in Greece and Rome, see Wiedemann (1981); for slavery in the context of Roman society, see Bradley (1984), especially 47–80 for the nature of the slave's life; Mouritsen (2011), 10–35; Gamauf (2016) for slaves in household business; for life as a Roman citizen, see in general Gardner (1993), especially 1–6.

Definition of Status: Free and Unfree

Gaius, *Institutes* 1.9

1. The main distinction in the law of persons is as follows, that all men are either free or slaves.

In Roman law the law of persons was closely related to the family (*familia*), the collection of persons who made up a household. The most important person (*persona*) in the household was the *pater familias*, who within the family had power and from that derived the law of persons relating to the family. To have the status of a person in law an individual required Roman citizenship, as the law applied only to citizens. Slaves were not Roman citizens and were excluded from the law of persons and treated as chattels. Therefore, in Gaius' definition they are not part of his subsequent discussion of the law of persons. For a text and translation of Gaius, see de Zulueta (1946; 1953); Gordon and Robinson (1988).

D 1.5.4 (Florentinus, *Institutes*, Book 9)

2. Freedom is the natural condition by which a person may do as he wishes except insofar as he is prevented by force or by the law. Slavery is a provision of the law of nations, by which someone is subjected to the ownership of another contrary to nature.

The Romans made a sharp distinction between freedom and slavery. Slaves as mere chattels were effectively dehumanized, with no rights as a citizen, no legitimate marriage or family, and no property ownership. For slaves as chattels, see also the aediles' edict on sale (p. 333). On the other hand, slaves did possess intellectual and moral qualities.

D 1.5.5 (Marcianus, *Institutes*, Book 1)

3. One condition is common for all slaves, but in the case of free men some are freeborn, some are freedmen. Slaves are brought into our ownership either through the civil law or the law of nations; by the civil law if someone more than twenty years old allows himself to be sold in order to share in the price; by the law of nations men become slaves if they are captured from the enemy or are born to a female slave.

Self-enslavement with fraudulent intent occurred when a person had an accomplice sell him as a slave to an unsuspecting third person, and then keep the money when his free status was established.

Suetonius, *Augustus* 21.2

4. In the case of those who rebelled frequently or in an especially treacherous way, he (Augustus) never exacted any more serious punishment than that the prisoners should be sold on the condition that they should not spend their time as slaves in a neighbouring country and should not be set free within thirty years.

Suetonius' biography of Augustus is one of the most important sources for his rule; it is detailed, generally objective, and enhanced by Suetonius' access to documentation through his position as an imperial secretary and his knowledge of how government worked. For Suetonius, see p. 481.

Varro, *De Re Rustica* 2.10.6

5. In respect of the breeding of herdsmen, it is a straightforward matter in the case of those who stay on the farm permanently, as they have a female fellow-slave in the house, and herdsmen's love does not look any further away than this. However, in respect of those who marshal the herds in valleys and wooded areas, and shelter from the rain not in a house but in temporary huts, many have thought it appropriate to send women with them to follow the flocks, make food for the herdsmen, and render them more efficient.

Children born to a slave mother in the master's household were one of the most important sources of new slaves (*vernae*), since, being illegitimate, they took the status of the mother. Sexual liaisons took place between slaves or sometimes with the master, voluntary or otherwise. Varro (see also Columella, *De re rust.* 1.8.19) suggests some deliberate encouragement of childbearing among their slaves. Informal associations that copied marriage could be tolerated.

Suetonius, *Claudius* 25.2

6. Since some people were abandoning their sick and worn-out slaves on the island of Aesculapius because of the trouble of treating them, he (Claudius) decided that all who were being abandoned should be free and should not return to the control of their master if they recovered. But if someone chose to kill such a slave rather than abandon him, he should be liable to a murder charge.

During the imperial period various pieces of legislation rather inconsistently extended limited protection to slaves, though to some extent emperors and their advisers aimed to achieve a balance in order effectively to maintain a valuable system and ensure a stable basis for the continuing structure of slavery. It is possible that Stoic philosophical ideas had some role in ameliorating the conditions of slavery. Seneca (*Letter* 47.1) congratulates a friend who lives on good terms with his slaves: 'They are slaves, people say. No, they are men'. Indeed, he likens them to fellow slaves since Fortune has equal power over slave and free. However, Seneca is principally concerned with the pernicious impact on the master's behaviour and intellectual health of his ability to lord it over and mistreat his slaves. For Seneca (the Younger), see p. 480.

D 48.8.6 (Venuleius Saturninus, *Duties of a Proconsul*, Book 1)

7. He who delivers a slave to be castrated shall be punished by a fine of half his property, under a decree of the senate enacted during the consulship of Neratius Priscus and Annius Verus (AD 97).

D 1.6.2 (Ulpian, *Duties of a Proconsul*, Book 8); cf. *Mosaicarum et Romanarum Legum Collatio* 3.3.1–6

8. If a master is cruel to his slaves and compels them to immodest behaviour or disgraceful depravity, the role to be played by the governor is made clear by a rescript of the divine Pius addressed to Aelius Marcianus, proconsul of Baetica. These are the terms of the rescript: 'It is correct that the power of masters over their slaves should remain unimpaired, and that no individual should be deprived of his rights. However, it is in the interests of masters that assistance against cruelty, starvation, or intolerable abuse should not be denied to those who justly demand it. Consequently, investigate judicially the complaints of those slaves from the household of Iulius Sabinus who fled to my statue, and if you discover that they have been more harshly treated than is reasonable, or have suffered outrageous abuse, order that they should be put on sale, on the basis that they should not be returned to the power of their master. And if he fraudulently evades my decision, he should know that I will punish him more severely'. Indeed, the divine Hadrian relegated a certain matron called Umbricia for five years because for the most trivial reasons she had treated her maids appallingly.

This decision of Antoninus Pius was an important development because it gave a slave the opportunity to invoke the law for his protection and compel a magistrate to respond, assuming that he could get the attention of anyone in authority; see Williams (1976), 76–7. (For an explanation of 'rescript' see pp. 416–17.) Gaius confirms that:

Among all nations without exception masters have the power of life and death over their slaves, and whatever is acquired by means of the slave is acquired for the master. But nowadays neither Roman citizens nor any other persons who are in the empire of the Roman people are permitted to behave with excessive and purposeless brutality towards their own slaves(*Institutes* 1.52–3).

Seneca, *De Ira* 3.40

9. To rebuke a man when he is angry and to get angry yourself is to provoke him; you should approach him in a varied and relaxed manner, unless you happen to be so important a person that you can reduce his anger, as the divine Augustus did when he was dining with Vedius Pollio. One of his slaves broke a crystal goblet. Vedius ordered him to be seized with the intention that he should die no ordinary death; he ordered that he was to be thrown in among the *murenae* fish, of huge size, which he kept in a pond. Who would not think that he did this because of dissipated extravagance? But it was the result of cruelty. The boy escaped from their hands and fled to the feet of Augustus hoping for nothing other than a different form of death and that he should not be fish bait. Appalled by this unusual cruelty Augustus ordered him to be released, all the crystal goblets to be smashed in his presence, and the pond to be filled in.

In this case the appeal was not to an imperial statue but to the emperor himself. Augustus, as in other matters, gave the lead which he would expect the upper classes to follow. The *De Ira* is one of Seneca's ethical treatises and was probably written early in the reign of Claudius.

Augustus, *Res Gestae* 25.1

10. In that war (against Sextus Pompey in 36 BC) I captured almost 30,000 slaves, who had fled from their masters and taken up arms against the state, and handed them over to their masters for punishment.

The *Res Gestae* consistently present Augustus as a bringer of peace and order to the state. If necessary, Augustus could treat slaves harshly. Sextus Pompey manned his fleet largely with slaves, and after his defeat Augustus crucified 6,000 of them; doubtless he argued that they were hostiles in a war against the Roman state.

D 48.8.11.2 (Modestinus, *Rules*, Book 6)

11. After the Petronian statute and senatorial decisions pertaining to that statute, the power was removed from masters of handing over on their own decision their slaves to fight against the animals in the arena. However, if

the slave is brought before a judge and the master's complaint found to be valid, he can be subjected to that penalty.

The *lex Petronia* is of uncertain date. Despite these well-intentioned efforts to moderate the treatment of slaves they faced many restrictions and an uncertain and abusive environment; see Wiedemann (1981), 167–87; Bradley (1984), 113–38 for the treatment of slaves. A master could grant to his slave any earnings, or a sum of money, or other items (*peculium*); the slave could make use of this though legally it belonged to the master. For the rights of slaves in respect of financial matters and the administration of *peculium* in business matters, see pp. 214–15.

Titles from Ulpian 5.5

12. There is no legal marriage with slaves.

Although liaisons between slaves were tolerated as mentioned earlier (no. 5), and although slaves might recognize family relations among themselves, these had no legal validity; and as slaves legally had no property, they could not make a will. But there was a degree of ambivalence in attitude, and many slaves carried on a kind of family life living as man and wife. Slaves of the emperor who also worked as public slaves had an additional status and performed significant administrative tasks.

CIL 6.5197 = *ILS* 1514

13. To Musicus Scurranus, (slave) of Tiberius Caesar Augustus, steward of the Gallic treasury in the province of Lugdunensis, dedicated to him, as was well-deserved, by those of his under-slaves who were with him in Rome when he died:

Venustus, agent	Agathopus, doctor	Facilis, attendant
Decimianus, treasurer	Epaphra, responsible for silver	Anthus, responsible for silver
Dicaeus, assistant	Primio, in charge of clothes	Hydelus, chamberlain
Mutatus, assistant	Cummunis, chamberlain	Firmus, cook
Creticus, assistant	Pothos, attendant	Secunda
	Tiasus, cook	

Musicus was a minor financial official of the emperor, and, perhaps suspiciously, amassed considerable wealth and status, having at least sixteen under-slaves in his own household, all with carefully designated functions, apart from the lady named Secunda.

CIL 6.5188 = *ILS* 1589

14. Alexander Pylaemenianus, slave of Gaius Caesar Augustus Germanicus in charge of the Greek library of the temple of Apollo, lived thirty years.

Pylaemenianus was slave of the emperor Gaius.

CIL 6.8669 = *ILS* 1617

15. To the spirits of the departed, in honour of Felix, slave of the emperor, steward of the Maiani gardens. Iulia Melitene to her well-deserving husband.

Pliny, *Letters* 10.29–30

16. Pliny to Emperor Trajan. Sempronius Caelianus, a splendid young man, has sent to me two slaves who were discovered among the recruits. I have postponed punishing them until I could consult you, as founder and bulwark of military discipline, about the type of penalty. I hesitate especially because, although they had already sworn the military oath, they had not yet been deployed to a unit. I request, sir, that you convey what course of action I should follow, especially since it may offer a precedent.

Trajan to Pliny. Sempronius Caelianus was acting in accordance with my instructions in sending those men to you, and you will need to investigate if they merit capital punishment; for it matters if they were volunteers, or conscripts, or indeed presented as substitutes. If they were conscripts then the recruiting process was to blame; if they were substitutes the blame lies with those who offered them; but if they volunteered knowing full well their status, they will have to be executed. It is not particularly relevant that they had not yet been deployed to a unit. For the day on which they were approved for military service should have brought out the truth about their status.

Pliny was consul in AD 100, and in 111 was appointed by Trajan to a special commission as *legatus* of Pontus and Bithynia, a position normally held by a proconsul of praetorian rank. Two previous proconsuls had been charged with corruption, and Pliny was to review the political and financial state of the province. This is an example of the official letters Pliny sent to Trajan, either passing on information or seeking advice, to which Trajan and his secretaries replied. Slaves were usually excluded from all branches of the army except occasionally at moments of crisis. In AD 6 and 9 Augustus in response to military reverses in Illyricum and Germany recruited freedmen, and slaves from rich families who were given freedom at once. But they were kept in separate units and not combined with freeborn soldiers (Suetonius, *Augustus* 25.2); Sherwin-White (1966), 598–602. For Pliny the Younger, see p. 480.

Tacitus, *Annals* 12.53

17. Among matters which he (Claudius) referred to the senate was the question of the punishment of women who married slaves. It was decided that if the master (of the slave) had been unaware of this she should descend into slavery, but if he had agreed, she should be considered as his freedwoman.

The government was concerned to control the association of citizens with slaves; the *senatus consultum Claudianum* was introduced under Claudius in AD 52 and very unusually permitted a Roman citizen to be enslaved. If a free woman formed a union with the slave of another person who, on discovering the liaison, disapproved and gave her three warnings which were not heeded, she would become his slave. If he gave his approval, she would become his freedwoman. In the case of illegitimate children from such a union, normally they would follow the status of the mother, but the decree laid down that they became the slaves of the owner of their slave father; see Gardner (1986), 141–2, Grubbs (2002), 145–6; Mouritsen (2011), 21–2 suggests government concern with the contamination of the highest social order; however, Crook (1967), 62–3 argued that free women might willingly pursue a liaison with an important imperial slave, and that the emperor would wish to keep control of the children of his slaves.

D 48.18.1pr-1 (Ulpian, *Duties of a Proconsul*, Book 8)

18. Torture is normally employed to discover crimes; but let us consider when and to what extent this should be carried out. The divine Augustus decided that the investigation should not begin with the inflicting of pain, and that complete trust should not be placed on torture. This idea is also contained in a letter of the divine Hadrian to Sennius Sabinus. The text of the rescript is as follows: 'The torture of slaves should be resorted to only when the accused is already suspected, and the case is so close to being proved by other evidence that only the confession of his slaves is lacking'.

In criminal cases the evidence of slaves could be given only under torture; Wiedemann (1981), 168–71.

Definition of Status: Male and Female

Women of the upper classes were normally held in great respect and their good name was certainly part of the Augustan ideal of a privileged group working with him to sustain the best traditions of Rome. But Roman law was androcentric, based on the traditional male role in politics, war, public business, and the management of the household. Being at the centre of every aspect of civic life, they were more involved with the law, and the legal process took more interest in them than in women and children. Women were regarded as physically weaker than men and to some extent intellectually deficient in respect of carrying on business, and their legal position was restricted. A woman whose *paterfamilias* was dead and who had not on marriage entered the power of her husband's family had to have a guardian (*tutor*); up to the age of puberty (twelve) this was a *tutor impuberum*, but thereafter a guardianship of women (*tutela mulierum*). A guardian would often be nominated by the father in his will, but if not, the woman's closest male relative on her father's side took the role, under which he had a responsibility to protect the paternal property; the guardian did not live with his charge; but various activities such as the manumission of slaves and selling property required his scrutiny and consent (Gardner (1986), 14–22). Augustus permitted free-born women who had borne three children, and freedwomen who had borne four, to conduct their business without a *tutor*; see Grubbs (2002), 23–37. For male views of the intellectual inability of women to deal with legal complexities and also the need to protect female feelings and modesty from the embarrassment of public business, see Grubbs (2002), 46–60; Gardner (1993), 89–97 argues that the continuing practice of *tutela* was largely intended to safeguard a woman's economic situation and prevent the reduction of her property to the detriment of potential heirs, rather than to protect her from any supposed feebleness of mind; for the *Senatus Consultum Velleianum* and women's modesty see further p. 212. It is not indeed clear how strictly financial guardianship was imposed, since Gaius expresses doubts about its necessity (no. 23), and although women were excluded as judges, in the view of Paul that was more a matter of custom and social inertia than lack of intellectual capacity (*D* 5.1.12.2). See the concise survey by Perry (2016).

D 1.5.9 (Papinian, Book 3 of Questions)

19. In many parts of our law the status of women is lower than that of men.

D 1.5.10 (Ulpian, Book 1 on Sabinus)

20. There is the question of intersex persons (hermaphrodites), namely how we class them. I incline to the view that they should be classed according to the sex that is physically prevalent.

Ulpian (*D* 28.2.6.2, book 3 on Sabinus) argued that the presence of *virilia* (male physical characteristics, presumably a penis) were decisive in the definition of a man. The characteristics of masculinity were recognized at birth and in legal terms remained unchanged even if physical conditions changed, for example, through impotence or castration. We can see this from the fact that men in this condition were permitted to make an adoption, a right granted only to men (Gardner (1998b)). Boys were deemed to reach adulthood at fourteen, or at the onset of puberty, girls at twelve whether or not they had attained puberty.

D 34.2.33 (Pomponius, Book 4 on Quintus Mucius)

21. There is no difference between the language 'clothing' for men and 'garments' for men. But the intention of the person making the will sometimes creates a difficulty if he was in the habit of using certain clothing that was also appropriate for women. Therefore, first and foremost it should be made clear if the clothing bequeathed was what the testator had in mind, and not that which was normally used by women or men. Indeed, Quintus Titius Mucius said that he knew of a senator who was accustomed to go to dinner wearing women's clothing, and who, if he made a legacy of women's clothing, could not be considered to intend that clothing which he wore as if it were male clothing.

The jurist is Quintus Mucius Scaevola. He is not interested in the senator's predilection for women's clothes but in the ramifications for the law in testamentary dispositions. The point about gender and clothing identity is that, although clothing was subject to male and female stereotypes, the senator remained a man, and whatever clothes he chose to wear to dinner had to be considered as male clothing. Therefore, if he bequeathed female clothing to someone, that bequest could not include the clothing he wore to dinner. The debate reinforced the concept of male status. The gender distinction in law between men and women also emerges clearly in the purchase of slaves; if a person was sold a female slave while expecting to receive a male, the sale was invalid (see no. 296).

Gaius, *Institutes* 1.144

22. Parents have been permitted to appoint by will guardians for the children whom they have under their power, in the case of male children those under puberty, in the case of female children those of any age, even if they are

married. For old-time lawyers believed that women, even if they were of full age, should be under guardianship because of their uncertain judgement.

Gaius accepted that it was essential that those of immature years should be under guardianship. But he questioned whether mature women should be subject to this imposition since experience showed that they were capable of managing their own affairs.

Gaius, *Institutes* 1.190

23. But there seems to be virtually no convincing argument to support the idea that women of full age should be in the charge of a guardian (in *tutela*). The argument, which is commonly accepted, that because of unstable judgement they are liable to be led astray and that accordingly it was reasonable for them to be guided under the authority of guardians, seems more specious than true. For women of full age deal with their own business, and in certain instances a guardian interposes his authority merely as a matter of routine. In fact, often a guardian is compelled by the praetor to interpose his authority even against his will.

Apuleius, *Apologia* 101.4–5

24. You have claimed that I bought a delightful estate in my name with a large sum of my wife's money. I say that it was a small, insignificant property worth sixty thousand sesterces, and that it was not I, but Pudentilla who bought it in her own name, and that the name of Pudentilla is in the records, and that the tax for this tiny property is paid in the name of Pudentilla. The public treasurer to whom the sum was paid, Cornelius Celer, an illustrious man, is present (in court). The lady's guardian and trustee is also present, Cassius Longinus, an impressive and venerable man, who must be mentioned by me with every honour. Ask him, Maximus, for whose purchase he gave permission, and for what a tiny price this rich lady bought her own little property.

Apuleius, who was well known as a public speaker, is defending himself against charges of using devious means to marry a rich widow for her money; for Apuleius and his appearance in court see also nos. 596–7; 670; 700; Summers (1970). Maximus is Claudius Maximus, proconsul of Africa, before whom the case is being heard. Pudentilla though rich and twice-married still requires a guardian.

Definition of Status: Citizenship

Citizenship by Birth

Gaius, *Institutes* 1.76

25. I am referring of course to those between whom there is no right of *conubium*. For otherwise, if a Roman citizen marries a non-Roman wife with whom he has *conubium*, a proper legal marriage is contracted, as I pointed out before, and therefore the child born from them is a Roman citizen and in the power (*potestas*) of his father.

The basis of Roman citizenship was the birth of a child of a legal Roman marriage where both parties had the right to marriage (*conubium*). In this the child followed the status of the father; on defining a Roman citizen see Gardner (1993), 2–6. *Patria potestas* was the power of the male head of a family over family members. In the imperial period it was of particular importance in respect of economic matters in that a son under paternal power (*filius familias*) could not own property and therefore not make a will or marry without his father's consent.

Citizenship by Grant

Suetonius, *Augustus* 40.3

26. Furthermore, considering it very important to keep the population pure and uncontaminated by any trace of non-Roman or servile blood, he (Augustus) granted Roman citizenship very sparingly and placed a limit on manumissions. He wrote to Tiberius when he asked for citizenship for a Greek dependant of his that he would not grant it unless this man came in person and persuaded him that he had good ground for seeking citizenship. He also refused when Livia requested the citizenship on behalf of a tribute-paying Gaul, but instead offered immunity (from tribute), claiming that he would more willingly accept a loss to the treasury than that the distinction of Roman citizenship should be cheapened.

Suetonius' explanation of Augustus' motivation is conventional but not necessarily untrue. Augustus will have been aware of the historical background of the motley Roman population, but as bringer of peace and order and a return to traditional Roman practices after the excesses of the civil wars, he needed to peddle the idea of a cleansed citizen body, law and order, and assurance that people of lesser degree would be kept in their proper place; hence also the expulsion of unworthy senators and attempts to control upper-class behaviour. For legislation on manumission, see no. 38. For the importance Augustus attached to the citizenship, see no. 788.

Pliny, *Letters* 10.6–7

27. Pliny to Emperor Trajan. Thank you, sir, for speedily granting full citizenship to the freedwomen of my friend Antonia, and Roman citizenship to my medical practitioner Arpocras. But when I was providing his age and property as you instructed, I was advised by those who are more knowledgeable than me that I ought first to have requested Alexandrian citizenship for him, and then Roman, since he is an Egyptian. However, because I did not think that there was any difference between Egyptians and other foreigners, I thought that it was enough to tell you merely that he had been granted freedom by a non-citizen and that his patron was for some time deceased. I shall not complain about my ignorance if it results in my being further obliged to you for the same man. Therefore, I request that you also grant him Alexandrian citizenship so that I may legally enjoy your benefaction. I have sent details of his age and property to your freedmen as instructed, to prevent any further hindrance to your generosity.

Emperor Trajan to Pliny. It is my policy, following the precepts of previous emperors, not to grant Alexandrian citizenship lightly. But since you have already obtained Roman citizenship for your therapist Arpocras, I am unable to refuse this second request. You need to tell me what his district (in Egypt) is, so that I can write you a letter for my friend, Pompeius Planta, prefect of Egypt.

This shows the patronage of well-connected Romans in the acquisition of citizenship. The freedwomen involved had the status of Junian Latins (see p. 35) and sought full Roman citizenship. In the case of Arpocras there was considerable bureaucracy involved because Alexandria with its dominant position and large Greek population was regarded as distinct from the rural areas of Egypt; see Sherwin-White (1966), 568–9; for Alexandrian citizenship in the Roman period see Delia (1991). Although citizenship was still a privilege, a significant extension of citizenship came about by grants to individuals (see no. 29). This was common in the imperial period and increasingly grants were made to whole communities.

Pliny, *Letters* 10.106–7

28. I have been asked, sir, by Publius Accius Aquila, a centurion of the sixth cavalry cohort, to forward to you a petition in which he begs your goodwill in respect of the citizen status of his daughter. I thought it difficult to

refuse, especially since I am well aware of how willingly you give a sympathetic response to the appeals of your soldiers.

I have read the petition of Publius Accius Aquila, centurion of the sixth cavalry cohort, which you sent to me. I am moved by his plea and have granted Roman citizenship to his daughter. I have sent to you the petition with my signature for you to return to him.

Aquila was a centurion in an auxiliary unit but seems already to have Roman citizenship. On his discharge he would expect to receive citizenship for existing children and *conubium* with a woman, which would ensure that future children were citizens. He was presumably hoping to obtain the benefits of citizenship as early as possible.

AE 1971.534; Sherwin-White (1973b), 86 (c. AD 168)

29. Copy of a letter of our emperors Antoninus and Verus to Coiiedius (*sic*) Maximus. 'We have read the petition of Iulianus Zegrensis attached to your letter, and although Roman citizenship is not normally bestowed on those peoples unless earned by the greatest services and through imperial goodwill, nevertheless since you confirm that he comes from the foremost of his own people and is very loyal and extremely supportive of our affairs, and since we think that few families among the Zegrenses can make similar claims about their services, and we wish to encourage as many as possible to emulate Iulianus through the honour conferred by us on his house, we have no hesitation in granting Roman citizenship, without prejudice to the rights of the tribe, to Iulianus himself, to Ziddina his wife, and also to his children, Iulianus, Maximus, Maximinus, Diogenianus'.

Coiedius Maximus was governor of Mauretania Tingitana c. 168. The inscription contains this letter and a second (AD 177) referring to a further grant of citizenship to the family of the children of Iulianus by Marcus Aurelius and Commodus in response to a petition; there is also a quotation from the imperial archives. The awards were recorded in an official register of grants of Roman citizenship to individuals by emperors, going back to Augustus. Reference is made to a file of documents kept by a freedman listing individual grants of citizenship with details of names and age, and Pliny's letter to Trajan (no. 27) also shows the importance of recording the prospective citizen's personal details. Grants of citizenship often specifically ensured that there was no infringement of the rights of the local community to require public service from its members who became Roman citizens and excluded any exemption from Roman taxation. See also Augustus' third Cyrene edict (no. 30).

FIRA I, no. 68, III (7/6 BC)

30. Imperator Caesar Augustus, chief priest, in the seventeenth year of his tribunician power declares: If any people from the province of Cyrene have been honoured with Roman citizenship, I order that they must nonetheless perform their local obligations in their turn as if part of the Greek community, with the exception of those to whom, in accordance with statute, or decree of the senate, or decision of my father (Julius Caesar) or myself, immunity from tribute was granted along with the citizenship. In the case of those people to whom immunity from tribute has been granted, it is my wish that they should have immunity in respect of that property which they had at that time but should undertake their obligations for everything they acquired subsequently.

Augustus' third edict from Cyrene emphasizes that those granted Roman citizenship were not exempt from liturgies unless they had also received immunity from tribute, which is taken to confer immunity from local obligations. Presumably it was tempting for new citizens to argue that they were exempt from local obligations, but that could have been disastrous for the financial situation of their home community (see Millar (1983), 84–5); newly created Roman citizens would retain the citizenship of their local community; see p. 35. For the disputed interpretation of the phrase translated here 'as if part of the Greek community' see Sherwin-White (1973a), 334–6.

FIRA I, no. 71 = Smallwood (1967), no. 368 (AD 46)

31. With reference to the status of the Anauni and Tuliasses and Sinduni, it is said to have been demonstrated by an informer that some of them are attributed to the Tridentini and some not attributed at all, and although I think that this group of people does not have a strong claim to Roman citizenship, nevertheless since they are said by usage over a long period to be in possession of it, and are so intertwined with the Tridentini that they could not be separated from them without serious damage to that outstanding community, through my generosity I permit them to retain the legal status which they thought they had, and all the more willingly because several from that category of people are said to be serving in my praetorian guard, and some have even been promoted to centurion, and several have been co-opted onto the jury panels in Rome and are serving as jurors.

I grant this benefaction to them on the basis that I confirm the legality of whatever business they conducted or transacted as if they were Roman citizens, either among themselves, or with the Tridentini, or others, and I permit that they should retain the names they previously had as if they were Roman citizens.

Claudius here makes a grant of citizenship to an entire community. The small settlement of the Anauni had been attached for administrative purposes to Tridentium, whose citizens had Roman citizenship, and over a period of years had come to assume that they enjoyed the same status; Sherwin-White (1973a), 374–5.

ILS 212 = *FIRA* 1.43 = Smallwood (1967), no. 369; Malloch (2020), (AD 48) (Extract)

32. (Claudius is referring to the history of innovation in Rome and the willingness to extend Roman citizenship) Indeed it was an innovation when my great-uncle, the divine Augustus, and my uncle Tiberius Caesar desired to admit to this senate house all the flower of the colonies and municipalities wherever they were to be found, provided of course that they were sound and wealthy men. But what is the next step? Is a senator from Italy not better than a senator from the provinces? I shall reveal to you by my actions what I think about that question when I begin to justify this part of my censorship. However, I do not think that even men from the provinces should be rejected, provided that they can bring distinction to the senate house.

Claudius' speech to the senate is reported and adapted by Tacitus (*Annals* 11.24). The council of the Gallic provinces had requested permission to stand for office and enter the senate, an indication of the extension of citizenship; the move was resisted by senators. Gaul beyond the Alps was Gallia Comata ('Long-haired' Gaul) and was not in the same position to provide senators as Narbonensis between the Mediterranean and Lake Geneva which was heavily Romanized, with its main centre at Narbo; see Malloch (2020), 26–41. Permission was initially granted to the Aedui (Tacitus, *Annals* 11.25), though senators from Gallia Comata were rare in the first century. Claudius himself had been born at Lugdunum. Lavan (2019) interestingly argues that the award of citizenship could be a way of control, and of differentiating between the various inhabitants of the empire, not necessarily of uniting them.

ILS 1986 = Smallwood (1967), 295 (AD 52)

33. Tiberius Claudius Caesar Augustus Germanicus, chief priest, in the twelfth year of his tribunician power, acclaimed *imperator* twenty-seven times, father of the fatherland, censor, consul for the fifth time, has granted to the trierarchs and oarsmen who served in the fleet which is at Misenum under the command of Tiberius Iulius Optatus, freedman of the emperor, and who were honourably discharged, and whose names are written below,

to them, their children, and their posterity, citizenship and the right of marriage (*conubium*) with the wives they had when citizenship was granted to them, or, if they were unmarried, with those whom they married afterwards, limited to one wife for each man.

11 December in the consulship of Faustus Cornelius Sulla Felix and Lucius Salvidienus Rufus Salvianus.

To the common sailor Sparticus Dipscurtus, son of Diuzenus, a Bessian.

Recorded and authenticated from the bronze plaque which has been affixed at Rome on the Capitoline, on the right-hand side of the temple of the Faith of the Roman people.

(There follow the names of witnesses.)

Auxiliary soldiers were generally non-citizens recruited from less Romanized provinces or areas on the periphery of the empire. On completion of twenty-five years' service or on discharge it became the practice to grant Roman citizenship to the soldier and any children he had; the grant of *conubium* with a woman, even if non-Roman, meant that subsequent children would also be citizens. In the 140s the award of citizenship to existing children was withdrawn for reasons that are not clear. The practice of awarding a bronze certificate (now termed a diploma) for these privileges dates at least from the reign of Claudius; see Campbell (1994), 193–203.

González (1986), *lex Irnitana*, Chapter 21

34. Concerning how they may acquire Roman citizenship in that *municipium*.

Whoever from the senators, decurions, or *conscripti* of the *Municipium Flavium Irnitanum* are appointed, or will be appointed, as magistrates, as is provided for in this statute, they, when they relinquish their office, are to be Roman citizens, along with their parents, wives, and children, who were born from legal marriage and have been in the power of their parents, and similarly grandsons and granddaughters born to a son, who both have been in the power of their parents, provided that there should be no more Roman citizens than the number of magistrates that it is right to appoint in accordance with this statute.

The *lex Irnitana* set out the rules governing the establishment of a *municipium* at Irni in Spain; the context is a grant of Latin rights (see p. 34) to Baetica by Vespasian probably in AD 73/4 (Pliny *NH* 3.30), though it was perhaps up to local communities to take up this offer (Sherwin-White (1973a), 360–7). In line with that grant each community received a statute setting out the relevant rules for its government. Sections of the municipal statutes of Malaca and Salpensa also survive and bear a close relationship to that of Irni. Clause 21 provides that existing and future magistrates of the community (and certain family members though excluding adopted children and the magistrate's brothers and sisters) will receive Roman citizenship on laying down their office (González (1986), 202–3); see no. 50. For local citizenship and the rights of those who did not become magistrates, see p. 35.

Suetonius, *Claudius* 25.3

35. He (Claudius) forbade men of foreign extraction to usurp Roman names at least in respect of clan names. Those who had usurped the rights of Roman citizenship he executed in the Esquiline field.

Clan names would be names such as Iulius, Claudius, Cornelius. Usurpation of citizenship had been a serious offence in the republic and the *lex Licinia Mucia* established penalties for non-citizens living in Rome who conducted themselves as citizens. Although citizenship was extended with increasing generosity, the rules governing its award had to be scrupulously observed.

***BGU* 1210 = *SP* no. 206, Sections 53 and 56 (*Gnomon* of the *Idios Logos*)**

36. Egyptian women who are married to discharged soldiers, if they present themselves as Romans, are liable to the rule on not adhering to status.

Soldiers who do not have a legal discharge, if they present themselves as Romans, are fined one quarter of their property.

The *Idios Logos* was a senior Roman official of equestrian status who was responsible for all financial activities in Egypt apart from regular taxation, including various fines and confiscations of property with particular attention to property that fell to the *patrimonium*, and also for measures to control status; the *Gnomon* was the schedule of regulations administered by this official; analysis in Swarney (1970). Although discharged Roman soldiers were granted certain rights of marriage so that any subsequent children were citizens, their wives were not formally citizens. Soldiers will normally have formed liaisons with women of non-Roman status in the provinces.

Citizenship by Manumission

Gaius, *Institutes* 1.10–11

37. Next, free men are either freeborn (*ingenui*), or freedmen (*libertini*). *Ingenui* are those who have been born free, *libertini* are those who have been set free from lawful slavery.

Slaves were set free from the power of their master by an act of manumission, most commonly before a magistrate in a trial which was a legal fiction, in which a third person proclaimed the slave to be free and his owner did not object (*manumissio vindicta*), or by a provision in his will by the owner, or by simple enrolment in the list of Roman citizens during the census with no objection from his owner. Another method of manumission was through a private ceremony before witnesses, though this informal process conferred rather uncertain rights on the ex-slave; see p. 35.

Gaius, *Institutes* 1.17

38. A slave in whom these three requirements come together, namely that he be more than thirty years old, be the Quiritary property of his master, and be set free by a proper and statutory manumission, that is by rod (*vindicta*), or census, or by will, becomes a Roman citizen. But if any one of these requirements is missing, he will be a Latin.

Quiritary refers to ownership acquired by a citizen through the *ius civile*. Augustan legislation attempted to control manumissions; the *lex Fufia Caninia* of 2 BC limited the number of manumissions possible in a will by establishing a ratio between the manumissions and the total number of slaves owned by the master, up to a maximum of one hundred. The *Lex Aelia Sentia* of AD 4 laid down that the slave manumitted had to be over thirty and the manumitting owner over twenty years of age. There was also provision to ensure that any creditors of the slave's master did not suffer any loss. The purpose of the legislation sponsored by Augustus is unclear. Since most slaves manumitted in Rome from large domestic establishments would probably stay in the city, Augustus may have aimed to limit the number of people from this source in Rome; discussion in Sherwin-White (1973a), 327–31; Bradley (1984), 91 argued that the measures were intended to prevent ostentatious display by the wealthy in freeing large numbers of slaves by their will, while Gardner (1993), 39–41 believed that the intention was to protect large estates and control the number of slaves manumitted by childless testators; such freedmen would have no bonds of loyalty to any Roman family. Mouritsen (2011), 80–92, while doubting that Augustan legislation was part of a broader cultural and ethnic policy to preserve the Italic population, notes that after the disturbance and social dislocation of the triumviral period, Augustus for political reasons wished to put a visible curb on the process of freeing slaves, and establish certain standards for manumitted slaves, as the rise of freedmen in defiance of social conventions could be seen as symbolic of the disorder of society. But the state had limited interest in manumission, and it was left to the owners to decide on who was worthy of freedom; for the practice of manumission see Wiedemann (1981), 50–60; Bradley (1984), 81–112; Mouritsen (2011), 120–205; for a survey of the number of manumissions in the context of Roman treatment of slaves, and the potential economic benefits to masters, see Hopkins (1978), 115–32.

Gaius, *Institutes* 1.42–3

39. Furthermore, by the *lex Fufia Caninia* a limit has been set on the manumission of slaves by will. (43) For the master who has more than two and not more than ten slaves, is permitted to manumit up to half that number (there follows a sliding scale for the number of slaves); finally the master who has more than one hundred and not more than five hundred slaves is permitted to manumit no more than a fifth ... but if a master has only one or two slaves he is not liable under this law, and therefore has unrestricted right of manumission.

Mouritsen (2011), 180–5 argues that for economic and other reasons slave-owners may have found it preferable to free slaves during their lifetime, and that manumission by testament was possibly fairly limited.

Gaius, *Institutes* 1.15

40. Slaves who have been disgraced in the way mentioned (that is, if they have been put in restraints by their master, or branded, or have been found guilty of wrongdoing, or have been sent to the arena or gladiatorial school), by whatever method and at whatever age they are manumitted, even though they were fully legally owned by their masters, never become either Roman citizens or Latins, but I reckon that they are always classed as *dediticii*.

In AD 212 or early 213 when the emperor Caracalla extended Roman citizenship to all the free population of the empire, only a particular class of ex-slave was excluded, the *dediticii*, who had committed a serious offence during their slavery. See Oliver (1989), no. 260 and this volume, no. 726.

Latins

Rome after the defeat of the peoples of Latium in 338 BC made peace settlements with individual Latin communities, often including the right of marriage (*conubium*) and commerce (*commercium*) with Roman citizens. After the Social War in 90 BC, they gained Roman citizenship and the term 'Latin' ceased to designate anything in linguistic or ethnic terms but did retain a legal significance in that the Latin right (*ius Latii*) was conferred on individual communities (*municipia*) in the provinces from the late republic onwards. The *lex Iulia Municipialis*, the work of Julius Caesar or Augustus, established a general framework for the constitution of *municipia*, which then received individual charters providing for local traditions and requirements; for the establishment and development of municipal charters in the late republic, see Bispham (2007), 205–46; 414–24. In these communities, ex-magistrates and certain other family members received Roman citizenship (see no. 34). Gaius, *Institutes* 1.96 distinguishes between grants of greater *ius Latii* to communities, which meant that town councillors (decurions) as well as high magistrates got Roman citizenship, and lesser *ius Latii* which meant only high magistrates received citizenship. Grants of greater *ius Latii* were probably no earlier than the time of Hadrian; the earliest clear indication is an inscription from the time of Antoninus Pius (see Millar (1977), 405–6; Lintott (1993), 165). It is possible that magistrates and decurions were the only people in these communities who had any citizen rights, and that the 'Latins' of Spanish charters such as that of Irni are Junian Latins (Millar (1977), 630–5). Gardner (2001) agrees with Millar that inhabitants of *municipia* granted Latin status did not become a kind of provincial Latin halfway between a non-Roman and a Roman citizen, and that *Latini* were effectively Junian Latins. She contends that the *ius Latii* could function only if those receiving Roman citizenship retained their local citizenship, including the right to vote and hold office and maintain private rights; otherwise, family arrangements would be disrupted, and it would be difficult to perpetuate the local elite from whom magistrates were drawn in the future and on which Rome relied for local administration.

Augustus' laws restricting manumission meant that slaves who had been set free in breach of proper procedures were in a nebulous status of being 'informally free'. The position of these Junian Latins (*Latini Iuniani*) was addressed by a *lex Iunia* of uncertain date but probably the work of Augustus or Tiberius, which provided a civil status for this category of freedmen (Crook (1967), 43–5; Sherwin-White (1973a), 328–34). Their status was based on the old *ius Latii* giving them Latin rights for their lifetime. There were opportunities for promotion to citizen status; one was through direct intervention by an emperor either as a favour or for services rendered. Another route led to full citizenship for descendants; if a son or daughter was born through legitimate marriage to a Roman citizen or a Latin, by application when the child reached the age of one, citizenship was granted to the *Latinus Iunianus*, the child, and his wife if necessary (*Tit. Ulp*. 3.1–3).

All other free inhabitants of the Roman empire were non-Romans (*peregrini*); see no. 43.

Gaius, *Institutes* 1.32 c-33

41. Furthermore, through an edict of Claudius, Latins obtain citizen status if they have built a sea-going vessel with a capacity of not less than ten thousand measures of corn, and that ship, or another substituted for it, has conveyed corn to Rome for six years. (33) Besides, it has been laid down by Nero that a Latin who has property to the value of two hundred thousand sesterces or more, and who has built a house in Rome, on which he has spent not less than half his resources, should obtain citizen status.

The grain supply was a particular concern to Claudius (Suetonius, *Claudius* 18) and various measures were introduced to ensure supply and storage; see Levick (1990), 111–12; and p. 79.

Pliny, *Letters* 10.104–5

42. Pliny to Emperor Trajan. My lord, Valerius Paulinus in his will has omitted Paulinus his son and appointed me as patron of his Latin freedmen (*Junii Latini*); I request that you grant Roman citizenship to just three of them for the moment. I fear that it might be unreasonable to call upon your goodwill for all alike, and I must use it in moderation, the more so in that I have benefitted so much from it. These are the names of the three for whom I am making the petition: C. Valerius Astraeus, C. Valerius Dionysius, C. Valerius Aper.

Trajan to Pliny. Since you have acted most commendably in speedily interceding with me on behalf of the freedmen entrusted to your care by Valerius Paulinus, I have ordered that it is to be entered in the official records that I have at this moment given Roman citizenship to those for whom you are now petitioning, and I am prepared to do the same for any others for whom you may petition.

Junian Latins could not make a will and consequently their property would revert to their former master. In this case Paulinus has left these patronal rights to Pliny rather than to his son; after the death of Paulinus, Pliny as heir requested that Trajan grant them full citizenship through a *beneficium*, and the response was generous. A Junian Latin who obtained full citizenship against the wishes or without the knowledge of his patron reverted to Latin status on his death (Gaius, *Institutes* 3.72).

Non-Romans (Peregrini)

Gaius, *Institutes* 1.78

43. In respect of what I said, namely that the child of a union between a Roman woman and a peregrine, unless there is *conubium*, is a peregrine, this is established by the *lex Minicia*, which states that the child follows the status of the peregrine parent. In the opposite case, where a Roman citizen takes as wife a peregrine woman with whom he does not have *conubium*, the same law states that the offspring of that union is a peregrine.

Proving Your Status

***FIRA* 3, no. 3 (AD 144)**

44. In the consulship of L. Lollianus Avitus and T. Statilius Maximus, 15 October, in the eighth year of Emperor Caesar Titus Aelius Hadrianus Antoninus Augustus Pius, month of Phaoph, eighteenth day, at Alexandria in Egypt.

Copied and verified from the tablet of the album of statements in which the births of children are attested, which was on display in the Great Atrium, on which was inscribed the entry written below.

In the consulship of L. Lollianus Avitus and T. Statilius Maximus, in the seventh year of Emperor Caesar Titus Aelius Hadrianus Antoninus Augustus Pius, L. Valerius Proculus being prefect of Egypt: Statements concerning the birth of children which were accepted without examination of the material, tablet two, and, after other items, page two, also in the eighth year of Emperor Antoninus, our lord, under the same consuls, and also on page three, 13 September:

M. Valerius Turbo (stated) that a son, M. Valerius Maximus, had been born to him from Antonia Casullute on 18 August just past. (He is) a Roman citizen in the ledger(?).

Regnal year eight appears in the second part of the document because the statements of that year had been included in the page relating to the previous year seven. It was important for proof of status as a citizen to have lodged a declaration of the birth of legitimate children. One possible and visible proof of citizenship was possession of three names: *praenomen*, *nomen*, and *cognomen*, the traditional form of Roman nomenclature; it was a serious matter to misrepresent yourself as citizen in this way, invoking the charge of forgery (*D* 48.10.13pr.); see also no. 36.

Tabulae Herculanenses 24

45. I, Gaius Petronius Telesphorus, have written and sworn by the spirit of Emperor Augustus (Vespasian) and his sons that I know that the girl Iusta, subject of the law suit, was born free, the child of my fellow-freedwoman Petronia Vitalis; and that it was I who reached agreement with Petronius Stephanus and Calatoria Themis that he should accept payment for the raising of the child and return her to her mother. From these facts I know that the woman Iusta, subject of the lawsuit, was born in freedom as the daughter of Petronia Vitalis, which is the matter at issue.

I, Quintus Tamudius Optatus, have written and sworn by the spirit of Emperor Vespasian Caesar Augustus and his sons that I was present when Petronia Vitalis discussed the girl, her daughter, with Calatoria Themis; and that I heard Stephanus the husband of Themis at that moment say to Petronia Vitalis: 'Why are you annoyed with us concerning the child, considering that we are treating her as our own daughter?' From this I know that the woman, subject of the lawsuit, is the daughter of Petronia Vitalis and is of free birth, which is the matter at issue.

I, (??), have written at the request of Marcus Calatorius Marullus and in his presence, because he stated that he was illiterate, that he has sworn by the spirit of Emperor Vespasian and his sons that: 'I know that Calatoria Themis manumitted both the girl and me; from this I know that the girl is the freedwoman of Calatoria Themis, which is the matter at issue'.

Pugliese Carratelli (1948), 168–80; Crook (1967), 48–50; Metzger (2005), 155–63; and see p. 347 for *vadimonium*. The case concerned the status of Petronia Iusta, illegitimate daughter of Petronia Vitalis, who had been manumitted sometime in the past by Calatoria Themis and Petronius Stephanus. Iusta, who was probably the plaintiff, had lived with Calatoria Themis and Petronius Stephanus for a period after her mother's manumission and was then taken back by her mother after the payment of expenses to Petronius for her upkeep. At the time of the lawsuit both Petronia Vitalis and Petronius Stephanus had died. The lawsuit was between Iusta and Calatoria Themis, the crucial issue being over the time of Iusta's birth; she was freeborn if born after her mother's manumission, but a freedwoman if born before (and subsequently manumitted by Calatoria); in which case Calatoria would have the rights of a patron over her. There are seven pieces of evidence (*testimonia*) from witnesses on both sides of the argument, and three *vadimonia* (*TH* 13–15) requiring an appearance before the magistrate. *Testimonia* were probably prepared unofficially, but the magistrate ordered their collection in order to be certain that there was some substance to the case before instructing the litigants to appear before the urban praetor in Rome.

BGU 1690 = *FIRA* 3, no. 5 (AD 131)

46. Epimachus, son of Longinus, soldier of the second cohort of Thebans, century of Octavius Alexander [affirmed ...] that a daughter, Longinia, had been born to him on 26 December just past, from Arsutis, daughter of Lucius, his concubine. Therefore, he said that he had made this declaration because of the restriction imposed by military service. Carried out at Philadelphia in the winter quarters of the second cohort of Thebans on 26 December, in the consulship of S [ergius Octavius] Laenas Pontianus and Marcus Antonius Rufinus, in the sixteenth year of Emperor Caesar Trajan Hadrian Augustus, month Chioak thirtieth day.

(In Greek) I, Epimachus, son of Longinus, the soldier mentioned above, have affirmed that my daughter, Longinia, was born, just as is written above.

Soldiers were not permitted to form a legally valid marriage. If they had a liaison with local women, the children would be illegitimate and not Roman citizens. They therefore made unofficial declarations before witnesses of their child's birth, which would establish the child's identity and assist future claims on the soldier's property, and on discharge when citizenship was granted to the soldier's children.

SP no. 315 (AD 188)

47. From the volume of records of examinations which have the outside title: Examinations of Longaeus Rufus, previous prefect, conducted by Allius Hermolaus, tribune of legion II Trajana Brave, from Epeiph 25 to Thoth 29, of year twenty-six of Aurelius Commodus Antoninus Caesar, the lord. After other entries, on the first page: Valerius Clemens, who wishes to live for a time in the Arsinoite nome, aged (left blank) years. The above-mentioned, a veteran, stated that he had served in the second cohort of Itureans, and presented a letter written in Latin from Pactumeius Magnus, the former commander, by which he demonstrated that having served in the above-mentioned cohort he had been officially discharged on 31 December in the consulship of Aurelius Commodus Antoninus Augustus Pius and Quintillus. He presented as his guarantors Marcus Aurelius Petesouchus, Serenus Petronius, and Iulius Gemellus, all three being veteran soldiers, who wrote out a declaration with him that he had not made use of concocted material. And the signature of Allius Hermolaus, tribune of legion II Trajana Brave, is attached to the above-mentioned name, Valerius Clemens, fifty-two years of age, with a scar

above the ankle of his right foot. I, Avius Callimachus, keeper of the records confirm that the original is here. Year twenty-eight of Aurelius Commodus Antoninus Caesar, the lord, Pauni 17.

Examination record of Valerius Clemens verified.

Soldiers serving in this auxiliary unit would normally not be Roman citizens but acquired citizenship on discharge. Valerius Clemens needs to demonstrate that he is honourably discharged and a citizen, in order to prove his status as a veteran and claim any rights to which he was entitled in the community in which he intended to settle; he had apparently not received or had lost a discharge diploma.

Rights and Responsibilities

The essential rights of Roman citizens were: to vote in the assembly of plebs or other assemblies on legislation (increasingly meaningless in the imperial period), to vote in the election of magistrates (also of much less importance), to form a legally valid marriage (*conubium*), to carry on business dealings under Roman law (*commercium*), to appeal to the emperor in certain circumstances against a capital sentence (see p. 446), which offered protection against arbitrary capital punishment by magistrates, provincial governors, and local officials. By the end of the second century AD the value of the citizenship had to some extent been superseded by the status of *honestiores* (members of the wealthy elite), who were distinguished from the *humiliores* (those of lesser station); see Garnsey (1970), 221–76, and this volume, p. 398. Some citizens also had the opportunity to obtain certain benefits depending on place of residence, such as a free corn distribution in Rome and provision of games and shows. Citizenship also brought responsibilities, notably that of service in the army during the republic. In the imperial era conscription in Italy was rare, though volunteers were welcome. For Roman citizens service was available in the praetorian guard (particularly favoured by Italians) and in the legions, though by the late second century they were also serving in the *auxilia*, which had originally been dominated by non-citizens. It was the upper classes who now shouldered most of the responsibilities of citizenship, while facing government interference with their family life and marital relations. Senators and *equites* were expected to make themselves available for magistracies or posts in the emperor's service, governing provinces, commanding soldiers, and administering the public services in Rome.

Acts of the Apostles 16.16; 18–24; 35–9

48. (16) When we were on our way to the place of prayer, we happened to meet a young girl who had the spirit of prophecy. By predicting the future she was providing a considerable profit for her owners ... (18) Paul becoming disturbed by this, turned and spoke to the spirit: 'I tell you in the name of Jesus Christ to come out of her'. And it came out of her immediately. (19) When her owners saw that their hope of profit had gone, they grabbed Paul and Silas and dragged them to the marketplace to the authorities. (20) They brought them before the magistrates and said: 'These men are Jews and are causing uproar in our city (21) by advocating practices which it is not right for us to accept to carry out, as we are Roman'. (22) The mob joined in the attack on them, and the magistrates, ripping off their clothes, ordered them to be flogged. (23) After they had inflicted many blows they threw them into prison and ordered the jailer to guard them carefully. (24) In response to these orders he lodged them in the inner part of the prison and secured their feet in the stocks ... .

(35) At daybreak the magistrates sent their attendants with the instruction: 'Release those men'. (36) The jailer reported these words to Paul: 'The magistrates have sent word that you are to be released. So, leave now and go in peace'. (37) But Paul said to them: 'They beat us in public without a trial, even though we are Roman citizens, and threw us in prison. And now they secretly throw us out. No! Let them come themselves and escort us out'. (38) The attendants reported these words to the magistrates. When they heard that they were Romans they were terrified, (39) and came personally to appease them, and bringing them out asked them to leave the city.

This incident took place at the Roman colony of Philippi in Macedonia. The *strategoi* (the leading magistrates in Greek cities) had the right to inflict flogging to protect the peace against interlopers. But Roman citizens were not subject to this since they had the right of appeal against a capital sentence. This is a good example of the status of Roman citizens in the early imperial period, and the respect in which that was held by local magistrates. In Egypt in AD 153 witnesses testify in a deposition to seeing a veteran and Roman citizen, Gaius Maevius Apellas, being flogged on the orders of a *strategos*; presumably the veteran was preparing to bring a case (*SP* 254).

CIL 2.159 = *ILS* 1978

49. In honour of Publius Cornelius Macer, of the Quirina tribe, granted citizenship individually by the divine Claudius, quaestor, member of the

board of two, in accordance with his will ... Quintius Capito, his heir, set this up along with Quintus his son.

This inscription from near Ammaia in the province of Lusitania proudly emphasizes the personal grant of citizenship by the emperor.

ILS 1982 = McCrum and Woodhead (1961), no. 480

50. To Emperor Domitian Caesar Augustus Germanicus, Lucius Munius Novatus of the Quirina tribe and Lucius Munius Aurelianus, son of Lucius, of the Quirina tribe, having acquired Roman citizenship through holding office as members of the board of two, erected this monument at their own expense.

This celebratory inscription from Iluro in Spain illustrates the value of citizenship to provincial notables, acquired in this case by holding a local magistracy. Plutarch, writing in the second century AD, notes sarcastically the ambitions of well-to-do Greek provincials not only to acquire Roman citizenship but to advance to high office.

Plutarch, *On Peace of Mind* 10 (*Moralia* 470 C)

51. But there is a different type of person, from Chios, or Galatia, or Bithynia, who finds no joy in winning the glory or power that are part of a certain standing among his fellow-citizens. He cries because he does not wear the shoes of a senator of patrician rank; but if he does wear them, because he has not yet become a Roman praetor; and if he has become a praetor, because he is not consul; and when he is consul, because he was not first to be declared as elected but came in later.

Plutarch's *Moralia* dealt with issues relevant to popular moral philosophy; here he notes the ambitions of many in the Greek east of the empire to be Roman citizens and move up in Roman social circles. For Plutarch, see p. 480.

Status and Social Groups

Senators

Dio 52.19.1–4

52. I argue, therefore, that right away you should pick out and choose the entire membership of the senate, since some unsuitable persons have become senators because of the civil wars, and retain those who have some merit while removing the rest from the roll. But do not remove any good man

because he is poor, but indeed give him the appropriate sum of money. In place of those who have been removed bring in the most noble, the best, and the richest, choosing them not only from Italy, but also from the allies and the subject peoples. By doing this you will have numerous assistants, and you will keep in security the leading men from all the peoples, who will not start revolts since they have no distinguished leaders, and whose leading citizens support you because they have come to share in the empire with you.

Follow the same procedure in respect of the *equites*. Select for the equestrian order those who hold the second rank in each area in birth, excellence, and wealth. Enrol as many members of both groups as you wish, and do not overly concern yourself with their numbers.

For Dio see p. 477. This is part of the fictional speech that Dio attributes to Maecenas in 29 BC, offering advice to Augustus on how to run the empire. In the speech Dio, as a senator, expresses his own views on what constituted an acceptable form of autocracy in the late second century, and it is notable that he emphasizes the importance of the status and responsibilities of senators and *equites* as being the best people in society; see Millar (1964), 111–18.

Dio 54.17.3

53. He permitted to stand for office all those who had property to the value of four hundred thousand sesterces and who were eligible according to the law to hold office. He laid down this as the first senatorial census requirement, but later raised it to one million sesterces.

See also 54.26.3; Tacitus, *Annals* 1.75. Suetonius (*Augustus* 41.1) mentions 1,200,000 sesterces raised from 800,000, perhaps indicating experimentation by Augustus. In their clothing senators had an indication of their rank, notably a broad purple stripe on their tunic, and by the early second century an honorific appellation *vir clarissimus* (distinguished man) was reserved for them; for the status of senators see Talbert (1984), 10–13; 493–5. The wife of a senator could be designated *clarissima* (see no. 54). Women of rank, however, could not vote, or take part directly in politics, or hold office, or participate in the business of the forum. Women could sometimes be influential, but that often came about through their membership of a wealthy upper-class family. For men, senatorial rank also provided an avenue to holding important offices in the service of the emperor. These privileges brought with them the expectation of behaviour consonant with the imperial image of upper-class respectability.

D 1.9.8 (Ulpian, *Fideicommissa*, Book 6)

54. The description 'most distinguished persons' includes those women who are married to men who are most distinguished. But the daughters of

senators are not described as 'most distinguished women', unless they happen to have husbands who are most distinguished. Husbands bestow on their wives the dignity of being most distinguished, but parents do so (on their children) only until they have undertaken marriage with a plebeian. Therefore, a woman will be most distinguished as long as she is married to a senator, a most distinguished man, or is separated from him but has not married another person of inferior rank.

See Grubbs (2002), 72 for the status of women married to senators.

D 1.9.1 (Ulpian, *Edict*, Book 62)

55. No one doubts that a man of consular rank must always take preference over a lady of consular rank. But we need to consider if a man of prefectorial rank takes precedence over a lady of consular rank. I incline to think that he does take precedence, because the greater status is inherent in the male sex. We apply the term consular to ladies who are married to men who have held the consulship. Saturninus also adds their mothers, but that is not mentioned anywhere and is not accepted practice.

Prefectorial rank must refer to *equites* holding senior positions such as praetorian prefect or prefect of Egypt.

D 50.17.2 (Ulpian, *Sabinus*, Book 1)

56. Women are excluded from all civil or public functions, and therefore cannot serve as judges, or hold a magistracy, or initiate a lawsuit, or intervene on behalf of another, or act as procurators. Similarly, a male who has not reached puberty should keep out of all civil functions.

For the limitations in legal matters imposed by gender, see Gardner (1986), 261–5; also, this volume pp. 23–5.

CIL 14.3608 = *ILS* 986 (Tibur)

57. To Tiberius Plautius Silvanus Aelianus, son of Marcus, of the Aniensis tribe, priest, *sodalis Augusti*, member of the board of two for striking gold and silver coinage, quaestor of Tiberius Caesar, legate of the fifth legion in Germany, urban praetor, legate, and companion of Claudius Caesar in Britain, consul, proconsul of Asia, governor with propraetorian power of Moesia, in which post he brought across (the river) more than one hundred thousand from the peoples who live on the other side of the Danube, along

with their wives and children, and their leaders or kings, for the payment of tribute. He suppressed a disturbance in the east among the Sarmatians, although he had dispatched a large part of his army for the expedition into Armenia. He brought kings previously unknown or hostile to the Roman people to offer obeisance to the Roman standards on the riverbank which he was guarding. He returned their sons to the kings of the Bastarnae and Rhoxolani, and to the king of the Dacians his brothers who had been captured or seized from the enemy. He received hostages from several of them by which he protected and enhanced the peace of the province. Furthermore, he forced the king of the Scythians to withdraw from his siege of the Chersonesus, which is beyond the Borysthenes (Dnieper). He was the first to assist the corn supply of the Roman people with a great quantity of corn from that province (Moesia). After he had been sent as governor of Spain, he was recalled to take up the prefecture of the city, and during his tenure the senate honoured him with the ornaments of a triumph, on the initiative of Caesar Augustus Vespasian, in the words of his speech which are set out below:

'His conduct as governor of Moesia was such that his honour of the ornaments of a triumph should not have been postponed for me to award, except that through the delay he has acquired even more renown as prefect of the city'.

During this prefecture of the city Emperor Caesar Augustus Vespasian appointed him consul for the second time (AD 74).

The honour and status of senators and *equites* were to some extent confirmed and expressed by holding magistracies and other offices, and by celebrating this in inscriptions erected either in their lifetime or after death. The inscription serves as an example of a senator who held routine magistracies but also as governor of Moesia achieved considerable military success. Vespasian's praise of the senator contains implicit criticism of Nero's failure to reward him. It is notable that the position of consul is still held in great respect. Senators were expected to accept any kind of responsibility if required, but some held more posts involving the command of soldiers while others, like Pliny the Younger, concentrated on civil administration; for a survey of senatorial office-holding see Birley (2005), 3–14.

Tacitus, *Agricola* 9

58. When Agricola returned to Rome from the command of a legion (in Britain) Vespasian enrolled him among those of patrician rank. Next, he appointed him governor of Aquitania, an important position in respect of its duties and carrying with it the expectation of a consulship, for which indeed he was marked out. Some people think that finesse is lacking in military

commanders because jurisdiction in the camp, being straightforward and rather blunt and to a large extent exercised summarily, does not develop the skills of the law courts in Rome. But Agricola, with his inherent good sense, conducted judicial business readily and fairly, even when dealing with civilians. He made a clear-cut division between time spent on business and on relaxation. When assize-courts demanded his attention, he was solemn and focused; he was rigorous but more often inclined to be sympathetic. When he had finished his duties, he dropped his official guise; and had long since put aside severity, arrogance, and greed. Affability did not diminish his standing, nor rigour affection for him, which is most unusual. It would be an insult to his noble qualities to emphasize the integrity and honesty of a man like this. Furthermore, he did not seek a reputation by parading his good qualities or by intrigue, a fault into which even some good men fall. He avoided rivalry with his colleagues and arguments with the procurators and considered it demeaning to override others but ignominious to be beaten down. He was retained in his position as governor for less than three years and was recalled to the immediate expectation of a consulship. The general view was that the province of Britain was earmarked for him, not because he himself had said anything about this, but because he was obviously up to the task. Rumour is not always wrong; sometimes it prompts the choice. During his consulship he betrothed to me, young as I was, his daughter, a girl of outstanding promise, and after the consulship he gave her to me in marriage. Immediately afterwards he was appointed governor of Britain and also received the office of a priesthood.

In his biography of his father-in-law Agricola, Tacitus obviously sets out what he considered to be the desirable and honourable qualities of a senator as he made his way through the various magistracies and offices available to those who had the confidence of the emperor. To display such qualities enhanced the status of a senator and his family. However, high-profile governorships brought their own risks, and the final years of Agricola's governorship of Britain were clouded by the uncertain attitude of Domitian towards his governor's achievements.

CIL 6.2086 = *ILS* 451

59. In this year a dinner was held on individual days at a cost of 100 denarii, on 17, 19, 20 May, and they made the acclamation: Most fortunate! Most fortunate! With you alive and victorious, most fortunate! Happy are we who see you as Emperor. May Jupiter take from our store of years to increase yours! Germanicus Maximus, may the gods preserve you! Britannicus Maximus, may the gods preserve you! With you safe we are safe and secure! With you as Emperor the senate is fortunate! Augustus, may the gods preserve you for

ever! You are youthful in war but mature in ruling. You are greater than Augustus, may the gods preserve you! Augustus, Augusta! May good fortune come to Iulia Augusta, mother of the Emperor! From you, Augusta, we see Augustus. May the gods preserve you for ever, Augusta, Augustus!

On 11 August the Arval Brethren convened on the Capitol before the shrine of Juno the Queen, because our lord the emperor, most revered, pious M. Aurellius Antoninus Augustus, chief priest, crossing the border of Raetia, has entered the (land) of the barbarians in order to destroy the enemy, so that this event may turn out well and fortunate for him, and carried out a sacrifice through L. Armenius Peregrinus.

Under the same consuls, on the sixth of October, the Arval Brethren convened on the Capitol before the shrine of Juno the Queen and sacrificed through L. Armenius Peregrinus, deputy-president acting in place of Flavius Alpinus, president of the college of arval brethren, for the safety and German victory of M. Aurellius Antoninus, Pious Fortunate Augustus, Parthicus Maximus, Britannicus Maximus, Germanicus Maximus, chief priest, in the sixteenth year of his tribunician power, acclaimed imperator for the third time, consul for the fourth time, proconsul, and Iulia Augusta, Pious Fortunate mother of our emperor Antoninus Augustus, and of the senate, the camps, and the fatherland … (the inscription goes on to list the details of the sacrifices made).

The Arval Brethren (*Fratres Arvales*) were an ancient priesthood probably revived by Augustus, consisting of twelve members one of whom was always the reigning emperor. They met in a sacred grove just outside Rome, and among other religious observances conducted rituals in honour of the emperor and imperial family. The records of this priesthood show what life was like for upper classes within the parameters of acceptable public conduct; they had the prestige of serving in a priesthood with the emperor but must also respect the imperial presence everywhere in public life and manifest their loyalty in solemn formality; see also pp. 317–21.

Equites

Senatorial ideals of service and respectability also applied to *equites*. They required a property valuation of four hundred thousand sesterces, Roman citizenship, and three generations of free birth. This wider group of people with equestrian status included the foremost citizens among the well-off in the communities of Italy, and, with the extension of citizenship, increasingly of the provinces. Strabo notes that there were 500 men of equestrian rank in Gades and Patavium (3.5.3 (169); 5.1.7 (213)). Augustus shrewdly exploited a group of wealthy, often ambitious men who were likely to be loyal supporters because of the opportunities he extended to them in junior army commands and other administrative roles. Men like the historian Velleius Paterculus had an avenue from equestrian military posts to more senior positions in the service of the imperial family, and eventually senatorial rank.

Arguably within this broad grouping there was a more limited number associated with the original 1,800 *equites Romani* in the *Comitia Centuriata*. At the discretion of the emperor certain gradations of honour were available. The *equus publicus* or public horse, apparently granted by the emperor, marked out a favoured group who in Augustus' time took part in a traditional parade or ride past. Augustus also established four panels of jurors, later increased to five by Gaius, and these served as a mark of distinction and a gesture of imperial goodwill and acceptance for those so favoured (discussion in Wiseman (1970); Millar (1977), 279–84; Davenport (2019), chapters 4–7, especially 157–203). For the most active and talented *equites* there was an increasing role in the emperor's service in imperial administration, including posts of high status, such as prefect of Egypt or praetorian prefect. In time, just like senators, *equites* acquired honorific titles, though these were more varied, depending on the rank they had achieved in government service: *vir egregius* for middling office-holders; *vir perfectissimus* for senior officials (first attested in AD 201 (*ILS* 1346)); *vir eminentissimus* exclusively for the praetorian prefect; see Millar (1983), 90–1.

CIL 2.1180 = *ILS* 1403

60. To Sextus Iulius Possessor, son of Sextus, of the tribe Quirina, prefect of the third cohort of Gauls, placed in charge of a detachment of Syrian archers, also of the first cavalry unit of Spanish, curator of the community of the Romulenses of the *municipium* of Arva, military tribune of legion XII Fulminata, curator of the colony of Arca Caesarea, added to the judicial panels by the best and greatest emperors Antoninus and Verus Augusti, assistant to Ulpius Saturninus, prefect of the corn supply, with responsibility for reviewing Africa and Spanish olive oil, and for transporting additional commodities, and for paying the freight money to the ship-operators, procurator of the emperors for the banks of the river Baetis, the Spanish boatmen (erected this) on account of his outstanding integrity and fairness.

As procurator of the banks of the Baetis (Guadalquivir) Possessor will have been responsible for ensuring the smooth passage of river craft and maintaining the towpath; the river was important for the export of oil and other materials to Gades (Cadiz) on the coast; see Pflaum (1960), vol. 1, no. 185; Campbell (2012), 260. It is notable that in Tacitus' description of his father-in-law's qualities, and in this inscription, honesty and fairness are emphasized; perhaps these qualities were not regularly found in Roman officials. See pp. 167–73.

ILS 9407

61. To Marcus Manlius Modestus Quietianus, son of Gaius, of the Quirina tribe, granted the public horse and admitted to the five judicial panels by the divine Pius, priest for life, member of the board of two and curator of the *alimenta*, responsible for (supervising) the town Poblicia, because of his outstanding generosity to his native community through the construction of a theatre at his own expense, to their patron, at public expense.

This inscription from Curubis in Africa celebrates a man who had been particularly honoured by Antoninus Pius, and who was generous to his local community; the *alimenta* is a local scheme in Curubis; see pp. 117–18 for *alimenta* in Italy.

Dio 68.32, 4

62. Later however, when the Dacian war had begun and Trajan needed the help of the Moors, he (Lusius Quietus) came to him on his own initiative and performed exceptional exploits. After being honoured for this, he carried out even more numerous and distinguished deeds in the second war, and in the end, he advanced to such a pitch of courage and good luck in this war that he was enrolled among men of praetorian rank, became consul (possibly in 117), and then governor of Palestine (Judaea). It was because of this especially that he was envied and despised and met his downfall.

Lusius Quietus commanded an auxiliary cavalry unit of Moors; if the situation demanded, men of talent from outside the senate could always be adlected into the order at whatever level pleased the emperor, though this might be resented by senators. Quietus was executed for allegedly plotting against Hadrian.

Decurions

Decurions (members of town councils) were responsible on behalf of Rome for local government in the colonies and *municipia* in Italy and the provinces. There was a minimum age of thirty, later twenty-five, and decurions would normally be men of substantial wealth and standing in the community; those who had been elected to a junior magistracy would become a decurion after their year of office; direct co-option was possible, for example, to replace someone who had died, and the list of decurions was revised every five years. The total number varied according to the rules of individual communities; they dealt with local finances, administration, tax-collecting, and relations with Rome and the emperor. Furthermore, they were expected to undertake local obligations (*munera*) in their community. The chief magistrates were usually the *duoviri* or board of two, but the status of a decurion was significant and is frequently mentioned on inscriptions; for discussion of the standing and personnel involved in local office-holding see Patterson (2006), 221–41; for access to Roman citizenship, see p. 26–34.

CIL 9.1654 = ILS 6497

63. To the spirits of the dead. In honour of M. Rutilius Aelianus, decurion of Beneventum, grammarian, who lived for seventy-five years, Rutilia Primitiva, his wife, with whom he lived for eighteen years.

Augustales

CIL 9.2475 = ILS 5583

64. To Marcus Annius Phoebus the inhabitants of the *municipium* of Saepinum (set this up), because in return for the honour of the position of Augustalis and an ornamented seat, (he rebuilt) the marketplace with columns, foundation, bronze, and marble.

In local communities the *Augustales*, a religious and social group often linked to the imperial cult, ranked below the decurions. Although many of them were ex-slaves they had a prestigious role in local life. Communities were able to exploit the wealth and civic goodwill of freedmen, who had resources and wanted to advance their family, by allowing them to participate in public life. *Augustales* were privileged above the rest of the plebs and their status and role reflected that of decurions and magistrates; see Patterson (2006), 242–52.

Social Responsibility and Changes in Status

Levick (1983), 97

65. M. Silanus and L. Norbanus Balbus the consuls announced that they had produced an account as regards the business [assigned to them concerning ...] or to those who, contrary to the dignity of their own order, appeared on stage or [were hiring out their services to fight] in the games, as provided for in the decrees of the senate which had previously been passed

concerning this matter, and by this deceitful practice impaired the majesty of the senate; in respect of what the senate might wish to be done about this matter, the senate decided as follows about this matter: that they resolved that no one should bring on to the stage a senator's son, or daughter, or grandson, or granddaughter, or great-grandson, or great-granddaughter, or any male whose father or grandfather, either paternal or maternal, or brother, or any female whose husband, or father, or grandfather, either paternal or maternal, or brother have ever had the right of sitting in the seats reserved for *equites*, or induce them with a payment to [fight to the death in the arena], or snatch the plumes of gladiators, or take part in gladiator training, or perform any similar role. [Nor if anyone] offers himself should he hire him; nor should any of them hire himself out; and for that reason special precautions are to be taken against that possibility, because those people who have the right of sitting in the seats reserved for *equites* ... for the purpose of mocking the dignity of this order have striven to incur public ignominy or to be condemned in a judgement involving infamy, and after they had [removed themselves of their own accord] from the seats reserved for *equites*, pledged themselves as gladiators or appeared on stage. Nor should any of those persons [mentioned above if they were doing this in violation of the dignity of their own order] receive burial unless they had already appeared on stage, or [hired out their services] for the arena, or were a son or daughter of an actor, or gladiator, or trainer of gladiators, or pimp. And in respect of what was written and laid down [in the senatorial decree] passed on the proposal of the consuls Manius Lepidus and Titus Statilius Taurus (AD 11), that it should be permitted to no freeborn girl under twenty years of age, or any freeborn boy under twenty-five years of age to pledge themselves as gladiators or hire their services for the arena or stage, except in the case of any of them who had been consigned by the Divine Augustus or by Tiberius Caesar Augustus to ... .

The inscription containing this *senatus consultum* of AD 19 was found at Larinum. It was intended to prevent members of the upper classes from performing publicly on the stage or in the arena. Previously the government had had a rather ambivalent attitude to such public performance. The civil wars at the end of the republic witnessed less respect for the dignity of the rank of senators, and measures were taken in 38 BC to ban senators from fighting as gladiators (Dio 48.43.2); appearance on stage may also have been prohibited, and in 22 BC the sons and grandsons of senators were banned from the stage (Dio 54.2.5). During Augustus' rule *equites* also were banned from appearing in the arena or on the stage, possibly in 22 BC. But gradually the restrictions had been disregarded and in AD 11 *equites* were allowed to fight as gladiators in contests witnessed by Augustus (Dio 56.25.7); the decree of AD 11, which forbade women under the age of twenty and men under the age of twenty-five from appearing publicly in any kind of performance, may have intended to close a loophole and protect younger people; see Levick (1983), 105–10; Lebek (1990); Gardner (1993), 140–8.

Suetonius, *Tiberius* 35.2

66. Infamous women had begun to profess openly that they were prostitutes, in order to evade the penalty of the law by surrendering the status and rank of matrons. Furthermore, the most wanton among the young men of both orders were voluntarily incurring *infamia* and degradation from their rank, so that they should not be prevented under the senatorial decree from appearing on stage or in the arena. He (Tiberius) sent into exile all these men and women so that there should be no escape for anyone through this ploy.

Tacitus, *Annals* 2.85 also refers to senatorial action against disreputable conduct by upper-class women, partly in response to the attempt of a lady of praetorian family, Vistilia, to register as a professional prostitute. Papinian (*D* 48.5.11(10).2) refers to a senatorial decree against women who set up a brothel or went on stage to avoid the penalty for adultery. The three writers probably refer to the same senatorial decree, though it is not clear if it is the decree from Larinum. Levick (1983), 110–14 argues that there might be two related but separate measures. The fraud which the Larinum decree tried to prevent concerned a deliberate attempt to incur temporary *infamia* which involved loss of rank for a time; those who then appeared in the arena could claim that they were currently without official rank, and so could avoid punishment, or in the case of women be free of the charge of adultery.

D 23.2.44pr Paul (*Iulian and Papian Law*, Book 1)

67. It is established by the lex Iulia: Let no senator, or son of a senator, or grandson by his son, or great-grandson by his son, who exists or shall exist, knowingly and fraudulently become betrothed to or married to a freedwoman, or a woman who is or has been an actress, or whose father or mother practise or have practised the profession of an actor. Let no daughter of a senator, or granddaughter by his son, or great-granddaughter by his grandson, knowingly and fraudulently become betrothed to or married to a freedman, or a man who practises, or whose father or mother practise or have practised, the profession of an actor. And let none of these people knowingly and fraudulently become betrothed to or married to such a woman.

Dio 56.10.1

68. Later, he (Augustus) increased the rewards for those with children and made a distinction between the married and the unmarried by imposing different penalties; he also granted a period of one year to both groups in which to obey him and avoid the penalties. Contrary to the *lex Voconia*, by whose provision no woman could inherit property valued at more than a hundred thousand sesterces, he permitted some women to do this. And he granted to the vestal virgins all the privileges held by women who had borne children. Later the *lex Papia Poppaea* was brought forward by Marcus Papius Mutilus and Quintus Poppaeus Secundus, who were consuls at that time for part of the year. As it happened, neither of them had children and were not even married. From this occurrence the necessity of the law was apparent.

Gaius, *Institutes* 2.111

69. Furthermore, unmarried persons, who by the *lex Iulia* are forbidden to receive an inheritance or legacies, and also childless persons, that is, those who do not have children, whom the *lex Papia* forbids to receive more than half of an inheritance or of legacies …

Augustus' laws on marriage and divorce aimed to move the upper classes in a direction approved by him: the maintenance of stable relationships and the siring of legitimate children with people of the requisite status, which would help to create a secure group from which his senior administrators could be drawn. A married man had seniority in office-holding (Dio 53.13.2); a woman with three or more children (*ius trium liberorum*) was freed from guardianship; a decree in the time of Tiberius (*Tit. Ulp.* 16.3) had established that if a man by the age of sixty and a woman by the age of fifty had not complied with the *lex Papia Poppaea*, the penalties continued to apply to them. But a senatorial decree issued under Claudius laid down that men over sixty could marry women under fifty, avoid penalties, and receive an inheritance or a dowry. However, another undated decree penalized as unsuitable a marriage between a man under sixty and a woman over fifty, and penalties were applied (*Tit. Ulp.* 16.4). Some resorted to astute devices for getting round the law; men were betrothed to infants and thereby got the privileges of married men even though they had no intention of consummating the marriage. Augustus provided that a betrothal was not valid if not followed by marriage within two years, and the girl had to be at least ten, since in Rome girls were considered marriageable at twelve (Dio 54.16.7). See Treggiari (1991), 60–80; Gardner (1993), 123–6; Rutledge (2001), 58–60 for the impact of Augustus' marriage legislation; Milnor (2005), 140–54. Augustus also initiated legislation to repress adultery and fornication with a married woman, virgin, widow, divorced woman of respectable background, or man; see Treggiari (1991), 277–80; this volume, p. 314.

CIL 11.6354 = *ILS* 6655

70. To Abeiena Balbina, daughter of Gaius, priestess at Pisaurum and Ariminum, patroness of the community of the Pitinatian Pisaurensians. To her in the year when her husband Petinius Aper was *quinquennalis*, the common townspeople of the community of Pisaurum (erected this) because of their meritorious activities. To her the emperor [...] granted the legal right of children. This location was granted by decree of the town councillors.

The name of the emperor (probably Commodus) who granted Balbina this privilege has been erased because his memory was condemned. The position of *quinquennalis* to which two of the decurions were elected every five years was responsible for the census. Many inscriptions demonstrate that women were keen to show that they had the *ius liberorum*, suggesting that, apart from any legal benefits, it was a significant badge of honour and status for women especially of the upper classes; see Dixon (1988), 88–91; Grubbs (2002), 37–43.

BGU 1210 = *SP* 206, Sections 30, 32

71. Inheritances left to Roman women who have property to the value of 50,000 sesterces and are unmarried and childless, are confiscated. 32. Roman men who have property to the value of 100,000 sesterces and are unmarried and childless, do not inherit. But if their property is less, they may inherit.

This extract from the Gnomon of the *Idios Logos* (see p. 32) suggests that the marriage legislation was aimed at the upper classes and exempted people of lower degree. Treggiari (1991), 78–9 suggests that some of these regulations applied only in Egypt; however, Egypt's supposed special status has been questioned, and there is no reason why all of Augustus' marriage legislation should not apply to Egypt.

Tacitus, *Annals* 3.53

72. For what shall I (Tiberius) deal with first if I impose controls and cut things back to old-fashioned practices? The enormous extent of our villas? The size and cosmopolitan variety of our households? The weight of our gold and silver? Our wonderful examples of sculpture and paintings? Our clothing which makes no distinction between men and women, or that

particular delight of women, precious stones, to pay for which our currency is transferred to foreign or even hostile peoples?

Excessive expenditure on banquets, exotic clothing, and jewels had long been a subject of legislation in the republic, leading to restrictions on the cost of elaborate banquets, limiting the number of guests, and controlling expenditure on women's clothing and jewellery. It was part of Augustus' policy that the upper classes should be sober and hard-working in his service and that of the state. A frivolous lifestyle and prodigious expenditure were frowned upon. Augustus set the example with his ostensible moderation and frugality. Livia and other family members allegedly made his clothes (Suetonius, *Augustus* 73). And the emperor set an example, as in the notorious case of Vedius Pollio (see no. 9). Tiberius took up this issue in more general moralizing terms in this speech to the senate in AD 22.

Adoption

Adoption into paternal power represented a change in status and was an aspect of social responsibility through the expansion and preservation of the *familia*. Where the adoptee was in the power of another, a process of emancipation had first to be undertaken to terminate that power; then in an undefended legal action the adopter claimed the adoptee as his son (*adoptio*). If the adoptee was legally independent (*sui iuris*), the process was called *adrogatio,* and all the adoptee's property and dependants passed into the power of his new *pater familias*. This meant that the family's traditional religious rites (*sacra*) were ended, and the family was terminated. Therefore, this procedure required an investigation by the priests and a vote by the *Comitia Curiata* and was permitted only if the adopter needed an heir and successor to the family property and was unable to produce one of his own. Those persons who had been adopted had the same rights of succession as the natural children of the *pater familias*. After the first century AD *adrogatio* could be brought about by imperial rescript. Adoption was subject to other regulations, notably that the adopter was supposed to be older than the adoptee. Women could not adopt since they did not have power over free persons. Permission for the *adrogatio* of persons who were not yet adult (*impuberes*) began to be extended only in the reign of Antoninus Pius, who wrote to the priests, and protection was offered for their economic interests. Adoption could sustain a family lacking an heir, and could be used to reconstitute family arrangements by, for example, emancipating a son and bringing in an adoptee. The attraction for adoptees in *adrogatio* was the prospect of a rich inheritance. For detailed discussion see Gardner (1998a), 114–208.

Gaius, *Institutes* 1.98–100

73. Adoption comes about in two ways, either by the authority of the people or by the power (*imperium*) of a magistrate, such as a praetor. (99) By the authority of the people we adopt those who are legally independent (*sui iuris*). This type of adoption is called adrogation (*adrogatio*), because both the adopter is asked (*rogare*), that is interrogated, if he wishes the person whom he is about to adopt to be his lawful son, and the person who is being adopted is asked if he wishes that to be done, and the people are asked if they instruct that to be done. By the *imperium* of a magistrate we adopt those who are under the power of their parents, whether they have the first rank of descent, such as a son or daughter, or a lower rank, such as grandson or granddaughter or great-grandson or great-granddaughter. (100) The former type of adoption that takes place by the authority of the people can take place nowhere but at Rome, but the latter type is indeed often carried out in the provinces by provincial governors.

In adoption by *adrogatio* the sanction of the people was through the *Comitia Curiata*, which was the earliest type of Roman assembly, consisting of thirty *curiae*, ten for each of the original three tribes. It gradually lost most of its legislative powers, but formally acted as witness to certain transactions including adoptions and wills under the chairmanship of the *pontifex maximus*.

Aulus Gellius, *Attic Nights* 5.19.5–9

74. However, adoptions by *adrogatio* are not undertaken lightly or without investigation. For the assembly which is called *curiata* is convened on the authority of the *pontifices*, and it is asked if the age of the person who wishes to adopt is not rather more suitable for begetting children of his own, and in respect of the property of the person who is being adopted, if precautions should be taken in case his property is being sought fraudulently. Furthermore, there is an oath which is said to have been devised by Quintus Mucius when he was *pontifex maximus* which is to be sworn during the adoption. But no one can be adopted by *adrogatio* unless they have reached the age of puberty. It is called *adrogatio* because this method of transmission to the family of another is achieved by a request to the people.

The language of this request is as follows: 'Express your wish and instruct that Lucius Valerius should be legally and justly the son of Lucius Titius just as if he had been born the son of that father and mother of his family, and that he (Titius) should have the power of life and death over him, as a father has over his son. I put this request to you, citizens, exactly as I have spoken it'.

Outside the Upper Classes

The Plebs

By Augustus' time the mass of the population, apart from senators and *equites* and local councillors, was the plebs. The plebs in Rome who were Roman citizens benefitted from imperial patronage; they were entertained by games and shows and gladiator contests, they had public baths, they received free or subsidized corn; amenities were improved by an increased water supply delivered through aqueducts; the administration of the city was better regulated, and it was marginally safer through the presence of the urban cohorts, the praetorian guard, and the *Vigiles* (fire brigade). In return the plebs were expected to keep the peace and acclaim the emperor on public occasions. They were of course looked down upon by upper classes, though in turn they could despise ex-slaves, however wealthy some became.

***CIL* 6.10227 = *ILS* 6067**

75. To the gods of the dead, in honour of Quintus Terentius Priscianus, who lived for four years seven months, and received the public corn for nine months. Terentia Sabina set this up for her son.

Juvenal, *Satires* 10.73–81

76. And what about the plebs at Rome? As always, they follow fortune and hate the losers ... Once upon a time they used to vote commands, elect consuls, assign the legions, everything, but now they have retreated into their shell and are fixated on only two things – bread and games.

For Juvenal, see p. 479. In this section he is discussing the fickleness of popular opinion, abusing the powerful now fallen from favour, but previously ready to flatter them. Courtney (1980, 446–54) offers a useful discussion of satire 10.

Dio 52.25.6–7

77. Furthermore some (*equites*) should be enrolled in the senate even if they have served as centurions in the citizen legions, except those who have served as rank-and-file soldiers. For it is a shameful disgrace that men of this type, who have acted as porters of wood and charcoal, should be found among the membership of the senate. But in respect of those who began

their service as centurions, there is nothing to prevent the most distinguished of them from belonging to the senate.

This is a further extract from the speech of Maecenas (see no. 52). Legionary soldiers were also from the lower classes of society, and military commanders of senatorial or equestrian rank tended to look down on them. Augustus also emphasized the importance of social order through the *lex Iulia Theatralis* which confirmed set rows in the theatre for the various sections of society, including soldiers, plebs, women, vestals, married men, *equites*, and senators; discussion in Rawson (1987); Dench (2018), 96–8.

Dio 75.2

78. Some particularly blamed him because he ended the practice of recruiting the praetorian guard exclusively from Italy, Spain, Macedonia, and Noricum, which produced men of more respectable demeanour and more restrained habits, and ordered that any vacancies in the ranks should be filled from all the legions equally. He did this so that he could have guards who had more experience of military life, and so that he could offer a reward to those who had shown themselves brave in war. But in fact, it became obvious that he had incidentally destroyed the youth of Italy, who turned to banditry and gladiator contests instead of their previous service in the army. And he also filled the city (Rome) with a motley mob of soldiers, who looked ferocious, spoke in the most terrifying way, and were vulgar in social contacts.

Septimius Severus, governor of Upper Pannonia, seized power in 193 in a civil war. Dio criticizes the soldiers from the Danubian legions who became Severus' bodyguard. Severus disbanded the existing praetorian guard, which had proved disloyal and betrayed the previous emperor. In opening the guard up to legionaries, he was mainly rewarding the soldiers in the Danube provinces who had first supported his bid for power. However, senatorial prejudice against rank-and-file soldiers is again apparent. Nevertheless, soldiers did have a status and significant privileges in law which in some ways raised them above the social group from which they came, and perhaps annoyed other members of society.

D 29.1.1pr-1 (Ulpian, *Edict*, Book 45)

79. (The context is disputes arising over wills made by soldiers if judged with the full rigour of the law) 'Therefore in response to the justness of my feelings for my excellent and most loyal fellow soldiers, I have decided that due consideration must be given to their simple-minded ignorance, so that, regardless of the way in which their wills have been drawn up, their wishes

are to be considered valid. Therefore, they may draw up their wills in whatever way they wish, and in whatever way they can, and the mere wish of the testator is to be sufficient for the division of his property'. Now the word 'soldier' is said to have been derived from *militia*, that is the hardship (*duritia*) which they endure on our account, or from the word 'multitude', or from the evil (*malitia*) from which soldiers customarily protect us, or from the number of one thousand men ...

See no. 742 for previous interventions on behalf of soldiers. Trajan's language, in particular the use of 'fellow soldiers', illustrates the special position of soldiers; apart from these concessions in making wills, they also had the right to own property related to their military service, which was not under the power of their father. Soldiers enjoyed regular pay and discharge benefits including a kind of pension, unlike the rest of the population. In addition, they had the possibility of promotion through the ranks, and especially in the case of centurions, opportunities for social advancement. It is interesting that Ulpian on rather doubtful etymological grounds tries to explain the privileged position of soldiers based on their services on behalf of the people of the empire. See also p. 468–73.

D 3.2.1 (Iulianus, *Edict*, Book 1)

80. These are the words of the praetor: 'That person is marked as infamous (*infamia*) who is dishonourably discharged from the army by the emperor or a person empowered to make that decision, who goes on stage to act or declaim, who has acted as a pimp, who has been convicted in a public jury court of false accusation or collusion in anything, who has been condemned in his own name in respect of theft, robbery with violence, insult, bad faith or fraud, or who has been compromised in such a case, who has been condemned in his own name and not in a counter-suit in an action regarding partnership, guardianship, a mandate, or a deposit'.

Gaius, *Institutes* 4.182 gives a slightly different list; the Tabula of Heraclea (see also p. 72) chapter 108 refers to those defined as unworthy persons who were prohibited from serving on the council or taking public office, including those dishonourably discharged from the army, or who had received reward for bringing in the head of a Roman citizen, or had been a prostitute, or trained gladiators, or run a brothel. Clearly within the ranks of the plebs there was a kind of social hierarchy, in that some activities or professions were regarded as morally reprehensible or disgraceful (Robinson (1992), 137–9; 200–6; (1995), 90–4; Gardner (1993), 126–40). *Infamia* or *ignominia* followed on conviction in a criminal trial and in consequence of some civil proceedings; it was a significant setback in upper-class society to lose the respect of your peers; it could be followed by a 'black mark' or *nota censoria* in the census lists; see Crook (1967), 83–5; Gardner (1993), 111–23 for the importance of the restrictions on *infames*. People could not appoint representatives at law or act as representatives because of *infamia* or *ignominia*; they could not act as a witness, for example, in the making of a will or the conveyance of property. Those who suffered exile and other punishments faced restrictions in making wills.

CJ 2.11(12).5 (AD 198)

81. Emperors Severus and Antoninus Augusti to Ambrosius. It is forbidden to beat town councillors with rods, or the sons of town councillors; but if the proconsul, distinguished man, declared that you had committed an outrage, you are marked with ignominy (*ignominia*).

For the practice of issuing a reply or rescript to a legal enquiry, and the approachability of emperors, see p. 450.

D 28.1.8 (Gaius, *Provincial Edict*, Book 17)

82. In the case of a person who is banned from fire and water, neither a will made by him beforehand, nor one made afterwards, is valid. Furthermore, the property that he had when he was condemned will be confiscated by the state, or, if it does not appear to be profitable, will be handed over to his creditors. Those deported to an island are in the same legal position; but those who are relegated to an island, and those who are banned from Italy and their own province, retain the right of making a will. But those who have been condemned to be beheaded, or to fight wild beasts, or to the mines, lose their liberty and have their property confiscated by the state. From this it is clear that they lose the right to make a will.

Ex-Slaves

D 47.10.7.2 (Ulpian, *Edict*, Book 57)

83. But we shall grant a patron the right of limited chastisement against his freedman, and the praetor will not accept a complaint from him on the ground that he has suffered abuse, unless he has been outrageously treated, for example, as if he were a slave. For the praetor should not have to permit someone who was a slave yesterday and today is free, to complain that his master spoke rudely to him, or lightly struck or disciplined him. But if the master chastised him with whips or rods, or seriously wounded him, it will be entirely proper for the praetor to come to the freedman's aid.

There were significant restrictions on freedmen; they were not permitted to join the army or marry upper-class women; they were excluded from office-holding at Rome and from being local town councillors. They might provide *operae*, or days of work, for their patron if that had been agreed in a contract when their manumission was discussed (*D* 38.1); see Waldstein (1986); Mouritsen (2011), 146–59, 224–6 considers the obligations on freedmen and the role of *operae*. Furthermore, the patron retained rights in the estate of the freedman after his death; under Augustan legislation the patron had a share in the estate if it was large, unless there were three or more children. The freedman also had certain responsibilities to behave respectfully towards his patron and to assist him if he fell on hard times (see no. 85); for freedman–patron relations see Crook (1967), 50–5; MacMullen (1974), 103–6; Gardner (1993), 20–32; Mouritsen (2011), 36–65. Lewis (2015) considers the status of slaves and freedmen in the context of legal provision for freeborn Roman citizens.

D 38.1.38pr-1 (Callistratus, *Monitoring Edict*, Book 3)

84. Only those services (*operae*) are agreed as properly imposed which can be provided without disgrace or mortal danger. For if a prostitute has been manumitted, she is not required to provide the same service for her ex-master even though she is still earning her living with her body. Similarly, a gladiator if manumitted should not provide these services since they cannot be provided without mortal danger. However, if a freedman practises a craft, he should provide services to his patron arising from it, even if he learned it after his manumission.

D 25.3.6.1 (Modestinus, *Manumissions*, Book 1)

85. A decision of the Emperor Commodus states: 'When it has been proved that patrons have been treated abusively by their freedmen, or that they have been disgracefully beaten up, or even have been abandoned when struggling with poverty or ill-health, firstly the freedmen should be returned to the power of their patrons and forced to provide services for their masters; but if they pay no heed even to this they should be handed over to a purchaser by the governor and the price given to their patrons'.

Tacitus, *Annals* 12.53

86. (The context is a proposal concerning the punishment of women who married slaves.) As for Pallas, whom the emperor had indicated was the originator of this proposal, the consul designate Barea Sonanus proposed

that he should receive the ornaments of a praetor and fifteen million sesterces. In addition, Cornelius Scipio suggested that he receive a vote of public thanks, because although he was descended from the kings of Arcadia, he had put his ancient noble rank behind his public duty and permitted himself to be included among the attendants of the emperor. Claudius intimated that Pallas was satisfied with the honour and content to remain in his former state of poverty. And so, a senatorial decree was publicly inscribed on bronze heaping praise for old-fashioned frugality on an ex-slave worth three hundred million sesterces.

See no. 17 for women and marriage to slaves. Pallas was the freedman financial secretary of Claudius and offended senators not only by his great wealth dubiously acquired, but through his role as an intimate adviser of the emperor in all aspects of his rule, a role to which senators thought that they were entitled. Among the upper classes it was convenient to make use of freedmen but also to sneer at those who rose above what was considered to be an acceptable station. Tacitus is contemptuously sarcastic, and that feeling is present in Pliny, who in two letters (7.29; 8.6) criticizes the senators who voted for the honours and complains of honours 'tossed away on such muck and filth', and 'that this vagabond should dare to accept and refuse them'. The whole episode was profoundly embarrassing for the upper classes; see Mouritsen (2011), 93–109 for the status of freedmen in the imperial entourage and the consequent political and social tensions.

CIL 6.8604 = *ILS* 1519

87. To Flavius Euschemon, freedman of the emperor, who served as imperial correspondence secretary and also as procurator of the tribute payments of the Jews. Flavia Aphrodisia made this for her well-deserving patron and husband.

Euschemon administered the poll tax of two drachmas imposed on Jews by Vespasian after the Jewish revolt (Josephus *BJ* 7.216–18; Suetonius, *Domitian* 12). Far away from the high-profile activities of Pallas and freedmen secretaries, other imperial freedmen, or indeed slaves, had roles in the emperor's and public service. They had the advantage of the emperor's personal patronage and enhanced opportunities; see, for example, Musicus (no. 13).

CIL 11.5400 = *ILS* 7812

88. Publius Decimius Eros Merula, freedman of Publius, clinical doctor, surgeon, eye-specialist, member of the board of six. He paid 50,000 sesterces for his freedom. He bestowed on the community 2,000 sesterces for his membership of the board of six. He contributed 30,000 sesterces for

the erection of statues in the temple of Hercules. He gave 37,000 sesterces to the public treasury for the paving of streets. On the day before he died, he left an estate worth ... sesterces.

Outside the world of the imperial entourage and amid the mass of the population in Rome and in the communities of Italy, ex-slaves would usually be largely indistinguishable in appearance from the freeborn population and could build a place in society according to their talents: 'For the mass of the population are now very mixed up with foreigners, freedmen have the same rights as citizens, and those who are still slaves in their way of dress are the same as their masters. Apart from those of senatorial rank, the dress of the rest of the population is the same as that of slaves' (Appian, *Civil Wars* 2.120). This inscription honours a wealthy freedman and successful doctor from Assisi. However, although Merula has a prominent part in local life, it is impossible to say whether he had been socially accepted in the town community, which may have been eager to exploit his wealth and medical skills while still looking down on him as an ex-slave. He would not have been eligible for a senior magistracy or membership of the council. However, there was nothing to prevent the sons of freedmen if wealthy enough from holding a magistracy and becoming decurion. Communities faced economic pressure to meet local obligations and maintain the *ordo* of decurions, and wealthy freedmen families could find advancement; see Patterson (2006), 236–41.

CHAPTER 2

Public and Private Interests

Rome and Italy

Introduction

The population of Rome probably reached one million in the imperial age; in this huge and potentially turbulent city Augustus as the bringer of peace and order needed the plebs on his side, and a peaceful Rome could help persuade the upper classes that his revolution did not threaten their accustomed lifestyle. Augustus gradually absorbed into his remit the city administrative functions, and the patronage of the plebs. New officials appointed or approved by him, who worked with or superseded the traditional magistrates, provided a consistent and coherent framework for city administration that had been beyond annual office-holders. When Augustus boasted that he had found Rome a city of brick and left it one of marble he may have had in mind his political accomplishments, but he did create or sponsor through his associates many new buildings and gardens for the benefit of the whole people. Augustus developed the idea, followed by his successors, that consequent upon the rights, duties, and legal obligations of a Roman citizen, there was a responsibility of care upon the emperor for the people, particularly those living in Rome. The steps taken by emperors for the management of the amenities and security of Rome were in a way linked to the legal status of being Roman. The introduction of urban amenities, such as corn, water, firefighting, and entertainment, was sponsored by legal enactment and managed by officials of the state.

Augustus aimed to extend the benefits of his stable rule to the whole of Italy, which was divided into eleven regions, and many colonies and *municipia* received imperial benefactions. The Italian municipal aristocracy were among his strongest supporters. Augustus' measures, regarded as precepts by his successor, were to offer a kind of template of government for future emperors. The needs and rights of individuals and communities had to be balanced against the requirements of the state as identified by the emperor. Robinson (1992) provides an excellent survey of the government and administration of Rome; rural and urban life in Italy has been impressively analysed by Patterson (2006), making full use of archaeological evidence.

This chapter deals with the state's assets and the management of buildings and public space to facilitate the government's activities in relation to the citizens; the regulation of the built environment involved citizens' rights and communal relations for the benefit of an ordered society. The government used public assets in the interests of the citizens, particularly the poorer ones, and controlled the city through the management of individuals and groups to preserve order (pp. 89–93). In Italy the state intervened to ensure efficient self-government in the colonies and *municipia*, and to oversee issues of jurisdiction between communities (pp. 101–7). Emperors also intervened directly to help individual communities, eventually developing a formal scheme to support poorer children that lasted until the third century (pp. 117–18).

Rome

Public Assets and the Citizen

D 43.8.2.21 (Ulpian, *Edict*, Book 68)

89. The land on which public roads run is public, either left (unmeasured) or with its breadth marked out between established boundaries by the man who had the right to make it public, so that people may go and travel along them.

See Campbell (2012), 90–8 arguing that the state had the power (similar to compulsory purchase) to acquire land and materials for the construction of public amenities, and also to maintain them; for discussion see Robinson (1992), 26–32, and Taylor (2000), 93–127, who holds that the government had no right of compulsory appropriation; for the state control of aqueducts, see Bannon (2017), 74–8. For the planning of aqueducts, see Hodge (2002), 171–214.

Frontinus, *Aqueducts* 125

90. When the consuls Quintus Aelius Tubero and Paulus Fabius Maximus (11 BC) had made a report concerning the repair of the channels, conduits, and arches of the aqueducts Iulia, Marcia, Appia, Tepula, and Anio, and enquired of the senate what it wished to be done in respect of that matter, it was resolved: That when those channels, conduits, and arches, which Augustus Caesar has promised the senate to repair at his own expense, shall be repaired, the earth, clay, stones, potsherds, sand, wood, and other

materials that are necessary for this task should be taken, removed, and transported from the fields of private individuals, each of them from the nearest place from which they could be taken, removed, and transported without injury to private individuals, their value having been determined on the judgement of an honest man, and that for the purpose of transporting all that material for repairing those works, as often as it should be necessary, roads and thoroughfares should be open and be granted through the fields of private individuals without injury to them.

For Frontinus' role in managing the aqueducts, see no. 128.

Frontinus, *Aqueducts* 127–8

91. When the consuls Quintus Aelius Tubero and Paulus Fabius Maximus had made a report that the routes of the aqueducts entering the city were being blocked by tombs and buildings, and planted with trees, and enquired of the senate what it wished to be done in respect of that matter, it was resolved: That since, in order to repair the channels and conduits [in respect of obstructions] through which public structures are being damaged, it is decided that a space of fifteen feet shall be kept on each side of water sources, arches, and walls, and that a space of five feet shall be kept on each side of channels which are underground, and conduits inside the city, and inside buildings adjacent to the city, so that after this time no one shall be permitted to erect a tomb or a building in these locations, or plant trees, and if there should now be any trees within that space, they shall be uprooted unless they are adjacent to country estates or enclosed by buildings.

(128) This decree of the senate would appear to be very fair, albeit that those areas were being laid claim to only in accordance with public need. However, our ancestors, with much more admirable fairness, did not even seize from private persons those areas that pertained to public requirements. Rather, when they were bringing water works through, if a possessor had been reluctant in selling a necessary part of a field, they paid money for the entire field, and after the necessary area had been measured, sold that field back again, on the understanding that the state and the private persons should have their proper legal rights within their own boundaries.

These passages show the involvement of the government in controlling the area round an aqueduct for construction and maintenance, though compensation was available for affected landholders. See also the *lex Coloniae Genetivae* (Crawford (1996), 408 and 427; this volume, no. 219).

CIL 10.4843 = *ILS* 5744 (Venafrum)

92. On the orders of Imperator Caesar Augustus, around that channel, which was constructed to convey water, a space of eight feet to the right and left has been left empty.

This is a marker stone near the aqueduct; Augustus' edict (*ILS* 5743) provided for the unobstructed channelling of water to Venafrum, and eight feet for maintenance and repair of the structure, and shows how the process for the effective management of the water supply was extended to other communities in Italy.

CIL 6.1266 = *ILS* 5939 (Rome)

93. T. Quinctius Crispinus Valerianus (cos. AD 2), C. Calpetanus Statius Rufus, C. Pontius Paelignus, C. Petronius Umbrinus, M. Crassus Frugi (cos. AD 27), curators for adjudicating public locations, in accordance with the decree of the senate examined the case and made a restoration from private to public (ownership).

For the demarcation of public and private space in respect of the river Tiber, see no. 132.

Suetonius, *Augustus* 56.2

94. He (Augustus) made his forum narrower than he wished because he did not venture to confiscate the neighbouring houses from their owners.

Augustus could have taken the land for his forum, but it is easy to see that for reasons of politics and public opinion he might refrain from doing this. Some have argued that the layout of the forum was in fact adjusted to avoid a large drain.

Regulating the Built Environment

Zoning the City

D 50.16.87 (Marcellus, *Digests*, Book 12)

95. As Alfenus says, the city is that part of Rome which is encircled by its wall, but Rome also consists of all the adjacent buildings. For Rome cannot be understood by everyday observance just to be the area enclosed by its wall, since we are in the habit of saying that we are going to Rome even if we live outside the city.

The *pomerium* was the official boundary of the city marked with stones and remained so for various religious observances. It was distinct from the city wall and did not mark the limit of habitation. It was extended on various occasions, for example by Claudius and Vespasian on the grounds that they had extended the territory of the Roman empire; but the existence of the *pomerium* did not affect administrative functions.

Suetonius, *Augustus* 30.1

96. He (Augustus) divided the area of the city into regions and districts (*vici*), on the basis that the former should be administered by magistrates drawn by lot each year, the latter by officials (*magistri*) elected from the people in each locality.

The fourteen regions into which Augustus divided the city in 7 BC were to be administered by aediles, tribunes, and praetors drawn by lot (Dio 55.8.7). The subdivisions (*vici*) of the regions numbered 265 in the time of Augustus, and were administered by *vicomagistri*, who among other things were responsible for the worship of the *Lares Compitales* (deities of the crossroads) and the celebrations linked with the crossroads. Later evidence suggests that the *vicomagistri* were often freedmen. It is possible that the *Lares* came to be associated with the emperor's ancestors – the *Lares Augusti* (see Beard, North and Price (1998), 184–7). Lott (2004), especially chapter 4, argues that while the *Lares* were not the deities of Augustus' household, the application of *Augustus* to the *Lares* 'pulled the neighbourhoods, their religion, and their inhabitants into the new system of the Principate and declared the active support of the city's lower classes to be one of the ideals of the new regime' (p. 110). For Augustus' further operations in Rome, see no. 133.

CIL 6.30960 = *ILS* 3621

97. To the *Lares Augusti* and the *Genius* of Emperor Caesar ... the masters (of the *vicus*) ... Pius and Lucius Calpurnius Felix restored in its entirety the shrine in the Vesta *vicus* of region VIII, [which had collapsed through age], using their own money, with the assistance of Gaius Iulius Paternus, prefect of the *Vigiles*, most eminent man, in the consulship of Lucius Marius Maximus for the second time and Lucius Roscius Aelianus (AD 223), under the charge of Marcus Servilius Crispus and Marcus Servilius.

The prefect of the *Vigiles* is mentioned probably because detachments of his men were stationed on fire-watch in the *vici*.

Building Regulations

Strabo 5.3.7 (235)

98. Augustus Caesar, being concerned about this kind of debasement of the city (of Rome), for protection against fires organized a force of freedmen to provide assistance, and to deal with collapses of buildings restricted the height of new buildings, imposing a limit of seventy feet for frontages on public roads.

For Strabo, see p. 481. Note also Suetonius, *Augustus* 30.1. Emperors continued to address these issues; after the great fire of Rome in AD 64 Nero decreed that street fronts must have a designated alignment with a height restriction. In addition, a fixed segment of each building had to be constructed of huge stones from Gabii or Alba without any wood, because that kind of stone was impervious to fire (Tacitus, *Annals* 15.43). Trajan reduced the height limit of houses to 60 feet 'because of their propensity to collapse and the ruinous expense when this happened' (*Epitome* 13.13).

Vitruvius, *De Architectura* 2.8.17

99. Public statutes do not permit party walls to be constructed more than one and a half feet thick. However, other walls are built of the same thickness so as not to narrow the space too much. Brick walls of a foot and a half thick, that is, not two or three bricks thick, cannot bear the weight of more than one storey. But in a majestic city with a huge population, it is necessary to provide innumerable places to live. Therefore, since level sites cannot cope with such a large number who need to live in the city, circumstances have compelled us to resort to using the height of buildings. Therefore, by employing stone piles, tile masonry, and party walls made of rubble, tall buildings have been erected and constructed with numerous floors, and beneficially create rooms using partitions. Consequently, with walls and various floors multiplied to reach a great height, the Roman people have outstanding dwelling places without any obstacle (of the law).

For Vitruvius, see p. 482. With his military and architectural background, he was employed to advise Augustus on his building projects in Rome and in the Italian colonies. Sun-dried bricks could not support more than one story and so other building materials had to be used, such as bricks baked in a kiln, and concrete. The relations between private citizens in respect of building, and the role of the state in managing this, are treated at pp. 239–42.

CJ 8.10.1

100. Emperors Antoninus and Verus Augusti to Taurus. You may build a bathhouse as you wish and add a structure on top of it, though you must follow the planning procedure by which others have been permitted to build on top of a bathhouse, that is, you should build the upper structure with vaulting and ensure that with the vault you do not exceed the customary limit on height.

D 8.2.14 (Papirius, *Imperial Decisions*, Book 1)

101. The emperors Antoninus Augustus and Verus Augustus replied that in a location that was not encumbered with a servitude to anyone, the owner or another person with the owner's permission may erect a building, provided that the legally required space is left between it and a neighbouring block of flats.

For servitudes, see p. 237. Any new construction had to conform to the appropriate building regulations and concerns for the appearance of the city (see no. 105).

D 39.1.1.17 (Ulpian, *Edict*, Book 52)

102. We give notice because we have the right to prevent something, either to protect ourselves against impending damage from a person who is perhaps building something on public or private land, or if something is being done against the laws and the edicts of the emperors issued in respect of the size of buildings, on a consecrated or religious location, or in a public river, or on the public banks of a river. For these reasons interdicts are also issued.

The heading of book 39 is: 'Concerning the giving of notice of a new structure'. See pp. 67–75 for the responsible use of buildings and space. Much was left to the initiative of private individuals to bring an action concerning a troublesome building; there was no procedure like the modern system of planning permission; see Robinson (1992), 33–46.

CIL 10.1401 = *ILS* 6043 = *FIRA* 1, no. 45 I (Herculaneum)

103. In the consulship of Hosidius Geta and Lucius Vagellius, 22 September, decree of the senate. Since the foresight of our excellent emperor has looked out for even the buildings of our city and the eternity of all of Italy, which he has personally benefitted not only through his most

revered precept but also by his own example, and since the proportionate preservation of public buildings and also of private buildings is in keeping with the happiness of the present age, and since everyone must refrain from an appalling form of speculation and not produce an appearance which is most injurious to a state of peace, through the destruction of houses and villas, it has been decided: if anyone should have bought a house in a business transaction so that by pulling it down he might make more than he paid for it, then he must pay to the treasury a fine of twice the sum for which he bought the house, and the matter should furthermore be referred to the senate. And since it is also as improper to sell a house with bad intentions as it is to buy it, in order that sellers should additionally be under restraint if knowingly and with malice they should sell property against the intention of this senatorial decree, it has been decided that such sales should be invalid. However, the senate stated that those owners were not liable who, intending to remain in possession of their own property, have changed some parts of it, as long as that was not done for a business deal.

Adopted. There were present in the senate three hundred and eighty-three.

This initiative of Claudius dealt generally with the practice of buying property, perhaps demolishing existing buildings, and selling the land, where in some cases a new apartment block would be built to exploit the rental market. Therefore, the government attempted to check unsuitable demolition of buildings because of what it considered to be speculation by greedy property developers (see also *D* 18.1.52). The second part of the inscription (no. 174) relates to a property at Herculaneum. The government's motive was perhaps mainly to preserve the appearance of the city rather than to maintain a supply of dwelling houses.

Historia Augusta, Hadrian 18.2

104. Among other rulings he decided that in no community should any house be demolished in order to transport cheap building material to another town.

For the *Historia Augusta* see p. 478. The life of Hadrian is considered to be a reasonably reliable source.

CJ 8.10.2 (AD 222)

105. Emperor Alexander Augustus to Diogenes. It is forbidden by an edict of the divine Vespasian and a senatorial decree to demolish buildings and

remove the marble for the purposes of business. But there is an exception by which it is permitted to transfer something from one house to another. However, owners are not permitted to transfer material in this way if by the destruction of viable buildings the public appearance of the area should be made less attractive.

Tabula Heracleensis Crawford (1996), p. 365, lines 68–72

106. Whatever public spaces or public porticos are or shall be inside the city of Rome or nearer to the city of Rome than one mile, the responsibility for which spaces and porticos belongs or shall under the statutes belong to the aediles or to those magistrates who shall be responsible for the cleaning of the roads and public spaces inside the city of Rome or nearer to the city of Rome than one mile, and no one in those spaces or in those porticos is to have anything constructed or built, and no one is to possess those spaces or any portico, and no one is to have any part of them fenced in or blocked off, with the result that people may not use those spaces and those porticos, or that they may not lie open, except for those to whom (it is or shall have been) granted and permitted by statutes and plebiscites or decrees of the senate.

The colony of Heraclea in the gulf of Tarentum had originally been a Greek city and received regulations for its government. Although these were not part of a general municipal law, it is possible that a *lex Iulia* in 45 BC dealt with some aspects of municipal government and is partly reflected in the material for Heraclea; see Crawford (1996), 358–60; and in this volume p. 99. Material relating to the buildings and roads of Rome has been used to provide a suitable model for a *municipium* like Heraclea, and consequently can illustrate the management of the city by Augustus and his successors. The *Curatores operum publicorum* were created by Augustus (Suetonius, *Augustus* 37) to look after the maintenance of public buildings, and the office was usually held by senators of praetorian rank. The cost of maintaining public buildings was normally funded by the state. Pertinax (AD 193) apparently put aside a fixed sum for public works (*Historia Augusta*, *Pertinax* 9.2).

D 43.8.2.17 (Ulpian, *Edict*, Book 68)

107. If someone has built on public land and no one has prevented him, he should not be compelled to demolish it, in case the city should be disfigured by ruins, and because the interdict is to prohibit not to restore. However, if that building impedes public use, then the official responsible for public buildings must have it demolished. Or, if it does not, he must impose a ground-tax (*solarium*), which is so-called because it is paid for the ground (*solum*).

City Streets

***Tabula Heracleensis* Crawford (1996), pp. 363–5, lines 20–3; 27–45; 53–5**

108. (20–3) Whatever roads are or shall be inside the city of Rome or nearer to the city of Rome than one mile, where there is continuous occupation of dwellings, in front of whatever building any of those roads is, he (the householder) is to maintain that road, according to the decision of that aedile to whom under this statute that section of the city has fallen; and that aedile is to ensure that, in front of whatever building and whatever road it is appropriate under this statute for anyone to maintain, they are to maintain that road according to his decision; and that water is not to stand at that location, with the result that the people may not conveniently use that road.

(27–45) Whatever part has in this way under this statute fallen to each aedile, the responsibility for repairing and maintaining the roads in those places which are in that part, is to belong to that aedile, as is proper under this statute.

(53–5) In front of whatever building a footpath lies in a (public) space, he is to keep that footpath appropriately paved, stretching along that whole building, with entire stones of good quality, according to the decision of that aedile whose responsibility for roads lies in that part (of the city) under this statute.

For the statute of Heraclea, see no. 106. These regulations concerning the maintenance of roads were derived from those operating in Rome and instruct the aediles concerning contracts for the maintenance and repair of roads where the householders had been negligent in their duty.

***CIL* 14.2922 = *ILS* 1420**

109. To Flavius Germanus, son of Titus, organizer of the second most fortunate German triumph (the name of Commodus has been removed), honoured with the magnificent office of a junior priesthood, procurator of the 5 per cent tax on inheritances, procurator of the emperor's private property, procurator of the *Ludus Magnus* (gladiatorial school), procurator of the morning games, procurator of a region of the city, in which he was given the additional duty of repairing the streets in two parts of the city, procurator of the 5 per cent tax on inheritances in Umbria, Tuscia, Picenum, and the (region?) of Campania, procurator of the *alimenta* in Lucania, Bruttium, Calabria, and Apulium, curator for repairing the roofs

of public buildings and temples, aedile, member of the board of two, priest of the divine Augustus, member of the board of two for the five-yearly census, patron of the colony, Cerdo, freedman, set this up in honour of his incomparable patron along with Flavius Maximus and Germanus and Rufinus, his sons, who have been honoured with the public horse.

Germanus held the position of procurator of a region of the city; procurators had replaced the praetors and tribunes of the time of Augustus. Germanus had also been given the duty of looking after some city streets, perhaps taking over some of the duties of the aediles. His curatorship of the roofs refers to his duties in his native community of Praeneste. For the *alimenta* see no. 187; public horse, p. 48 and no. 61.

D 43.11.1pr-1 (Ulpian, *Edict*, Book 68)

110. The praetor declares: 'I forbid force to be used to prevent a person from opening up or repairing a public street or road, provided that that street or road is not made worse'. To open up a street is to restore it to its original depth and breadth. Cleaning a street is part of the repair. To clean it, described in proper terms, is restoring the original surface by removing what was on top of it. For the person who opens up a street and the person who cleans it repair it since they all restore it to its former condition.

D 43.7.1 (Pomponius, *Sabinus*, Book 30)

111. Anyone must be permitted to claim for public use that which is designated for the use of everyone, such as public roads and public highways. Consequently, on the demand of anyone at all interdicts are available concerning them.

For interdicts see p. 247.

Martial 7.61

112. The reckless shopkeeper had taken over the entire city, and a citizen's doorstep was no longer his own. Domitian, you ordered that the narrow streets should grow wider, and now where there was a narrow path a thoroughfare has been created. No pillar is now festooned with wine jars chained together, and the praetor is not forced to wade in the middle of mud. The barber's razor is not flourished blindly in the middle of a dense throng and the sooty cook shops do not take up entire streets. Barbers, innkeepers, cooks, and butchers stay within their own thresholds. Now Rome exists, whereas it was formerly a huge shop.

For Martial see p. 479. His epigrams, at times satirical, often comment vividly on life in Rome; he suggests the limitations of city planning regulations despite the best efforts of emperors, because of the encroachments of shopkeepers.

Juvenal, *Satires* 3.234–48; 254–9

113. What sort of lodging permits you to get to sleep? Only the wealthy can get a good sleep in Rome. That is the cause of the trouble. The racket of the waggons making their way through narrow, twisting streets, and the yells of the drivers stuck in the traffic would snatch away sleep from even that drowsy seal Claudius. If a business meeting summons the rich man, he is carried above the crowd by foreign slaves, and on the way he reads or writes or sleeps inside, as the litter with its drawn blinds allows him to sleep. And he still gets there before us. As we hurry forward a great wave of people blocks us, and the people behind crowd on our heels. One hits me in the ribs with an elbow, another hits me with a hard pole, another strikes me on the head with a wooden beam, another with a barrel. My legs are covered in mud, big feet kick me from every direction, and a soldier's hobnail boot lands on my toe ... (254) A great fir-tree wobbles along on its waggon, and other waggons carry pine-logs, nodding threateningly high above the heads of the crowd. If an axle were to break in the waggon carrying a load of marble and upended it over the heads of the crowd, what would be left of the bodies?

D 21.1.40–1 (Paul, *Edict of the Curule Aediles*, Book 2)

114. Then the aediles declare: No one is to keep a dog, a hog, a small boar, a wolf, a bear, a panther, a lion, or generally any animal likely to be dangerous, whether they are on the loose or chained up, to prevent them causing harm where there is a commonly used path, with the result that injury or damage could be caused to someone.

Tabula Heracleensis Crawford (1996), p. 365, lines 56–61

115. Whatever roads are or shall be inside the city of Rome within those places where there is continuous occupation of dwellings, no one, after 1 January next, in the day-time, after sunrise or before the tenth hour of the day, is to bring or drive a cart on those roads, unless it is appropriate for anything to be conveyed or carried in order to build sacred temples of the immortal gods, or carry out work (for that purpose), or unless it is appropriate for any of those materials, for which a contract has been let for their public demolition, to be

publicly removed from the city, or from those areas, and in those circumstances where it is permitted for particular individuals for particular reasons to drive or lead waggons under this statute.

For the relevance of the statute of Heraclea to Rome, see nos. 106, 108.

CIL 6.31615 = *ILS* 8208

116. Lucius Sentius, son of Gaius, praetor, by decree of the senate, has instructed that boundaries should be established. For the public good. No one is to seek to construct a place for burning corpses or seek to dump dung or corpses within the boundary markers closer to the city. (Painted on one of the boundary markers) Take dung far away, unless you want trouble.

Two stones marking the boundary of a communal dump for corpses near the Esquiline gate probably date from the late first century BC. Burials and cremations were normally prohibited inside a community (Cicero, *Leges* 2.23.58; *Paul. Sent.* 1.21.2). Hence the better-off constructed their tombs along the approach roads. See in general Toynbee (1971). For poorer citizens burial often occurred in a communal pit which could then be covered over; Robinson (1992), 124–6.

Urban Life

Emperor and City

Suetonius, *Augustus* 37

117. To enable more men to participate in the administration of the state he (Augustus) created new offices: the responsibility for public buildings, for the roads, for the water supply, for the bed of the Tiber, for the distribution of corn to the people, and also the prefecture of the city, a board of three for choosing senators, and another for assessing the companies of *equites* whenever that should be necessary.

The office responsible for public buildings consisted of two senators – *Curatores aedium sacrarum et operum locorumque publicorum*, though the title is subject to variation. They were responsible for maintenance and restoration.

Augustus, *Res Gestae* 19; 20.1–4; 21.1

118. I built the senate house and next to it the Chalcidicum, the temple of Apollo on the Palatine with its porticoes, the temple of the divine Julius, the Lupercal, the portico at the Flaminian circus, which I permitted to be

named the portico of Octavius after the person who had built the previous portico on the same site, the *pulvinar* at the Circus Maximus, the temples of Jupiter Feretrius and Jupiter the Thunderer on the Capitol, the temple of Quirinus, the temples of Minerva and Juno the Queen and Jupiter the Liberator on the Aventine, the temple of the Lares at the top of the Sacred Way, the temple of the Di Penates on the Velian hill, the temple of Youth, the temple of the Great Mother on the Palatine.

(20) I restored the Capitol and the theatre of Pompey, both tasks at great expense, but did not inscribe my own name on either. I restored the channels of the aqueducts, which in several places were collapsing through age, and I doubled the supply of water of the Marcia aqueduct by bringing water from a new spring into its channel. I completed the Julian Forum and the basilica which was between the temple of Castor and the temple of Saturn, works begun and almost completed by my father, and when this same basilica was destroyed by fire I began the rebuilding on a bigger site to be dedicated in the name of my sons, and if I should be unable to complete it in my lifetime, I have given instructions that it is to be completed by my heirs. During my sixth consulship I restored eighty-two temples of the gods in the city on the authority of the senate, passing over none that needed to be restored at that time.

(21) I built the temple of Mars the Avenger and the Augustan Forum on private ground from the proceeds of booty.

Augustus' account of his building in Rome serves as an example of imperial building in the city; numerous public buildings boosted imperial standing and provided public amenities and employment. The contribution of the imperial entourage was also important, notably Agrippa (Dio 53.27); in addition, Augustus encouraged private individuals to build for the public good (Suetonius, *Augustus* 29.4). Other emperors followed this example as inclination and funds permitted; see Robinson (1992), 51–3; for Augustus' impact on the architecture of Rome, see Favro (1996), 79–142; Walker (2000).

Suetonius, *Augustus* 100.4

119. This building (the Mausoleum) he had constructed in his sixth consulship between the Flaminian way and the bank of the Tiber, and at the same time he laid open to the public the woods and walks which surrounded it.

See also Strabo 5.3.8 (236). Augustus had also planted a wood at the site of his Naumachia built to stage naval battles (Tacitus, *Annals* 14.15).

Dio 54.29.4

120. And indeed he (Agrippa) left to them (the people) the gardens and the baths named after him, so they could bathe free of cost, and for this purpose he left several estates to Augustus. He not only turned these over to the state but distributed to the people one hundred denarii each, stating that Agrippa had ordered this.

For public gardens in Rome, often provided through imperial benefaction, see Farrar (1998), 179–86.

The Corn Supply

Augustus, *Res Gestae* 5.2

121. I did not refuse in a great shortage of corn to undertake responsibility for the corn supply, which I administered in such a way that within a few days I freed the entire state from anxiety and the immediate danger, using my own money and by my own work.

In 22 BC because of a serious shortage of corn Augustus accepted a *cura annonae*, which gave him responsibility for obtaining corn and making sure that those entitled to a free distribution received it. Augustus also records (*RG* 15.1–2; 4) a special grant of corn purchased with his own money, and generous cash handouts to the plebs, up to 250,000 people, and in 5 BC to 320,000. Therefore, Augustus met his responsibilities to the citizens, and in return could expect loyalty and obedience to his authority. The corn was handed out to adult males and probably amounted to five *modii* a month, which was not enough for a family, but the government also aimed to supplement this by ensuring a plentiful supply of cheap corn. Cassius Dio (55.26.3) remarks that in AD 6 during a famine Augustus gave as much again to recipients of free corn. Augustus' acceptance of responsibility for the free corn distribution and for ensuring the availability of sufficient corn which the plebs could buy at a reasonable price created a permanent imperial obligation which had political implications. An emperor could acquire great popularity if things went well but face potential disorder and hostility if the corn supply was affected by adverse weather or other problems. For example, in 51 during a grain shortage Claudius was surrounded by a mob in the forum and pelted with pieces of bread, only with difficulty escaping to the place by a back door (Suetonius, *Claudius* 18.2). Therefore, great attention was given to the administration of the corn supply of Rome.

Between AD 8 and 14 Augustus appointed a prefect of the corn supply of equestrian rank to be responsible for the entire system and report to him. The prefect, of senior equestrian rank, monitored the corn supply market, storage facilities, assessed supply and demand, and tried to plan for a consistent supply at a reasonable price. His office was in Rome and his duties were for the benefit of the citizens of Rome, but his remit extended to corn supply areas throughout the empire, particularly Egypt and North Africa. Corn distribution was organized by prefects of senatorial rank, the *praefecti frumenti dandi*, and took place from gates in the *Porticus Minucia* at which recipients presented themselves with their token. Although much of the corn-shipping business was essentially a free market, the government to some extent intervened, offering privileges to encourage the participation of ship-owners, and attempting to check speculators and fraud. Rickman (1980) offers an excellent overview of the corn supply; see also Mattingly and Aldrete (2000); Erdkamp (2005), 206–57; for the problem of corn shortages in the empire see Garnsey (1988), 218–43. At Oxyrhynchus there was a corn dole apparently modelled on that at Rome but issued not to the destitute but to the better-off (*P. Oxy.* Vol 40).

D 50.5.3 (Scaevola, *Rules*, Book 3)

122. Those persons who have built a sea-going ship and have provided it for the corn supply of Rome, each with a capacity no less than fifty thousand measures of corn or more, or five or more each with a capacity of at least ten thousand measures, provided that these ships sail, or others in their place, receive exemption from public service for providing the ship.

Corn measurers in Rome also had exemption – *D* 27.1.26 (Paul, *Exemptions*, book 1). For Claudius' concessions to encourage participation in shipping corn to Rome see no. 41. In addition, Claudius offered citizens who built merchant vessels exemption from Augustus' marriage legislation, and to women the privileges granted to women with four children (Suetonius, *Claudius* 18–19). The emperor celebrated his attention to the corn supply with an issue of coins where Ceres, the goddess of grain, was presented as *Ceres Augusta*.

D 47.11.6 (Ulpian, *Duties of a Proconsul*, Book 8)

123. Speculators habitually disrupt and disturb the corn supply, and their greed has been combatted both by imperial instructions and constitutions. In the instructions to governors the following guidance is given: 'Furthermore, you must ensure that there are no speculators in any kind of merchandise, and that the corn supply is not imperilled by those who buy up supplies and then hoard them, or by the rich who are reluctant to sell their own produce at a reasonable price while they wait for a less bountiful crop'. Various penalties are laid down for these men.

Generally, if they are in business they are merely prohibited from that business, though sometimes they are deported, and if of lower social rank sent to the public works.

BGU 27 = *SP* no. 113

124. Irenaeus to Apollinarius, dearest brother, many greetings. I am continually praying for your good health, and I myself am well. I want you to know that I made land on the sixth of the month Epeiph (30 June) and we unloaded the cargo on the eighteenth of the same month (12 July). I travelled up to Rome on the twenty-fifth of the same month and the place gave us a welcome that the god wished, and every day we expect our note of discharge (*dimissoria*), as right up to today no one from the grain fleet has been released. I send all good wishes to your wife and to Serenus and by name to all those who love you. Farewell.

Until the *dimissoria* was issued the corn shippers from Alexandria were not allowed to leave Italy after unloading their grain, presumably to ensure that everything was in order and that all the ships were ready.

D 48.2.13 (Marcian, *Criminal Proceedings*, Book 1)

125. The divine Severus and Antoninus stated in a rescript that a woman who brought information relating to the grain dole was to be heard by the prefect of the grain supply for the public good.

Women were not normally allowed to initiate legal action in criminal courts except where they had a direct personal interest.

Aqueducts and Water Supply

Frontinus, *Aqueducts* 104; 106

126. (In respect of the number of public fountains established by Marcus Agrippa) … the senate has resolved that the number of public fountains which are reported to exist at this moment by those who were instructed by the senate to inspect the public aqueducts and record the number of public fountains, shall neither be increased nor decreased. It was further resolved that the curators of the aqueducts whom Caesar Augustus appointed on the authorization of the senate shall ensure that the public fountains gush out water as continuously as possible day and night for the use of the people. (106) The senate has resolved that no private person shall be

permitted to draw water from the public conduits, and all those persons to whom the right of drawing water has been granted, shall draw it from the cisterns, and the curators of the aqueducts shall indicate at which locations inside the city private persons can appropriately construct cisterns in order to draw from them the water which they have received from a public reservoir through the action of the curators.

For the protection and maintenance of the aqueducts, see no. 127.

Frontinus, *Aqueducts* 129 = *FIRA* 1, no. 14 (Extract)

127. Titus Quintius Crispinus, consul, properly put the question to the people and the people properly gave its vote in the forum before the Rostra of the temple of the deified Julius on 30 June. The Sergian tribe voted first. Sextus Varro, son of Lucius, cast his vote first on behalf of his tribe: Whoever after the passage of this statute knowingly and maliciously pierces, or breaks, or arranges for the piercing or breaking, of the conduits, arches, pipes, tubes, reservoirs, or basins of the public waters, which are brought to the city, or who degrades them so as to prevent those waters or any part of them from going, plunging, flowing, coming, or being conducted into the city of Rome, or to prevent their movement, distribution, division, or pouring into reservoirs or basins in the city of Rome, or in those places and buildings, which places and buildings are adjacent or will be adjacent to the city, and in those gardens, estates, and properties of owners or possessors, to whom water is given or granted now or in the future, that person shall be condemned to pay one hundred thousand sesterces to the Roman people. Furthermore, whoever does any of these things wrongfully and maliciously shall be condemned to patch up, repair, restore, rebuild, or replace (what has been damaged), or speedily demolish (any construction) in good faith [...]. (There follows a statement of the responsibilities of the curators for enforcement.)

This measure was voted by the senate in 9 BC; it goes on to note that pasturing cattle and cutting hay is permitted within the enclosed area round the aqueducts, but the curators have the right to remove trees or vines and other undergrowth that might threaten the aqueducts; see nos. 90–2.

CIL 5.1245 = *ILS* 98

128. Imperator Caesar M. Aurellius Antoninus Pius Felix Augustus, greatest conqueror of the Parthians, greatest conqueror of the British,

chief priest, arranged for the Aqua Marcia which had been blocked by various impediments, to be brought into his very own revered city, by clearing out the source, cutting and digging through hills, restoring the channel, and even adding a new source, the Antoniniana.

This inscription from the Aqua Marcia celebrates the work of Caracalla, and this aqueduct was intended to supply his new baths. The inscription also cites work by Augustus and Titus. The ethos is that the state accepted an obligation to provide running water even if the citizens had to come to fountains or cisterns to use it. The *Curatores Aquarum* were established by the senate on the authority of Augustus. They were headed by a consular and had a gang of 700 slaves; their job was not just to run the system but to guarantee the water supply. Consequently, the curators had control over private water lines and acted as judge in cases concerning aqueducts and water supply (see Frontinus, *Aqueducts* 17, 103, 105, 109). Frontinus, a senator of consular rank (see also p. 478), was appointed by Nerva in 97 as curator of the aqueducts and wrote the *De Aquis* (*Aqueducts*) as a kind of guide to their management. One of his duties was to protect the system against interference and interruption: 'I discovered that these (pipes) had been perforated in various places by these men described as "puncturers" and provided water by special pipes to all the businesses in the vicinity, with the result that only a limited amount was getting through for public use' (*Aqueducts* 115).

It has been surmised that of water available in Rome c. 17 per cent went to public baths, c. 44 per cent to military and official establishments, including theatres, fountains, and baths, and c. 38 per cent to private houses and industries (Dodge (2000), 187; Hodge (2002), 246–72; 273–303). For firefighting see p. 89–93. From the start emperors had an important role in building and repairing aqueducts; a large proportion of the water went to the baths which came to be seen as a subsidized public amenity, which will also have contributed to cleanliness and perhaps better health. Agrippa built public baths; in 33 BC during the year of his aedileship he provided free bathing in all the baths (Dio 49.43; and no. 142), and in his will provided for the upkeep of the baths. Similarly, Agrippa and Augustus ensured that gardens and open spaces were available to the plebs (see p. 78).

Frontinus, *Aqueducts* 98

129. Marcus Agrippa, after holding the office of aedile, which he did after his consulship, was the first to hold a virtually permanent curatorship of the works and service which he had created. When the supply of water was sufficient, he decided how much water should be assigned to public buildings, how much to basins, and how much to private individuals.

He also maintained a private squad of slaves to maintain the channels, the reservoirs, and the basins. Augustus gave this squad, which had been left to him in Agrippa's will, to the state.

The aedileship was a junior magistracy, and it is a mark of the importance attached by Augustus to these public amenities that Agrippa held it after his consulship.

The Tiber

D 1.8.5 (Gaius, *Everyday Matters or Golden Words*, Book 2)

130. By the law of nations there is public use of the banks just as of the river itself. Therefore, anyone is free to bring a boat up to the bank, tie it up with ropes attached to the trees growing on the bank, to dry nets and haul them up from the water, and to put any cargo on them, just as he is free to navigate the river. But the ownership of the banks belongs to those on whose property they are. For this reason, any trees that grow on the banks also belong to them.

D 43.12.1.7 (Ulpian, *Edict*, Book 68)

131. (If a river leaves its bed and flows in another direction) it certainly ceases to be public property. Furthermore, that (new) bed which the river made for itself, although it was previously private property, nevertheless begins to be public, because it is impossible that the bed of a public river should not be public property.

All significant rivers were defined as public property although private landholders could own the land up to the water's edge; for riverine definitions see Campbell (2012), 86–90. There were restrictions on what could be done on or near a river, so as not to impede the water flow. The Tiber was particularly important as a route for imports to Rome transported upstream from the port of Ostia. In the city itself substantial harbour facilities existed. Although many private properties fronted onto the river, the government took stretches of bank into public ownership and marked them with boundary stones. The city was plagued by flooding, as the river, swollen by rainwater from its course in the upper valley, burst its banks. In 23 BC the situation was so bad that people had to travel about the city by boat for three days (Dio 53.33.5). In the next year there was another serious flood (Dio 54.1). In AD 5 the Tiber destroyed the Sublician bridge, and the city was navigable for seven days (Dio 55.22.3), and in AD 12 the Circus was flooded (Dio 56.27.4); for the Tiber floods see Aldrete (2007).

ILS 9376

132. Gaius Caninius, son of Gaius, urban praetor, adjudicated the public area in accordance with the decision of the senate.

This stone dating from the last century of the republic is one of five erected by Caninius in Ostia to demarcate public ownership of an area between the town's main street and the Tiber; another stone possibly set up independently by a landholder marks the limits of public control: 'private land to the Tiber, right up to the water' (*CIL* 14.4703). In AD 23–41 boundary stones were erected along the Tiber at Ostia by the curators of the beds and banks of the Tiber, Gaius Antistius Vetus and his colleagues; inscribed on the rear: 'without prejudging the rights of the state or private individuals' (*CIL* 14.4704 a–c); see Campbell (2012), 87.

Suetonius, *Augustus* 30.1

133. Augustus, in order to prevent flooding, widened and cleared up the bed of the Tiber, which over a period of time had been filled with rubbish and narrowed by projecting buildings.

Suetonius believed that Augustus established a formal commission for controlling the river, but Tacitus (*Annals* 1.76) and Dio (no. 134) ascribe the action to Tiberius. For Augustus' arrangements in Rome, see no. 96.

Dio 57.14.8

134. (Tiberius) however thought that the flood had resulted from the huge quantity of surface water and established five senators chosen by lot as permanent curators with the task of looking after the river, so that it did not flood in the winter or run dry in the summer, but as far as possible always maintained a consistent flow.

From the time of Vespasian, the board of curators was replaced by one curator of consular rank.

CIL 6.31553 = *ILS* 5932 (AD 161)

135. [Emperor Caesar T. Aelius Hadr]ianus An[toninus] Pius, chief priest, in his twenty-fourth year of tribunician power, acclaimed imperator for the second time, consul for the fourth time, father of the fatherland, when Aulus Platorius Nepos Calpurnianus was curator of the bed and banks of the Tiber and the sewers of the city, built up and restored the boundary

markers, which had collapsed through age, in a straight line, ... feet from the next stone, which had been set up on the authority of Emperor Caesar Nerva Trajan Augustus Germanicus, son of Nerva, chief priest, in his fifth year of tribunician power, consul for the fourth time, father of the fatherland, under Iulius Ferox, curator of the bed and banks of the Tiber and the sewers of the city.

Calpurnianus restored stones set up by a previous curator, Iulius Ferox, in 101. See Campbell (2012), 309–20 for the management of the Tiber. The job of the curators was to control as far as possible the water level in the river and try to moderate flooding, and to supervise the course of the river downstream to Ostia. The boundary stones marked the public area, which was consistently maintained.

Tacitus, *Annals* 1.79

136. The next subject for discussion, introduced by Lucius Arruntius and Gaius Ateius Capito, was whether, in order to control the Tiber floods, the rivers and lakes by which its flow was increased should be diverted. Deputations from the municipalities and colonies received a hearing, and the people of Florentia begged that the river Clanis should not be diverted from its normal bed into the Arnus since that would be disastrous for them. The people of Interamna made a similar case; the most fertile land in Italy would be ruined if the river Nar (for that was planned) was scattered into channels and its flow dissipated. The people of Reate also spoke vigorously, arguing that the Veline Lake, at its outlet into the Nar, should not be damned, as it would burst its banks and flood the surrounding countryside. Nature had looked after humans very well by giving every river its own source, outlet, and limits. They should take account of the religious views of local people, who had honoured the rivers close to their homes with sacred rites, groves, and altars. Even Tiber himself would not take kindly to flowing with his majesty diminished if he were deprived of the tributary rivers. Either because of the pleas of the townspeople, or technical problems, or superstitious feeling, the senate adopted the proposal of Cnaeus Calpurnius Piso, who voted that nothing should be changed.

Quite apart from the potential disruption to local riverine hydrology, small communities had a strong emotional connection to their local rivers, which often received offerings and sacred groves; these communities felt strongly enough to incur the expense of a deputation to the senate; see Campbell (2012), 118–19.

D 39.2.9.1 (Ulpian, *Edict*, Book 53)

137. The question is asked if an interdict can be granted in respect of items which have been brought into your property by the force of a river. Trebatius notes that when the Tiber had flooded and moved many possessions of a great number of people to the houses of others, an interdict was granted by the praetor that no force should be used against the owners to prevent them from collecting and taking away their property, provided that they gave security for any possible damage.

This indicates the legal response to frequent flooding, outlined by the jurist Trebatius, who wrote in the late republic.

Sewers

The main sewer was the *Cloaca Maxima* and in the early imperial period responsibility for the upkeep of the sewers in Rome probably fell mainly on the aediles; however, Trajan extended the duties of the curators of the bed and banks of the Tiber to include supervision of the sewers (see for example *ILS* 5930). There was limited provision of latrines, though some will have been available in the public baths. Public urinals would often consist of jars provided in streets; the contents were collected under public contract and sold to fullers. Excrement could be collected and removed by carts during the night (and see no. 116). The aediles were responsible for making sure the streets were cleared of any kind of rubbish; see Robinson (1992), 85–6.

Strabo 5.3.8 (235)

138. The Romans exercised foresight in maters which the Greeks ignored, for example, the construction of roads and aqueducts and sewers capable of flushing out all the filth of the city into the Tiber ... Water is brought into the city in such amounts by means of aqueducts that a virtual river flows through the city and the sewers.

At the direction of the emperor redundant water was not to be drawn off but retained to flush the sewers (Frontinus, *Aqueducts* 111).

Pliny, *NH* 36.104

139. The ancients marvelled at the vast extent of the constructions and the foundations of the Capitol, and particularly the sewers, reportedly the greatest of all the works, with mountains excavated and, as I pointed out

before, buried below the city hanging above them; they were navigated by Marcus Agrippa in his aedileship, which he held after his consulship. There are seven streams channelled (in the city) and under the impulse of their surging current they snatch and carry away everything, and driven on by rainwater they batter the sides and bottom, and sometimes the waters of the Tiber are backed up and all the contending streams of water battle one another inside, but the walls despite the assault remain firm.

See also no. 142. For Pliny, see p. 480.

D 43.23.1.1–2 and 15–16 (Ulpian, *Edict*, Book 71)

140. Under this heading the praetor provides two interdicts, one to prohibit, the other to restore. The first prohibits. The praetor ensures by these interdicts that the drains are cleaned and repaired, and both these operations contribute to the health and security of communities. For the filth of drains if they are not repaired brings a threat of pestilence in the air, and ruin. This interdict is provided in respect of private drains. For public sewers require the attention of public officials. (15–16) Next the praetor declares: 'Whatever you have done in or introduced into a public drain so its effectiveness is or will be reduced, you must restore. And I will issue an interdict prohibiting the doing or introducing of any such thing (into the drain)'.

For interdicts see p. 247.

Macrobius, *Saturnalia* 3.16.13–14

141. (Macrobius is referring to the quality of fish in the Tiber) Varro says this about all the fish in the river. But as I pointed out above, the pike has pride of place, and especially the one which is caught between the two bridges.

For Macrobius, see p. 479. The two bridges are the *pons Aemilius* and the *pons Sublicius* south of the Tiber Island and adjacent to the mouth of the *Cloaca Maxima*, which was not thought to undermine the quality of the fish.

Baths

After the substantial generosity of Agrippa emperors had large bathing complexes built, notably Nero, Trajan, and Caracalla. Entry to the baths was free or heavily subsidized and this imperial generosity was another important link between emperor and plebs in Rome. Both men and women used the baths but at different times, although the idea of mixed bathing did develop by the end of the first century, to the extent that Hadrian had to forbid it; for a brief survey see Robinson (1992), 113–16; also, in general, Nielsen (1993).

Dio 49.43.1–2

142. In the next year (33 BC) Agrippa agreed to be appointed aedile, and, without withdrawing anything from the treasury, repaired all the public buildings and all the streets, cleaned out the sewers and sailed underground through them to the Tiber ... In addition, he distributed olive oil and salt to everyone and throughout the year provided the baths free of charge to both men and women.

See also Dio 54.29.4. For the operation of the baths, we can compare the baths at Vipasca in Portugal; see no. 234.

Dio 69.8.2

143. He (Hadrian) distributed gifts by means of little balls in the theatres and in the circus to men and women separately. And he instructed that they should bathe separately.

See also *Historia Augusta, Hadrian* 18.11. Augustus' mother apparently attended the baths regularly (Suetonius, *Augustus* 94.4).

Seneca, *Letters* 86.9

144. But once upon a time baths were few and not elaborately decorated; for why should something that cost a quarter of an *as* and was devised for use not pleasure be decorated?

For the younger Seneca see p. 480. If there was a charge for entry to the baths it was a *quadrans* (see also Martial 1.59), and children probably entered free.

Amphitheatres

Amphitheatres and other venues for games, shows, and performances provided pleasure and escape for the mass of the people in a crowded city, but the emperor had to be the principal benefactor in providing the games. For a time, the only permanent structure for games and animal hunts had been built by a senator, Statilius Taurus; temporary structures were also employed before Vespasian built the Colosseum on the site of Nero's golden house from the spoils of war, probably the Jewish war, emphasizing his concern for the people and success in war; it was dedicated by Titus and completed by Domitian. The games could be a useful focal point for expressions of support for an emperor, although the opposite was also possible, as occurred in AD 193 when the audience adopted a rhythmical chant against the short-lived Didius Iulianus. The preservation of order was also important, as the excitement and betting caused frequent disturbances; for a useful summary see Coulston and Dodge (2000), 227–40; on the place of gladiators in imperial ideology, see Wiedemann (1992), 165–83; for sources on the games, see Futrell (2006).

CIL 6.40454a; Alföldy (1995)

145. Emperor T(itus) Caesar Vespasian Augustus ordered a new amphitheatre to be built from the spoils of war.

Alföldy restored the inscription partly based on the position of the peg-holes on the stone; it may have been first dedicated to Vespasian who died before its dedication; the letter T was then added for Titus. The use of booty in the construction symbolized an emperor powerful in war; Augustus had built the temple of Mars the Avenger 'from booty' (*Res Gestae* 21).

Security and Control

The last days of the republic were notorious for political violence and disorder in Rome. The annual magistrates were unable or unwilling to keep order, and state-sponsored armed force was inadequate to maintain control. Augustus transformed life in the city, not just by his buildings and benefactions, but also by his establishment of units of armed men and the appointment of officials to take command, serving for several years in each post. The emperor's own guards, the praetorian guard, had three cohorts (probably 3,000 men) permanently stationed in the city, and the remaining six in neighbouring communities, from 2 BC commanded by prefects of equestrian rank. From early in the rule of Tiberius all nine cohorts were stationed in a camp in Rome itself. By the time of Septimius Severus, after the reorganization of the praetorians, larger forces were present in Rome and a legion was based at Albanum north of the city. The *Vigiles*, who kept a watch throughout the city for fires, numbered 7,000 and were commanded by an equestrian prefect. The three urban cohorts (probably 3,000 men) served essentially as para-military police and were under the direction of the prefect of the city. The officials in control of these forces between them controlled fire safety, gatherings either at public spectacles or in private clubs that might lead to disorder, the marketplace, and aspects of jurisdiction, including summary jurisdiction. As appointees of the emperor, they were directly responsible to him for maintaining good public discipline. The plebs could express their feelings by demonstrating and chanting at the games, but sometimes popular fervour had to be checked by an imperial edict, or even the use of force, as when Nero had his guards drive out of the palace people voicing their support for his divorced wife Octavia who was facing exile (Tacitus, *Annals* 14.61). In the reign of Severus Alexander relations between the plebs and the praetorians had deteriorated to the extent that there was a three-day battle in Rome which ended when the soldiers set fire to parts of the city (Dio 80.2.3); see Robinson (1992), 181–95; for the maintenance of order in Rome see Nippel (1984); (1995); Fuhrmann (2012), 49–52; 113–21; 124–30.

Policing the City

Dio 53.11.5

146. Immediately he (Augustus) arranged to have voted to his bodyguards double the pay of the other soldiers so that he might be securely guarded. Therefore, in truth he was eager to establish a monarchy.

Dio refers to 27 BC and Augustus' speech to the senate in which he apparently claimed to hand over to them responsibility for affairs of state; Dio sarcastically regarded it as part of a plan to get the senate to urge Augustus to take on a leading role.

***D* 1.11.1.1 (Charisius, *Duties of the Praetorian Prefect*, Sole Book)**

147. The power of the praetorian prefects from its infancy deservedly developed to the extent that no appeal was possible from the prefect. For although the question had been raised earlier whether an appeal could be made from the prefect, and although it was legally possible and there were examples of those who had appealed, later the right to appeal was rescinded through an imperial decision publicly pronounced. For the emperor believed that those who had been promoted to such a lofty position because of their outstanding diligence and proven loyalty and seriousness, could

not possibly reach a judgement on behalf of his wisdom and the shining glory of his eminence, other than he would have reached himself.

The origins of the praetorian prefect's jurisdiction lie in the fact that the prefect controlled the only substantial source of military power close to the emperor in Rome; he could exercise summary jurisdiction in respect of people detained by the praetorians for offences, probably originally of a minor nature. He also was responsible for organizing executions and the application of torture. Furthermore, the prefect was responsible for receiving prisoners sent to Rome for trial (see p. 115). It was a short step for him to be given responsibility for hearing some of these cases since he was already exercising limited jurisdiction. Prefects by their position were closely associated with the emperor, who, being burdened with legal business, would find it convenient to pass certain cases to them. Since there were often two prefects in office, twice as much could be passed on. This was an ad hoc arrangement and, as we have seen, other officials also exercised jurisdiction in Rome, such as the praetor and the prefect of the city. But beyond the hundredth milestone from the city the praetorian prefect had unchallenged jurisdiction (see no. 186).

D 1.12.1.1–14; 2 (Ulpian, *Duties of the Prefect of the City*, Only Book; Paul, *Duties of the Prefect of the City*, Only Book; Ulpian, *Edict*, Book 2)

148. The jurisdiction of the city prefect claims for its remit all criminal offences, not only those that are committed inside the city but also those which take place outside the city within Italy, as a letter of the divine Severus to Fabius Cilo, prefect of the city, makes clear. He is to give a hearing to slaves who have fled to statues, or who have used their own money to pay for their manumission, when they make a complaint about their masters. He is also to give a hearing to impoverished patrons who complain about their freedmen, especially if they claim that they are ill and want to be supported by their freedmen. He has the power to relegate and deport to an island which the emperor has designated. At the beginning of the same letter is the following: 'Since we have entrusted our city to you', whatever crime is committed within the city evidently pertains to the jurisdiction of the prefect of the city. Furthermore, if any offence is committed within the hundredth milestone, it is within the remit of the prefect of the city, but anything beyond that milestone is outside the jurisdiction of the prefect of the city … (9) Furthermore, the prefect of the city should ensure that moneylenders conduct themselves honestly in all their business and avoid activities that are prohibited. When a patron claims that he has been insulted by his freedman or complains that a freedman has acted abusively towards him, or states that he or his wife

and children have been outrageously insulted or something similar, the prefect of the city is usually approached and punishes the freedman in proportion to the seriousness of the complaint … (11) Responsibility for the meat business, so that all of it is sold at a fair price, pertains to the prefect of the city, and the pig market is also under his remit. Furthermore, all herds of sheep and cattle which are part of provision of this kind are the responsibility of the prefect of the city. Responsibility for the peaceful behaviour of the citizens and good order at public spectacles evidently pertains to the prefect of the city. Indeed, he ought to have soldiers positioned strategically to maintain public order and to inform him of what is happening and where. Furthermore, the prefect of the city has the power to ban someone from the city and from any other of the usual districts, from business, from professions, from advocacy, and from the forum, temporarily or in perpetuity. He also has the power to ban people from public spectacles, and if he banishes a person from Italy, he can even ban him from his own province. (14) The divine Severus stated in a rescript that those who allegedly form an illegal club (*collegium*) were to be accused before the prefect of the city.

2. Applications may be made to him either by bankers, or against them, and he can act in all pecuniary cases, according to a letter of the divine Hadrian.

Despite the prefect of the city's control of the pig market, the curule aediles had jurisdiction over general sales in the markets. To ensure fair play for the citizens a system of standard weights and measures operated, and fraudulent activities were dealt with (see p. 333 for the role of the aediles). For discussion of the jurisdiction of the prefect of the city, see Bauman (1996), 100–6. The jurisdiction of the prefect of the city sat side by side with that of the praetorian prefect, which applied particularly to the actions or arrests of praetorian guardsmen.

D 1.15.3pr-1; 3–5 (Paul, *Duties of the Prefect of the Vigiles*, Book 1)

149. For he (Augustus) believed that the protection of the safety of the state was the responsibility of no one other than Caesar, and no other person was competent for that task. Therefore, he established seven cohorts in suitable locations, so that one cohort was responsible for two regions of the city; each cohort was commanded by a tribune, and in overall command was a senior official who was called prefect of the *Vigiles*. The prefect of the *Vigiles* tries cases involving arsonists, burglars, thieves, robbers, and harbourers of criminals, unless the culprit is so outrageous and notorious that he is remitted to the prefect of the city. And because fires generally break out because of the carelessness of the residents, he either beats with rods

those who have kept a fire negligently or gives them a severe reprimand and remits the punishment of a beating (3–5). It must be recognized that the prefect of *Vigiles* should keep watch for the entire night and, wearing appropriate shoes, patrol in company, equipped with hooks and axes, and warn all residents to take care that they do not cause an outbreak of fire through their negligence. Furthermore, he should order that every resident should keep water in his apartment. He has also been given jurisdiction over the functionaries (*capsarii*), who undertake for a fee to look after people's clothes at the baths, so that he can undertake a hearing if they have acted fraudulently in keeping the clothes.

D 1.15.4 (Ulpian, *Duties of the Prefect of the City*, Only Book)

150. The emperors Severus and Antoninus issued a rescript in the following terms to Junius Rufinus, prefect of the Vigiles: 'You may order those who live in apartments, and those who keep fires carelessly in their premises, to be beaten with rods or flogged. However, in the case of those who are convicted of deliberate and malicious arson you will send to our friend, Fabius Cilo, prefect of the city. You ought also to search for fugitive slaves and return them to their masters'.

Challenges to Law and Order

Despite the large numbers of military or semi-military personnel in Rome, satirists such as Juvenal and Martial suggest that walking in the streets was not necessarily safe, unless you were a rich man with a large retinue of slaves. Apart from individual footpads there were other elements in society that the government at times considered at least potentially disruptive, including astrologers, actors, some religious cults, and particularly *collegia.*

CIL 6.2193 = *ILS* 4966

151. To the gods of the dead: in honour of the *collegium* of bandsmen who perform at public rituals, whom the senate has allowed to meet, be summoned, and be gathered under the Iulian law, by the authorization of the emperor, for the purpose of festivals.

The right of free association for citizens had been established in the Twelve Tables. Thereafter this right was increasingly subject to interference by the government depending on the current political situation. In 186 BC the so-called Bacchanalia conspiracy saw action against the clubs or groups of worshippers whom the senate saw as perhaps an alternative source of authority, or a cause of social disturbance (see no. 599). In the late republic any organized group of poorer citizens had the potential of being a political club and a weapon that could be used to stir up trouble and disrupt the established upper-class consensus. In 64 BC nearly all *collegia* were banned, an excessively harsh measure which Clodius as tribune of the plebs in 58 reversed; in 56 in the aftermath of Clodius' murder the senate brought in a more limited ban. But the tendency was to restrict public association in the cause of suppressing dissent and disorder; see MacMullen (1966), 173–80.

In the imperial period, to have a *collegium* was a concession permitted under a *lex Iulia* (either of Julius Caesar or Augustus) for a particular purpose, after scrutiny by the senate and the emperor. While the authorities wanted to prevent groups from establishing a focus of loyalty outside their control and inciting violence, certain *collegia* could provide useful services. Obviously, those concerned with shipping had a vital role in supplying Rome with corn. But humbler *collegia* (*collegia tenuiorum*) served a useful social purpose in that such societies provided for the proper burial of their members, offered an outlet for social interaction among the members including slaves and freedmen, and provided limited scope for the ambitious, in that they were administered like a miniature version of local councils or the Roman state, with treasurers, officers, and masters. Therefore, the government accepted *collegia* likely to be beneficial but kept tough legislation available in case of need; see in general Meiggs (1960), 311–36; Aubert (1999); Coulston and Dodge (2000), 277–80; Perry (2011); Ascough et al. (2012); Verboven (2017). At times the law dealing with *collegia* was not strictly enforced, and the ambivalence of the government attitude is also seen in the eventual willingness to accept a corporate identity for *collegia* (see pp. 95–7).

D 47.22.1–3 (Marcian, *Institutes*, Book 3; Ulpian, *Duties of a Proconsul*, Book 6; Marcian, *Public Courts*, Book 2)

152. Governors of provinces are ordered in the imperial instructions not to permit political societies to exist, nor permit soldiers to have societies in the military camps. However, people of the lower classes are permitted to make a monthly contribution provided that they meet only once a month, in case under a pretext of this kind an illegal society may meet. The divine Severus also provided in a rescript that this rule applied not only in Rome but also in Italy and the provinces. Furthermore, they are not prevented from meeting for religious purposes, provided that in this nothing is done in contravention of the senatorial decree by which illegal societies are prohibited. However, a person is not permitted to be a member of more than one

legal society, as was decided by the divine brothers (Lucius Verus and Marcus Aurelius). If someone belongs to two societies, it was stated in the rescript that he is to choose the one of which he prefers to be a member and is to receive from that society from which he resigns the sum that was due to him as his share of the communal fund.

(2) Whosoever carries on an illegal society is liable to the penalty that is applied to those who have been convicted of occupying public places and temples with armed men.

(3) All illegal societies are dissolved by imperial mandates and decisions and senatorial decrees. But when they are dissolved, the members are permitted to divide common funds if they have any and apportion the money among themselves. Most importantly, unless a society or any similar body meets with the authorization of a decree of the senate or of the emperor, it meets in contravention of the decree of the senate and imperial mandates and decisions. It is also permitted for slaves to be admitted into a society of the lower classes, provided that their masters agree. Therefore, the officials of these societies should be aware of this lest they admit to a society a slave without the agreement or knowledge of his master, and in future become liable for a penalty of one hundred gold pieces for each man (admitted in this way).

These regulations show the ambivalent attitude of the government. On the one hand, there was tough legislation, in that to run an illegal society was tantamount to occupying public places with armed men, that is, rebellion and treason; on the other hand, when an illegal society was dissolved its members could claim their share of the funds. The government aimed to prevent violence while seeking to exploit the benefits of *collegia* in society.

D 3.4.1.1–2 (Gaius, *Provincial Edict*, Book 3)

153. Neither a partnership nor a *collegium* nor any other body of the kind is freely allowed in all cases to have a corporate capacity. For this right is controlled by statutes, decrees of the senate, and imperial decisions. Indeed, in only a few instances are bodies of this type permitted, for example, partners in the collection of public revenue, and in gold, silver, and salt mining, have been permitted to have a corporate status. There are also some associations in Rome whose corporate status has been confirmed by senatorial decrees and imperial decisions, for example, the bakers and some others, and the ship-owners who exist also in the provinces. In the case of any association or partnership or indeed either one of these which

has been permitted to have a corporate status, it is correct on the analogy of the state that they should have common property, a common treasury, and a representative or syndic, through whom, just as in the state, business that needs to be done and conducted in common may be done and conducted. Because if no one comes forward in their defence in respect of whatever is owned in common, and, having been warned they do not make a move in defence of their property, the proconsul declares that he will order it to be sold.

A legal *persona* has a capacity to receive rights and carry out obligations. In Roman law there was some acceptance of the concept that entities apart from human beings could be legal persons and have a status of their own, although the exact significance of the term *persona* is disputed. Of particular importance, apart from the state itself, are *collegia*, the government of local towns, religious institutions, tax-collecting companies, and eventually the Christian church. But there is a significant problem in establishing exactly what corporate rights these institutions had. The interpretation of this passage is disputed; it is difficult to make sense of the opening sentence: *Neque societas neque collegium neque huiusmodi corpus passim omnibus habere conceditur*. The translation (no. 153) follows the amendments suggested by Duff (1938), 141–8: *Neque societati neque collegio neque huiusmodi aliis corpus passim omnibus habere conceditur*. If property belonged to a corporate body, it was not owned by the individuals in that body; Duff thinks that Gaius restricts *corpus habere* to a limited number of semi-public organizations; he was not referring to poor men's burial clubs and dining clubs but describing the privilege of a few. The examples he mentions relate to people who were important contributors to the working of the empire, particularly tax-collecting companies, and the provision of foodstuffs for Rome. The power to have corporate identity was probably given sparingly; it was not until Marcus Aurelius that all *collegia* acquired attributes of personality, allowing them to receive legacies and free slaves. The interests of a *collegium* could be pursued by a representative (*actor*). For *collegia* outside Rome, see nos. 241–3. For the corporate identity of towns, see p. 111. For tax-collecting companies, see p. 198. For the Christian church and the ownership of property, see pp. 344–6.

D 40.3.1–2 (Ulpian, *Sabinus*, Books 5 and 14)

154. The divine Marcus granted to all associations who have the legal right to meet together the power of manumitting. Therefore, these bodies may claim the lawful inheritance of their freedmen.

Collegia now had the right to own slaves and other property in a corporate capacity (not in common), to sue, and be liable, as well as take legacies and manumit. 'Since the senate in the time of the divine Marcus permitted the making of legacies to associations, there is no doubt that if a legacy has been left to a corporate body that has the legal right to meet together, it is entitled to it' (*D* 34.5.20(21)). These rights are based on those of *municipia*.

Other groups from time to time attracted the government's attention as potential sources of disorder, especially at public events. Although the theatre and public performance were popular among the upper classes and emperors, actors had a persistently disreputable or salacious reputation either because of their personal conduct or because partisan support led to violence in the theatre. They were frequently expelled from Rome, and then recalled according to the public mood; for a summary see Robinson (1992), 202–6; see also p. 59. For astrologers and magicians, see pp. 325–8. Keepers of places of amusement for the lower classes such as brothels and gambling houses were closely observed by the authorities.

Suetonius, *Tiberius* 37.2

155. He severely punished outbreaks of popular disturbances and made strenuous efforts to prevent any outbreak. When blood was shed because of a fight in the theatre, he banished the leaders of the supporter groups and the actors who had caused the disagreement, and he could never be persuaded by any prayers of the people to recall them.

Tacitus, *Annals* 4.14 indicates that actors were expelled from Italy as well; but Caligula recalled them (Dio 59.5).

D 3.2.4.2 (Ulpian, *Edict*, Book 6)

156. The praetor declares: 'Someone who has kept a brothel'. A person who keeps a brothel is a man who has kept slaves for hire as prostitutes. Furthermore, a man who carries on this business with free persons is in the same position. He is liable for keeping a brothel whether he pursues this as his main occupation or as a secondary occupation to another business, for example if he was an inn-keeper or tavern-keeper and kept slaves of this type in his employment who took advantage of this employment to carry on their business (prostitution), or if he was the owner of a bathing establishment, and, as happens in many provinces, employed slaves to look after the clothes in the baths who carried on this business in their work place.

The brothel-keeper would be liable for *infamia*; see p. 59.

Italy

The last years of the republic and the civil wars that eventually saw the emergence of Augustus as emperor brought disruption to Italy, with new settlements, confiscation of land, and sometimes the addition of new settlers to existing communities. This usually meant the drawing or re-drawing of boundaries, and division of land into measured areas suitable for distribution to settlers. The boundaries of the community had to be marked and recorded, and jurisdiction confirmed in relation to neighbouring communities. Nevertheless, the rule of Augustus saw greater involvement and interest in the administration of Italy than had been the case in the republic. He divided Italy into eleven regions (Pliny, *NH* 3.46), aiming for stability and order, and settled relations between communities; for the emperor's management of the geography of Italy, see Laurence (1999), 162–76. Augustus also injected manpower and resources, founding twenty-six colonies of military veterans with which he maintained connections, sometimes sponsoring new buildings; naturally they were a focus of local support for him; for the pattern and impact of settlement, see Keppie (1983), 49–133; Patterson (2006), 125–69 examines the extent of public building in Italian communities up to the second century AD. Since good communications for the movement of troops were also vital, there was investment in road building. Roads were also a bulwark of economic development, and their supervision and maintenance became increasingly important (nos. 171–3). Augustus was much involved in the process of managing and recording land arrangements (see Campbell (1996), 94–8), and relations between landowners in Italy remained an issue for his successors. The concern of the state was to regulate the behaviour of its citizens to encourage stability and an equitable resolution of disputes. This included the management of water resources and control of buildings, just as in Rome. The government made few social interventions to assist the rural population, though, as noted, *collegia* were tolerated where some public benefit was to be expected. However, apart from occasional imperial assistance, local rich men who controlled the government of communities often contributed in various ways to benefit their fellow-citizens; see Johnston (1985); Patterson (2006), 169–76. It was Nerva at the end of the first century who probably undertook the first significant attempt by the government to assist poorer citizens in rural areas through the alimentary scheme of grants to children, though similar provision had previously been made through private generosity (nos. 187–8). For a useful survey of the unresolved debate over the size of Italy's population (between seven and fourteen million) in the imperial period, see Patterson (2006), 25–32.

State and Citizen in Italian Communities

Mechanisms for organizing communities in Italy and providing rules for their government developed in the last century of the republic and were applied in the imperial period. The *lex Tarentina* relating to the *municipium* of Tarentum can probably be dated soon after the Social War in 90 BC, and is taken as an example of a general law which has been adapted and amended to suit the particular circumstances of the local community; see Crawford (1996), 302–3; Bispham (2007), 208–9; no. 157; for a survey of the establishment of *municipia* and the rules for their governance after 90 BC down to Augustus see Bispham (2007), especially 205–46; 436–42; he raises the question of how far Rome was proactive, enforcing the adoption of the *ius civile* in the new *municipia*, or perhaps leaving it to the communities themselves to follow the *ius* as best they could. It seems likely that statutes relating to *municipia* were passed in Rome and then delivered to individual communities for specific local application. The arrangements for *municipia* were flexible and 'allowed for the preservation of local and traditional elements within the structure of the *municipium* … the municipal *leges* allowed for the individual characteristics and strengths of each community to be retained, even if transformed to some degree, within a conceptual system that was firmly rooted in Roman juridical practice' (Bispham (2007), 438). However, by the Flavian period Rome may have been operating more with the idea of a standard *lex* aimed at being as comprehensive as possible; see Crawford (1998), 32–3, and no. 34 (Irni). In the imperial period the title of *colonia* came to be conferred on existing *municipia* as an enhancement of their status and civic honour; see Sherwin-White (1973a), 350–2.

Lex Tarentina **Crawford (1996), p. 304, lines 1–6, 21–5, 39–42**

157. And no one is to steal or take away whatever public, sacred, or religious monies that belong to or will belong to that *municipium*, nor is anyone to act in such a way through which either of these happens, nor is anyone by fraudulently dealing with public records to harm public property with malicious deceit. In respect of whoever shall have acted in this way, there is to be a fine of four times the amount involved, and he is to be condemned to pay that money to the *municipium*, and there is to be legal action and

exaction of that money by whatever magistrate there is in the community (lines 1–6).

And whatever business shall have been publicly delegated to anyone in the *municipium* in accordance with the decision of the senate, or whatever public business he shall have carried out, or whatever public funds he shall have spent or recovered, the person to whom that business shall have been delegated in this way, or who shall have carried out some business publicly, or who shall have spent or recovered public funds, must produce and present to the senate an account of that business within the next ten days from the time when the senate of that *municipium* shall have taken its decision, without malicious deceit (lines 21–5).

And whatever roads, ditches, or drains a member of the board of four, a member of the board of two, or aedile in the service of that *municipium* wishes publicly to make, to insert, to change, to build, or to repair, within those boundaries which are part of that *municipium*, whatever of it may be done without harm, it is to be permissible for him to do that (lines 39–42).

The *lex Tarentina* illustrates aspects of life in an Italian *municipium* in the republic, and the procedures for safeguarding and managing the community's resources and amenities.

Tabula Heracleensis Crawford (1996), pp. 368–9, lines 142–56

158. Whatever *municipia*, colonies, or prefectures of Roman citizens are or shall be in Italy, and whoever in those *municipia*, colonies, or prefectures holds the senior magistracy or the greatest office there, at that time when a censor or some other magistrate in Rome carries out a census of the people, that person, within the next sixty days from the time when he is aware that the census is being conducted in Rome, is to carry out a census of all the inhabitants of his *municipium*, and colonists, and whoever belongs to that *praefectura*, who are Roman citizens. And he is to receive from them once they have taken an oath, their names, their forenames, their fathers or patrons, their additional names (*cognomina*), and the years of age that each has reached, and an account of their property according to the rules of the census, which shall have been published at Rome by the person who is at that time about to carry out the census of the people. And he is to ensure that all this material is entered in the public records of his *municipium*. And he is to send those books in the keeping of envoys, whom the larger part of the decurions and *conscripti* shall have decided should be sent as envoys for that purpose, at the time when that matter shall have been discussed, to

those who are to carry out the census at Rome. And he is to ensure that, when there are more than sixty days left before that day on which whoever shall carry out the census at Rome may terminate the census of the people, they approach them and present the books of that *municipium*, colony, or prefecture; and that censor, or whatever other magistrate shall carry out the census of the people, within the five days next after the envoys of that *municipium*, colony, or prefecture shall have approached (him), is to receive without wrongful deceit those books of the census which shall have been given to (him) by those envoys; and he is to ensure that from those records, whatever shall have been written down there is entered in the public records, and that those records are stored in the same place, where there are other public records, in which the census of the people is written out (lines 142–56).

For this statute relating to the government of Heraclea see nos. 106, 108, 115. Originally a community without voting rights was administered by a praetor who operated through a *praefectus*; hence it was called a *praefectura. Praefectura* was also the name given to an area in one community which had been allocated to the ownership of a colony. The clause translated ensures that the local magistrates conform to the procedure established by the censors in Rome, and that the whole process is correlated to the census in Rome.

Augustan Settlements

Augustus, *Res Gestae* 16.1; 28.2

159. I paid cash to the communities for the lands that I granted to soldiers in my fourth consulship (30 BC) and subsequently in the consulship of Marcus Crassus and Gnaeus Lentulus (14 BC). This sum amounted to about 600,000,000 sesterces which I paid for land in Italy, and 260,000,000 sesterces for land in the provinces. I was the first and only person among those who founded colonies of soldiers in Italy or in the provinces who did this in the memory of my contemporaries (16.1).

Italy also has twenty-eight colonies founded on my instructions, which during my lifetime were renowned and heavily populated (28.2).

Augustus is keen to emphasize that in contrast to his earlier career as triumvir when there had been much disruption and confiscation of land in Italy in 41/40 BC, now as bringer of peace and order he would ensure that private property was safe. It is impossible to say if Augustus was correct to boast of the success of his colonies.

***Liber Coloniarum*, Lachmann (1848–52), p. 219.6 = Campbell (2000), p. 173.8**

160. The colony of Graviscae was founded by the orders of Augustus. Its land was held without survey. Later, the emperor Tiberius Caesar, in order to preserve the area allocated in *iugera*, made measurements, set up boundary stones, and allocated some areas to the community. In addition, between the lands of private individuals he positioned conspicuous boundary markers, which are separated from one another by such a short distance that they can easily be found. Ditches were placed along the straight lines (of the boundaries), and by common agreement these protect the rights of individual (landholders).

The Book of Colonies (*Liber Coloniarum*) is an anonymous compilation probably of the fourth century AD, offering descriptions of the territorial layout of colonies mainly in Italy, with their important characteristics and boundary-marking techniques. In part at least it goes back to a commentary produced in the time of Augustus, to which other material was added. It is therefore potentially an important source for the history of land settlement and landholding in Italy. A colony of Roman citizens had been founded at Graviscae in 181 BC, but there is no other evidence for an Augustan settlement.

Velleius 2.81.2

161. About the same time (after a mutiny in the army in 36 BC) a significant addition (that is of veteran soldiers) was made to lands in the colony in Campania (Capua) which had been left public. In return for these, much more fertile land on the island of Crete was granted with an annual revenue of 1,200,000 sesterces, and an aqueduct was promised which today is an outstanding contributor to health and a beautiful ornament to the environment.

For Velleius' historical work see p. 482. In 36 BC Octavian needed land for his veteran soldiers; Dio 49.14.5 names the aqueduct as the Aqua Iulia and claims that the Capuans still made use of the land at Cnossos in Crete in his day; several large boundary stones have been found near Capua attesting Octavian's activity: 'on the orders of Imperator Caesar where the plough was brought round' (*ILS* 6308); this refers to the traditional ploughing of a furrow at the perimeter of a new settlement.

***CIL* 11.6218 = *ILS* 104 (Fanum, AD 9–10)**

162. Emperor Caesar Augustus, son of a god, chief priest, consul for the thirteenth time, in his thirty-second year of tribunician power, imperator for the twenty-sixth time (*sic*), father of the fatherland, provided the wall.

For Augustan benefactions in support of his settlements see Keppie (1983), 114–22. Land settlements often caused uncertainty, but Augustus tried to reassure communities, made a speech on the rights of towns (T 7.9–10 = Campbell (2000), p. 7.13–15), and instigated other measures (see nos. 163–4). There is a mistake in the number of *imperator* acclamations; Augustus received only twenty-one. For Fanum see also no. 169.

Management of Land and People

Hyginus Gromaticus (T, p. 136.17 = Campbell (2000), p. 139.7)

163. The divine Augustus in his land allocations ordered that stones inscribed with the number of the *limites* should be placed at all corners of *centuriae*. In the contracting out of this task he not only gave instructions concerning public *limites*, but also took care that between holdings there should be no lack of wooden boundary markers.

See also T, p. 157.9 = Campbell (2000), p. 153.25 – Augustus had laid down appropriate regular widths for the various *limites*. The *limites* marked the boundaries of the units of land division (*centuriae*) and also provided access; for a general survey see Dilke (1971), 82–97. Hyginus Gromaticus (see p. 478) was one of the writers on surveying whose work was collected in the *Corpus Agrimensoum Romanorum* of the sixth century AD (see p. 251); he was writing probably in the second century.

Hyginus, *Categories of Land* (T, p. 82.28–83.6 = Campbell (2000), p. 87.30)

164. There are also several edicts of the divine Augustus in which he makes clear that whenever he had taken land away from the territory of another community and allocated it to veterans, nothing other than whatever was granted and allocated to the veterans should belong to the jurisdiction of the colony. Therefore, it is not always the case that whatever land has been divided passes to (the jurisdiction of) a colony, but only what has been granted and allocated. Nevertheless, there are some *municipia* that have no jurisdiction outside their walls.

For Hyginus (to be distinguished from Hyginus Gromaticus), see p. 478. Here he is explaining jurisdiction in Italian communities; when land was taken from a community for the benefit of a colony of veterans, only that which was formally allocated to the new settlement came under its jurisdiction; however, some communities had lost all their land and so had no jurisdiction outside their walls.

Commentary on Land Disputes **(T, p. 64.31–65.4 = Campbell (2000), p. 67.24)**

165. A dispute about territorial jurisdiction occurs when some private individual wishes improperly to impinge on the *pomerium* of a city with private works, or greedily tries to usurp land from public areas, that is, areas belonging to the city itself. The *pomerium* of a city is a space measured out with definite dimensions in front of the walls. Moreover, in some cities a space of similar area is established inside the walls in order to protect the foundations.

This is an anonymous commentary of the fifth or sixth century AD on the surveying work of Iulius Frontinus, probably to be identified with the author of the *Stratagems* and the *Aqueducts* (see p. 478).

FIRA **1, no. 75 = McCrum and Woodhead (1961), no. 462 (AD 82)**

166. Emperor Caesar [Domitian] Augustus, son of the divine Vespasian, chief priest, with tribunician power, imperator for the second time, consul for the eighth time, designated for the ninth, father of the fatherland, expresses greetings to the board of four and the decurions of the people of Falerium in Picenum.

I have ordered to be appended to this letter what I have decided concerning unsurveyed land, after the case between you and the people of Firmum had been heard, so that you may be aware of it.

P. Valerius Patruinus consul … 19 July

I, Emperor Caesar [Domitian] Augustus, son of the divine Vespasian, after assembling eminent men of both orders, and hearing the case between the people of Falerium and the people of Firmum, pronounced the judgement that is written below.

The antiquity of this suit which, after so many years, the people of Firmum have revived against the people of Falerium, disturbs me greatly, since far fewer years than this should guarantee security of those in possession, and also the letter of Augustus, an exceptionally meticulous and indulgent emperor in respect of the men of his own fourth legion, in which he advises them to collect and sell all their unsurveyed land (*subsecivum*), wise advice which I have no doubt they obeyed. Therefore, I confirm the rights of the possessors. Farewell.

Given on 22 July at Albanum, with T. Bovius Verus supervising, and P. Bovius Sabinus and P. Petronius Achilles acting as envoys. By decree of the town councillors, publicly.

Veterans of the IV Macedonica legion were settled at Firmum probably in 44 BC, and the settlement may have extended into the land of Falerio. *Subsecivum* was land left out of the original survey, either on the periphery of the allocated areas, or an unsuitable location within the surveyed area, such as a marsh. The people of Firmum had brought a case against the neighbouring Falerienses, probably trying to exploit a ruling of Vespasian that communities should repossess *subsecivum* that had been occupied. But Domitian was reluctant to see the disturbance of long-term possession and cited the evidence of Augustus' letter in support of his view that the people of Firmum had long ago sold the land currently at issue; discussion in Keppie (1983), 181–3.

Agennius Urbicus, *Land Disputes* (T, p. 41.4–26 = Campbell (2000), p. 39.6)

167. When the allocation was taking place in allocated lands not all the area of land enclosed by four *limites* could be allocated to the veterans. Some land remained (unallocated) in it and got the name *subsecivum* from the line which cut it off. Some (of the colonial founders) sent out more settlers to whom land was to be allocated in these *subseciva*; others granted the *subseciva* to colonies. Therefore, this type of dispute is always pursued by communities. For, over a long period of time, neighbouring landholders encroached on unoccupied land, as if the availability of the idle ground had prompted them, and over a long period of time attached it to their land with impunity. Even if many communities were late in reclaiming the area of these *subseciva*, they made no small contribution to their treasury. Indeed, the emperor Vespasian demanded money from several colonies on the grounds that they had not had the *subseciva* (which they were exploiting) granted to them; for it was impossible that that land, which had not been allocated to anyone, could belong to anyone other than the person who had the power to allocate it. By selling off the *subseciva* he brought no small amount of money to the treasury. Subsequently, however, he was moved by the distress of delegations, because all the landholders in Italy were in turmoil, and intermitted his ruling, but did not yield (that is revoke the policy entirely). Similarly, the emperor Titus repossessed some *subseciva* in Italy. Later the excellent emperor Domitian speedily conferred this benefaction and with one edict freed all Italy from fear.

For the little-known writer Agennius Urbicus, see p. 477. This passage demonstrates the continuing problem of unsurveyed land and its exploitation by neighbouring landholders; the availability of due process for settling land disputes of all kinds was an important aspect of an equitable relationship between state, citizens, and communities. Vespasian took the view that in the case of land improperly exploited by colonies it should revert to the original allocating authority, that is imperial authority, and by extension, him.

CIL 10.1018 = *ILS* 5942

168. On the authority of Imperator Caesar Vespasian Augustus, Tiberius Suedius Clemens, tribune, examined the issues, completed measurements, and restored to the community of Pompeii the public areas that had been possessed by private individuals.

For a typical boundary description, see introduction, p. 11.

Agennius Urbicus, *Land Disputes* (T, p. 45.6 = Campbell (2000), p. 43.4)

169. Disputes of this kind between communities are initiated so that they may argue that certain areas belong to the jurisdiction of their territory, even though they are within the territory of another community, and claim that the yield from these places is due to their colony or *municipium*. However, some colonies, either through the generosity of the founders, like the people of Tuder, or subsequently by appeal to emperors, like the Fanestres, gained this (concession), namely, that the inhabitants who dwelt inside the territory, even if they belonged to another community, should be liable for the performance of all obligations in the colony. The Fanestres have gained this right recently, the people of Tuder hold it through the generosity of their founder.

The *colonia Iulia Fida Tuder* was possibly founded after 36 BC by Octavian, by whose goodwill it had this special privilege from its foundation. The other community is Fanum Fortunae, which Augustus made a colony and granted the title *Iulia*. The privilege for example allowed Fanum to make citizens of another community living in an enclave within its territory pay appropriate dues and perform duties in Fanum; for these settlements see Keppie (1983), 176–7; 184–5.

CIL 11.3003a = *ILS* 5771

170. Mummius Niger Valerius Vegetus, of consular rank, brought his own water, the Vegetiana, which rises in the bigger Antonianus farm of P. Tullius Varro, along with that place in which (ownership of) that spring has been transferred, over 5,950 paces to his villa Calvisiana, which is located at his Aquae Passeris, having obtained and transferred to his ownership places, and routes of that water from the possessors of each

individual farm through which the above-mentioned water was conducted, to a width of ten feet for structures, six feet for the width of pipes, through … (there follows a list of farms) and along the left-hand border of the public highway of Ferentium, through the Scirpianum farm of Pistrania Lepida, and along the Cassia road to his villa Calvisiana, and also along public roads and *limites* by permission of a decree of the senate.

Vegetus had to manage private and public rights in order to bring water to his own estate over a distance of nearly six miles, using a precise survey of the area; with permission of the senate he was able to make use of public *limites*, which would normally be kept clear of any obstructions.

Roads

Denarius (*EJ*, no. 287) (16 BC)

171. Obverse: Head of Augustus. Augustus, holding the tribunician power for the seventh time.

Reverse: Boundary stone with inscription: The senate and people of Rome in honour of Imperator Caesar because the roads were repaired from that money which he lodged in the treasury.

Outside the boundary stone: Lucius Vinicius, son of Lucius, member of board of three.

Lucius Vinicius was the moneyer responsible for the minting of the coins. Suetonius attests Augustus' concern for the roads of Italy: 'To make the approach to the city easier from all directions he took upon himself the task of repairing the Via Flaminia as far as Ariminum and assigned the remaining roads to men who had held a triumph, with the responsibility for paving them using the money gained from their booty' (*Augustus* 30.1). In 20 BC Augustus established a board of curators of praetorian rank to look after the roads in Italy (Suetonius, *Augustus* 37; Dio 54.8.4); for a survey of imperial road building in Italy see Chevallier (1989), 131–40; Laurence (1999), especially 39–57.

CIL 11.365 = *ILS* 84 Arch at Ariminum (27 BC)

172. The senate and people of Rome in honour of Imperator Caesar Augustus, son of a god, acclaimed imperator on seven occasions, consul for the seventh time and designated for the eighth, because he repaired the Via Flaminia and the other busiest roads of Italy under his direction and at his expense.

Siculus Flaccus, *Categories of Land* (T, p. 109.19–110.14 = Campbell (2000), p. 113.11)

173. When roads demarcate a boundary, we shall have to examine what kind of roads and how (they mark the boundary). Now, roads often occur on boundaries, and landholders often have some parcels of land on the other side of a road. Some roads, therefore, sometimes cut across the boundaries of landholdings. However, not all roads have the same status. There are public thoroughfares, which are maintained at public expense and bear the name of the men who initiated them. They have curators and are maintained by contractors. For the maintenance of some roads a set sum is regularly exacted from landholders. By contrast, local roads, which turn off the public highways into fields and often lead back to other public highways, are maintained in a different way, by *pagi*, that is, by the officials of the *pagi*, who normally demand labour from the landholders for their upkeep. Or, as I discovered, set lengths of road running through individual fields are assigned to each landholder, which they are to maintain at their own expense. They even have inscriptions erected at specified intervals, recording which owner of which piece of land is responsible for which length (of road).

For Siculus Flaccus and his treatise on the technical operations of land survey, see p. 481. Although in this passage Flaccus initially refers to roads in Italy he probably has in mind roads throughout the empire (see Campbell (2000), 373–4); for the definition of a road see Laurence (1999), 58–62.

Buildings

***FIRA* 1, no. 45. II (Herculaneum, AD 56)**

174. In the consulship of Quintus Volusius and Publius Cornelius, 2 March, by decree of the senate. In respect of the statement that Quintus Volusius and Publius Cornelius made concerning the petition of the friends of Alliatoria Celsilla, as to what they wished to be done about that matter, they decided as follows about that matter: Since the decree of the senate which was passed in the consulship of Hosidius Geta and Lucius Vagellius, most distinguished men, on September [...], on the authority of the divine Claudius, laid down that no one should demolish a house or a villa in order to acquire greater profit for himself, or to buy or sell any of these for the purpose of business, and since it was decided that the purchaser, who acted against the decree of the senate, was to be liable for the penalty, to the effect that the person who had bought anything should be compelled to lodge in the treasury twice the value of his

purchase, and in respect of the person who had made the sale, that sale was to be void; however, in respect of those who, intending to remain in possession of their own property, have changed some parts of it, as long as that was not done for a business deal, no new measure had been taken. And since the friends of Alliatoria Celsilla, wife of Atilius Lupercus, a man of excellent reputation, had explained to this body that her father Alliatorius Celsus bought some farms with their buildings in the vicinity of Mutina, called the *Campi Macri*, in which a market used to be held in previous times, but which had ceased to be held for several years, and that the buildings were slipping into decay through long neglect and were not going to be repaired for future use since no one was living in them, and nor did anyone wish to move to an area which was a deserted ruin, liability for a fine or penalty for fraud should not lie with Celsilla, if those buildings, which had been the subject of discussion in this body, were to have been demolished, or sold, either themselves or with the fields, on the condition that the purchaser should be permitted without incurring personal liability to demolish and remove them.

A decision of Claudius (no. 103) had attempted to check unsuitable demolition of buildings for financial gain by property developers. In this inscription which immediately follows that containing the emperor's decision, Alliatoria Celsilla claims exemption on the grounds that her property was unsustainable in light of changing economic and social conditions. It was normally up to the government of local communities in Italy to enforce suitable building regulations.

Lex Tarentina Crawford (1996), p. 304, lines 33–5

175. No one is to remove the roof or demolish or dismantle a building in the town that shall belong to that *municipium*, or demolish it, or dismantle it, unless he is about to rebuild it in no worse condition, or unless in accordance with a decision of the senate. If anyone shall have acted contrary to these provisions, however much that building shall have been worth, he shall be condemned to pay an equivalent amount to the *municipium*, and there is to be suit for that amount available to whomever shall wish.

For the *lex Tarentina*, see p. 99, and no. 157.

Tacitus, *Annals* 4.62–3

176. In the consulship of Marcus Licinius and Lucius Calpurnius (AD 27), an unexpected disaster brought a number of casualties equal to those of great wars. It started and ended in an instant. A freedman called Atilius had

begun an amphitheatre at Fidenae in order to stage a gladiatorial contest but did not establish the foundations on solid ground or construct the wooden superstructure with firm attachments. He had undertaken this venture not from an abundance of financial resources or to court local public opinion, but simply for sordid profit. Those people who loved such shows, deprived of this pleasure during the rule of Tiberius, flocked to the venue, both men and women, people of all ages, in greater numbers because of the proximity of the town. Therefore, the disaster was even more severe because the huge structure was packed and then collapsed, both falling inwards and bending outwards; it pulled down and buried a vast number of people, who were concentrating on the show or standing around.

(63) When they came to remove the debris, they rushed up to the dead, embracing and kissing them. There was often an argument over them if the face had been maimed but similar age or appearance had caused mistaken identity. Fifty thousand people were maimed or crushed in that disaster. For the future it was established in senatorial decree that no one should stage a gladiatorial show if his resources were fewer than four hundred thousand sesterces, and that no amphitheatre should be built except on ground that was demonstrably solid. Atilius was sent into exile. But in the immediate aftermath of the disaster the houses of the leading citizens were thrown open, and bandages and doctors were provided for everyone; in those days despite the sad aspect of the city, Rome behaved in a way similar to the practices of our ancestors, who after a great battle used to support the wounded with their generosity and care.

The extent of the disaster was so great (however, Suetonius, *Tiberius* 40 places casualties at 20,000) that the senate intervened directly with a regulation that applied throughout Italy. For public building in Italian communities see the excellent survey by Patterson (2006), 125–69 examining amphitheatres, baths, and market buildings. Local communities tended to copy Rome in buildings that emphasized local dignity and civic identity, and were supported by the generosity of wealthy citizens of the community, and by those families that had acquired senatorial status in Rome, and sometimes by imperial benefactions. In the amphitheatre the seating arrangements confirmed distinctions in status although amphitheatres and public baths were for the enjoyment of the entire population.

CIL 10.5183 = *ILS* 5628

177. Ummidia Quadratilla, daughter of Gaius, with her own resources constructed an amphitheatre and temple for the people of Casinum.

Pliny, *Letters* 7.24 notes that Quadratilla lived to the age of seventy-nine and kept a troupe of pantomime actors in her house.

The Legal Status of Towns

Land which was owned in the corporate capacity of the community, for example pastureland (*compascua*), was used generally by those nearby, though no idea of common ownership was ever developed. But the idea of a legal personality was important. At some point a right was recognized in the town as a body distinct from its members; therefore, a town could have rights and duties that were not considered to be the rights and duties of individual members; it could own things: land, slaves, and houses in which the townsmen might have no part; it could take part in legal transactions not directly concerning the townsmen, and was allowed *restitutio in integrum* (reinstatement to a former legal position to prevent loss), and could be sued. If a town was legally recognized as distinct from its members, its juristic personality had been established. The town could not act for itself but could appoint a representative (*actor*) to act for it in court and protect its interests. See in general Duff (1938), 62–94. In what follows I do not deal with constitutional and legal distinctions between various types of community, such as *municipia*, *coloniae*, and *civitates liberae.*

Hyginus Gromaticus, *The Establishment of Limites* (T, p. 160.22 = Campbell (2000), p. 155.45)

178. Similarly, if something has been allocated to a territory, it will belong to the city itself, and it may not be sold or alienated from public ownership. We shall write this down as follows: 'such and such granted to the territory for its support', as in the case of woods and public pastureland.

As regards something that has been granted to the government of a colony, we shall enter it on the map as follows: 'the woods and pastureland', say for example, 'of Sempronius, the government of the colony'.

The colony has corporate ownership of certain assets determined in the original establishment of the colony or granted subsequently. It was up to the community to decide on what way it wanted to exploit pastureland.

***D* 10.4.7.3 (Ulpian, *Edict*, Book 24)**

179. Furthermore, a community can be sued with an action for production, since it has the power of restoring something; for it is agreed that it can possess and acquire by *usucapio*.

Not all lawyers agreed; Paul argued that communities could not themselves possess because all the citizens could not consent, but nevertheless made free use of public buildings, temples, and so on, which they did not possess (*D* 41.2.1.22). However, Ulpian was emphatic that municipal citizens could possess and obtain things by *usucapio* (*D* 41.2.2).

D 4.3.15.1 (Ulpian, *Edict*, Book 11)

180. But there is doubt as to whether an action should be granted against the citizens of a community collectively for fraud. I think that an action cannot be granted simply on the grounds of their own fraud or malice, for what fraudulent or malicious action can a community commit? But if any profit came to them because of the fraud or malice of those who were administering the community's affairs, I think that an action should be granted. However, an action for fraud committed by town councillors will be granted against the councillors as individuals.

The question for lawyers in these issues was whether a community as a corporate unit could do wrong or only its agents. So, for example, an action for fraud could not be brought against a community since all the individual members of the community could not have participated in the fraud. Where an act was not attributable to the town itself but to its agents, the town was liable only as far as the profits of the unlawful action had accrued to it. No clear view or statement emerged on a community's corporate liability for wrongs committed. Although there was no corporate responsibility for fraud, redress was given to a community for loss caused by the actions of its own fraudulent or bankrupt officials; see Duff (1938), 92–4.

D 4.2.9.3 (Ulpian, *Edict*, Book 11)

181. But I know on the basis of a real case that when the Campanians by intimidating someone had extracted from him an obligation including a promise to pay over money, our emperor said in a rescript that he could seek restitution from the praetor, and the praetor with me in attendance as assessor, issued an interlocutory declaration that, if he (the plaintiff) wanted to take an action against the Campani, that was available, or if he wanted to make a defence against a suit brought by them, that was available.

Duff (1938), 92 suggests that Campani probably refers to the community of Capua. If so, this may suggest that corporate responsibility for wrongful action by a community was recognized. *Pollicitatio* normally refers to a promise of money to a community, which in this case may have been under some form of duress; the community was perhaps required to pay it back. An *interlocutio* is a statement or preliminary decision by a magistrate during a trial.

Titles from Ulpian 24.28

182. It is possible for all communities that exist under the rule of the Roman people to receive legacies. That was instituted by the divine Nerva, and later was established in more detail by the senate under the guidance of Hadrian.

In Roman law a person whose legal existence was uncertain (*incerta persona*) could not be instituted as heir or receive legacies, and Ulpian maintained that *municipia* could not be instituted as heirs (*Tit. Ulp* 22.5). In respect of Nerva's decision on legacies, it seems likely, based on inscriptions and other legal passages, that Roman communities already had the right to receive legacies and that the emperor simply extended this to peregrine communities; for discussion of the issue, see Johnston (1985), 106–10. As for the senatorial decree under Hadrian, this may be a *senatus consultum Apronianum* mentioned by Paul (*D* 36.1.27), which seemingly gave peregrine communities the right to sue for *fideicommissa hereditatis* (wishes expressed in a will for conveyance of property); before this they would have had to rely on the good faith of the fiduciary; see also Duff (1938), 86–90; p. 437 for *fideicommissa*.

Collegia in Italian Communities

CIL 14.2112 = *ILS* 7212 = *FIRA* 3, no. 35 (AD 133)

183. In the consulship of Lucius Ceionius Commodus and Sextus Vettulenus Civica Pompeianus, 28 May.

At Lanuvium in the temple of Antinoüs in which Lucius Caesennius Rufus, patron of the municipality, had instructed that a meeting be held through Lucius Pompeius … senior officer (*quinquennalis*) of the worshippers of Diana and Antinoüs, he promised that he would in his generosity give and donate to them the interest from a sum of 15,000 sesterces, namely 400 sesterces on the birthday of Diana on 13 August, and 400 sesterces on the birthday of Antinoüs on 27 November, and laid down that the by-laws established by them should be inscribed on the inner side below the four columns of the temple of Antinoüs, as written below:

[In the consulship of Marcus Antonius Hiberus] and Publius Mummius Sisenna, 1 January, the benevolent association of Diana … and Antinoüs was established, with Lucius Caesennius Rufus, son of Lucius, of the Quirina tribe being chief magistrate for the third time and also patron.

Clause from the decree of the senate of the Roman people.

The following are permitted to meet and assemble and have an association: those who wish to make a monthly contribution for burial expenses may meet in that association, and they are not permitted under the auspices of that association to meet more than once a month for the purpose of making contributions for the burial of the dead.

May this be happy, lucky, and beneficial to Emperor Caesar Trajan Hadrian Augustus and the entire imperial house, to us, to our people, and to our association, and may we have properly and carefully arranged that we can decently carry out the funerals of the dead. Therefore, we all should agree to make contributions loyally so that we can remain established for a long time. You who wish to join this association as new members must first read the by-laws before joining, so that you do not bring complaints later, or bequeath a lawsuit to your heir.

As discussed (pp. 93–4), those associations that in the view of the government performed a useful social or economic function were permitted to function. The inscription sets out the by-laws of this religious and burial society and they show an interesting social interaction, with membership consisting of freeborn, freedmen, and slaves, and an emphasis on convivial social intercourse with dinners, plentiful wine, and strict rules to avoid disturbance or disruption; discussion in Dench (2018), 101–4; detailed analysis in Bendlin (2011). Patterson (2006), 252–63 suggests that the members of *collegia* had an important role in civic life, increasingly took part in communal activities, and could contribute to municipal finances. Furthermore, by the time of Marcus Aurelius *collegia* had acquired greater respectability and their corporate identity was recognized; see p. 96.

CIL 11.970 = *ILS* 7216 = *FIRA* 3, no. 39 (AD 190)

184. In the consulship of Emperor Caesar Marcus Aurelius Commodus Antoninus Augustus Pius Felix for the sixth time, and Marcus Petronius Septimianus, 23 March, in the shrine of the association of labourers and rag men of Regium.

In respect of the proposal of the treasurers, Publius Saenius Marcellinus and Gaius Aufidius Dialogus, noting that Tutilius Iulianus, a generous man distinguished for his way of life, his decorum, and inherent modesty, ought to be adopted as patron of our association, in order that the evidence of our decision may serve as an incentive to others, in respect of what it pleased them should be done concerning this matter they decided as follows:

We think both individually and collectively that a most proper proposal has been put forward by the treasurers and officers of the association with excellent advice, and that we should offer apologies to that honourable man Iulianus for the unavoidable delay in our belated consideration, and that we should beseech him to undertake willingly the position of patron of our society, and that a bronze plaque containing the words of this decree should be placed in his house. Adopted.

The *collegium* of rag men had some prestige as they were sometimes employed in firefighting, since rags were used to smother the fire. The process of appointing a patron illustrates the interaction between rich citizens and associations of poorer men; this offered the possibility of financial assistance for the *collegium*, and for the patron a boost to his local status. It is interesting that the decision is couched in language appropriate to the decision-making process of the Roman senate. This could give ordinary people some sense of doing something important. Three *collegia* seem to have been particularly important: rag men, *fabri*, and *dendrophoroi* (tree-carriers), who were associated with a religious cult.

Tacitus, *Annals* 14.17 (AD 59)

185. At the same time from a minor incident a ferocious fight broke out between the inhabitants of the colonies of Nuceria and Pompeii at a gladiatorial contest organized by Livineius Regulus, whose expulsion from the senate I have described. The rowdy townsfolk exchanged insults, then threw stones, then drew swords, with the people of Pompeii coming off the better, since the show was held there … The emperor asked the senate to investigate the affair, and the senate passed it over to the consuls. When they reported to the senate, the people of Pompeii were prohibited from holding any public gathering of this kind for ten years, and the societies, which they had set up against the laws, were dissolved. Livineius and others who had instigated the disturbance were punished with exile.

Collegia in local communities were often suspected as a likely contributory cause of violence at large gatherings of people. It is also notable that in this case at Pompeii supervision had been lax and societies had been set up in defiance of regulations. For *collegia* outside Italy, see no. 241.

The Role of the Praetorian Prefects in Italy

CIL 9.2438 = *FIRA* 1, no. 61 (AD 169–172)

186. Bassaeus Rufus and Macrinius Vindex to the magistrates of Saepinum greetings. We have attached a copy of the letter written to us by Cosmus, freedman of the emperor and financial secretary, along with that which was

added to his, and we warn you to stop inflicting loss on the lessees of the flocks of sheep with consequent substantial loss to the imperial treasury, in case we have to investigate the matter and punish the act, if the situation is as stated.

Letter of Cosmus, freedman of the emperor and financial secretary, to Bassaeus Rufus and Macrinius Vindex, praetorian prefects, most eminent men. I have attached a copy of the letter written to me by Septimianus, my fellow-freedman and assistant, and I ask that you be so good as to write to the magistrates of Saepinum and Bovianum that they should cease from inflicting loss on the lessees of the flocks of sheep, which are under my responsibility, so that through your assistance the treasury should suffer no loss.

Letter written by Septimianus to Cosmus. Since the lessees of the flocks of sheep, which are under your responsibility, are now frequently complaining to me that they are suffering loss on the mountain pathways and tracks at the hands of the military police (*stationarii*) and magistrates at Saepinum and Bovianum, to the effect that they detain in transit the animals and shepherds that the lessees employ, claiming that they are runaway slaves and are in possession of stolen animals, and on this pretext even sheep belonging to the emperor are lost in this uproar. We considered it necessary to write repeatedly that they should behave more responsibly lest the imperial property should suffer loss. But since they are persevering with the same impertinence, saying that they will not pay any attention to my letters and that it will make no difference if you write to them, I request, my lord, if you agree, that you inform Bassaeus Rufus and Macrinius Vindex, praetorian prefects, most eminent men, to send letters to these same magistrates and police.

This inscription from Saepinum is an excellent illustration of the process of Roman government in Italy, the hierarchy of authority, and the difficulty of protecting even the imperial treasury, in this case exacerbated by the truculence of the local magistrates. The *stationarii* had originally been established by Augustus to curb bandits (Suetonius, *Augustus* 32.1). The praetorian prefects had legal jurisdiction beyond the hundredth milestone (see p. 91) and the right to reach a judgement, as they state that they will punish the culprits if the situation is as claimed. In the reign of Septimius Severus, when the notorious bandit Bulla was captured, he was interrogated by the praetorian prefect Papinian (Dio 77.10.7).

The alimenta *Scheme*

***CIL* 11.1147 = *ILS* 6675 = *FIRA* 3, no. 116 (AD 109/112) (Extract)**

187. Mortgages on properties amounting to 1,044,000 sesterces, so that through the goodwill of the best and greatest emperor, Imperator Caesar Nerva Trajan Augustus, conqueror of the Germans, conqueror of the Dacians, boys and girls may receive support: legitimate boys to the number of 245 at 16 sesterces each (per month), making a total of 47,040 sesterces, legitimate girls to the number of thirty-four at 12 sesterces each (per month), making a total of 4,896 sesterces, one illegitimate boy at a total of 144 sesterces (per year), one illegitimate girl at a total cost of 120 sesterces (per year). The total is 52,200 sesterces, which amounts to 5 per cent interest on the sum noted above.

Gaius Volumnius Memor and Volumnia Alce, through Volumnius Diadumenus their freedman, declared the farm Quintiacus Aurelianus, the Muletas hill and its woods, which is in the territory of Veleia, in the Ambitrebius district, bounded by Marcus Mommeius Persicus, Satrius Severus, and the public road, to the value of 108,000 sesterces. He should receive 8,692 sesterces and put forward the farm noted above as security.

The *alimenta* scheme was probably initiated by Nerva, carried through by Trajan, and lasted until the third century. Inscriptions show alimentary schemes in about fifty Italian towns. Landholders in Italian communities were persuaded or instructed to borrow a sum of money from capital put up by the government against the value of their property (roughly twelve and a half times), and then paid 5 per cent interest on the loan into the *alimenta* fund from which the children could be supported. There is no explicit contemporary evidence for the purpose; some have supposed that the scheme was intended to boost Rome's manpower, which might explain the privileged treatment of boys (though that may be mere prejudice), others that it was a genuine attempt at poor relief. Most scholars now agree that it was not intended to boost Italian agriculture, and indeed landholders may not have welcomed the loans, which then became a charge on their property. The antecedent to the scheme can be found in many private acts of benevolence to their community by rich men (see no. 188). For government intervention and demographic policy see Duncan-Jones (1964), (1974), 288–319; Hands (1968), 108–15; Woolf (1990) argues that alimentary schemes were not aimed specifically at the poor, but in part represented imperial patronage and the popular presentation of the role of the emperor. For the similar scheme at Ligures Baebiani, see *FIRA* 3, no. 117; Patterson (2006), 50–3 for patterns of landholding in these communities.

CIL 10.5057 = ***ILS*** 977

188. To Titus Helvius Basila, son of Titus, aedile, praetor, proconsul, legate of Caesar Augustus, who bequeathed to the people of Atina 400,000 sesterces in order that from the interest their children might be given corn until they reached maturity, and subsequently 1,000 sesterces each. Procula his daughter set this up.

Any government activity was supplemented by private generosity based on enthusiastic local loyalty, in this case the beneficence of a distinguished senator (possibly in the reign of Nero) and government official, to his native community.

CHAPTER 3

Public and Private Interests
The Provinces

Introduction

This chapter deals with the framework and practice of provincial government, in which the state mediated its relations with its subjects through a blend of control, and co-operation with the local elite, whose interests and aspirations had to be taken into account to promote stable rule and minimize the need for a large presence of Roman administrators and soldiers. The Romans had acquired territory in a piecemeal fashion and without a coherent plan, to secure military and strategic interests, for economic exploitation, to prevent the aggrandizement of other states, and establish a diplomatic framework; personal ambition, military glory, and political advancement also played a part. In the administration of newly acquired provinces many diverse existing practices were adopted or adapted. For example, in the Greek east the provincial setup was based on the city and its territory, which the city government in the traditional format of people, council, and magistrates administered in the interests of Rome, whereas in Egypt the Romans retained part of the Ptolemaic structure, with the innovations and supervision that suited them.

The provincial governor was the primary representative of the state and the principal point of contact for the local population and their magistrates. In the Roman system, which went back to the arrangements of Augustus, largely based on the presence or otherwise of a military garrison in the province, responsibility for appointing the governor lay either with the emperor or the senate. Crucial to the effective government of the empire was the position of *legatus Augusti*, of consular rank, directly appointed by the emperor to serve at his pleasure, often for three years or more, in provinces of high status usually containing a substantial deployment of legionary and auxiliary troops (lesser provinces were governed by legates of praetorian rank). The governor was responsible for commanding troops in his province, for supervising the administration, and for juridical matters (nos. 189–201). He had a small staff and was mainly supported by legionary legates, senators of praetorian rank, who commanded individual legions, and military tribunes. However, financial responsibility in the province lay with the equestrian procurator appointed as the emperor's agent (nos. 200 and 203). In those provinces to which the senate appointed the governor (proconsul), usually by lot from eligible senatorial candidates, tenure was for one year. Proconsuls in the plum provinces of Asia and Africa were of consular rank and operated like *legati Augusti*, except that they had no military functions. Quaestors, again serving for one year, looked after financial affairs in these provinces. In all provinces the emperor's personal estates were administered by procurators. Certain smaller provinces were governed by men of equestrian rank. The one exception (up to the creation of the province of Mesopotamia by Septimius Severus) was the rich and strategically important province of Egypt, governed by an equestrian prefect from its inception, by decision of Augustus. The administration of this province was anomalous in other ways in that it was divided into three *epistrategiae*, administrative areas subdivided into districts called *nomes*. An equestrian official, the *dioketes*, looked after finance, but there was another senior equestrian official, the *idios logos*, who administered the so-called special account dealing with confiscated or sequestered assets (nos. 202–4); for a valuable discussion of the administration of Egypt, see Bowman (1986), 56–88; Bowman and Rathbone (1992).

Governors served as an avenue of communications from provincials to the emperor and vice versa, and had to deal with numerous local interest groups, such as city councils and magistrates, rich and influential individuals, and the provincial council (*koinon*), amid the rivalries and aspirations of ambitious communities (pp. 122–5). The governor was responsible not only for ensuring that Roman economic interests and assets in the province were safeguarded, but also that local communities fulfilled their expected role and dealt responsibly with their buildings and financial resources (pp. 138–51).

Above all, it was not in a governor's interest to have discontent openly expressed in his province, and disorder would catch the emperor's eye; this could take various forms, such as the tumultuous meetings of the assembly at Prusa, which led to its being suspended (Dio Chrysostomos, *Discourse* 48), or the disruption caused by striking bakers at Ephesus (no. 243), or the riots arising from racial and social tension in Alexandria in the reign of Claudius (no. 729), or the simmering religious and nationalistic tensions in Judaea. Therefore, communication between the governor and the various pressure points in his province was essential. In this, the judicial circuit was of great importance, in which the governor followed a defined itinerary to hear legal cases. He supervised jurisdiction relating to citizens under the procedures of Roman law, and when required applied a version of these procedures to the local inhabitants, who might also use their own courts. The differing status of various communities, and the presence of Roman colonies and *municipia* with their own rules of procedure, made his task more difficult. Ulpian, in the *De Officio Proconsulis et Legati*, provided the classic exposition of the duties and responsibilities of a governor. The correspondence between Trajan and Pliny, governor of Bithynia, gives a vivid illustration of how the administration dealt with real issues ranging from the routine to the challenging.

The emperor had an important role in establishing or confirming the style of government. In the first place he needed to choose his appointees carefully, balancing competence, reliability, and loyalty. The instructions (*mandata*) given to a governor before he set out for his province might initially be more effective than the inevitably slow process of consulting the emperor while in post. Personal intervention and supervision by the emperor could ensure that principles of fair government and recognition of the Romans' responsibility for the welfare of subject peoples were clearly impressed upon the governor; he should publish in a clearly visible location edicts righting wrongs, set out definite rules of government procedure, and respond positively to complaints (pp. 160–7). Particularly sensitive issues were the interface between Roman and local law, and effective procedures for redress of abuse involving Roman officials (pp. 167–73). Routine Roman bureaucratic procedures did offer a mechanism by which those with complaints could hope that approaches and appeals would be heard, though the actual operation of the law was frequently far removed from the good intentions of the legislators.

Lendon (1997), 201–22 provides a good general survey of the relationship between Roman officials and their subjects. Ando (2000) deals in general with the nature of Roman government procedures and the process of stimulating loyalty among provincial subjects; Dench (2018) examines local peoples and their experience of change under Roman rule; see also Lintott (1993), especially 111–53 for Rome's relations with the provinces; for the nature of provincial government see Richardson (2016) and also Humfress (2021). For the network of policing in the provinces including military police (*stationarii*) and out-posted centurions, see Fuhrmann (2012), 151–7; 201–38; for examples of senatorial and equestrian office-holding, see nos. 57–8; 60–2.

Provincial Government

Defining the Governor's Role

D 1.16.7.2; 8 (Ulpian, *Duties of a Proconsul*, Book 2; *Edict*, Book 39)

189. Since the proconsul has the fullest jurisdiction, all the authority of those at Rome who exercise jurisdiction, either magistrates or those exercising extraordinary power, lies with him. (8) Therefore, in his province he has greater authority than everyone except the emperor.

D 1.18.3 (Paul, *Sabinus*, Book 13)

190. Furthermore the governor of the province has authority only over people in his province, and that only while he is present in the province. For as soon as he leaves it, he is a private citizen. Sometimes he has the power also to act against men from outside the province if they have committed an assault; for it is laid down in the emperor's instructions that the person in charge of the province should see to it that it is cleared of evil men, and does not specify their origin.

D 1.16.4.4 (Ulpian, *Duties of a Proconsul*, Book 1)

191. The governor will act properly and correctly if he sends the edict to his predecessor and indicates the day on which he is going to enter the province; for uncertain and unanticipated actions especially disturb the provincials and disrupt business activities. For his arrival the governor ought to observe the following protocol, namely that he should enter that part of the province which it is the custom to enter and adhere to what the Greeks call a 'place of sojourn' or a 'port of arrival', in whatever community he should arrive at or sail into first. For the provincials esteem it of great importance that this tradition and privileges of this kind should be preserved. Some provinces even have the protocol that the governor should arrive in the province by sea, for example, in Asia, and indeed this was taken even to the extent that our emperor Antoninus Augustus issued a rescript in response to a request from the people of Asia that the governor was absolutely obliged to arrive by ship and to disembark first at Ephesus of all the metropolitan places.

Government and its representative had to respect the sensitivities of the local population and their rivalries. Well-ordered arrangements were an important aspect of co-operating with local elites who had a role to play in administering cities and their territory on behalf of the Romans and facilitating tax-collection.

Sylloge[3] no. 849 (AD 140–144)

192. Imperator Caesar, son of the divine Hadrian, grandson of the divine Trajan Parthicus, great-grandson of the divine Nerva, Titus Aelius Hadrian Antoninus Augustus, chief priest, holding the tribunician power for the … time, acclaimed imperator for the second time, father of the fatherland, to the magistrates, council, and people of Ephesus.

I am informed that the people of Pergamum in their letter to you use the titles which I stated that your city should use. But I think that the people of Smyrna have by mistake left them out of the decree about the common sacrifice, but will in the future willingly conform, if you too, in your letters to them, allude to their city in the terms which are appropriate and have been agreed. Sulpicius Iulianus, my procurator, dispatched the decree. Farewell.

Publius Vedius Antoninus, secretary, made the decree.

This demonstrates the sensitivities of Greek cities; Pliny (Letters 8.24) wrote to a man who was about to govern Achaea, advising him to show respect to the cities under his care and to remember their distinguished heritage and past achievements and legends, while not forgetting the importance of well-ordered government.

D 1.16.7pr (Ulpian, *Duties of a Proconsul*, Book 2)

193. If the governor visits a populous community or the leading city of the province, he should permit it to offer a commendation of itself and listen politely to speeches in his own praise since the provincials regard this as a mark of their honour, and also grant holidays according to the practice and custom that applied before.

D 1.16.10pr (Ulpian, *Duties of a Proconsul*, Book 10)

194. The proconsul should remember that he must deal with all business up to the arrival of his successor, since there is only one governorship, and the welfare of the province requires that there be someone through whom the provincials can conduct their business. Therefore, up to the arrival of his successor he must administer justice.

There is an important recognition here that the governor was expected to facilitate the activities of the provincials, and also that he was a crucial figure in the life of the province.

D 1.16.6.3 (Ulpian, *Duties of a Proconsul*, Book 1)

195. The governor should not entirely refrain from accepting gifts but use moderation so that he does not glumly decline all presents or greedily exceed what is reasonable in the way of gifts. The divine Severus and the emperor Antoninus regulated this issue most elegantly in a letter, whose words are as follows: 'With respect to gifts, hear what we think: the old proverb has it – "neither everything, not every time, nor from everyone". For it is entirely discourteous to accept gifts from nobody, but to accept them without discrimination from everyone is despicable and avaricious'.

See p. 312. The governor was expected to find a delicate balance in his relations with the provincial communities and display polite fastidiousness.

D 1.18.6.4 (Ulpian, *Opinions*, Book 1)

196. The governor of the province should personally ensure that no one is prevented from carrying on lawful business activities, and that nothing unlawful is permitted, and that no punishment is inflicted on innocent persons.

For the concept of responsible government, see p. 160.

D 1.16.6.1 (Ulpian, *Duties of a Proconsul*, Book 1)

197. Just as it lies in the governor's remit to delegate jurisdiction or not delegate it, so he may also take away delegated jurisdiction, but he ought not to do this without first consulting the emperor.

The governor was permitted to delegate jurisdiction only after he had entered his province (*D* 1.16.4.6).

D 1.18.6.8 (Ulpian, *Opinions*, Book 1)

198. Those who govern entire provinces have the right to impose the death penalty (power of the sword), and authority is also granted to them to condemn people to the mines.

The *ius gladii* enabled provincial governors to punish criminal individuals (*D* 2.1.3) with a variety of punishments including the death penalty.

D 1.18.9 (Callistratus, *Judicial Enquiries*, Book 1)

199. In general, when the emperor refers business to provincial governors by rescripts, for example, 'you can approach the person who is governor of

the province', or by adding: 'he will consider what role he ought to play', there is no compulsion upon the proconsul or legate to undertake the case personally. But even when the words 'he will consider what role he ought to play' have not been added, the governor should consider whether he should hear the case or appoint a judge.

For the administration of justice in the provinces see p. 152.

D 1.16.9pr (Ulpian, *Duties of a Proconsul*, Book 1)

200. There is no business in the province that the governor cannot conduct personally. But if the business relates to public finance, which is within the remit of the emperor's procurator, it will be better if the governor keeps away from it.

See also no. 203.

D 1.18.13pr (Ulpian, *Duties of a Proconsul*, Book 7)

201. It is appropriate for a competent and efficient governor to ensure that the province he governs is quiet and peaceful.

It was established that provincial governors could bar from shows people, described as 'young', who stirred up uproarious behaviour among the populace (*D* 48.19.28.3). A peaceful province was important for the governor's reputation, but also contributed to efficient administration for the benefit of the provincials.

Equestrian Officials

D 1.17.1 (Ulpian, *Edict*, Book 15)

202. The prefect of Egypt does not lay down his prefecture and power, which, just like that of a proconsul, was given to him by statute under Augustus, before his successor has entered Alexandria, even though he has already entered the province. This is provided for in his instructions.

The legal position of the prefect was essentially like that of other governors; for the background and career of prefects of Egypt, see Brunt (1975).

D 1.19.1; 3 (Ulpian, *Edict*, Book 16; Callistratus, *Judicial Enquiries*, Book 6)

203. Whatever is done or transacted by the emperor's procurator, those actions acquire the same validity from him, just as if they had been

transacted by the emperor himself. (3) The emperor's procurators do not have the right of deportation, for they do not have the right to decide on this penalty. However, if they prevent from entering the emperor's estates someone who is violent and likely to cause damage to the imperial tenants, that person must keep away, as the divine Pius stated in a rescript to Iulius. (3) Furthermore, procurators may not permit anyone to return (after deportation), as our emperors Severus and Antoninus stated in reply to the petition of Hermias.

At section 3 I follow Mommsen's reading of 'procuratores' for 'curatores' in the MSS.

BGU 1210 = *FIRA* 1, no. 99pr = *SP* no. 206pr (AD 150–161)

204. Of the rules which the divine Augustus entrusted to the supervision of the *idios logos*, and the material added to it on various occasions, either by emperors, or the senate, or the prefects, or *idioi logoi* of the time, I have set out for you a summary of the most relevant items, so that by applying your mind to the brief form of notation you can readily master the issues.

This guide to the *gnomon* of the *idios logos* was perhaps arranged by a holder of that office. See p. 120 for the financial officials in Egypt. Both the *dioketes* and the *idios logos* were equestrians, of equal rank and subordinate to the prefect. The *idios logos* was also responsible for the revenues of temples and holy places, since Augustus had confiscated all temple land, granting the priests a small stipend or plot of land. The papyrus of the rules administered by the *idios logos* lists some of the most important clauses and shows in unusual detail the meticulous and grasping nature of Roman provincial government in Egypt (see also no. 213); for a summary of the officials in Egypt, see Bowman and Rathbone (1992), and, briefly, Lintott (1993), 126–8.

The Management of Rome's Provincial Assets: the Census

Augustus was responsible for instituting a regular census of the provinces as a duty of the central government: 'And it happened in those days that there went out a decree from Caesar Augustus that all the world should be registered for the census. And all went to be registered, each one to his own city' (Luke 2.1; 3). There seems to have been no specifically prescribed period between each census; Egypt was a special case with a census period of fourteen years (see Bagnall and Frier (1994), especially pp. 1–30). The object was to make an inventory of property and people that should then inform the fair apportionment of tax liability for landed property (*tributum soli*) and individuals (*tributum capitis*). The provincial governor was responsible for the census in his province, though special officers were appointed from time to time. The co-operation of local communities was essential, and in this exercise the impact of the state on individuals was considerable. Furthermore, local communities through their magistrates and officials were responsible for much of the collection of Roman taxes, supervised by Rome. In the eastern provinces, from the late first to early second century boards of the 'first ten' and later the 'first twenty' appear (*dekaprotoi*; *eikosaprotoi*) with the role of regulating local finance; in some communities they also had some responsibility for collecting the tribute; see Burton (2001), 207–9; for Roman taxes see in general Brunt (1981).

D 50.15.4 (Ulpian, *Census*, Book 3)

205. The census document provides that land should be entered in the census in the following way: the name of each property, the community and district (*pagus*) in which it is situated, its two closest neighbours; how many acres (*iugera*) of land have been sowed in the previous ten years; how many vines there are in vineyards; how many acres of olive plantations there are and how many trees; how much hay has been cut in the previous ten years, how many acres of pasture and how many trees suitable for felling. The person completing the return must estimate everything. The census officer ought to display sufficient fairness, insofar as it is appropriate to his duties that when someone who has declared a certain area of land in the record has been unable to enjoy the fruits of it for attested reasons, for example, if a part of his land has been destroyed in an earthquake, he can be assisted by the census officer.

D 50.15.4.2 (Ulpian, *Census*, Book 3)

206. But the person who has land in another community ought to make the census declaration in that community where the land is; for the land tax should be levied in respect of that community in whose territory the land is possessed.

See Ando (2000), 353–6 for census documentation; in Egypt see Bagnall and Frier (1994), 179–312 for a catalogue of census returns; for some census rules of the *idios logos* see no. 213.

D 50.15.3 (Ulpian, *Census*, Book 2)

207. In making the census entry it is necessary to indicate age, because the age of certain individuals means that they do not pay tax; for example, in Syria, males from age fourteen and females from age twelve, both up to age sixty-five, are obliged to pay the poll tax. The relevant age is that when the census is being taken. Immunity conferred on property should not lapse, as was correctly stated in a rescript of our emperor to Pelignianus, for immunity granted to persons lapses with the death of the person, whereas immunity granted to objects never lapses.

CIL 2.4188 = *ILS* 1393

208. To Gaius Aemilius Galerius Fraternus, son of Gaius, prefect of engineers for the second time, military tribune of legion v Alaudae, priest of the province of Nearer Spain, this man conducted the census in the province of Gallia Aquitanica, province of Nearer Spain.

British Museum Papyrus 904, lines 18–38 = *SP* no. 220 (AD 104)

209. Gaius Vibius Maximus, prefect of Egypt, declares: Since the house-to-house census has begun, it is essential that all those people who for any reason at all are absent from their local areas (*nomes*) are told to return to their own home, so that they may complete the usual business of the census and carry on the work on the land that is their responsibility. However, I know that our city (Alexandria) needs some of the people from the country areas, and I wish all those who believe that they have an acceptable reason for remaining here to register the reason … Those who have demonstrated that it is necessary they remain will receive from Festus, cavalry squadron commander, whom I have appointed for this purpose, signed permits in accordance with this edict, up to the thirtieth of this month Epeiph.

P. Mich. no. 176 (AD 91)

210. To Horus son of Haryotes, officer in charge of the census of Bacchias, and Apynchis son of Onnophris and the other elders, from Peteuris son of Horus, of the village of Bacchias. In the village I own one fourth of a house in which I live, and I register both myself and those in my household for the census of the past ninth year of the Emperor Caesar Domitian Augustus Germanicus: myself, Peteuris son of Horus (son of Horus) and

my mother being Herieus (daughter of Menches), cultivator of state land, about thirty years of age, with no identifying marks, and also my wife Tapeine, daughter of Apkois, twenty-five years of age, and my brothers born of the same father and mother, Horus, about twenty years of age, and another, Horion, about seven years of age. And my brother also owns one fourth of the house mentioned above and the courtyard in which we live.

[Signatures] I, the above-mentioned Peteuris, have submitted this, and I swear by the Emperor Caesar Domitian Augustus Germanicus that the foregoing is true and that I have not made a false statement. Aphrodisios, village secretary, wrote for him since he is illiterate. Year ten of the Emperor Caesar Domitian Augustus Germanicus, Pachon 15.

This is the first of three census returns for this family, in 91, 104, and 119, by which time Peteuris had died, and Horos signed the return.

Lewis (1989), no. 16 (AD 127)

211. A verified and exact copy of a document of registration set out in the basilica here, and it is as attached below.

In the reign of Emperor Caesar Trajan Hadrian Augustus, son of the divine Trajan Parthicus, grandson of the divine Nerva, chief priest, in the twelfth year of his tribunician power, consul for the third time, in the consulship of Marcus Gavius Gallicanus and Titus Atilius Rufus Titianus, 2 December, and according to the reckoning of the new province of Arabia, year twenty-two, sixteenth of the month Apellaios, in the city of Rabbath-Moab. Since a census of Arabia is being conducted by Titus Aninius Sextius Florentinus, legate of the emperor with propraetorian power, I, Babtha daughter of Simon, from Maoza, in the Zoarene district of the administrative region of Petra, living in my own property in the said Maoza, register what I own, in the presence of my guardian, Judanes son of Elazar, from the village of En-gedi, in the district of Jericho in Judaea, who lives in his own property in the said Maoza, within the confines of Maoza, namely, a date orchard called Algiphiamma, the area of sowing being one *saton*, three *kaboi* of barley, paying in tax fifteen *sata* of Syrian and mixed dates, ten *sata* of 'splits', and as crown tax one 'black' and thirty sixtieths, which a road and the sea abut; and within the confines of Maoza a date orchard called Algiphiamma, the area for sowing being one *kabos* of barley, paying in tax half of the crops produced there each year, which the *moschantic* estate of our lord the emperor and the sea abut; within the confines of Maoza a date orchard called Bagalgala, the area of sowing being three *sata* of barley, paying in tax one *koros* of Syrian and Noaran(?) dates, one *koros* of 'splits', and as crown tax three 'blacks' and thirty sixtieths, which abuts the heirs of Thesaios, son of Sabakas, and Iamit, son(?) of Manthanthes; within the confines of Maoza a date orchard called Bethphaaraia, the area of sowing being twenty *sata* of barley, paying in tax three kaboi of Syrian and Noaran(?) dates, two *koroi* of 'splits', and as crown tax eight 'blacks' and forty-five sixtieths, which Tamar, daughter of Thamous, and a road abut.

Translation of the subscription. I, Babtha, daughter of Simon, swear by the good fortune of our lord the emperor that I have in good faith registered what is written above. I, Judanes son of Elazar, acted as her guardian and wrote for her. Translation of the subscription of the prefect: I, Priscus, prefect of cavalry, have received (this) on 4 December in the consulship of Gallicanus and Titianus.

(Names of five witnesses)

Babatha (her name appears as Babtha in this document) was a Jewish woman who lived in the small community of Maoza on the southern shore of the Dead Sea, which had become part of the Roman province of Arabia in AD 106. A dossier wrapped in a leather bag of documents relating to her activities was found in a cave in the Judaean Desert, and since she failed to retrieve these records, it is likely that she perished in the Bar Kokhba revolt in AD 132–135/6. For other documents of Babatha see nos. 255–7. This document refers to a census declaration which had to be delivered in person. Babatha has travelled to Rabbath, about forty kilometres from Maoza. There she hired a scribe to write the return in Greek; her attestation in Aramaic was also translated into Greek; the witnesses signed in Nabatean. The document shows the precise detail required in the census declaration.

Saton is the Greek version of the Hebrew unit of measurement se'ah (perhaps about 13 litres); *kabos* (Hebrew *kab*) is one sixth of a *saton*; *koros* (Hebrew *kor*) amounted to thirty se'ahs, about 400 litres. 'Splits' Lewis explains by reference to Pliny, *NH* 13.45 – a date filled with so much juice that it split while still on the tree. Crown tax was an imperial money impost. 'Black' is a form of recognized currency perhaps deriving from the pre-Roman currency of the area. *Moschantic* is obscure, but Lewis conjectures may refer to an estate with 'young growth'. Babatha's claim to register the date-palm orchards as her property was challenged by Besas, who was guardian of Babatha's second husband's children by his first wife (Lewis (1989), no. 24).

P.S.I. 1064 = *SP* no. 310 (AD 129)

212. To Herminos, royal scribe of the area of Heraclides in the Arsinoite nome, from Sabinus, son of Sabinus, ex-gymnasiarch, from the quarter of the district of Dionysios, acting in my absence through Nemesianos, also called

Artemidoros. My grandson Serapion, who is registered in the same quarter of the district of Dionysios and subject to the poll tax, died in the month of Mecheir in this current thirteenth year of Hadrian Caesar, the lord. I ask therefore that he be recorded in the list of those in this status. I, Sabinus son of Sabinus, ex-gymnasiarch, acting in my absence through Nemesianos, also called Artemidoros, have presented this statement, and I swear by the fortune of Emperor Caesar Trajan Hadrian Augustus that the foregoing statement is true. In the thirteenth year of Emperor Caesar Trajan Hadrian Augustus, Mecheir 24. To the scribes of the metropolis (from royal scribe): if it is true that the person noted above has died, perform the requisite actions. In the thirteenth year of Emperor Caesar Trajan Hadrian Augustus, Mecheir 24. I, Philoxenos, scribe, have signed this. District of Dionysios.

Since the census registered people as well as property, it was important for the local population to register the death of someone liable to the poll tax; but the government officials needed to check to prevent fraud.

BGU 1210 = *FIRA* 1, no. 99 = *SP* no. 206 *Gnomon* of the *Idios Logos*, sections 58–63

213. Those who have not registered themselves in the census of the household and other persons whom they ought (to register), are fined a quarter of their property, and if they are reported as not registering themselves on two occasions of the census, they are sentenced to pay the same fine doubled.

Romans and citizens of Alexandria who do not register those whom they ought, whether this is one person or more, are sentenced to a fine of one quarter (of their property).

Those who have not registered slaves have only the slaves confiscated.

The children of slaves who are unregistered are given to their masters, if they have no means of support except for the slaves alone.

Soldiers on active service are not deemed responsible if they are unregistered, but their women and children are liable.

Those who are liable on the grounds that they did not register at the previous census are excused if the person requiring to be registered was less than three years old.

The precise rules in Egypt give an idea of the impact of the census procedure on the local population. Bagnall and Frier (1994), 57–74 analyse the nature of Egyptian households revealed in the census returns.

The Management of Rome's Provincial Assets: Bridges and Roads

CIL 2.4697 = *ILS* 5867 (AD 79)

214. Emperor Caesar Vespasian Augustus, chief priest, in the tenth year of his tribunician power, acclaimed imperator on twenty occasions, consul for the ninth time, father of the fatherland, censor, repaired the via Augusta from Ianum to the Ocean, constructed bridges, and restored the old ones.

This refers to the remedial work of Vespasian in Baetica in Spain.

D 43.7.3 (Ulpian, *Sabinus*, Book 33)

215. Local roads which have been constructed from contributions from the lands of private individuals and of which there is now no record, are numbered among public roads. But there is this difference between them and other, military roads, namely that military roads terminate either at the sea, or in cities, or at public rivers, or at another military road. The situation of these local roads is different since some of them lead into military roads, others peter out with no exit.

For the definition and maintenance of roads and the provision of access to landholdings, see pp. 108; 238.

Mitchell (1976), p. 106 (Extract)

216. The people of Sagalassus are to provide a service of ten carts and the same number of mules for the essential use of people passing through, and should receive from those who make use of them, ten asses per *schoenum* for each waggon, and four asses per *schoenum* for each mule; but if they prefer to provide donkeys they must give two for one mule at the same price. Or, if they prefer, for each mule and waggon they may pay to the people of another community or village who undertake the responsibility, the same price as they would have received, were they themselves providing the service, so that these people provide the same service. But they are to provide vehicles as far as Cormasa and Conana.

A *schoenum* was a Persian unit of measurement, approximately four or five miles according to Pliny, *NH* 6.124; 12.53. This inscription from Burdur in Galatia relates to the operation of the public post, which was a particular burden to each of those communities through whose territory a main road passed. The locals were obliged to provide *angareia*, that is, animals, guides, and hospitality. Libuscidianus the governor was attempting to manage as fairly as possible an essential element of Roman administration in the face of abuse by local officials; see also no. 265. A third century inscription from Phrygia illustrates a dispute between two villages over obligations to the imperial post (Frend (1956)). Roads in the provinces facilitated not just trade but the movement of Roman troops and were a visible symbol of Roman control.

The Management of Rome's Provincial Assets: the Watery Environment

Agennius Urbicus (T, p. 44.5–20 = Campbell (2000), p. 41.28–40)

217. I know that Lusitania in the territory of Augusta Emerita, the substantial river Ana flows right through the middle of the colony's territory, and lands were allocated around it as far as the soil appeared useable at that time. Because of the huge extent of the lands, the founder settled veterans for the most part round the outer boundary just like boundary markers, but very few round the colony itself and round the river Ana; the residue remained to be filled up later. Even though a second and third allocation took place, the quantity of land could not be exhausted by distribution, and an amount remained unallocated. In these lands, when unsurveyed areas were being claimed back, the landholders obtained an undertaking from the governor of that province to designate a specific width for the river Ana. Since individuals were being compelled to buy back the unsurveyed area that they had occupied, it was judged unfair that anyone should buy the river, which was public property, or unfertile land which the river had deposited.

An area was assigned to a river marking property boundaries, usually encompassing the greatest extent to which the river had ever been known to flood. There was no settlement in that area, though adjacent landholders could make use of it at their own risk. In this instance in the original survey no width had been assigned to the river; the land along the bank was unsurveyed, and over time the neighbouring landholders had occupied it. When the river overflowed this land was damaged and presumably rendered less fertile. The landholders could accept this since they had taken over the land for nothing, but circumstances changed when they were forced to buy the land they had occupied. We may compare Vespasian's instructions to local communities to reclaim unsurveyed land that had been occupied by neighbouring landholders (see no. 168). Government intervention with rivers, which of course affected individual landholders, was intended to minimize disruptive disputes, avoid the flooding of productive and taxable land, and safeguard local finances.

Oliver (1989), no. 108 (AD 125)

218. Emperor Caesar Trajan Hadrian Augustus, son of the divine Trajan Parthicus, chief priest, in the ninth year of his tribunician power, consul for the third time, to the archons, council, and people of Koronea, greetings.

I ordered dykes to be constructed for the Kephisos and the Erkynne and the other rivers along the stretch where they flow together before passing into Lake Kopais. Work will commence as soon as possible, so that they flow within their banks and do not turn aside from their course and, as happens now, flood much of the agricultural land. I shall also bring you a water supply. I shall provide the money, a sum of 65,000 denarii, which the experts in these matters say will be necessary. You should choose those who are to supervise [the project].

[Emperor Caesar] Trajan [Hadrian Augustus], son of the divine Trajan Parthicus, grandson of the divine Nerva, chief priest, holding tribunician power for the [... time], father of the fatherland, to the archons, council, and people of the Koroneans, greetings.

The work on the Phalaros has turned out for you [to have been well worth my enthusiasm], not only because of its usefulness but also because of its appearance. In order that [in the future] any damage can never avoid notice, it is now your responsibility [to be watchful?]. It is indeed appropriate that the outsiders who have acquired land, since they use the water [for ...], take proper care of the dykes [...], and not drive stakes into them. [It is necessary for those with land along the banks] to put their embankments and bulwarks into the river, but [they should do so] without [... or] constructing a barrier in it. One who is caught [... shall] himself rectify the damage to the structure [and] shall pay the city [a fine of one thousand] five hundred denarii. Farewell.

A wall in the city of Koronea was inscribed with a series of letters addressed to the city by emperors: Hadrian, Antoninus Pius, Marcus Aurelius, and Lucius Verus. The Hadrianic letters were part of his initiative to control Lake Kopais in Boeotia by channelling some of the local rivers to prevent the flooding of arable land and to guarantee a water supply; Hadrian funds the cost (no. 108); a subsequent letter (n. 110) celebrates the success of flood control measures on the Phalaros river, and reminds the city of its responsibility for supervision, especially of those who were not citizens of Koronea, even establishing the amount of fine.

Local Government

In the records and constitutions of colonies and *municipia* in the provinces we can trace part of the process of self-regulation and management of resources which established a platform for dealing with the Roman government for the benefit of the community and its individual citizens. Indeed, the management of *municipia* in the provinces illustrates the interface of Roman overall administrative objectives and the requirements of individual communities; good order and efficient management must fit in with the living and working arrangements of the citizens, for example, in keeping the streets clean and useable, managing public spaces and watery resources, and ensuring the corn supply.

Municipal Regulations

Lex Colonia Genetiva **Crawford (1996), p. 424, Chapters 73–4 (Extracts)**

219. No one is permitted to bring a dead person inside the boundaries of a town or of a colony, where (a line) shall have been marked around by a plough, nor may he bury him there, or cremate him, or construct a tomb for a dead person (penalties follow for the infringement of these rules). 74. No one is permitted to prepare a new *ustrina*, where a dead person has not (before this time) been cremated, nearer the town than 500 paces (penalties follow for the infringement of these rules).

Ustrina was a dedicated space for burning corpses. The *lex Coloniae Genetivae* sets out the rules for municipal government at Urso in Spain, which was founded by Julius Caesar; its municipal statute dates from 44/43 BC, but some of its provisions derive from precedents in Italian *municipia* and overlap with constitutions established in Spain in the Flavian period, such as at neighbouring Irni; see Lintott (1993), 137–45.

Lex Coloniae Genetivae **Crawford (1996), p. 425, Chapter 79**

220. Whatever rivers, streams, fountains, lakes, waters, ponds, or marshes there are within the land, which shall have been divided out among the colonists of this colony, there is to be a right of way for men and animals and access to water in respect of those streams, fountains, lakes, waters, ponds, or marshes, for those who will have or will possess that land, in the same way as there was for those who had or possessed that land. And the rule and law for the passage to water is to be applicable in the same way for those who have or possess or shall have or shall possess that land.

Lex Coloniae Genetivae **Crawford (1996), p. 427, Chapter 99**

221. Whatever public waters shall be brought in, in the town of the Colonia Genetiva, the board of two who are then (in office) are to raise with the decurions, two-thirds being present, through which lands it may be permitted to bring water. In that place where the majority of the decurions

who shall then be present shall have decreed for it to be brought, there is to be legal right and power to bring water through those lands, provided that the water is not brought through that building, which has not been built for that purpose; and no one is to act to prevent water being brought in this way.

This clause indicates the right of the community to bring a water channel along a chosen route provided that the water moving through the channel did not damage any adjacent building; clause 104 provided that boundary ditches should not be blocked. See also *ILS* 5749 (a boundary stone near Lugdunum): 'On the instructions of Imperator Caesar Trajan Hadrian Augustus no one has the right to plough, sow, or plant within that area of land that is appointed for the safeguarding of the aqueduct'.

Lex Irnitana González (1986), Chapters 19–20 (Extracts) (AD 82/84)

222. (19) They (the aediles) ... are to have the legal right and power of dealing with the corn supply, the sacred buildings, the sacred and religious places, the town, the roads, the districts, the drains, the baths, and the market, and of examining and checking weights and measures, and of organizing the fire-watch when the situation requires, and of arranging and doing whatever else the decurions or *conscripti* (local senators) decide has to be done by the aediles, and also of seizing a pledge from the *municipes* and other inhabitants, which is not to exceed 10,000 sesterces per person per day, and also of imposing a fine on them or giving a judgement against them, not over 5,000 sesterces per person per day.

(20) And they (the quaestors) ... are to have the legal right and power of collecting, spending, safe-keeping, administering, and dealing with the common funds of the *municipes* of that *municipium*, in line with the decision of the duumviri. And they are to be permitted to have common slaves of the *municipes* of the *municipium* with them in that *municipium* to attend them.

These clauses set out the wide-ranging local rights and powers of the aediles and quaestors in Irni in Spain, carefully noting that those elected in the future are to have the same powers. For the constitution of Irni, see p. 154.

Lex Irnitana González (1986), Chapter 74

223. No one may take part in an illegal gathering in that *municipium*, or have a society or association for that purpose, or conspire that it (a gathering) be held, or act in such a way that any of these things is brought

about. Anyone who acts contrary to these rules is to be condemned to pay ten thousand sesterces to the *municipes* of the *Municipium Flavium Irnitanum*, and the right of taking action, bringing a suit, and pursuing that money and concerning that money, is to belong to any *municeps* of that *municipium* who wishes to, and who is permitted by this statute.

This provision did not necessarily ban associations or burial societies of poorer citizens; it is primarily aimed at any illegal gathering for whatever purpose; see p. 113 for *collegia*.

Lex Irnitana González (1986), Chapter 75

224. No one in the *municipium* may buy up or hoard anything, or work with another, or agree to enter into a partnership so that something may be sold more expensively, or not be sold, or an inadequate amount be sold. Anyone who acts contrary to these rules is to be condemned to pay ten thousand sesterces to the *municipes* of the *Municipium Flavium Irnitanum* for each action, and the right of taking action … (as in no. 223).

This provision banned speculation that was likely to damage the corn supply; it seems to be related to Roman legislation: 'Under the *lex Iulia* on the corn supply a penalty is established for the person who has done anything against the interests of the corn supply or has formed an association in order to make corn more expensive' (*D* 48.12.2pr).

FIRA 1, no. 24 = *ILS* 6089 = McCrum and Woodhead (1961), no. 454; Chapter 63 (AD 82–84)

225. Concerning public contracts, the publication of the rules that govern the contracts, and their entry in the public records.

Whoever is in office as duumvir responsible for jurisdiction must lease the public revenues, or anything else that is appropriate to be leased in the corporate name of the citizens of that *municipium*. And the contracts he has made, and the rules that he has established, the amount which has been paid for each contract, the personal sureties accepted, the landed property which has been offered as security, warranted, and mortgaged, and those who have been accepted as vouchers of the properties, he shall ensure that they are entered in the corporate records of the citizens of that *municipium*, and he shall keep them on display for the remainder of his magistracy, so that they may be read clearly from the ground level, in whatever place the decurions or the senators may determine that they are to be displayed.

This is part of the Flavian municipal law of Malaca (Malaga) in Baetica in Spain, which has many common features with those of Salpensa and Irni.

Supervising Local Administration and Infrastructure

In addition to overseeing regulations for *municipia*, in respect of all local communities the Romans were involved directly or indirectly in the provision of buildings, streets, roads, the maintenance of water channels and water supply, the supervision of local finance, social affairs, and organizations such as *collegia*, which were an important part of the fabric of community life; the generosity of rich members of communities was also a factor in maintaining local life. For an excellent survey of the involvement of the Roman state in the public finances of provincial communities, see Burton (2004). The relationship between state and citizen is revealed in Rome's responsibility for orderly and effective local government, in which she would expect co-operation from city councils and magistrates who could be cajoled and if necessary brought under legal compulsion.

***D* 1.16.7.1 (Ulpian, *Duties of a Proconsul*, Book 2)**

226. The governor should make a tour of inspection of temples and public buildings to see if they are in good order in respect of their walls and roofs, or require some repair, and to ensure that buildings that have been begun should be completed as far as the resources of that community permit, and formally appoint efficient supervisors of public works and, if necessary, deploy some military personnel to assist the supervisors.

***Sylloge*[3] no. 850 (AD 145)**

227. Imperator Caesar, son of the divine Hadrian, grandson of the divine Trajan Parthicus, great-grandson of the divine Nerva, Titus Aelius Hadrianus Antoninus Augustus, chief priest, in the eighth year of his tribunician power, imperator for the second time, consul for the fourth time, father of the fatherland, to the magistrates, council, and people of Ephesus, greetings.

I learned of the generosity which Vedius Antoninus displays toward you not so much from your letter as from his, since, wishing to obtain assistance from me for the adornment of the public buildings which he had promised you, he made clear the number and type of large buildings that he is adding to the city. But you do not appreciate him appropriately. I have granted everything he asked for and have noted that he prefers not to act in the accustomed manner of politicians, who, to gain immediate favour, expend their generosity on shows, and distributions, and prizes for the games, but to choose a course of action by which he hopes to make your city more distinguished for the future. Claudius Iulianus, the honourable proconsul, sent the letter. Farewell.

Vedius Antoninus came from a family that had been long-term benefactors of Ephesus and had built a gymnasium and *bouleuterion*; see Kalinowski (2002); Kokkinia (2003). Elsewhere, however, Pius was concerned that benefactions should be spent on repairs, not new buildings (no. 233).

D 43.10.1 (Papinian, *Care of Cities*)

228. Those in charge of the city will take care of the streets throughout the city ensuring that they are kept level, and that overflows of water do not damage the buildings, and that bridges are in place where they are needed. They should also take care that the walls of private houses or those round the house which touch the road should not be dilapidated, ensuring that the owners of the houses where necessary clean and repair them.

This treatise written by Papinian perhaps suggests an attempt by the Romans to ensure that Greek cities of the east had a framework in which to maintain procedures for the care of public roads and buildings. This might explain why it was translated into Greek.

Pliny, *Letters* 10.23

229. Gaius Pliny to Emperor Trajan. Sir, the people of Prusa have a public bath which is dirty and old. Therefore, they are very keen for it to be rebuilt. In my view you can properly accede to their wishes. The money will be available, firstly from the sums that I have already begun to call in from private people, and secondly because the citizens are ready to transfer for building the bath the money normally set aside as a grant for providing olive oil. Furthermore, the prestige of the town and the glory of your regime require this project.

Trajan accepted the proposal provided that there were no new taxes or disruption of money for public services (10.24). See also *Letters* 10.37–8 where Nicomedia had wasted 3,518,000 sesterces on two failed aqueducts. At Nicaea a theatre costing ten million sesterces had been built on insecure foundations on unsuitable ground; a gymnasium of poor design had also been begun; at Claudiopolis a bath was being constructed in an unsuitable location (*Letters* 10.39). It seems that the emperor had instructed Pliny not to permit new buildings without reference to him. It was subsequently laid down that new buildings to be funded from municipal monies needed imperial approval (*D* 50.10.3.1).

Pliny, *Letters* 10.90–1

230. Pliny to the Emperor Trajan. Sir, the community of Sinope lacks a water supply. There is apparently a good and bountiful source which could be brought from sixteen miles distant. However, there is a dubious, marshy area stretching about a mile from this source. Meanwhile, I have ordered that this be surveyed (at moderate expense) to see if it will bear and support the weight of the construction. There will be no shortage of money assured by me if you, sir, will agree to this kind of work so beneficial to the health and lifestyle of a very thirsty community.

My dear Pliny, diligently carry on the survey which you have begun to discover if the area that concerns you can sustain the weight of the aqueduct. I have no doubt that a water supply must be brought into Sinope provided that the community can cope with the cost from its own resources. It will make a large contribution to the health and pleasure of the people.

Among other important projects discussed by Pliny and Trajan was the plan to cover a sewer at Amastris (*Letters* 10.98–9), and to build a canal from Lake Sophon, about eighteen miles east of Nicomedia, to the Black Sea in order to improve the movement of goods (*Letters* 10.41–2); for the context see Campbell (2012), 224–5. A papyrus of roughly contemporary date from Oxyrhynchus also shows central control and supervision of public building:

Copy. Flavius Titianus (prefect of Egypt) to the city of the Oxyrhynchites, greeting. I congratulate you on your plans to beautify your city and I permit you to equip the baths with the funds already collected, as you assert, and from those which may be contributed by … I pray for your health. Year twelve of Imperator Caesar Traianus Hadrianus Augustus(P. Oxy. 43. 3088; c. AD 128).

In 10.54 Pliny suggested to Trajan compulsory personal short-term loans at a rate of 12 per cent interest as a form of investment (land not being available) for public finances. Pliny suggested the possibility of lowering the interest rates to make the loans more attractive. The idea of compelling town councillors to undertake loans was unusual and Trajan rejected it, pointing out that some would have no use for a loan of this type and that the whole notion was 'incompatible with the justice of our times' (*Letters* 10.55). See Sherwin-White (1966), 635–6.

CIL 8.2728 = *ILS* 5795 (Lambaesis)

231. Endurance Hope Courage

[To Marcus Valerius] Etruscus (Legate of III Augusta): the most illustrious community of Saldae and I, along with the citizens of Saldae, ask you, sir, that you request Nonius Datus, veteran of legion III Augusta, surveyor, to come to Saldae to complete what remains of his work.

I (Nonius Datus) set out and on the way encountered bandits; stripped and wounded, I got away with my companions and came to Saldae. I met the procurator, Clemens. He took me to the mountain, where they were bemoaning the tunnel as a doubtful piece of work which they thought would have to be abandoned.

(Here there is a description of the technical difficulties with the tunnel.) When I was allocating the work so that they should know who was responsible for each section of the tunnelling, I arranged for there to be rivalry in the work between men from the fleet and the auxiliary troops, and on this basis they came together at the meeting point of their tunnelling through the mountain. Therefore I, who had originally conducted a survey and marked out the course, decided that it should be done in accordance with the plan which I had given to the procurator Petronius Celer (procurator of Mauretania Caesariensis in AD 137). When the work was completed and the water was sent through the channel, Varius Clemens the procurator (AD 152) dedicated it. Five *modii*.

I have appended some letters so that my work on this water channel at Saldae may emerge more clearly.

Letter of Porcius Vetustinus (procurator of Mauretania, AD 150) to Crispinus (Legate of III Augusta, AD 147–50): You acted very kindly, sir, and in keeping with your consideration and goodwill on other occasions, in sending me Nonius Datus, reservist, so that I could discuss with him the work which he undertook to look after. Therefore, although I was pressed for time and was hurrying to Caesarea, nevertheless I made the journey to Saldae and inspected the water channel which had started well, although it is a large undertaking and could not be completed without the attention of

Nonius Datus, who has dealt with the matter both carefully and conscientiously. I was therefore going to ask that we be permitted to detain him for several months to take charge of the work, unless he should be taken ill.

This illustrates the role of Roman technical expertise in assisting a local community, with the good offices of the legionary commander and the procurator. The commander of legion III Augusta, stationed at Lambaesis, had sent Nonius Datus a soldier and surveyor, to Petronius Celer, procurator of the adjacent province of Mauretania Caesariensis, to assist the town of Saldae in building an aqueduct. Nonius' involvement seems to have begun in AD 137 when he gave to the procurator Celer a plan for the route of the aqueduct; this project required a tunnel (428 metres long), and between 146–50 Porcius Vetustinus, the new procurator, asked for Nonius to be sent again to sort out construction problems. Then, in the early 150s the current procurator Clemens asked the commander of the III Augusta to send Nonius yet again in order to complete the project; the aqueduct was finally opened in 152/153; discussion in Cuomo (2011).

D 50.10.2pr (Ulpian, *Opinions*, Book 3)

232. Anyone who through generosity and not indebtedness has devoted his own resources temporarily to completing public works, should not be prohibited by envy from receiving the fruits of his munificence by inscribing his name on the work he has done.

D 50.10.7pr (Callistratus, *Judicial Enquiries*, Book 2)

233. The divine Pius stated in a rescript that money which had been bequeathed for the construction of a new building should be transferred into maintaining buildings that already existed rather than for starting a new building. This was particularly the case if the community had enough public buildings and money could not easily be found for repairing them.

The government was trying to manage the generosity of local rich citizens and preserve a balance, to avoid the addition of more and more buildings while existing constructions fell into disrepair. However, in the case of Vedius Antoninus at Ephesus, Antoninus Pius encouraged his expenditure of his funds on new buildings (no. 227).

ILS 6891 = FIRA 1, no. 105, lines 19–31 = Smallwood (1966), no. 440

234. The concession for the baths. The lessee of the baths or his partner must at his own expense heat on every day the bath for which he has contracted up to the next 30 June, and keep the bath open from dawn up to the seventh hour for women, and from the eighth hour to the second hour of the night for men, according to the decision of the procurator who presides over the mines. He must ensure that water flows abundantly [into the bath(?) right up to] the topmost level for the tanks of the boiler and into the tub, equally for women and men. The lessee should demand from each man half an *as* and from each woman an *as* in payment. Exempt are freedmen and slaves of the Emperor who are in the service of the procurator, or people who receive such benefits, also children and soldiers. The lessee, or his partner, or his agent must, when the lease has been completed, return undamaged the equipment of the baths and all the items which were entrusted to him, unless they have been worn out with age. He must properly wash, clean, and anoint with fresh grease the bronze vessels which he uses, at least once every thirty days. [If a need for repair] prevents the proper use of the bath, the lessee should calculate a proportionate deduction from his rent for that time. Apart from this, if he incurs any other expenditure to facilitate the operation of the said bath, he is not entitled to make a deduction. The lessee is not permitted to sell wood, unless taken from cuttings of branches not suitable for burning. If he does anything in contravention of this, he must pay to the treasury a fine of 100 sesterces for each [sale]. If this bath is not properly available for use, then the procurator of the mines is permitted to impose a fine of up to 200 sesterces on the lessee on every occasion when the bath is not available. The lessee must keep wood stored all the time, enough for ... days.

This extract from an inscription of the second century AD provides for the leasing of a public bath in the vicinity of the mines at Vipasca in Portugal which fell under the general supervision of the procurator of the mines in a kind of administrative district; the government did not operate them directly but leased them to private contractors. It illustrates the interface of state-organized activities and the life of local inhabitants who had use of the baths; for contracts and lease, see p. 190.

***Lex rivi Hiberiensis*, Beltrán Lloris (2006) I lines 21–46; III lines 44–7**

235. To the clearing and repairing of the channel *Hiberiensis Capitonianus* from its highest part as far as the bottom dam, which is at the (property) of the centurion Rectus, all the inhabitants of the district (*pagus*) must contribute, each in proportion to his share.

They should clean out and repair the channels that they use in common, so that up to the boundary of where each person has access to water, as far as this he should supply his labour. When the channels are intact, from that dam from which each takes water, to the next dam, (he is to) clean twice a year, when the officials of the district (*magistri pagi*) shall have named a day for him and announced it. And whatever it would be an act of malice and deceit for someone to omit, that must be done at all times.

And if anyone installs a canal or bridge, that must be looked after as if it were a dam, and he must supervise and clean that place, in particular in respect of how far the channel has been blocked by that object, so that the proper flow of water is prevented.

The officials of the district will hold their magistracy from 1 June to the following 1 June, and from the time when they shall have been appointed, within the next five days they will assemble the district in a meeting, and in accordance with the view of the majority of the members of the district they should divert the water from the *Hiberiensis* channel, from that day that the members of the district decided, until they divert the lowest portion of the water supply. And from 15 July they are to prepare the labour for repairing and cleaning that channel.

[–]ndanus Augustanus Alpinus legate [propraetore(?) of the Emperor Caesar] Trajan Hadrian Augustus, approached by the *magister pagi* of the *pagani Caesaraugustani*, Lucius Man[lius(?) Mate]rnus(?), [the son of Lucius (?), from the Aniensis tribe(?)], established [this law] and ordered it to be binding.

This inscription of Hadrianic date sets out regulations for the administration of a canal shared by several communities on the river Ebro in Spain. Important points include the costs, and labour to be provided by those who received water, the decision-making process, a system to ensure that all contributors carried out their duties, protection from interference with the system, and provision of a procedure for settling any legal issues before the municipal magistrates. All this was arranged by agreement, but under the supervision probably of the provincial governor. The government intervenes to facilitate an equitable distribution of water among several communities.

For another case in Spain dated to 87 BC involving a disagreement among several local peoples, over the construction of a canal, which was settled using formulae suggesting a familiarity with Roman law, see Richardson (1983).

CIL 8.18587 = *ILS* 5793 (Lamasba in Numidia)

236. To Imperator Caesar M. Aurelius, Unconquered, Pious Fortunate Augustus [… and] Valentinus, to whom the matter was delegated by

decree of the council and the colonists, [when an assessment was made of the water which previously] had been customarily provided, decided that the water ought to flow down in the following arrangement ...

Level 1 from 25 September, first day, early morning, on which the Claudiana stream descends into the main irrigation channel, first hour

Mattius Fortis – 408 K (an area of land) – from the first hour on 25 September to hour 5½ of the same day, for his own section, four and a half hours

Flavius Adiutor, veteran – 350 K – from hour 5½ on 25 September to hour 10½ of the same day, for his own section, five hours

Heir of Apuleius Faustinus – 117 K – from hour 10½ on 25 September to hour 12 of the same day, for his own section, 1½ hours

Apuleius Rogatianus – 110 K – from hour 12 on 25 September to hour 1½ of the same night, for his own section, 1½ hours.

This is an extract from a long inscription recording water allocations at Lamasba in Africa which had come into dispute; the landholders approached the government of the community to resolve the issue. Although it was a local matter the emperor was included in the dedication, showing Rome's general concern; the scheme worked by means of time units, and the water was provided to the landholders in order of sequence from a main canal; discussion in Shaw (1982); (1995), chapter V.

Pliny, *Letters* 10.108–9

237. Gaius Pliny to Emperor Trajan. Sir, I ask that you tell me what kind of legal rights you wish the communities of Bithynia and Pontus to have in respect of recovering money which they are owed as a result of hire, or sale, or some other reason. I have discovered that priority to the claims of the community was granted by several proconsuls and that this has acquired the force of law. However, I think that through your consideration something should be decided and established permanently to look after their interests for the future. For their concessions, even if wisely bestowed, are ephemeral and uncertain, unless your authority confirms them.

Trajan to Pliny. The legal right to which the cities of Bithynia and Pontus should resort in respect of money that is owed to a community for any reason, must be established by considering the law of each community. If they have the right by which they are given priority over other creditors, that should be maintained, but if they do not have such a right, it is inappropriate for me to grant it to the detriment of the interest of private creditors.

In respect of provincial financial matters and the recovery of debts, the imperial treasury was normally first in line – 'It is the right of the imperial treasury to have the first place among all the creditors' (*Opinions of Paul* 5.12.10). In this case, in respect of local finances, several previous governors of Bithynia had given priority to the interests of local governments. Now that the province was governed by a direct appointee of the emperor, it was legitimate to ask about a definite policy. Trajan is prepared to let local law and custom prevail and seeks to protect individuals against pressure from imperial and city administration.

CIL 2.6278 (Near Italica) = *ILS* 5163 (Extracts)

238. O mighty emperors who know how to find deep-seated remedies which take account of those troublesome people (gladiator trainers), who indeed have made themselves indispensable. And now the fruit of your great foresight emerges. For your speech has just now been read to us, but when rumour revealed that the profits of the owners and trainers of gladiators had been cut, and that the imperial treasury had rejected all money from that source as if it were contaminated, the priests of your most loyal Gallic provinces immediately met together, expressed their delight, and held a discussion.

There was one individual, who, when he had been elected priest, lamenting the loss of his fortune, had decided to seek help by making an appeal to the emperors. But when first he discussed the matter with his friends, he said: 'Why do I need to appeal now? The most sacred emperors have removed the entire burden that was threatening my property. Now I wish and choose to be a priest, and I welcome the duty of putting on the games, which once we detested'.

(Line 30) However, in the case of those who produce games costing more than 30,000 sesterces up to 60,000 sesterces, gladiators are to be provided for them with equal numbers in three classes; the maximum price for the first class is to be 5,000 sesterces, for the second class 4,000, and for the third 3,000. When the cost (of games) is from 60,000 sesterces up to 100,000 sesterces, the group of gladiators should be divided into three categories; the maximum price for a gladiator of the first category is to be 8,000 sesterces, for the middle category 6,000, then 5,000. When the cost (of games) is from 100,000 sesterces up to 150,000 sesterces, there are to be five groups, and the price of the first is to be 12,000 sesterces, the second 10,000, the third 7,000, the fourth 6,000, and the last 5,000. Then finally when the cost (of games) is from 150,000 sesterces up to 200,000 sesterces or whatever cost beyond this, the cost of a gladiator of the lowest rank is to be 6,000 sesterces, of the one above him 7,000, of the third counting backwards 9,000, of the fourth 12,000, up to 15,000. This is to be the fixed price for the top and most renowned gladiator. Furthermore, in all the games in which limits have been established, the gladiator-trainer must provide as half of the entire number (of gladiators), a number of general fighters, and from these (known as *gregarii*) one who is superior who will fight under a standard at a cost of 2,000 sesterces, and no one from that group is to fight for less than 1,000 sesterces.

See Oliver and Palmer (1955); Carter (2003); Birley (1966), 275–6; Talbert (1984), 291–2. The inscription records part of a speech made by a senator who spoke first on the imperial proposals which were embodied in the subsequent senatorial decree, and even suggested amendments. It was the duty of one member of the council of the three Gallic provinces, chosen through annual rotation as high priest, to provide entertainment at the annual festival at Lugdunum in honour of Rome and Augustus. The person mentioned in the first paragraph had been appointed high priest for 177 and was appalled at the likely cost of putting on a gladiator contest. But Marcus Aurelius ordered that criminals condemned to death could be cheaply supplied as gladiators, and proposed the abolition of a tax on gladiator shows, probably paid by the gladiator trainers and passed on to customers. The senatorial decree fixed the price of gladiators throughout the empire. Amid a shortage of trained gladiators, the decree aimed to reduce the overall price of individual gladiators for those organizing shows; if a gladiator was killed, they were required to pay the full price. Gladiators were ranked according to their perceived skill and status (the *palus* system) and an upper limit was set on the cost of obtaining them. The cost of leasing a gladiator was to be calculated at 1 per cent of his total value. The content is known from inscriptions found at Sardis in Asia and Italica in Spain, indicating that the government had ordered widespread publication.

D 27.1.6.8 (Modestinus, *Exemptions*, Book 2)

239. There is included in the decisions of the emperor Commodus a section from a letter of Antoninus Pius which makes clear that philosophers are exempt from serving as tutors. It is worded as follows: 'Similarly in all these matters, my divine father, as soon as he assumed power, confirmed honours and exemptions by edict, writing that philosophers, rhetoricians, grammarians, and doctors were exempt from serving as gymnasiarch, *agoranomos*, and priest, and from the burden of providing hospitality and the responsibility of buying corn and olive oil, and that they cannot be compelled to act as a judge, serve on embassies, be enlisted for military service against their wishes, or for any other local duty whatsoever'.

The provision of services in local communities was undertaken and paid for by the communities themselves through the imposition of *munera*, which often involved personal expense. Exemptions from these requirements were strictly monitored (see further p. 459). Grammarians could be salaried officials. Lollianus, the public *grammaticus* at Oxyrhynchus, approached the emperors Valerian and Gallienus complaining about his salary and asking for an additional consideration; he notes that the emperors' ancestors had ordered that salaries should be given to *grammatici* (*P. Oxy.* 3366).

Pliny, *Letters* 10.65–6

240. Gaius Pliny to Emperor Trajan. Sir, a significant problem which pertains to the entire province concerns the status and support of those persons described in Greek as foundlings. I have consulted the decisions of emperors but found no individual case or anything generally applicable that could be referred to Bithynia, and so I decided to consult you as to your wishes. I did not think that I should be satisfied with using precedents in a case that required your authority. (Pliny goes on to mention that he had found a few imperial decrees or edicts which for various reasons were not helpful.)

Trajan to Pliny. This question, which relates to those persons who were exposed at birth and then taken by some people and brought up as slaves, has often been examined, but I can find nothing in the archives of my predecessors as emperor which was established as a rule for all the provinces. There are indeed the letters of Domitian to Avidius Nigrinus and Armenius Brocchus of which perhaps we ought to take account. But Bithynia is not among the provinces to which he referred. Therefore, I think that we should not prevent those persons who wish to claim emancipation on this account from making a public assertion of their right to freedom, and that they should not have to buy their freedom by paying back the cost of their support.

Persons referred to as foundlings fall into three types: foster children of free birth, adopted children, those of servile status exposed at birth and then brought up in a household. The foundlings described by Pliny belong to the third type. Under Roman law the foster father or master of an exposed child of servile status was entitled to the costs of upbringing. But Greek custom waived the costs of upbringing and maintenance when they were able to assert their freedom. Pliny was under some pressure to permit recovery of costs, and consulted the emperor because he could not find a clear rule, only the individual decisions of previous proconsuls. Trajan preferred to uphold the local rule; importantly it is also accepted that an imperial decision does not necessarily have universal application, but could be limited to the circumstances, people, or area for which it was issued.

ILS 7215a = *FIRA* 3, no. 41 (AD 167)

241. Copied and certified from the notice which was posted at Alburnus Maior at the office of Resculum, in which was set out what is written below:

Artemidorus, son of Apollonius, master of the association of Jupiter Cernenus, and Valerius, son of Nico, and Offas, son of Menofilus, treasurers of this association, by publishing this notice publicly bear witness:

That of the fifty-four members who belonged to the association noted above, no more than seventeen now remain at Alburnus, and even Iulius, son of Iulius, his co-master from the day of his inauguration has not come to Alburnus or been present at the association; and that he rendered his accounts to those who were present concerning what he had of theirs and was returning, what he had spent on funerals, and that he had recovered the security that he had established for these sums; and that there was now insufficient for burial expenses and that he did not possess a single coffin, and throughout all this time no one had been willing to come to meetings on the days established by the by-laws, or provide burial dues or contributions; and that they publicly bear witness by this notice that no one is to think that he has a burial association if he dies, or that any claim on them for funeral expenses will be accepted.

Posted at Alburnus Maior, 9 February, in the consulship of Emperor Lucius Aurelius Verus for the third time and Quadratus. Carried out at Alburnus Maior.

Associations (*collegia*) to provide proper burial for their members existed throughout the empire with government approval. Given the supervision of these associations (see p. 94), the ending of this *collegium* in Dacia had to be formally recorded.

Pliny, *Letters* 10.92–3

242. Gaius Pliny to Emperor Trajan. The free and allied community of Amisus by your goodwill uses its own laws. In this place a petition was presented to me relating to mutual benefit associations which I have appended to this letter, so that you, sir, may consider whether, and to what extent, you think these are to be permitted or prohibited.

Trajan to Pliny. In respect of the people of Amisus, whose petition you appended to your letter, if it was granted to them in their laws which they enjoy through the treaty to have a mutual benefit association, I am unable to prevent them from having one, particularly if their contributions are aimed not at the instigation of trouble or illegal assembly, but to support those who are in need. In other communities, which are bound by our laws, gatherings of this kind are prohibited.

This exchange of letters and the correspondence about establishing a fire brigade at Nicomedia (*Letters* 10.33–4) show the government concern about potential disorder associated with *collegia*. The Greek *eranos* was a kind of social club for subscription dinners; Trajan places it in the category of a *collegium tenuiorum* which was normally permitted under Roman law. Amisus was originally granted its free status by Julius Caesar, which preserved its freedom from interference by the governor in its local administration and jurisdiction. Trajan also confirmed a privilege perhaps from the time of Augustus, which allowed it to describe itself as an ally of Rome. Trajan is once again unwilling to upset local arrangements (see also no. 240).

Abbott and Johnston (1968), no. 124

243. [...] and in compliance with agreements [...] it happens occasionally that the people are precipitated into uproar and rioting by the reckless [deceptive?] rhetoric of the bakers' clubs in the marketplace, for which they should already have been detained and brought to justice. However, since the welfare of the city must rank higher than the punishment of these men, I have decided to bring them back to their senses through an edict. Consequently, I order the bakers not to meet as a club and not to be the leaders in reckless conduct. They must in every way obey those who have been appointed to represent the interest of the community and must supply a reliable source of bread for the city. Henceforth, whenever one of them is caught attending a meeting in contravention of the pronouncement, or starting a riot or group disturbance, he will be detained and suffer the appropriate punishment. If someone who is plotting against the city goes to the extent of hiding himself, he is in addition to be [marked?] by branding of the word '*decuria*' on the foot, and the person who shelters such a man is to be subject to the same penalty.

Under the presidency of Claudius Modestus, on the fourth day after the start of the month Clareon, when the council had been convened [... ?] another part: Marcellinus said: 'Hermias, the man attached to the treasury ... yesterday gave an outstanding example of the insanity of the foremen of the shop'.

This is an edict of the proconsul of Asia c. AD 200 followed by a decree of the council at Ephesus. The bakers had instigated a riot and apparently deprived the city of bread, either because of the disturbance or deliberately through a strike; for measures against *collegia*, see no. 185.

BGU 646 = *SP* no. 222

244. Mantennius Sabinus to the *strategoi* of the Heptanomia and of the Arsinoite nome, greetings. I have ordered that a copy of the edict sent by me to the most splendid Alexandria to be attached, in order that all should know that you may hold a festival for the same number of days. I wish you good health. Year one of Emperor Caesar Publius Helvius Pertinax Augustus, Phamenoth 10.

Copy of the edict. O Alexandrians, it is appropriate that you, as you are holding a festival in honour of the accession of our lord, Emperor Publius Helvius Pertinax the Augustus, leader of the holy senate, father of the fatherland, and Publius Helvius Pertinax, his son, and Flavia Titiana Augusta (his wife), should in full strength make sacrifice and offer prayers on behalf of his eternal rule and all his family, and wear garlands for fifteen days, starting from today.

This edict of the prefect of Egypt requiring the celebration of the accession of the emperor Pertinax in Egypt in AD 193 illustrates the interaction of central government with the administrative authorities in local communities for the purpose of organizing a co-ordinated festival throughout the region. Yet Pertinax ruled for only three months before he was murdered by the praetorian guard.

CIL 3.6866 = *ILS* 6090

245. We have noted that the people of Tymandus with outstanding eagerness and the greatest zeal wish, dearest Lepidus, to obtain through our decision the legal right and dignity of a city. Therefore, since it is our wish that throughout our entire empire the status and number of cities should be increased, and since we see that they vehemently desire the status and dignity of a city and have given a strong undertaking that they will have a sufficient supply of city councillors in the future, we have decided to give our assent. Therefore, we wish that you should endeavour to encourage the said people of Tymandus, now that they have attained their wish, to work loyally along with our other cities to implement all those duties that they are required to recognize now that they have attained the status of a city. Now, in order that, as other cities have the right to meet in a council, make decrees, and conduct other business that is permitted by law, this city also may do this by our permission, they should see to the election of

magistrates, aediles too, and also quaestors, and any other business that needs to be done. It will be right to preserve this framework of doing business in perpetuity, as long as the city deserves it. Meanwhile, however, you ought to enrol men as city councillors, to the number of fifty. The support of the immortal gods will ensure that as their resources increase, a more plentiful supply of councillors can be obtained.

This letter from an unknown emperor addressed to an imperial official authorizes the establishment of a city council and the election of officials in Tymandus in northern Pisidia. There was competition in status among local communities, and city status was an incentive that could be offered, if the locals paid for it by holding office and running the local government. It is clear that the imperial government controlled the process by which a local community could become a city.

Administration of Justice

Public and private interests intersected in the relationship between the representatives of the state and locals, both citizens and non-citizens, in respect of the administration of justice in the provinces. Three categories of legal proceedings existed. First, the entire apparatus of Roman law applied only to Roman citizens; the governor could deal with them or delegate the matter to a subordinate official. Second, provincials who were non-Romans had their own laws and customs and local courts, which normally operated in private transactions. Third, the law of the province ('*ius provinciae*') set up at the formation of a province would apply to all inhabitants whatever their status.

In the process of jurisdiction, the role of the governor was crucial in mediating the interests of the state and the expectations of individual litigants. Assizes in each province were probably held annually by the governor who travelled round the province to the assize cities. Those who wished a hearing would have to make their way there (see Pliny, *Letters* 10.58 on holding an assize at Prusa). This was not easy for poorer citizens, and the cost might be prohibitive. A litigant would need to petition the governor, and if the governor subscribed the petition, then a summons would be issued. Even if you made it to the assize there was no fixed order for the presentation of cases and no guarantee that your case would be heard. Although it is likely that local courts remained important in many provinces for minor civil suits or where only non-citizens were involved, the governor will have had a large amount of legal work. The interface of Roman law and local courts in the provinces involved some tolerance by the Romans of other legal practices.

Roman legal practice had originally gained currency in the empire because there were many communities of Roman citizens in the provinces, both colonies and *municipia*, which operated under Roman law. Over time the operation of the legal system in the provinces was increasingly flexible in respect of cases involving Roman citizens and non-Romans, or non-Romans alone. Many non-Romans might wish to have their case heard by a Roman judge, who would often apply the methods and rules of the *ius civile*. Indeed, the prefect of Egypt, Subatianus Aquila, dealt with 1,804 petitions from the Arsinoite *nome* over three days in AD 209 (*P. Yale* 1.61). This is not surprising since the Roman approach represented respect for property, due legal form, properly formulated agreements and contracts whose formality and precision commanded attention, and appropriate redress. Therefore, aspects of Roman law could be especially advantageous for the elite, who had most to gain at law.

Gradually there was a blurring at the edge of Roman law and some local legal practices could be accepted in the form of a custom and interpreted in the Roman courtroom, though the general view was that to have legal respectability the custom had to be long-standing and well-established. Local litigants could work Roman legal mechanisms into their pleadings to give at least the appearance of a proper Roman legal mechanism acceptable to a judge. After Caracalla's edict of universal citizenship in 212, nearly every free person in the empire was a Roman citizen, with, theoretically, access to the full panoply of Roman law, while local laws were eventually either adopted into the Roman system or dropped. For discussion see Burton (1975), 100–6; Oliver (1979); Lintott (1993), 154–60; Garnsey (2004); Czajkowski and Eckhardt (2020), pp. 3–4 speak of 'legal pluralism'; for Egypt see Bryen (2008); Kelly (2011), especially chapter 3 for the organization of the legal system; Keenan, Manning and Yiftach-Firanko (2014), especially chapter 3.3; Cotton (1993) (Arabia); Cotton and Eck (2005) (Judaea); for an analysis of local and Roman law under Hadrian, Cortés-Copete (2019); Rutledge (2001), 71–8 on informers and prosecutors (*delatores*) in the provinces; for a summary of the evidence of papyri see Yiftach-Firanko (2009), especially 550–60; he notes that in Egypt whereas Romans and non-Romans wrote their contracts in Greek, shaping them according to procedures and mechanisms in use before the advent of Rome, in the writing of wills and the law of succession much of the practice of the *ius civile* was maintained; this influenced the practice of non-Romans; for the importance of Egyptian customs in respect of transactions in property and contracts, see Alonso Rodríguez (2016). However, this is an area of continuing debate, and Dolganov (2019) has argued that we should not underestimate the hegemonic character of Roman jurisdiction dependant on the governor's *imperium*, and the application of Roman legal practice to Egypt (see pp. 375–96 for court cases).

Local Legal Practice and Roman Law

Lex Irnitana **González (1986), Chapter 84 (Extract)**

246. Rubric. Over what matters and up to what amount there may be jurisdiction in that *municipium*.

Whichever *municipes* or residents of that *municipium* wish privately within the boundaries of that *municipium* to bring a legal action against, or sue, or bring a claim against each other on any matter, either in their own name or in that of another who is a *municeps* or resident, as long as the matter is worth one thousand sesterces or less and has not been divided or is not divided in order to defy this statute, and as long as there will not be a *praeiudicium* concerning a free person or a larger sum than one thousand sesterces, ... the member of the board of two who is in charge of the administration of justice in that place is to have jurisdiction and the right of granting or assigning a judge or arbiter or *recuperatores* from those whose names are displayed there, and a trial.

The *lex Irnitana* shows the influence of Rome mediated through local requirements. It gave Irni a new legal system, and in legal practice local judges are on several occasions (chapters 71; 89; 91) instructed to give judgement following what would apply if the case were being tried at Rome, that is, not as if a peregrine were on trial at Rome, but as the praetor judged between Roman citizens. Chapter 84 of the statute sets out how if the parties agree a civil case can be settled locally without reference to the governor; there is a long list of exceptions, including cases involving the use of force, or fraud especially the defrauding of under-age persons, and issues of freedom; *praeiudicium* was a judicial hearing to resolve a preliminary issue that might have a bearing on the dispute at issue, which, for example, could raise the sum beyond the limits set in this clause, or predetermine the guilt of a free man in a capital case; the statute aimed to prevent any attempt to circumvent the law by separating a legal action so that each was worth less than one thousand sesterces.

Lex Irnitana **González (1986), Chapter 93**

247. Rubric. Concerning the law of the *municipes*.

In respect of whatever matters in this statute there is no specific provision or statement, concerning the law (*ius*) under which the *municipes* of the

Municipium Flavium Irnitanum should deal with each other, in all these matters they are to deal with each other under the civil law (*ius civile*) under which Roman citizens deal or will deal with each other. Whatever is not done contrary to this statute, and whatever is done so that it is not carried out or done with wrongful intent, is to be legal and valid.

In the absence of a specific rule in the statute, members of the *municipium* wishing to sue one another must behave as if they were Roman citizens, and as if the civil law of Rome applied to them. It is imagined that the *municipes* were all citizens following Roman legal practice even though in reality they were not; see Gardner (1993), 188–9; Lintott (1993), 140–1; Richardson (2016), 120–1; also, Chapter 1, no. 34.

FIRA 1, no. 68, I (Extract): 7/6 BC

248. Imperator Caesar Augustus, chief priest, in his seventeenth year of tribunician power, declares: Since I discover that all the Roman citizens in the province of Cyrene number 215, of every age group, being in possession of property to the value of 2,500 denarii or greater, from whom the judges are chosen, and that among these there are conspiracies, as embassies from the provincial communities have complained, which have oppressed the Greeks in capital cases, by taking in turn the roles of accusers and witnesses for each other, and since I myself have discovered that some innocent people have been badly treated in this way even to the extent of a capital penalty, until the senate reaches a decision about this matter or I myself find some better solution, in my view the future governors of Crete and Cyrene would act fairly and appropriately if they established a list in the province of Crete and Cyrene of Greek jurors of the highest property valuation equal in number to the Roman jurors.

Roman citizens in Cyrene had a monopoly of the jury panels in local courts dealing with capital cases and it seems that they had exploited this for personal gain, either to dispose of enemies or appropriate their property. Augustus' solution was to prescribe mixed juries of Romans and Greeks when the case involved a Greek.

FIRA 1, no. 68, IV: 7/6 BC

249. Imperator Caesar Augustus, chief priest, in his seventeenth year of tribunician power, declares: In respect of whatever legal disputes shall arise between Greeks in the province of Cyrenaica, with the exception of those involving a capital charge, in relation to which the person who is governor

of the province should himself investigate, and give judgement, or appoint a panel of judges, I have decided that Greek judges should be appointed in all other cases, unless a plaintiff or defendant wishes to have Roman citizens as judges. However, I do not wish, in the case of those to whom Greek judges will be granted under this edict of mine, any judge to be granted from the same community from which the plaintiff or accuser shall come, or from which the defendant or accused shall come.

Augustus sets out rules in cases involving Greeks (that is, non-Romans) which did not involve a capital charge; it is not clear if in these cases local Greek law could be used. The possible presence of Roman judges may suggest that Roman legal practice was to be employed. Of course, at any time the governor could hear any case he chose in whatever way he deemed appropriate.

D 1.3.34 (Ulpian, *Duties of a Proconsul*, Book 4)

250. When someone seems to be relying on the customary practice of a community or province, I think that it first ought to be established whether that customary practice has been confirmed in contended legal proceedings.

Ulpian here suggests that provincial governors should check that a local custom had been established as acceptable through a previous dispute. The conventional Roman view was that such a custom had to be of long standing and well-established and should not compromise existing law.

D 22.1.1pr (Papinian, *Opinions*, Book 2)

251. When the case concerns a good faith action, in the assessment of the judge the rate of interest is established according to the custom of the region where the agreement was undertaken, though only in so far as it does not compromise statute.

Menander Rhetor, *Treatise* 1.363 lines 7–14

252. For if the citizens do not mistreat foreigners or do ill to one another, and use customs that are equitable and fair and laws that are just, they will administer their cities very properly and justly. But in current times the question of the laws is not relevant since our affairs are administered under the common laws of the Romans. On the other hand, customs vary from city to city.

See Russell and Wilson (1981), 66–7, and p. 474 in this volume for Menander; this passage relates to the possibility that local laws could be transformed into provincial Roman customs in the field of private law. Roman officials had to judge non-Roman legal practices and principles brought before them by litigants; some were accepted such as the guardianship of minors and women; wills and marriage were accepted as provincial customs and then could be used as a precedent (Russell and Wilson, 40–1).

Petsas (2000), Inscription no. 63 (AD 212)

253. In the Augustan year 244, which is also Macedonian year 363, at the temple of the goddess Autochthonous, in compliance with the instructions of the mighty governor, Marcus Ulpius Tertullianus Aquila, I, Aurelius Poseidonios, formerly son of Mestys, also called Pantakianos, donate a slave by the name of Ammia and her children Poseidonios and Nikon, whose documents of manumission I have deposited in the arms of the goddess.

See also Petsas, no. 68 (AD 218). Inscriptions from the sanctuary of the Mother of the Gods at Leukopetra in Macedonia belonging to the city of Beroia give evidence of manumissions in the sanctuary. Procedures governing manumissions in Macedonia were different from the Roman legal practice; they were performed at temples and took the form of a donation of the slave as a gift to the goddess. Furthermore, no specific legal terminology was required for the act to be valid. Marcus Ulpius Tertullianus Aquila, proconsul of Macedonia in 212, issued a proclamation by which this manumission procedure was adapted to the principles of Roman law. He introduced some compulsory steps, notably the public display of a manumission deed for thirty days prior to manumission (this would give an opportunity to interested parties such as creditors who might object to alienation of property). Therefore, an institution of Greek private law became official Roman law within the province of Macedonia, and local manumission practice was validated by the authority of Roman law because it did not contravene the principles of that law; see Youni (2010). Kantor (2013), 165 examines similar practices in Phrygia; for the mix of Roman and local legal practices in Phrygia, see Kantor, 162–7.

Gaius, *Institutes* 1.193

254. Among non-Romans, women are not under guardianship in the same way as with us. Nevertheless, they are usually in a kind of virtual guardianship. For example, a law of the Bithynians requires that, if a woman undertakes any form of transaction, her husband or fully-grown son must be the authorizer.

For *tutela* of women see p. 23. This was the kind of tradition that Rome could accept.

Lewis (1989), no. 14 (11 or 12 October AD 125)

255. In the ninth year of Imperator Trajan Hadrian Caesar Augustus, in the consulship of Marcus Valerius Asiaticus for the second time and Titius Aquilinus, 11 October, and according to the reckoning of the province of Arabia, year twenty, on the twenty-fourth of month Hyperberetaios called Thesrei (12 October), in Maoza, district of Zoara, before the witnesses present, Babatha, daughter of Simon, son of Menahem, through her guardian for this business, Judah, son of Khthousion, summoned John, son of Joseph Eglas, one of the guardians appointed by the council of Petra for her son Jesus, the orphan of Jesus, saying: On account of the fact that you did not give ... to my son ... the orphan mentioned above ... just as Abdoöbdas son of Ellouthas, your colleague, has given by means of receipt, therefore I summon you to attend at the court of the governor Iulius Iulianus in Petra, the metropolis of Arabia, until we are heard at the tribunal in Petra on the second day of the month Dios(?) or at his next sitting in Petra.

(List of witnesses)

Probably through a scribal error two different dates are given in the papyrus, which is written in Greek. The legal issue concerned the guardianship of Babatha's son (Jesus) by her first husband (now deceased). Babatha now had a second husband, Judah, though he had another wife living. Babatha under Roman law could not be a guardian for her orphaned son and had brought a case before the governor of Arabia at Petra complaining that the guardians of her son were not providing enough money for his upkeep; for the details of her struggle against the guardians, see Hanson (2005); Chiusi (2005). This document is a summons to attend court; the substance of Babatha's complaint is found in Lewis (1989), no. 15, with flattery of the benefits of Roman rule. Babatha was preparing to use documents in Roman legal form (no. 256). Goodman (1991), 172–3 argues that it is likely that in Arabia after its annexation by Trajan a variety of legal systems continued in operation in private law; appeals were made to the Roman governor and Roman legal forms were used, but local practice was also observed, as for example in the appointment of two guardians for an orphaned child; Roman law required at least one, though in a will more could be nominated; also Lintott (1993), 157; Cotton (1993) argues that recourse to Roman law and Roman courts was voluntarily adopted by the locals, who take the trouble to prepare Roman legal arguments; also Cotton and Eck (2005). Meyer (2007) argues that in the documents from the Judaean Desert the format, method of dating, language (Greek, Aramaic, or Hebrew), and number of witnesses serve as guidelines for the attitude of those involved and their choice of legal practice; personal preference prevailed, not dictation by the Romans. Czajkowski (2017) discusses the legal culture and perception of the law in the community of Maoza based on the archives of Babatha and another lady, Salome Komaise; litigants not fully trusting Roman courts may have resorted to private negotiations; see also Dench (2018), 43–5. For Roman practices in *tutela*, see Saller (1994), 181–203; for Babatha's census declaration see no. 211; for her sales document, see no. 257. See e.g. no. 677 for Roman and local legal process in the courtroom.

Lewis (1989), nos. 28–30

256. Between a plaintiff X son of Y and a defendant A for up to 2,500 denarii there shall be [local?] judges. Since A son of B has carried out the role of guardian of orphan X, concerning which issue the suit lies, whenever by reason of this issue A is obliged to give or to do [something] for X in good faith, the judges of this shall give judgement against A in favour of X up to 2,500 denarii, but if [such obligation] does not appear, they shall absolve.

This is a Greek version of the praetor's formula for judgement; see also Gaius, *Institutes* 4.47. They were prepared for Babatha in the presentation of her case for her son.

Lewis (1989), no. 22

257. In the fourteenth year of Imperator Trajan Hadrian Caesar Augustus, in the consulship of Marcus Flavius Aper and Quintus Flavius Catullinus, 11 September, and according to the reckoning of the new province of Arabia, year twenty-five, on the twenty-fourth of month Gorpiaios, in Maoza, district of Zoöra, Babatha, daughter of Simon, to Simon, son of Jesus, son of Ananias(?), both living in Maoza, greeting: I acknowledge that I have sold to you the date crop of the orchards that formerly(?) belonged(?) to Judah, son of Khthousion, my late husband, in Maoza. I hold in place of my dowry and the debt (owed to me) the said properties called Pherora orchard and Nikarkos orchard and the third one of Molkhaios, for the current year, and you are to pay me for this year for the said orchards forty-two talents of first and second 'splits', weighing them in (my) house using the scales of Maoza at drying time, and also of Syrian and Naaran(?) (dates), delivering them to (my) house, two *koroi* and five *sata* using the measure of Maoza. If you do not pay me the dates mentioned above, the total as stated above, you are to give me for each talent of 'splits' two

denarii, and of Syrian and Naaran(?) one 'black'. I shall ensure your right to the orchards mentioned is clear of every counterclaimant, and if anyone brings a counterclaim against you because of your purchase and I do not resolutely validate (it) for you as previously stated, I shall owe you in return for your work and expenses twenty silver denarii, raising no objection. Whatever is (produced) over and above in the previously mentioned orchards, those dates ... you are to take for yourself in return for your work and expenses. Through(?) her guardian who also subscribed, John, son of Makhouthas of this Maoza, the formal question having in good faith been asked and acknowledged in reply.

(Babatha's confirmation of sale; names of witnesses)

The seller's declaration in the sale of a date crop is seemingly based on the Roman concept of *emptio venditio*; see Lintott (1993), 156–7; for another sale document, see no. 295. Babatha's confirmation of sale is appended in Nabatean; for the measurement of dates, see no. 211.

Responsible Government: Theory and Practice

Good Intentions

Florus 2.30.29

258. But it is more difficult to keep than to create provinces; they are acquired by force but maintained by justice.

Florus (see p. 478) in his survey of Roman history with especial emphasis on warfare normally maintained a belligerent attitude against Rome's enemies.

***FIRA* 1, no. 68, v (5/4 BC)**

259. Imperator Caesar Augustus, chief priest, in the nineteenth year of his tribunician power declares: the decree of the senate which was passed in the consulship of Gaius Calvisius and Lucius Passienus in my presence, and in the writing of which I participated, which pertains to the safety of the allies of the Roman people, I have decided to send to the provinces so that it may be known to those in our care, and to attach my edict so that it may be clear to everyone living in the provinces the extent of our concern, both mine and that of the senate, that none of our subjects should suffer any unjust harm or extortion.

Augustus here emphasizes the application of the concept of responsible government. The context is the decision to introduce a modified procedure, involving simple reparation, for dealing with non-capital charges against corrupt provincial governors.

SEG 4.516 = Smallwood (1967), no. 380, cols. i–ii

260. Paulus Fabius Persicus, priest, priest of Augustus, Arval brother, quaestor of Emperor Tiberius Caesar Augustus, praetor ... consul ..., proconsul of Asia, has proclaimed (the governor announces a decree of the emperor Claudius relating to Ephesus): In this I am above all things certain that the governors of provinces should steadfastly and honestly administer the position entrusted to them, so that they consider the permanent benefit of individuals, and of the entire province, and of individual cities, and not just for their year of office alone. Nevertheless, I am glad to say that I am inspired to this view by the example of the greatest and truly just ruler, who has made the entire human race his concern, and among his first acts of benevolence, all most welcome, has granted the benefaction of restoring what is their own.

After this introduction the proconsul proceeded to set out proposals to reform the administration of the temple of Artemis at Ephesus; for this aspect see no. 583. Persicus had been consul in AD 34 and the emperor in question is Claudius; see also Johnson, Coleman-Norton, Bourne (1961), no. 171.

D 1.16.4pr (Ulpian, *Duties of a Proconsul*, Book 1)

261. It is right for the governor to ensure that he does not burden the province through the provision of hospitality.

Note also Antoninus Pius' comment that the retinue of even a frugal emperor was a burden to the provinces (*HA Vit. Antonini Pii* 7.11). However, Pius while a provincial governor had quartered himself in the house of a provincial, and later found himself ejected by the irate owner (Philostratus, *Lives of Sophists* 534). See also Septimius Severus' advice on receiving gifts (no. 195).

D 1.18.6.5–6 (Ulpian, *Opinions*, Book 1)

262. The governor of the province should ensure that poor people are not deprived of their single lantern or meagre furniture, taken for the use of others under the pretext of the arrival of officials or soldiers. The governor of the province should also ensure that, in the name of the military,

property which does not pertain to the common usage of the soldiers is not taken by some people improperly claiming it for their own purpose.

Augustus had apparently issued a kind of guide, probably to provincial governors about military discipline (*D* 49.16.12.1): For in the treatise on discipline by Augustus the following warning appears: 'Although I realize that it is not inappropriate for soldiers to be occupied in building activities, nevertheless I fear that if I grant some leeway in what might be done for my or your benefit, that a restraint that would be acceptable to me would not be exercised'.

SEG 17.755 = McCrum and Woodhead (1966), no. 466

263. From the instructions of imperator Domitian Caesar Augustus, son of Augustus, to Claudius Athenodorus, procurator. In these vital matters that require careful consideration, I find that my divine father, Vespasian Caesar, was greatly concerned with the welfare of the cities. When he had investigated the matter, he ordered that the provinces should not be weighed down with the burden of hiring out beasts of burden or the annoyance of strangers (travellers). But nevertheless, this has not been observed, either because of complicity or lack of punishment. For there still persists long-standing and continuing behaviour, which will bit by bit become established practice if it is not by force prevented from increasing. I therefore order that you take thought to ensure that no one takes a beast of burden unless he has my certificate. For it is most unjust that through the favour or standing of certain individuals that certificates are produced which no one but me has the right to grant. Therefore, permit nothing to occur that will impede my order and frustrate this decision which will be most helpful to the cities. For it is proper to help the provinces, which are struggling and barely have enough for the necessities. No one is to use force against them against my wish. And no one is to take a guide unless he has my certificate. For if the country folk are dragged away the fields will remain untilled. And you yourself will conduct yourself properly if either you use your own animals, or hire them.

The compulsory provision of animals, carts, and guides to facilitate the movements of imperial officials, messengers, and others on government business (*vehiculatio*) was a constant source of abuse; some demanded more than was permitted, while others forced the locals to put them up even though they had no authority. It is notable that Domitian adds a note to his procurator reminding him of his obligations. This kind of abuse was present in the time of Augustus, who issued instructions (*mandata*) to the governor of Galatia; Tiberius then intervened on the same issue: Sextus Sotidius Strabo Libuscidianus, legate of

Tiberius Caesar Augustus with propraetorian power, declares: 'It is the most unfair thing of all for me to tighten up through my own edict what the emperors, one the greatest of gods, the other the greatest of emperors most carefully laid down, namely that no one should make use of vehicles without paying. But since the abusive behaviour of certain people demands immediate punishment ... ' (Mitchell (1976); this volume no. 216); for Germanicus in Egypt see no. 269. Claudius in an edict of AD 49–50 about the burden of the public post lamented that it had 'proved impossible to cope adequately with the evil of men' (Smallwood (1967), 375); for Hadrian, see no. 264. For a detailed discussion of the transport system, see Kolb (2000).

Hauken and Malay (2009)

264. Good fortune. Emperor Caesar Trajan Hadrian Augustus, son of the divine Trajan, grandson of Nerva, chief priest, in his thirteenth year of tribunician power, consul for the third time, father of the fatherland, proconsul, declares: During my visit when I stayed among your people, I noticed that the town and villages are being bothered more than the regulations permit by soldiers passing through. So that they know in the future what they must refrain from, and that you know what you must fulfil, and what you will not tolerate even if it is requested, I found it necessary to pronounce this by edict: A waggon must be given only to those who have a diploma. The person who uses the waggon must pay what is laid down in the diplomas. No one is to be entitled to take a guide since soldiers have no need to depart from the public roads, and since they do not depart from them, they do not require anyone to guide the way. If the roads become invisible because of a heavy snowfall, only in this case is it permitted to take a guide. It is not permitted to demand breakfast, dinner, barley, or fodder without paying, and no one should provide these items when asked to do so. No soldier travelling on private business is permitted to take lodging without paying. However, if someone is passing through while on duty, or conveying imperial monies, or moving prisoners or wild animals, public lodgings are to be provided for them alone, and provisions at the price prevailing in the market ten days earlier. And if anyone thinks fit to act in contravention of this or uses force, the names of those who take (anything) are to be sent to the governor of the province and to my procurator and forwarded to me, since nothing is insignificant which will help the cities in the future so that they do not suffer any abuse. Let it be posted.

This intervention by Hadrian in the province of Asia shows continuing problems with the operation of the *vehiculatio* and abusive conduct by Roman officials despite vigorous imperial intervention. The emperor presumably refers to his personal visit to Asia in 124 during his travels round the provinces of the empire.

P. Oxy. 705; Johnson, Coleman-Norton, Bourne (1961), no. 273

265. The Emperor Caesar Lucius Septimius Severus Pius Pertinax Augustus Arabicus Adiabenicus Parthicus Maximus and the Emperor Caesar Marcus Aurelius Antoninus Pius Augustus to Aurelius Horion, greeting. We approve of this benefaction also which you request permission to confer upon the villages of the Oxyrhynchite nome, giving (to different persons) a succession in the enjoyment of it. The same rule shall be observed in this case also, and, as you wish, no change shall be introduced which would divert the gift to any other purpose.

The request is as follows:

To the most gracious Emperors, Severus and Antoninus, the saviours and benefactors of the world, Aurelius Horion, formerly *strategos* and *archidikastes* of the most illustrious city of Alexandria, greeting. Certain villages in the Oxyrhynchite nome, most humane Emperors, in which both I and my sons own estates, are utterly exhausted by the burdensome demands of the annual liturgies required both for the treasury and the protection of the districts, and there is a danger of them being ruined as far as the treasury is concerned and leaving our (?) land uncultivated. Accordingly, since I aim to be both humane and useful, I wish, in order that they may recover, to make a small benefaction to each (village) for the purchase of land (?), the income of which shall be devoted to the maintenance and support of those who are annually subject to the liturgies, on the condition that (?) … .

The emperors implicitly recognize the economic problems in Oxyrhynchus, while accepting and endorsing this euergetism by a rich landowner. Horion had made a previous donation to support contests for the young men of the villages.

SP no. 216 = Oliver (1989), no. 275 (AD 222)

266. Edict of Emperor Caesar, son of the divine Magnus Antoninus Pius, grandson of the divine Septimius Severus Pius, Marcus Aurelius Alexander Pius Felix Augustus, chief priest, holding the tribunician power, consul, father of the fatherland.

In case, in order to make an (annual?) demonstration of their delight at my accession to imperial power, they should be forced to contribute more than they can afford. Therefore I have come to this conclusion, that does not lack precedents, and I intend to follow the example of Trajan and Marcus, my own ancestors, emperors particularly worthy of respect, and indeed in other areas I have decided to emulate them, so that, if the current poverty of national resources did not prevent me, I would have produced much clearer evidence of my goodwill. Also, I would not have hesitated to remit anything that was owing from previous contributions of this kind, and whatever monies had already been voted for my acclamation as Caesar under the name of crowns or might still be voted by cities under the same name. However, I think that this will not be possible for the reason I mentioned a little earlier. Yet I have not failed to notice that as far as I can see this is all that the cities can pay at this time. Therefore, everyone in all the cities both in Italy and in the other regions is to know that I remit to them the money due in lieu of the gold crowns in recognition of my accession to imperial rule, which I have achieved accompanied by the wishes and prayers of everyone. I do this not because of an abundance of wealth, but by my own policy, which I have followed since becoming emperor, of restoring our declining resources, not by collecting taxes but by restraint alone and avoidance of spending money for personal motives. For I did not intend to gather money from every source, but rather to develop the welfare of this empire by means of goodwill and kindness, so that my governors whom I have sent to govern provinces and whom I scrutinized and selected with the greatest care before I sent them out, should also have the purpose of behaving with great restraint. For more and more the provincial governors will appreciate how eagerly they should spare and be considerate to the people over whom they have been put in charge, when they can see the emperor conducting imperial business with such decency, moderation, and self-restraint. The magistrates in each city are to ensure that copies of my edict are displayed in public fully visible to those who wish to read it. Year one, Pauni 30.

Severus Alexander had already received gold crowns in the previous summer to celebrate his appointment as Caesar. The gold crown was originally a gift of gold to celebrate an imperial event but had become virtually a regular tax. Alexander had become emperor after the overthrow of his cousin, the unpopular Elagabalus, and it was his advisers' policy to present him as a complete contrast to his predecessor.

AE 1931.38 (AD 144)

267. In the consulship of Lollius Avitus and Statilius Maximus, 27 October, in the Ulpian senate house, with the officials from Sala present. Insofar as Gaius Valerius Rogatus and Publius Postumius Hermesander,

members of the board of two, have stated that a successor has been appointed for the excellent and unique prefect, Sulpicius Felix, to whom, because of the outstanding example he has set, although he has already received an expression of public support, it is now necessary to provide even clearer tokens of our esteem, since it is appropriate to repay him at once for his new favours, both to the community and to individuals, with new honours, and to offer the hope of similar expectations to those who in the future may act in the same way. (His various beneficial acts are listed.) Now, in respect of those qualities which indicate a spirit of exceptional integrity, he surpassed the standard of his predecessors in moderation, modesty, gentleness, self-control, reverence for the local senate, affection for the people, and diligence, in that he provided us with free access to our woods and fields, going so far as to stay out at night to safeguard those working there … Furthermore, the benevolence which he displays is very delightful now, and in the future will bring benefits for us because of the example he has set. Because of his deeds and his character, we previously voted Sulpicius Felix the position of local senator, with a rank of a member of the board of two, and the excellent governor delightedly welcomed this decree. And now, as we hear that a successor has been appointed to him, and since we consider his imminent departure with such trepidation that we can hardly assuage the feeling of our intense longing with the most extensive expectations of his future progress, we have decided not to decree something unseemly for this man, since he did not take unseemly actions, and we beg the very indulgent governor, who delights in the praise and laudation of his prefects, and indeed himself makes them deserving of praise, to favour us, since we wish to owe him our thanks in this matter, by permitting the erection of a statue to the prefect … and to send ambassadors to celebrate him before the most sacred emperor.

This inscription from Mauretania is a useful illustration of the Roman concept of responsible government and a welcome provincial response. Felix, prefect of the auxiliary cohort stationed at Sala, had behaved with great energy and propriety and the city welcomed this enthusiastically; this was mutually beneficial; the community got peace and quiet and various advantages, while Felix was likely to get the favourable attention of the emperor; the city's honour and elaborate flattery of Felix was part of a circular process; it would be an incentive for other officials to conduct themselves with moderation and integrity. However, the tone of inscription may suggest that such honourable conduct by officials was not all that common.

AE 1988.723, from the Estuary of the River Baetis (Guadalquivir) in Spain, c. 5–2 BC

268. When Publius Petronius, son of Publius, Turpilianus was proconsul and Marcus Alfius, son of Gaius, Laches was [quaestor (or legatus) with propraetorian power], Titus Quinctius, son of Titus …, the magistrates and senate and people of the Conobarians swore the following oath: I swear that I, on behalf of the salvation, honour, and victory of Imperator Caesar Augustus, son of a god, his son, the *princeps* of the youth, consul designate, priest (Gaius Caesar), and on behalf of Lucius Caesar, son of Augustus, and Marcus Agrippa, grandson of Augustus, shall assuredly take up arms, and shall consider my friends and allies those whom I see to be their friends and allies, and I shall consider as my enemies those whom I perceive to be enemies of their interests. And if anyone commits any act against them, they must realize that I shall pursue them to destruction by land and sea.

This inscription illustrates the relationship between the expectations of the rulers and the response of the ruled. Proper fulfilment of the requisite expressions of respect for the imperial family would place a community in a good position to communicate with the government and perhaps seek benefits in return. In this case the provincials needed to be up to date with imperial politics, since Tiberius who had seemed to be Augustus' likely successor had retired to Rhodes, and Gaius and Lucius Caesar, Augustus' adopted sons, and their younger brother Agrippa Postumus, were now to the forefront in the imperial family.

Seeking Redress

The following examples have been selected to illustrate how in the government of the provinces the Romans often failed to achieve acceptable standards; emperors and senior officials recognized this failure and the need to provide a clear line of contact so that the local population could seek redress of grievance. The evidence for good intentions is often double-edged in that it also indicates that abuse inflicted on provincials was widespread, repeated, and frequently at the hands of the emperor's own officials or soldiers; therefore, benevolent initiatives were often frustrated. Taxation was a burden, and imperial goodwill extended only so far. Notably, Tiberius responded to a governor who recommended heavier taxes for the provinces that a good shepherd should shear his flock, not flay it (Suetonius, *Tiberius* 32.2). For consideration of these topics, note Brunt (1961); Mitchell (1976); Campbell (1984), 246–54; Isaac (1992), 269–310;

Fuhrmann (2012), 177–81; 228–38; Hauken (1998) usefully collects petitions to the emperor. It is important to note that at the interface of citizens and army there were opportunities to make profit, not just in selling to army camps but also in contracts transporting military supplies; for Egypt see Adams (2007), 210–19.

SP 211 = *EJ* 320

269. Germanicus Caesar, son of Augustus, grandson of the divine Augustus, proconsul, declares: Since I hear that on account of my visit the requisition of boats and animals is taking place, billets for accommodation are being seized by force, and ordinary people terrorized, I thought it essential to clarify that I do not wish either boat or animal to be seized from anyone, unless on the order of Baebius, my friend and secretary, or billets to be seized. Furthermore, I order that for the requisition of either boats or animals payment should be made according to my schedule. I wish those who disobey to be brought to my secretary, who will either himself prevent the abuse of ordinary people or refer the matter to me. I wish to stop those who seize by force animals they encounter going through the city. For this is nothing other than an act of clear-cut robbery.

The visit of Germanicus as a prince of the imperial house to Egypt in AD 19 during his eastern command will have put numerous legitimate demands on local communities. But abuse made the situation much worse. In his tough response Germanicus recognizes the importance of establishing a point of contact so that people had an avenue of complaint. Problems with the rules for requisitions were to be long-standing; see nos. 216; 263; 270–6; see Adams (2007), 135–55 for an excellent survey of the requisitioning of animals in Egypt. Germanicus also declined excessive honours in Egypt (*SP* 211, second edict).

Pliny, *Letters* 10.78

270. Trajan to Pliny. It is a feature of the community of Byzantium that huge crowds of people flow into it from all directions, and therefore in accordance with previous practice we considered that we should assist its magistrates with a guard under a legionary centurion. If I decide that the people of Juliopolis should be assisted in the same way, I shall burden myself with a precedent, for other communities, and in particular the weaker ones, will ask for the same assistance. I have confidence in your competence and believe that you will take every action to ensure that they are not exposed to abuse. However, if someone behaves in contravention of

my ruling they are to be arrested immediately; but if their actions are so serious that they cannot be appropriately punished summarily, in the case of soldiers you should inform their commanding officer of what you have discovered against them, or if they are passing through on their way to Rome, you should write to me.

Pliny had pointed out to Trajan that Iuliopolis was a frontier town in Bithynia with a large transit traffic. The emperor suggests a mechanism for protecting provincials from recognized risks. This is a useful indication of Trajan's attitude to the role of the government in the welfare of his subjects. For serious offences involving soldiers or imperial functionaries Pliny had to refer the case to the appropriate official. As we have seen, soldiers and officials on move along major roads were often a source of oppression of the local population. For the important position of Byzantium see Sherwin-White (1966), 667.

SP 221 (AD 133–7)

271. Marcus Petronius Mamertinus, prefect of Egypt, declares: I have discovered that many soldiers passing through the country requisition unfairly boats and animals and men without a certificate, in some cases seizing them by force, in others obtaining them from the *strategoi* through favour or fawning on them. The result of this is that ordinary people are subjected to insults and abuse, and the army has come to be blamed for greed and injustice. I therefore order the *strategoi* and royal secretaries in no circumstances to provide to anyone without a certificate, either travelling by boat or by land, any material for the trip, on the understanding that I will punish severely anyone, who, after this edict, is found receiving or providing any of the items mentioned. Year ... of Hadrian Caesar, the lord, Thoth 8.

It is striking that the prefect of Egypt recognized that the abusive behaviour of soldiers had turned local opinion against the army. The movement of soldiers and officials continued to cause serious problems despite imperial good intentions.

SEG 38, no. 1244

272. Since you say that even soldiers on the march stray off from the main road and make their way to you for no other purpose than to take what are called *supplementa*, the most illustrious governor of the province shall be informed about this too, and he will correct the apparent offences committed against you by the soldiers. Aemilius Iuncus, proconsul, to the magistrates, council, and people of Tabala, greetings. If you prove that any

soldier, not belonging to those sent to Aizanoi, has strayed off to your city, wandering about to enrich himself, he shall be punished. For it is not necessary to hand over such things under the pretext of hospitality. For it is clearly stated and determined by all proconsuls that soldiers are not allowed to leave the main road. [You can display this in a public place in your town.] Farewell.

Mitchell (1993), vol. 1, 228–9, and n. 16; *SEG* 43 (1993), 313, no. 870. The letter was written by Pertinax in 193 and published after his death by Aemilius Iuncus, proconsul of Asia. *Supplementa* refer to illegal exactions in lieu of recruits to the army. For Hadrian's similar action, see no. 264.

IGR 3.1119 = *OGIS* 609 (AD 185–186)

273. Iulius Saturninus (governor of Syria) to the people of Phaine, chief village of the district of Trachonitis, greetings. If any soldier or private person establishes a billet for himself by force in your houses, contact me and you will receive redress. For you are not obliged to provide any contribution for visitors, nor, since you have a public hostel, can you be compelled to receive visitors into your homes. Publish this letter of mine in a conspicuous location in your chief village, so that no one can argue that he did not know of it.

Once again, the government, this time in the person of the governor of Syria, tries to ensure that official instructions are carried out. Of course, for the villagers it may not have been easy to contact the distant governor. Phaine was on the busy road that led from Bostra to Damascus, and the public hostel was perhaps installed so that soldiers and travellers did not ask the inhabitants for accommodation.

CIL 3.12336 = Abbott and Johnston (1926), no. 139 (AD 238) (Extract)

274. To Emperor Caesar Marcus Antonius Gordian Pius Fortunate Augustus, petition from the villagers of Scaptopara and of Gresa (?) … We live and have our property in the village mentioned above which is exposed to harm because it has the advantage of hot springs and is located between two of the army camps which are in your (province of) Thrace. Previously, as long as the inhabitants remained undisturbed and free from oppression, they reliably paid their tribute and met their other obligations. But when at times some persons started to become insolent and to use force, then the village started to decline. A famous festival is held two miles from our village, and those persons who stay there for fifteen days for the festival do not remain in the vicinity of the festival itself, but leave it and

descend on our village, forcing us to provide them with hospitality and purvey many other items for their enjoyment without payment. In addition to these persons, soldiers too, who have been dispatched somewhere else, leave their proper routes, and come to us, and similarly intimidate us into furnishing them with hospitality and provisions, and pay no money. Moreover, the governors of the province, and indeed your procurators, are regular visitors here to use the hot springs. We unceasingly receive those in authority, as we are required to do, but being unable to put up with the others, we have repeatedly approached the governors of Thrace, who in accordance with the letters of the divine emperors have ordered that we are to remain undisturbed. For we made clear that we could no longer put up with it but intended to leave our ancestral homes because of the violence of those who descend on us.

Scaptopara by its position attracted many visitors; the inscription illustrates the extent and long-term nature of the abuse. The villagers' previous appeals to the governors of Thrace and emperors had brought some relief, but the abuse started again and had become so bad that they threatened to leave their ancestral homes. They had succeeded in getting their petition to the Emperor Gordian III with the assistance of a soldier in the emperor's praetorian guard. Gordian's response was to order them to approach the governor's court and seek a settlement. In view of their previous experience this may not have seemed very helpful to the villagers; see Connolly (2010), 167–74.

SEG 37, no. 1186

275. Imperator Caesar Marcus Aurelius Pius Augustus Parthicus Maximus Britannicus Maximus to the people of Takina through Aurelius Andronicus and Hilarianus. My procurator and freedman shall take every care that soldiers neither rush ahead prematurely on the pretext of (orders of) the most illustrious proconsuls and harass you or leave the towns and ravage the fields. You will also have the help of the same person in receiving the set rate for waggons per mile, and in that the oxen are given back to you in good time without any dispute. I have issued the rescript. I, Ofillius Theodorus, have read. There were present . . . .

This rescript of Caracalla is followed by a letter of the proconsul of Asia Gavius Tranquillus indicating that soldiers are still acting against imperial instructions. The only solution is (as usual) to urge the community of Takina in Phrygia to have the imperial instruction displayed in a public place in their town.

CIL 3.14191; Rostovtzeff (1957), p. 741, n. 26 (AD 246)

276. With good fortune. Emperor Caesar Marcus Iulius Philippus Augustus, son of Philippus, and the most noble Caesar Marcus Iulius Philippus, to Marcus Aurelius Eclectus, through the soldier Didymus, with special police duties (?):

When the proconsul, most distinguished man, has investigated the truth of what you allege, if anything has been done unjustly, he will take it under his personal care. Farewell.

Petition to Marcus Iulius Philippus Pius Felix Augustus and the most noble Caesar Marcus Iulius Philippus from Aurelius Eclectus on behalf of the community of the dwellers at Arague and your tenant farmers in the Appian district, and on behalf of the community of the Totteani-Soenians in the area of Phrygia, through the soldier Titus Ulpius Didymus.

Most pious and serene of all emperors, although in this most blessed era of yours everyone enjoys a peaceful and untroubled life since all wickedness and corruption have ceased, we alone are suffering something greatly at odds with these most happy times, and we make this appeal to you. The gravamen of the petition is this. Most holy emperors, we are your property, an entire community, which has fled and become suppliants before your divinity. We are subject to improper abuse and are oppressed by those whose duty it is to protect the public good. For although we have remote dwellings and have no military presence, we suffer abuse at odds with your most happy times. Commanders and soldiers, and powerful people among the leading men in the city, and your agents, passing through the Appian district, come upon us and leaving the main road take us from our work and requisition our ploughing oxen, and exact from us what is certainly not due to them. And therefore, as a result of this, we are oppressed and wronged. Once before, Augustus, we approached your greatness, when you were praetorian prefect, and made clear what was happening. And the attached letter shows that your divine spirit was moved by this, 'We have sent the material you included in the petition to the proconsul, who will ensure that there is no further ground for complaint'. Since therefore no benefit has come to us from that petition, and since improper exactions are being made in respect of our agricultural activity, when people descend on us and trample on us unjustly, and since we are oppressed improperly by your agents, our property is expended on them, our land is stripped and destroyed, for we live in a remote area far from the main road.

This is a response by the emperor Philip to a petition from the Araguenians who lived in a village on an imperial estate in Phrygia and had suffered oppression from soldiers and imperial agents, who seem to have assisted in tax-collection. The petition was in Greek, and the rescript in Latin. Philip had been praetorian prefect in 242. See also Johnson, Coleman-Norton, Bourne (1961), no. 289; Williams (1986). Imperial response to petitions about abusive conduct by officials often seems limited, if not feeble. Emperors tend to refer the issue to the provincial governor, even though this had not previously produced a solution, or place their hopes in a visible display of the written version of their instructions. We do not usually hear of any institution of special measures to deal with persistent problems, though Pliny's appointment in Bithynia can be seen as a response to incompetent administration in that province. Hadrian's perambulations in the provinces may have served to keep governors on their toes.

CHAPTER 4

Economic Life

Introduction

This chapter discusses the role of legal regulation and practice in facilitating orderly and measured relationships in respect of contracts, buying, selling, hiring, agency, and labour. Of course, resort to the legal process will often have been a last step and many will have tried to settle disputes or malpractice by private negotiation. Evidence in legal texts and other sources has naturally inspired debate about the extent to which legal institutions helped determine the forms within which economic activity was organized, and how they regulated the relationship between state and subject in respect of the accumulation of wealth and business dealings between the various groups in society, where the elite might be thought to have a natural advantage. In general terms many factors contributed to a positive and helpful background for economic activity. Public law would reasonably be concerned with social stability and smooth money dealings, on which, ultimately, taxes depended. The Roman legal system provided a consistent and authoritative framework that offered ways to resolve disputes and was capable of innovative solutions in areas relevant to economic activity. Access was available to some form of controlling authority, either a magistrate, or, in the provinces, the governor, who had control over jurisdiction and could hear cases and petitions; papyri and inscriptions show that many people did take their case to the governor. But the Romans also permitted local courts which increased the opportunity to seek redress, perhaps less expensively. It was crucial that the Romans maintained a legal framework to enforce judgements. There were also in Roman ideology informal but well-established social customs and upper-class conventions about honouring debts that could often prove more effective than official sanctions in business (Kehoe (2012a), 189–205).

The evidence of papyri indicates the widespread availability of lawyers in the provinces (see p. 350), and the meticulous keeping of records, accredited receipts, contracts, mortgages, and loans which conformed to

Roman practice. The implication is that people involved in business expected that this was a valuable exercise and that any contract or receipt would be honoured, or if not, that there was an avenue for redress. The government too meticulously kept records, as for example in the records of land distribution and holdings, and it was in the interests of emperors to sustain the economic basis of taxation, as we see in Domitian's concern in his instructions to his procurator of Syria (no. 263).

More precisely, in some respects Roman commercial law may have contributed to economic development. Commercial transactions appear in the twelve tables of Roman law in the fifth century BC, and the first treaties between Rome and Carthage (508 and 348 BC) included the idea that goods might be exchanged between Romans and Carthaginians, and that such transactions would have the same legal validity as those between citizens (Aubert (2015), 216–18). The edict of the aediles (*FIRA* 1.66 and in this volume no. 291), which probably merged eventually with the praetorian edict, was helpful in the regulation of Roman business. Furthermore, the urban praetor's edict contributes considerably to our knowledge of Roman business law, and nine titles out of forty-five and more than forty rubrics out of 292 deal with legal issues concerning commerce (Aubert (2015), 221–5). We can also see how grain traders exploited legal, social, and economic institutions to operate on a large scale (Kessler and Temin (2007)). However, it is difficult to establish how far economic and social concerns influenced the Roman attitude to contracts. In the early period *stipulatio* allowed interested parties to agree to any kind of obligation, provided that it was lawful. Subsequently this very general approach to contract changed, but the emergence and form of distinct contracts were also bound up with legalistic practice. Presumably a specific contract arose whenever a *stipulatio* proved to be ineffective or when society exerted certain pressures. Lawyers had to deal with a set of complex social and economic issues in the expanding Roman world.

Contracts and Obligations

In the modern business world the formal, written contract is crucial. Things were different in Rome. The basis of Roman contractual activity was the *stipulatio*, which was a formal though oral mechanism for making a contract (pp. 177–9). The practice arose in a period when ability in writing was not common. Through it you could ensure that any undertaking became actionable. The terminology used decided the nature of the agreement. Despite the drawback that both parties had to be present in person, the *stipulatio* was enormously flexible in that it could be applied to any kind of agreement that the parties wanted, for example, sale, hire, or protection of property, and became the basis of the contractual system. By contrast, other contracts had no set form, but each type had a function and clear legal definition that applied only to the exactly relevant circumstances. As each contract was an individuality, it took its name and attributes from the activity in question, for example, *mutuum* referred to contract for a loan for consumption, which therefore did not have to be returned (p. 200). Consensual contracts relating to activities such as selling (pp. 179–90), hiring (pp. 190–3), partnership (pp. 197–9), and mandate (p. 199) had developed by the second century BC, and such contracts required mere agreement with no special formulae or the personal presence of the interested parties (we may compare the motto of the London Stock Exchange: *Dictum meum Pactum:* 'My word is my bond'). Consensual contracts were bilateral, establishing rights and obligations on both parties; each contract had a definition and rules on what needed to be included. Most Roman contracts either involved the payment in money of what was due in law, or not. There is no case where goods or services were offered in return for other goods and services.

The Romans therefore had no general principle of contract but rather law relating to contracts in their various forms. Since consensual contracts were technically made of 'good faith' (*bonae fidei*), the judge dealing with a dispute had some leeway to take account of relevant or mitigating factors. Furthermore, the law eventually established crucial guarantees which were inherent in the contract of sale, such as the quality of goods and the seller's title to them. But if the contracting party wished to have formal guarantees not provided by the law, he could apply a *stipulatio* setting them out. Those with substantial business interests would perhaps find it inconvenient to turn up in person frequently to complete a *stipulatio*, and might therefore prefer other types of contract, although they could use an agent such as a slave or a *filius familias* (see p. 214). There was another kind of contract set out in writing (*litteris*); it normally consisted of formal entries in a record of accounts, for example, to the effect that one man was owed money by another for a particular reason; this of course would require the acknowledgement of the debtor (p. 199). The Romans did not have a contract that created obligations by the writing itself, though see no. 282. It can be argued that consensual contracts especially sale, lease, and mandate were economically efficient in that all damages for breach of contract were monetary (Kehoe (2015), 235–7).

In general, contracts of all kinds belonged to the area of private law and were one important source of obligations, in the sense that by committing to a contract an individual incurred an obligation in law to do or provide something. Therefore, an important aspect of the law of obligations was associated with commercial and financial dealings. This law of obligations was an area of private law that, together with property and succession, came under the category of 'things' in the basic threefold division of Roman law (along with the law of persons and the law of actions).

D 44.7.3pr (Paul, *Institutes*, Book 2)

277. The essential element of obligations does not consist in making some object or servitude our own, but in binding another person to give, do, or provide something in our interest.

Gaius, *Institutes* 3.89

278. First let us examine those (obligations) that arise from contract. There are four categories (*genera*) of these: an obligation through contract arises either by the handing over of something (a real contract), or by words, or by writing, or by consent.

Formal Verbal Contracts: Stipulation (*stipulatio*)

Gaius, *Institutes* 3.92

279. A verbal obligation is made by question and answer, such as: 'Do you solemnly promise to convey?' 'I solemnly promise.' 'Will you convey?' 'I will convey.' 'Do you promise?' 'I promise.' 'Do you promise on your honour?' 'I promise on my honour.'

One party had to ask a question in specific terms and the second party had to reply in exactly the same words. If the two statements matched precisely, this constituted a binding agreement with formal legal requirements (*stricti iuris*). The *stipulatio* would be specific, for example, 'Do you solemnly promise to convey to me twenty denarii for the gold chain I gave you?' In this way it could be adapted to suit almost any situation or transaction. Its origin goes back to the fifth century BC and the twelve tables of Roman law and shows that in the early period the state was prepared to enforce at law private agreements between citizens. By the imperial period we find that, presumably in a context of developing commerce, the limitation to citizens and certain Latin words had been removed. The Roman verbal *stipulatio* could apply to the whole empire.

Gaius, *Institutes* 3.93

280. This verbal obligation 'Do you solemnly promise to convey?' 'I solemnly promise' is particular to Roman citizens. But other formulations belong to the law of nations (*ius gentium*) and are therefore valid between all men, whether they are Roman citizens or foreigners. And although they are expressed in Greek ... nevertheless, even these are valid between Roman citizens provided that they understand the Greek language.

D 45.1.1.6 (Ulpian, *Sabinus*, Book 48)

281. It does not matter if the reply is made in the same or another language. So, if someone poses the question in Latin and the reply is made to him in Greek, provided that it is consistent, the obligation is established; and it is the same the other way round. But it is open to doubt if we should extend this only to the Greek language or even to another, possibly Punic or Assyrian or some other language. In his writings Sabinus accepts the truth of the idea that every language contains a means of expressing an obligation verbally, provided that both parties understand the other's language, either through their own efforts or through a reliable interpreter.

Ulpian here suggests a further relaxation of the strict rules, confirming the recognition that a verbal agreement could be applied throughout the empire, facilitating wider commercial contacts (see du Plessis (2012a), 75). Ulpian was writing at the height of the empire's power in territory and contact with other peoples, which perhaps has influenced his wide interpretation of the rules.

Gaius, *Institutes* 3.105

282. It is obvious that a dumb man cannot stipulate or promise. It is accepted that the same applies to a deaf man because the man who stipulates must be able to hear the words of the man who promises, and the man who promises must be able to hear the words of the man who stipulates.

This confirms the original verbal nature of the *stipulatio*. However, Meyer (2004, chapters 8–9, especially 253–61), on the basis of waxed wooden tablets discovered at Pompeii and Herculaneum (first century AD), and also at Alburnus Maior in Dacia (second century AD), recording private legal and financial actions, has argued that over time such tablets put together as records of transactions, and other types of written evidence, came to serve as written contracts and could complement, or indeed serve as a substitute for, a verbal *stipulatio*, and as such could be recognized and cited in court; see also no. 292.

What legal remedy provided for invalidation of contract in the case of duress, fraud, or the impossibility of fulfilling it? In the *stipulatio* the form of words bound the parties even if improper pressure had been brought to bear, or if they had been fraudulently misled. In the first century BC the praetor had begun to provide a defence against the strict procedure of the *stipulatio*, by granting an action for duress (*actio quod metus causa*; see *D* 4.2.1). He could also grant an *exceptio* if the person who had used duress attempted to bring an action on the contract. The *exceptio* was a defence that enabled the defendant, while accepting the accuracy or validity of the *stipulatio*, to argue that special circumstances should be considered, for example, that he had been subject to intimidation (see Watson (1991), 54–5).

D 4.3.1pr-2 (Ulpian, *Edict*, Book 11)

283. In this edict the praetor offers relief against untrustworthy and deceitful people who damage others through some kind of trickery, so that the former do not profit from their wickedness and the latter do not suffer because of their simplicity. The terms of the edict are as follows: 'Wherever something is alleged to have been done with malicious or fraudulent intent, if there is no other action available concerning these matters and the grounds seems just, I will grant an action'. Servius indeed defines malice or fraud as a scheme for the purpose of deceiving a third party where someone pretends one thing but does another.

In any legal case the praetor could grant an action based on the facts presented by the plaintiff, even if no formal avenue were available.

Consensual Contracts: Sale

Sale replaced barter (*D* 18.1.1) and in the contract of sale (*emptio venditio* – literally buying and selling) the crucial characteristics were the consent of the parties, acceptance of bilateral obligations, and the absence of deceit or fraud, that is, the contract was of good faith (*bonae fidei*). The origins of consensual sale may have had something to do with economic motives in the expansion of foreign trade and a willingness to work with foreign merchants. An effective contract of sale required (as well as consent) an item that was capable of being sold, a definite price, which had to be in money, and a clear intention that it would be paid. There was no formal framework and no procedure in front of witnesses (Zimmermann (1996),

230 emphasizes the importance of consensual contracts). The consequent *actio venditi* (action on sale) was against the buyer for payment of the price, while the *actio empti* (action on purchase) was against the vendor if he did not meet his obligations.

Cicero, *De Officiis* 1.7.23

284. The foundation of justice is trustworthiness (*fides*), that is, adherence to and the truth of words and agreements.

For Cicero, see p. 477. The *De Officiis* gives advice derived from Stoic principles on problems of personal conduct, and here gives a late republican definition of *bona fides*.

D 50.17.116pr (Ulpian, *Edict*, Book 11)

285. Nothing is so opposed to consent, which is the basis of good faith cases, than force and duress, and to approve this is contrary to proper procedure.

Gaius, *Institutes* 3.135–6

286. Obligations in sale, hire, partnership, and mandate are made by consent. (136) We say that obligations are contracted by consent in these cases because no formality either in words or writing is required, but it is enough that those who are conducting the business have consented. Therefore, contracts like this can be arranged between parties who are at a distance, for example by letter or messenger, although a verbal obligation cannot be contracted by parties at a distance.

This kind of contract would meet the need to establish wider trade opportunities with a large range of contacts.

D 18.1.2.1 (Ulpian, *Sabinus*, Book 1)

287. Without a price no sale is possible. However, it is not the counting out of the money but the agreement that completes a sale contracted without writing.

See de Zulueta (1945), 17–18 for the exclusion of barter from the concept of price. A definite price was required, or at least one that could be defined in respect of established facts or circumstances. There must also be intent to pay the price; in other words, the sale must not be a concealed gift, although this was subject to interpretation.

Gaius, *Institutes* 3.146

288. Furthermore, if I provide you with gladiators on the condition that for each gladiator who comes out unharmed twenty denarii should be paid to me for his efforts, but one thousand denarii for each one who is killed or disabled, the question is whether this is a contract of sale or of hire. The majority view is that for those who come out unharmed the contract is one of hire, but for those who have been killed or disabled it is one of sale.

Gaius is here explaining the distinction between sale and hire, using a vivid example where the definition of sale or hire depended on the outcome of the event for which the original purchase had been intended.

D 18.1.20 (Pomponius, *Sabinus*, Book 9)

289. Sabinus replied that if I want something to be made for me, such as a statue or a vase or clothing, in such a way that I hand over nothing except money, it is to be considered a purchase, and there cannot be any form of hire if the material is not being handed over by the person for whom the item is to be made. But the situation would be different if I provided an area of land on which you were to build a block of flats, since in this case the substantive material is coming from me.

This discussion relates to a complication relating to sale in respect of goods made by the seller; if, for example, you supplied your own gold to a goldsmith for the manufacture of a bracelet, it was a contract of hire. The sale of non-specific goods, that is, goods of which the seller produced a sample or representation and agreed to supply according to his own arrangements or from his own resources, raised difficulties. This was not recognized as a contract of sale in classical Roman law, but of course in these cases the parties could proceed by *stipulatio*. There were other ways round the problem; it was possible through a consensual contract of sale to purchase a future crop on the expectation of what would be produced. And a seller could promise future delivery of goods with contractual penalty for non-compliance (see Zimmermann (1996), 236–41).

D 19.1.47 (Paul, *Responses*, Book 6)

290. Lucius Titius received money for the sale of materials, with a fixed penalty to the effect that if he did not present the materials in good condition within the appointed time, he would suffer the penalty. He died when only some of the materials had been handed over. Since therefore the testator (Titius) had incurred the penalty and his heir has not provided the remaining materials, can he (the heir) be sued for the

penalty and also the interest, especially if the purchaser has borrowed the money at a punitive rate of interest?

The response was that the heir did have to pay the penalty and the interest from the moment when the vendor defaulted.

D 21.1.44.1 (Paul, *Edict of the Curule Aediles*, Book 2)

291. An action is offered under this edict against the person who has the greatest part in the sale, because slave-dealers generally form a partnership, so that whatever business they transact is held to be done in common. It seemed equitable to the aediles that the actions under their edict should be brought against the person among the slave-dealers who had the greater part of the property, or at least did not possess a smaller part, lest the purchaser should be compelled to enter litigation with many people. Normally an action on purchase is carried on with individuals in proportion to their share as partners. For this kind of man tends to be prone to profit and to base practice.

The general responsibility of the aediles was to exercise care over the city of Rome (see pp. 86; 92). They also supervised trade and the marketplace, and their edict aimed to establish rules for fair dealing. Slave-dealers, having a reputation as smart operators, came under special scrutiny, since they apparently formed cartels among themselves to fob off customers who complained about the quality of their merchandise. Cattle-dealers were also strictly regulated. For protection against defects see p. 188. The law aimed to facilitate the buying and selling market by offering a framework to provide confidence in contracts of sale.

CIL 4.3340.1 (AD 15)

292. M. Cerrinius Euphrates is stated to have realized 520 sesterces as the result of the sale of a mule to [M.] Pomponius Nico, freedman of Marcus, and this money is in the *stipulatio* of L. Caecilius Felix.

M. Cerrinius Euphrates, freedman of Marcus, stated that he had received, counted out, all that money, which is written above, from Philadelphus, slave of Caecilius Felix.

Executed at Pompeii on 28 May in the consulship of Drusus Caesar and C. Norbanus Flaccus.

L. Caecilius Iucundus was a banker in Pompeii who regularly offered credit, in some cases to a prospective purchaser, by paying the vendor; he kept his records in a chest which was carbonized during the eruption of Vesuvius in AD 79. This example is a wooden tablet containing a receipt and release from obligation under a *stipulatio* (given probably to Iucundus' father, L. Caecilius Felix) for money paid to the seller of the mule on behalf of the purchaser. See Andreau (1999), 35; Meyer (2004), 126; 142–3; for banking, see p. 206. It is possible that this and other tablets from Campania are simply private records made as evidence of transactions. See also no. 282.

The Contract of Sale in Operation

There were several crucial elements in the operation of contracts of sale, which in some respects went through a process of development. First, implicit in the vendor's offer to sell was his title to the goods in question. Originally the purchaser could by *stipulatio* ensure his specific rights if he was subsequently deprived of possession by the true owner. Later, under the consensual good faith contract the vendor had to give the promise of good title and could be sued for breach of contract. Finally, this promise came to be regarded as inherent in the very contract of sale. Second, by the same kind of process it came to be accepted that the vendor guaranteed the quality of the goods he was selling; this arose partly from the aediles' edict relating to certain defects in respect of the sale of cattle and slaves in the market in Rome and requiring vendors to reveal any problem. Subsequently this guarantee was implied in all contracts of sale. Third, at some point in the sale responsibility for goods sold passed to the purchaser. In Roman law this point occurred when the contract was perfected or completed, in so far as the necessary conditions of sale had been fulfilled. Potentially, therefore, the purchaser was responsible for loss or damage to the goods before he had taken delivery of them. But the seller could evade responsibility only if the damage to the goods occurred in circumstances not preventable by him; on aediles and sales see Crook (1967), 181–6. For the aediles' edict – *D* 21.1.1.1; Aulus Gellius, *Attic Nights* 4.2.1 notes that the description of a slave for sale had to make clear any illness or defect and whether he had been a fugitive or guilty of a misdemeanour; for Aulus Gellius, who wrote c. AD 180, see p. 477; Holford-Strevens (2003).

***D* 21.2.8 (Iulianus, *Digests*, Book 15)**

293. The vendor of a slave must offer a guarantee to the purchaser in respect of what it is worth to him that the slave belongs to the vendor. Therefore, if the purchaser is evicted from possession of either the offspring of a slave girl or an inheritance that he had ordered the slave to accept, he can bring an

action in respect of purchase. And just as the vendor is required to present free and continuous possession of the slave whom he has sold, he also must be liable to the purchaser for everything he could have acquired through him.

This kind of guarantee became implicit in the contract of sale itself by the early second century AD (see Johnston (1999), 81). For examples of the operation of the contract of sale with guarantees against future legal action see nos. 294–6.

P. Oxy. 1707 = *SP* no. 33 (AD 204)

294. Apollonios, son of Hephaestion son of Ammonios, of the Sosicosmian tribe and the Althaean deme, to Apollonios, son of Apollonios son of Serapion, of the Euthenodian tribe and the Althaean deme, greetings. I acknowledge the sale to you of a female ass, which has lost its first teeth, is mouse-coloured and unbranded, for the price that we agreed between us of 600 drachmae of silver imperial coinage, that is, six hundred drachmae, which the acknowledging person, Apollonios, received on the spot from Apollonios; and he will guarantee it with every guarantee against the action of any person, just as it is, and not capable of repudiation. If anyone lays claim to it, Apollonios will rebuff him at his own expense. This deed of sale is valid. Year thirteen of emperors Lucius Septimius Severus Pius Pertinax Arabicus Abiabenicus Parthicus Maximus and Marcus Aurelius Antoninus Pius Augusti, and Publius Septimius Geta Caesar Augustus, Phaophi 5. I, Apollonios, mentioned above, have sold as noted above.

This receipt for sale contains a careful description of the item sold and an affirmation of its saleability. The silver denarius was the principal coin in the Roman world and was the equivalent of the Attic drachma, which continued to be widely used in the east. The gold *aureus* was worth twenty-five denarii. Other widely used coins were the silver *sestertius* (four to the denarius) and the bronze *as* (sixteen to the denarius).

FIRA 3, no. 87

295. Maximus, son of Bato, bought and acquired ownership of the girl by the name of Passia or any other name she is known by, roughly about six years old, who had been bought as a foundling, from Dasius, son of Verzo, a Pirusta from Kavieretium (?) for 205 denarii.

He (the vendor) declares her to be healthy, not acquired by theft or any offence, not a fugitive or prone to wander. And if anyone should acquire possession of this girl or any share of her with the result that Maximus, son of Bato, or anyone else to whom it may be a concern should not have full possession and enjoyment, then for the price for which the girl was bought and as much again Maximus, son of Bato, duly requested a promise to be given, and Dasius, son of Verzo, a Pirusta from Kavieretium duly gave the promise.

For the girl, who is noted above, Dasius, son of Verzo, declares that he has received into his possession from Maximus, son of Bato, 205 denarii.

Transacted at Kartus, on 17 March in the consulship of Titus Aelius Caesar Antoninus Pius for the second time and Bruttius Praesens for the second time (AD 139).

There follow the names of witnesses.

The warranty is given by *stipulatio*; it may be that at this time warranty was not implied in the contract of sale, or perhaps the buyer simply wanted to be sure; see Johnston (1999), 82.

FIRA 3, no. 136 (AD 77)

296. C. Valerius Longus, cavalryman of the squadron Apriana, bought a black Cappadocian horse for 2,700 Augustan drachmas from C. Iulius Rufus, centurion of legion XXII. (It is agreed that) this horse eats and drinks as veterinary animals normally do, apart from [...] which has been described and is clearly visible on its body. Furthermore, if someone brings about an eviction of him, then that [double(?)] (the value of the horse) should be properly and appropriately paid in good coin, as is normal, C. Valerius stipulated and Iulius Rufus, centurion, promised on oath. C. Iulius Rufus, centurion, has declared that he received and holds the said 2,700 Augustan drachmas from C. Valerius Longus, the purchaser, and [to have handed over to him the above-mentioned horse].

In this receipt of purchase the saleability of the animal is affirmed with a record of distinguishing marks (see Crook (1967), 216). It is worth pointing out that these soldiers are sufficiently wealthy to own and buy a horse.

D 18.1.35.5 (Gaius, *Provincial Edict*, Book 10)

297. In respect of items that are established by weight, number, or measure, such as corn, wine, oil, and silver, the same practice is sometimes observed as in other cases, namely that as soon as the price has been agreed, the sale is held to have been perfected, and sometimes the practice that even if a price has been agreed it is accepted that the sale is not perfected unless the items

have been measured, weighed, and counted. Now, if all the wine, or oil, or corn, or silver, irrespective of how much there is, is sold for a single price, the same rule applies as in other things. But if it is the case that the wine is sold by the amphora, the oil by the cask, corn by the bushel, or silver by the pound, the question arises: when will the sale be considered to have been perfected?

Sale at a price to be established by counting the units is deemed conditional on the actual counting (see de Zulueta (1945), 32). The transfer of risk occurs when the contract of sale is completed (see no. 298). This provision rather oddly seems to penalize the buyer as he becomes responsible on conclusion of contract before the goods are transferred to him. Originally in earlier times the law may have envisaged a cash sale with two transactions almost simultaneously. Why did the law not change? Perhaps there was not much pressure to do so since the outcomes for which the buyer was responsible were ones that the vendor could not prevent, like floods and earthquakes (see Zimmermann (1996), 281–4; Johnston (1999), 82). A contract might include an opportunity for the prospective purchaser to take the goods on approval, for example to taste wine or exercise horses. Parties could negotiate their own contract as suited, based on the essential law of sale, as the further examples show.

CJ 4.48.2 (AD 223)

298. Emperor Alexander Augustus to Gargilius Iulianus. Since it is agreed that individual jars of wine should be sold for a definite price, before they are handed over, when the sale is therefore incomplete, the purchaser is not liable for the risk of a change in the wine's character provided that he did not cause the delay in measuring it. Since however you claim that the entire stock of wine, which had been stored in a granary, was sold without being measured, and the keys had been handed over to the purchaser, then with the sale complete, the purchaser is liable for the loss incurred by the change in the wine. This is entirely the case not only in respect of wine but also if oil or corn or other similar things are on sale, and they deteriorate or are completely destroyed.

D 19.5.20pr (Ulpian, *Edict*, Book 32)

299. Labeo considered this question: If I give you horses that are for sale so that they can be tried out, on the condition that you will return them if after three days they have not satisfied you, and you ride them in a circus jumping from one to another, and win a prize, but then decline to buy them, is there an action on sale against you? I think that a better course is to

proceed on the words of the contract. For here it was laid down between us that you should have a free trial of the horses not that you should compete with them.

Labeo recommends an action based on the agreed contract, which was precisely worded, rather than on sale.

D 19.1.48 (Scaevola, *Responses*, Book 2)

300. Titius, heir of Sempronius, sold a farm to Septicius on the following terms: 'The farm of Sempronius and whatever legal right Sempronius had in it will be sold to you for such and such a price'. He handed over vacant possession of the land but did not formally point out its boundaries. The question is whether he should be compelled by an action on purchase to demonstrate on the basis of documents relating to the inheritance what rights the deceased had, and to point out the boundaries. I replied that he ought to be responsible for whatever the parties understood to have been intended in accordance with what had been written. If this is not clear, then the vendor must show both the documentation relating to the farm and the boundaries. For this is consistent with a contract of good faith.

Titius had sold a farm as part of the estate which he had inherited without a formal *demonstratio* (pointing out) of boundaries; if the contract of sale had been vaguely worded, he is now under an obligation to provide documents relevant to the title of the farm and its boundaries.

D 18.1.9pr (Ulpian, *Sabinus*, Book 28)

301. It is obvious that in sales and purchases agreement must be present. But if there is no agreement over the sale contract, in the price, or in anything else, then the sale is invalid. For example, if I thought that I was buying the Cornelian farm and you thought that you were selling me the Sempronian farm, because we disagree over the object of the transaction it is clear that there is no sale.

D 18.1.11 (Ulpian, *Sabinus*, Book 28)

302. Well then, what do we say if the purchaser were blind, or if an error were made in the material or through the purchaser's lack of skill in understanding the material? Or do we say that the parties have agreed to the object? And how does a man agree who is not able to see it? However, if I think that I am buying a virgin slave, when in fact she is a woman, the sale

will be valid, for there is no mistake in respect of her sex. But if I were selling a female slave and you thought that you were buying a boy, because there is an error in respect of sex, the purchase and sale are invalid.

The fact that the sale was deemed invalid if the slave was a girl instead of a boy shows the importance of the gender distinction in law between men and women; the female slave was not only held to be inferior but a completely different entity.

D 21.1.4.3 (Ulpian, *Edict of the Curule Aediles*, Book 1)

303. Pomponius also declares that although the vendor should not be responsible for a slave being properly intelligent, nevertheless if he sells one who is so stupid or moronic that he is of no use, this is held to be a defect. But we seem to employ the rule that the terms defect and disease apply only to the physical condition. For a mental defect the vendor will be liable only if he makes a specific guarantee concerning it, but if he does not, he will not be liable. It is for this reason that a specific reservation is made (in the edict) in respect of wandering or fugitive slaves. For these are mental not physical defects.

What about defects not obvious at point of sale? A warranty for concealed defects could be arranged through *stipulatio*. Later, as previously noted (p. 183), there was an implied warranty (independent of the seller's knowledge) through the act of selling, and in the aediles' edict more severe penalties were laid down for sellers who knew of the defect. The *actio redhibitoria*, if successful, allowed a purchaser to return a slave and receive back the purchase price within six months of a defect becoming apparent, or reimbursement of part of the purchase price (Zimmermann (1996), 317–19; see no. 305). There was a move towards generalized liability for latent defects based on the *actio empti* (action on purchase) and the good faith clause inherent in it; gradually the principles of the aediles' edict were received into the *ius civile*. These procedures tried to address the problem that the seller and purchaser might have different information on the item, or a different understanding of its condition. Again, the law offers a framework to promote confidence in the contract of sale and so perhaps facilitate transactions, though a poor man might be daunted by the prospect of going to law to secure his interests.

D 19.1.13pr (Ulpian, *Edict*, Book 32)

304. Iulianus in book 15 with reference to condemnation in an action on purchase distinguishes between a person who knowingly made a sale and the person who did so in ignorance. For he says that the person who sold a diseased flock or a defective beam, as long as he made the sale in ignorance, would be responsible in an action on purchase only in respect of how much

less I would have paid if I had known the facts. If, however, he knew but kept silent and deceived the purchaser, he must be responsible for all the loss that the purchaser incurred from that sale. Therefore, if a building collapsed because of the defective beam, he (the vendor) must be responsible for the assessed cost of the entire building, or if a flock died from infection by diseased animals, he must be responsible for the purchaser's interest in a property in good condition.

D 21.1.23pr (Ulpian, *Edict of the Curule Aediles*, Book 1)

305. When rescission (annulling of sale) takes place, if the slave's intellectual or physical condition has been impaired by the purchaser, the purchaser must make restitution to the vendor, for example, if a slave has been raped or become a fugitive because of the purchaser's cruelty. Therefore, as Pomponius says, whatever the reason for the slave's impairment, that should be assessed on the decision of a judge and consequent restitution made to the vendor.

To sum up the options open to the purchaser: a serious error would render a sale contract void, for example, if someone contracted to buy wine and it turned out to be olive oil. In a case where the character of the item sold had changed before the purchase was completed (for example wine that had deteriorated), it was a question of who was responsible for the delay in completing the deal. If a mistake had been made in the contract that was not considered serious enough to invalidate the sale, the purchaser had no remedy unless the vendor had in some way misrepresented the item to be sold. If the vendor's inaccurate statement was innocent the purchaser was entitled to an action (*actio empti*) for the difference between what he paid and the real value of the item. If it was fraudulent the purchaser could also be entitled to recover any incidental losses. If the vendor did not have legal title to the item sold, he was liable to compensate the purchaser if he was evicted from ownership of the item.

D 18.2.1 (Paul, *Sabinus*, Book 5)

306. Reservation (*addictio*) up to a defined date is made in the following terms: 'Let that estate be sold to you unless by the first of January next someone makes a better offer, in which circumstances the estate is to depart from the owner'.

Addictio was a clause inserted into the contract of sale affecting its operation; the vendor had the right to annul the sale if he received an offer of a higher price. If the vendor had handed over the item to the purchaser, he had the right to reclaim it (see Zimmermann (1996), 735). Furthermore, a contract of sale could be cancelled if, before any delivery or payment, both vendor and purchaser agreed to this (de Zulueta (1945), 53–4).

Fraudulent Measurement in Sales

D 11.6.5.2 (Ulpian, *Edict*, Book 24)

307. The praetor extended the scope of this action (relating to surveyors measuring land) even further, and if it is claimed that someone made a false declaration of the measurement of any other thing, this action will apply, such as the false measurement of a house or of corn or of wine.

D 48.10.32.1 (Modestinus, *Penalties*, Book 1)

308. If a vendor or purchaser interferes with weights that have been publicly verified, for corn, wine, or anything else, or with malicious intent commits a fraud, he will be condemned to pay twice the value of the object concerned. And by the decree of the divine Hadrian, it has been laid down that those who falsify weights or measurement should be relegated to an island.

Consensual Contracts: Letting and Hiring Out of Services and Objects

Hiring of specialized services was brought about under a consensual contract, where crucial issues concerned risk, and loss of items entrusted to the person hired, who might be liable for carelessness or incompetence while in charge of an item. According to Gaius (*Institutes* 3.205–6) cleaners and repairers of clothes (who were possibly intended to represent typical cases of hiring services) were responsible for custody (*custodia*), which might also include vigilance against theft, and due care and attention (*diligentia*). However, no one was responsible in the case of force majeure (*vis maior*), major acts of nature such as floods and fires, and significant disruption by passing armies. Contracts of letting and hiring had wide-ranging applications; see pp. 260; 272 for renting land or apartments; for hire of labour see p. 219. In general, it is not clear how far juristic practice in the matter of such contracts was conditioned by a response to social pressures and increasing business activity throughout the empire. For examples of contracts to hire workers, see nos. 371–3, 375–6, 378–80.

Letting and Hire Contracts

P. Fay. 93 = *SP* no. 44 (AD 161)

309. To Castor, son of Antiphilos, of the Sosicosmian tribe and the Althaean deme, from Serapion, son of Artemidoros son of Ptolemaeos, of the Second Goosefarm quarter. I wish to lease from you the perfume and spices business, desiring a fourth part of the half share granted to you in the area of Themistes, excluding markets and festivals, for the present second year only, for a total rent of forty-five silver drachmae, which I will pay each month in equal instalments, if it happens that you give the lease to me. I, Castor, son of Antiphilos, have granted the lease on the above-mentioned terms. Year two of Antoninus and Verus the lords Augusti, Thoth 5.

This perfumery business was probably a government monopoly from which Castor is sub-letting part of the operation.

FIRA 1, no. 104 = Smallwood (1966), no. 439 (Extract)

310. (2) Silver mines must be operated according to the rules which are set out in this law. Prices will be charged in accordance with the liberality of the most revered emperor Hadrian Augustus, so that possession of that part which belongs to the treasury will pass to the person who first pays the price to operate a mine and pays four thousand sesterces to the imperial treasury.

(3) The person who from a total of five mines strikes a vein of silver in one, must keep working the others without a break, as is set out above; if he fails to do this another shall have the right to take over the mine. If a person begins work immediately after the twenty-five days permitted for the accumulation of funds, but then for ten days in succession ceases to work (the mine), another shall have the right to take over the mine. When a mine has been sold by the imperial treasury and then left unworked for six months in succession, another shall have the right to take over the mine, on the basis that when silver is produced from it, half should be kept for the imperial treasury according to the usual rule.

(4) The person working a mine is permitted to have whatever partners he wants, on the basis that each one contributes to expenses in proportion to his role in the partnership. If anyone does not do so, then the man who has incurred the expenses is to post a notice of the expenses incurred by him in the most conspicuous place in the forum for three days in succession and make a declaration by herald to his partners that they should each contribute towards expenses in proportion to their role in the partnership.

Whosoever does not do this and acts in any way fraudulently to avoid paying the expenses and to cheat one or more of his partners, is not to have a part of the mine, and that part is to belong to the partner or partners who have incurred the expenses.

This is part of a series of regulations concerning the imperial silver mines at Vipasca in Lusitania; an imperial procurator supervised their administration, but they were worked by independent contractors. This is analogous to property and farm leases. The contract for operating the mines laid down that by established custom half of any output belonged to the treasury; the person who bid to operate a mine had to buy a licence and pay four thousand sesterces to the treasury, which secured him the other half of the mine. Hadrian's liberality was presumably in establishing the price at four thousand sesterces. However, there were strict rules requiring the mines to be continuously operated. Partnerships were permitted as long as the government was protected against any default of the partners. For the operation of the baths in the vicinity, see no. 234.

D 19.2.13.3, 5, 6 (Ulpian, *Edict*, Book 32)

311. If anyone enters a contract to train a slave and takes him abroad and he is either captured by the enemy or perishes, it is accepted that there is an action on lease, provided that it was not part of the lease agreement that he should take the slave abroad. (5) If a precious stone was given (to a craftsman) in order to be set or engraved, and it was broken, if this occurred because of a fault in the stone, there is no action on lease, but this action would lie if it happened because of the incompetence of the craftsman. (6) If a fuller receives clothes for cleaning and mice nibble them, he is liable under an action on lease because he ought to have taken precautions against this happening.

The Romans had no general rule of liability, though lawyers recognized a variety of circumstances, such as negligence by inaction, or carelessness in taking action, or cases where two or more parties had contributed to the incident that incurred liability. Issues of liability were dealt with in civil courts for a penalty; see pp. 281–7.

D 19.2.30.2 (Alfenus, *Digest, Epitomized by Paul*, Book 3)

312. A man leased out mules to carry a load comprising a definite weight, and when the lessee injured them with a heavier load, asked advice about bringing an action. He (Servius) replied that he could properly sue either under the *lex Aquilia* or on the basis of the contract of lease, but under the *lex Aquilia* he could bring an action only against the man who had driven

the mules at that time, whereas on the basis of the contract of lease, even if someone else had injured the mules, he could properly take action against the lessee.

The *lex Aquilia* was the statute dealing with wrongful damage done to the property of a third party and the resulting liability. Under the *lex Aquilia* the consequence of the action had to be traced directly to the actions of the wrongdoer; if the consequence was too remote, as through the actions of someone delegated by the hirer, no action might be possible under that statute (see further p. 280).

D 19.2.25.7 (Gaius, *Provincial Edict*, Book 10)

313. If someone contracted for the transportation of a column, and it was broken when it was being raised up or transported or repositioned because of his own fault and that of the people whose labour he was using, he is liable for any risk. No fault however is present if everything was done in the way that a most careful man would have done. We recognize that the same point applies if someone has contracted to transport jars, or a wooden beam, and it can be applied in respect of the transport of other objects.

Zimmermann (1996), 399–401 translates the first sentence (*si qua ipsius eorumque, quorum opera uteretur, culpa acciderit*) as 'or that of the people whose labour he was using' and argues that this is an example of vicarious liability where the contractor is liable for the fault of his assistants.

Building

D 19.2.60.4 (Labeo, *Posthumous Works Epitomized by Javolenus*, Book 5)

314. I instructed you to estimate how much you would charge to build a house. You replied that you worked out that it would cost two hundred *aurei*. I leased the job to you for this fixed payment but afterwards discovered that the house could not be completed for less than three hundred *aurei*. I had already given you one hundred *aurei* of which you had spent a part, and I forbade you to carry on with the work. I stated that if you were to continue with the building work, I would sue you on the basis of the contract of lease for the restitution of the remainder of my money.

Building contracts raised particular issues because they tended to involve large sums of money, might extend over a long period, were subject to substantial risk, and potentially involved complicated checks on the quality of the work. A contract of hire for building work meant that the builder was the contractor (*conductor*) and the person who commissioned the work was the hirer or leaser (*locator*). A contract would normally specify the total cost of the building work and often contained a clause establishing the date on which it was to be completed. The full extent of the period set out in the contract had to elapse before the *locator* could sue for default. But it was not essential to set a completion date. A common method was part payment at the beginning of the work with the remainder on completion. But it was also possible to pay by instalments as segments of the building were completed and duly measured to check if they were in accord with the original specification. The contract was a means to resolve in an ordered way potential conflicts of interests; the *locator* wanted work of good quality in line with the architect's plans and completed on time; he also wanted the work to be on budget or at least with only a limited over-spend; the builder wanted to exercise his skill without interference or major changes of plan, to keep the timescale originally agreed, and to obtain his payment (*merces*) promptly. It is possible that the increased volume of building activity in the early empire inspired interest in a more standardized form of building contract in which the concerned parties could establish clear rights and responsibilities. An important area was the assessment (*probatio*) of the completed building, and this was to be carried out on the basis of the judgement of a reasonable man. A builder was liable if faults were found in his work, and he would not receive payment until they were rectified. If the builder failed to complete on time without a reasonable excuse, the *locator* might bring in a second builder. A further issue concerned problems with the building site during construction. The builder was not responsible for natural events like a landslide or flood and could expect extra time if he had to start rebuilding. After the final payment the *locator* was entirely responsible for the building unless the builder had knowingly concealed defects in the work (see also Martin (1989), 136–50).

D 19.2.36 (Florentinus, *Institutes*, Book 7)

315. If a job has been leased out on the basis of its entire completion, it is at the risk of the contractor until it has been approved. But if the contract specifies that it should be paid for according to feet or units of measurement, the contractor is at risk only for the time when the measurement is not completed. In both instances it will be damaging to the lessor's case if he is responsible for preventing the approval or measurement of the work. If, however, the work is destroyed by some superior force before it can be approved, it will be at the risk of the lessor, unless another agreement has been made. For the lessor should not obtain any more than what he would have achieved through his own care and labour.

It was intended that approval of building work should be assessed reasonably, and changes demanded to the original plan by the hirer absolved the contractor from responsibility for non-compliance with the original agreement (*D* 19.2.60.3).

D 45.1.124 (Papinian, *Definitions*, Book 2)

316. 'Do you promise to build an apartment block within two years in that location?' This stipulation does not come into effect before the end of the two years, although the person who made the promise has not built it and there is insufficient time remaining for a building to be constructed. For the provisions of the stipulation, which named a definite date, cannot be changed by something that happens afterwards. And the same holds good in respect of a stipulation in order to secure appearance in court. It is agreed that the stipulation does not come into effect before the appointed day, even if it is clear that there is insufficient time remaining to comply with the terms of the stipulation.

In this case the jurist emphasizes the importance of the terms of the stipulation in the contract, and no action can be taken before the appointed time even if it is clear that the builder is unlikely to keep his part of the agreement.

D 46.3.31 (Ulpian, *Disputes*, Book 7)

317. Among craftsmen there is a great difference in skill and talent and learning and experience. Therefore, if someone has promised to construct a ship, or build an apartment block, or excavate a ditch, and it has been specifically agreed that he should complete this work with his own labour, and then the surety builds it himself or digs the ditch without the agreement of the stipulator, this does not free the person who made the promise from liability.

This text illustrates the use of a surety (a person who promised to underwrite the completion of an action for a third party) for a contract, including building work, and the possibility that, some problem having arisen in the completion of the task, the surety would complete it himself. The jurist is reluctant to permit this since it contradicted the original contract in which the employer arranged to engage the skill of a specific artisan; there was no guarantee that the surety could provide work of the same standard as he might well be intent on keeping down his own expenditure. Therefore, the builder remains liable for the cost of ensuring the completion of the contract at the level of skill previously negotiated. It is up to the individuals contracting for building or other services to draw up and supervise the appropriate legal format. The state offered no direct assistance.

Travel

D 14.2.2 (Paul, *Edict*, Book 34)

318. If cargo was jettisoned because a ship was in difficulties, the owners of the jettisoned goods should sue the captain of the ship on the basis of the

hire contract, if they made a contract for the transport of goods. The captain can sue the others, whose goods were saved, on the basis of his contract so that the loss is shared in proportion. Servius indeed stated that they (those who have lost goods) should sue the captain of the ship on the basis of the contract to ensure that he keeps the goods of the other shippers until they provide their share of the loss. But even if the captain does not retain their goods, he will still have an action against the passengers based on the contract. But what if there are passengers who have no baggage? Plainly it is more convenient to keep baggage if it exists. But if he has not hired the entire ship, he may sue based on the contract, just like the passengers who hired space in the ship. For it is most equitable for there to be a proportional loss for those who through the destruction of the property of others saved their own goods.

This refers to a contract for hiring the means of travel and the issue of liability for those providing the means. The proportional responsibility was to be observed even in the case of those whose cargo had no weight (for the principle of community of risk, see Zimmermann (1996), 407–8). The owners of jettisoned goods had the right to sue the captain if they were legal owners of the goods in question, and if they had established a contract with the captain for the transport of the goods, and if the action of jettisoning the goods was the result of a crisis, which might include a storm; this was one way in which a form of insurance against loss was available in support of trade and commerce. The captain in turn could sue those whose goods had been saved to recover a proportion of the overall loss. An *actio exercitoria* was available against the owner of a ship for the actions of his agent, its captain (see p. 215). In respect of liability in the case of innkeepers (*cauponae*) and keepers of stables (*stabularii*) for any property they had received (*receptum*), they were liable for the actions of their servants or employees; see Crook (1967), 224–7.

D 4.9.1pr-1 (Ulpian, *Edict*, Book 14)

319. The praetor declares: 'If sailors, innkeepers, and owners of stables have received someone's property for safe-keeping, I shall grant an action against them unless they restore it'. This edict is extremely valuable because it is often essential to trust people like this and commit property to their safe keeping. And no one should think that this is a harsh imposition on them, for it is their decision whether they receive someone, and if this provision were not in force, they would have the opportunity of conspiring with thieves against those whom they receive as customers, since even now they do not abstain from this kind of fraud.

Consensual Contracts: Partnerships

FIRA 3, no. 157 (AD 167)

320. A partnership for moneylending was undertaken by Cassius Frontinus and Iulius Alexander from 23 December just past in the consulship of Pudens and Pollio (AD 166), up to 12 April next, on the condition that whatever profit or loss should accrue arising from the business of that partnership, they will accept in equal proportion. Into this partnership Iulius Alexander contributed 500 denarii either in cash or through interest, and Secundus, the slave representative of Cassius Palumbus, contributed 267 denarii on behalf of Frontinus …

In this partnership if anyone is detected practising a fraud with malice aforethought, he must pay one denarius for each *as* and twenty denarii for each denarius. When the period is up, when the debts have been deducted, each partner is to recover the sum set out above, or, if there is a profit, to divide it. Cassius Frontinus made a *stipulatio* for this to be provided, done and arranged, and Iulius Alexander duly responded. Concerning this matter two pairs of tablets have been signed. Furthermore, fifty denarii are owed to Cossa, which he is to receive from the said partners. Carried out at Deusaris, on 28 March, in the consulship of Verus for the third time and Quatratus.

This partnership arrangement in Dacia is supported by *stipulatio* and presumably there was a reciprocal *stipulatio* by Alexander. This seems unnecessary since shares in profits and loss were equal unless another arrangement was specifically stated (see no. 321). However, it is possible that the partners in this case did not have adequate legal advice available and were ignorant of the law, or simply wanted to take no chances.

Gaius, *Institutes* 3.150

321. This point is certain, namely if the partners have made no specific agreement in respect of their shares in profit and loss, their shares in both good and bad outcomes will be equal.

Gaius, *Institutes* 3.148

322. We normally enter a partnership either in relation to our entire fortune or for one particular business undertaking, such as buying or selling slaves.

There was usually a specific agreement in setting up the partnership (*societas*), which in classical law was based on good faith; the partnership agreement by establishing shares in profit and loss would in general facilitate business arrangements. Lawyers debated whether one party could be immune from losses; this was deemed acceptable if he provided exceptional services to the partnership. The partnership lasted as long as the parties remained in agreement, but when one withdrew the partnership was dissolved; if there were more than two members the rest could agree among themselves to continue (Gaius, *Institutes* 3.151; Crook (1967), 230–2; Zimmermann (1996), 454). In terms of economic development, it was problematic that the *societas* did not have a corporate identity or juristic personality allowing it to function as a legal entity distinct from its members (*socii*), though one partner could act as an agent for the other partners. The provision of *peculium* for sons and slaves to act as agents (see p. 216) allowed the wealthy to engage in economic activity and protect themselves against excessive risk (see Kehoe (2011), 145–7).

D 17.2.52.4 (Ulpian, *Edict*, Book 31)

323. Some men entered a partnership for the manufacture of cloaks. One of them having set out to obtain materials fell in with thieves, his money was stolen, his slaves were wounded, and he lost his own property. Iulianus states that this loss was suffered in common, and therefore in an action based on partnership the (other) partner should be responsible for half the loss of the money as well as the other property, which the first partner would not have brought with him had he not set out for the purchase of materials in the name of the partnership. Furthermore, if there were any medical expenses Iulianus very properly agrees that the other partner should accept these in proportion.

D 17.2.59pr (Pomponius, *Sabinus*, Book 12)

324. A partnership is dissolved so totally by the death of one of the partners that we cannot make an initial agreement that an heir can succeed to a position in the partnership. He (Sabinus) says that this is the situation in private partnerships. However, in a tax-collecting partnership, the partnership continues in existence even after the death of a partner, provided that the share of the dead man has been assigned to an heir, so that the partnership too should come to him. This should be worked out in relation to the circumstances of the case.

A special type of partnership was the tax-collecting company, a group of associates (*publicani*) who bid for contracts to collect Roman state taxes of various types.

These were still prevalent in the early empire though gradually the government moved to direct collection. The purchaser of the contract was the *manceps* and he had partners (*socii*) who contributed financially and expected a share of the profits; the company employed a variety of other officials such as *magistri* (business managers). Pledges and guarantees had to be given. It is not clear if these companies unlike most others had some kind of corporate identity (see discussion in Chapter 2, no. 153). At any rate, tax-collecting contracts were usually let to individuals, the contractor remained personally responsible for the contract, and on his death the partners, guarantors, and heirs would be responsible (see Duff (1938), 159–61; Nicolet (1979); Lintott (1993), 90–1). However, a tax-collecting company, unlike other companies, was not dissolved by the death of one of its members.

Consensual Contracts: Mandate

D 17.1.1 (Paul, *Edict*, Book 32)

325. The obligation of mandate exists through the agreement of the contracting parties. Therefore, mandate can be undertaken by messenger, and by letter. Also, whether the phrase written down is 'I ask', or 'I wish', or 'I instruct', or any other expression, it is a mandated action. Furthermore, a mandate can be contracted to be deferred for a time or to be subject to conditions. There is no mandate unless it is gratuitous, for it has its origin in duty and friendship, and payment for a service is the opposite of duty. For when money is involved the issue is more a case of lease or hire.

If two parties willingly agreed that one should act on behalf of the other, this was termed *mandatum* (mandate). This private arrangement, involving no payment, was perhaps most at home in an upper-class social world where the wealthy felt bound by family and class honour to carry out tasks at the request of friends. In this context it would be inappropriate to request a *stipulatio*, and so the need for a separate contract emerged; see Crook (1967), 237; Buckland (1975), 514–21; for a detailed analysis see Zimmermann (1996), 413–30.

Contract *litteris* (by Writing)

Gaius, *Institutes* 3.137

326. Furthermore, in these contracts the parties are liable reciprocally in respect of what each one is obliged in a fair and equitable manner to perform for the other. However, in verbal obligations one party stipulates

and the other promises, while in literary contracts one party imposes an obligation by recording the debit and the other is brought under the obligation.

This form of contract was strict law and very specific, relating only to formal entries in a record of accounts, to facilitate the transfer of an existing debt; it had probably faded out of use before the end of the classical period (see Watson (1991), 57–9). The debtor would need to consent to this contract.

Real Contracts: Delivery of an Object by One Party to Another

Real contracts were initiated when an item was delivered: *mutuum* (loan for consumption, including money), *commodatum* (loan for use), *depositum* (deposit), *pignus* (pledge). In the last three contracts the lender expected the same object to be returned, and the arrangement involved no payment, since originally this was a free-will agreement between relatives or friends or even neighbours. For discussion see Buckland (1975), 462–81; Zimmermann (1996), 188–229.

Gaius, *Institutes* 3.90

327. A real obligation arises by contract, for example by the conveyance of a loan for consumption (*mutuum*). [Conveyance of a loan for consumption] properly takes place in respect of objects that are calculated by weighing, counting, or measuring, such as money, wine, oil, corn, bronze, silver, or gold. We convey these objects by counting, measuring, or weighing, so that they become the property of those receiving them, and in due course not the same objects but others of the same type are returned to us. Hence this is called *mutuum* because the object given to you by me in this way becomes yours having previously been mine.

This contract came into being through the action of handing over objects into the ownership of the borrower with the expectation that they would be used up. With that comes the obligation on the recipient to return an equivalent amount of similar objects. The agreement might name a date and place for payment and the consequence of the contract was to impose on the borrower an obligation to pay up. In the event of non-payment, the lender had an action known as *condictio*, which was applied to a definite sum of money or objects (see Watson (1991), 125–6). If the arrangement involved the lending of money, under the *mutuum* contract no interest could be charged since it provided only for the return of an equivalent sum of money, was gratuitous, and was not a business agreement. However, those parties to the contract could by *stipulatio* make arrangements about interest payments (de Zulueta (1953), 148–50; Zimmermann (1996), 153). In these circumstances the *mutuum* contract could play a role in banking and moneylending (see nos. 328–9). For transfer of ownership of money and its importance for commerce see Johnston (1999), 54–5.

At *D* 45.1.122.1 Scaevola discusses an example of a contract setting up a special loan (*nauticum faenus*), namely a bottomry loan, so that the recipient could purchase a cargo and transport it to sell in another location. The loan would then be paid back from the profits. The security would normally be the cargo (and sometimes also the ship), and so the creditor was undertaking a high-risk venture, since if the ship sank, he lost his money. A slave usually went with the ship to collect the creditor's money when the contracted voyage was completed (see Buckland (1975), 466–7). Since the creditor was offering a kind of insurance for the voyage interest rates were high, beyond the usual rules. See Jones (2006), 180–2. Aubert (2015), 225–6 argues that in the question of insurance and liability in transportation the law struck a balance between customers and people in business.

TPSulp 67 (Camodeca (1999)) (29 August AD 38)

328. I, C. Novius Eunus, have written that I owe Hesychus Evenianus, slave of C. Caesar Augustus Germanicus, 1,130 sesterces, which I have received from him as a loan (*mutuum*) and will repay either to him or to C. Sulpicius Faustus, as soon as he demands them.

Hesychus Evenianus, slave of C. Caesar Augustus Germanicus, stipulated that the 1,130 sesterces noted above are to be duly paid back in good coin, and I, C. Novius Eunus, have promised that I shall do so. Transacted at Puteoli.

Names of five witnesses.

See also Jones (2006), 97–8. In this case the loan in the form of a *mutuum* has been backed up by a *stipulatio*. This raises the question whether the *stipulatio* superseded the *mutuum*, or whether they existed concurrently (see Johnston (1999), 85). The Sulpicius Faustus mentioned as another payee of the loan was a banker in Pueoli among whose records the tablet of the loan was found.

FIRA 3, no. 122

329. Iulius Alexander asked in good faith that sixty good denarii should be handed over on the day that he requested them, Alexander, son of Cariccius, promised in good faith that they would be handed over, and that he had received those sixty denarii mentioned above counted out as a

loan (*mutuum*) and that he owed them. Iulius Alexander asked in good faith that the interest on this principal, at 1 per cent from this day for the next thirty days, should be given to Iulius Alexander or to whom that business shall concern, and Alexander, son of Cariccius, promised in good faith that it would be conveyed. Titius Primitius stated that this was at his risk in respect of the principal written above, which was to be correctly and properly paid along with the interest.

Concluded at Alburnus Maior, 20 October, in the consulship of Rusticus for the second time and Aquilinus (AD 162).

The *stipulatio* between the parties allowed the loan contract to be concluded with provision for interest. A common interest rate was 1 per cent per month or 12 per cent per annum, which seems to have been regarded as a legal maximum, though parts of the empire had different practices in establishing interest. Primitius provided surety for the loan.

P. Lond. 332 = *SP* no. 75 (AD 166)

330. Year seven of Emperor Caesar Marcus Aurelius Antoninus Augustus and Emperor Caesar Lucius Aurelius Verus Augustus, Thoth 13, by means of the bank of Sarapion in the Treasuries district. Didymos, son of Didymos also called Demetrios, of the Sosicosmian tribe and the Althaean deme, and Tesenouphis, son of Tesenouphis, and another Tesenouphis son of Tesenouphis, and Panephremis son of Stotoetis, and Pabous son of Satabous, inform Claudianus also called Serenus son of Musthes, ex-cosmetes, that he has received from those listed above all the amount that they owed to him according to the record of the said bank, which he has handed over to them to be rescinded and cancelled, in respect of one thousand one hundred and twenty-four drachmae, a total of 1,124 drachmae, and that he has no claim lying against them up to the present day. I Serenus, also called Claudianus, received the sum as noted above.

Serenus, apparently an agent of the bank of Serapion, endorses the repayment of a sum loaned through the bank; for banking see pp. 206–14.

D 13.6.5pr (Ulpian, *Edict*, Book 28)

331. If it was agreed that a loan for use (*commodatum*) should be returned at a certain location or time, it forms part of the duty of the judge to take account of the location.

Commodatum, which shares aspects of *mutuum*, was the term applied to fungible material lent out gratuitously for use and return at some later date; in this arrangement ownership did not pass to the borrower and he was liable for the safe-keeping and maintenance of the object, though he was not responsible for the loss if the object was destroyed by an accident over which he had no control. The lender of the object could pursue an *actio commodati* for return of the object or compensation for its misuse; if the borrower believed that he had incurred expenses because of a borrowed object (for example, the medical cost of a sick slave) an action was available to him.

D 13.6.9-10pr (Ulpian, *Edict*, Book 2; *Sabinus*, Book 29)

332. For no one by lending something for use makes it the property of the person to whom he lends it.

In respect of the party who receives an item on loan, it is correct that if he uses that item only for the purpose for which he borrowed it, he is not liable if he caused it to deteriorate but in no respect was to blame for this. But if he was to blame for its deterioration then he will be liable.

D 16.3.1pr (Ulpian, *Edict*, Book 30)

333. A deposit is whatever is given to someone to look after, and the word (*depositum*) is derived from the word to place (*ponere*) while the preposition *de* adds to the meaning, indicating that everything which pertains to the safe-keeping of the item is committed to the good faith of the party who receives it.

Depositum referred to the gratuitous lodging of an item with a third party for safe-keeping. The person who received the item had to return it at the request of the owner. Since the receiver was willingly helping, the depositor could hardly impose a contract demanding return of the item. But an action for the simple value of the deposit was available in respect of its fraudulent non-return, though double damages would be awarded in cases where the deposit had been made as the result of a calamity like an earthquake or shipwreck (see Watson (1991), 127). These three distinct contracts, *mandatum*, *commodatum*, and *depositum*, would all become a contract of hire if payment was promised.

D 16.3.1.45 (Ulpian, *Edict*, Book 30)

334. If I make a deposit with you on the terms that it will be returned after your death, I can pursue an action on deposit against you and against your heir, for I can change my mind and demand the return of the deposit before your death.

D 16.3.1.8 (Ulpian, *Edict*, Book 30)

335. If clothing given to the bath attendant to look after has disappeared and if he received no fee for looking after the clothing, I think that he ought to be liable for an action on deposit (*depositum*), and that he should be responsible only for fraud; but if he did receive a fee then he is liable on the basis of a contract of hire.

Juvenal, *Satires* 13.14–17

336. You are blazing and seething with anger because a friend refused to return your sacred deposit. Can a man of more than sixty really be surprised at this?

P. Oxy. 1039 = *SP* no. 71 (AD 210)

337. Apollonios, son of Serapion, whose mother is Sintheos, from the community of Oxyrhynchus, to Theon, son of ... also called Chaeremon, whose mother is Apia, from the same community, greetings. I acknowledge that I have received by hand from you on deposit 600 silver drachmae of imperial coinage, which I will return to you whenever you wish without any delay or sophistry, otherwise I will forfeit them to you in accordance with the law relating to deposits, and you will have the right of execution on me and all my property. This deed of deposit which has been set out in duplicate by me, Apollonios, is valid wherever it should be produced and whosoever produces it on your behalf. Year nineteen of Emperors and Caesars Lucius Septimius Severus Pertinax Arabicus Adiabenicus Parthicus Britannicus Maximus and Marcus Aurelius Antoninus and Publius Septimius Geta, Britannici Maximi Pii Augusti, Phaophi 13.

For *depositum* with interest and its role in banking see pp. 208–9.

Lewis (1989), no. 17 (AD 128)

338. In the consulship of Publius Metilius Nepos for the second time and Marcus Annius Libo, ten days before the kalends of March (21 February), and on the calculation of the new province of Arabia, year twenty-two, on the sixth of the month Dystros, in Maoza of the district of Zoara, Judah, son of Eleazar also known as Khthousion, from En-gedi, acknowledged of his own free will and agreement to Babatha, daughter of Simon, his own

wife, with her guardian, Jacob son of Jesus, being present for the purpose of this business, all of them being resident here, that Judah has received from her on account of a deposit 300 silver denarii of proper legal coinage, on the basis that he retains and owes them on deposit until such time as Babatha may decide, or whoever is acting through her or on her behalf, to request the return of the above-mentioned denarii of the deposit from the said Judah. And if Judah does not promptly return this sum when requested, in accordance with the rules of deposit he shall be liable to repay double the deposit with damages, and he shall be open to a charge of illegal behaviour in this business, since Babatha or anyone who brings forward this contract on her behalf shall have the right of execution on Judah and all his property everywhere, both that which he possesses now and that which he may also validly acquire, by whatever method the person conducting the execution may decide to carry it out. In good faith the question was formally put, and in reply it was agreed that the business in this way was properly done.

(Confirmation by Judah in Aramaic; witnesses)

This is a double document written both on the outer and inner side of the papyrus. As we see also from Egyptian papyri, people used the contract of deposit in Roman form as a convenient means for a variety of transactions (Lewis, p. 35); in this case the money involved seems to be a loan, which would normally be for a fixed term; here the date is left open in the form of a deposit. Babatha's guardian would normally be her husband, but Judah cannot act in this case as he is party to the agreement. For Babatha see also nos. 211; 255–7. Double penalty may have been the practice under the Nabatean kings; see Lewis, p. 40.

D 20.4.21.1 (Scaevola, *Digest*, Book 27)

339. A loan was made to a dealer in marble on the basis of a pledge (*pignus*) of the blocks of marble, the vendors of which had been paid by the money provided by the creditor. The debtor (that is, the marble-dealer), who was also the lessee of granaries belonging to the emperor, had not paid the rent of these for several years, and the procurator who was charged with recovering this money took it within his remit to sell the blocks of marble. The question was asked whether the creditor could retain them in accordance with the pledge. The reply was that on the basis of the information supplied he could (retain them).

Pignus was a consensual contract where a debtor transferred possession but not ownership of an object to a creditor (for possession and ownership, see p. 234). It was returned when the debt was paid. The debtor no longer had use of the property, but as he retained ownership, he could in theory recover the item if the creditor disposed of it. In practice the debtor would not pledge property that he needed to make ends meet, for example to till his land. *Pignus* (along with *fiducia* and *hypotheca*) related to the question of security for debt and the practice of banking in the Roman world, and to some extent *pignus* offered protection to the debtor against a potentially dishonest lender (for banking see pp. 206–14). The passage shows the working of the pledge and an aspect of moneylending; the marble-dealer had borrowed the money to purchase marble blocks in the expectation of selling them on at profit before his debt became due; he could therefore trade in marble without using his own money. The procurator was deputed to recover monies owing to the emperor, but Scaevola upheld the validity of the original pledge by which the marble blocks guaranteed the creditor's loan.

D 13.7.8pr (Pomponius, *Sabinus*, Book 35)

340. If I incur essential expenses in looking after a slave or a farm which I received as a pledge, I shall be entitled not only to retain the pledge but also to a counteraction on pledge. Suppose for example that I spent money on doctors when a slave was ill and he then died, or that I propped up or repaired a building and it then burned down, and I now have nothing which I could have retained.

An action was available for the recovery of necessary expenses incurred in looking after the object that had been pledged, especially if it had ceased to function as a pledge.

Banking: Security, Debt, and Insolvency

Banks

In the Roman world, both in society and in business, loans were important. The tendency of the rich to base their wealth in land ownership might make it difficult to raise money quickly, apart from a loan. Lending money and other services associated with banking were at first provided by relatively high-status financiers, though from the second century BC an increasing role was played by *argentarii*, who offered services in money-changing, assaying of coins, taking deposits, and advancing credit, especially for buyers at auction sales. The assaying procedure verified the value and quality of coins; money-changing was necessary in the imperial period because various Greek cities minted their own coins. Another group, *nummularii*, appeared in the early first century who also acted as money-changers and assayers, took deposits, and lent money. It can be argued that both *argentarii* and *nummularii* effectively played the role of bankers

(Andreau (1987); (1999), 30–40). For example, the *argentarius* would typically receive money in an unsealed deposit, keep it, or lend it to others. Or he could invest the money, provided that he returned an equivalent amount to the depositor. No interest could be charged for keeping the deposit for in that case it would be classed as a loan. However, the *argentarius* and depositor could contract for payment of interest through *stipulatio* (see nos. 341–5). The banker was required to keep an account (*ratio*) for each client. The bankers were in the main small-time businessmen, often freedmen, operating from a table in a shop; they might have several assistants of lower status, for example, slave *institores* who acted as business agents (Andreau (1999), 66). It is unlikely that most Roman bankers, who dealt entirely with private clients on an individual basis, were aiming in any coherent way to provide a specially created route to further economic investment. Each deal was an individuality suiting the wishes and circumstances of certain parties, and there was little distinction between loans for consumption and loans for production, that is, for economic investment. The praetor's edict set out the rules of private law that could be applied to financial transactions, but there is no sign that the law was intended to encourage or facilitate management of financial matters by the government. Nevertheless, at Pompeii the Sulpicii bankers looked after documents and business contracts, acted as creditors, offering credit for business activities in the port of Puteoli, provided security for loans, and invested money for others including senators. Indeed Harris (2006) has argued strongly for the importance of credit in Roman finance, and that the role of coined money has been overestimated. Von Reden (2012, especially 279–83) discussing credit and banking argues that bankers made legal principle adjust to their financial reality; for example, bankers could make a payment on a client's behalf even if the client's account did not show sufficient funds.

CIL 6.9182 = *ILS* 7502

341. P. Caucilius Salvius, freedman of Publius, P. Caucilius, [freedman of Publius] Helles ..., bankers from the wine market, by decision of Lysimachus and Callippus, freedmen.

TPSulp 60 (Camodeca (1999)) (20 March AD 43)

342. Tablets of Titinia A[ntracis]

Paid out.

To Euplia, the Melian, daughter of Theodoros, on the authority of her tutor Epichares, son of Aphrodisios, the Athenian; she sought and received [1,600 sesterces] counted out from the strongbox in the house.

Received.

From the strongbox [1,600 sesterces].

Those 1,600 sesterces [which are written out above, when Titinia Antracis] asked the question, Epichares, son of Aphrodisios, the Athenian, promised with good faith on behalf of [Euplia], the Melian, daughter of Theodoros, to Ti[tinia Antracis].

Executed at Puteoli on the thirteenth day before the kalends of April in the consulship of Sex. Palpellius Hister and L. Pedanius Secundus.

This tablet from the household accounts refers to a loan made by one woman (Titinia) to another (Euplia); the process involved the actual counting out and handing over of the money followed by a *fideiussio* (a version of *stipulatio* used by non-citizens) indicating formal acceptance of the loan and an obligation to repay by Euplia and her tutor; see Meyer (2004), 137–8; see also *SP* 70.

FIRA 3, no. 123 (AD 162)

343. Anduenna, wife of Bato, put the question in good faith if, in respect of 140 denarii, capital and interest thereon from that day at a rate of 12 per cent per year as long as she does not withdraw it, she had handed over the money properly and correctly. Iulius Alexander in good faith gave his promise that the money had been handed over, which money he will return to her on the day she requests it, along with the interest noted above. The said Anduenna put the question in good faith if the capital subject to appropriate interest had been handed over correctly, and Iulius Alexander gave his promise in good faith that they have been handed over.

Executed at Deusara, on 20 June, in the consulship of Rusticus for the second time and Aquilinus.

140 denarii to Iulius Alexander.

This refers to a deposit of money lodged by Anduenna with Iulius Alexander, who acts as a banker. The *stipulatio* provided for the payment of interest on the deposit.

D 16.3.28 (Scaevola, *Replies*, Book 1)

344. Quintus Caecilius Candidus wrote a letter to Paccius Rogatianus in the following terms: 'Caecilius Candidus to his friend Paccius Rogatianus, greetings. I confirm by this letter that the twenty-five sesterces that you

wished to be deposited with me have been entered in my accounts. I shall make sure that as soon as possible they will not lie idle, that is, I shall take care that you will receive interest from them'. The question was asked whether on the basis of this letter interest can also be demanded. I replied that on the basis of a good faith action interest was due whether the party stored the money or used it in his own business.

The point is that the letter served as an agreement to pay interest on a deposit.

P. Oxy. 507 = *SP* no. 62 (AD 169)

345. Harmiusis … To Diogenes, son of Serapion … ex-*agoranomos*, current gymnasiarch of the community of Oxyrhynchus, priest of Fortune, greetings. I acknowledge that I have received from you a sum of 260 silver drachmae, to which nothing has been added, subject to interest of one drachma per mina for each month, starting from the current month of Pharmouthi. I will pay back the principal with the interest on Phamenoth 30 of the coming year ten of Aurelius Antoninus Caesar the lord, without delay, and if I do not pay I shall forfeit to you the sum increased by one half, with the same interest for the time over the limit at one drachma per mina each month, and you shall have the right of execution on me and all my property. I have expended the above-mentioned 260 drachmae on the purchase of hay, which is to be stored in the camel-yard of Similis in the community of Oxyrhynchus, on which I have taken a lease; it will not be permitted for me to remove or sell or pledge this hay until I repay to you the principal and interest, as it is mortgaged to you. And if any mishap occurs to this hay, no loss shall accrue to you, since the money along with all the interest is guaranteed to be entirely without risk of any kind. This agreement, written in duplicate, is valid wherever it should be produced. Year nine of Emperor Caesar Marcus Aurelius Antoninus Augustus Armeniacus Medicus Parthicus Maximus, Pharmouthi.

The sum of money borrowed was used to purchase hay, which was to be stored and acted as a surety for the creditor against the non-payment of the debt. The debtor presumably wished to purchase the hay at an attractive price for a future project.

CJ 4.25.3 (AD 230)

346. Emperor Alexander Augustus to Marcia: An *actio institoria* will be available to you against the party by whom, as you allege, a slave was appointed in charge of his banking house, provided that it can be proved that in respect of that business which the slave was conducting, money was deposited (with him) and not returned.

The *institor* was the manager of a business appointed by its owner; an *actio institoria* was available against the owner for actions taken by his manager. For agency see p. 214.

D 16.3.7.2 (Ulpian, *Edict*, Book 30)

347. Whenever bankers become bankrupt, normally account is taken of depositors first, that is, those who have made deposits of money with them, but not those who deposited money with the bankers for interest, or who invested the money co-operating with the bankers, or who left money for the bankers to use. And if the bankers' goods are sold up, account is taken of the depositors before privileged creditors, provided that those involved did not subsequently receive interest payments, as they will be held to have renounced their deposits.

Simple money deposits with bankers had priority if the bank failed. In the case of those who deposited their money for interest it was no longer a contract for deposit, since a *depositum* was gratuitous.

Security for Loans

Various forms of security facilitated the process of lending, and the law's intervention came eventually to protect both the creditor and debtor. In this area the Romans preferred personal security and there were various methods of achieving this:

Pignus – see p. 206.

Fiducia – when the debtor offered an item (*res mancipi*) as security for a loan, the ownership of the item passed to the creditor by mancipation (conveyance of ownership; see p. 233), though he might allow the debtor to keep it and make use of it (for example, it might help to pay off debt); but the debtor could not use it as collateral for raising further loans. This action included a pact of *fiducia* involving a pledge that the creditor would re-convey the item when the debt was paid.

Hypotheca – the item offered as security remained in the possession and ownership of the debtor and he could make use of it or pledge it to raise further funds. If he failed to pay the debt it could be sold up by the creditor.

The problem of obtaining a loan could also be addressed by having a third party offer himself as surety; debtor and surety then became equally liable for the debt. Some sureties were linked to the *stipulatio* procedure, so the *sponsor* or *fideipromissor* would support the formal promise made by the debtor. By the early first century AD the *fideiussor* had emerged as a surety for various kinds of contracts, deals, and sales. There are problems about how this worked out in practice. It is likely that if the creditor brought an action against the debtor for recovery of the loan, the sureties were released from their obligation. Another option was for the creditor to sue the sureties first, though it is not clear if such a suit, while implying the debtor's insolvency, would release him from obligation. Among upper-class parties a relevant factor would be reputation, in that both debtors and sureties would be reluctant to impair their social standing by defaulting on a debt (Crook (1967), 246–8).

Tabulae Herculanenses 65 (Arangio-Ruiz and Pugliese Carratelli (1954), 64)

348. M. Nonnius Fuscus swore by Jupiter and the spirits of the gods and the spirit of Nero Claudius Caesar Augustus that the said slave woman Nais is his and is owned by him, and that he possesses her and does not own her jointly with anyone else and that she is not pledged publicly or privately. Then M. Cominius Primus accepted the said slave woman Nais through mancipation for one sesterce through a process of *fiducia* for a debt of six hundred sesterces. Balance-holder was T. Blaesius Saturninus.

Before Nais can be offered as security for a debt, her owner Fuscus must swear that she has not been pledged to another party. The balance-holder was the person who held the scales as if to weigh the money at a nominal transaction.

Lewis (1989), no. 11 (AD 124)

349. In the consulship of Marcus Acilius Glabrio and Torquatus Tebanianus, on 6 May, in En-gedi, village of lord Caesar, Judah, son of Elazar Khthousion, Engedian, to Magonius Valens, centurion of *Cohors I Miliaria Thracum*, greetings. I acknowledge that I have received and owe to you in a loan sixty denarii of Tyrian silver, which amount to fifteen staters, on hypothec of the courtyard in En-gedi which belongs to my father, Elazar Khthousion, of which I have from the said Elazar authorization to hypothecate and to lease out, the neighbours of this courtyard being, on the east the camp, and Jesus, son of Mandron, on the west the camp, and the factory of the said Elazar, my father, on the south a market, and Simon, son of Matthew, on the north a street, and the headquarters of the camp;

this money I will repay to you on 1 January in the same year during the said consulship, and the interest of the said money I will convey to you each month at the rate of one denarius per hundred denarii per month. If I do not repay you on the specified final date as written above, you will have the right to acquire, employ, sell, and administer this hypothec without any opposition(?), and the right of execution both on me and on all the possessions everywhere of my father Elazar, both those which we have obtained and those which we may additionally obtain, will be open both to you and to your representative, and to every other person who legally produces this document through you or for you, provided that they are acting validly, in whatever manner the one conducting the business chooses, with the lease which I hereby(?) leased to you remaining valid.

Translation. I, Judah, son of Elazar Khthousion … have hypothecated according to the terms written above … It was written by Justinus.

(On the back are the names of seven witnesses)

This is a double document written both on the outer and inner side of the papyrus; it served as the borrower's copy in Greek of the transaction; the original which he signed in Aramaic was retained by the lender. The Judah mentioned was Babatha's second husband (see no. 255), and he had borrowed sixty denarii from a centurion for a period of slightly less than eight months. As security for the loan he uses a courtyard belonging to his father but entrusted to him to use at his discretion. The amount of the loan was originally written as forty denarii, which was erased and sixty written in above. This may be a simple mistake, but Lewis (p. 41) speculates that Judah was perhaps forced by the greedy centurion to accept only forty denarii while contracting to pay interest on sixty. Judah did repay the loan, as he is found in possession of the courtyard in AD 128 (Lewis (1989), no. 19).

D 16.1.1 (Paul, *Edict*, Book 30)

350. The decree of the senate called the Velleianum very comprehensively provided that women should not offer surety for anyone. For just as by custom the undertaking of civil duties is closed to women, and many of these actions are invalid through the operation of law, it is even more necessary that they should be deprived of that action through which not only their work and simple employment are involved, but also a risk to the family property. It seemed reasonable therefore to assist women in this way, so that an action should be granted against the original debtor, or against the person who had made a woman liable on

his behalf; for in fact this party, rather than the creditor, led the woman astray.

Legislation by Augustus and Claudius had prevented women from giving security on behalf of their husbands, presumably guarding against exploitation of wives' property. The *Senatus Consultum Velleianum* of the mid first century (for the text see *D* 16.1.2.1) aimed to prevent women from offering security for the debts of other people. In fact, the decree did not actually prohibit women from standing surety; it encouraged a magistrate to review carefully claims of creditors against female guarantors and permit the woman to lodge an *exceptio* if he thought that she had genuinely been misled by her inexperience in legal and financial matters; discussion in Gardner (1993), 97–107; Grubbs (2002), 55–8. Therefore, a creditor might be able to recover a surety if he could demonstrate to the praetor that the woman was experienced in business and aware of the situation. The purpose of the decree was probably to prevent the dissipation of family property by unwise guarantees.

The Defaulting or Insolvent Debtor

Gaius, *Institutes* 3.78

351. The estates of the living are sold if they abscond with fraudulent intent and are not defended in their absence, or if they cede their estates under the Iulian statute, or if, after suffering judgement, the period granted to them for paying the money, partly through the law of the Twelve Tables and partly through the praetor's edict, has elapsed.

This refers to *emptio bonorum*, which involved selling up or auctioning off the debtor's entire property (not just what was required for the debt). The whole procedure was embarrassing for the debtor and was partly aimed at punishing him; he was declared *infamis* (see p. 59). An alternative was the *cessio bonorum*.

D 42.3.3 (Ulpian, *Edict*, Book 58)

352. The man who has ceded his property in bankruptcy (*cessio bonorum*) is not deprived of his property before its sale. Therefore, if he is ready to present a defence his property will not be put up for sale.

This process was introduced by Julius Caesar or Augustus and made life rather easier for the debtor, perhaps reflecting difficult times for the upper classes in the aftermath of the civil wars. Although the debtor still lost control of his property he was not rendered *infamis*. At some stage a further concession was made specifically to spare the embarrassment of the upper classes, with the result that only certain parts of their property could be taken as required to meet the debt.

D 27.10.5 (Gaius, *Provincial Edict*, Book 9)

353. By decree of the senate a curator is established when a person of distinction, either a senator or his wife, is in the position that their property must be sold. For the curator is established, either by the praetor or in the provinces by the governor, for the purpose of selling off their property, so that from their property as much as possible is properly paid to the creditors.

Agency

It is a normal part of business for a person to act on behalf of another, with the result that items are acquired or a contract agreed. For example, if X, acting on behalf of Y, deals with Z, can this produce a binding contract between Y and Z? This was not possible in Roman practice, and a man could not act as a 'conduit-pipe' between two other men (Crook (1967), 241). Therefore, the idea that an agent could take on a contract with a third party on behalf of his principal, and so create obligations between principal and the third party in which the agent had no part, did not develop in Roman law. The guiding ideology was that obligations were personally binding and usually contracted in a face-to-face meeting. However, various exceptions allowed a form of agency transaction and facilitated business arrangements. The hierarchical structure of the Roman family was important, with sons (*filii familias*) still under the legal power of their father, and slaves, and to some extent freedmen, under the direction of their owner or patron; such people could engage in activities that promoted the interests of the principals. However, the problem was that a third party would be unwilling to deal with either the son or the slave of the principal, because the *pater familias* would not be liable under any such contract. A slave had no *locus standi* to appear in court and could not be sued personally. It is difficult to estimate how restrictive this was in business dealings, and in any case the Romans developed a series of practical legal remedies based on the *peculium*, which was a (revocable) grant of property (money, land, movables) to a son or slave over whom the father or owner had legal control. In commerce the development of this concept of indirect agency, which also applied to collective organizations, is important (see Aubert (1994), especially 40–116; Johnston (1998), 55–7; Kehoe (2015), 244–8). For the complexity of Roman business management in the Mediterranean world, see Harris (2006).

The recipient of *peculium* could administer this fund as if it were his own, and a third party involved in business dealings could then sue the father of a *filius familias* or owner of a slave as being liable for their actions. In this way a son or slave acted as a means for the principal to conduct business at a distance. Presumably this happened more often in the case of slaves since they were more numerous. The praetor could grant an *actio de peculio* to the creditor for recovery of claims up to the amount of the *peculium*. This was usually applied if the father or owner did not know or claimed not to know what his son or a slave was doing. If he did know then an *actio tributoria* (administered by the praetor) was available, though liability was limited by the proportion of the *peculium* used in the business in question. This produced a kind of compromise in that in many cases the liability of a father or slave-owner was restricted; this is not surprising since in law he owned all the property. For the creditor a difficulty was the vague definition of the principal's intentions (*voluntas*) in respect of his business dealings. Furthermore, in seeking to recover his loss he would have to obtain an accurate analysis of the resources in the *peculium*, from which the owner might be tempted to transfer money. It was of some assistance in this that accounts relating to the *peculium* were kept separately from the rest of the owner's property.

However, if the owner of a business had specifically instructed someone, a *filius familias* or a slave or free person, to carry on certain related activities then he was subject to unlimited liability, and the praetor could make available other actions that permitted a creditor to sue the principal rather than the person representing him with whom he had dealt directly. One action applied specifically to shipping contracts (*actio exercitoria*) and permitted claims against the owner of the ship for the actions of its captain (see no. 318). The *actio institoria* related more generally to agency and allowed a third party to sue the principal for actions done by his agent (*institor*) in the business that he had deputed him to transact (for the legal issues of agency see nos. 359–65). In assessing the legal process, the degree of involvement by the principal in the business was important, and the terms of the agreement by which he had appointed an *institor*. By extending this concept of indirect agency imperial jurists helped to remove restrictions on some types of commercial activity. The *institor* appears frequently in legal texts operating as an agent for another party; he could be slave, freedman, or freeborn, and would often be in charge of a shop or tavern or other business. For the operation of the *peculium* see Johnston (2002); Gamauf (2009); (2016), 389–91; for the economic significance, see Kirschenbaum (1987). For agency and the role of freedmen as agents in business, see Crook

(1967), 189–92; Treggiari (1980), 54–6; Johnston (1998), 58–65; (1999), 101–5; Mouritsen (2011), 206–47; Holleran (2012), 32; 44–5. See also Kehoe (2012a), 207–10 for the development of remedies offering protection for people engaging in contracts with agents, such as freedmen, representing principals.

Gaius, *Institutes* 2.95

354. This is what is meant by the common saying that we can acquire nothing through an extraneous person.

D 15.1.5.4 (Ulpian, *Edict*, Book 29)

355. Tubero, as cited by Celsus in book 6 of the *digesta*, defines '*peculium*' as whatever a slave with his master's permission keeps separately from the master's accounts, having deducted anything owed to the master.

D 15.1.21pr (Ulpian, *Edict*, Book 29)

356. The praetor was entirely right to attribute to the *peculium* the assets which the owner had fraudulently prevented from being in it. We must consider it fraud if the owner removed the *peculium*, but it is also fraud, as Mela writes, if he allows the (slave) to complicate the *peculium* to the detriment of the interests of the creditors. Furthermore, if someone suspects that he is about to be sued and alienates the *peculium* to somebody else, he is guilty of fraud. But if he pays a creditor, I have no doubt that in this case he is not liable, since the money is being paid to a creditor and creditors are entitled to be vigilant in their own interests.

Clearly those who tried to sue a *pater familias* or slave-owner for the *peculium* might encounter clever though dishonest countermoves, such as obscuring the amount of the *peculium*, transferring monies from it surreptitiously, or creating a complicated arrangement of delegated agents all operating with part of the original *peculium*. For the possible business complications of a slave operating through several under-slaves (*vicarii*) see *D* 15.1.17; also, Gamauf (2009).

In the reign of Vespasian there was a notorious case where a son had conspired to murder his father in order to inherit his estate and pay off his creditors. The senatorial decree (*senatus consultum Macedonianum*) forbade loans to a son who was under his father's power; a creditor could not recover from the father money lent to his son, even after the father's death. However, in terms of business dealings this was less restrictive than it at first seems, since it did not apply where the *pater familias* had clearly arranged for his son to represent him in business using his *peculium*.

D 14.6.1pr (Ulpian, *Edict*, Book 29)

357. The text of the *senatus consultum Macedonianum* is as follows: 'Since among the other incentives to crime with which nature had endowed him, Macedo had contracted debts, and since the person who lends money under doubtful security (to say no more) often provides material for wrongdoing to those of bad character, it has been resolved that no action or claim should be granted to the person who has lent money to a *filius familias*, even after the death of the father in whose power he was, so that aggressive moneylenders will realize that in no case may the debt of a *filius familias* be recovered by waiting for the death of the father'.

D 14.5.1 (Gaius, *Provincial Edict*, Book 9)

358. The governor makes every effort to ensure that the person who has contracted with someone who is under the power of another, even if the other actions mentioned do not apply, such as those related to the conduct of a ship's captain, or agency, or a praetorian action, may nevertheless recover what belongs to him, in as far as circumstances permit this fairly and equitably. If the business was conducted on the instructions of the person in whose power the agent was, an action will be offered for the whole amount. If it was not done under his instructions, but nevertheless the business was to his advantage, he (the governor) will begin an action up to the extent of that advantage. But, if neither of these applies, then he initiates an action on the *peculium*.

Gaius argued that the *actio exercitoria* or *institoria* (see p. 215) was more effective than an action on the *peculium* since in that action the plaintiff would have the trouble of proving that the person with whom he had made a contract possessed *peculium* and that his claim could be satisfied out of it (*Institutes* 4.74).

D 14.3.1 (Ulpian, *Edict*, Book 28)

359. It seemed equitable to the praetor that since we gain advantage from the actions of agents that we should also be bound by and liable to be sued on the contracts they make.

D 14.3.3 (Ulpian, *Edict*, Book 28)

360. An agent is so-called because he is responsible for the conduct of business, and there is not much difference whether he is in charge of a shop or any other kind of business.

D 14.3.7.1 (Ulpian, *Edict*, Book 28)

361. It is of little matter who the agent (*institor*) is, male or female, free man, or slave, one owned by you or by another. Also, it does not matter who placed (the agent) in charge; for if a woman placed him in charge, she will be liable for an action on the agent, on the analogy of an action for the conduct of a ship's captain; and if a woman has been placed in charge she will be liable. Furthermore, if a daughter in paternal control or a slave girl is put in charge the action for the conduct of the manager will apply.

D 14.3.5.3–7 (Ulpian, *Edict*, Book 28)

362. If someone appointed a slave to have charge of his banking business, he will be liable on his account. And it is accepted that those to whom clothes-dealers and linen-sellers give clothing to take round and sell should also be described as agents, though we commonly call them pedlars. Also, it is appropriate to call muleteers agents, and those placed in charge of a fuller's or tailor's business. And those in charge of a stable must also be considered agents. Furthermore, Labeo states that if a shopkeeper dispatched his slave to obtain merchandise and send it to him, he must be considered as an agent.

D 14.3.5.2 (Ulpian, *Edict*, Book 28)

363. Labeo declared that if someone put an agent in charge of lending money, administering a farm, engaging in commercial activities, and undertaking contracts, he should be liable to the full.

D 14.3.5.9 (Ulpian, *Edict*, Book 28)

364. Labeo declares: if a baker normally sent his slave to a particular place to sell bread and he received money in advance for supplying someone with bread on a daily basis, and then became insolvent, there is no doubt that the baker should be liable if he permitted money to be given to him on this basis.

D 3.5.1 (Ulpian, *Edict*, Book 10)

365. This edict is necessary since it deals with a matter of great benefit for those who are absent, so that they do not suffer loss of possession, or the selling up of their property, or the alienation of a pledged item, or an action for incurring a penalty, and unjustly lose their property through being undefended.

In addition to the actions of agents, it was possible for a friend or neighbour to act unofficially on someone's behalf without their knowledge or express permission. This could serve a useful social purpose in preventing loss of or damage to property or the infringement of the rights of an absent party. Originally this arose from upper-class ideology that a man should help another man of the same social class who was facing an unexpected problem, although there was no legal obligation to do so. The praetor therefore made available an action on transacted business (*actio negotiorum gestorum*), which protected those whose business had been transacted from incompetence, or duplicity, or unreasonable profit-taking by their friend, and also offered reimbursement for those who had legitimately expended funds on protecting the interests of an absent party.

D 3.5.10 (11) (Pomponius, *Quintus Mucius*, 21)

366. If you transact the business of someone who is absent and unaware that you are doing this, you must answer for both negligence and fraud. But Proculus held that you ought sometimes to be liable for an accident, for instance if, acting in his name, you carry on new business which the absent person did not normally transact, for example, by buying up recently imported slaves or entering some business venture. For if any loss results from that, it is your responsibility, while any profit falls to the absent party. But if in some dealings a profit is made, while on others a loss, the absent party ought to weigh the profit against the loss.

The Labour Market

Much labour in Rome was dependent, that is, supplied by people who were dependent on the employer, like his children or slaves. Also, there was increasing employment of the labour of freedmen, who might act as a general agent (procurator) or acquire rights on the patron's behalf (see Johnston (1999), 106; Crook (1967), 237–9; Mouritsen (2011), 216–20). However, there is good reason to think that there was a significant need for independent freemen as unskilled workers in Rome, to labour in tasks for which slaves were unsuitable because they were seasonal or short-term, in which case it would not be profitable to provide keep for slaves (Brunt (1974), 87–91; (1980), especially 88–96). There is very limited evidence in the legal writers for litigation by persons who were in paid employment, or for actions involving the hire of freemen, but that is not necessarily surprising since it would not be worth suing humble men who had few resources; it would be more effective simply not to pay them if their work was in some way deficient. By contrast, there is much more about work done by freedmen or slaves; the former were often men of some wealth who could defend their rights, while in the case of slaves their owners could be sued as already described. For a useful summary of the range of jobs in Rome, see Treggiari (1980), 56; Joshel (1992), 173–82; according to this study of occupational inscriptions from Rome, only 2.9 per cent are certainly freeborn and 22.6 per cent are uncertain but perhaps freeborn (Joshel (1992), 46–7; 127). For freedmen, see Treggiari (1969), 74–81; Joshel (1992), 56–61; Mouritsen (2011), 206–47. For a summary of the labour market see Temin (2013), 114–38. In respect of terminology, *operarius* denoted a day-labourer and *operae* workdays. The person promising to hire another's services is the *conductor operis*, the person hiring out his labour is the *locator operis*. For building contracts, see p. 193.

Paul, *Sententiae* 2.18.1

367. A free man, who has his own status under his control, can make it worse or better; and so, he hires out his services for work both day and night.

Paul probably means not that the labour of a free man was *necessarily* degrading but that in certain circumstances a free man might feel compelled to take on work under conditions that were more suited to slaves.

Varro, *De Re Rustica* 1.17.2

368. All land is cultivated by men, slaves, or free men, or both. Free men are either those who till their land themselves, as do many poor people with their own children, or hired workers, when more demanding work such as the vintage and the cutting of hay is carried out by hiring free men.

D 45.1.137.3 (Venuleius, *Stipulations*, Book 1)

369. The man who has contracted to build an apartment block ought not to hurry, assembling builders from all sides and employing a huge number

of labourers, but nor should he be satisfied with one or two; rather he should have a measured approach in accordance with the sensible policy of a careful builder, taking account of the time and location.

The implication in this case is that the builder in order to complete a large commission might hire a large number of labourers or builders lacking desirable skills, whereas in normal circumstances he retained only a few permanent employees.

D 19.2.38 (Paul, *Rules*, Single Book)

370. The man who has hired out his labour should receive his wages for the entire period if it was not his fault that he could not provide his labour. In the same way advocates, if it was not their fault that they could not plead a case, are not obliged to return their fees.

P. Cornell 9 = *SP* 20 (AD 206)

371. To Isidora, castanet-dancer, from Artemisia of the village of Philadelphia. I wish to engage you with two other castanet dancers to give a performance at the festival in my house for six days beginning on the twenty-fourth of the month Pauni on the old reckoning, and you are to receive in payment thirty-six drachmae per day, and for the entire number of days four *artabai* of barley and twenty pairs of loaves of bread. In addition, whatever clothing or gold ornaments you bring down, we will keep these safely, and we will provide you with two donkeys when you travel down to us, and the same number when you return. Year fourteen of Lucius Septimius Severus Pius Pertinax and Marcus Aurelius Antoninus Pius, Augusti, and Publius Septimius Geta Caesar Augustus, Pauni 16.

This contract of hire of free labour precisely defines payment, maintenance, and the arrangements for travel for the dancers. Papyri from Egypt show a wide range of contracts for the hire of various kinds of service, labour, or training; see pp. 190–5.

FIRA 3, no. 150a (AD 164)

372. In the consulship of Macrinus and Celsus, 20 May, I, Flavius Secundinus at the request of Memmius Asclepius because he said that he was illiterate, have written down the fact that he stated himself to have hired out, and has indeed hired out, his labour as a gold miner to Aurelius Adiutor, from this day to 13 November next, for seventy denarii and his

food. He is to be entitled to receive his wages in stages. He is to provide his labour as able-bodied and fit to the employer mentioned above. But if he wishes to resile or cease working against the wishes of the employer, he is to pay five sesterces for every day, deducted from his total wages. But if a flood prevents (work) he is to calculate in proportion. If, when the period of work has been completed, the employer delays in paying the wages, he will be liable to the same penalty after three days' grace.

Enacted at Immenosum Maior.

In this contract for labour in Dacia, since the miner was illiterate it is doubtful if he understood fully his rights under the contract. He could seek legal advice, but that was likely to be beyond his means, and his rights therefore would be difficult to enforce. Although there was a general ruling on labour rights when work was interrupted by outside circumstances (no. 370), it is likely this could be offset by a specific agreement negotiated by the parties.

D 19.2.19.9 (Ulpian, *Edict*, Book 32)

373. When a certain scribe had hired out his services and then the man who hired him died, the Emperor Antoninus and the divine Severus replied by rescript to the petition of the scribe in the following terms: 'Since you argue that it was not your fault that you did not provide the services leased to Antonius Aquila, and if in the same year you did not receive payment from anyone else, it is equitable that the good faith of the contract should be honoured'.

Petronius, *Satyricon* 117

374. The hired man (*mercennarius*), Corax, a constant complainer about his job, kept throwing the luggage down and cursing us for hurrying, saying that he would throw it away or abscond with it. 'Do you think that I am a beast of burden or a ship for carrying stones? I hired out the services (*operae*) of a man, not a carthorse. And I am just as freeborn as you are, even if my father left me a pauper'. Not content with these curses he kept lifting his leg up high and filled the street with a revolting noise and smell.

For Petronius see p. 479.

St Matthew 20.1–8; 13–14

375. For the kingdom of heaven is like a man who is a householder and who went out early in the morning to hire labourers for his vineyard. 2 And

when he had agreed with the labourers for a denarius a day, he sent them into the vineyard. 3 And going out about the third hour he saw others standing idle in the marketplace, 4 and said to them: You also go into the vineyard, and I will pay you whatever is fair. And they went on their way. 5
Again he went out about the sixth and ninth hour and did the same. 6 And about the eleventh hour he went out and found others standing idle, and said to them: Why are you standing here all day idle? 7 They said to him: Because no one has hired us. He said to them: You also go into the vineyard. 8 So when evening came, the master of the vineyard said to his steward: Call the labourers and give them their wage, beginning from the last to the first. Those who had started work last came forward and received a denarius. Those who had started work first came forward expecting that they would get more. But they also received one denarius each. (These labourers then dispute the payment suggesting that they should get more than those hired later in the day.) 13. But he answered one of them, and said: Friend I am not doing you an injustice: did not you agree with me on a denarius? 14 Take what is yours and go. But I wish to give the last man (hired) the same as you.

This parable reflecting life in the Roman near east illustrates that this contract of labour is consensual and bilateral, agreeing services and wages for the service. The contract is verbal, but the hirer and the hired men cannot change its terms later.

Cato, *De Agricultura* 144

376. The gathering of olives should be contracted out on the following terms: the contractor must properly gather the entire harvest according to the wishes of the owner, or the person whom he has put in charge, or the person who is intending to buy the crop. Olives should not be picked or beaten down without the instructions of the owner or his representative. If anyone contravenes this rule, in respect of what he has harvested on that day, no one will pay him for that and there will be no liability. All gatherers of the olives will swear an oath before the owner or his representative that they have not stolen olives, and that no one with their connivance has stolen olives from the farm of Lucius Manlius during that harvest. If any of them will not swear the oath in this form, in respect of everything that that person has picked, no one will give him any pay and there will be no liability for pay. He (the contractor) must give adequate security for the harvesting of the crop, according to the instructions of Lucius Manlius. Ladders are to be returned in the same condition as when they were issued, except where they have been broken through age. If they are not returned, a

reasonable sum will be deducted according to the determination of a fair arbitrator. If the owner suffers loss through the actions of the contractor, it will be made good through deduction according to the determination of a fair arbitrator. He (the contractor) is to provide as many gatherers and pickers as are required. If he does not provide them, a deduction will be made for the cost of hiring or contracting (them), and the total (bill) will be less by that sum. He is not to remove firewood or olives from the farm. If any gatherer removes olives, a deduction of two sesterces will be made for each act, and there will be no liability for this. All olives are to be measured, clean, in an olive-measure. He (the contractor) is to provide fifty diligent men, two-thirds of whom are to be pickers. No one is to leave to travel to where a higher price is paid for picking olives and making oil, unless he names a replacement team member at the time. If anyone contravenes this, if the owner or his representative wishes, the rest of the group must swear (not to follow suit). If they do not swear in these terms, no one will pay for the picking of olives or the making of oil and there will be no liability for pay in respect of the person who has not sworn. Bonuses: for a harvest of 1,200 *modii* the bonus is five *modii* of salted olives, nine pounds of pure oil, and five *quadrantals* of vinegar for the entire harvest. In respect of that proportion of the salted olives that they do not receive during the harvest, their allowance will be five sesterces per *modius*.

For Cato see p. 477. His writing on agriculture offered advice to farm owners, especially those producing olive oil or wine. In this passage he describes a contract for the harvesting of an olive crop (see also Varro, *De Re Rustica* 1.55). The farm provides the equipment. The contractor must work out in advance the likely size of the harvest in order to assemble his team. Of the employed workers, two thirds are to be pickers, the purpose of which was probably to encourage the picking of the olives as opposed to knocking them off the tree with a stick; this helped to protect next year's crop. Among the benefits for the workers is the provision of relish. In the contract Lucius Manlius is used as an example of an owner. Once the contract has been established, the contractor and his employees must abide by it, even though a higher price for picking olives is paid elsewhere.

CIL 8.11824 = *ILS* 7457 (Maktar in Tunisia)

377. I was born in an impoverished environment to a humble father who had no resources and no household. From the time of my birth, I lived in the country dealing with my affairs, and there was no respite in the country and never any for me. When the year had brought crops to ripeness then I was the first to harvest the stalks. When a crew of men equipped with

scythes went out into the fields, making for either the Nomads of Cirta or the lands of Jupiter, I went first into the fields as a harvester in front of all the others, leaving a large throng behind my back. I reaped twelve harvests under the blazing sun, and afterwards was made leader instead of a labourer. I led crews of harvesters for eleven years and our crew harvested the plains of Numidia. This work and my restrained way of life made me master of a household, and a house has been got ready and this house lacks no rich fittings. Our life has received the fruits of public reward and I was enrolled among those who had been chosen as councillors. Having been elected by the council I took my seat in the meeting house of the council, and starting from my humble country background I too came to hold the position of censor. Furthermore, I begat children and saw them grow up, and also saw my darling grandchildren. In accordance with the merits of my life I enjoyed years of distinction which no acidic tongue has slandered with any reproach. Men, learn to live your life free from reproach. The man who has lived without deceit has deserved to die in this way.

See Parkin and Pomeroy (2007), 39–40; Shaw (2013), 281–98. In this interesting story of social mobility a peasant from Maktar served twelve years as member of a crew of harvesters. Then he contracted to lead workers to carry out harvesting in Numidia. The record of his life illustrates the hire of labour for limited tasks and the entrepreneurial possibilities. In a similar case we hear that Vespasian's grandfather had an annual contract to bring labourers from Umbria to the Sabine country (Suetonius, *Vespasian* 1.4); see Garnsey (1980a), 42.

P. Oxy. 275 = *SP* no. 13 (AD 66)

378. Tryphon, son of Dionysios son of Tryphon and of Thamounis daughter of Onnophris, and Ptolemaeos, son of Pausirion son of Ptolemaeos and of Ophelous daughter of Theon, weaver, both inhabitants of Oxyrhynchus, have mutually agreed that Tryphon has apprenticed to Ptolemaeos his son Thoonis, whose mother is Saraeos daughter of Apion, and who is not yet of age, for a period of one year from the present day, to work and follow all the instructions given to him by Ptolemaeos in respect of the entire skill of weaving as he himself knows it, with the boy to be fed and clothed for the entire time by his father Tryphon, who is also to be liable for all the taxes on the boy, on the condition that Ptolemaeos will pay him every month five drachmae for food, and at the end of the entire period twelve drachmae for clothing; and it shall not be right for Tryphon to remove the boy from Ptolemaeos until the time span has been completed; and in respect of whatever days the boy shall be absent, he (Tryphon) shall send him to work

for an equal number at the end of the period, or will forfeit one silver drachma for each day, and if he removes him within the period he will pay a penalty of one hundred drachmae, and an equal amount to the treasury. But if Ptolemaeos does not instruct the boy properly, he is to be liable to the same penalties. The contract of apprenticeship is valid. Year thirteen of Nero Claudius Caesar Augustus Germanicus Emperor, the twenty-first of the month Sebastos. I, Ptolemaeos, son of Pausirion, son of Ptolemaeos and of Ophelous daughter of Theon, will fulfil everything in the one year. I, Zoilos, son of Horus son of Zoilos and of Dieos daughter of Sokeos, have written for him as he is illiterate. Year thirteen of Nero Claudius Caesar Augustus Germanicus Emperor, Sebastos 21.

Fines for non-compliance with the terms of the contract would be paid into the treasury of the nome-capital, Oxyrhynchus. As in other contracts, clarity was important, and the participants are carefully identified.

P. Fay. 91 = *SP* no. 17 (AD 99)

379. Phaophi 18. Agreement of Thenetkouis with Lucius. Year three of Emperor Caesar Nerva Trajan Augustus Germanicus, Phaophi 18, at Euhemeria, in the division of Themistes of the Arsinoite nome. Thenetkouis, daughter of Heron, olive-carrier, Persian, about twenty-six years old, with a scar on her right shin, with her guardian and kinsman Leontas, son of Hippalos, about fifty-four years old, with a scar on the right side of his forehead, acknowledges to Lucius Bellenus Gemellus, discharged legionary soldier, Bellenus Gemellus, about sixty years old, with a scar on his left wrist, that she has received directly by hand from his house sixteen silver drachmae as pledge money that cannot be repudiated. Therefore Thenetkouis is required to carry at the olive press of Lucius Bellenus Gemellus at Euhemeria from whatever day he gives her an order, the olive crop for this current third year, performing all the duties of an olive-carrier until all the olive oil manufacture has been completed, and receiving from Lucius Bellenus Gemellus her daily wages at the same amount as the other olive-carriers in the village; and Lucius is to deduct the sixteen silver drachmae in instalments from the wages to be paid. If Thenetkouis does not act in accordance with the conditions set out above she is to pay back to Lucius double the pledge money, and Lucius Bellenus has the right of execution against the one who entered the agreement and against all her property, as if by a legal decision. Signatory for Thenetkouis: the above-mentioned Leontas. I, Thenetkouis, daughter of Heron, Persian, with my guardian and kinsman Leontas, son of Hippalos, agree that I have received from Lucius the sixteen silver drachmae as pledge

money, and I will be an olive-carrier at the olive press from whatever day you order me, receiving from you, Lucius, my wages at the same amount as similar carriers, and I will carry out everything as set out above. I, Leontas, have written for Thenetkouis also as she is illiterate. Registered in year three, Phaophi 18, by Heron keeper of the records at Euhemeria. I, Lucius Bellenus Gemellus, have received by way of Epagathus the sixteen silver drachmae mentioned above, and I have no complaint. Year five of Emperor Caesar Nerva Trajan Augustus Germanicus, Tubi 12.

Gemellus' receipt for the sixteen drachmae is dated two years after the original contract. In this arrangement the sixteen drachmae act as a partial advance payment guaranteeing employment and an obligation to work for a set period, and are recouped from the employee's wages. At the end of the period of employment if everything is satisfactory on both sides the sixteen drachmae are returned, as in this case.

P. Hamb. 74 = *SP* no. 78 (AD 173 or 174)

380. Inhabitant of Acho ... in the nome, helmsman of a boat for carrying bodies, to ... greetings. I acknowledge that I have received from you the bandaged body of ..., whom I shall transport to the harbour of Kerke in the Memphite nome and hand over to Thakaris, the undertaker, and for the freight and the toll, and all expenses of the boat the fee that was agreed, which I have received. Year thirteen (or fourteen) of Emperor Caesar Marcus Aurelius Armeniacus Medicus Parthicus Germanicus Maximus, Pharmouthi.

This refers to the hire of a helmsman and boat for transport of a mummified body for a fee negotiated in advance.

Protection of an Employee

D 9.1.3 (Gaius, *Provincial Edict*, Book 7)

381. (On injuries caused by animals) ... No price can be put on the body of a freeman, but consideration can be given to the expenses incurred in treatment of an injury, or the loss of working days, or future employment because of disablement.

There is comparatively little evidence relating to Roman labour law and regulations to protect employees unjustifiably dismissed or provide compensation for injury (see Crook (1967), 198–200). Action was possible under the *lex Aquilia* for damage or injury by a third person to your slaves, and deliberate injury to a freeman constituted *iniuria*, which the injured party had to pursue. These actions would not cover damage through the negligence of an employer. However, there are some indications of concern to provide redress for those injured by the careless actions of others (nos. 382–3). Indeed Ulpian (*D* 9.2.13pr) suggests that a freeman could have an *actio utilis* (an action for a legal situation not covered by existing law) on the analogy of the *lex Aquilia* for an injury, though he could not take direct action under that *lex* because 'he did not own his own limbs'. However, this may be a post-classical interpolation. In any case, the chance of a poor man successfully suing his employer was limited. Freedmen had some protection against the unreasonable demands of their patrons (no. 384).

D 9.2.5.3 (Ulpian, *Edict*, Book 18)

382. Iulianus put forward the following case: a cobbler while instructing his apprentice, who was a freeborn *filius familias*, and who made a mistake in carrying out what had been demonstrated, struck him about the neck with a last and put out his eye. Iulianus observed that an action for outrage (*iniuria*) was not appropriate because he had not struck the boy in order to cause outrage, but in order to advise and teach him. He was uncertain whether an action on contract (for his teaching) was possible because the teacher has the right to punish only to a limited degree. However, I do not doubt that an action under the *lex Aquilia* is possible.

This case refers to a freeborn boy in a low-grade activity; Ulpian, contra Iulianus, argued that an action under the *lex Aquilia* was possible, presumably based on the loss of earning power of the man's son injured as an apprentice (see p. 281).

D 38.1.50 (Neratius, *Replies*, Book 1)

383. The performance of services depends on the status of the person who offers them, for they must be consistent with his rank, his resources, his character, and his skill. Not only a freedman but anyone who is providing services must be given food or sufficient time to purchase comestibles, and in every respect time for essential bodily requirements.

D 38.1.17 (Paul, *Rights of Patrons*, Only Book)

384. A patron should not receive a hearing if he demands services that the freedman's age cannot permit, the infirmity of his body endure, or by which his condition and lifestyle would be undermined.

Freedmen and freedwomen could be required by an agreement at manumission to provide certain services including labour for their former master (see p. 61); the praetor could enforce this but was prepared to intervene to prevent undue exploitation of this right; see also *D* 38.1.2 on the praetor's edict controlling what could be demanded of freedmen by their patrons.

CHAPTER 5

Government, Citizens, and Property

Introduction

Justinian proclaimed in the *Institutes* that the general precepts of the law were: 'to live honourably, to do no harm to another person, and to give each person his own' (1.1.3). Undoubtedly the Romans vigorously believed in the importance of securing private property. However, there was also a level of sophistication in recognizing that your title to an object might in some way relate to the activities and indeed rights of other people, and that there were potentially many definitions of what was yours. In the probably unstable social conditions of early Rome and uncertain intervention by state authorities, tough measures protected against loss of property by theft. In the Twelve Tables of Roman law (fifth century BC) you were entitled to kill without state retribution a thief who lurked in the night; a thief who came by day could be killed if he was armed (Crawford (1996), 611–12). Later, in the last century of the republic, threats to wealth and property might be more sophisticated and involve agents of the state. Cicero affirmed the principle of property rights as a state responsibility: 'Above all, the man who administers the state must see to it that each man keeps his own and that the property of private persons is not reduced by inroads of the state' (*De Off.* 2.73). Indeed, part of the basis of the Roman commonwealth was sound management of wealth and property, and Cicero spoke of the 'government founded by extraordinary labour, liberty established by courage, fortunes increased and augmented by the goodwill of the gods' (*Cat.* 4.19). In this context the good citizen was not just morally upright: 'Good citizens are made by nature in the first place, but wealth helps. It is to the benefit of all good men if the state is secure, but particularly so in the case of men of wealth' (*Phil.* 13.8).

The emphasis on wealth helps to explain the political struggles over the subsidized dole of corn to large numbers of the Roman plebs. As a drain on the treasury this could be seen as undermining the ability of the rich to enjoy and preserve the fruits of empire without hindrance. In his speech in defence of Aulus Caecina Cicero cleverly merges the personal interests of his client with the social interests that the state should protect:

> Therefore my point is, what is the advantage in having a farm if the rules so properly laid down by our forefathers concerning boundaries, possessions, waterways, and roads can be disturbed and changed on any argument? … An estate can be bequeathed to a man by his father, but secure possession of the estate, that is, freedom from anxiety and the threat of legal action, is bequeathed not by his father but by the law.

He goes on to say that if his client loses it will cast doubt on the cause of the Roman people, the rights of the state, and the 'property, wealth, and claims to possession of all of us' (*Pro Caecina* 74).

This rousing defence of property rights was particularly relevant in the last century of the republic, when in political turmoil and eventually civil war, the property of political opponents was arbitrarily confiscated and distributed to the supporters of the military dynasts, and often indeed to their veteran soldiers. After his victory at Actium in 31 BC Augustus set out to bring peace and order, where men of settled respectability could have confidence that their property would not be plundered. Above all, he established clear service conditions for the army and the provision of funds to pay the soldiers. Cassius Dio, writing in the third century AD, observed that as a result people began to hope that 'they would no longer be robbed of what they owned' (54.25.6). Later, in AD 6/7 the cost of the army began to exceed resources, and Augustus set up the military treasury in order to pay soldiers their gratuity after twenty-five years' service. He then asked the senate to suggest ideas on how to fund the treasury. Needless to say, there was no agreement. Augustus then introduced his own idea, as he had probably intended all along, a 1 per cent tax on auctions and a 5 per cent tax on inheritances and bequests except those from close relatives, or those relating to poorer citizens. In AD 13 Augustus responded to senatorial objections to the levy by threatening to impose a tax on land and houses and began a survey and assessment (Dio 55.25; 56.28.4). This was enough to persuade senators that the inheritance tax was not so bad after all. Indeed, this tax may also have been intended to encourage the keeping of money within the family (Nicolet (1984), 110).

Augustus knew his audience and their concern for maintaining family property. Velleius Paterculus, enthusiastically supportive of the government, gives us the contemporary view that 'mankind was free from anxiety, and each person had indisputable property rights' (2.89.4). Public opinion responded positively; as Augustus sailed past Puteoli he was publicly lauded by the crew and passengers of a ship, since 'because of him they were alive, sailed the seas, and enjoyed their liberty and fortunes' (Suetonius, *Augustus* 98.2). We also hear rather vaguely how Augustus was praised and held in reverence by everyone when he lent sixty million sesterces for three years without interest to 'all who needed it'. The cash apparently came from the property of the condemned and was lent to those who could offer security for double the amount (Dio 55.12.3a; Suetonius, *Augustus* 41.1). Augustus was apparently helping the property-owning upper classes by providing funds for those who were temporarily embarrassed (Nicolet (1984), 114–15).

Dio cited Augustus' approach as an exemplar of what he hoped would be imperial practice in his own day under the Severan emperors. In the fictitious speech of advice offered by Maecenas to Augustus, he recommended a policy of choosing as senators the noblest, the best, and the richest in society (52.19.2). Furthermore, an equitable tax system would ensure Augustus' popularity since senators then could confidently enjoy the rest of their property (52.29.1). Dio's principal complaint against Caracalla (AD 211–217) was the emperor's financial indulgence of the army, financed by a series of new taxes, which hit senators hard: 'He made it his task to strip, plunder, and crush all the rest of mankind, and particularly senators' (78.9). Among other things, Caracalla increased to 10 per cent the tax on bequests and legacies and abolished the exemption on those from close relatives. Furthermore, throughout the imperial period a new factor was the confiscation of property by the emperor.

Landed property was the basis of wealth in Rome. We see this in the career of the rich freedman Trimalchio: 'What the gods want soon comes to pass. On one voyage I made a profit of ten million sesterces. I immediately bought up all the estates that had belonged to my master. I built a house, I bought slaves and cattle, and whatever I touched grew like honeycomb' (Petronius, *Satyricon* 76). In the context of large private estates and the increasing role of the emperor as a landholder, it is important to ask to what extent if any the Roman government intervened in the rural economy by using the law to guarantee property rights and protect the landed elite. The situation was not entirely one-sided, since even a rich landholder needed contented tenants to provide a steady income and to help manage his property that might be in different parts of Italy. For example, Pliny, noting that nearly all his capital was in land, wondered if it was wise to buy a single large estate rather than protect against uncertain weather by having land in separate localities (*Letters* 3.19; see Kehoe (1988)).

The government perhaps had an interest in mediating the landlord and rural tenant relationships in a way that took account of seemingly beneficial local customs and dealt with problems in an orderly way through the courts to produce the stable occupation of land by competent farmers capable of producing crops, and of course of paying any taxes the state or local communities required (see in general Kehoe (2007), 1–18). The clear definition of property rights and the availability of legal procedures to enforce them would give confidence to landholders and tenants and contribute to economic stability. Furthermore, the possession of property opened the way to many commercial transactions, including buying and selling, loans, mortgages, and the availability of credit.

Ownership of urban properties was also important. Urban rents could be a valuable element of upper-class wealth in the letting out of apartments managed through middlemen. In some locations the clientele might be from the same social class. The state perhaps had an interest in enabling the profitable exploitation of urban property, which could assist the availability of affordable rooms for the plebs, and in avoiding the disruption caused by the expulsion of tenants. In some ways the law can be viewed as an element of social control, in that jurists responded to legal issues by weighing up the interests of the protagonists. This process over time could guide the rental market towards practices considered socially desirable (Frier (1980), especially 206–19).

The following extracts illustrate definitions of property, ownership, and possession (nos. 385–93), servitudes (easements), (nos. 394–401), and the regulation of living space between residents in towns and cities (nos. 402–9). *Usufruct* permitted the exploitation of property and its benefits for a limited time (nos. 410–12). The acquisition of ownership by having possession of a thing for a set time (*usucapio*) indicates the importance in Roman law of the stable occupation of property and the protection of the status quo (nos. 413–22).

If possession of land or other objects was lost or challenged, the best defence was to make use of an interdict (an order issued by a magistrate) to defend or recover possession (nos. 423–32). Much of the evidence relates to land, notably the categories of land in the Roman state, and the acquisition and division of land for distribution to communities, citizens, and veteran soldiers; this was the work of the Roman land surveyors (nos. 433–52). Land disputes and the role of law in their resolution were common issues in local communities, especially in respect of disruption caused by river floods (nos. 443–52). The acreage under cultivation was also relevant to the census, taxation, and fund-raising schemes like the *alimenta* (see pp. 117–18).

Well-off landowners often required smaller farmers to work their land as tenants for a rent, and in Roman law this was a form of contract (see p. 175 on obligations and contract); in addition, local communities and the Roman state rented out public land. The law was invoked to sort out disputes over leases or rents, and in this way became involved in social issues and mediated between the interested parties (pp. 266–70). Urban property owners and renters also had similar issues involving leases and legal rights (pp. 270–4), and the law had a role in ensuring a stable market where problems that could not be resolved by agreement were settled through court procedures.

Definition of Property

In the property-conscious society of the Roman world it is not surprising that elaborate definitions of property emerged. By the end of the first century BC one fundamental classification set apart divine and human law. Divine law included *res sacrae*, property belonging to the deities of the upper world, and *res religiosae*, belonging to deities of the underworld (Gaius, *Institutes* 2.2–4). In terms of human law, objects were classified as either public or private; public things, such as rivers, harbours, roads, and state-funded aqueducts, belonged to no individual; private things could theoretically belong to individuals, and according to *ius naturale* some things were common to all, such as air, running water, and the seashore. There were further distinctions between items that could be touched, and those that could not be touched, such as a right of way, and between immovable property, such as land, and movables (Gaius, *Institutes* 2.10–14). For a very useful collection of examples with analysis see Hausmaninger and Gamauf (2012).

Gaius, *Institutes* 2.14a

385. There is a further division of things: they are either *res mancipi* or *res nec mancipi*. *Res mancipi* are things such as a farm on Italic land, also houses on Italic land, also slaves and those animals that are normally broken for draught or for carrying burdens, such as oxen, horses, mules, asses; also, rustic praedial servitudes. But urban praedial servitudes are *nec mancipi*. *Nec mancipi* are also stipendiary and tributary lands.

This definition relates to the means of conveyance of ownership; *res mancipi* could be transferred only by the formal procedure of *mancipatio*, or by *in iure cessio*. The property defined in this way probably reflects the concerns of early Roman society, with emphasis on the crucial importance of essentials for farming and the means to attain self-sufficiency in a relatively primitive rural economy: land, slaves, cattle, horses, asses, and mules. When such items were acquired by *mancipatio* the person who acquired them became the formal owner. Stipendiary and tributary lands were those lands in the provinces subject to a money tax. For praedial servitudes, see p. 237.

Ownership and Possession

There was an important distinction between ownership (*dominium*) and possession (*possessio*) of a thing. In *dominium* the owner was in complete control of the property with full title, provided that he or she had the legal right to carry out a valid transaction (*commercium*), the item involved was capable of private ownership, and the item had been transferred in an appropriate way as already described. *Commercium* was associated with Roman citizenship, and *dominium* was often called *ex iure Quiritium* (according to the right of citizens). Although the owner had complete control of his property, he was not entirely free to do what he liked with it. There were restrictions requiring an owner to use his property in such a way that the rights of others were not infringed, for example by overhanging trees or drainage channels pouring excess water onto another's land. One important limitation of ownership was a servitude (see no. 395).

On many occasions a property might be in the possession (*possessio*) of someone who had physical control and might, for example, have use of land and enjoy its fruits even though the property was formally owned by another. To have possession of an object brought significant benefits; it was an important (though not sufficient) step to proving and acquiring ownership by *usucapio* (that is, having it in your possession for at least two years in the case of immovables, one year for movables). Possession involved intent and direct physical control of an object and therefore could be applied only to touchable things. Furthermore, being the possessor, you were the defendant in any legal case, and the onus was on the plaintiff to prove his title to the property in question. The rules on *possessio* were important for keeping the issue in the legal process, respecting the status quo, avoiding attempts at violent self-help, and limiting the amount of litigation. See Johnston (1999), 56–8; also, Capogrossi Colognesi (1998). For *usufruct* and the definition of fruits see p. 242.

D 41.2.12.1 (Ulpian, *Edict*, Book 70)

386. Ownership has nothing in common with possession.

D 41.2.13pr (Ulpian, *Edict*, Book 72)

387. Pomponius asks whether, in the case of stones that were immersed in the Tiber because of a shipwreck and subsequently recovered, ownership was retained intact for that period during which they were immersed. I think that I retain ownership of them but do not possess them. This is not analogous to the case of a fugitive slave, since a fugitive slave is considered to remain in our possession, so that he cannot by himself deprive us of possession. But the case with the stones is different.

Ulpian argues that stones sunk in the Tiber had been lost from the control of their owner and the physical relationship broken even though no third party was involved. But he retained ownership of them because the location was known and there was a chance of recovery assuming that the river was not too deep. In the case of the fugitive slave, possession by intent alone is (exceptionally) defended because the slave cannot be physically watched all the time and can actively plan an escape. For a valuable analysis of the legal arguments, see Hausmaninger and Gamauf (2012), 83; 324–5.

D 41.2.3pr-1 (Paul, *Edict*, Book 44)

388. Those things that are corporeal can be possessed. And we take possession both physically and mentally, not just mentally or just physically.

Because of the requirement to possess mentally, there were restrictions on the ability of some people to acquire possession. Furthermore, possession could be lost, for example, through theft or carelessness or through lack of interest in continuing to possess; Hausmaninger and Gamauf (2012), 70–1.

D 41.2.1.3 (Paul, *Edict*, Book 54)

389. A madman, and also a child without the approval of his tutor, are not able to begin to possess because they do not have the intention of holding, however vigorous their physical contact with the object, just as if someone placed something in the hands of a person who was asleep. But a child with the approval of his tutor may begin to possess.

D 41.2.17.1 (Ulpian, *Edict*, Book 76)

390. There is this difference between ownership and possession, namely that ownership remains with a person even though he does not wish to be owner, whereas possession ceases when someone decides that he does not wish to possess.

Gaius, *Institutes* 2.73

391. Besides, whatever is built on my land by anybody becomes mine by natural law, even if he built it for himself, because a superstructure (*superficies*) goes with the land.

Ownership of land in Roman law also meant ownership of anything built on the land, even if built by someone else; see Crook (1967), 143.

CJ 3.32.2 (AD 213)

392. Emperors Severus and Antoninus to Aristaenetus. If you can prove that the lower part of the building, which touches the ground, belongs to you, there is no doubt that the part which your neighbour added above it has accrued to your ownership. Furthermore, whatever is built on your land, provided that it remains in the same condition, legally belongs to you.

In law, rights of property moved upwards; so, if you owned one floor of a building you owned all floors above. On the other hand, it was possible to divide a house into two separate entities by a party wall. However, *superficies* also described a right by which the constructor of a building acquired the position of a lessee if he paid a rent (*solarium*) to the owner of the land; this arrangement had no time limit and could be left to an heir. A vivid example concerns the freedman curator of the column of Marcus Aurelius in Rome who was granted the right to build a small dwelling place in the vicinity (no. 393).

CIL 6.1585b = *ILS* 5920 = *FIRA* 3, no. 110

393. Copies of the letters written by the financial officials (*rationales*) of our lords relating to Adrastus, freedman of our Emperors, in which he is permitted to build a cottage from scratch at his own expense and under his legal control and is to pay a *solarium* (rent) as others do.

Aelius Achilles, Claudius Perpetuus Flavianus Eutychus to Epaphroditus, greetings. Assign to Adrastus, the procurator of the column of the divine Marcus, all the tiles and building material from huts, cottages, and suitable buildings, so that he can construct a dwelling for himself to his own satisfaction, which he may have under his legal control and bequeath to his heirs. Letter issued on 6 August at Rome in the consulship of Falco and Clarus (AD 193).

Aelius Achilles, Claudius Perpetuus Flavianus Eutychus to Aquilius Felix (procurator of public works). We request you to instruct that there be given to Adrastus, freedman of the emperor, for the building which he is about to construct at his own expense for the custodianship of the one-hundred-foot column (of Marcus Aurelius), ten waggon loads of wood at the price paid by the treasury when it was necessary to construct a bridge. Letter issued on 19 August at Rome in the consulship of Falco and Clarus.

Financial officials to Seius Superstites and Fabius Magnus. The procurator of the one-hundred-foot column of the divine Marcus who has been instructed to construct a dwelling in the vicinity, will undertake the work if he receives your authorization. We therefore request that you order that the area which Adrastus, freedman of our lord, has pointed out, be assigned to him on the basis that he will pay the *solarium* as others do. Letter issued on 7 September at Rome, returned on 11 September at Rome, under the same consuls.

In this bureaucratic process, the officials of the public treasury (*rationales*) wrote to Epaphroditus, an imperial freedman in the public works office, to provide basic building materials, and then to the procurator of public works to organize timber at cost price, and finally to the curators of public works to confirm the location for Adrastus' dwelling; discussion in Moore (2012).

Praedial Servitudes

A form of proprietary right was the servitude (equating to the English 'easement'). It permitted the owner of neighbouring land (the dominant) to use the property of another (the servient) in a defined way, for example, a right of way across someone's land, or the right to have access to water. The servitude was required to offer a specific benefit, and although you were entitled to enjoy its fruits, the servitude was not personal but was attached to the immovable itself, either land or a building. These were known as praedial servitudes. Rustic praedial servitudes and urban praedial servitudes were distinguished by how they were used to benefit the dominant immovable for agricultural or for commercial and building purposes (Johnston (1999), 68–70; 75–6).

D 8.4.1.1 (Ulpian, *Institutes*, Book 2)

394. These servitudes are called praedial servitudes since they cannot be established without estates (*praedia*). For no one can acquire either a rustic or urban praedial servitude unless he has an estate, and no one can be required to respect such a servitude unless he has an estate.

D 8.3.1pr (Ulpian, *Institutes*, Book 2)

395. The following are rustic praedial servitudes: *iter*, *actus*, *via*, *aquae ductus*. *Iter* is a man's right to proceed on foot and to walk, but not to drive a beast of burden as well. *Actus* is the right to drive either a beast of burden or a vehicle. Therefore, whoever has an *iter* does not have an *actus*, while whoever has an *actus* also has the right to walk (*iter*) even without a beast of burden. *Via* is the right to proceed on foot, to drive, and to walk, for *via* subsumes within it both *iter* and *actus*. *Aquae ductus* is the right to bring water through another person's land.

This was very important for rural farming communities since it allowed effective and secure use of land and resources. As well as the right to channel water, servitudes also covered the right to draw water and to water animals; see in general on servitudes Bannon (2017), 67–71.

D 8.1.4.1 (Papinian, *Questions*, Book 7)

396. It is agreed that specific limitations can be added to servitudes, such as the type of vehicle that may or may not be driven (for example that only a horse is permitted), or that only a defined weight may be carried, or that a particular flock may be driven through, or that charcoal may be carried.

D 8.3.8 (Gaius, *Provincial Edict*, Book 7)

397. The width of a road (*via*) in accordance with a law of the Twelve Tables is eight feet when it runs straight, but at a curve, that is when it bends, sixteen feet.

Gaius is here referring to servitudes. For the width assigned to various *limites* see Hyginus, *Establishment of Limites* (Campbell (2000), p. 153.25, and pp. 364–5); for *limites* as a perpetual right of way see nos. 436–7.

Siculus Flaccus, *Categories of Land* (T, p. 110.14 = Campbell (2000), p. 113.25)

398. There is always right of way to all lands. Sometimes, for lack of local roads a right of way is provided through another person's land. Indeed, some landholders make a specific agreement to concede a servitude in respect of those fields to gain access to which they are obliged to allow a right of way through their land.

CIL 5.2547 = *ILS* 6004 (near Ateste)

399. The right of way (*iter*) of Q. Critonius. The right of way is due to Q. Critonius, son of Quintus, and … Pomponius Silo, and to no one else.

This boundary stone marked a local right of way specifically for two individuals.

D 8.1.9 (Celsus, *Digest*, Book 5)

400. If someone has been ceded or left without reserve a right of way (*via*) across the land of another, he will have the right to walk and drive over it entirely freely, that is, through any part of the estate he likes, provided that he does so in a reasonable way; for general statements have unspoken reservations. For he is not to be permitted to walk or drive through the house, or through the middle of the vineyards when he could equally conveniently do this through another part of the estate with less damage to the servient land. In fact, it was established that whatever route he first took, he ought to go or drive by that exclusively, and had no right to make further changes to it. This was also the opinion of Sabinus, who used the analogy of a water channel, so that in whatever direction a man had first been permitted to establish it, after it had been established, he was not able to change it. It is correct that the same principle should be observed in the case of a right of way.

A servitude had to confer a specific benefit. It was a requirement that those benefitting from a servitude conducted themselves in a reasonable and considerate way. Furthermore, the nature of servitudes was essentially passive. The owner of the servient land was required to allow some kind of action by another, but not actually to do or construct anything.

D 8.1.15.1 (Pomponius, *On Sabinus*, Book 33)

401. It is not part of the character of servitudes that someone (that is, the person whose land is subject to the servitude) should be compelled to do something, for example to remove trees or make the view more pleasant, or for the same purpose to paint something on his estate. He may only be required to permit something to be done or to refrain from doing something.

Urban praedial servitudes helped to regulate relations between residents in the more crowded environment of towns or cities. Irresponsible treatment of party walls and interference with a neighbour's normal way of life could be controlled in an organized way (nos. 405–6). There were other ways of dealing with nuisance or antisocial behaviour, for example through an action for damage by negligence under the *lex Aquilia* provided that the plaintiff could prove that the defendant was solely responsible and that he was not simply making normal use of his property (see p. 278). There was also provision under *damnum infectum* (relating to a potential threat to a property) to provide protection against supposed future damage, either a security (*cautio*) against the expected damage or the right to take possession (*missio in possessionem*) of the offending property (see nos. 408–9). There was a further provision to compel the removal of work already completed if it had been carried out without due notice or in contravention of an existing ruling; see Johnston (1999), 71–6.

Seneca, *Letters* 56.4

402. Among the uproar that throbs around me without distracting me, I include passing chariots, an engineer in the same block, a sharpener of saws situated nearby, or some man who is demonstrating pipes or flutes by the Meta Sudans and is bawling rather than singing.

This is a good example of the possible nuisance of living in a big city with many neighbours. In fact, Seneca claims that he had an apartment above a bath house in Rome and was disturbed by the medley of sound from there as well as the racket from the neighbouring streets: heavy breathing of the exercise-conscious, the splashing of those jumping into the bath, the slapping sounds as bathers were rubbed down, the yells and calls of vendors and others in the baths. Possibly Seneca was emphasizing the noisy environment of Rome rather than relaying his personal experiences. It may be questioned that, as a very wealthy man, he found it necessary to live above a bathhouse.

D 8.2.2 (Gaius, *Provincial Edict*, Book 7)

403. These are the rights relating to urban praedial servitudes: the right to build higher and thus block a neighbour's light, or the right to prevent this; the right to direct water dripping from eaves onto the roof or ground of a neighbour, or the right to prevent this; the right to insert wooden beams into the wall of a neighbour, and finally the right to have a roof or building projecting, and other rights similar to these.

D 8.5.8.5 (Ulpian, *Edict*, Book 17)

404. Aristo, in a legal opinion to Cerellius Vitalis, said that he did not think that smoke from a cheese factory could be legally released into higher buildings, unless a servitude to that effect was admitted. The same man also said that it is not permissible to send water or anything else from the higher level to the lower. For a man is permitted to conduct his business on his own property to the extent that he does not send anything into another's property, and an influx of smoke is the same as an influx of water.

Therefore, the person on the higher level (that is, the one who suffers from smoke) can bring an action against the person on the lower level, claiming that he has no legal right to act in this way. Finally, he says that Alfenus notes that a man does not have the legal right to break up a boulder on his property in such a way that the fragments fall on my land. Therefore, Aristo says that the person who leased the cheese-making factory from the community of Minturnae can be prevented by the person on a higher level from having smoke permeate to the higher level, but that he has an action on the lease contract against the community of Minturnae.

The owner of the cheese factory can sue the community of Minturnae on the grounds that he cannot operate his business as intended in the lease.

D 8.2.13pr (Proculus, *Letters*, Book 2)

405. A man called Hiberus, who owns an apartment block behind my warehouse, constructed a bath house against our party wall. A person is not permitted to attach pipes transmitting smoke to a party wall, just as he is not permitted to build his own wall along the party wall. This rule is even more important in the case of smoke pipes since because of them the wall may be scorched by the fire. I should like you to speak to Hiberus about this to prevent him from doing something illegal.

D 8.2.12 (Iavolenus, *From Cassius*, Book 10)

406. When buildings are subject to a servitude to the effect that no part of them can be raised any higher, they can have shrubs higher than that level. But if the servitude applies to the view and the shrubs are likely to obstruct it, this is not permitted.

D 8.2.6 (Gaius, *Provincial Edict*, Book 7)

407. These rights (urban servitudes), in the same way as rustic praedial servitudes, are lost through lack of use after a specified time has elapsed.

Damnum infectum

D 39.2.2 (Gaius, *Provincial Edict*, Book 28)

408. An anticipated injury (*damnum infectum*) is an injury that has not yet been brought about but which we fear will happen.

P. Fouad 30

409. To Demetrios, *strategos* of the Oxyrhynchus district, from Tasionys also known as Dionysia, daughter of Dionysios, of Oxyrhynchus, and Ammonios, son of Paseis, of the Little Oasis, Tasionys being with her guardian, Demetrios Theon, son of Theon, of the Oxyrhynchus district: We own adjoining houses in the Metroon quarter, and an adjoining house is owned by Philo, son of Dionysios and (other names). This house is in danger of collapse because of its great age. Therefore, as we foresee danger for ourselves and our families, especially since the house described overlooks both our yards, we ask that a copy of this statement be served on each of them by the court messenger, so that having a written warning they may take measures to make their house safe, or else be aware that they will be responsible for all danger in the future and resulting loss.

This is a *hypomnema* or petition to the local administrative official in Egypt. It is in line with Roman legal process to prevent possible damage, but the petitioners, who are not Roman citizens, do not request a security (*cautio*) or to enter possession (*missio in possessionem*); Taubenschlag (1955), 254 describes this action as a kind of 'administrative intervention'.

Usufruct

A servitude attached to the person and not land could relate to movable property and was for a limited time. One of the most important was *usufruct*, which allowed the beneficiary to make use of the property of another and take its fruits over an agreed period, though without damaging or diminishing the property. A man making a will would often make use of a usufruct to provide an income within the family; for example, family property might be left to the testator's children, but his wife could be granted use of it during her lifetime. Owners were anxious to protect their property and stop the holder of the usufruct from changing its character, especially in the case of houses. Lawyers debated exactly what could be classed as an improvement and what as a significant change of character, and what constituted fruits.

D 7.1.1 (Paul, *On Vitellius*, Book 3)

410. Usufruct is the right to make use of and enjoy the property of another, but at the same time preserving its substance.

D 7.1.13.7 (Ulpian, *On Sabinus*, Book 18)

411. If a usufruct of a house has been bequeathed as a legacy, the younger Nerva argues that the usufructuary can install windows. He can also paint the walls, bring in paintings, pieces of marble, statuettes, and anything that will serve to decorate the house. But he may not change the rooms, join them together or separate them, or reverse the front and rear entrances, or open up places that have been partitioned off, or change the entrance hall, or change the layout of the gardens. Therefore, he may do anything to improve what he finds without changing the character of the house.

D 7.8.12.2 (Ulpian, *On Sabinus*, Book 17)

412. If the usufruct of a flock is left to him (the beneficiary), for example, a flock of sheep, Labeo argues that he can use them only for their manure and not for their wool, or lambs, or milk; for these are more part of the fruits. However, I think that he can go a little further and use a moderate amount of milk, for the last wishes of the deceased should not be interpreted so strictly.

Acquiring Ownership

Ownership could be acquired in several ways: original ownership, for example, by *usucapio*, and derivative ownership because of action taken by the previous owner. In the second case the previous owner had to hand over or transfer the property into another's keeping, either by *mancipatio* or *traditio*.

D 41.3.3 (Modestinus, *Pandects*, Book 5)

413. *Usucapio* is the acquisition of ownership through continued possession for a period of time defined by law.

Usucapio helped to deal with the problem of people who genuinely thought that they owned something but found that there was some impediment to their title. As early as the Twelve Tables we find that land could be acquired through possession and use. The essential requirements were full possession and also uninterrupted possession for the time fixed by law (two years in the case of immovables and one year for other objects). Acquisition by *usucapio* could be achieved only if possession was the result of lawful activity and not violence. The good faith of the possessor was important, in that he reasonably believed that he was in the right. Goods originally stolen could not be acquired by *usucapio*, which served to protect the interests of the original owner. The legal system had to strike a balance between protecting ownership, and the rights of the possessor or someone who had purchased an object. If commerce was to function, everyone had to have confidence in retaining their purchases and in knowing that there was a process to enforce this. There was a special provision in respect of land in the provinces (no. 419).

D 41.3.1 (Gaius, *Provincial Edict*, Book 21)

414. *Usucapio* was introduced for the public good to prevent the ownership of some things from being uncertain for a long time or indeed almost permanently, provided that the amount of time laid down was sufficient for owners to inquire about their property.

See Justinian, *Inst.* 2.6; de Zulueta (1953), vol. 2, 68–9; Crawford (1996), 658–60.

D 41.10.5.1 (Neratius, *Parchments*, Book 5)

415. But a man may take by *usucapio* something that he possesses and believes that he owns, even if that belief is mistaken. This, however, should be interpreted in the following way, namely, that a reasonable error will not obstruct *usucapio* by a possessor, as for example if I possess something which I mistakenly believe my slave, or the person in whose place I now stand by the law of succession, purchased; for ignorance of a third person's action is a reasonable error.

D 43.17.2 (Paul, *Edict*, Book 65)

416. In the case of this interdict (an order issued by a magistrate) it does not matter if the possession is just or unjust against the other parties involved. Whosoever the possessor is, by the very fact that he is the possessor he has more legal right on his side than the person who does not possess.

In any legal case the possessor would be the defendant and the onus would be on the plaintive to prove his ownership; see no. 425.

D 6.1.23.3–4 (Paul, *Edict*, Book 21)

417. Whatever is written on my paper or painted on my tablet immediately becomes mine. However, some have taken a different view on account of the value of a painting. But since one thing cannot exist without the other it inevitably must accede to it. 4. Therefore, in all these cases where my

property by predominance brings the property of another with it and makes it mine, and I undertake a suit to recover it, I may be compelled by an action on fraud to pay the price of the item that has accrued to me.

What happened if something in your possession was modified by the work of another, for example, if one party provided parchment to a second party who inscribed it with gold letters, or a wooden tablet on which another painted a picture? An important principle applied, namely that one object could not exist without the other; therefore, when two movables were combined the thing added gave way to the existing thing. In the examples cited writing cannot exist without parchment or a painting without a tablet, and therefore the parchment or tablet remained with the original possessor. The law offered a defence to the party that proved they had an interest in an object that was now in the possession of another, ensuring that suitable compensation was available. Therefore, the owner of the tablet had action to recover it, but subject to payment of a price for the picture. Or the painter could sue for return of the painting if he was willing to pay the value of the tablet; see Buckland (1975), 208–11.

D 41.1.26pr (Paul, *Sabinus*, Book 14)

418. But if you build a ship using my planks, it is your ship because the nature of the cypress wood does not remain, just as in clothing made of wool. There is now an object made of wood or wool. Proculus states that we are to use the rule of which Servius and Labeo approved. In their view we must examine the overall quality, so that if anything is added to them it merges with the whole; therefore, if a foot or hand is added to a statue, a base or handle to a cup, a bedpost to a bed, a plank to a ship, stone to a building, the whole belongs entirely to the previous owner.

This ruling applied to objects composed of disparate parts, for example if a new head was added to an existing statue; the statue with its new head was deemed to belong to the statue's previous owner, though the owner of the head could expect to be compensated.

CJ 7.33.1 (AD 202) (Extract)

419. Emperors Severus and Antoninus Augusti to Iulianus. When after a legal action has been launched and completed and property in good faith has passed to a new owner and then twenty years have passed without any interruption in his possession, the party now in possession should not be disturbed.

The provision of *praescriptio longi tempori* applied to land in the provinces, which could not be acquired by *usucapio* under the *ius civile*. Someone who was in possession of provincial land could use the *praescriptio* to oppose a plaintiff who sued him for the land, if he had been in possession of it for ten years (if both parties lived in the same locality) or twenty years (if they lived in different localities). The provision first appears in this rescript of Septimius Severus and Caracalla and laid down that a possessor of provincial land who had obtained it lawfully could be protected from being sued by someone claiming ownership. Originally, therefore, it was defensive in intent.

Gaius, *Institutes* 1.119

420. Now *mancipatio*, as I said earlier, is a kind of imaginary sale. It is a legal institution reserved for Roman citizens.

In the case of *res mancipi* (see no. 385) the process involved was a complicated formal procedure involving five Roman citizens as witnesses and the pronouncement of a solemn formula of transference. Alternatively, *cessio in iure* was a fictitious trial before a magistrate or provincial governor during which the transferee claimed that the property was his and the transferor did not deny it. This was carried out face to face, with the property to be transferred (land could be represented symbolically by a piece of earth). Otherwise changes of ownership could be effected by *traditio*, when the owner handed over the property directly to the new owner. This was accompanied by a 'just cause', normally the preceding act of sale. If someone received *res mancipi* through simple *traditio* then he was considered to hold the object *in bonis* (bonitary and not full ownership); however, he might expect to acquire full ownership through *usucapio*. The *actio Publiciana* (see p. 247) provided legal protection for the bonitary owner.

D 41.2.1.21 (Paul, *Edict*, Book 54)

421. For he (Priscus) says that it is not necessary to take possession by touch and physical contact, but that it is possible by sight and intention is demonstrated by those objects, which, because of their great weight, cannot be moved, such as columns, which are held to have been delivered if both parties agree in the presence of the object. Similarly, wine is held to have been delivered when the keys of the wine cellar have been given to the purchaser.

This describes an act of delivery or handing over (*traditio*), in which possession of something that was not *res mancipi* was transferred in a convenient way. The law flexibly accommodated items that could not physically be handed over.

Gaius, *Institutes* 2.66

422. It is not merely those things that we obtain by delivery that become ours through natural law, but also those that we acquire by occupation (*occupatio*) because they were previously without an owner, for example anything that is captured on land, in the sea, or in the air.

These rights were open to all people of empire and not just Roman citizens through Roman law. It relates to the concept of 'finders keepers' in the taking hold of something that has no obvious owner. Natural law as defined by Paul (*D* 1.1.11pr) was a kind of ideal concept of 'what is always just and right'.

Protecting What You Have

Loss of possession could occur by simple physical means, for example, if you lost something or it was stolen. But in terms of intent, possession could be deemed to be lost if you ceased to be interested in possessing an object for whatever reason. In respect of recovering or protecting possession, interdicts had an important role. An interdict (*interdictum*) was an order issued by a praetor or other Roman official (under *ius honorarium*) and served to protect private possessors by offering a means of self-help within a legal structure. The two most important interdicts were *utrubi* for movables and *uti possidetis* for immovables, ensuring that someone could retain possession and protecting them against the use of force. The interdict *unde vi* provided for the recovering of possession in cases where it had been lost by force. It had to be applied for within one year. The interdict *de vi armata* dealt with cases where possession had been lost because of armed force. The process of applying for interdicts was easier than another procedure, the *rei vindicatio*, through which a person who claimed ownership of an object could assert his rights and sue its possessor for its return; he was therefore in the position of plaintiff and had to prove ownership in order to advance his case, which might mean proving that the person from whom he acquired the object was the owner. Ownership was also protected by the *actio Publiciana*, which originally offered a remedy for those who had obtained a *res mancipi* but not through the proper procedure, or who had in some way a defective title, and whose possession was challenged before they had acquired ownership by *usucapio*. It permitted the plaintiff to argue that he had previously possessed the thing in dispute under conditions that would have led to his eventually acquiring it by *usucapio* (see Johnston (1999), 58–61). A settled framework for retaining or recovering possession was important for the commercial arena of buying and selling.

D **41.2.3.9 (Paul, *Edict*, Book 54)**

423. If I hand an object over to someone else, I lose possession. For it is established that we are in possession until we of our own free will give it up or are removed by force.

D 41.2.25pr (Pomponius, *Quintus Mucius*, Book 23)

424. If we have lost control of something that we possess to the extent that we do not know where it is, we cease to possess it.

D 6.1.24 (Gaius, *Provincial Edict*, Book 7)

425. Anyone who intends to bring an action to recover property should consider whether he can obtain possession through some interdict, because it is more convenient for him to have possession and compel his opponent to undertake the burden of the plaintiff, than for him to sue someone who is already in possession.

See no. 428.

Gaius, *Institutes* 4.148

426. An interdict for retaining possession is normally issued when there is a dispute launched by two parties concerning the ownership of something, and the first question relates to which of the litigants should be in possession and which should be the plaintiff. For this matter the interdicts *uti possidetis* and *utrubi* have been made available.

D 43.17.1 (Ulpian, *Edict*, Book 69)

427. The praetor says: Since you do not possess the property about which there is this dispute either by force, or stealth or by grant (*precarium*), the one from another, I forbid force to be used to prevent you from possessing it.

Precarium was a gratuitous grant of the use of land or movables (see Borkowski (2010), 308–9).

D 41.2.35 (Ulpian, *All Courts*, Book 5)

428. The outcome of a dispute about possession amounts merely to this, namely that the judge makes a preliminary statement as to which one (of the parties) is in possession. Therefore, the result is that the party who was defeated on the issue of possession now assumes the role of plaintiff when the issue of ownership is argued.

D 43.16.3.2–5 (Ulpian, *Edict*, Book 69)

429. What do we mean by 'dispossessed by arms'? Arms are all weapons, that is, clubs and stones, not just swords, spears, lances, and missiles. Obviously if one or another brandished a club or a sword the possessor is held to have been ejected by arms. But this should be extended, namely, if men came unarmed, but in the dispute the unarmed men proceeded to take up clubs or stones, this constitutes armed force. In the case of those who came armed, even if they did not use the arms to eject someone but nevertheless ejected him, then it is held that armed force was used. For, to terrorize with arms is sufficient to be held as ejection by arms.

D 43.16.1.31 (Ulpian, *Edict*, Book 69)

430. Whoever has been ejected by force should recover damages for whatever loss he encountered by his ejection. For his previous status must be restored which he would have had if he had not been ejected.

D 48.7.7 (Callistratus, *Judicial Enquiries*, Book 7)

431. The terms of the decree are as follows: 'It is very important that, if you think that you have a claim, you should press it through legal action. Meanwhile the man in possession should remain in possession; you are the plaintiff'. And when Marcianus replied 'I used no force', the emperor replied: 'Do you think that force is used only when men are wounded? Force is used whenever a man demands what he thinks is owed to him other than through the work of a judge'.

This relates to creditors moving against debtors, but the principle of the definition of force and the right of the person in possession to remain in possession against threats apply to land and property disputes.

Euphrates Papyrus 1; Feissel and Gascou (1989) (1995)

432. In the consulship of Emperor Caesar Marcus Iulius Philippus Augustus and Messius Tittianus, five days before the kalends of September (28 August), in the year 293 (of Antioch), on Loos 28, at Antioch, colony and metropolis, in the baths of Hadrian.

To Iulius Priscus, most excellent man, Prefect of Mesopotamia, exercising proconsular power, from Archodes, son of Phallaios, Philotas, son of Nisraiabos, Vorodes, son of Sumisbarachos, and Abezautas, son of

Abediardas, from the imperial village of Beth Phouriaia, the one that is near Appadana:

Being in dispute with our fellow-villagers, Lord, concerning land and other things, we have come here to plead our case before Your Goodness, and, after we attended on your tribunal for eight months our case was introduced, as Your Goodness remembers, on the ninth day before the kalends of September (24 August), the day that has just passed. Your Goodness, our benefactor, having heard part of the case, decided that you would give judgement when with good fortune you would be in the area. Since, therefore, the case has not so far been resolved, and our fellow-villagers are attempting to expel us from the land on which we live, and to employ violence before the judgement, and since the divine constitutions, which you more than others are aware of and venerate, lay down that those who find themselves in possession (of land) should remain so until judgement, for this reason we have fled to you and we ask you to order through your subscription that Claudius Ariston, outstanding man, procurator in the region of Appadana, with whom the jurisdiction lies, should maintain the status quo, and should forbid the use of force before your fortunate visit to the area, when, if we realize our desire, we will be able to render Your Fortune our eternal thanks.

I, Aurelius, Archodes, son of Phallaios, have submitted the petition, and also on behalf of the others.

Subscription of Iulius Priscus, most excellent man, Prefect of Mesopotamia, exercising proconsular power: Ariston, outstanding man, will examine your petition.

I have read.

Petition of Archodes, son of Phallaios, and Philotas, son of Nisraiabos.

This petition was addressed to Iulius Priscus, brother of the emperor Philip, in AD 245, who seems to have had overall responsibility for the east. The villagers of Beth Phouriaia, a village belonging to the emperor, had been in Antioch from the end of 244 and it was not until 24 August 245 that their case came before Priscus after a wait of eight months. Priscus declined to reach a decision and postponed the case until his arrival for the judicial *conventus* at Appadana. Between 24 and 28 August the villagers drafted the above petition aiming to preserve the status quo. It is striking that the villagers had gained access to one of the most senior officials in the empire though his answer was not especially encouraging. It is also interesting that the humble villagers know the principle of Roman law, in that those in possession should not be dislodged by force pending the hearing of a court case (*interdictum uti possidetis*) and expect it to be applied in their case. If they had been dispossessed by force the interdict *unde vi* would order restitution. Presumably they had some kind of legal advice or a powerful patron; see Millar (1993), 155–6; Ando (2000),

73–80. Stolte (2001), 170–2; 175–9 observes that the interdicts are not mentioned specifically; in fact, the villagers request a decree identical with an interdict. He notes that although there was no concerted effort by the authorities to bring in Roman law at all levels of legal activity, 'Roman private law was finding its way through the courts into daily practice'. Local people obviously wanted to resolve legal issues and would adopt what they thought were Roman practices or terminology if they believed that would help, perhaps hoping that the Roman governor would favour a claim that he could understand. But this was an inconsistent process depending on knowledge of Roman law and the strength of local legal practice, and the result was a mixed system of Roman law and indigenous rules; see also p. 154.

Landholding: Defining, Measuring, and Using Land

The practice of land survey in Rome developed gradually and eventually acquired a semi-professional status. Surveyors offered magistrates or governors expert advice on the measurement of land, boundary marking, and the resolution of disputes. Military surveyors, as well as dealing with camps and logistical matters, were sometimes also available to help local communities. Surveying lore and expertise were passed on from surveyor to surveyor and eventually set down in a series of texts by various authors (*Corpus Agrimensorum Romanorum*), partly didactic and partly a historical celebration of the achievements of surveying. Most of the texts date from the first to the third centuries AD and are very useful in offering an unusual view of technical expertise in the Roman world, and the acquisition and distribution of land in Italy and elsewhere. This large body of Roman technical literature illustrates the relationship between state, citizens, law, and the management of land. The state was in control through the various stages of conquest, settlement, and colonization, in all of which public resources were invested. In the beginning, land was occupied in a haphazard way depending on what the first conquerors or settlers thought they could hold or cultivate. But once the state had decided the status of the land, it then interacted with the citizens. Some of the land was distributed to settlers in an organized and fair way in a system which became the pattern of future landholding. The surveyors' methodology of a regimented system with broad straight lines (*limites*), intersecting at right angles and forming large units (*centuriae*) often containing 200 *iugera*, distinctively marked the Italian and provincial landscape, and the *limites* served as rights of way and provided access (see also no. 437). In a society where landholding and the cultivation of the land were so important, the surveyors tried to control the rural environment for the benefit of individual citizens and manage disruptive elements, particularly turbulent rivers which changed the layout of the land. More generally, the careful demarcation of land, clear procedures of boundary-marking, the experienced judgement of surveyors, and the keeping of detailed records in stone or bronze inscriptions on the site with a copy in the record office in Rome helped to establish a framework for settling disputes in a land-owning economy, without resort to self-help or violence. Texts and discussion can be found in: Blume, Lachmann and Rudorff (1848–52); Thulin (1913); Clavel-Lévêque et al. (1996); Behrends et al. (1998); Campbell (2000); Guillaumin (2010); (2014); Lindermann, Knobloch and Möller (2018); Dilke (1971) offers an excellent introduction.

Frontinus, *Types of Land* (T, p. 1.1–3 = Campbell (2000), p. 3.3–4)

433. There are three types of land: firstly, land that has been divided and allocated; secondly, land that has been contained in a survey throughout its extent; thirdly land of uncertain boundary, which is not contained within any survey.

For Frontinus see p. 478. Frontinus here describes land that had been measured by means of straight lines and allocated; land not included within a survey was bounded according to local practice by rivers, mountains, roads, and so on.

Siculus Flaccus, *Categories of Land* (T, 102.1–8 = Campbell (2000), p. 105.27–33)

434. Land described as occupied, which some call *arcifinalis*, is land to which a victorious people has given the name by occupying it. For after wars had been fought, the victorious peoples confiscated all lands from which they had expelled the conquered, and generally gave the name 'territory' to them, with the intention that there should be a right of jurisdiction within their confines. Then, whatever a man occupied through his skill in cultivation, he called *arcifinalis* from the action of keeping off neighbours.

Hyginus, *Categories of Land* (T, p. 80.14–17 = Campbell (2000), p. 85.21–5)

435. Divided and allocated lands are those that have been granted or returned to veteran soldiers or other people in *centuriae*, with a specific

area written down, or that have been returned to previous landholders, or exchanged for their own.

On some occasions, for example after confiscations of land or disruption of established holdings by river action, officials and surveyors might arrange for an equivalent portion of land in a different location to be given in exchange to a possessor who had lost some of his own land.

Siculus Flaccus, *Categories of Land* (T, p. 117.22–5 = Campbell (2000), p. 121.7–8)

436. All *limites* divide up land and demarcate *centuriae*. As I said before, in land which has been divided and allocated, they must always be passable for rights of way and for conducting a survey.

Frontinus, *Land Disputes* (T, p. 10.7–13 = Campbell (2000), p. 9.16–22)

437. According to the law establishing a colony, all *limites* ought to serve as public rights of way. But many *limites*, because of the demands of the overall plan, run through uneven or woody areas, which are impassable for a road, and are indeed used as fields in those places where an adjacent landholder, whose wood perhaps occupies a *limes*, impudently prevents passage, although he ought to provide a *limes* or its equivalent width for a right of way.

For rights of way and servitudes see p. 237.

Agennius Urbicus, *Land Disputes* (T, p. 41.1–7 = Campbell (2000), p. 39.4–9)

438. There are two types of *subseciva*: one, where a *centuria* on the outer boundaries of allocated lands is not completed; and one which occurs within whole *centuriae*. It is this type that produces the greatest disputes. When the allocation was taking place in allocated lands, not all the area of land enclosed by four *limites* (that is, the *centuria*) could be allocated to the veterans. Some land remained unallocated in it and got the name *subsecivum* from the line that cut it off.

Not all land assigned for distribution to settlers could be included within the survey. Areas too rough for cultivation or habitation were excluded (*subseciva*), and other land served as common pasture areas that adjacent landholders could enjoy.

Liber Coloniarum (Lachmann (1848), p. 213.6 = Campbell (2000), p. 169.4–13)

439. The colony of Florentia (Florence) was founded by the triumvirs; the land was allocated under a *lex Iulia* and the *centuriae* of Caesar contain 200 *iugera*, divided by *kardines* and *decumani*. The boundary stones are circular, measuring one foot, and the intervals between them are 2,400 feet. There are also midpoint boundary markers, which are called 'flat', 1 foot long and 1 foot thick, and the intervals between them are 1,200 feet. Other boundary markers are placed proportionately and demarcate intermediate *limites*. Veteran soldiers preserve these markers, which were established to delineate individual holdings; they are not relevant to the overall plan or the straight lines of the *limites*, but to safeguarding the area of each holding, and are 600 feet apart from one another.

For the *Book of Colonies* see p. 102. In the case of Florentia its foundation date is uncertain; it may have been founded as a colony by Caesar in 59 BC and subsequently strengthened by more settlers; see Keppie (1983), 175–6. The *kardo* was the *limes* normally running from north to south, the *decumanus* from east to west. These arrangements by the state were crucial for future landholding in these communities, the relations between individuals, especially settlers and previous landholders, and the settlement of disputes.

Land and the Law: Disputes

Frontinus, *Land Disputes* (T, p. 4.2–11 = Campbell (2000), p. 5.5–12)

440. There are two causes of disputes: boundary and site. Any disagreement that arises from land is confined to one of these. But since even in these categories individual disputes have different characteristics, each dispute must be specifically defined. As far as I have been able to establish, there are fifteen different types of dispute: the position of boundary markers, a straight line boundary, boundary, site, area, ownership (of land), possession (of land), alluvial land, territorial jurisdiction, *subseciva*, public places, places omitted and not enclosed, sacred and religious places, control of rainwater, rights of way.

Alluvial land was land whose position or shape had been altered by river action; territorial jurisdiction related to inter-community disputes over allocated land; for *subseciva* see no. 438; public places were areas owned by the communities, such as common pasture land; places omitted were those not included in the original survey; ownership of a sacred site might be important for a community because of the revenue that accrued from festivals; rainwater should not be allowed to flow into a neighbouring property and cause damage.

Siculus Flaccus, *Categories of Land* (T, p. 118.26–119.1 = Campbell (2000), p. 121.33–6)

441. The only evidence should be whatever is laid down in the bronze tablets. But if anyone raises an objection it is normal to turn to the emperor's record office. For the imperial government keeps in the record office maps of all allocated and divided lands, and registers of land divisions and allocations.

For the keeping of records and land division see Moatti (1993), especially 63–78.

Agennius Urbicus, *Land Disputes* (T, p. 24.17–22 = Campbell (2000), p. 21.29–33)

442. Now it will greatly benefit our technique in speaking in someone's defence if we have studied the law with every care. We should not intervene in a dispute using any method of approach but must examine which proposition is most likely to be vindicated, lest by some intricacy we both impede the judge and make the dispute even more obscure.

***Commentary* on *Land Disputes* (T, p. 61.21–4 = Campbell (2000), p. 61.42–6)**

443. If there is a dispute about site, and the enquiry has the following procedure, namely, that there is no reference to a map or any written evidence, merely a statement by one party: 'I declare that this site begins here', while the other party makes a similar statement opposing this, in this case a comparison is made on the basis of similarities in types of cultivation.

The procedure involved trying to establish where one property ended and another began, for example, by comparing adjacent vineyards to see if the vines were the same and the rows matched.

***D* 10.1.2 (Ulpian, *Edict*, Book 19)**

444. This action relates to country estates, even though buildings may also come between them. For it does not much matter whether someone places trees or a building on a boundary. The judge in a case of deciding boundaries is permitted, where he is unable to determine the boundary, to settle the dispute by adjudicating. And if the judge indeed wants to remove a long-standing difficulty by establishing the boundaries in a

different direction, he can do this by adjudication and deciding that one party is in the wrong.

Hyginus, *Land Disputes* (T, p. 90.19–24 = Campbell (2000), p. 93.41–5)

445. Marks on trees belonging to a particular property are placed on the side away from the property, so that the marks leave the trees untouched on the side facing the owner's property. If the trees stand between two properties and are owned by both, they are marked on both sides, so that the marks belong to both parties and make it clear that the trees are owned in common.

For boundary-marking techniques see Campbell (2000), 468–71.

D 10.1.8 (Ulpian, *Opinions*, Book 6)

446. If after a river has burst its banks an inundation has disturbed the boundaries and provided an opportunity for some people to occupy that to which they have no legal right, the governor of the province orders that they should keep off the land of another, that the owner's land should be restored, and that boundary markers should be established by a land surveyor. It is part of his duty in a case involving boundaries to send surveyors and by means of them settle the issue of boundaries, in accordance with what is right, and if necessary to examine the locality with his own eyes.

Rivers caused special problems because of flooding and disruption of boundaries. Alluvial activity transferred quantities of land from one location to another, either gradually, or more dramatically after a large storm; and the deposition of soil and debris led to the formation of islands in midstream, which, as new land, raised questions of ownership; see Campbell (2012), 109–16. For the management of rivers and the protection of boat traffic, see Bannon (2017), 79–84.

Siculus Flaccus, *Categories of Land* (T, p. 121.26 – 122.15 = Campbell (2000), p. 125.14–28)

447. In some regions the area of rivers was included in the allocation. In some it was omitted, just like *subsecivum*; in others an area was excluded with the notation: 'so much for this or that river'. For example, in the territory of Pisaurum I discovered: 'granted and allocated' for instance 'to a veteran', then, 'his own property restored to the previous possessor', 'so much for the river Pisaurus, in which the bed … '. Then, even beyond the

riverbanks on both sides, an area is sometimes written in, throughout all the *centuriae* through which that river flows. In doing this the author of the division and allocation exercised a most equitable foresight. For the river, swollen by sudden and violent storms, breaks its banks and flows over the land, going even beyond the area assigned to it and damaging the land of its neighbours. Since the landholders suffer this inconvenience through a succession of storms, it seems fair that when the river has been again confined within its own bed and banks, those who suffered any loss should trace their land right up to the bed of the river. However, the people of Pisaurum officially sold off their area of land, and we must suppose that it was bought by the nearest neighbours who had lands adjoining it.

The width assigned to the Pisaurus was the furthest point to which it had ever flowed beyond its banks; for the river Ana and the problems caused by selling off the river environs, see no. 217.

Agennius Urbicus, *Land Disputes* (T, p. 42.3–17 = Campbell (2000), p. 39.28–41)

448. The dispute (about alluvial land) concerns the soil that a river deposits, and complex questions are thereby produced, namely whether it should belong to the person on the opposite bank whose land has been augmented on the retreat of the river water, or whether the man who lost some of his land should cross over and take possession of that soil that the river deposited. But against this is raised a very subtle point, namely, that the soil that one man lost does not immediately cross over to the other bank but is removed and washed away (by the river). On the other hand, the neighbour receives a very different type of soil, because, while the former lost soil that was perhaps cultivated and fertile, the latter was left with a residue of sand, stones, and mud washed up by the flood water. There is a further point, namely, that the river always marked the boundary between them, and should also do so now.

Gaius (*Institutes* 2.70–2) distinguished between gradual alluvial action (where land was added so gradually that the property holder could not tell how much was added at any particular moment), and more dramatic river action when a substantial portion of land was transferred to another property; it theoretically continued to belong to the original owner if he could identify it, unless it had remained in its new location so long that trees carried with it had taken root; see also no. 449.

Commentary on Land Disputes (T, p. 64.8–18 = Campbell (2000), p. 65.45–67.10)

449. Now, when there was a dispute in the area of the Po, because the river surges down sometimes in such a raging torrent that it changes its course and carries across its bank, so to speak, the land of many people over a wide area, and often even creates islands, Cassius Longinus, a very wise man and legal expert, decided that a landholder should lose whatever soil the river gradually eroded, since he ought to look after his own stretch of river bank without inflicting any loss on a third party. But if the river had surged down with unusual force and changed its course, everyone should claim his own area of land since it had obviously been swept away not through the carelessness of the landholder but by the vehemence of the storm. If, however, the river had created an island, he decided that the person from whose land it had been fashioned should possess it; on the other hand, if the island had been fashioned out of land owned in common, each person should recover his own portion.

It is not clear how landholders were to be compensated in the circumstances described. It is likely that surveyors with the help of the map of allocations could work out what a landholder had lost, and another had gained. The profiting landholder could then either make over to the losing landholder another equivalent piece of land or provide appropriate financial compensation. This was another means of land acquisition, which was important in an agricultural community at the mercy of turbulent rivers. But the landowner was responsible for taking reasonable precautions to protect his land.

D 39.3.1.2 (Ulpian, *Edict*, Book 53)

450. Neratius noted that a man constructed a ditch to keep out the water which used to overflow from a marsh and come across his land; if the marsh should be filled up with rainwater and this water is deflected by the ditch he built, with the result that it damages the fields of a neighbour, he will be compelled to remove it by an action for rainwater.

Disputes over rainwater took different form in different regions; in Italy it was a serious offence to divert water onto someone's land, but in Africa to prevent water from crossing another's land.

FIRA 1, no. 72 = McCrum and Woodhead (1961), 460 (AD 77)

451. Emperor Caesar Vespasian Augustus sends greetings to the magistrates and senators of the Vanacini:

I am delighted that Otacilius Sagitta, my friend and procurator, has governed you in such a way that he earned your testimonial. In respect of the border dispute which you have with the Marians, which related to those lands which you bought from my procurator, Publilius Memorialis, I have written asking my procurator Claudius Clemens to fix the boundaries and have sent a surveyor. I confirm the privileges granted to you by Augustus after his seventh consulship (27 BC), which you retained to the time of Galba.

The ambassadors Lasemo, son of Lecunus and priest of Augustus, and Eunus, son of Tomasus and priest of Augustus, presented the case, in the consulship of Gaius Arruntius Catellius Celer and Marcus Arruntius Aquila, 12 October.

This inscription from Corsica relates to dispute between a local people and the Marians, who are presumably descendants of colonists originally settled by Gaius Marius. Vespasian was keen to realize the value of unsold *subseciva* (see p. 105), and the Vanacini may have encountered problems with the exact dimensions of the lands they had purchased from the emperor's procurator.

D 11.6.1 (Ulpian, *Edict*, Book 24)

452. The praetor offers an action on the facts (*in factum*) against a land surveyor, by whom we should not be misled. For it is in our interests that we should not be deceived in the statement of area, if perhaps the dispute concerns boundaries, or the purchaser or the vendor wishes to know the area of the land for sale. He offers this action because the ancients did not believe that in the case of a surveyor there was a process of hire of services, but rather that he offered a service as a favour, and whatever was given to him was given as remuneration and therefore was called an honorarium. If, however, a suit is begun on the basis of hire, it must be stated that the claim cannot be upheld.

This relates to the increasingly important role of land surveyors in land disputes. Over time they came to assume a professional status; see Campbell (2000), xlv–liii. Because the surveyor was not considered to hire out his services he could not be sued on hire; but the praetor on his authority allowed a suit, which was based not on a contract or established law, but on the actions of the defendant which had caused harm or loss to the plaintiff.

Making Use of Rural Property

In an economy where agriculture was particularly important, land was the basis of the wealth of the upper classes, but much of that land was conveniently tilled by tenant farmers from a lower social class. Since large numbers were employed in farming one way and another, it is reasonable that it figured prominently in government policy, especially since emperors depended on the well-off landed proprietors in Italy and the provinces to hold offices and administer the towns and their territories for Rome's benefit. In this context it is worth asking if the Roman state developed and used law-making to develop the rural economy generally, or more particularly to guarantee the social and economic interests of the upper classes. In this the issue of farm tenancy 'was an economic institution of fundamental importance to both the private agrarian economy and to the state' (Kehoe (2007), 2). This should be seen in the context of the development of large-scale private estates and of tracts of land owned by the state or the emperor. In fact, the action taken by the imperial government in organizing its estates in Africa can show us something about its efforts to encourage tenants to ensure that the land was cultivated, and, if possible, that more be brought into cultivation, perhaps in competition with private landlords, and also to protect their tenants where necessary from the abusive behaviour of officials (Kehoe (2007), 53–62).

In some ways the upper-class landholders needed the same kind of stability from their tenants. The crucial issue was the nature of the farm lease and the circumstances in which legal procedure could be invoked if disputes could not be settled informally at local level. It was in everyone's interest that the land should be looked after in the long term by tenants who were confident enough to be productive farmers. Therefore, it might be thought that the government would seek to encourage this, foster security of tenure and protection from excessive rent demands, take account of customary practices in various areas, and adjudicate disputes relating to possession of land and debt, with the intention of avoiding violence, while at the same time ensuring the profitability of estates for landowners. To what extent could this be achieved through the operation of the law, especially since the balance of power seemed to lie with the owner? Farm leases were traditionally of five years' duration; the tenant was required to cultivate the land usually for a money rent, and any crops from the land became his only when they had been harvested; he was entitled to keep any profits beyond his rent; for negotiating the lease see nos. 460–7.

Kehoe (2007, 18–25; 2012b, 115–21) has argued effectively that the law was not just interested in the richest. Three factors intersected: the agrarian economy, the law, and the social concerns of the government. In several areas it seems that jurists did respond to social concerns and were not operating in a closed intellectual tradition. Landholders and the legal authorities were willing to adapt the classical farm lease to provide tenants with greater security, thus offering an incentive to invest for the long term. Leases could be enforced through legal institutions, and furthermore the classical farm lease provided a set of legal conventions within which the authorities in resolving disputes interpreted leases whose terms were based on local practice. Leases also took account of the impact of natural disasters and loss of crops (see pp. 267–70). Importantly it was recognized that a lease was tacitly renewed if the tenant remained on a farm without the landlord's objection (Kehoe (2012b), 118). Jurists would respect contracts and operate on the basis that a tenant could sue his landlord, though of course a poor man might find that intimidating; see also Frier (1980), 174–95; Johnston (1999), 62–7 (on leases). For land ownership see Temin (2013), 139–49.

Farm Tenancy

Pliny, *Letters* 9.37

453. I must remain here because of the necessity of renting out my farms on long leases, and I need to adopt a new policy for this. During the previous five years, although I granted generous remission of rent, the arrears grew, and so many of my tenants have lost interest in reducing their debt since they have no hope in paying off the entire amount … I must deal with this increasing problem and find a cure. One method would be to rent the farms not for a cash sum but for a set share of the produce, and then to install some of my men as overseers of this to keep an eye on the harvest.

This shows how important it was for Pliny to find suitable tenant farmers to work his estates. Faced with the problem of increasing tenant debt he considers moving to a system in which the tenants became sharecroppers, who paid over in kind to the owner a proportion of whatever they produced. Pliny is planning to use his own employees to manage this system. Passage no. 454 shows Pliny obtaining a tenant farmer of some means to take over a more substantial farm; Sherwin-White (1966), 519–21 discusses the advantages of the share-cropping system for the tenant; Kehoe (2007), 106–9.

Pliny, *Letters* 6.3

454. Many thanks for taking over the cultivation of the small farm which I gave to my nurse. It was worth 100,000 sesterces when I gave it to her, but subsequently its returns declined, and its value has been reduced; it will recover with you in charge. But do remember that I am entrusting to you not only the woods and vines, though these are included, but my little gift. For I, the donor, am as concerned that it should be as profitable as possible, as is my nurse who received it.

The farm was intended to serve as a kind of pension for Pliny's nurse but had been badly managed.

Siculus Flaccus, *Categories of Land* (T, p. 100.13–19 = Campbell (2000), p. 105.3–7)

455. Afterwards, as larger areas captured from the enemy began to become available, they divided up and allocated some of the land; other land remained, but in such a way that it was the territory of the Roman people, for example, in Picenum in the region of Reate, where there are mountains called 'Roman'. They are the territories of the Roman people and the rent (*vectigal*) from them belongs to the public treasury.

A large quantity of land was owned by the Roman state or by individual communities (*municipia* or colonies), and this was often leased to tenants for a rent. In the colony at Urso in Spain founded by Julius Caesar, the land was leased for up to five years (see no. 456), but in the imperial period land was let for much longer periods or in perpetuity; consequently, it is likely that the tenant was virtually the owner and could leave the property to an heir (Gaius, *Institutes* 3.145). See de Zulueta (1953), vol. II, 173. The emperors also owned estates and were keen to recruit tenants and keep or bring land into production (see no. 457).

***Lex Colonia Genetiva* Crawford (1996), p. 405, Chapter 82**

456. Whatever lands and woods and buildings shall have been granted or attributed to the colonists of the *Colonia Genetiva Iulia*, so that they may make public use of them, no one is to sell those lands or those woods, or lease them for a period longer than five years, nor is anyone to refer to the decurions or pass a decree of the decurions, through which those lands or those woods may be sold, or leased in any other way.

For the colony at Urso, see no. 219.

FIRA 1, no. 102 = Johnson, Coleman-Norton, Bourne (1961), no. 268 (Ain-Ouassel in the Bagradas Valley) (Extract)

457. Because our Caesar in his tireless care, by which he is without cease looking out for the advantages of mankind, orders all kinds of land to be cultivated, both that which is suitable for olive trees or vines as well as that which is suitable for grain, and for that reason by the grace of his foresight the right is given to all persons to occupy areas of that kind, even in the surveyed parts, which have been leased, of the Blandian Estate and the Udensian estate, and also those parts of the Lamian Estate and the Domitian Estate, which adjoin the Thusdritan Estate and are not cultivated by the leaseholders.

The date is between AD 198 and 212 and the enactment permits the cultivation of unoccupied public land and neglected allocated land on the imperial estates in Africa and establishes the obligations and rights of those who occupied them; it quotes extensively from previous regulations of Hadrian, and the 'Mancian formula' probably dating from the first century AD. The leaseholders were responsible for managing the affairs of the estate.

Abbott and Johnson (1968), no. 142 (Extract)

458. If then some redress for these disgraceful outrages is not granted us from your heavenly right hand, and support for the future, it is inevitable that those of us who remain, being unable to bear the avarice of the collection men and of our enemies, who use the pretexts we have already described, shall even abandon the hearths of our forefathers and our ancestral burial areas and move to private land for our own safety (the men who are carrying out this life of crime ignore those who live there, preferring instead your own farmers), and become refugees from the imperial estates in which we have been both born and brought up and have continued since the time of our forefathers to farm, carrying out our agreement with the imperial treasury.

This inscription from Philadelphia in Lydia dates to the third century, probably in the reign of Septimius Severus and Caracalla. Government officials had been corrupt in the administration of the imperial estate and had abused the tenant farmers, even murdering some. Municipal officials had also attempted to force the farmers to accept obligations in neighbouring towns. The men making this appeal claim to be long-term tenants of the emperor and make the interesting claim that private landholders were better able to protect their tenants than the emperor; for the abusive behaviour of officials see pp. 167–73.

P. Oxy. 1279 (AD 139)

459. To Petronius Dionysius, *strategos*, from Ophelas also called Corax, freedman of Apia also called Dionysia, daughter of Dionysios, of Oxyrhynchus. I agree to lease from the state for five years from the current third year of Antoninus Caesar the lord, three *arurae* of unproductive land in the vicinity of Senao, in the holdings of Heraklides and Heraklides, of which the neighbouring areas are, on the south, a field, on the north and east a public dyke, on the west, the land of Didymion, son of Demetrios, on condition that every year I may sow and plant the land with any crops that I choose except wheat, woad, and (?), and may have the pastures and additional pastures at the yearly rent for the pastures of four drachmas in total, and this sum I shall pay annually in the month of Caesareus. If any part should come to lack water, an allowance is to be granted to me, and at the end of the period of five years I shall not be compelled to take the lease. The third year of the Emperor Caesar Titus Aelius Hadrianus Antoninus Augustus Pius, Hathur 11. I, Ophelas also called Corax, presented this application. Written by Hermes, *nomographos.*

The rent for this unproductive land owned by the state seems comparatively low; the government perhaps aimed to stimulate interest in bringing more land under cultivation. The lessee attempts to protect himself against the possibility that government officials might compel him to continue with an unprofitable lease. In the context of the problem of abuse in the management of land, the government wanted to make sure that issues in the rural economy were settled under the authority of the Roman courts (see Kehoe (2007), 160). This did help to establish the property rights of estate owners but also served to protect smaller landholders against arbitrary actions by the more powerful.

Negotiating the Lease

D 19.2.22.3 (Paul, *Edict*, Book 34)

460. The nature of buying and selling is that it is accepted that you can buy for less what is worth more and also sell for more what is worth less, and so there is reciprocal advantage; the same rule applies in leases and hires.

D 19.2.23 (Hermogenianus, *Epitome of Law*, Book 2)

461. And so, when a lease has been set up it cannot be rescinded on the ground that the rent is too low, unless the opponent can be proved to have engaged in fraud.

CJ 4.65.9 (AD 234)

462. Emperor Alexander Augustus to Fuscus, soldier. The purchaser of a farm is not obliged to permit the tenant, to whom the previous owner rented the property, to remain (until the expiry of his lease), unless he bought the property under this condition. But if it is proved that he made some kind of agreement, even if not written, that the tenant could remain under the same lease, under an action of good faith he is obliged to accept what he (the original owner) agreed.

CJ 4.65.16 (AD 260)

463. Emperors Valerianus and Gallienus Augusti and Caesar Valerianus to Aurelius Timotheus. It is right to observe the lease agreement and not in the name of rent to demand more than was agreed. If, however, the term for which the farm was leased has expired and the tenant has remained with the same lease, it is accepted that by tacit agreement this serves to renew the lease along with the pledge obligation.

The principle of tacit renewal of lease was a mechanism by which the government could encourage long-term lease arrangements. If a tenant remained on the land and cultivated it without a specific objection from the landowner, then the lease was considered renewed for one further year on the same terms as before. This arrangement would encourage a tenant to continue to invest in cultivating the land effectively, which was also to the benefit of the landowner and the government, which had an interest in tax revenues; Kehoe (2007), 125–6.

CJ 11. (49)50.1

464. Emperor Constantine Augustus to Maximus, Vicarius of the east. If a tenant is forced by the owner to pay more than he had been accustomed to, and which was previously demanded, he should approach a judge as quickly as he can gain access and prove the offence, so that the man who is convicted of demanding more than he had been accustomed to receive should be prohibited from doing this in the future, having first returned the sum that he is shown to have illegally extorted.

Constantine's response is equitable, but a plaintiff could not always expect benevolent imperial intervention. There follow several examples of agricultural leases from Egypt (nos. 465–7).

P. Ryl. 172 = *SP* 43 (AD 208)

465. To Flavia Petronilla, also called Titanias, with her guardian, her husband Gaius Valerius Pansa, ex-gymnasiarch, from Kan[.]ereos, and Heries his brother. We wish to lease from you the palm grove called the grove of Herennios, which belongs to you, in the vicinity of the village of Hephaestias, at a total rent of one thousand silver drachmae, and an extraordinary payment of two *artabae* of dates on single stems, assessed by the *dromos* date measure of the village, and of twelve *salotia* (meaning unclear). And I will pay you the rent promptly at the time of picking. I, the lessee, will be liable for all the works, namely, picking, fertilizing, irrigating, constructing basins, and a third share of banking up canals, and a half share of cleaning them. I will also pay two *artabae* of *sabautia* (meaning unclear). I, Gaius Valerius Pansa, have let it as is set out above, and as long as no one bids higher, you will retain the lease set out above. Year seventeen of Lucius Septimius Severus Pius Pertinax Arabicus Adiabenicus and Marcus Aurelius Antoninus Pius, Augusti, and Publius Septimius Geta Caesar Augustus, Thoth 17.

In the procedure of buying and selling it was possible to cancel a deal within a time limit (see no. 306); for the guardianship of women, see p. 23.

P. Oxy. 499 = *SP* 42 (AD 121)

466. Tryphon, son of Aristander and Sarapion, son of Herodes of Oxyrhynchus, have leased to Apollonios, son of Horos, of the village of Senepta, Persian of the Epigone (a legal status), for the current sixth year of Hadrian Caesar the lord, from their property in the village mentioned, in the holding of Dion, the ten and a half *arurae* recently planted with corn, of which the boundaries are on the east the property of Didymos, on the south that of the lessors mentioned above, on the north the same, on the west that of Seuthes, son of Potamon, which is to be planted with grass for cutting and grazing, at a rent for each *arura*, without any further measurement, of thirty-six silver drachmae, free of every risk, with the lessor to be liable for the taxes on the land, who is also to be the owner of the crop until he receives the rent. If the lease is confirmed, the lessee is to pay the rent in the month of Pauni of the said year, and if he is in arrears, he is to forfeit what he owes increased by one half, and the lessor is to have the right of execution on the said Apollonios and all his property, as if by legal judgement. This lease is valid. Year six of the Emperor Caesar Trajan Hadrian Augustus, Thoth 25. (Signed) I, Serapion, son of Herodes,

have undertaken the lease of the above-mentioned ten and one half *arurae*, without any further measurement, at thirty-six silver drachmae for each *arura*, as is set out. The same date. Lease of Apollonios for year six.

Mitteis and Wilcken (1912), no. 176 = *SP* 280

467. To Philoxenos, ex-*cosmetes*, *strategos* of the division Themistes in the Arsinoite nome, from Herieos, son of Satabous, from Socnopaei Nesos. As long ago as year thirteen of the divine Claudius I leased an olive oil factory from the former estate of Narcissus, for a rent of two hundred drachmae and three *choes* of oil. Subsequently, however, since those supervising the estate did not give me the iron receptacles or the other equipment necessary for the oil-press, I myself was compelled to provide them by purchase at my own expense, and also a lever and mortars and other essential material, all also at my own expense, as they took no account of me. Since therefore the factory itself was ruinous I was compelled to install beams and supports, and for two years, although unable to use the factory, I have been compelled to pay the rent from my own funds, I beseech you, since I am no longer able to sustain the losses, to force the supervisors to refrain from harassing me concerning the rent.

This situation in the reign of Nero resembles the case of those who rented a farm of which some aspects did not function properly; the tenant in such circumstances could avoid paying rent (see nos. 468–71). Narcissus was the freedman confidant and adviser of Claudius after whose death he was forced to commit suicide and his estate was added to the imperial properties.

Remission of Rent

Columella, *De Re Rustica* 1.7.1–4

468. The landholder should deal civilly with his tenants and show himself pleasant. He should be keen to get work from them rather than payments since this tends to be less offensive and overall is more profitable. For when the land is carefully cultivated it usually produces a profit, and never brings any loss, unless a serious storm or robbers attack it, and in that case the tenant does not dare seek a remission of rent.

See Kehoe (2007), 106 for Columella's attitude to his tenants; he preferred tenants with whom he could establish a mutually beneficial relationship over time; to this end he was prepared to be flexible.

D 19.2.15.1–2 (Ulpian, *Edict*, Book 32)

469. The lessee is given an action on hire. It comes about for reasons such as the following: imagine if he is not allowed to enjoy what he had leased, for example because possession of the entire farm or part of it is not granted to him, or the villa is not repaired, or the stable, or a place where he needs to keep his animals, or if they came to an agreement on something in the contract of hire, and this is not provided, there will be a legal action on hire. 2. Let us consider if the lessor should be responsible in any way to the lessee if a storm has done a great deal of damage. Servius thinks that the owner should indemnify his tenant farmer for any kind of force that could not be resisted, for example through river action, or various types of birds such as starlings and jackdaws, or some similar event, or if there was an enemy invasion. But if the problem arose from the property itself, for example if the wine becomes sour or if the crops are ruined by worms or weeds, this loss should be borne by the lessee. But if there was a landslide that destroyed the entire crop, the tenant should not bear the loss since he should not be compelled to pay the rent for the land on top of the loss of his seed. Furthermore, if frost destroys an olive crop, or this occurs because of unusually high temperatures, the owner will be liable for the loss; but if nothing unusual happens, the tenant is liable. And we must agree that this is true if a passing army brazenly steals something. However, if an earthquake demolishes the land so comprehensively that nothing exists, the owner is liable for the loss. For he must provide land for the lessee so that he can enjoy it.

The contractual remedy of remission of rent (*remissio mercedis*) was probably first introduced in the late republic; it arose from a generally accepted agricultural custom that if force majeure caused failure of crop the loss lay on the landlord. The remedy was available when force that could not be resisted so damaged the crops of a tenant farmer that his ability to make his annual rent payment to the landowner was impaired. The tenant was legally entitled to the agreed rent for the year in which the damage to the crops occurred. This ensured that the landowner bore some or all of the cost of significant crop failure. The legal authorities therefore showed some flexibility in a willingness to modify the allocation of risk under the classical lease contract, and landowners could go beyond the contract to help a tenant either for social reasons or to retain tenants, for example in offering remissions of rent for infertility (*sterilitas*); lawyers accepted this and defined the rights and obligations of both parties when a remission was granted; it was like a renegotiation of the contract (Kehoe (2012a), especially 197–205), though the landowner was responsible only for the most unpredictable of risks, and when remission was granted the basic terms of the contract were preserved (Kehoe

(2007), 110–13; (2015), 238–43; (2016), 649–52). It was in the interests of the legal authorities to promote private bargaining.

Frier (1989–90) analysed the economic impact of *remissio mercedis*. Noting that *remissio mercedis* transgressed the rule of contract law that the parties' agreement on price or rent could not subsequently be altered because the amount proved to be too high or low in respect of the value received, he argued that jurists intervened in the free market, by granting a special contractual remedy in cases where the parties themselves had not provided for catastrophic crop losses, because *remissio mercedis* was economically efficient since it made contract negotiations easier, and a tenant who expected to be granted *remissio* could, if necessary, be asked for a higher rent (Frier, op. cit., 260–9); see also Foxhall (1990), 111–12. Where a no remission clause had been inserted in the contract, the tenant could seek lower rent.

D 19.2.15.4 (Ulpian, *Edict*, Book 32)

470. Papinian in the fourth book of responses said that if someone grants one year's remission of rent to his tenant farmer on the grounds that the land is infertile, and then there is plenty during the following years, the remission of the rent is not prejudicial to the landowner, and he can even demand the rent for the year in which he granted a remission.

D 19.2.25.6 (Gaius, *Provincial Edict*, Book 10)

471. Superior force, which the Greeks describe as the 'power of god', should not cause a loss to the lessee if the crops have suffered damage to an unacceptable level. But the tenant farmer should equitably endure moderate loss since he is not being deprived of a significant profit. However, I am obviously referring to a tenant farmer who rents for a set amount of cash. But where the tenant farmer is a sharecropper, he must share the profit and loss with the owner of the land, as in the law of partnership.

D 19.2.55.1–2 (Paul, *Views*, Book 2)

472. On a farm that has been leased, if the lessee by his own labour has developed it, or has built or established anything in a way that was necessary or beneficial, then even though this was not part of the (leasing) agreement, he can take an action on hire against the owner of the farm to recover his expenditure. If, in contravention of the terms of his lease, a man abandons a farm before the term has expired without a just or reasonable cause, he can be sued based on his lease for the payment of the rent for the

remaining time, to the extent that compensation can be secured for the lessor to the amount of his interest.

D 19.2.9.3–4 (Ulpian, *Edict*, Book 32)

473. If it was stated in the leasing contract that the tenant farmers of an estate could have a harmless fire, and if some accidental occurrence should cause a fire, the lessee will not be held responsible for this risk. But if the carelessness of the lessee has caused the loss, for which he must be held responsible, then he will be liable. 4 The emperor Antoninus and his father, when a herd which a man had leased was driven off, issued a rescript in the following terms: 'If it can be proved that robbers drove off the goats without any fraudulent action on your part, you will not be compelled to take responsibility for this misfortune by an action on lease, and you will receive the payment, as being un-owed by you, for the period that followed (after the loss of the animals)'.

Pliny, *Letters* 3.19

474. Now, the chief point of debate is the following. The land is fertile with rich and well-watered soil; the farm consists of fields, vines, and woods, the produce of which provides a steady though admittedly modest income. But the richness of the land is being exhausted by incompetent cultivation. The previous owner more than once sold off the pledged possessions of the tenants, with the result that while he temporarily reduced their rent arrears, he also left them debilitated for the future. This weakness caused their debts to increase again.

Pliny is preparing to buy a neighbouring estate which is in poor condition; the existing occupiers are tenant farmers; the previous owner had sold up the possessions the tenants had pledged for the rent. Pliny dealt with rent arrears on his own estates by granting a remission and moving to a share-cropping system (see no. 453). Sherwin-White (1966), 254–9 estimates that he was dealing with between fifty and seventy tenants. For the issue of pledged possessions, see pp. 275–6.

Making Use of Urban Property

There was no Roman law specifically dealing with landlords and tenants (see in general Frier (1980), 21–34; 174–95). Urban leasehold was based around two actions relating to contract: *actio locati* (by the landlord) and *actio conducti* (by the tenant). Several issues arose at law and produced some rules of procedure: justified expulsion, abandonment, justified deduction from rent, the landlord's right to retain the tenant's possessions in lieu of rent, damage to property, and tenants who remained beyond their lease. Leases were normally for a fixed period, and a property owner could rent an entire apartment block (*insula*) to an intermediary who might sublet to tenants; July 1 was the normal start of the rental year (see no. 487). Although the law did not offer possessory protection to tenants, casual expulsion would be deterred by the contractual element of the deal. Then the tenant would have to sue the owner of the property. The state preferred to have issues involving abandonment, expulsion, and compensation under the remit of the courts. Jurists were particularly interested in how the contracts were executed and fulfilled; it is possible that pre-existing social conditions in respect of rental property were adapted by jurists as a basis for establishing and applying the legal institutions of urban leasehold. It is plausible that jurists would have certain attitudes in line with upper-class thinking, and perhaps assume a capacity to litigate among the protagonists. However, Frier (1980, especially 39–47) goes further, arguing that much of classical Roman lease law related to flats that were erected for tenants who had means at their disposal and were able to stand up for themselves in social terms and at law. He takes account here of the discovery at Pompeii of an apartment block seemingly constructed for superior and discerning customers (see also no. 480). On his view there was a clear distinction between *cenacula* (multi-roomed apartments for the well-off) and *meritoria* (single rooms for rent for poorer citizens). There is certainly evidence for upper-class renters, but it is important not to generalize from a few notable cases which we happen to hear about. Crook (1983) casts some doubt on Frier's arguments for upper-class tenants, pointing out that some of the rules about tenants' rights and duties 'are rather implausible as examples of law directed at upper-class tenants'. For example, he notes the lack of a right of possession, and the ability of a landlord to seize the tenant's possessions if he defaulted in the rent. Indeed, Ulpian notes that if a tenant died without having enough resources to pay for his funeral, the landlord had to pay his burial costs out of his effects and keep the rest against the rent owed, which hardly suggests an upper-class environment (*D* 11.7.14.1). The priorities of the legal establishment were to manage equitably the rental market between upper-class landlords and tenants, and perhaps on a long view to help provide a supply of housing for the population of Rome and other bustling towns like Ostia and Pompeii; in part they could achieve that by day-to-day interest in the routine working of the urban lease and dealing with the consequences of disputes (nos. 478; 483; 485–6). Although legal provision protected rent and the landlord's property and enforced the agreed terms of contracts, in some respects the law was even-handed between landlord and tenant, with a certain balancing of interests (Frier (1980), 207–12; Johnston (1999), 62–3); see also du Plessis (2016) who notes the commercial aspects of urban rental contracts; rental of a tenement block could produce a substantial income through letting to a principal or primary tenant who could then sublet the property. For the importance of urban renting as a source of wealth, see Garnsey (1976).

In respect of the seizure of movable items the interdict *de migrando* available to tenants of urban property allowed a tenant to remove such items held by a landlord on account of unpaid rent (Frier (1980), 105–35); there were four grounds for this remedy: the items detained did not form part of the original agreement as pledged; they did, but the rent had been paid; the rent had not been paid but adequate additional security had been established; it was the landlord's fault that security had not been provided. The interdict was introduced to deal with the difficulties arising from a contractual clause that came to be inserted in contracts of urban tenancy and that served to pledge the tenant's current and future assets for the payment of rent. This clause was included alongside one listing specific goods to be pledged and would come into effect only if the specific goods did not raise enough money to pay the rent arrears. It is not clear how effective the interdict *de migrando* was and the extent to which all tenants (not just the upper classes) had access to it (du Plessis (2012b), especially 131–47).

Urban Property Owners

Aulus Gellius, *Noctes Atticae* 15.1.1–3

475. Therefore we friends of his (Antonius Iulianus, the orator) gathered all round and were following him home, when, as we were travelling up mount Cispium, we caught sight of a block of flats on fire; it was built with many lofty floors and all the neighbouring buildings were engulfed in a vast conflagration. Then one of Iulianus' companions said: 'There is a great return on urban properties, but the risks are by far the greatest. If, however, some remedy could be found to prevent houses in Rome from going on fire so frequently, then by heavens I would have put my rural properties up for sale and bought urban ones'.

D 5.3.27.1 (Ulpian, *Edict*, Book 15)

476. Furthermore, the rents obtained from leasing out urban properties will come (into the claim for inheritance), even if they are obtained from a brothel; for brothels are operated on the property of many respectable men.

D 7.1.13.8 (Ulpian, *On Sabinus*, Book 18)

477. In the case where the usufruct of a house (*domus*) has been bequeathed, the beneficiary of the usufruct must not rent rooms (*meritoria*) in it or divide the house into apartments (*cenacula*). He can certainly rent it, but he must rent it as an entire house.

See Frier (1980), 27–8 on the distinction between *meritoria* or *cellae* and *cenacula*, and p. 271 in this volume. However, the jurists make no distinction in the legal process applied to both types of accommodation.

D 19.2.30pr (Alfenus, *Digest Summarized by Paul*, Book 3)

478. A man rented an apartment block for thirty gold pieces and then leased out the individual rooms in such a way that he collected forty gold pieces from them all together. The owner of the apartment block said that the building had a defect and demolished it. The question was: what amount of damages should be calculated if the renter of the entire block took an action on the basis of the lease?

This illustrates the practice of sub-letting and the debate over appropriate compensation for the lessee; the owner presumably argued that the building was unsafe and liable to collapse.

CIL 6.65; 67 = *ILS* 3500; 3501a

479. M. Vettius Balanus ordered the sanctuary of Bona dea to be restored. Cladus placed the image of the restored Bona dea in the protection of the Bolanus apartment block, and also willingly and properly bestowed the shrine. (On the side) Belonging to Bolanus.

This seems to refer to apartments owned by Vettius Bolanus in Rome; this is possibly the man who was consul c. AD 66 and subsequently governor of Britain (Tacitus, *Histories* 2.65; *Agricola* 8), or he may be the consul of AD 111.

FIRA 3, no. 143 (Pompeii)

480. The apartment block called Arriana Polliana belonging to Cn. Alleius Nigidius Maius. Shops are let from 1(?) July next along with their porticoes, also superior apartments and a house. Potential tenants should apply to Primus, slave of Cn. Alleius Nigidius Maius.

For the issue of more expensive apartments at Pompeii see p. 271. See nos. 103 and 174 for Claudius' attempt to control the reckless demolition of buildings by speculators who perhaps sought land or materials to build profitable rentable accommodation. The usual rental period began on 1 July, but the inscription mentions the i(des) (15 July); an amendment to k(alends) is suggested.

Landlords and Tenants

D 19.2.35pr (Africanus, *Questions*, Book 8)

481. This distinction corresponds to the one introduced by Servius, and which has been approved by nearly everyone, namely that, if an owner rents an entire apartment block and then prevents his tenant's enjoyment by rebuilding it, we must consider if it was necessary to demolish the building.

This relates to the balance of legal responsibility; the owner should keep his building in good repair, but also keep the building work under control, so as to provide a reasonable environment for the tenants.

D 43.17.3.3 (Ulpian, *Edict*, Book 69)

482. When a tenant prevented an owner who wished to repair his house, it was agreed that an interdict for possession should equally be applied, and that the owner should make a witnessed statement that he was not preventing the tenant from living there, but from having possession.

The lessor needs to assert his right to possess the property in order to make repairs in the face of opposition from his tenant, but without denying the tenant the right to reside there. By preventing the lessor from making use of what he possessed, the tenant was effectively disputing his possession.

D 19.2.27 (Alfenus, *Digest*, Book 2)

483. The occupants, if their use of some part of their apartment is somewhat less comfortable, should not immediately make a deduction from the

rent. For the condition applying to the occupant is that if something untoward happened which made it necessary for the owner to demolish some part, he should put up with some small element of inconvenience, but not to the extent that the owner could lay open that part of the flat of which the resident made most use. A further question was: if someone abandoned their flat because they were afraid, did they owe the rent or not? The reply was if there was a genuine reason why he should fear some danger, even though in reality there was no danger, he did not owe the rent. But if the reason for his fear was not legally justified, he did still owe the rent.

Juvenal, *Satires* 3.193–202

484. We live in a city propped up to a large extent by feeble supports; for in this way the landlord prevents the collapse of his building and plasters over the gaping hole of an old crack and invites his tenants to sleep sound in a tottering ruin. I would prefer to live where there are no fires and no panics during the night. Your next neighbour is already shouting for water and removing his scanty possessions and your third floor is already smouldering, but you are unaware; for if the alarm is raised on the ground floor the last to burn will be the man on the top floor, who is protected from the rain only by the tiling where the gentle doves lay their eggs.

Not every owner was eager to make repairs, according to Juvenal's caustic view of living in Rome. And fire was an ever-present danger.

D 19.2.11.1 (Ulpian, *Edict*, Book 32)

485. If it was agreed in the lease that the tenant should not have a fire and he nevertheless had one, he will be liable, even if a fire starts accidentally, because he should not have had a fire.

D 2.14.4pr (Paul, *Edict*, Book 3)

486. Because tacit agreements are considered valid, it is agreed that in the letting of urban properties the movable effects of the tenant are held to be pledged to the lessor, even if there was no specific agreement to this effect.

See p. 267 for the issue of rent arrears.

Martial 12.32.1–5

487. O great disgrace of the first of July, Vacerra, I saw, I saw your luggage, the part which had not been confiscated in lieu of two years' rent, carried away by your wife with her seven red hairs, and your grey-haired mother and enormous sister.

The first of July was the normal date for the start of a rental contract unless other arrangements had been made (see no. 480); Martial imagines an eviction and seizing of pledged possessions.

***P. Mich.* 1355**

488. And no one knew whether the house belonged to me or you because there was no disagreement between me and you. But now I am the victim of violence by your very own Ptolema, who contacted me in the following words: 'Give up the house or your household furnishings will be thrown out'. I ought not to have been subjected to this treatment. For I have assurances for the time from the Amesysia to the Amesysia, and the god willing I owe you nothing on the rent except for the current semester only. I pray for your good health.

The Amesysia was an Egyptian celebration usually held in mid summer. This refers to an eviction notice where the tenant had an oral rental agreement running for a year between the festival dates, which was divided into two payment periods of six months. The tenant had paid the rent for the first six months but would not yet have been in arrears for the second period. He argues that there are no grounds for his eviction (which could be the basis of legal action on his part), and points to previous good relations with his landlord and his unjustifiably poor treatment in the current circumstances, which might serve to embarrass the landlord; see Frier (1980), 221–2.

***D* 19.2.24.2 (Paul, *Edict*, Book 34)**

489. If a house or a piece of land has been rented for a five-year period, the owner can immediately bring an action against the renter or tenant farmer, if the one abandons the house and the other gives up cultivating the land.

***CJ* 4.65.3 (AD 214)**

490. Emperor Antoninus Augustus to Flavius Callimorphus. If you have paid the entire rent to the owner of the apartment block for the dwelling which you say you have rented, it is not right for you to be expelled against

your will, unless the owner proves that the dwelling is necessary for his own use, or he wishes to repair the house, or you have infringed the rental agreement.

For the tenant seeking compensation on the grounds of the loss of his accommodation much depended on the issue of justified or unjustified expulsion. Other major questions involved the circumstances in which rent could be withheld, such as the inconvenience caused by building modifications; see nos. 481–3; 488.

CHAPTER 6

Crime and Punishment

Introduction

This chapter considers how the legal system dealt with theft, damage to property, personal insult and violence, and the means for citizens to obtain redress. The law of obligations had a prominent place since, for example, theft, the most common action that modern law defines under criminal law, was under Roman law a delict, prosecuted through action taken by the injured party on the basis of an obligation on the wrongdoer to make restitution, often in the form of a monetary penalty paid to the plaintiff. Therefore, the Romans distinguished between a delict and a *crimen*, which was punished by public penalty after formal trial. However, although delicts were not pursued under the criminal law, in the imperial period the distinction tended to become blurred, in so far as a delict that had a significant degree of public interest could be classed as a *crimen*. Delict as an obligation had a strong penal element, since in the popular view such actions required requital and revenge as well as compensation; there was also a social presumption that a householder had a right of self-defence. For a survey of obligations in Roman legal practice, see McGinn (2012); also Metzger (2012b).

The origins of delict probably lay in an attempt in the early state to deter those who felt that they had unjustly suffered loss or injury from seeking violent personal retribution, and to maintain public peace in the community. There were four delicts of this kind defined by Gaius: theft, robbery, causing loss, and outrage (*Institutes* 3.182). Theft, robbery, and outrage were dealt with under the Twelve Tables of Law, and subsequently developed through the praetor's edict. The delict of wrongful loss had its origins in the *lex Aquilia*, probably dated to the early third century BC, which dealt with compensation for damage to property; it was limited in that the damage had to be wrongful, directly the result of action by the third party, and with no reasonable legal excuse (nos. 491–8). Over time, action by the praetor further extended the scope of the *lex Aquilia*, notably through the grant of an *actio utilis* ('analogous action'), in which he adapted an existing formula to allow an action beyond the intention of the original, or an *actio in factum* ('action on the fact'), accepting not statute but a particular fact as the basis for someone's liability, and consequently the issue of liability for damage and the precise line of causation and responsibility for an incident came to the fore, and the need to measure loss (nos. 500–8).

Routine criminality perpetrated in the main by the lower classes would be dealt with by a magistrate by virtue of his *imperium* or right of *coercitio*, permitting him to enforce obedience and chastise as he thought appropriate in the circumstances. The operation of this does not leave much trace in our sources. However, there were precise legal definitions of delicts such as theft and robbery (nos. 509–19), which provided a framework for litigation. Originally, *iniuria* or outrage was concerned with physical assault on citizens, but the law was developed through the praetor's edict to include a wide range of activity involving abuse and insult (nos. 520–6). The praetor could also by his edict grant other delicts on the analogy of statute to deal with issues of deceit and duress (nos. 527–30). The legal activity of the praetors contributed to the development of so-called quasi-delicts which for example concerned the consequences when objects were suspended from a building or material thrown from it so as to cause damage to others; discussion in Buckland (1975), 585–9; Kolbert (1979), with a useful introduction and translation of texts; Frier (1989), especially 29–107, with numerous examples; Johnston (1999), 71–2; 116; du Plessis (2012a), 86–101; Cursi (2012).

The most serious criminal acts usually involved the upper classes and were brought to trial in the permanent jury courts (*quaestiones perpetuae*) with tribunals specifically empanelled for particular charges, including forgery (nos. 539–41), violence (nos. 542–54), treason (nos. 555–61), extortion (nos. 562–6), electoral bribery (nos. 567–8), and public morality (nos. 569–75).

In the jury courts penalties were fixed by the relevant statute and followed automatically on conviction, either monetary or capital. Penalties in the *cognitio* procedure (see pp. 348–9) took the form of exile, either relegation, that is, usually temporary banishment from Rome or a province and a fine or partial confiscation of property, or the more serious deportation, which involved permanent removal to a specific place, loss of citizen rights, and confiscation of property. These penalties were generally inflicted on people of higher status. People of lesser status could be condemned to public works or to the mines. The death penalty was available, or in certain cases an aggravated death penalty, which might involve crucifixion or being sent to the beasts in the arena. Imprisonment was not normally employed, though people might be detained while awaiting trial; for discussion of penalties see Robinson (2007), 187–93.

On the periphery of society beyond convention and the religious establishment (nos. 576–87) were those who by their actions or beliefs caused the government to be suspicious of them, leading to occasional repression and prosecution (588–616).

Lex Aquilia: Chapter 1

Unlawful Killing

D 9.2.2pr-1 (Gaius, *Provincial Edict*, Book 7)

491. The first chapter of the *lex Aquilia* lays down that: 'If someone unlawfully kills a male or female slave belonging to another, or a four-footed animal from a herd, he is to be condemned to pay to the owner as much money as its greatest value in that year (that is, before the killing)'. It further lays down that the action should be for double against the person who denies it.

Four-footed herd animals include sheep, cattle, goats, horses, mules, asses, pigs, elephants, and camels. For discussion of clauses 1 and 3 of the *lex Aquilia*, see Frier (1989), 3–27.

D 9.2.7.1–2 (Ulpian, *Edict*, Book 18)

492. We should agree that the victim is 'killed' if someone struck him by means of a sword, or club, or other weapon, or by his hands (if he strangled him), or kicked him with his foot, or butted him with his head, or by any other similar means. However, if someone who is burdened more than is reasonable throws down his load and kills a slave, the *lex Aquilia* comes into play. For it was up to his judgement not to burden himself to this extent. Even if someone slips and kills another person's slave with his load, Pegasus says that he is liable under the *lex Aquilia* provided that he burdened himself more than was reasonable or walked carelessly over slippery ground.

D 9.2.7.6–7 (Ulpian, *Edict*, Book 18)

493. Celsus states that there is a significant difference between killing and providing the means of death. The person who provided the means of death is liable not under the *lex Aquilia* but for an *in factum* action. Therefore, he cites a person who administered poison instead of a

medicine, stating that he provided the cause of death, just like the man who handed a sword to a lunatic. For this person is not liable under the *lex Aquilia*, but to an action *in factum*. But if someone knocks a person off a bridge, Celsus states that whether he died as a result of the impact itself, or was immediately drowned, or died from exhaustion when overcome by the force of the river, the perpetrator is liable under the *lex Aquilia*, just as if someone had crushed a boy against a rock.

The definition of 'killing' includes providing the means that caused the death, and the possible distinction between killing and furnishing the means of death raised for lawyers the issue of causation and the chain of events that led to a death; unless the consequence could be directly connected to the deliberate action of the wrongdoer the *lex Aquilia* would not be appropriate; but the praetor could grant an alternative remedy, such as an *actio in factum* to offer redress.

Chapter 2 of the *lex Aquilia* dealt with the rights of creditors in respect of the fraudulent release of a debtor from his debt by one creditor.

Lex Aquilia: Chapter 3

Loss Unlawfully Caused

D 9.2.27.5 (Ulpian, *Edict*, Book 18)

494. In the third chapter the *lex Aquilia* states: 'In respect of other property apart from the killing of a slave or an animal from the herd, if anyone brings about damage to another by wrongfully burning or breaking or tearing asunder, he is to be condemned to pay to the owner as much money as that loss will be worth in the next thirty days' (that is, after the incident of damage).

In the Latin text *rumpere* implies destruction of some kind – to wreck, spoil, rend, pull, or tear asunder.

Gaius, *Institutes* 3.217

495. Therefore, not just burned or broken, but also cut, and smashed, and poured out, and all kinds of damage, wrecking and spoiling are expressed by this word *ruptum*.

Gaius, *Institutes* 4.6, 9

496. Sometimes we bring an action merely in order to attain our right, sometimes in order to obtain a penalty, sometimes to obtain both our right

and a penalty … (9) We obtain our right and a penalty in those cases in which we sue for double against a defendant who denies liability; this occurs in an action … for wrongful damage under the *lex Aquilia*.

To pursue your right meant financial recompense for the value of property stolen or damaged; any penal element for wrongful conduct meant a further financial penalty. The *lex Aquilia* was eventually to include the two aspects of penalty and compensation; compensation was linked with the concept of negligence on the part of the perpetrator (Cursi (2012), 296–301).

Culpa *and* dolus

D 9.2.31 (Paul, *Sabinus*, Book 10)

497. If a trimmer of trees threw down a branch from a tree and killed a passing slave (the same applies to a man working on a platform), he is liable only in so far as it fell down in a public area, and he did not shout a warning in order to avoid the accident. But Mucius said that even if the incident occurred in private land an action for fault (*culpa*) could be pursued. For there is fault when what could have been foreseen by a diligent man was not foreseen, or when a shout of warning was too late to avert the danger. In line with this reasoning, it does not much matter if the slave was walking through public or private land, since commonly the general public walk through private land. But if there was no path there, he should be liable for *dolus* (intentional fault), in so far as he should not aim at someone whom he sees passing. But fault should not be imputed to him when he could not have guessed that someone was going to cross through that place.

Once the praetor had decided that there was a case to answer under the *lex Aquilia*, the appointed judge (*iudex*) had to decide the crucial issues. Foremost among these was the question of the wrongfulness of the perpetrator's actions, that is, the loss he had inflicted had to be the result of fault (*culpa*) and sometimes of *dolus* (malice or intentional fault). Lawyers assessed these issues objectively based on the responsibility on individuals to exercise care in their behaviour, in line with what would be expected of a Roman in normal circumstances. This would ensure reasonable protection of the interests of others. Fault was often identified with carelessness or negligence (*neglegentia*), which could be applied in cases where the perpetrator failed to assess properly his own ability to carry out a task (see nos. 498–9).

D 9.2.39pr-1 (Pomponius, *Quintus Mucius*, Book 17)

498. Quintus Mucius writes: A mare was grazing in another person's land and lost her foal when she was forcibly driven off, as she was pregnant. The

question was raised if her owner could sue under the *lex Aquilia* the man who had driven her off, because he had injured the mare in striking her. If he had struck her too hard or deliberately driven her off too violently, it was apparent that he could sue. Pomponius says: Even the person who finds someone else's cattle on his land must drive them off in the same way as if he had found his own, since if he has suffered any loss from that incident, he has available appropriate (legal) actions. Therefore, the person who finds another's cattle on his land may not lawfully close them in, and, as I said above, he must not act otherwise than if they were his own. But he must either drive them away without causing injury or warn the owner to collect his animals.

_D_ 9.2.8.1 (Gaius, _Provincial Edict_, Book 7)

499. If a mule-driver through inexperience is unable to control the movement of the animals and they trample over a slave belonging to someone else, it is generally agreed that he is liable for fault (*culpa*). The same point is made if through weakness he is unable to cope with the movement of the animals. And it does not seem unjust if weakness is counted as fault, since no one should take part in an activity if he knows, or ought to know, that his weakness is likely to be a danger to others. The same legal position applies to the person who is unable to restrain the movement of a horse that he is riding either through lack of skill or weakness.

Causation

_D_ 9.2.52.2 (Alfenus, _Digest_, Book 2)

500. On the Capitoline Hill mules were pulling two laden carts. As the first cart had tipped back, the mule-drivers lifted it up so that the mules could pull it easily. But the first cart began to roll backwards, and when the mule-drivers who were between the two carts got out of the way, the rear cart was stuck by the first one and, careering backwards, crushed someone's slave boy. The boy's owner asked me which person he should sue. I replied that it depended on what had actually happened. If the mule-drivers who were in charge of the first cart had of their own accord removed its support and therefore brought it about that the mules could not hold the cart and were pulled back by its weight, there is no action against the owner of the mule, but under the *lex Aquilia* it is possible to sue the men who were holding up the cart. For a man nonetheless causes damage if he voluntarily lets go of

what he was holding back with the result that it strikes someone. In the same way, if someone who was driving an ass did not keep control of it, or someone hurled a javelin or something else from his hand, he would be liable for any damage. However, if the mules stopped because they took fright at something, and the mule-drivers, fearful of being killed, abandoned the cart, there is no suit against these men, but there is against the owner of the mules. However, if neither the mules nor the mule-drivers were to blame, but the mules were unable to sustain the load, or when they tried they slipped and fell, with the result that the cart rolled down the slope and the men were unable to hold the weight of the cart that had been tipped backwards, there is no suit against either the owner of the mules or the men. This point is certain: in whatever way the accident happened, it is not possible to sue the owner of the mules of the cart in the rear since they did not initiate anything, but it, being struck, rolled backwards.

This shows the subtleties of the chain of causation, which could become so tenuous and remote that there might be no remedy for the plaintiff.

D 9.2.11pr (Ulpian, *Edict*, Book 18)

501. Furthermore Mela writes that when some people were playing with a ball, and one of them threw the ball violently against a barber's hands, with the result that the throat of a slave he was shaving was cut by the razor thrust against it, then with whichever one of them the fault (*culpa*) lies, that person is liable under the *lex Aquilia*. Proculus thinks that the fault lies with the barber; and indeed, if he was carrying on his barber's business in a place where there was usually a game or where there was a lot of traffic, the fault can indeed be imputed to him. However, a reasonable point is made that if someone entrusted himself to a barber who had his chair in a dangerous place, he ought to blame his own actions.

This hypothetical case offered guidance for the judge in establishing the circumstances in which the ballplayer would be liable. If the ballplayers had started their game near to the barber's stall, they would be more to blame. Ulpian also raises the issue of contributory negligence by the injured party; see no. 502.

D 9.2.9.4 (Ulpian, *Edict*, Book 18)

502. But if a slave is killed by people throwing javelins in a game, there is a place for action under the *lex Aquilia*. But if, when other people were already throwing javelins in the field, the slave walked through the place,

the *lex Aquilia* does not apply, because he should not have been walking at an inappropriate time through a field set aside for javelin-throwing. However, if someone deliberately threw a javelin at him, he is liable under the *lex Aquilia*.

D 9.2.30.3 (Paul, *Edict*, Book 22)

503. In this action, which arises under this chapter, intention (*dolus*) and fault (*culpa*) are punished. So, if someone starts a fire in his own stubble or thorns in order to burn them away, and the fire escapes, and, spreading further, damages someone else's crops or vineyard, we should consider if this came about through his inexperience or negligence. For if he did this on a windy day, he is guilty of fault, since the person who provides the opportunity is regarded as having brought about the damage. Equally liable is the person who did not take precautions that the fire should not spread more widely. But if he took all appropriate precautions and a sudden gust of wind spread the fire more widely, he is free from fault.

Self-Defence and Necessity

D 9.2.52.1 (Alfenus, *Digest*, Book 2)

504. One night a shopkeeper had placed a lantern on top of his counter beside a pathway. A passer-by picked it up and the shopkeeper followed him, demanded the return of the lantern, and restrained him when he ran away. The passer-by, to make him let him go, began to beat the shopkeeper with a whip which he was holding in his hand, and which had a spike in it. As a result, the fight became more intense, and the shopkeeper knocked out the eye of the person who had taken the lantern. The shopkeeper asked me if he could be held to have inflicted wrongful damage, given that he had been struck first with the whip. I replied that unless he had deliberately knocked out his eye it did not appear that he had inflicted wrongful damage, but the fault (*culpa*) lay with the party who had hit out first with the whip. But if the shopkeeper had not been struck by him first and had begun the violence because he wanted to get the lantern back from him, the shopkeeper would be considered responsible for what happened.

Apart from the assessment of responsibility and the possible defence of contributory negligence by the plaintiff, there were other matters for the *iudex* to consider such as self-defence, mitigation, measurement of loss, damages, and indirect damage. Roman law strongly supported the right of self-defence, and it was legitimate to kill a thief caught in the act at night. Alfenus is trying to find a way forward in the rather murky facts of this brawl, supporting the right to defend property but not to inflict disproportionate violence on the perpetrator.

D 9.2.29.3 (Ulpian, *Edict*, Book 18)

505. Similarly Labeo writes that when a ship was driven by the force of the wind into the anchor ropes of another ship and the sailors cut the ropes, if the ship could not be extricated in any other way except by cutting the ropes, no legal action should be granted. Labeo and Proculus took the same view in the case of fishermen's nets in which a fishing boat had been caught. Clearly, if this happened because of the fault of the sailors, action should be brought under the *lex Aquilia*. But when an action for wrongful damage is being brought in respect of the nets, no calculation is made in respect of the fish which were consequently not caught, since it is not clear if they would have been caught.

This is the defence of necessity. The case also relates to measurement of loss and unprovable future profits. See further (no. 508).

Measurement of Loss

D 9.2.27.17 (Ulpian, *Edict*, Book 18)

506. We will certainly agree that a person has 'ripped apart' (*rupisse*) a slave, if he has wounded him, or struck him with rods or whips or fists, or with a weapon, or anything else, with the result that he cuts his body or causes a swelling, provided that the loss was caused wrongfully. But if the action has not made the slave cheaper in price or of less value, action will not lie under the *lex Aquilia*, and only an action for outrage (*iniuria*) should be brought in respect of this case. Under the *lex Aquilia* are pursued those damages that cause loss. Therefore, even though a slave has not been made less valuable in terms of price, if expense has been incurred in ensuring his welfare and health, in my opinion in this respect a loss has been inflicted, and so action is possible under the *lex Aquilia*.

D 9.2.27.30 (Ulpian, *Edict*, Book 18)

507. When a husband has given unstrung pearls to his wife for her use, and she pierces them, either against her husband's wishes or without his knowledge, so that when they had been pierced, she could wear them as a necklace, she is liable under the *lex Aquilia*, whether she is divorced or still married.

This refers to loss through damage. The pearls remained the husband's property and the wife had a duty of care. If the husband had known that she was going to pierce the pearls and did not prevent her, there might have been a case for arguing that he had given consent.

Indirect Loss

D 9.2.23.2 (Ulpian, *Edict*, Book 18)

508. The same Iulianus writes that if I should be instituted as heir under the condition that I should manumit Stichus, and Stichus is killed after the death of the testator, in the calculation of my loss I can pursue the value of the inheritance, for the condition failed because of the killing. But if he is killed when the testator is still alive, the inheritance does not come into the evaluation because the highest value is assessed by counting retrospectively.

This concerns related or indirect loss. Ulpian (*D* 9.2.21pr) explains that loss was calculated on the basis of the maximum the property was worth in that year (counted backwards from when the slave was slain). Therefore, in this case the plaintiff can pursue an action under the *lex Aquilia* concerning the killing of the slave which resulted in the loss of his inheritance; but on a retrospective calculation, if the testator was still alive when the slave was killed, the inheritance had not come into play and therefore could not be attached to the slave's value in any calculation of loss.

Theft

Definition of Theft

Gaius, *Institutes* 3.195–6

509. However, theft is committed not only when a person removes an object belonging to someone else in order to purloin it, but generally when a person interferes with an object belonging to someone else against the owner's wishes. Therefore, if a person makes use of an object deposited with him, he commits a theft. And if a person has received an object for a particular use and then uses it for another purpose, he is liable for theft, as for example when a person receives silver plate on loan on the basis that he is going to invite friends to dinner but then takes it abroad with him, or if a person borrows a horse for a ride and takes it rather further (than was understood).

D 47.2.52.7 (Ulpian, *Edict*, Book 37)

510. Mela says that a creditor who, when the money has been paid over, does not return the surety, is liable for theft, if he keeps the object with the intention of concealing it. I think that this is correct.

In early law the physical removal of the object was necessary for the definition of theft and that idea remained in the word 'interference' or 'handling' (*contrectatio*) in respect of another's property, though in classical law the definition had been widened so as, for example, to include attempted theft or handling of stolen goods. There also had to be a clear intent to steal. There was a rather inconclusive debate about circumstances where a thief stole part of a larger quantity. Paul argued that in an action for theft the culprit was liable only for what he had taken (*D* 47.2.21pr).

Remedies and Compensation for the Plaintiff

Gaius speaks of 'hatred of thieves' and deals with remedies available to the plaintiff (*Institutes* 4.4). The action on theft (*actio furti*) allowed the victim of theft to sue for a monetary penalty, the amount of which depended on whether the theft was manifest, that is, the thief was caught in the act, or non-manifest, the former bringing fourfold damages, the latter twofold. The thief also suffered *infamia* (loss of standing and reputation and certain legal disabilities). These penalties demonstrate the penal element in the treatment of thieves. The plaintiff would also want the return of the stolen object, which could be attempted through *vindicatio* and a possessory interdict (see p. 247). This posed difficulties since such an action lay against the actual possessor of the object, which might have passed through several hands. However, the plaintiff could make use of the *condictio furtiva*, a personal action against the thief or his heirs for the value of the object. The *actio furti* and the *condictio* were cumulative, so that the thief had to return the object or its equivalent and pay damages.

D 47.2.3.1–2 (Ulpian, *Sabinus*, Book 41)

511. A manifest thief, whom the Greeks call *ep'autophoros*, is one who is caught in the very act of theft. It little matters by whom he is caught, whether by the victim of the theft or by someone else. But is a thief defined as manifest if he is caught in the act, or if he is caught somewhere else? The preferable view, as Iulianus also has written, is that he is nevertheless a manifest thief even if he is not caught where he committed the theft but is

apprehended with the stolen object before he has taken it to the place which he had planned.

On this analysis, if the thief managed to get to his destination and dispose of the stolen object, he would no longer be a manifest thief, although if you tried to apprehend him and he escaped, throwing away the stolen goods, it was still manifest theft. Furthermore, if stolen items were found on his property, he was also a manifest thief, though the search had to be carried out under a seemingly archaic ritual in which the searcher wore only a loincloth and carried a platter, presumably to prevent the planting of evidence (Gaius, *Institutes* 3.192–3).

D 47.2.50pr (Ulpian, *Edict*, Book 37)

512. In an action on theft the actual value of the (stolen) object is quadrupled or doubled, not the interest of the plaintiff.

However, other jurists held that the full amount of the interest the plaintiff had in the stolen object should be taken into consideration including any potential gain to be expected from it. Furthermore, any loss resulting from the theft could be recovered. It would be up to the plaintiff to suggest appropriate compensation.

D 47.2.68.1 (Celsus, *Digest*, Book 12)

513. If something was stolen from you which you had offered as a surety if you did not deliver by a designated day, and consequently you had to suffer that penalty, in the action on theft this too can be included in the calculation (of compensation).

Accomplices

In the Roman view an accomplice was either someone who was present at the theft or someone who merely offered advice, provided that they had acted with dishonest intention.

Gaius, *Institutes* 3.202

514. Sometimes a person is liable for theft even if he has not himself committed the theft, for example, a person by whose assistance and advice a theft has been committed; this is the case when a person knocks coins out of your hand so that someone else can remove them, or who obstructs you so that someone else can remove them, or who scatters your sheep and cattle so that another can get hold of them.

The whereabouts of coins were important; if they rolled away into a river or drain so that no one else could obtain them, then an action for outrage (*iniuria*) was possible, but if they came into another's possession, an action for abetting theft could be brought (*D* 9.2.27.21). Jurists note that there was a distinction between advising a thief and actually assisting in a theft; malign intention in an accomplice was also important; *D* 47.2.50.2–3; 50.16.53.2.

D 47.2.48.1 (Ulpian, *Sabinus*, Book 42)

515. The person who knows the identity of a thief, whether he points him out or not, is not himself guilty of theft, since there is a great difference between someone who conceals a thief and someone who does not point him out. The person who knows who the thief is, is not liable for theft, but the person who conceals him is liable for this action.

Concealing a criminal amounted to negative complicity, and accomplices were held as equally liable with the principal offender.

P. Oxy. 1408 lines 11–21 = *SP* 224 (c. AD 210–214)

516. Baebius Iuncinus to the *strategoi* of the Heptanomia and the Arsinoite nome, greetings. I have already in an earlier letter instructed you to make a diligent search for robbers, warning you of the risk if you neglect this, and now I wish to confirm my decision through a decree, so that everyone living in Egypt may know that I am not treating this business as a matter of secondary importance, but indeed am offering rewards to those of you who work with me, while warning about the danger to those who chose to disobey. Therefore, I wish this decree to be posted in the *metropoleis* and the most conspicuous parts of the nomes, and you will be in line for a penalty and personal risk if any wrongdoer is able to commit violent acts undetected. I hope that you will be in good health. Year …, Phaophi 28.

Lucius Baebius Aurelius Iuncinus, prefect of Egypt, proclaims: [It is clear] to all that it is impossible to destroy robbers without the co-operation of those who shelter them, but when they are stripped of those who help them, we will speedily [bring them to justice?]. Some shelter them because they connive at their crimes, others while not participating in … .

This text written on the back of a papyrus containing another document is a circular from the prefect of Egypt, Iuncinus, to local officials emphasizing the hostile government attitude towards those who harboured bandits for any reason; see no. 517.

D 47.16.2 (Paul, *Civilian Penalties*, Only Book)

517. Those persons who conceal a robber who is related to them by blood or marriage should neither be absolved nor yet suffer severe penalty. For their offence is not on the level of those who harbour robbers who have no relationship with them.

See no. 692; the future Antoninus Pius, when he was governor of Asia, instructed the local magistrates in charge of law and order (*eirenarchs*), when they had arrested bandits, to interrogate them about their henchmen and those who had harboured them.

Robbery

Gaius, *Institutes* 3.209

518. The person who violently takes the property of another is also liable under theft. For who perpetrates greater interference with the property of another against the wishes of its owner than the person who takes it by force? Consequently, this person has been correctly described as a wicked thief. But the praetor has introduced a particular action in respect of this delict, which is called an 'action for goods taken by violence' and is for fourfold compensation within a year and after a year for simple value of the object.

For fourfold damages see Robinson (1995), 30; the punishment probably reflects the concerns of the upper classes. See Riess (2011) on *latro* (bandit) as outsider and acts of aggravated robbery; for bandits and rural order, see Hopwood (1989).

D 47.18.1.1–2 (Ulpian, *Duties of Proconsul*, Book 8)

519. Robbers, who are more appalling thieves (that is plunderers), are usually condemned to perform forced labour, either permanently or for a set period; however, those of high rank are removed from their social rank for a time or ordered to leave the boundaries of their native land. No special penalty is laid down for these persons by imperial rescripts, and consequently once their case has been heard, their punishment lies within the discretion of the person who conducted the enquiry. Purse-stealers and pickpockets are punished in the same way, and those who break in. For the divine Marcus ordered that a Roman *eques*, who had broken and bored through a wall and stolen money, should keep out of the province of Africa, of which he was a native, and also from Rome and Italy for five years.

Outrage (*iniuria*)

The original scope of *iniuria*, perhaps going back to the Twelve Tables of Roman law, probably was concerned with deliberate physical assaults on citizens, with fixed money payment for lesser injuries. These penalties over time had become derisory, as Lucius Veratius demonstrated publicly (see no. 520). But the law was then developed through the praetor's edict, which offered an action for damages, and over time widened the framework to embrace a more extensive range of remedies for non-physical outrage such as defamation, abuse, insulting behaviour, which might include a man's family or slaves, unauthorized entry of property, interference with normal citizen rights, raising uproar, and compromising the reputation of a matron. Therefore, this delict offered a secure area defended by the law in which citizens could carry on their personal activities in society without affront to their dignity and reputation, or, if necessary, assert their status by legal action. Family members could sue since the outrage might affect them too, but the action could not be taken up by an heir since outrage was considered to be personal. The action had to be brought within one year (after which the outraged feeling presumably could be considered to have worn off). Damages were set by the judge as penalty rather than compensation. Although the issue in this delict was personal, the state had an interest in maintaining orderly government and ensuring that antisocial behaviour did not upset established norms. The *lex Cornelia* of 81/80 BC added criminal liability (with the penalty of a fine) for three specific outrages: beating another person, or thrashing them, or forcibly entering someone's home. Therefore, the defendant in this case would be subject to both civil and criminal actions; see Robinson (1995), 49–51; Harries (2007), 46–50 on the *lex Aquilia* and *iniuria*. For outrage and the use of force (*vis*), see p. 320.

Aulus Gellius, *Noctes Atticae* 20.1.13

520. There was one L. Veratius who was particularly disreputable and irresponsible. He used to find fun in slapping free men in the face with the palm of his hand. A slave followed him carrying a bag full of asses; as soon as he had slapped someone, he ordered twenty-five asses to be immediately counted out to him in accordance with the Twelve Tables. Therefore, according to Labeo the praetors decided that this provision should be abolished and abandoned and announced that they would appoint assessors to assess the outrage.

The Twelve Tables said: 'If he shall have done an injury (*iniuria*) to another (?), let there be a penalty of twenty-five' (Crawford (1996), 578, I.15). Labeo held that the statute was defective and permitted an affront to the individual dignity of citizens, in this case purely for fun.

Gaius, *Institutes* 3.220–1

521. Outrage is committed not only if someone strikes a man with a fist or a club, or flogs him, but also if he verbally abuses him, or if he lists a man's property for sale as that of a debtor though well aware that he owes nothing, or if he writes a pamphlet or poem defaming someone, or if he stalks a matron or a young man, and furthermore in many other ways. We are considered to suffer outrage not only through our own person, but also through the person of our children whom we have in our power, and our wife. Therefore, if you commit outrage against my daughter who is married to Titius, I can take an action against you for outrage, not only in the name of my daughter, but also in my name and that of Titius.

Horace, *Satires* 2.1, 81–91

522. Horace: Unless you, learned counsel, wish to give a dissenting view. Trebatius: I think that I cannot object to that, but still be advised that you need to beware, in case ignorance of our revered laws catches you out. The law states that whosoever writes wicked poems against another person must himself face the law and the court. Horace: Fair enough if someone writes badly, but what if someone writes good verses and receives the praise of the emperor as judge? If he has yelped his disapproval at someone who has deserved it by his bad behaviour, then the yelper himself is surely free from blame? Trebatius: The court will break up in a torrent of laughter and you will depart with the case dismissed.

Horace (see p. 478) in the *Satires* examines various types of personal conduct; here he debates the wisdom of writing poetry critical of others. Gaius Trebatius Testa was a distinguished jurist and friend of Cicero, who recommended him to Julius Caesar.

D 47.10.15.15, 20–2 (Ulpian, *Edict*, Book 77)

523. If someone accosts young girls he is less at fault if they are dressed as slaves, still less if they are dressed like a prostitute and not in the garb of a matron. Nevertheless, if a woman was not dressed as a matron and

someone accosted her or took away her companion, he is liable to an action for outrage. (20–2) To accost means making use of alluring conversation to try to undermine someone's chastity. It does not involve causing uproar, but it is against good morals to make an attempt. The person who is verbally abusive does not undermine a woman's chastity but is liable for outrage. There is a distinction between accosting and stalking. A man accosts if he tries to undermine (a woman's) chastity by conversation; he stalks if he silently follows close behind her. For constant lurking virtually denotes something disreputable.

Actions available for *iniuria* show a range of social and cultural attitudes in Rome; women are assumed to face a sexual threat which might reflect badly on their reputation and the standing of their family; men face physical assault. Furthermore, status and context affect the legal outcome, and, for example, respectable women have more impact with the law.

D 47.10.3pr-3 (Ulpian, *Edict*, Book 56)

524. It is generally accepted that those who can suffer outrage can also inflict it. Certainly, there are some who cannot inflict it, for example the insane and minors, who are not capable of wrongful intent. For these people can suffer outrage but not inflict it. For, since outrage depends on the intention of the person who inflicts it, it follows that we must agree that these people, whether they commit battery or raise uproar, have not inflicted outrage. Therefore, a person can suffer outrage even though he does not realize it, but no one can inflict it unless he realizes he is inflicting outrage, even though he does not know on whom he is inflicting it. Therefore, if a person strikes someone as a joke or while in a competition, he is not liable for outrage. If someone knocks down a freeman thinking that he is his own slave, he is in the position of not being liable for an action on outrage.

D 26.10.1.7 (Ulpian, *Edict*, Book 35)

525. Furthermore, even women are admitted (to bring a charge of untrustworthiness of tutors), but only those who come to this point compelled by duty, for example a mother. Also, a nurse and a grandmother can bring a charge. So too can a sister, for in respect of a sister a rescript of the divine Severus is extant. And if there is any other woman whose proper sense of duty the praetor has recognized, and who is not transgressing the sense of

modesty of the female sex but is compelled by duty not to endure an outrage done to the minors, he will permit her to bring an accusation.

See Grubbs (2002), 48–60 for the modesty and weakness of women as expressed in Roman law. Legal writers often refer to female modesty (*pudor*) or sense of shame (*verecundia*). The idea of preserving a woman's good reputation was associated with the idea of keeping her away from engagement with public activities, and hence there was a reluctance to see women involved in legal suits (see p. 23–5). They were prohibited from taking legal action on behalf of others except in special circumstances, of which this was one; see Gardner (1986), 161–2; also no. 351.

Gaius, *Institutes* 3.225

526. An outrage is considered to be heinous either by the very deed itself, for example if a man is wounded or flogged or beaten with clubs by someone, or by the location, for example if an outrage is perpetrated on someone in the theatre or forum, or by the person, for example if a magistrate suffered an outrage, or an outrage was perpetrated on a senator by a person of humble status.

To some extent the severity of the penalty for outrage depended on the status of the victim and the perpetrator; see Garnsey (1970), 199–203.

Praetorian Delicts

Praetorian delicts were designed to deal with circumstances and issues not covered by statute, and the most important were deceit (*dolus malus*) and duress (*metus*), both of which were probably developed in the late republic. The first allowed a plaintiff to recover the value of losses suffered through the defendant's deceit, while the second provided for the recovery of property that had been extorted, or its equivalent value. Furthermore, these delicts could be offered as a defence (*exceptio*) by a defendant against a plaintiff who was taking advantage of some kind of fraud or threats perpetrated by him or by someone else on his behalf.

D 4.3.8 (Gaius, *Provincial Edict*, Book 4)

527. Therefore, if when you knew that a man was in financial difficulties, for the sake of your profit you claimed to me that he was sound, justly an

action for fraud should be granted to me against you because you falsely praised another person in order to deceive me.

D 4.3.9.1 (Ulpian, *Edict*, Book 11)

528. But if you persuade me to reject an inheritance on the grounds that it is insolvent, or to choose a slave on the grounds that there is none better in the household, I state that an action should be granted for fraud if you did this deceitfully.

D 4.2.1; 3pr (Ulpian, *Edict*, Book 11)

529. The praetor states: 'Whatever has been done because of duress (*metus*) I shall not consider valid'. The edict once referred to (what was done): 'by force or as a result of duress'. Force was mentioned as compulsion imposed against the will; duress was the fear caused in the mind by a present or future threat. Later the reference to force was removed, because whatever was done as a result of outrageous force was regarded as also done under duress. (3pr) Therefore, this clause comprises both force and duress, and if anyone has done something under forceful compulsion, his rights are restored by this edict.

For distinctions in the types of force used see also pp. 303–6.

Damage Caused by Animals

D 9.1.1pr-3 (Ulpian, *Edict*, Book 18)

530. If a four-footed animal is alleged to have caused loss (*pauperies*), an action depends on the law of the Twelve Tables. This statute provided that either whatever had done the harm should be handed over, that is, the animal that had actually caused the harm, or that a financial calculation of the damage should be offered. The harm constitutes the delict. This action pertains to all four-footed animals. The praetor states: 'have caused *pauperies*'. *Pauperies* is a loss brought about without wrongful action by the perpetrator. For an animal cannot have acted wrongfully since it lacks reasoning.

This action, which had originated in the early Roman state, was then enshrined in the praetor's edict. Wild animals were excluded. There had to be a direct link of causation between the animal and the harm inflicted, for example, if an ox knocked something over on someone (*D* 9.1.1.9).

Criminal Offences and Penalties

The *lex Calpurnia* of 149 BC established a permanent court of senators to deal with charges of extortion in the provinces. This was a *quaestio* and subsequently additional permanent jury courts were created (*quaestiones perpetuae*), which were extended and reinforced by Sulla in 82–81 BC. Each court was set up to deal with a particular offence and acted as an individuality (see p. 279). The imperial period saw the decline of the *quaestiones*; those dealing with political crimes or treason are likely to have disappeared first, while those concerned with less controversial offences continued. Since there was no public prosecutor and the state did not undertake prosecutions, it was up to individuals to bring an accusation and approach the consuls or the emperor, who also had jurisdiction (see pp. 360–1; 414), and in these circumstances the senate often in practice acted as the court. In this role it had serious deficiencies since it could accept several charges at once, take an additional charge after the hearing had begun, vary penalties at will, and was potentially subject to intimidation by the emperor, who was often present.

In the definition of criminal liability there had to be a guilty party, that is, someone capable of committing an offence; therefore, children and lunatics were excluded. There had to be an intention to commit a criminal act, and an act, since a thought could not normally constitute a crime. Prosecutions had to be brought within a certain time span. Defences of various kinds were available and pleas in mitigation (Robinson (1995), 15–22). There was also an interesting debate about the nature, function, and value of punishment (nos. 531–4), though this was conducted in a rather remote, philosophical manner by scholars and jurists, and it is uncertain how much attention the average judge or juror paid to it.

On the Nature of Punishment

Aulus Gellius, *Noctes Atticae* 7.14.1–4

531. It is understood that there should be three motives in punishing misdeeds. The first, which in Greek is called *kolasia* (correction) or *nouthesia* (advice), is when a penalty is applied in order to correct or admonish someone, so that the person whose misdeed was thoughtless, may be made more observant and careful. The second is that which those who have precisely defined those words call *timoria* (retribution). That is the reason

for punishment when the standing and influence of the person against whom the offence was committed must be protected, in case failure to punish might bring contempt on him or reduce his prestige. Therefore, they think that this word was attributed to it from the protection of a person's honour (*timoria* retribution is derived from *time* – 'honour'). The third reason for punishment is what is called *paradeigma* (example) by the Greeks, when a penalty is necessary to set an example, so that others may be deterred from similar offences, which it is in the public interest to prevent, through fear of the penalty which they recognize. Therefore, our own ancestors too spoke of 'an example' for very serious and weighty penalties. When, therefore, either there is considerable hope that the person who committed the offence will reform himself before a penalty is imposed, or by contrast no hope that he can be changed or reformed, or if there is no need to fear a loss of standing of the person against whom the offence was committed, or if the offence is not of the kind that punishment needs to be imposed in order to instil the necessary fear, then in an offence of that kind it was held that it was not worthwhile imposing a penalty.

Aulus Gellius (see p. 477) sheds some light on Roman attitudes to the function of punishment; see Harries (2007), 37–8.

Seneca, *De Clementia* 1.2.2

532. Consequently, when the distinction between bad and good men is removed, confusion follows and an outbreak of vice. Therefore, a moderate attitude should be applied which knows how to distinguish between personalities that can be reformed from those that are incurable. And it is not right to extend clemency in an indiscriminate and commonplace way, or to exclude it all together. For it is just as cruel to pardon everyone as it is to pardon none. We must exercise moderation; but because a balanced attitude is difficult, if in the future we move beyond this balance, we should incline to the more humane.

For Seneca, see p. 480. For the context of the *De Clementia* in the reign of Nero and the administration of justice, see Griffin (1976), 148–51; 158–65; also Bauman (1996), 78–81; in *De Ira* 1.6.2–4 Seneca discusses how the ideal judge will be rational and act without anger, taking into account the circumstances of each case, but also ensuring the safety of the state and recognizing the value of punishment as a deterrent; see Griffin, pp. 168–71. The purpose of punishment and the nature of penalties were issues of increasing importance in relation to trials by the *cognitio* procedure in which the judge had the responsibility of deciding the penalties where previous decisions could be a precedent but not a firm rule. Cowan (2016) discusses the role of *clementia* in the emperor's decisions in the reign of Tiberius.

Seneca, *De Clementia* 1.22.1–2

533. Let us move on to crimes inflicted on others, in punishing which the law has followed three objectives, which the emperor himself ought to observe: either to reform the person whom it is punishing, or that his punishment should make others better, or that with evildoers removed the rest can live more securely. You can reform wrongdoers more readily with a moderate punishment; for a man will live more carefully if he has some part of his status remaining. No one cares about respect once it has been lost. It is a kind of impunity to have nothing on which punishment can be inflicted.

Justification of punishment is defined as: reform, deterrence by encouragement of others in good conduct, public safety; but use of tough measures should be moderate, or they lose their effectiveness; see Bauman (1996), 141–60, especially 151–9 for attitudes to appropriate punishment and its purpose and value; Robinson (2007), 179–97.

D 48.19.28.15 (Callistratus, *Judicial Enquiries*, Book 6)

534. Many officials have approved the practice of hanging notorious bandits on a pole in the location where they carried out their banditry, so that others would be deterred by the sight from carrying out similar crimes, and the relatives and friends of those who had been murdered could find consolation in the fact that punishment was administered in the same place where the bandits had committed murders. But some condemned these people (brigands) to the beasts.

D 48.19.13 (Ulpian, *Appeals*, Book 1)

535. Nowadays the man who is judging a criminal case *extra ordinem* may bring in whatever verdict he wishes, whether more severe or more lenient, provided that in either case he does not exceed whatever is reasonable.

Marcianus (*D* 48.19.11) recommended that a judge should not be seduced by a reputation for severity or clemency but assess each case on its merits. In general, in less severe cases they should incline towards leniency, in more serious ones exercise the rigour of the law with a leavening of mercy.

Criminal Intention

D 48.8.12 (Modestinus, *Rules*, Book 8)

536. Neither an infant nor a lunatic is liable under the *lex Cornelia* if they kill a man, since inability to form criminal intent protects one and his unfortunate condition excuses the other.

It must be possible to identify a potentially guilty party before an action could be brought, and that required a guilty intention; see Robinson (1995), 16–17.

CJ 9.16.1 (AD 215)

537. Emperor Antoninus Augustus to Aurelius Herculianus and the other soldiers. Your brother would have acted more appropriately if he had presented himself to the governor of the province. If he proves to him that he struck Iustus with no intent to kill him, he will remit the penalty for murder and bring a judgement in accordance with military discipline. For a criminal act is construed only if an intent to harm is present. But actions that occur by chance rather than through malicious intent are generally considered accidental and not deliberately harmful.

This definition of manslaughter seems sympathetic to the soldier, whose brother had apparently persuaded his comrades to join him in approaching the emperor; for the advantages of military service in respect of the law see Campbell (1984, 207–67).

D 48.8.1.3–5 (Marcian, *Institutes*, Book 14)

538. The divine Hadrian stated in a rescript that the person who killed a man can be acquitted if he committed the act without the intention of killing, and the person who did not kill a man but wounded him with the intention of killing him, should be found guilty as for murder. The matter should be considered on the facts; for if he drew a sword and struck him there is no doubt that he did this with the intention of killing him, but if he struck him with a key or a saucepan during a quarrel, although he struck him with metal, he did not have the intention of killing him. A lesser penalty should be inflicted on the person who committed a murder by accident rather than design during a quarrel. Furthermore, the divine Hadrian stated in a rescript that the person who killed a man who was forcibly carrying out a sexual assault on him or a member of his family should be acquitted. And the divine Pius wrote that a lighter penalty

should be inflicted on the man who killed his wife caught in the act of adultery and instructed that a man of humble status should be sent into permanent exile, but that a man of any standing should be relegated for a fixed time.

For the treatment of sexual offenders see p. 314.

Forgery

D 48.10.1pr-2 (Marcian, *Institutes*, Book 14)

539. The penalty provided in the *lex Cornelia* is applied to the person who has with malicious intent instigated the presentation of false depositions or false evidence. Similarly, the person who receives money to provide legal assistance or evidence, or who makes a deal or enters a conspiracy to entrap the innocent, will be punished in accordance with the decree of the senate. Furthermore, if somebody receives money to suppress or withdraw evidence, and for the delivery or non-delivery of evidence, he is punished under the *lex Cornelia.* In addition, whoever corrupts a judge or arranges for him to be corrupted (is liable under this law).

This statute introduced by Sulla concerning forgery (*falsum*) included interference with wills, and also applied to forging seals (*D* 48.10.9.3); it may also have dealt with counterfeiting coinage, though it is possible that there was a second statute for this offence against the state; see Robinson (1995), 36–9; 86–8.

CJ 9.23.3 (AD 223)

540. Emperor Alexander Augustus to Martialis. According to the decree of the senate and the edict of the divine Claudius, anyone who is summoned to write out a will is forbidden to include any advantageous bequest to himself, even if the testator dictates it to him, and anyone who does so has the penalty laid down by the Cornelian statute invoked against him. Even if he begs for remission because of ignorance of the law and promises not to accept the legacy left to him, the senate and the divine emperors have rarely extended remission.

CJ 9.23.5 (AD 235)

541. Emperor Alexander Augustus to Gallicanus, soldier. Since you were summoned to write out your comrade's will, and on his instructions assigned a slave to yourself in the will, it is considered as if it had never

been written, and you cannot take up that legacy. But in line with my usual tendency to display benevolence, I grant that you should be exempt from the penalty of the Cornelian statute, into which you have strayed more through inadvertence, in my opinion, than with fraudulent intent.

This response to a soldier is in stark contrast to the blunt statement of the law in no. 540. In dealing with soldiers emperors sometimes adopted a more understanding tone or extended the benefit of the doubt; see no. 537, and pp. 468–70.

*Violence (*vis privata *and* vis publica*)*

Violence or force (*vis*) emerged as a crime originally associated with forms of sedition in the republic. Subsequently a *lex Iulia de vi* was introduced either by Julius Caesar or Augustus, though it is likely that there were two laws, as argued by Cloud (1988); (1989). The legislation embraced both *vis privata* and *vis publica*, and the differences between the two are not always clear in the *Digest* texts which discuss them (*D* 48.6 and 7). In fact, a clear distinction between *vis privata* and *publica* was probably made by jurists in the late second century on the basis that private persons committed the former, magistrates and officials the latter (Robinson (1995), 29; 79). In the classical period *vis* in private law was viewed broadly and referred to actions by private persons which used or threatened physical force or moral pressure amounting to intimidation, even if falling short of actual violence; for example, theft committed employing violence, or the threat of violence, was classed as *rapina* and pursued as delict.

It is likely that types of serious physical assault were dealt with under statute, the *lex Cornelia de iniuriis*. The distinction between *vis* and *iniuria* is not always clear and it is possible that in cases of serious assault on an individual the public interest would require a prosecution for *vis*, as well as the private penal action (see p. 212 for suits involving *iniuria*). In cases of *iniuria* prosecuted as assault, the object of the legal process was more to punish than to seek reparation. Statute was primarily concerned with murder as it might affect public order, for example, through criminal gangs or bandits, and the specific use of poison, which might be thought of as domestic crime, but was often associated with magic and other unwholesome practices. The relevant statute was the *lex Cornelia de sicariis et veneficiis* (Crawford (1996), 749–53); see in general Robinson (1995), 28–30; 41–6; and in this volume nos. 543–50. Violence against the person also included castration, which had been banned by Domitian (Suetonius,

Domitian 7); a senatorial decree had laid down a penalty under the *lex Cornelia* for a person who castrated someone for lust or profit (*D* 48.8.3.4); see Robinson (1995), 51–3.

In respect of *vis publica* (see nos. 553–4), at one level this might constitute an assault where the state had an interest, such as to preserve public order, or maintain public morality, or control the actions of magistrates or officials that might undermine the interests of the state. At a more serious level *vis* was defined as sedition. The *lex Plautia* dated between 78 and 63 BC confirmed the earlier *lex Lutatia* (see Lintott (1968), 110–23), which dealt with attacks on the senate or magistrates or the seizure of public places, and extended it in treating as *vis* actions against private individuals that were deemed contrary to the interests of the *res publica*. For legislation against the potential threat to public order from *collegia* see pp. 94–5.

D 43.16.1.2 (Ulpian, *Edict*, Book 69)

542. It is provided by the Iulian statutes relating to public and private cases, and also by decisions of the emperors, that force (*vis*) shall not be employed.

D 50.17.152pr (Ulpian, *Edict*, Book 69)

543. We operate by this rule, namely that whatever is done by force, is prosecuted as a crime either of public or private force.

D 48.7.2 (Scaevola, *Rules*, Book 4)

544. The man is liable under this statute (the *lex Cornelia* concerning private force) who assembles a group of men and uses force (*vis*) to flog or beat up someone, even though no one is killed.

D 48.7.5 (Ulpian, *Edict*, Book 69)

545. If someone expels a person from their land by assembling a group of unarmed men, he can be prosecuted for *vis privata*.

This law also applied if a mob was gathered to prevent someone's appearance in court. Punishment was the confiscation of a third of the property of the guilty party; he was not permitted to become a senator or decurion or attain any mark of distinction.

D 47.10.5pr (Ulpian, *Edict*, Book 56)

546. The *lex Cornelia* concerning outrage (*iniuria*) is applicable to the person who wishes to sue for outrage because he claims that he has been struck and beaten up or that his home has been invaded by force.

Tacitus, *Annals* 4.22

547. Round about this time (in AD 24) the praetor Plautius Silvanus for no apparent reason threw his wife Apronia out of a window, and when hauled before the emperor by his father-in-law Lucius Apronius, replied incoherently saying that he had been fast asleep and did not know what had happened, and that his wife must have committed suicide. Tiberius went immediately to his house and examined the bedroom, where evidence of a struggle and violence were detectable. He referred the matter to the senate, and it was sent for trial. Then Urgulania, Silvanus' grandmother, sent a dagger to her grandson. Because of Urgulania's friendship with Augusta (Livia) this was generally taken to be a hint from the emperor. The accused, after an unsuccessful attempt to stab himself with the dagger, arranged for his veins to be opened. Soon after, his first wife Numantina was accused but acquitted of driving her husband mad by magic spells and poisons.

In the early imperial period murder within the family was often the responsibility of the *paterfamilias*; in this case Silvanus' father-in-law was *paterfamilias* of Apronia and he chose to take the case to the emperor; the court presumably heard a case for *vis privata* with ramifications of public interest because of the status of those involved; for the senate as a court, see p. 297.

Tacitus, *Annals* 13.44

548. (In AD 58 a tribune of the plebs, Octavius Sagitta, had seduced a married woman, Pontia, promising marriage. Pontia agreed, but having got free of her husband, reneged because she had the chance of a richer husband.) He (Octavius) demanded one night (with her) to console himself and to teach him to be more restrained in future. A night was agreed on, and Pontia had a maid who knew of the affair on watch in the bedchamber. Octavius arrived with one ex-slave, and with a dagger concealed under his clothing. Then, as usually happens in the case of love combined with anger, they argued, appealed, insulted one another, and made up; they made love for part of the

night. Then, apparently on fire with passion, he stabbed the unsuspecting woman with his dagger, wounded the maid when she ran up, and rushed out of the bedchamber. Next day the murder was discovered and there was no doubt about the perpetrator since the evidence was unambiguous that they had been together. But the ex-slave claimed that he had done the deed in order to avenge the wrongs done to his patron. This striking example of devotion convinced some people, but the maid recovered from her wound and disclosed the truth. The father of the deceased brought him before the consuls, and after he had resigned from the tribunate, he was condemned by vote of the senators in accordance with the *lex de sicariis*.

Again, the high social status of the protagonists meant a degree of public interest in the prosecution which took place under the relevant statute.

D 48.8.1pr-1 (Marcian, *Institutes*, Book 14)

549. Under the *lex Cornelia* concerning murderers and poisoners, whoever kills a man, or whoever maliciously causes a fire, or whoever goes armed with a weapon in order to kill or commit robbery, or whoever, being a magistrate and presiding over a criminal court, arranges for false testimony to be produced so that an innocent person is ensnared or condemned, is liable. Furthermore, whoever prepares and administers poison in order to kill someone, or whoever maliciously offers false testimony so that someone is condemned on a capital charge in a criminal case, or a magistrate or judge in a jury court who receives a bribe so that someone should be arraigned on a criminal charge, is liable.

D 48.8.3.5 (Marcian, *Institutes*, Book 14)

550. Under the *lex Cornelia* concerning murderers and poisoners, the penalty of deportation to an island and confiscation of property is laid down. But nowadays execution is the normal punishment, unless the convicted are of too high social status (*honestiores*) to be subject to the penalty of the law; those of lower social status (*humiliores*) are either crucified or sent to the beasts, but people of higher rank are deported to an island.

For the double penalty system and access to justice see pp. 396–412.

Tacitus, *Annals* 14.42–3

551. Not long afterwards the prefect of the city, Pedanius Secundus, was murdered by one of his own slaves, either because Pedanius had refused to grant freedom after agreeing a price, or because the slave, infatuated with someone or other, could not tolerate his master as a rival. But when traditional practice required that all the slaves who lived under the same roof should be executed, a crowd of the common people assembled in order to protect so many innocent victims, which led to a riot and the besieging of the senate house. Indeed, there were different views among the senators since some disapproved of excessive severity while the majority believed that there should be no change. (There followed a speech by Caius Cassius Longinus, arguing that the traditional custom should be maintained:)

'Today this has come about (that the state needed his advice) since a man of consular rank has been murdered in his own home through an attack by his own slave. None of his fellow slaves prevented the crime or revealed the identity of the murderer, although the senatorial decree threatening the entire household with execution is still valid. You may indeed decide to exempt them from the penalty. But whose status will be enough to protect him if the status of the prefect of the city was not enough? How many slaves will offer protection when the four hundred of Pedanius Secundus could not protect him? Will a man's household bring assistance if they do not protect us from danger even when they fear for their own lives?'

The death sentence could not be executed immediately because the mob was threatening to use stones and firebrands (Tacitus, 14.45). Nero rebuked the plebs in an edict. Crimes of violence by certain types of persons, such as slaves and bandits, occasioned special measures. This notorious murder of a senior senator by one of his own slaves in AD 61 brought into play the traditional practice of executing all the slaves in the household. The state clearly had an interest in preserving public order and social control. The *senatus consultum Silanianum*, dating probably from AD 10, laid down that slaves of the household were tortured to find the culprit, and until this had been achieved the dead man's will could not be opened; therefore, manumissions of slaves would not happen (*D* 29.5; *D* 49.14.14; *CJ* 6.35.3 (AD 222); Talbert (1984), 438, no. 13). Slaves who fled and deserted their master when he was attacked by bandits on the road, when caught, were to be put to torture and executed (Paul, *Sententiae* 3.5.6–8).

***P. Tebt.* 333 = *SP* no. 336 (AD 216)**

552. To Aurelius Iulius Marcellinus, centurion, from Aurelia Tisais, whose mother is Tais, previously described as an inhabitant of the village of

Tebtunis, in the division of Polemon. Sir, my father Kalabalis, who is a hunter, left home with my brother Nilos as long ago as the third of the current month, to hunt hares, and up to this time they have not returned. Therefore, I suspect that they have come to a lethal end, and I present this declaration making this issue clear to you, so that if they have come to a lethal end, those who are shown to be guilty may be liable to me. I have also presented a copy of this declaration to the *strategos* Aurelius Idiomachos (?), to be kept as a record. The year twenty-five of Marcus Aurelius Severus Antoninus Caesar the lord, Choiak 26.

Bryen (2008) notes the importance of making a complaint, as in this case about suspected murder; the visibility of words and the putting of things on record are part of due process of seeking redress through proper channels against the use of force; for violence and legal response in Egypt see Bryen (2013); for the judicial role of centurions, see Campbell (1984), 431–5.

D 48.6.1; 6.3pr-5; 6.5pr (Marcian, *Institutes*, Book 14)

553. Under the *lex Iulia* concerning public violence (*vis publica*) a man is liable if he collects weapons and arms in his house, land, or farm building beyond what is needed for hunting, or travelling by land, or by sea.

(6.3pr) In the same position are those who form a plan to stir up a mob or sedition or who keep slaves or freemen under arms. A man is also liable under this statute if, having reached maturity, he appears in public with a weapon. In the same position are those who hold a seditious assembly with evil intentions and attack country houses with arms and weapons and steal property. The man who grabs something from a fire is also liable, unless it is building material. Furthermore, whoever forcibly violates a boy, woman, or anyone else at all, is liable to punishment under this statute. Whoever approaches a fire with a sword or spear with the purpose of stealing or preventing the owner from saving his property, is liable to the same penalty. Also liable under this statute is anyone who with armed men ejects someone from possession of their house, farm, or ship, and attacks him.

(6.5pr) Whoever by means of a gathering, crowd, mob, or sedition starts a fire, or whoever maliciously confines or imprisons a man, or whoever takes action to prevent a burial or to disrupt and plunder a funeral, or whoever uses force to obligate someone to him (for the law rescinds that obligation), is liable.

Lintott (1968), 107–8 and 126 argues that the *leges Iuliae* in the *Digest* (*D* 48.6.1ff.) belong to the principate.

Pauli Sententiae 5.26.1

554. Under the *lex Iulia* concerning public violence is condemned whoever, while in a public office, executes, orders to be executed, tortures, beats, or condemns to be publicly put in chains a Roman citizen who has appealed, in former times to the people, but nowadays to the emperor. The penalty to be applied in this case is execution for a person of lower status, and deportation to an island for a person of higher status.

For appeals to the emperor see pp. 359–60 and pp. 446–50; for distinctions in penalty see nos. 711–14; for the prosecution of extortion and misbehaviour in office see nos. 564–6.

Treason

The *crimen laesae* (or *inminutae*) *maiestatis* was a charge of diminishing the majesty of the Roman people, and subsequently the emperor. The first permanent court for treason was established by the *lex Appuleia*, probably in 103 BC. This will have been confirmed by Sulla before the *lex Iulia maiestatis* (introduced by either Caesar or Augustus) established a formulation specifically aimed at misconduct by those in public office and powerful positions, particularly army commands. This was associated with other provisions on *vis publica* and the *lex de sicariis*, aimed at violent sedition or actions likely to endanger the state or its agents. But the *maiestas* law came particularly to be associated with actions or conspiracies against the emperor. For a useful summary, see Robinson (1995), 74–8; Williamson (2016), 337–42; for the trial of Gnaeus Piso see pp. 361–2.

Cicero, *De Inventione* 2.53

555. To diminish the majesty (of the Roman people) is to detract something from the standing, or the greatness, or the power of the people, or of those to whom the people has given power.

The *De Inventione* was a handbook of oratorical method.

D 48.4.1.1 (Ulpian, *Duties of a Proconsul*, Book 7)

556. The crime described as treason (*maiestas*) is closest to sacrilege. The crime of *maiestas* is what is done against the Roman people or against its security.

Pauli Sententiae 5.29.1

557. Under the *lex Iulia* concerning treason that person is liable by whose assistance or advice an armed rebellion is raised against the emperor or the state, or his army is led into an ambush, or whoever without instructions from the emperor wages war or conducts a levy of soldiers, or prepares an army, or seduces it in order to betray the emperor. Previously the penalty was permanent banishment (interdiction from water and fire). Nowadays people of lower social rank are thrown to the beasts or burned alive, while people of higher social station are executed. This crime lies not only in actions but is particularly exacerbated by impious words and curses.

Tacitus, *Annals* 1.72

558. For he (Tiberius) revived the law of *maiestas*. In earlier times the same name was used but other offences were prosecuted if someone had diminished the majesty of the Roman people by betraying an army or fomenting sedition among the plebs and therefore damaged the state. Actions were brought to book; mere words went unpunished. Augustus was the first under cover of this law to investigate libellous pamphlets, irritated by the wantonness of Cassius Severus, who had defamed distinguished men and women with offensive writing. Then Tiberius, when asked by the praetor Pompeius Macer if he should empanel the jury court for treason, replied that the laws must be enforced.

Tacitus alludes to a sinister development of the treason law, begun by Augustus, by which it was applied to words or thoughts. This could lead to frivolous charges assimilated to the original intention of the law. Tiberius tried to weed out such charges, but this depended on his vigilance. It was also possible that the treason law could become a vehicle for private quarrels or rivalries as senators sought to win the emperor's favour. Furthermore, a law originally intended to protect the safety of the state became identified with the safety of the emperor. In a sense, the *maiestas* law offered emperors protection against various forms of *iniuria*. Charges were frequently heard in the senate acting as a court, which will not often have helped the cause of justice since the senate was a docile political court. See Harries (2007), 77–81. In this case Tiberius is not encouraging the bringing of charges of treason, he is merely telling the praetor that the proper procedures must be followed if there are accusations of treason.

D 48.4.5pr-1 (Marcian, *Rules*, Book 5)

559. The person who repairs imperial statues decayed by age does not incur the charge of treason; similarly, the person who hits a statue (of an emperor) by accident with a stone hurled at random does not commit the crime of treason. Severus and Antoninus issued a rescript to Iulius Cassianus to this effect. The same emperors issued a rescript to Pontius that selling images of the emperor that had not yet been consecrated did not contravene the law of treason.

This shows how the law could potentially be used oppressively for trivial offences. Modestinus (*D* 48.4.7.3) urged care in identifying those who were mentally impaired and not responsible for their actions; and mere slips of the tongue should not be punished.

Tacitus, *Annals* 1.73

560. Falanius was accused of introducing among the worshippers of Augustus, who had been established in all households like associations, the actor Cassius who was also a male prostitute, and getting rid of a statue of Augustus when selling his gardens. Rubrius was charged with violating the divinity of Augustus by perjury. When Tiberius heard of this, he wrote to the consuls that his father had not been granted a place in heaven so that the honour could be the ruin of Roman citizens. He observed that Cassius the actor, along with others in this profession, had regularly taken part in the games that his mother had organized in honour of Augustus. Furthermore, it was not sacrilegious that statues of Augustus, just like other statues of deities, should be part of the sale of gardens and houses. In respect of the perjury, they should consider it to be like a false oath in the name of Jupiter; injustices done to the gods should be a matter for the gods.

Tiberius sarcastically dismissed these charges, but in another case Clutorius Priscus, an *eques*, was accused of writing a poem about Tiberius' son Drusus when he was ill, in the hope of profitable publication if he died. Priscus was immediately executed before Tiberius could intervene; he was absent from the senate and Drusus was presiding. From this emerged the rule of a ten-day interlude between sentence and execution; Tacitus, *Ann.* 3.49; for the context see Cowan (2016).

Dio 76(77).8

561. After this came the end of the business about Apronianus, strange as it is to hear. He was accused because his nurse was reported once to have had a dream that he would be emperor, and because he had apparently used magic of some kind to bring this about. He was condemned in his absence while governor of Asia. (When evidence statements were read out it appeared that a witness had been asked who had heard the story of the dream.) He said among other things: 'I saw a bald-headed senator peering in'. Hearing this we were in a terrible state; for although the man had not mentioned and Severus had not written down anyone's name, such was the consternation that even those who had never frequented Apronianus' house, and not only the bald-headed but even those with just a bald forehead, were frightened … I shall not conceal my experience at this time even if it is laughable. I was so flustered that I felt with my hand to check that I had hair on my head.

This treason charge under Septimius Severus was heard in the senate. Severus who seized power after a civil war had a difficult relationship with the senate, especially in the early part of his reign. This is a vivid illustration of the consternation caused among the senior governing class by even vague accusations of treason.

*Extortion (*res repetundae*)*

There were several statutes dealing with extortion by magistrates in office, going back to the *lex Calpurnia* of 149 BC; the *lex Acilia* included extortion directed at non-Romans. In 59 BC Julius Caesar introduced the *lex Iulia* which laid down new procedures and confirmed or extended the scope of the extortion law to deal with any kind of wrongful exaction from provincials by magistrates or others in authority, including peculation, taking bribes, and improper exercise of jurisdiction. The wives of public officials and those serving under them were also included. The penalty was exile, with possible disgrace, and as far as possible reparation for the victims. Augustus had sponsored in 4 BC a decree of the senate (*Senatus Consultum Calvisianum*), which was disseminated to the provinces prefaced by his own edict (see no. 259) proclaiming his concern for his subjects. The decree provided for a special procedure to appoint five assessors from the senate in cases involving no capital charges but only simple reparation of extorted funds. The object was to offer a more straightforward process and speedier settlement. The perennial problem remained of the trial of senators by senators, who were likely to be sympathetic to members of their own order; see p. 664; also, Robinson (1995), 81–2; Harries (2007), 65–8.

D 48.11.1pr-1 (Marcian, *Institutes*, Book 14)

562. The *lex Iulia* relating to extortion applies to those funds taken by anyone holding a magistracy, power, curatorship, embassy, or any other public position, responsibility, or function, and it applies if he belongs to the entourage of these people. The law makes an exception for those people from whom it is permitted to receive money, such as cousins, or blood relatives of a closer degree, or a wife.

D 48.11.3 (Macer, *Criminal Proceedings*, Book 1)

563. Under the *lex Iulia* relating to extortion is liable whoever, when holding some power or other, receives money for the purpose of giving a judgement or not giving a judgement or making an adjudication.

D 48.13.1 (Ulpian, *Sabinus*, Book 44)

564. Under the *lex Iulia* concerning embezzlement (of public money) it is laid down that no one should remove anything from sacred, religious, or public monies, or intercept it, or divert it for his own purposes, or arrange for someone to remove, intercept, or divert it for his own purposes, unless in the case of someone who is authorized by statute. Nor should anyone add anything to or mix anything with gold, silver, and bronze belonging to the state, nor knowingly and with malicious intent arrange for anything to be added or mixed, by which its value is reduced.

For the law and the embezzlement of public funds, see Robinson (1995), 81–3. The best evidence for the conduct of *repetundae* cases in the senate is provided by Pliny, who was involved in several instances for the prosecution and the defence. Marius Priscus had been proconsul of Africa in 97–98, and the community of Lepcis and several individuals brought charges of corruption against him; he was first condemned for the lesser form of extortion; Pliny and Tacitus had acted for the prosecution at that stage. But more information emerged leading to capital charges, which resulted in a trial in the senate, in which Pliny and Tacitus appeared again for the prosecution. Priscus was found guilty and exiled from Rome and Italy; a bribe of 700,000 he had accepted was confiscated to the treasury. Hostilius Firminus, who had been *legatus* of Priscus, was subsequently condemned as being implicated in the governor's corruption (*Letters* 2.11–12). Caecilius Classicus, governor of Baetica, was charged with aggravated extortion involving violence and was tried before the senate (*Letters* 3.9). Prosecution had been initiated by the provincial council of Baetica. Classicus had died before the trial began and the object was to establish his guilt and then move against his friends and associates who had colluded in his corruption; Pliny established that carrying out orders was no defence; see Robinson (2007), 86–91. In the trial of Iulius Bassus Pliny appeared for the defence; Bassus was charged with inappropriately accepting gifts as governor, and Pliny rather dubiously pleaded mitigation (*Letters* 4.9); although convicted, he escaped comparatively lightly, but his acts as governor were later rescinded; see Robinson (2007), 91–4.

D 1.16.4.2 (Ulpian, *Duties of a Proconsul*, Book 1)

565. It is better if a proconsul sets out (for his province) without his wife. But he may be accompanied by his wife provided that he is aware that the senate in the consulship of Messalla and Cotta decided that for the future if the wives of those who were on their way to hold public office committed any offence, they would be called to account and face retribution.

Messalla and Cotta were consuls in AD 20; Tacitus (*Annals* 4.20) places the senatorial decree in 24, after the case of Gaius Silius and his wife, both charged with extortion; at *Annals* 3.33 (no. 566) he describes an earlier debate at which no decision was taken.

Tacitus, *Annals* 3.33

566. During the debate Aulus Caecina Severus proposed that no magistrate who had been chosen for a provincial governorship should be accompanied by his wife, noting that he got on well with his wife and had six children by her, and that he maintained in his own household what he was advising in public affairs, since he had kept her in Italy although he had completed forty years' service in numerous provinces ... They should reflect on whenever officials are charged with extortion most of the charges are directed against their wives. For the women attract all the worst elements in the provinces, and they undertake and negotiate business.

*Electoral Bribery (*ambitus*)*

This was a common offence in the republic and many laws were passed in an attempt to control it (Robinson (1995), 84–6; Lintott (1990)). In the imperial period, although Augustus ensured that the men he approved of were elected (Dio 53.21.6–7; Tacitus, *Annals* 1.15), he did not control everything and elections still witnessed great excitement, bribery, and even violence. In 18 BC Augustus sponsored the *lex Iulia de ambitu* which debarred from office for five years those who had used bribery to get elected (Dio 54.16). Nevertheless, in AD 7 no elections could take place because of partisan outbreaks and Augustus appointed all the magistrates (Dio 55.34.2). In AD 14 elections to the consulship and praetorship were moved to the senate, as were elections to other magistracies subsequently. Even in the senate there were disorderly scenes at elections and further measures were taken by the senate against bribery. Eventually, as Modestinus (no. 568) points out, such measures became irrelevant with increasing imperial control.

Pliny, *Letters* 6.19

567. During the last election the senate expressed a very proper opinion, namely: 'Candidates should not be permitted to give dinners, send gifts, or place money on deposit'. The first two of these were carried on openly and unrestrainedly; the third although carried on in secret was well known.

Money left on deposit if not reclaimed could serve as a bribe; Sherwin-White (1966), 377; see also *Letters* 2.9, 3.20, 4.15, 4.25, 6.6 which show vigorous competition for office.

D 48.14.1pr (Modestinus, *Punishments*, Book 2)

568. This statute (*lex Iulia* on electoral bribery) is no longer operative in Rome since the creation of magistrates lies within the remit of the emperor and not the favour of the people.

Public Morality and Sexual Offences

Augustus made strenuous efforts to legislate in order to direct personal conduct and encourage the families of citizens (especially the upper classes) to behave in a way that supported the public interest (see pp. 50–5). He aimed to control the incidence of adultery, and the *lex Iulia* (with at least nine chapters) created a court for sexual offences, aimed at improper sexual relations including incest. In cases of adultery the government was particularly concerned that another man's child might be introduced into the male family line with a consequent threat to family property rights. Bigamy was not a criminal offence since the Romans did not accept that two marriages could exist. Homosexuality was not illegal unless it amounted to *stuprum* (attempted rape or sexual assault). Sex with an unmarried but marriageable woman also came under this offence. As the law was extended, some trials subsequently came to be held in the senate. See in general Robinson (1995), 54–73; Treggiari (1991), 262–98; Bryen (2016).

Gaius, *Institutes* 1.59; 62

569. A marriage cannot be contracted and there is no *conubium* (right of marriage) between those persons who have the status of ascendant and descendant to each other, as for example between father and daughter, or between mother and son, or between grandfather and granddaughter [or grandmother and grandson], and if persons of this status form a union, they are considered to have contracted a wicked and incestuous marriage. (62) A man is permitted to marry the daughter of his brother, and this was first introduced when the divine Claudius married Agrippina, daughter of his brother. However, it is not permitted for anyone to marry the daughter of his sister. And these rules are set out in the imperial decisions.

Iulia Agrippina was the eldest daughter of Germanicus and had been exiled by her brother Caligula; she was recalled by Claudius who married her in AD 49. Claudius persuaded some members of the senate to suggest that the marriage was in the interests of the state, 'and that others should be allowed to form similar marriages, which previously had been considered incestuous' (Suetonius, *Claudius* 26.3).

CJ 9.9.1 (AD 197)

570. Emperors Severus and Antoninus Augusti to Cassia. The *lex Iulia* declares that women do not have the right of bringing a charge of adultery before a jury court even though they wish to make complaint about the betrayal of their marriage. For the law, when it established for men the right of bringing a charge according to the prerogatives of a husband, did not extend the same privilege to women.

The Iulian law on adultery was proposed by Augustus himself and was probably linked to the marriage law of 18 BC; Dio 54.16; Suetonius, *Augustus* 34; Treggiari (1991), 264–90; McGinn (1998), 140–215, especially 140–7; 207–15. Under the legislation adultery had become a criminal offence; a married woman was guilty if she had sexual relations with any man other than her husband; but a man was not guilty if he pursued a liaison with another woman, provided that she was not married. The woman could not prosecute her husband for adultery, for in the Roman legal view he had not committed an offence against the marriage, and women could litigate in the criminal courts only for offences against themselves; for a useful summary see Gardner (1986), 127–31.

Pauli Sententiae 2.26.5

571. A husband who kills his wife caught in the act with an adulterer, since he committed this because he was unable to endure his justified grief, should be punished more leniently. When the adulterer has been killed the husband must divorce his wife immediately and make an announcement within the next three days of the identity of the adulterer with whom, and the location in which, he caught his wife.

A husband had the right to kill the man whom he surprised in an adulterous relationship with his wife, but only if he was caught in the husband's own house and was of low social degree. The husband was not permitted to kill his wife, but the law required him to divorce her and to bring a prosecution. If he had failed to do this within sixty days, third parties could launch a prosecution. If the husband did not divorce his wife or prosecute her, he was open to a charge of making gain out of sexual activity (*lenocinium*). Prostitution itself was not illegal. See Treggiari (1991); Robinson (1995), 58–68; prostitution – McGinn (1998), 320–37.

D 48.5.24 (Ulpian, *Adulteries*, Book 1)

572. The words of the statute stating 'If he finds the adulterer in his daughter' do not seem to be redundant. For it indicates that the father has this power only if he actually catches his daughter in the act of adultery. Labeo also agrees with this view, and Pomponius writes that the man caught in the very act of lovemaking is killed.

The legislation of Augustus was intended to place some restriction on the father's right to kill. Apart from the immediacy of the act, a further impediment to the father's right to kill his daughter and the adulterer was that it had to be done in his own house or that of his son-in-law. The emphasis here is on the family honour and morality.

CJ 9.9.4

573. Emperor Alexander Augustus to Iulianus, proconsul of Gallia Narbonensis. If, in the case of Gracchus, whom Numerius caught committing adultery during the night and killed, his status was such that he could be killed without penalty according to the *lex Iulia*, he does not merit any punishment because he acted in accordance with the law. Indeed, the same right must be granted to his sons who acted under their father's instructions. But if, without the authority of the law, through his intemperate grief he killed the adulterer, although a murder has been committed,

nevertheless the fact that it occurred at night, and his legitimate grief bring mitigation to his deed, and he may be sent into exile.

See also no. 538.

Pliny, *Letters* 6.31.4–6

574. Next day the case of Gallitta charged with adultery was heard. Married to a military tribune who was about to stand for civilian office she had stained her own and her husband's reputation by a love affair with a centurion. The husband had spoken to the governor about it, and he had written to the emperor. The emperor after considering the evidence dismissed the centurion from military service and also banished him. There remained the other part of the punishment since the charge could only have been made against two people. But love for his wife had made the tribune delay, although there was criticism of his restraint. For he retained her in his house even after the adultery was revealed, as if he was happy enough to have got rid of his rival. When he was told to proceed with the accusation he did so unwillingly. However, it was essential for her to be condemned even if the accuser was reluctant, and she was indeed condemned and punished under the *lex Iulia*. The emperor added to the verdict the name of the centurion and a statement on military discipline, as he did not want all cases of this type to be referred to him.

The governor had probably referred this case to Trajan because of the status of the tribune (who was of senatorial rank) and his wife. The procedure here is by *cognitio* in which the emperor investigates with chosen advisers and establishes a penalty; Sherwin-White (1966), 393–4. The penalty for adultery was normally pecuniary, though banishment was available (no. 575). See no. 748 for other legal cases considered at this session.

Pauli Sententiae 2.26.14

575. It is agreed that women convicted of adultery should be punished with the loss of half their dowry and one third of their property, and removal to an island. In the case of the man convicted of adultery he also should lose half his property and be relegated to an island, though to a different island.

The Religious Establishment

Ius divinum referred to laws created by gods and concerning the relations of men to gods; *res sacrae* were things consecrated to the gods. The relationship of priests, sacral law, and the individual is an important theme. *Pontifices* dealt with sacrilege, damage to sacred places, burial, and the movement of bodies; they also supervised adoption practices, the calendar, and the maintenance of the *pomerium*, the sacred boundary of the city, along which they conducted a lustration for purification in times of crisis and uncertainty (Pliny, *NH* 10.35; Beard, North and Price (1998), 177–8). In the early period the *pontifices* were expected to be available to advise citizens, and this could extend beyond issues of religious practice. In the fourth century BC a specific formula was invoked before legal actions could be initiated, and this was the preserve of the *pontifices* (Livy 9.46.5). Doubtless, therefore, they came to advise on legal issues (no. 577). Since priests invariably were members of the upper classes this will have helped to confirm their domination in society and government. The law was used by the Roman state to regulate various aspects of religion; whereas in the republic limits were established to recognize the agency of gods, post-classical law tended to mobilize religion as a source of legitimation of the ruler and the empire (Ando and Rüpke (2006), 11–12). Regulations dealt with two aspects of religious affairs: public rituals, which were officially organized and financed, and more personal matters, such as burial rights and the cult of ancestors.

Among other notable priesthoods were the *quindecimviri sacris faciundis* (no. 589); the augurs, whose task it was to establish the will of the gods by interpreting various signs such as the flight of birds and natural phenomena; they assisted the appropriate magistrate who was required to take the auspices; the *haruspices* interpreted portents and inspected the entrails of animals at sacrifices; the fetials supervised procedures by which a war could be declared properly and justly; the arvals originally celebrated an ancient agricultural rite (for their hymn see no. 59). The vestal virgins were the only significant female priesthood at Rome; the six priestesses were chosen in childhood and were responsible for keeping the sacred fire in the temple of Vesta, in a way symbolizing the continuation of the Roman race. In religious activity also the emperor was dominant, and Augustus held most of the major priesthoods (*Res Gestae* 7.3). For a summary of priesthoods, see Beard, North and Price (1998), 18–30.

Gaius, *Institutes* 2.2–9

576. The principal division of things places them in two classes: some are subject to divine right, others to human. Things subject to divine right are for example *res sacrae* and *res religiosae*. *Res sacrae* are those consecrated to

the gods above, *res religiosae* are left to the gods of the underworld. But only something consecrated by the authority of the Roman people is considered *sacrum*, for example by a statute carried or a senatorial decree introduced concerning that matter. But we can make a thing *religiosum* by our own volition, by burying a body on our land, provided that the funeral of the dead man is our responsibility. But it has been generally accepted that in the provinces land does not become *religiosum*, because ownership of provincial land lies with the Roman people, or the emperor, and we apparently have only possession or usufruct. However, even if it may not be *religiosum*, it is held to be such. *Res sanctae* also, for example walls and gates, are to some extent subject to divine right. Now, whatever is subject to divine right is not part of anyone's property. But whatever is subject to human right is generally part of someone's property, though it is possible that it belongs to no one. For things that are part of a deceased person's estate belong to no one before someone is established as heir.

The distinction between public and private related to spaces owned by the community and those owned by individuals, and the nature of the religious practices conducted there either for the benefit of the entire community or for an individual or family.

Rights and Duties of the pontifices

D 1.2.2.6 (Pomponius, *Textbook*, Only Book)

577. However, in respect of all these statutes, the knowledge of how to interpret them and execute legal actions lies with the college of pontiffs, from whom one priest was designated every year to be responsible for private individuals.

Roman religious authority applied throughout Italy. Calendars were set up in Italian towns, which were mutually compatible and part of the same system of religious time keeping; see Beard, North and Price (1998), 321–3.

Tacitus, *Annals* 3.71 (AD 22)

578. Then a religious issue intervened in respect of the temple in which should be placed the gift which the Roman *equites* had vowed to Equestrian Fortune for Augustus' recovery from illness. For although there were many shrines of that goddess in the city, there was none with such a cult title. But a temple was found at Antium which had this title, and furthermore all religious observances in Italian towns and temples and statues of gods were

subject to the authority and jurisdiction of Rome. Therefore, the gift was established at Antium. Since religious affairs were under discussion, the emperor related his recently postponed decision concerning Servius Cornelius Lentulus Maluginensis, the priest of Jupiter, and read out a decision of the college of pontiffs that, whenever the priest of Jupiter was afflicted by illness, on the decision of the chief priest he could be away for more than two nights, provided that this was not on days of public sacrifice and did not happen more than twice in a year. This ruling, established under Augustus, demonstrated that priests of Jupiter could not be absent for a year and hold provincial governorships. The precedent was noted of L. Metellus the chief priest who had prevented the departure of Aulus Postumius (in 242 BC).

Servius had applied to have his name added to the lot for the proconsulship of Asia.

CIL 6.2120 = *ILS* 8380 (AD 155)

579. Velius Fidus sends greetings to his colleague Iubentius Celsus.

My dear brother Desiderius (another name for Celsus), I have sent to you the petition of Arrius Alphius, freedman of Arria Fadilla, mother of our emperor Antoninus Augustus, a man whom I have known for a long time from my earliest youth. Indeed, I was astonished that, when I was absent from home, he followed me to the same place and I learned from him that he had made an urgent petition to our lord the emperor, both for the sake of his own peace, and particularly for religious reasons. Therefore, so that we do not appear to have caused delay for him, please return the signed petition to me without delay by the same public slave. I hope that you are well and happy.

Copy of the petition submitted:

Since a while ago I lost my wife and son, and burdened with poverty committed their remains to an earthenware coffin, until a tomb could be constructed at the location which I had bought on the Via Flaminia, between the second and third milestone on the left-hand side as you leave the city, the tomb being under the guardianship of Flavia Thumele, in the burial ground of Marcus Silius Orcilius. I request, my lord, that you allow me to place their remains in the same place in a marble tomb that I have just purchased, so that when I die, I may be laid to rest next to them.

Resolved: agreed. I, Iubentius Celsus, deputy master have signed, 3 November, in the (suffect) consulship of Antius Polio and Opimianus, and the ordinary consulship of Severus and Sabinianus.

Dates are usually given by the ordinary consuls alone who took office first in the year, being replaced by the suffects later. The right to relocate or transport bodies was granted by the *pontifices* in accordance with the regulations of burial in Rome (see Crook (1967), 133–8). Alphius had first approached the emperor because he was senior priest in the college, *pontifex maximus*; but as a freedman of the emperor's mother, Alphius was particularly well-connected.

D 11.8.1; 6–7 (Ulpian, *Edict*, Book 68)

580. The praetor declares: 'In respect of whosoever has the right to transport a dead man to any location by any route without your permission, I forbid you to use force to prevent that person from transporting a dead man by any route and burying him in any location. (6–7) Furthermore this interdict was issued because it is in the interests of religious practice for tombs to be constructed and adorned. No one is prevented from building a tomb or monument in the location in which he has a right to do so'.

Administration of Religious Practice in the Provinces

D 48.13.4.2 (Marcian, *Institutes*, Book 14)

581. It is set out in imperial instructions on sacrilege that governors are to search out those who commit sacrilege, bandits, and kidnappers and punish them as the offence of each deserves. And it is set out in imperial decisions that those who commit sacrilege are to be punished suitably by judicial examination (*cognitio*).

Governors were generally responsible for sacred places in their province.

Agennius Urbicus, *Land Disputes* (T, p. 48.4–12 = Campbell (2000), p. 45.21–34)

582. According to the legislation of the Roman people, the great religious aura and guardianship of sacred places must be preserved; even provincial governors receive no more important exhortation in their instructions than that those places which are sacred should be safeguarded. This is more easily maintained in the provinces. In Italy, however, the multitude of landholders acts with a great deal of dishonesty, and they appropriate sacred groves whose land undoubtedly belongs to the Roman people, even if they are within the territory of colonies or *municipia*. Concerning

these places, no small dispute normally arises between a community and private individuals.

Agennius gives an example of a dispute in Africa between Hadrumetum and Thysdrus over a temple of Minerva. Ownership of a temple might have economic benefits because religious festivals could attract large numbers of people.

Smallwood (1967), no. 380 cols. iii–iv; Johnson, Coleman-Norton, Bourne (1961), no. 171

583. Paulus Fabius Persicus, priest, *Sodalis Augustalis*, Arval Brother, quaestor of Emperor Tiberius Caesar Augustus, praetor … consul … proconsul of Asia, has proclaimed:

Since Emperor Tiberius Claudius Caesar Augustus Germanicus has announced a decree which is beneficial to the city of Ephesus and the entire province, and which he published at Ephesus and instructed that it be inscribed on a column before 28 March … (cols. iii–vi) For many buildings have been destroyed by fire or collapsed in a pile of disordered ruins, and the temple of Artemis herself, which is an adornment for the whole province, and which, because of the size of the building and the antiquity of the observances for the divinity, and the wealth of the funds that Augustus restored to the goddess, is being deprived of its special funds, which could be sufficient for the maintenance and embellishment of the offerings. For this money has been spirited away for the corrupt purposes of those in charge of the common fund according to what they think will profit their own interests. For every time any uplifting news comes from Rome, they exploit this for their own gain. They make the outer shape of the divine house a screen, sell the priesthoods as if they were dealing in a public auction, and invite all kinds of men to purchase them. Then, they do not select the most suitable candidates on whose heads the proper crown is to be placed, and they divide the revenues among the priests taking part, as much as they are willing to take, so that they can appropriate as much as possible for themselves … It seems essential to me that the city undertakes these expenses in order that the most suitable person will be thought worthy of this honour from the people. I am pleased that an enormously heavy burden will be removed by this decree. Since I realize that the payment of the money will be difficult for the city, or indeed entirely impossible, if it should be compelled to pay out now the sum they received from those who purchased (the priesthoods), it is my wish that the city should pay to the priests no more than 1 per cent of the sum paid at that time for a priesthood, in accordance with the practice of Vedius Pollio, which was confirmed by the divine Augustus. I do not wish the priests to give anything to the senate, or in turn, to receive anything from it.

For the governor's preamble to this decree, see no. 260. Around AD 44 the Romans regulated the religious finances of the temple of Artemis in Ephesus, which had suffered a recent earthquake; it had been the practice that priests had to buy their office, which had led to corrupt practice and the choice of unworthy people. The governor is revising an earlier intervention in the reign of Augustus. The city could not repay in one tranche all the money paid out by those purchasing priesthoods, and so only 1 per cent of the sum was permitted. In the future the city was to take over priestly expenses. This ensured that the temple finances would be in order, and perhaps made it easier for Roman supervision of religious practice. However, Roman sacral law did not apply in alien land (that is, in the provinces) and so governors had to use their initiative and identify established precedent.

Lex Colonia Genetiva Crawford (1996), p. 401, Chapter 66

584. Whoever shall be appointed *pontifices* and *augures* from the *colonia Genetiva* by Caius Caesar, or by whomever sets up the colony on Caesar's instructions, they are to be *pontifices* and *augures* of the *colonia Genetiva Iulia*; they are to be *pontifices* and *augures* in the colleges of *pontifices* and *augures* in the said *colonia*, in the same way as those who are or shall be *pontifices* and *augures* in every colony with all the best conditions and rights. Those *pontifices* and *augures*, who are members of each college, and their children, are to be exempt by sacred provision from military service and obligations to the community, in the same way as for a *pontifex* at Rome, and all their military service shall be considered to have been completed. Concerning the auspices and whatever matters relate to them, the jurisdiction and power of adjudication is to belong to the *augures*. These *pontifices* and *augures* are to have the right and power to wear the *toga praetexta*, both at the games which the magistrates celebrate publicly, and at public sacrifices of the *colonia Genetiva Iulia* conducted by the *pontifices* and *augures*; and these *pontifices* and *augures* shall have the right and power to watch the games and the gladiatorial contests (seated) amongst the town councillors.

For the colony at Urso, see p. 135; this inscription was re-inscribed in the first century AD and shows the continuing importance of the Roman context of the priesthoods (see Beard, North and Price (1998), 328–30). Chapters 64–72 deal with religious practices, which were to be part of the new community's self-definition; these related to large-scale public rituals organized by the community, and private observances connected with burials and remembrance; see Rüpke (2006), who considers that religious practice in the colony was based round rituals and the role of magistrates.

Pliny, *Letters* 10.49–50

585. Before my arrival, sir, the people of Nicomedia had begun to add a new forum to the existing one, in the corner of which is an ancient temple of the Great Mother goddess, which must either be rebuilt or moved to another place, mainly because it is far below the new building which rises to a great height. When I asked if any special law had been passed for the temple, I discovered that their usual practice of dedicating a temple is different from ours. Consider therefore, lord, if you think that the temple for which no special law has been passed, can be moved without offending religious scruple; in other respects, it would be most convenient to do so, if no religious scruple prevents.

My dear Pliny, without any concern for religious scruple you may move the temple of the Great Mother to a more suitable site if the nature of the location seems to require this. You need not worry if no law relating to the dedication of the temple can be found, since land in a non-Roman community cannot receive dedication, which is carried out according to our law.

In Roman practice the person or authority dedicating a temple established a formula setting out the extent of the shrine, the religious practices to be observed, and how it was to be administered; see *Letters* 4.1 where Pliny dedicates a shrine at Tifernum. The formula was probably under the supervision of the *pontifices*. However, according to Gaius (see no. 576) since in the provinces only the Roman people or the emperor could own land, provincial ground could not become truly religious, only quasi-religious. Governors had to assess how far pontifical law could be applied.

Pliny, *Letters* 10.68–9

586. Certain people have requested that in accordance with the precedent of previous proconsuls I should permit them to move the remains of their relatives, either because of decay (of the tombs) through age, or the incursion of a river, or some other similar reason. Because I am aware that in our city it is usual to approach the college of pontiffs in respect of issues of this kind, I thought that I should consult you, sir, as chief priest, as to what you think that I should do.

It is unfair to impose on provincials the requirement of approaching the pontiffs if they wish to move the remains of relatives from one location to another for any good reasons. Therefore, it would be better if you followed the precedents set by those who were governors of that province and granted or refused each request on its merits.

In Roman sacral practice the burial of a body made a site *religiosum* and plans to redesign the area or move the body required investigation and approval by the pontiffs. Trajan advises a compassionate, equitable approach based on local practice. Augustus made much of his election as *pontifex maximus* in 12 BC (*Res Gestae* 10.2); for the significance of the role, see Beard, North and Price (1998), 188–90.

CJ 3.44.1 (AD 213)

587. Emperor Antoninus Augustus to Dionysia. If the remains of your son are being threatened by the force of a river, or some other just or essential reason intervenes, you can through the judgement of the governor of the province move them to another location.

Magicians, Astrologers, and Prophets

Magical practice was thought to use supernatural methods to influence or change natural events and to affect individuals. Poisons, drugs, and curse tablets were employed, accompanied by incantations, often to bring about illness (or sometimes a cure), or to arouse feelings of love. The state's desire for order came into conflict with the individual's wish to know the future or influence events. The secretiveness and association with criminal enterprises of those involved with magic caused the authorities to be suspicious; see in general MacMullen (1966), 95–162; Robinson (1995), 92–4; Beard, North and Price (1998), 153–6; 231–6; since magic was thought to use deviant religious acts to bind or direct people in various ways, the law was used to police such quasi-religious activities; Rives (2011) in a useful survey of magicians and astrologers argues that the connection between astrology and imperial rule gave astrology considerable social power but also made it potentially dangerous, as was demonstrated by the case of Marcus Scribonius Libo Drusus, accused of subversion in AD 16. He seems to have been empty-headed and harmless but was accused of consulting fortune-tellers and having information on members of the imperial family; he committed suicide while awaiting the outcome of his trial, though Tiberius said that he would have ruled out the death penalty; the trial was followed by the expulsion of astrologers and magicians from Italy (Tacitus, *Annals* 2.27–32). Further expulsions occurred under Nero (Tacitus, *Annals* 12.52), Vitellius (Suetonius, *Vitellius* 14.4), and Vespasian (Dio 65.9.2); Domitian expelled philosophers (Suetonius, *Domitian* 10.3). By the early third century it was established that making enquiries about the emperor or political events was a capital offence. For the law and marginalized groups in Roman society, see in general Taylor (2016).

Dio 56.25.5

588. Apart from these events, seers were forbidden to utter prophecies to a lone person, or concerning death even if others were present. But Augustus was so far from being concerned about these issues in his own case that he revealed to everyone in an edict the location of the stars at the time of his birth. However, he prohibited this practice.

Augustus also burned more than two thousand works of prophecy in Greek and Latin, which were either anonymous or by authors of low repute. See MacMullen (1966), 129–30 on secret divinatory consultations. A senator under Septimius Severus in AD 205 whose nurse dreamed that he would one day be emperor was accused of using magic to bring this about (see no. 561).

Tacitus, *Annals* 6.12

589. Quintilianus, a tribune of the plebs, now put a proposal to the senate concerning a Sibylline book, which Caninius Gallus, a member of the college of fifteen, demanded should be included among the other books of that prophetess, and that the senate should issue a decree on the matter. This had been passed without discussion when the emperor sent a letter only mildly criticizing the tribune since because of his youth he was ignorant of ancient practice. But he upbraided Gallus because despite his long experience of religious lore he had on uncertain authority anticipated the decision of the college, and in defiance of usual practice had introduced the matter into a poorly attended senate meeting before the poem had been read and analysed by the members of the college. At the same time, he pointed out that because many false works were being circulated under the famous name, Augustus had established a day by which they were to be brought to the urban praetor, and that private ownership was to be illegal.

The college of the *quindecemviri sacris faciundis* was responsible for the Sibylline books, or Greek oracles bought according to tradition by king Tarquinius

Superbus; they consisted of ritual practices to be adopted, notably in time of difficulty. The college consulted the books when requested by the senate.

Tacitus, *Annals* 12.22

590. In the same year, Agrippina, who had fierce hatreds and was hostile to Lollia Paulina because she had been her rival for marriage to the emperor, arranged her prosecution and a prosecutor on the charge that she visited Chaldaean astrologers and magicians, and had inquired at the image of Clarian Apollo about the emperor's marriage. Claudius without hearing the defendant made a long speech to the senate ... (about her distinguished ancestry and marriages). He added that the plots were dangerous to the state and that the means of her wickedness should be removed. Therefore, it was right to confiscate her property and expel her from Italy.

Lollia was subsequently forced to commit suicide; her dealings with magicians were a convenient excuse for Agrippina's hostility. The Chaldaeans from the area of Babylon were noted for their study of astrology, associating planetary movements with life on earth, and casting horoscopes.

Tacitus, *Histories* 1.22

591. The astrologers also exerted pressure, asserting from observation of the stars new opportunities and a glorious year for Otho. These men are untrustworthy towards the powerful and mislead the ambitious, and in our state will always be banned yet always retained.

After the murder of Nero in 68, Otho, governor of Lusitania, supported Galba, but was disappointed in his hope of becoming his heir and was encouraged by members of his entourage including astrologers to win over the praetorian guard and seize power. Cassius Dio in the invented speech of Augustus' henchman Maecenas set out desirable principles of autocratic government for the management of society in the late second century AD; although divination and augury are necessary, 'there should not be any magicians at all. For such men, sometimes speaking the truth but usually telling lies, often persuade many into revolutionary behaviour. Not a few of those who pretend to be philosophers do the same thing' (52.36.2–4).

Pauli Sententiae 5.21.1–3

592. It has been decided that prophets, who pretend that they are full of the divine, should for this reason be expelled from the state, in case

through human credulity public morals are corrupted through a longing for something, or indeed because of this the minds of the people should be disturbed. Therefore, they are first beaten with clubs and then expelled from the state. If they persist, they are publicly put in chains or deported to an island or indeed relegated. (2) Those who introduce new sects or religions lacking all reason, by which men's minds are disturbed, are deported if of higher social rank, and executed if of lower social rank. (3) Those who consult mathematicians, astrologers, haruspices, or soothsayers about the emperor's well-being or public business are executed along with the person who gave a response.

Pauli Sententiae 5.23.14–19

593. Those who administer a potion to bring about an abortion or to act as an aphrodisiac, even if there is no malicious intent, nevertheless, because the action creates a bad example, should be sent to the mines if they are people of low status, or banished to an island with confiscation of property if they are people of high status. But if as a result of the potion a woman or a man dies, they are to suffer capital punishment. Those who have conducted or have had conducted for them impious or nocturnal rites in order to enchant, bewitch, or bind someone, are to be crucified or thrown to the wild beasts. Those who have sacrificed a man or have conducted rites with his blood or have polluted a shrine or a temple, are to be thrown to the beasts, or executed if they are of high status. It has been decided that those who have experience of the magical arts suffer capital punishment, that is, they are crucified or thrown to the beasts. However, magicians themselves are to be burned alive. No one is permitted to have books on the magical arts in his possession. If such books are found in their possession, their property is confiscated, the books burned in public, and they are to be deported to an island, while those of low status are executed. Not only is the practice of this art forbidden, but also knowledge of it. If a man dies because of a drug administered to him to promote his health or as a cure, the man who administered it is relegated to an island if he is of high status, or executed if he is of low status.

For distinctions of status, see pp. 411–12; providing the means of death, see no. 493; for the *lex Cornelia* and the administration of drugs, see Rives (2006).

Mosaicarum et Romanarum Legum Collatio 15.2.1 (Ulpian, *Duties of a Proconsul*, Book 7, Under the Heading: Concerning Mathematicians and Soothsayers)

594. Furthermore, there is legal provision against the clever conceits and the persistent conniving of mathematicians. But today is not the first occasion on which it has been decided to take action against them; rather this prohibition is of long standing. Indeed, there is extant a decree of the senate issued in the consulship of Pomponius and Rufus (AD 17), in which it is laid down that mathematicians, Chaldaeans, prophets, and others, who undertake similar activities, should be exiled and all their property confiscated, and if anyone from foreign peoples does these things, he should be executed. However, a question was asked whether the learning of men of this type should be punished, or the exercise and profession of it. Among older authorities the view was that it was the profession not the actual knowledge that was prohibited. Later that view was amended.

For this text, see p. 6.

Historia Augusta, Marcus Aurelius 13.6

595. (On the emperor's clemency) In the case of one fraudster, who with several accomplices was looking for an opportunity to plunder the city and made public orations from a fig tree in the Campus Martius, prophesying that fire would fall from heaven and bring about the end of the world if he fell from the tree and turned into a stork. At the set time he fell from the tree and released a stork from his clothing. He was brought to Marcus Aurelius and made a confession but was pardoned.

For the *Historia Augusta*, see p. 478.

Apuleius, *Apologia* 47

596. This magic, as I have been told, is forbidden by statute, indeed in ancient times by the Twelve Tables because of incredible attempts to entice away crops (from one owner to another). It is therefore a secret rite, and also appalling and disgusting, usually requiring watches throughout the night, hidden away in the dark with private actions and muttered incantations, to which few free people never mind slaves are admitted. But you claim that fifteen slaves were present? Was it a marriage ceremony or some other crowded occasion or a summer banquet? Fifteen slaves took part in a

magic ritual just like fifteen men elected to conduct public sacrifices. Would I have had so many involved in this business if they were too many to be accomplices?

Apuleius delivered this speech before the proconsul of Africa in AD 158–9 to defend himself against the charge of having bewitched a rich widow, Pudentilla, to fall in love with him. To procure this by magic was a capital charge. Pudentilla's family was outraged at the thought that her fortune might end up with Apuleius. In arguing in defence of his actions Apuleius does not claim that the use of magic was impossible, but that he was not a magician and that various incidents brought up by the plaintiffs had an innocent explanation. See MacMullen (1966), 121–4; Bradley (1997); Harries (2007), 121–7 for the trial of Apuleius; Rives (2003), 322–7; (2006); see also nos. 597; 670.

Apuleius, *Apologia* 53; 61

597. Furthermore, although I had omitted to mention this, there are matters that you admit you know nothing about but use the same matters to bring a charge as if you do know them. You allege that I kept some objects wrapped in a handkerchief among the household gods in the home of Pontianus. You admit that as these objects were wrapped up you did not know their nature or purpose, and that there is no one who has seen them. Nevertheless, you claim that they were instruments of magic. (61) Out of all this they have produced one charge, after reading Pudentilla's letters, concerning the making of a seal. They allege that I had this made by a secret method from an exotic type of wood for magical black arts. And, although it is in the shape of a disgusting and horrible skeleton, (they claim that) I worship it lavishly and address it by the Greek word *basileus*, 'my king'.

P. Coll. Youtie I, no. 30; Rea (1977) (AD 198–199)

598. [Since I have encountered many people] who believe that they have been deceived by the practice of divination, I immediately thought it necessary, so that no danger should come from their foolishness, to announce here clearly to everyone that they should halt a fascination that brings danger. Therefore, no one is to pretend that he knows about the supernatural or make statements about the uncertainties of the future, whether that is by means of oracles (namely written documents allegedly emanating in the presence of the divine), or by means of a parade of images or similar skulduggery, nor is anyone to assist those who want to know about it or offer any response at all. But if anyone is detected persisting in

this kind of announcement, he must be certain that he will be sentenced to the ultimate penalty.

Each of you is to ensure that a copy of this letter, written in clear and legible letters, is set up on white boards in public in the chief towns (*metropoleis*) and in each village, and you must continually carry out investigations; if you find someone acting in defiance of the prohibitions, you are to send him under guard for my examination. For you too will not be free of risk if I learn again that such activity is being disregarded in the areas for which you are responsible. In fact, you will suffer the same punishment as those who have been detected. For each of those people, even if he dares to do what has been forbidden, is only one individual; but an official who fails to repress this behaviour everywhere is himself responsible for bringing danger to many.

During the seventh year of Emperors Caesars Lucius Septimius Severus Pius Pertinax Arabicus Adiabenicus Parthicus Maximus and Marcus Aurelius Antoninus Augustus.

This is a letter from the prefect of Egypt to local officials. In Egypt divine images carried in a procession could give an answer to a petitioner by turning towards or away from him, or by becoming heavier.

Religious Outsiders

Bacchus and Isis

The worship of Bacchus was an early example of the intervention of the state to control aspects of the worship of a divinity outside the accepted Roman pantheon. The cult of Bacchus had been previously established and tolerated in Italy, but in 186 BC the senate took action to suppress it; the Roman governing class seem to have objected to its organization, with small cells of worshippers, priests, oaths, and common treasury; it offered potentially a strong focus of influence on the worshippers, apart from the Roman state. The worship of Bacchus as such was not prohibited; see Beard, North and Price (1998), 92–6; Baudy (2006).

ILS **18 =** ***ILLRP*** **511 (186 BC)**

599. The consuls Quintus Marcius, son of Lucius, and Spurius Postumius, son of Lucius, consulted the senate on 7 October in the temple of Bellona. Present for the writing (of the decree) were Marcus Claudius, son of

Marcus, Lucius Valerius, son of Publius, and Quintus Minucius, son of Gaius.

In respect of the Bacchic orgies, they decided that a proclamation should be made to those who are linked by treaty.

Let none of them seek to have a place for Bacchic worship. If there should be those who say that they must have a place of Bacchic worship, they must come to the urban praetor at Rome, and our senate, when it has heard their statement, shall make a decision in respect of these matters, provided that no fewer than one hundred senators be present when that matter is discussed. Let no man, either a Roman citizen, or someone of the Latin name (i.e. someone from a Latin town or colony), or one of the allies, seek to attend a meeting of Bacchic women, unless they shall have approached the praetor and he has given his approval, in accordance with the opinion of the senate provided that one hundred senators be present when that matter is discussed. Adopted.

No man is to be a priest. No man or woman is to be a master. No one of them may seek to hold money in common. No one may seek to appoint a man or a woman as master or deputy master. After this time, they are not to make oaths, or vows, or pledges, or promises with one another, and no one is to seek to present or receive sureties. No one may seek to perform religious rites in secret. No one may seek to perform religious rites in public, or in private, or outside the city, unless he has approached the urban praetor and obtained his permission, in accordance with the opinion of the senate, provided that no fewer than one hundred senators were present when that matter is discussed. Adopted.

No one may seek to carry out religious rites in a group containing more than five men and women. No more than two men and no more than three women may seek to be present there, unless through the permission of the urban praetor and the senate as set out above.

You are to announce these measures in a public meeting over a period of no fewer than three market days, and in order that you may be aware of the decision of the senate, their decision was as follows: If there are any persons who act contrary to the decision set out above, they decided that they must face capital charges. The senate decided that it was right and proper for you to inscribe this on a bronze table, and that you should order it to be erected where it can most easily be read; and that any Bacchic shrines which may already exist you are to dismantle within ten days of your receiving this letter, except if there is anything holy within them, as noted above. For the Ager Teuranus.

This is a letter of the consuls setting out the decree of the senate about associations in honour of Bacchus in Italy. The letter was inscribed on bronze by the community of Ager Teuranus in southern Italy.

D 21.1.1.10 (Ulpian, *Edict of the Curule Aediles*, Book 1)

600. Vivianus says that although at some stage in the past a slave participated in Bacchanalian revels around the shrines and gave responses, nevertheless, if he does not do this now, he has no defect. And on that account, there will be no more liability in respect of his actions than if at some time he had a fever. But if he persists in that defect so that he regularly dances round the shrines and gives responses as if out of his mind, even though this is done through self-indulgence, it is still a defect, but an intellectual not a physical defect, and so there is no legal basis for rescission, because the aediles decide on physical defects; however, an action on sale is possible.

For rescission see p. 189. Defects in purchased items could result in their return and refund of the purchase price; for the distinction between physical and intellectual defects, see no. 303.

Josephus, *AJ* 18.65–80

601. (A Roman of equestrian status, Mundus, was enamoured of a beautiful Roman lady, Paulina, wife of a senator, but she was immune to his approaches and offers of money. However, she was a devotee of the worship of Isis and Anubis, and Mundus persuaded the priests in the temple of Isis to reveal to Paulina that Anubis would like to have dinner and spend the night with her. It was then arranged so that in the darkened temple Mundus could seduce her during the night. The trick worked but Mundus subsequently boasted to Paulina about what had happened.) He departed after saying this and she for the first time came to recognize the appalling nature of her actions and tore her clothes; she revealed the extent of the trickery to her husband, begging him not to omit to help her. He told the emperor about the business. Tiberius, after a rigorous enquiry and examination, crucified the guilty priests, and also Ide (freedwoman of Mundus), who had been the cause of their ruin and the instigator of everything which was so damaging to the lady. Furthermore, he demolished the temple and ordered the statue of Isis to be thrown into the river Tiber.

During the last three centuries of the republic several deities were introduced into Rome from the Greek east through vote of senate and people. Notably, in 205 BC *Magna Mater* was invited on the advice of the Sibylline books of oracles and eventually had a temple on the Palatine hill. Although the deity was accepted there was a significant amount of control because the cult had orgiastic elements not to Roman taste, with wild music, furious dancing, and self-castrating priests (Dionysius Halicarnassus, *Roman Antiquities* 2.19; see Beard, North and Price (1998), 96–8). These aspects were largely confined within the temple.

Isis can serve as an example of Roman treatment of foreign cults in the imperial period. The worship of Isis arrived from Egypt in the republic through the medium of the Hellenistic Greek east. With its distinct priesthood and a deity who cared for individual worshippers, Isis often caused the Roman hierarchy to be worried about a separate focus of religious loyalty and expertise, which could seem to be beyond Roman control. Therefore, there were periodic attempts to expel Isis from Rome and Italy especially if there were incidents or disturbances. Augustus had banned worship of Isis within the sacred boundary of Rome (Dio 53.2.4); the story recounted by Josephus may be distorted or exaggerated, but for whatever reason Tiberius was provoked into taking decisive action in AD 19 (see Beard, North and Price (1998), 230–1). The government also restricted religious life in Egypt after its annexation in 30 BC. Priesthoods with their lucrative temple lands had been important throughout Egyptian society and politics, and Augustus sought to control this powerful group, which could be a focus of opposition to Rome, by confiscating some temple land and extending Roman supervision through the *idios logos* and the governor over religious funds and the composition of the priesthood. For Roman treatment of priesthoods in the east, see Beard, North and Price (1998), 339–42.

Jews and Christians

Among religious outsiders in the Roman world Jews and Christians stood out as monotheists who found it difficult to fit in with their polytheistic neighbours and to conform to social and civic conventions of community life. The Romans had come to recognize the Jewish religion as ancient and legitimate, and there was a reasonably large Jewish population in Rome in the first century AD; a synagogue has been identified in Ostia, and there may have been as many as eleven synagogues in Rome during the imperial period. Julius Caesar had permitted Jews to follow their ancestral customs and rites, meet together, and contribute money for meals (no. 602). Augustus upheld this through a decision taken by him and his advisers (no. 603). There were occasional expulsions of Jews from Rome, for example, in AD 19 under Tiberius, though this was more to do with disorder in the city and does not seem to have affected their general standing. But the Jews were deeply attached to their traditional practices and tended to be exclusive, with a fierce nationalistic tradition, which combined with strong religious belief came to be a danger to the Romans, or at least was believed to be in Judaea. The Romans were indeed rather suspicious of the high priesthood in Jerusalem, and when Judaea became a province in AD 6 the governor had the power to appoint and remove the high priest (tenure was now for one year though reappointment was possible) and supervised the finances of the temple. The rebellion of AD 66 in Judaea, which was partly religious and partly nationalistic, confirmed the suspected danger. The Romans put down the revolt as that of a dissident subject people and remained suspicious of Jewish intentions. This allowed the enemies of the Jews, especially the Greeks in the east, to move against them. Certainly, the Jews of the diaspora may have found things more difficult for a time after the great rebellions in AD 66 and the Bar Kokhba revolt in the reign of Hadrian. For a concise survey of Rome's relations with Judaea up to AD 70, see Goodman (1987).

The emerging Christian sect, unlike Judaism, was not recognized as ancient or legitimate and had no tradition of dealings with Rome. Christians seemed different; they had unusual observances which could be misunderstood, like the Eucharistic ceremony and brotherly kisses which encouraged allegations of unnatural activities. They seemed to be outside the normal run of city life and obligations. Furthermore, some tended to be disrespectful towards other cults and therefore could be seen as a threat to the favour of the gods. The forms of Christian worship did not seem likely to promote the *salus* of the Roman state. Innocent references to Christ as king or to the end of the world could be used against them before a magistrate nervous of failing to protect the emperor's interests. Indeed, to many Roman governors Christians were probably seen as another of the warring Jewish factions that had fomented rebellion. Furthermore, some Christian defendants were willing to seek martyrdom, and persistent obstinacy once in court could annoy the presiding official. Although there was no specific legal enactment that forbade people to be Christians, the circumstances described could contribute to the creation of an atmosphere in which they could be brought to trial by ambitious prosecutors exploiting the popular mood. Over time the name of being a Christian became sufficient to encourage a prosecutor and get a magistrate's or governor's attention. It is debatable how extensive were Nero's actions against Christians in 64 BC, perhaps aimed at deflecting attention from rumours that he had started the disastrous fire in Rome, and how far they acted as a precedent for others to bring a prosecution against a noticeably vulnerable group; see no. 609.

Roman legal procedure also played a part. Since there was no public prosecutor, individual citizens had to come forward with information to bring Christians to trial. But only a limited number of actions were defined by statute as crimes that could come before a jury court, or a magistrate, or a provincial governor. In other cases, like the actions against Christians, it was up to the discretion of an individual magistrate how to proceed or whether to proceed at all. That decision would be influenced by several factors, such as his personal feelings towards traditional worship, his previous experience, and the prevailing circumstances in his province, especially if there was agitation against Christians. The Roman governing class was in general indifferent to Christians. For example, Tacitus knew of the existence of Christ, but had little detailed knowledge of what Christians believed, though he subscribed to the general hostility towards them (no. 609). But it is clear that Christian practices were regarded as a *superstitio*, not a true or legitimate *religio,* and therefore were always liable to criticism and suspicion. The government was generally passive, responding to stimulation from below. This explains why there was no persecution before the mid-third century. Instead, there were spasmodic actions against Christians in response to local conditions. There is no space in this book for detailed exposition of the place of Christians in the empire and their subsequent persecution; for useful and approachable accounts of the early Christians, see Whittaker (1984); Lane Fox (1986), especially 265–492, with the review by Fowden (1988), especially 174–6; Stark (1996), applying social science theory to the history of early Christianity; Humphries (2006); Jacobs (2006).

Josephus, *AJ* 14.213–16

602. Iulius Gaius (?), consul of the Romans, to the magistrates, council, and people of Parium, greetings. The Jews of Delos and some neighbouring Jews, with your ambassadors also present, met me, and disclosed that you by decree are preventing them from carrying on their traditional customs and religious practices. I am displeased that such decrees should be issued against our friends and allies preventing them from living according to their own customs and making contributions to their common meals and religious rites, which even in Rome they are not prevented from doing. For Gaius Caesar, our imperator and consul, in the edict forbidding religious associations in the city exempted these people alone in not prohibiting them from making contributions to a common fund or holding common meals. Similarly, I, while prohibiting other religious

associations, grant to these people alone to meet and hold feasts in accordance with their traditional customs and laws. Therefore, it would be well for you, if you have issued decrees against our friends and allies, that you cancelled them, because of their decency and goodwill towards us.

The odd arrangement of the name of the man at the start may be a mistake by Josephus or a muddle in the text; he was the proconsul of Asia during the time of Caesar. Despite Roman goodwill towards the Jews of Asia Minor (promoted by Julius Caesar who had been helped by Jewish leaders in Egypt), local Greek communities continued to be intolerant of Jewish traditions.

Josephus, *AJ* 16.162–5

603. Caesar Augustus, chief priest, with tribunician power, declares: Since the race of the Jews and their high priest Hyrcanus have been found to be friendly towards the Roman people, not only in current times but also in the past, and especially in the time of my father, Imperator Caesar, I and my council have decided under oath, and by vote of the Roman people, that the Jews may carry on their own practices in accordance with their ancestral law, just as they did in the time when Hyrcanus was high priest of the most high God; their sacred funds are not to be violated and are to be sent to Jerusalem and given to the treasurers at Jerusalem; they are not to be bailed to appear in court on the Sabbath, nor in the time of preparation for it from the ninth hour. If anyone is caught stealing their sacred books, or the sacred funds from a synagogue or hall, he is to be judged as sacrilegious and his property is to be forfeit to the treasury of the Roman people. The vote that they passed in my honour on account of the goodwill that I have for all mankind, and on behalf of Gaius Marcus Censorinus, and this decree, I order to be set up in Ancyra in the most eminent place granted to me by the council of Asia. If anyone contravenes any of the measures set out above, he will pay a significant penalty. It was inscribed in the temple of Augustus.

Censorinus was proconsul of Asia in AD 2/3. Despite this goodwill, concessions to Jewish practice and tradition granted in particular circumstances and locations may have had limited application throughout the empire. See also Philo, *Embassy to Gaius*, 155–8 for Augustus' goodwill towards the Jews.

Josephus, *AJ* 19.307–9

604. I have given orders that those who dared to take such actions (putting a statue of Claudius in a synagogue) in contravention of the emperor's

edict, at which those among them who have a leading reputation expressed annoyance, claiming that this was not a personal decision but done at the insistence of the people, should be brought to me by the centurion Proclus Vitellius to give an account of their actions. And I warn the chief magistrates that, unless they wish it to be seen that this wrongdoing was committed with their approval, they must point out the guilty men to the centurion, and must permit no opportunity for strife or riot, which in my view seem to be the purpose of such actions.

At Dora in Phoenica some young men had provocatively set up a statue of Claudius in the local synagogue; King Agrippa wrote to complain to Petronius, governor of Syria, who in turn wrote to the local magistrates reminding them of Jewish rights, which Claudius had confirmed in an edict. In 41 Claudius had written a letter to the city of Alexandria dealing with the conflicts involving Greeks and Jews in the city, and the question of Jewish rights; see no. 729.

Tacitus, *Annals* 2.85

605. Action was taken for the expulsion of Egyptian and Jewish religious cults and the senate passed a decree that four thousand men of ex-slave status who were contaminated by that superstition and who were of suitable age should be sent to the island of Sardinia to suppress the bandits there; if they should perish because of the unhealthy climate it would be no great loss; the rest were to leave Italy unless they abandoned their unholy rites before a set date.

The expulsion of the worshippers of Isis was the result of a scandal in Rome (see no. 601); the expulsion of the Jews may have been partly the result of an incident when a Roman matron who had converted to Judaism was allegedly swindled by four Jews.

Acts of the Apostles 18.12–18

606. When Gallio was proconsul of Achaea the Jews (in Corinth) attacked Paul in a body and brought him to court. 'This man', they argued, 'is urging the people to worship God contrary to the law'. When Paul was about to speak, Gallio said to the Jews: 'If there was some crime or wrong done, I would quite properly make time for you Jews, but if the issue concerns a word, or a definition, or your law, you must look after it yourselves. I do not wish to be a judge of these matters'. And he ejected them from the court. But then they all grabbed Sosthenes, one of the

officials of the synagogue, and beat him right in front of the court. But Gallio took no interest in this. Paul remained for some time.

Iunius Gallio, brother of Seneca the Younger, was proconsul of Achaea in 52. Tensions between Jews and Christians did much to promote hostility in government officials. It is not clear if Sosthenes was a convert to Christianity or a Jewish leader abused by his own people because he failed to persuade the governor. Gallio's unwillingness to get involved encouraged Paul to stay in Corinth.

Acts of the Apostles 23.26–30

607. Claudius Lysias to his excellency the governor Felix, greetings. This man had been arrested by the Jews who were preparing to kill him when I came on the scene with the troops and rescued him. I discovered that he is a Roman citizen, and, wishing to find out the reason for their accusations against him, I brought him to their council. I discovered that he was being accused in respect of issues in their law, but that there was no charge that merited a death sentence or incarceration. However, when I discovered that there was a plot against the man, I immediately sent him to you, ordering his accusers to make their case about him before you.

Felix was governor of Judaea AD 52–60. Lysias was in command of the detachment of Roman soldiers in Jerusalem; since Paul was a Roman citizen he had to be treated with care and guarded with a strong escort, but the Jews are given a further opportunity to make their case. Felix conducted a reasonably amicable examination of Paul, but after two years nothing had been decided and Felix's successor, Festus, once again heard vague charges from the Jews. Paul exercised his right as a Roman citizen to be tried in a Roman court of his choice, if the governor assented; in fact, he appealed for trial before the emperor in Rome, where he was kept under house arrest for two years. All this helps to show the ambivalent attitude of the government to the activities of the early Christians and the difficulty of separating them from other Jewish groups. In his letters to the Romans Paul urged respect for the authority of officials, particularly in their judicial activities.

St Paul, *Letter to the Romans* 13.1–6

608. Every person must be subject to the supreme authorities. For no authority exists except by the will of God, and the existing authorities have been established by God. Therefore, the person who resists authority is fighting against a divine ordinance. And those who have fought against it will bring judgement upon themselves. For the rulers are not an object of fear to those doing good, but to those doing wrong. Do you wish to have no fear of the authorities? Then carry on with doing good and you will

receive their praise. For the authorities are representatives of God and they work for your good. But if you do wrong you should fear them. For it is not without a reason that they have the power of the sword. Indeed, they are agents of God and will bring punishment and retribution on the one doing wrong. Therefore, you must submit to them, not only because of fear of retribution, but also because of your conscience. This is also why you pay taxes. The authorities serve God, and they strive constantly in this task.

Tacitus, *Annals* 15.44

609. But neither human efforts, nor the generosity of the emperor, nor offerings to the gods could dispel the hostile feelings based on the belief that the fire had been started by command. Therefore, to quash this rumour Nero substituted victims and punished most severely those people generally called Christians who were hated for their abominable practices. The founder of this name was Christ, who in the reign of Tiberius had been executed by the procurator Pontius Pilate. This execrable superstition was suppressed for the moment but broke out again not only in Judaea, where the plague had originated, but even in Rome, to which all abominations and repulsive activities flow from every direction and thrive. Therefore, first those who confessed were arrested, and then on their evidence a huge number was convicted, not so much on the charge of arson than for their hatred of humanity. As they died, mockery was added, so that they were clad in animal skins and torn apart by dogs, or nailed to crosses and set alight, and when daylight faded, they were burned as lamps for the nighttime. Nero provided his own gardens for the spectacle and put on a carnival like the games, joining the people in the dress of a charioteer or driving a chariot. Consequently, compassion began to emerge, although it was for guilty people who deserved exceptional punishment; it was as if they were being killed not for the public good but for the cruelty of one man.

In the opinion of Tacitus after the great fire in Rome in AD 64 Nero tried to divert suspicion from his suspected involvement by pursuing Christians in the city. The fact that they could be singled out like this with little popular opposition may suggest that they were already a group subject to suspicion and dislike. However, Brent Shaw (2015) has argued that there is no evidence to support the notion that Christians were martyred under Nero as a recognized group, and that Tacitus was influenced by events in his own day when the Roman government had become aware of a distinctive group known as Christians. If so, this would make it less likely that events in Rome in 64 could serve as a precedent for subsequent prosecutions of Christians.

Pliny, *Letters* 10.96–7

610. It is my established practice, sir, to refer to you all matters about which I am in doubt. For who is better able to relieve my doubts or guide my ignorance? I have never been present at any legal investigation of the Christians, and so I do not know how or to what extent they should be punished or sought out. I have considerable doubt over whether there should be any distinction on the basis of age, or if the young should be treated the same as grown-ups; whether a pardon should be extended to those who repent, or whether a person who was once a Christian should gain no benefit by renouncing it, or whether the mere name of Christian should be punished even if free from wrongdoing, or the crimes associated with the name.

At the moment, in the case of those who are brought before me on the grounds that they are Christians, I have adhered to the following procedure. I have asked them individually if they are Christians. If they confess it, I ask them a second and third time, giving them a warning of the penalty. If they persist, I command that they be taken away for execution. For I had no doubt that whatever the nature of their confession they should be punished for their clear defiance and inflexible obstinacy. There were others who, similarly deranged, were Roman citizens, and I have added them to the list of people to be sent to Rome.

Now that the matter is being dealt with, as usually happens, the bringing of charges has become more widespread and of greater variety. An anonymous document has been published containing the names of many people. Those who denied that they were or ever had been Christians I thought should be dismissed, if they called upon the gods at my dictation, and made offerings with incense and wine to your statue, which for this purpose I had ordered to be brought in along with the images of the gods, and reviled Christ, since genuine Christians, so it is said, cannot be compelled to do any of these things. Others who were named by an informer first confessed that they were Christians and then denied it, saying that that they had been but had ceased to be Christians, three or even more years ago, some even as long ago as twenty years. All these people also reverenced your statue and the images of the gods and reviled Christ. Furthermore, they claimed that the limit of their fault or error had been that on an arranged day they had the practice of meeting before daybreak, to recite together alternately a prayer to Christ as to a god, and to bind themselves by an oath not for criminal purposes, but to refrain from theft, banditry, and adultery, not to break their word, and when summoned not to deny that they had received a deposit. When this had been completed it was their custom to depart and assemble again to take food of a common and harmless kind; and they had refrained from this after my edict by which in accordance with your instructions I forbade political clubs. Therefore, I decided that it was all the more necessary to find out the truth under torture from two servant girls, which they call deaconesses. All I found was a depraved superstition carried to fanatical lengths.

Therefore, I postponed further investigation and hurried to consult you. In my view the matter is worthy of consideration principally because of the number of people in danger (Pliny goes on to say that Christianity seems widespread even in rural areas, but that now traditional rites were being observed and sacrificial meat was on sale again).

You have followed the appropriate course of action, my dear Pliny, in dealing with the cases of those persons who are charged before you with being Christians. For no definite rule can be established with a clear-cut formula. They should not be hunted out. If they are brought before you and are convicted, they must be punished. But in circumstances where a person denies that he is a Christian and proves this by offering reverence to our gods, although he may incur suspicion over what he has done in the past, through his repentance he should be pardoned. Documents published anonymously must have no place in any accusation. For this sets the worst kind of precedent and is no part of our age.

This exchange of letters confirms that there was no law or imperial ruling outlawing Christianity. Instead, there were private prosecutions brought by individuals on their own initiative and heard in the *cognitio* procedure that was subject to the personal judgement by the holder of imperium. Although various vague crimes were associated with the practice of Christianity, the mere name or identification as a Christian could be sufficient to secure conviction if the judge was so minded, as these people were viewed as potentially divisive and troublesome and a threat to public order. In court there was often a procedure of repeated questions and threats followed by sentence. Many Christians, when offered the chance to recant, persisted in their defiance. For a Roman governor this *contumacia* or contempt of court would seem an intolerable affront to his authority and confirm his decision to convict. Pliny used the test of introducing divine images and emperor's statue only for those who denied the charge of Christianity. It is also clear that the Christians are not being charged with forming an illegal *collegium* (see also no. 612). Trajan emphasizes that Christians should not be sought out; there must be a formal accusation, and those who demonstrably recanted were to be released. See Corke-Webster (2017) who argues that this exchange of letters was aimed at the resolution of a specific local problem and downplays their significance in dealing with the wider issue of Christianity; for a useful account of the various explanations of the legal treatment of Christians, see Robinson (1990–2), especially 270–5 on Pliny and Trajan.

Eusebius, *History of the Church* 4.8.6–8; Stevenson (1987), pp. 21–2

611. Indeed the same writer (Justin) says that Hadrian received a message from a most distinguished governor, Serennius Granianus, supporting the Christians, namely that it was not just to execute them without proper charge or trial simply to indulge the uproar of the mob, and that the emperor replied to Minucius Fundanus, proconsul of Asia, instructing him to try no one without a charge and proper hearing. A copy of the letter is added which preserves the original Latin … I have translated it to the best of my ability into Greek, and it runs as follows:

'To Minucius Fundanus. I have received a letter from your predecessor, Serennius Granianus, distinguished man. I think that the issue should not be left without investigation, so that people should not be harassed, and a route be provided for the wickedness of informers. Therefore, if on this basis the provincials can make a strong case against the Christians, namely, to plead it in the courtroom, they should turn to this procedure alone, and not petitions or outcries. If someone wants to bring a charge it is much better for you to adjudicate the issue. Therefore, if someone brings a charge against them and demonstrates that they have acted in some way contrary to the laws, you must enter a judgement in accordance with the seriousness of the offence. But if someone initiates these proceedings for reward, then in the name of heaven arrest him and work out a penalty in keeping with the seriousness of the offence'.

Eusebius (see p. 478) in his *History of the Church* recounts the struggles of the early Christians from the Christian point of view, with great emphasis on martyrs. In the manuscripts of Justin (*Apol.* 1.68) there is no Latin text for Hadrian's rescript, just the Greek of Eusebius, and there is a considerable question about its authenticity; see Minns (2007). It must be doubtful if Hadrian would have limited action against Christians simply to demonstrable crimes, and not the name or profession of Christianity. The text can still form part of the debate about the standing of Christians in Roman legal practice.

Eusebius (*History of the Church* 5.1.7–10) claimed that there were significant moves against Christians in the reign of Marcus Aurelius in AD 177, and he quotes a letter from the churches in Gaul to those in Asia and Phrygia describing their experiences. The governor at Lyon gave the alleged Christians a hostile reception and did not follow proper legal process; torture was used, those who recanted were not released, and many were strangled in prison; see Harries (2007), 40–1. For another example of the interrogation of Christians by a governor, see no. 673.

Tertullian, *Apologia* 38.1

612. Should this group (Christians) not have been viewed more leniently and placed among permitted associations, since it takes no action of the type that is usually feared from illegal associations? For, unless I am mistaken, the reason for banning associations derived from a concern for public order, lest the state be split into factions, a situation which would disturb elections, public meetings, local senates, speeches, and even the games with the competing rivalry of partisans, especially since men had begun to consider their violence as a marketable and profitable source of money.

Tertullian (see p. 481) defended Christians from common charges made against them, including atheism and subversion. Although *collegia* were permitted for religious purposes, the Romans were suspicious of Christian gatherings; see no. 610.

Tertullian, *Letter to Scapula* 4.2–4

613. If you intend to destroy us it is innocence that you are attacking. For how many governors, more resolute and cruel than you, have disassociated themselves from cases like this! For example, Cincius Severus at Thysdrus provided his own solution by which the Christians made a response that allowed them to be acquitted. Similarly, Vespronius Candidus, who acquitted a Christian on the grounds that it might cause disturbance to satisfy his own citizens. Similarly, Aper who, in the case of man who after slight torture gave up his faith, did not compel him to offer sacrifice, having previously admitted to the lawyers and legal assessors that he was sorry that he had become involved with this case in the first place. Pudens even dismissed one Christian who had been sent to him; realizing that the accusation was malicious, he tore up the charge sheet and said that to interview the man without an accuser would not be in line with his instructions (*mandata*).

Tertullian's *Letter to Scapula* was addressed in AD 212 to a local governor in Africa and advocated religious freedom.

Lactantius, *De Mortibus Persecutorum* 48.9 (Creed (1984))

614. Furthermore, since these same Christians are known to have had not only those places in which they normally met but others also, which legally belong to their body, that is, to their churches, not to individuals, you will

order that all this, under the terms of the law I set out above, without any further doubts or argument, is to be restored to these Christians, that is, to their body and congregations, though of course preserving the principle set out above that those who, as I laid down, restore this property without charge may expect to be indemnified through my generosity.

Lactantius as a Christian apologist vigorously extolled Constantine's support for Christianity. The context is AD 313 and the aftermath of the victory of Constantine and Licinius; Constantine's letter was intended to confirm freedom of worship for Christians, and to pursue vigorously the restitution of property to the church to make good the losses resulting from previous persecution. The emperor recognizes the proprietary rights of the church, and by extension the individual congregations that made up the body of the church. These congregations would then be able to own property, manumit slaves, and sue.

Codex Theodosianus 16.2.4

615. Let every individual at his death have the freedom to leave any property he wishes to the most holy and venerable congregation of the catholic church.

Constantine's law of AD 321 addressed the issue of legacies and inheritances and established the right of anyone to institute a Christian church as *heres*. Previously this had been limited to a small number of pagan gods. Duff (1938), 171–5 thinks that the church was treated rather like a licensed *collegium*; for the rights of *collegia* and towns, see pp. 111–14. These decisions by Constantine were the beginning of vast private wealth for the church, and the basis of many church-sponsored charitable institutions. Constantine was generous in his donations, and from the fourth century onwards the scale of munificence to the church was striking.

Liber Pontificalis (Davis (1989), pp. 18–20)

616. Then the emperor Constantine built (at bishop Silvester's request) a basilica to St Peter the Apostle at the temple of Apollo where he buried the tomb with St Peter's body in this way ...

Also, for revenue the presentation made by the Emperor Constantine to the apostle St Peter:

in the diocese of the east in the city of Antioch:
the house of Datianus, revenue of 240 solidi
a small house in Caene, revenue 20 solidi, 1 tremiss
rooms in Aphrodisia, revenue 20 solidi
a bath in Cerataea, revenue 42 solidi

a bakery in the same place, revenue 23 solidi
a tavern in the same place, revenue 10 solidi
the garden of Maro, revenue 10 solidi
a garden in the same place, revenue 11 solidi

in the suburbs of Antioch:

the property Sybilles, presented to the emperor, revenue 322 solidi, 150 decads of paper, 200 lb spices, 200 lb nard-oil, 35 lb balsam

in the suburbs of Alexandria:

the property of Timialica, given to the Emperor Constantine by Ambronius, revenue 620 solidi, 300 decads of paper, 300 lb of nard-oil, 60 lb of balsam, 150 lb spices, 50 lb Isaurian storax

the escheated property of Euthymius, revenue 500 solidi, 70 decads of paper

in Egypt, in the suburbs of Armenia:

the property of Agapius, which he gave to the Emperor Constantine

the property of Passinopolimse, revenue 800 solidi, 400 decads of paper, 50 medimni of pepper, 100 lb saffron, 150 lb storax, 200 lb cassia spices, 300 lb nard-oil, 100 lb balsam, 100 sacks of linen, 150 lb cloves, 100 lb cyprus-oil, 1000 clean papyrus stalks

the property which Hybromius gave to the emperor Constantine, revenue 450 solidi, 200 decads of paper, 50 lb cassia spices, 200 lb nard-oil, 50 lb balsam

in the province of Euphratensis, in the suburbs of Cyrrhus:

the property Armanazon, revenue 380 solidi
the property Obariae, revenue 260 solidi.

The *Liber Pontificalis* is the name given to a collection of biographies of the Roman bishops; the early part of the work was probably compiled in the mid sixth century and contains much information on church property and endowments. For a survey of the value of the text see Davis (1989), vii–xv. We have here an idea of the amount of property owned by the Christian church as a body and the generosity of Constantinian endowments. For the reliability of the *Liber* for the work of Constantine, see Davis, xix–xxvi. The solidus was the standard gold coin in the reign of Constantine and subsequently; the tremiss was one third of a solidus.

CHAPTER 7

Appearing in Court

Introduction

Crucial to any legal system is the plaintiff's ability to get the defendant into court, and the supervision of the process in civil suits. In Rome this was the job of the praetor. The method of civil litigation underwent several changes over time. In the early period, *legis actio* involved the employment of precisely designated verbal phrases, and deviation from these could result in the loss of the case. It remained a feature of Roman law to define precisely a legal act so as to proceed in the correct form (Watson (1995), 90). From about 150 BC the formulary system came into use (see Kaser (1967), 130–7). This operated in two stages: first before the praetor, whom the plaintiff must persuade that there was a case to answer, and second before a judge. The proceeding before the praetor (*in iure*) produced a formula, which was not an adjudication but a summary of the claims of the contending parties and the legal context, and appointed a judge (*iudex*). The defendant needed to be present to provide his input into the formula. The plaintiff could send him an announcement of a lawsuit and invite his attendance on a specific day before the praetor. If the defendant was reluctant the praetor could impose a penalty (Gaius, *Institutes* 4.183; see nos. 618–19 in this volume). Alternatively, the defendant could be bound by formal promise (*vadimonium*) to appear at a set day, time, and place; this was supported by a surety, usually a sum of money, which was forfeited if the defendant did not appear. On the arrival of the defendant the formal summons before the praetor could take place (*in ius vocatio*). In circumstances where a case was delayed and litigants could not complete their legal business on the day, the magistrate ordered them to make a *vadimonium*. The defendant had to make a promise to appear on a subsequent day, at a place and time. The plaintiff was entitled to demand a penalty from the defendant in the event of his non-appearance. Those who could not agree a date for return were ordered to return on the third day, that is, one day was established between the appearances of the litigants. In these circumstances the *vadimonium* was therefore employed with magisterial authority to ensure that the defendant was brought back to resolve the case. The monetary penalty was left to the plaintiff to set, though there were certain restrictions in amount (the absolute limit was one hundred thousand sesterces). Municipal judicial regulations at Irni have offered further evidence on the process of *vadimonium* and postponements to the third day; see González (1986), 178, chapter 90 lines 27ff; Metzger (2005), 7–10; 66–76; 81; 95–135, especially 112–14; 123–34, and in this volume nos. 621; 623; (2007) examines postponement procedure in the light of the banking records from Puteoli. At Irni there were fines against magistrates who failed to grant appropriate postponements.

A judge might be appointed on the recommendation of the litigants; otherwise, he was chosen from an approved list, generally of the well-to-do. It was up to the plaintiff to collect relevant evidence and keep the defendant informed of his intentions so that he had an opportunity to prepare his defence. The second stage of the procedure was the hearing before the judge (*litis contestatio*), whose responsibility was to examine the facts as set out in the formula, and to convict if the facts were as the plaintiff claimed or absolve. The formula was effectively his authority to reach a decision, and he could not deviate from it, which is understandable given that judges were usually lay people with no detailed experience of the law. However, the formula might be relatively complicated if it had to take account of the defendant's pleas of exculpation or mitigation. Documentary evidence and witnesses might also need to be considered. If the judge convicted, the reparation was monetary even though in the case of theft a plaintiff might be more interested in getting his property back, which however could perhaps be achieved by social pressure. There was no formal procedure for execution of the judgement and there was no appeal against it. These formulae associated with various aspects of the law were included in the praetor's edict (nos. 626–7). In some cases the dispute might be directed to a board of arbiters (*recuperatores*), who were people entitled to act as judges. It is not clear what categories of cases could be dealt with in this way. A judge who failed to give a judgement, or gave a judgement when it should not be given, was himself liable (discussion in Metzger (2012a), 180–7). In Rome the praetor offered relief of *restitutio* to litigants whose suit had been lost because of delays on the part of the judge, that is, granting too many postponements, or corruption or bias (*D* 4.6.26.4; Metzger (2005), 118–19).

The formulary system was gradually superseded though not replaced in the first century AD by *cognitio*, in which there was only one stage, before a magistrate; the procedure was therefore based directly on the *imperium* of a magistrate, or indeed of the emperor. The magistrate heard the case himself including initial pleadings and assessment of evidence and reached a judgement; he could consult whomever he chose or delegate the case to a suitable deputy. He could compel attendance at court and had discretion in how he tried the case and applied the law. Effectively the judge was now an official and his decision could be appealed; in practice many appeals went to the emperor. This system may have emerged from the procedure in the provinces where the governor if he chose to hear a case had complete responsibility for reaching a decision. For the operation of the civil law procedure, note fundamentally Metzger (1997); (2005), especially 65–135; (2015), 278–89; also, Burton (1996); Johnston (1999), 112–18; Robinson (1997), 79–90; for the *cognitio* procedure, see Robinson (1997), 90–6; Turpin (1999); Harries (2007), 21–33; and Rüfner (2016); for appeals, see pp. 359–60; 446–50.

In serious criminal offences, usually involving members of the upper classes as defendants and prosecutors, permanent jury courts were gradually superseded by the *cognitio* procedure, and more cases were heard in the senate or by the emperor.

Roman society was litigious, and it is useful to try to recover the experience of appearing in court, the place of the litigant, the availability and role of advocates, and the extent to which the state could ensure fairness in the context of changing views of citizenship and social status. State and citizen came in contact through the legal process and the courts. Writers on oratory and rhetorical method can help to show how material was presented in legal cases and what methods were used in getting the judge's attention and winning him over, which is a useful commentary on society and legal procedure. Advocates, experts in forensic rhetoric, might themselves have a working knowledge of the law or rely on legal experts for guidance on how to conduct their client's case. Tacitus in the *De Oratore*, written at the beginning of the second century AD, explored the idea that contemporary oratory was in decline and has useful observations on oratorical method. Quintilian, born about AD 35 in Spain, wrote the *Institutio Oratoria*, which was published in the reign of Domitian (see Tellegen-Couperus (2003); (2021); Crook (1995), 167–71). He examined the education and training of an orator with many valuable insights on the preparation of a case, consultations with a client, and the advocate's role in a courtroom. In the opinion of Tellegen-Couperus (2021) Quintilian was well-acquainted with Roman law. But for a note of caution on the value of Quintilian for recovering the substantive law of his own time, see Robinson

(2003). The elder Seneca's *Controversiae* (fictional legal cases that served as exercises in the rhetorical schools) may not be entirely removed from the reality of pleading in a courtroom (Crook (1995), 163–7). Pliny the Younger has valuable evidence on his performance in the courtroom, at least for high-profile cases before the senate or the Centumviral Court. Furthermore, there is useful material in papyri from Egypt for the conduct of local court cases at a mundane level (nos. 675–88). Crook (1995, 58–118) argues that this is a reliable indication of the role of advocates, the interaction of the litigants, and courtroom experience in the Roman world, and is not peculiar to Egypt. For the nature of petitions and litigation in Roman Egypt, see in general Kelly (2011), especially chapter 3; Keenan, Manning and Yiftach-Firanko (2014). For the training of lawyers, see Harries (2016); for the role of rhetorical training in constructing legal arguments, see Kacprzak (2016), 202–7.

Civil Cases

Getting the Defendant into Court

***Twelve Tables* 1, 1–3**

617. If (anyone) summons to trial, he (the defendant) is to go. If he does not go, he (the plaintiff) is to call witness to it. Then he is to take him. If he (the defendant) hesitates or drags his feet, he (the plaintiff) is to lay hands on him. If there be illness or age, he (the plaintiff) is to provide a yoked beast of burden; if he is unwilling, he is not to arrange a carriage.

For the reconstruction of these sections of the Twelve Tables managing relations between citizens in Rome of the fifth century BC, see Crawford (1996), 584–8. This action could take place in any public or private location, but not in the home of the defendant (Gaius on the Twelve Tables, in *D* 2.4.18; 20; 22pr-1). The last sentence is ambiguous and may mean that if the plaintiff is reluctant to arrange a carriage he is not compelled to do so.

Gaius, *Institutes* 4.183

618. Finally, we should observe that the person who wants to start legal proceedings against someone must summon him into court, and the person who has been summoned will incur a penalty by the terms of the praetor's edict if he does not come. However, it is not permitted to summon certain people to court without the permission of the praetor, such as your parents, patrons, patronesses, also the children and parents of

a patron or patroness, and the person who acts against this rule will incur a penalty.

D 2.13.1pr (Ulpian, *Edict*, Book 4)

619. Where any person wishes to bring an action, he should give notice of that; for it seems most equitable for the person who is about to bring an action should give notice of it so that consequently the defendant may know whether he ought to concede or contest the case, and, if he thinks that he ought to contest it, so that he may arrive suitably prepared to conduct the suit, as he knows the action by which he is sued. Giving notice also involves offering an opportunity to make a copy, the completion and provision of a document, or dictation. Labeo points out that a person also gives notice if he brings his opponent to the tablet of the praetor's edict and points out the action which he is about to conduct or states the one which he is intending to use.

CJ 3.9.1 (AD 202)

620. Emperors Severus and Antoninus Augusti to Valens. An issue has not been brought to trial if there has been only an initial examination of it, or an account of the type of action given to the defendant before a trial. For there is a considerable difference between a hearing before a judge and an announcement of an action. The hearing is considered to be underway only when the judge begins to hear the case according to the statement of the business at issue.

TPSulp 15; *AE* 1986.182

621. Bail is given by Gaius Publicius Carus for 16 (or 19?) November next, in Rome, in the forum of Augustus, in front of the altar of Mars the Avenger, at the nearest step, at the fourth hour, for ? sesterces, being about to act on the basis of a sale. Quintus Castricius Fructus made the stipulation and Gaius Publicius Carus responded. Done in the consulship of … .

See Camodeca (1999), 68–9; Metzger (2005), no. 24. The tablets from Herculaneum and Puteoli show the form of the *vadimonium*; it served as a record of proceedings and evidence of what had been promised about a future appearance by the defendant and the amount of any penalty, and that both sides in the dispute had acted in accordance with the magistrate's directions; in this case the document explains the nature of the action: sale. For a *vadimonium* relating to the case of Petronia Iusta (no. 45), see *Tabulae Herculanenses* 14 (Pugliese Carratelli (1948), 169–70).

FIRA 3, no. 169

622. An extract from the records.
Year eight of Domitian, month Caesareus 10.
Since several people from those names cited for court procedure did not respond, Mettius Rufus instructed the herald to make an announcement: 'Those cited before me who have not responded should be aware that they will be summoned for a second time, and if on this occasion they still have not responded they are to be condemned in their absence'.

Apollodoros the advocate: 'After your announcement, Menelais, Posidonia, and Posidonios, whom I represent, gave the necessary security that they can present their case only if they have received letters from their tutors, and they request that their presence be noted in the court record'.
Mettius Rufus: 'Let it be so noted'.

A Roman magistrate had the right to summon litigants before him; non-appearance could lead to condemnation by default; a plaintiff who did not appear would lose his suit; in this case the advocate notes that his clients have complied with the magistrate's order to attend a hearing but need to acquire further authorization from their tutors before proceeding; for the role of tutors see, for example, no. 342.

Gaius, *Institutes* 4.184–5

623. When a defendant has been summoned to court and the business cannot be completed on that day, he must give bail (*vadimonium*), that is, he must undertake to appear on a definite day. (185) In some cases simple bail is taken, that is without security, in some cases with security, in some cases with an oath, and in some with the addition of recoverers (*recuperatores*), so that the person who does not appear is immediately condemned by the recoverers for the amount of the bail.

This illustrates *vadimonium* in a case of delay in proceedings, to ensure that the litigants returned for the next session; for *recuperatores* see p. 348.

FIRA 3, no. 167 (AD 99)

624. To Tiberius Claudius Areius, *strategos* of the Heraclides district in the Arsinoite locality from Tabus, daughter of Teseis, inhabitant of the Socnopaean Island, village in the same district, with Stotoes, son of Apynch, acting as tutor.

There is a major dispute between me and my full brother Satabos, which requires the justice that Pompeius Planta, the most distinguished prefect, displays throughout his entire administration of the law. Satabos malevolently began this dispute when he enlisted as his associate Harpogathis, the son of my other brother, now deceased, and took possession of all the property of Teseis my mother, now deceased. Therefore, I request that a copy of this petition which has been entered in your records be served to Satabos by one of your officials so that he is aware that he, along with Harpogathis, must attend wherever in this locality Pompeius Planta, the most distinguished prefect, shall hold the assizes, and thus through you I may be able to receive assistance.

Served by Ammonios, son of Ammonios, official of the court. Year two of Imperator Caesar Nerva Trajan Augustus Germanicus, month Phamenoth 1.

In the *cognitio* procedure the plaintiff backed by the court issued a summons (*denuntiatio*) to the defendant; in this case a petition, concerning wrongful appropriation of property, lodged with the local *strategos* leads to a summons, conveyed by the court officer, to the prefect of Egypt's court.

P. Hamb. 4 = *SP* no. 249 (AD 87)

625. Copy of bond. Lucius Vettius Epaphroditus to Nemesion, royal scribe of the Heraklides district. I swear by Emperor Caesar Domitian Augustus Germanicus that I will be in attendance at Alexandria no later than the twenty-third of the month Pharmouthi in this sixth year of Emperor Caesar Domitian Augustus Germanicus, and will be present at the most sacred tribunal of the most excellent prefect, Gaius Septimius Vegetus, until I have dealt with the suit which Marcus Antonius Tituleius, soldier, has brought against me, in accordance with the letter conveyed to Claudius Chares, late *strategos*; otherwise may I be subject to the penalty of the oath. Isidoros, public scribe, has written on his behalf since he claims to be illiterate. Epaphroditus, thirty-five years old, with a scar on the small finger of the right hand, viewed by Tebulos, assistant. The sixth year of Emperor Caesar Domitian Augustus Germanicus, Pharmouthi 3.

The Formula

Gaius, *Institutes* 4.39–43

626. These are the parts of formulae: *demonstratio*, *intentio*, *adiudicatio*, *condemnatio*. (40) The *demonstratio* is that part of the formula which is inserted at the beginning to make clear what the issue is about ... (41) The *intentio* is that part of the formula in which the plaintiff sets out his claim

… (42) The *adiudicatio* is that part of the formula which permits the judge to assign property to one of the litigants, for example, if the case involves the division of an inheritance among co-heirs … (43) The *condemnatio* is that part of the formula which grants the judge the power to condemn or absolve.

The formula was constructed through several sections, some of which were essential, others optional, treating in one sentence all the relevant issues in the case.

Gaius, *Institutes* 4.47

627. (After discussion of a formula *in ius*) But a formula framed on the action (*in factum*) is as follows: Let X be the judge. If it appears that Aulus Agerius deposited a silver table with Numerius Negidius, and that through the fraud of Numerius Negidius it was not returned to Aulus Agerius, the judge is to condemn Numerius Negidius to pay to Aulus Agerius an equivalent sum of money as that object shall be worth. If it does not appear, absolve.

The formula begins with the appointment of the judge and this clause gives him his authority to judge. Aulus Agerius and Numerius Negidius are stock names for the plaintiff and defendant in legal cases. The praetor could also issue a formula framed on the law (*in ius*); in the example here the issue would then be not whether a table had been deposited and not returned, but assuming that it had been deposited, the legal consequences of that action. For further discussion see de Zulueta (1953), vol. 2, 261–3.

Appointment and Role of Judge

D 50.5.13pr; 3 (Ulpian, *Edict*, Book 23)

628. The praetor undertakes that he will excuse from duty those whom he thinks cannot give their attention to serving as judge, perhaps because someone is unable permanently to give their attention, because he has suffered a state of health which makes it certain that he is unable to undertake civic office; or it may be that he suffers from another illness so that he is unable to conduct his own affairs; or some people may have obtained a priesthood of the type that they cannot resign from without causing religious offence. For these too are permanently released.

3. If a judge begins to ask for release after the case has been undertaken, this cannot be entertained if he asks for release on the basis of an exemption

that he had before he undertook his role as judge; for he renounced his exemption by undertaking his role as judge. But if afterwards a just reason appears for a judge to be released, perhaps temporarily, the case must not be transferred to another if that will take place to the discomfiture of another person. Overall, it will be more acceptable to wait for some time for a judge who has already had experience of the case, rather than entrust the case to a new judge to be judged again.

It was laid down in the *lex Iulia* that no one under the age of twenty should be compelled to act as a judge; others were excluded by their physical condition: the deaf, those incapable of speech, and the mentally impaired. Women and slaves were also excluded not because they lacked an ability to judge, but because they were not regarded as participating in public life (*D* 5.1.12.2 (Paul, *Edict*, book 17)).

Lex Irnitana González (1986), p. 177, Chapter 87

629. Concerning the rejecting and granting of judges.

If it is not agreed between two people, between whom there is a suit or disagreement in a private matter, in which it is proper for a judge or arbiter to be granted under this statute, whom they should have as judge or arbiter, the person who is responsible for the administration of justice is to ensure that in a rejection of *decuriae*, the person who is bringing the case or suit, or if both are bringing the case or the suit, the person who is bringing the case over the greater matter, or suing for the greater amount, should have the first right of rejection; and that from the remaining *decuria* they should have the right of rejection in turn … Or, if either of them is unwilling to reject *decuriae* or judges, he is to grant as judge or arbiter between them for that business, and allot and order to judge, the person whom his opponent wishes to have as judge or arbiter from the judges whose names are displayed.

Decuriae were the lists of people qualified to serve as judges or jurors. It is likely that procedural rules in a Roman colony reflected normal Roman practice; see Metzger (1997), 61–76 for the evidence of the *lex Irnitana* and the appointment of judges; also, Rodger (1991) on legal procedure and the role of local magistrates and judges; Johnston (1999), 125–7. For the limits of the jurisdiction of local magistrates, see Rodger (1990); cases beyond their remit would normally go to the proconsul of Baetica, as argued by Burton (1996), rather than the praetor in Rome, as suggested by Rodger; on the jurisdiction of the governor see also Garnsey (1968).

D 22.5.1.1–2 Arcadius Charisius (*Witnesses*, Only Book); 2 Modestinus (*Rules*, Book 8); 3pr Callistratus (*Judicial Enquiries*, Book 4)

630. Evidence by word of mouth is frequently essential and should be sought from those particularly whose reliability is not in doubt. Witnesses can be summoned not only in criminal cases but also in litigation involving money, as circumstances require, as long as they are not prohibited from giving evidence nor excused from giving evidence by any statute. Although in some statutes a large number of witnesses is set out, nevertheless in imperial decisions this excess is reduced to a sufficient number of witnesses, so that judges should show restraint and permit to be summoned only that number of witnesses that they consider sufficient, lest an uncontrolled freedom to summon unnecessary witnesses may prolong things vexatiously.

(2) In the giving of evidence, respectability, reliability, morals, and gravity must be examined. Therefore, witnesses who waver in the consistency of their evidence should not be heard.

(3pr) The reliability of witnesses must be carefully examined. Therefore, in researching their background you must first consider their status: are they decurions or plebeians? Do they live a decent and blameless life, or have they received a mark of shame and are disreputable? Are they rich or poor, so that they may do something for profit? Are they enemies of the person against whom they give evidence, or friends of the person for whom they give evidence? For if evidence is not subject to suspicion either because of the person who gave it (because he is honest), or because of the context (it was not given because of gain, favour, or hostility), it should be accepted.

This is interesting advice for the treatment of witnesses by judges and the kind of guidance that judges were thought to need. See nos. 731, 776, 777 for rescripts of Hadrian on the treatment of witnesses.

***Tabulae Herculanenses* 76 (Arangio-Ruiz and Pugliese Carratelli (1955), 449–51)**

631. In respect of the dispute between L. Cominius Primus and L. Appuleius Proculus over the boundaries of the estate called 'Numidianus', property of L. Cominius Primus, and that called 'Stratanicianus', property of L. Appuleius Proculus … In respect of that dispute they stipulated and agreed as follows: that Tiberius Crassius Firmus is to be arbiter through agreement between L. Cominius Primus or his heir and L. Appuleius Proculus or his heir; and he is

to give a decision, either publicly or in private, or order that a decision be given openly with both parties being present; and provided that he gives the decision or orders that it be given before 1 February next, or postpones the day of agreement or orders that it be postponed, then if anything is done or not done contrary to the agreement, one thousand sesterces are to be paid. It is agreed that fraud is absent or shall be absent from this matter and arbitration.

The appointment of an arbiter by agreement was extra-judicial and did not involve a suit in court, though legal rules were applied to the procedure.

Quintilian, *Institutio Oratoria* 10.1.32

632. Therefore, as I said, the well-known brevity of Sallust, which cannot be surpassed for the ears of those with leisure and education, should be avoided by an advocate before a judge who is distracted by many considerations and often uneducated.

Quintilian did not have a high opinion of judges with no legal training or even education; for criticism by jurists see *D* 21.2.51pr; 24.3.17.2; Johnston (1999), 126–9; nos. 633–4 for examples of judges in action.

Ovid, *Tristia* 2.93–6

633. The fate of those on trial was not injudiciously granted to me, and cases to be tried in the Centumviral Court. As judge I also settled private suits without objection, and even the defeated party accepted my good faith.

Ovid (see p. 479) was of equestrian status, a social class probably supplying many judges in Rome and Italy. For the Centumviral Court, see no. 749.

Aulus Gellius, *Noctes Atticae* 14.2.1–11

634. At the time when I was first chosen by the praetors as a judge to hear cases described as private, I collected books written in both Greek and Latin about the duty of a judge, so that as a young man summoned from the stories of the poets and the speeches of orators in order to judge legal cases, I could learn judicial business from what we call silent teachers, since, as it is said, there is a shortage of contemporary voices. I received advice and guidance in respect of postponements and adjournments and other legal practices from the Iulian law itself, and from the commentaries of Sabinus Masurius and several other legal experts. However, when, as usually

happens, there was ambiguity in these matters, or the uncertainty of differing opinions, books of this kind were no help at all to me. For although judges should form their views on the basis of the cases before them, there are some general precepts and principles with which a judge ought to familiarize himself before a case and prepare for the uncertain impact of future difficulties, as for instance, I once encountered the unsolvable complexity of reaching a verdict.

The suit in my court involved the recovery of money, which allegedly had been handed over and counted out. But the plaintiff seeking the recovery could not prove the facts with either records or witnesses but relied entirely on meagre arguments. But it was established that he was a truly good man of tried and trusted good faith and blameless life, and many striking examples of his trustworthiness and honesty were produced. On the other hand, the defendant from whom he was seeking the money was demonstrated to be a man possessed of no good quality, living a base and sordid life, and who had been publicly convicted of lying and was steeped in deceit and fraud. However, this man kept shouting with his many supporters that it had to be proved before me by the normal methods that money had been given to him, namely, by an entry of money paid, an account book, demonstration of signature, a signature on records, and the testimony of witnesses. If the suit could not be proved in any respect by all these methods, then he should be absolved, and his opponent convicted of false accusation. Everything that was being said about the life and actions of each man was taking place and being said pointlessly, for the issue was about recovery of money and was being conducted before a civil judge, not before the censors about morals.

My friends whom I had asked to advise me and who were well-versed and distinguished in pleading cases and the work of the courts, and who were always rushing about dealing with cases pressing on them from all sides, immediately said that I should not prolong the session and that there was no doubt that the defendant should be acquitted, since it had not been demonstrated by any proper evidence that he had received the money. But when I considered the two men, one trustworthy, the other full of wrong-doing, and with a disgusting and reprehensible lifestyle, I could not be persuaded to bring in an acquittal. I therefore ordered a postponement, left the courtroom, and went to visit Favorinus, the philosopher, of whom I was a great follower at that time in Rome. I told him everything said in my presence about the case and about the two men, as the matter stood, and asked that he make me wiser in these matters, both the particular problem on which I was stuck, and also the other things that I would have to follow in my role as judge.

Aulus Gellius was acting as judge in a civil suit and was free to consult whomever he chose. Favorinus advised that when a dispute between two litigants could not be resolved by appropriate proofs and evidence, then the judge should normally consider who was the better man; in this case since the plaintiff was an excellent man, whereas the defendant was a rascal, he should bring in a verdict against the defendant. However, in the end Aulus Gellius could not persuade himself to bring in a verdict based on character and not on the evidence, and concluded that the issue was not clear, which will have meant referral to another judge.

Appeals

D 49.6.1 (Marcian, *Appeals*, Book 2)

635. After the appeal has been lodged, letters must be sent by the person from whom appeal is made to the person who will hear the appeal, whether that is the emperor or someone else; these are known as letters of appeal or report. The nature of these letters is as follows: for example, Lucius Titius has appealed against the judgement of such and such a person, which was given in the case involving such and such. However, it is sufficient for the appellant to have asked for the letters of report immediately and on several occasions within the time limit, so that even if he does not receive them, this point may be put forward as evidence. For imperial constitutions require that the person seeking letters of report does so at once. It is therefore equitable that, if the fault lay with the person who ought to have sent the letters but did not do so, this should not prejudice the person who was to receive them.

In the *cognitio* procedure appeal was possible against the decision of an appointed judge and was made to the magistrate who had appointed him, for example, a provincial governor. Appeals from the court of a senior magistrate would go to the emperor. Appeals had to be made within strict time limits and there were monetary penalties to discourage frivolous appeals; see also p. 398. There was no appeal from a decision of the emperor, or any judge appointed by him. There was no appeal against the *iudex* in formulary procedure, though appeal was possible against the choice of a particular judge or the content of the *formula*.

AE 1974.629 = Oliver (1979), 551–4

636. Gnaeus Domitius Corbulo, proconsul, to the archons, council, and people of Cos, greetings. I have often thought that it is not without point to remind even cities in respect of matters that lie within my remit, that it has

been laid down in my instructions (*mandata*) that whatever matters might be thought appropriate for the sacred decision of the emperor [should first be sent] to those in charge of the provinces. But now, [on the basis of your decree] [someone] has made an application [to the emperor], and I discovered that he had done this defying [the rule]. Therefore, if the appeal comes to the emperor, it will be necessary for me to find out the reason first. But if it does come to me, the quaestor must require the guarantee to the value of 2,500 denarii according to my edict issued in respect of those people who do not appear for trial. If he does not comply with this requirement ... .

Corbulo was proconsul of Asia under Claudius. The inscription is badly damaged, and Oliver interprets the circumstances to be that a litigant in Cos had failed to notify the governor in advance about his intention to appeal to the emperor from a judicial decision and has not lodged the necessary deposit as surety. The city government conveyed notice of appeals to the governor who scrutinized their suitability for imperial adjudication; in Asia in the first century a deposit of 2,500 denarii had to be lodged by the appellant; these measures would protect the emperor and stop frivolous appeals aimed at intimidating an opponent who could not afford another trial. See also Burton (1976).

Criminal Cases

See p. 279 for the role of the permanent jury courts (*quaestiones perpetuae*), and how they were gradually superseded by the developing jurisdiction of the emperor, the senate, the prefect of the city, and the praetorian prefect. These magistrates exercised jurisdiction by *cognitio*. Provincial governors exercised *cognitio* and all had the right to inflict capital punishment (*ius gladii*) and to condemn to the mines (*D* 1.18.6.8). The *quaestiones* were usually presided over by a praetor chosen by lot but excluding the urban and peregrine praetor, and the panels of jurors (*decuriae*) were taken from the top social classes – senators, *equites*, and *tribuni aerarii*, who were socially linked to the *equites* through their census qualification. Augustus confirmed this framework of jury courts in 17 BC by the *lex Iulia iudiciorum publicorum*, which probably simplified the previous procedure. Jurors had to be between thirty and sixty years old and to live in the vicinity of Rome. In this procedure a citizen could approach the president of the relevant court to seek permission to prosecute; if permission was granted, there was a formal statement of charge at which the defendant had to be present; from this point the prosecutor was bound to proceed. Time was granted for the preparation of the case by the prosecution (*inquisitio*) and the defendant could use this opportunity to prepare a defence. Prosecution witnesses could be compelled to appear, up to a certain number, and written statements and documentary evidence were used; the defence could also call witnesses, and all witnesses were subject to cross examination. Jurors swore an oath before the trial and they could acquit or condemn or declare *non liquet*, in which case another trial was required. Penalties were fines and loss of rights in various ways; forced labour could be imposed on people of lesser rank. There was no appeal against the verdict.

Since the launching of a criminal prosecution required an accuser (*delator*) and a formal charge, the *delator* acquired a bad name because of some questionable prosecutions by unscrupulous individuals aimed at enrichment and political advancement (no. 639). Although some people were prohibited from bringing accusations, anyone could bring a charge of treason (*D* 48.4.7–8). For court procedure see Jones (1972), 91–118; Robinson (1995), 1–14; for the senate, Robinson (1996).

Bringing an Accusation

Dio 56.24.7

637. Germanicus was becoming popular with the people for many reasons, and especially because he acted as advocate for several people, not only before other judges but also before Augustus himself. Therefore, on one occasion when a quaestor was facing a charge of murder and Germanicus was preparing to speak on his behalf, the accuser, fearing that he would for this reason lose his case before the jurors before whom such cases were usually tried, wished Augustus to hear the case. But this was in vain, for he lost his case.

This illustrates the variety of courts on offer: the public jury court or in this case the emperor; it was up to the prosecutor whom to approach; the emperor of course could decline to hear a case. It is also important to note the potential impact of influential people in court; see further p. 397.

Tacitus, *Annals* 3.10

638. On the next day Fulcinius Trio approached the consuls for permission to bring an accusation against Piso. But Vitellius, Veranius, and the rest of Germanicus' companions objected to this, claiming that Trio had nothing to do with the matter; they said they were not accusers but witnesses to

what had happened, and conveyed Germanicus' instructions. Trio abandoned the prosecution of Piso on that charge but obtained permission to bring accusations about his previous career, and the request was made that the emperor (Tiberius) should assume responsibility for the investigation. Even the accused did not object to this, fearing the feelings of the people and the senate; on the other hand, he thought that Tiberius was tough enough to ignore rumours and also was aware that his mother was implicated in the affair. Furthermore, he thought that a single judge could more easily distinguish facts from hostile assumptions, whereas hatred and envy thrive among a large audience. Tiberius was aware of the importance of the investigation and that his own reputation was suffering from the rumours. Therefore, consulting a few close associates, he reviewed the arguments of the accusers and the appeals of the defence, and referred the entire case to the senate.

The trial of Gnaeus Piso who had been governor of Syria and special adviser to Tiberius' adopted son Germanicus, who was in overall charge in the eastern provinces, was an important public occasion. Piso was initially charged with the murder of Germanicus, though this charge did not proceed; the gravamen of the prosecution was that he had attempted to re-enter his province without permission, suborned the soldiers, and committed treason. The accusers first approached the consuls for leave to bring an accusation and the issue was referred to the emperor. The business was too sensitive for the public jury court, and after a preliminary hearing Tiberius referred the entire case to the senate where the trial eventually took place in his presence. In his opening address to the senators Tiberius emphasized that Germanicus had received special treatment only in that 'his death is being investigated in the senate house rather than in the forum, by the senators rather than the jury in a law court' (Tacitus, *Annals* 3.12). Richardson (1997) argued that under the *lex maiestatis* the senate could not pronounce the judicial verdict, but instructed the praetor in charge of the jury court to deliver the verdict in accordance with the *lex* ('by that praetor who is to conduct trials under the *lex maiestatis*'); see also Robinson (2007), 56–77; this volume pp. 308–11 for treason trials.

Tacitus, *Annals* 4.30

639. And because Cornutus had committed suicide it was proposed that the accuser's reward should be forfeited in cases where someone accused of treason committed suicide before the trial had been completed. That proposal was about to be adopted, when the emperor aggressively and more frankly than usual sided with the accusers and complained that the

laws would be rendered useless and the state would be at the edge of a cliff; it would be better to overturn the laws than to remove their guardians. Consequently, those bringing accusations (*delatores*), a group of men associated with public ruin and insufficiently controlled even by penalties, were now being enticed into action by rewards.

The context is prosecution of Vibius Serenus by his son on charge of conspiracy against the emperor, in which Cornutus had been implicated; Cornutus committed suicide at an earlier stage of the trial and the question concerns the reward for the prosecutor, normally entitled to part of the assets of those convicted on his charge. Any citizen had a right to bring a prosecution, was responsible for seeing it through, and false accusations were liable to punishment. Tiberius upholds the importance of due process in legal procedure. See also p. 424. For the role of *delatores* in senatorial society, see in general Rutledge (2001), especially 54–71; 78–84; for this case, pp. 161–2.

Having Your Day in Court

Finding a Lawyer

Crook (1995) discussed the role and status of advocates, emphasizing their importance in the imperial period in court procedures, as against legal experts. Advocates ranged from well-connected men from the upper class pleading high-profile cases often before the emperor or senate, to men of lesser standing pleading more run-of-the-mill cases for which there is much evidence in Egyptian papyri; as noted (p. 350) this evidence may be taken as fairly typical of court procedure and the prominent role of advocates throughout the empire. Increasingly Greek speakers were drawn to the study of Roman law (there were law schools in Berytus) and could provide a source of advocates for local courts; some like Licinius Rufus became distinguished jurists and participated in imperial councils (see Millar (1999), especially 105–8). Advocates may have been plentiful; paying them was another matter. The remuneration of advocates varied enormously and obviously you got the quality you could afford. Although magistrates were seemingly concerned that vulnerable people should have representation, there is no clear evidence that the state paid for advocates through a kind of legal aid (an idea raised by Crook (1995), 63–4). For some reflections on life as a lawyer, based on the ancient *Colloquia* (collections of materials to assist children to learn Latin and Greek, in use from the first century AD), see Dickey (2017), 48–57; for the texts: Dickey (2012–15), 1, 3–56.

D 3.1.1.3–4 (Ulpian, *Edict*, Book Six)

640. In respect of disability he (the praetor) forbids an application to him by a person who is deaf and entirely unable to hear. For a person could not be allowed to make an application who was unable to hear the praetor's statement since that would be hazardous to him, because if he did not hear the praetor's statement, he would suffer punishment as being contumacious if he did not obey. The praetor declares: 'If they do not have an advocate, I will appoint one'. The praetor normally provides this humane solution not only for these people, but for anyone else who for definite reasons, either through the influence of his opponent, or through fear, cannot find an advocate.

This relates to consideration for those who were disabled and had to appear in court; it is not clear if the state paid for the advocate appointed by the praetor in these circumstances; see Gardner (1993), 155–60; 167–8. Ulpian notes that improper influences might be brought to bear in the courtroom, perhaps through the social disparity of the litigants (see no. 646).

D 1.16.9.4 (Ulpian, *Duties of a Proconsul*, Book One)

641. He (the governor) should make sure that there is some plan for the legal proceedings, ensuring that the petitions of everyone receive a hearing, in case proper respect is given to those of high rank or some concession granted to the unscrupulous among those making applications, while people of moderate means cannot put forward their petitions, inasmuch as they either do not obtain advocates at all, or they find ones who are less prominent and not held in any esteem. He should also in general grant advocates to those making petitions, women, or wards, or those who are debilitated for other reasons, or those who are not in their right mind, if someone enters a petition for them. But if there is no one to make a petition, he should grant one on his own accord. But if someone claims that he cannot obtain an advocate because of the influence of his opponent, the governor should also grant him an advocate. It is not right for anyone to be overwhelmed by the influence of his opponent. For it will reflect badly on the governor of the province if someone conducts himself so intemperately that everyone is afraid to be retained as an advocate against him.

We see again the important role of senior magistrates, in this case the provincial governor, in helping litigants get representation. For improper influence in court, see also p. 397.

Martial, *Epigrams* 8.17

642. Sextus, I pleaded your case for the agreed sum of two thousand sesterces and you have sent me as far as I can see one thousand sesterces. What is going on? You say: 'You did not make a statement and you lost the case'. Sextus, you owe me that much more because I was embarrassed.

Martial makes useful observations on contemporary Rome and the cost of employing advocates and the likely profits or otherwise of that profession, as the following examples indicate.

Martial, *Epigrams* 2.30

643. I happened to ask for a loan of twenty thousand sesterces, which was not a great burden, even as a gift. The person I asked is an old and wealthy friend and his strongbox struggles to contain his spreading wealth. He said to me: 'You will become rich if you plead legal cases'. Give what I ask for, Gaius; I am not asking for advice.

Martial, *Epigrams* 8.16

644. You, Cyperus, who were a baker for a long time now, plead legal cases and ask for two hundred thousand sesterces. But you spend it all and borrow more. You have not stopped being a baker, Cyperus. And you make bread and flour.

Martial, *Epigrams* 3.38

645. What motive or what pledge drags you to Rome, Sextus? What are you hoping or looking for there? Tell me. You say: 'I shall plead legal cases more eloquently than Cicero himself, and no one will be my equal in all three of the courtroom venues'. Atestinus and Civis pleaded cases (you know both), but neither made enough for their rent. 'If nothing comes from that source, I shall compose poetry. You will hear it and you will say that it is the work of Virgil'. You are mad … .

For the limited income of some advocates see also Martial, *Epigrams* 12.72; Crook (1995), 129–31; also note 4.46, indicating a lawyer being paid in kind. But Martial also suggests that lawyers were in demand (12.68): Clients come round to the door early in the morning: 'I am not a pleader or suited for bitter legal disputes'.

Quintilian, *Institutio Oratoria* 12.7.8–11

646. It is open to debate if he (a lawyer) should always offer his services without a fee. It would be unwise to decide this prematurely. For who is unaware that it is by far the most respectable course for the liberal arts, and most worthy for that attitude of mind which we require, not to sell our services, or to undermine the value of such a great gift as eloquence, since many things can appear cheap simply because they have a price. This point is clear enough even to the blind, as the saying goes, and no one who is sufficiently well-off (and that is only a modest amount) will try to obtain an income in this way without the charge of meanness. But if his domestic finances require a little more for essential expenses, in accordance with the precepts of all the philosophers, he may certainly allow appreciation to be expressed to him, since collections were made even for Socrates for his maintenance, and Zeno, Kleanthes, and Chrysippos received payment from their pupils. Furthermore, I do not see a more reasonable means of acquiring income than through most honourable labour, and indeed from those for whom they have given outstanding service, and who, if they proffer nothing in return, would have been unworthy of legal defence. Indeed, this is not only just but essential, since the task of being a lawyer and the time spent on the affairs of others remove the opportunity of acquiring income in any other way. But even so a balance must be preserved, and it is of paramount importance from whom he accepts a fee, how much he charges, and for how long he continues to charge.

See no. 651 for a senatorial debate on lawyers' fees.

Quintilian, *Institutio Oratoria* 12.9.7

647. Furthermore a genuine advocate will not disdain to plead lesser cases, as if they are beneath him or might detract from his reputation because their substance is insufficiently elevated. For the most compelling reason for undertaking a case is duty to our client, and indeed we should even hope that our friends have legal cases as unimportant as possible. Anyway, the advocate who presents his case appropriately will have spoken exceptionally well.

Juvenal, *Satires* 7.106–14

648. But what about lawyers? What benefit do they get from all their activity in court and the bulging notebooks they carry around with them?

They talk big and especially when a creditor is listening or if someone pokes them in the ribs with a great ledger as he chases up a bad debt. Then they spew out enormous falsehoods like a great bellows and fire spittle all over themselves. But if you examine their genuine incomes, you can weigh the income of a hundred lawyers against that of one jockey of the red team at the circus.

Juvenal sneers at life as a barrister; but some came from a wealthy background and could offer their services in an altruistic way, while others could earn enormous sums and star in high-profile cases.

Philostratus, *Lives of the Sophists* 519

649. In the law courts he (Scopelian) displayed a character that was neither greedy nor abusive. He offered his services without a fee to those who were in danger of a capital sentence, and when speakers became abusive in their address and thought that they should make a great display of anger, he used to call them drunks and raving old women.

Scopelian of Clazomenae was a sophist and orator of the late first century AD.

Pliny, *Letters* 6.29.1–3

650. Avidius Quietus, who is a dear friend of mine and holds me in high regard (which pleases me even more), along with many other comments of Thrasea Paetus, whose friend he was, often used to communicate this point, namely that he used to advise that three types of legal cases should be undertaken: those of friends, those that were spurned by others, and those setting a precedent. It needs no explanation why we should undertake a case for a friend. But what about cases spurned by others? Because in such cases the resilience and compassion of the advocate come strongly into public view. And what about cases setting a precedent? Because it is of great importance whether a good or bad precedent is established. To these categories, perhaps presumptuously, I would add those cases that are famous and bring public attention. For it is reasonable occasionally to plead for renown and reputation, that is for your own case.

Tacitus, *Annals* 11.5–7

651. There was no public business so obviously corrupt as the deceitful behaviour of lawyers; indeed Samius, a distinguished Roman member of the equestrian order, who had paid four hundred thousand sesterces to

Suillius Rufus and then discovered that he was in collusion with his opponents, committed suicide in Suillius' house. Therefore, on the initiative of Gaius Silius, consul designate, whose power and destruction I shall describe at the appropriate time, the senators were galvanized and demanded that the *lex Cincia* should be invoked, with its ancient provision that no one should receive either money or a gift for pleading a legal case.

6. Then amid the objections of those against whom the criticism was directed, Silius violently denounced Suillius, whom he detested, citing the precedent of old-time orators who had reckoned that current and future reputation was sufficient reward for eloquence: 'What would otherwise be the leading and finest of the respectable arts was defiled by grubby service for money. Neither trust nor integrity remained when the size of the fees took centre stage. But if the cases were carried on without anyone making a profit there would be fewer of them. As it was, feuds, accusations, hatred, and injustice were fomented, so that just in the way that the impact of disease brings in money for doctors, similarly the plague of the courts brings money to lawyers. They should remember Asinius, Messala, and more recently Arruntius and Aesernius. They reached the top of their art without besmirching their life or their eloquence'. (Several lawyers objected to this and made their case:)

7. 'What man was so proud that he should assume hopefully that his reputation would endure for ever? It was of benefit to defendants that assistance was made ready for them, so that no one should be left vulnerable to the powerful through lack of a lawyer. But eloquence does not just happen without a cost; domestic business is neglected as a man applies himself to the affairs of others. Many supported themselves by military service, some by running their estates; no man follows a calling unless he has worked out in advance its returns. It was easy for Asinius and Messala, fat with the rewards that came with the war between Antony and Augustus, or people like Aesernius and Arruntius, scions of rich families, to adopt a high-minded attitude. There are ready precedents in Publius Clodius and Gaius Curio who often delivered speeches for huge fees. But we are senators of moderate resources who live in a tranquil state and seek nothing but the rewards of peace. He should consider the ordinary people who stand out by pleading cases. If the emoluments of the skill which they studied are removed, then the skill itself will perish'. The emperor (Claudius) thought that these views, though not high-minded, made a valid point, and established a maximum fee of ten thousand sesterces, with those who exceeded it to be subject to the law on extortion.

After this scandalous abuse of the advocate's position and deception of his client, there was an attempt to revive the *lex Cincia* of 204 BC, which had placed a limit on the amount of donations, and specifically forbade advocates from accepting any gifts from their clients in return for their professional services.

Tacitus, *Dialogus de Oratoribus* 7

652. Anyway, to describe my own situation, I did not have more pleasure on the day when I received my senatorial toga, or as an outsider from an insignificant community I was elected to a quaestorship or a tribunate or a praetorship, than on those days when it was granted to me, as far as my limited skill in oratory allowed, successfully to defend a client or to speak persuasively before the Centumviral court or in the presence of the emperor to protect and defend the imperial freedmen and procurators.

For the date of Tacitus *De Oratoribus* see Barnes (1986); it was probably written after the *Agricola*, that is, after AD 98. See no. 661 for Tacitus' complaints about the context of contemporary oratory.

Lawyer and Client: Preparation and Presentation

Advocates had to prepare for appearing in court, school their client, and work out the best way to influence the judge in their favour, sometimes with lawyerly ruses, in the challenging environment of a noisy courtroom. The advocate faced the challenge that he could not always humour all his clients' wishes or expectations. The following passages help to illustrate some of the issues facing lawyers and litigants as they prepared for a court appearance, and to interact with the state's legal framework; for the relationship between lawyer and client and the value of advocacy, see Crook (1995), 120–31; on the litigant in the courtroom, see Bablitz (2007), 71–88; (2011), 321–2. For the Centumviral Court see no. 749.

Quintilian, *Institutio Oratoria* 12.8.7–11

653. Therefore above all we should allow generous time and an undisturbed space for those involved in the case, and we should encourage them to tell their story, no matter how long-winded and repetitious they are and how far back they go. For it is less of a problem to listen to superfluous material than to miss the essential. Frequently in these sessions the advocate will find a problem and its solution in a matter which the client thought was of no importance in any respect. Furthermore, the advocate who is going to

plead a case should not be so confident in his memory that he disdains to make a note of what he has heard.

It is not enough for the advocate to hear his client just once. The client must be compelled to repeat his story and indeed more than once, not only because points can be missed in the first statement, especially, as often happens, if he is an uneducated man, but also so that we can discover if he is saying the same thing. For many clients lie and speak not as if they were explaining the case to their advocate, but actually pleading it before a judge. Therefore, the advocate must never believe them too readily, but in every way must pursue them, disturb them, and draw them out ... After the advocate thinks that he has given a sufficiently patient audience to his client, he must adopt another character and conduct himself like opposing counsel, putting forward whatever point that could conceivably be raised in opposition, such as the nature of this kind of contest might suggest. He must be questioned in the most hostile way and put under pressure. For by examining everything we sometimes hit upon the truth where we least expected it.

Quintilian illustrates the relationship between lawyer and client; preparation of the case with the client was crucial, although some advocates did not bother to study the case in advance. He vividly describes what it was like for a litigant to be prepared for his day in court facing the legal system. He notes that some clients will be uneducated and presumably poor.

Quintilian, *Institutio Oratoria* 12.9.10–11

654. Litigants often demand a disgusting and improper kind of indulgence that no good man in the audience will welcome, because they are determined on vengeance rather than protection. But in this and in many other issues an advocate must not give way to the judgement of his clients. For what man of a liberal disposition could bear to be rude according to the opinion of another person? But there are some who willingly abuse opposing counsel, which, unless they have deserved it, is improper and disrespectful to the duties of the profession, and furthermore pointless to the speaker because his opponent is given the opportunity to reply in the same way, and against the interests of his case because his opponents become hostile and however little their talent is, it will be increased by the insults they have suffered.

In a case in which Fronto had to appear against Herodes Atticus, Marcus Aurelius (who knew both men) asked him to be moderate in his court speech and avoid reviling his opponent. Fronto accepted the advice, provided that it was consistent with being true to his brief (Haines, *Loeb* vol. 1, pp. 62–6); see Bowersock (1969), 93–100; Champlin (1980), 63–4; for the possibly damaging effect of influence (*gratia*) in court cases see p. 397. Quintilian also emphasized that sometimes a lawyer needed to go against the wishes of his client present in court (4.5.20).

Quintilian, *Institutio Oratoria* 4.2.45

655. For perhaps this (brevity) does not incommode the leisurely reader, but flies past the listener, who does not wait to recover what was said, especially since someone who reads is normally well-educated, while they generally appoint to the jury panels a rustic judge who will deliver a verdict based on what he understands, as perhaps happens everywhere. Therefore, in presenting material above all a mid-course of speaking should be maintained: 'As much as the task requires and as much as is necessary'.

Quintilian is emphasizing the importance of making things clear to the judge, who as already noted might have limited education and knowledge of the law. Quintilian also observed that an orator had to develop a style suitable to whatever case he was pleading (12.10.70). See further for examples of inappropriate presentation by advocates (nos. 659–70).

Quintilian, *Institutio Oratoria* 6.2.3–5

656. There certainly are and always were a reasonable number (of advocates) who could with adequate skill discover what was helpful to establishing arguments. I certainly do not despise these people, but I think that they are valuable as far as making sure that through their efforts nothing escapes the judge's attention, and (to speak frankly) in that they are suitable for teaching the eloquent the nature of a case. But the man who could sweep a judge along and bring him whatever point of view he wanted, and who by his speaking could inspire pity and anger, was indeed rare. But this is what takes control in court, this eloquence rules. For arguments generally arise out of the case, and most of them are on the side of the stronger party, so that the person who wins through them merely knows that his advocate did not fail him. But when you must apply some pressure to the mind of the judge and take his thoughts away from contemplation of the truth – that is the real task of an advocate. The client does not teach this, and it is not contained in books of legal cases. For arguments can bring it about that the judges think our case is superior, but playing on the emotions makes them want it to be so; and what people want they also believe.

This is an interesting analysis of techniques of advocacy, which the advocate's client might not always appreciate.

Quintilian, *Institutio Oratoria* 6.1.39

657. Once an advocate carried a girl, whom he claimed was the sister of his opponent (this was the subject of the suit), across the courtroom to the benches opposite as if he was going to leave her in the lap of her brother. But he had been warned by me in advance and had left. The advocate, usually an eloquent man, was struck dumb by this unexpected occurrence and very slowly carried back what was his own child.

The Roman courtroom was rather an undisciplined and noisy environment with people able to come and go, and with scope for various demonstrations and ploys by enterprising advocates.

Quintilian, *Institutio Oratoria* 6.1.32–3

658. But I do not approve of what has been done, as I have read or indeed as I have occasionally seen myself, namely that a picture of the defendant by whose pitiful condition the judge was to be influenced, was displayed on a tablet or a screen. What foolishness is it in an advocate to think that a silent portrait will speak better for him than his oratory? But I know that mourning garments and unkemptness and also a similar demeanour of the relatives (of the defendant) have been beneficial, and that prayers have brought a great impetus for acquittal. Furthermore, an entreaty to the judges through pledges of love will assuredly be useful, if they, like the defendant, have children, wife, and parents, and also an appeal to the gods, as this is usually the result of a clear conscience.

Martial, *Epigrams* 6.19

659. My suit concerns not violence or murder or poison, but three little goats. I am contending that my neighbour has stolen them. The judge requires that this is proved to his satisfaction. But you bellow about Cannae, the war with Mithridates, mad Punic treachery, and all about Sulla, Marius, and Mucius while waving your hands about. Postumus, please speak now about the three little goats.

A lawyer's inappropriate argument illustrates one kind of mistaken pleading, which undermined the client's case.

Aulus Gellius, *Noctes Atticae* 1.22.6

660. I recall that I was once present in the court of the praetor, a learned man, and that a not undistinguished lawyer was pleading in such a way that he roamed outside the case and suit he was representing and did not stick to relevant material. Then the praetor said to the person whose suit it was that he did not have a lawyer, and when the lawyer who was talking expostulated 'But I speak for this distinguished man', replied wittily: 'Well you certainly speak a lot, but you do not represent your client'.

The joke is in the possible meanings of *superesse*, 'to be present for' and 'to be superfluous'.

Pliny, *Letters* 6.2.7

661. Indeed whenever I am acting as judge, which I do rather more often than I plead, I grant however much time anyone requests. For I think it rash to guess how much time a case which I have not yet heard is going to take, and to set a time for the business before its extent is known, especially since above all a judge who has been sworn in must display patience, which is an important element in justice. But of course, some irrelevant material is said. I accept this, but it is better for this to be said rather than essential material to be excluded. Furthermore, you cannot tell if material is irrelevant until you have heard it.

The context here is that Pliny complains about a lack of respect for oratory; advocates wanted to get their speeches over and done with, and judges were too eager to finish the case rather than make an informed judgement. Tacitus (*Dialogus de Oratoribus* 19.5) complained that some judges 'conduct the case by force and authority, not by legal practice and the law, and do not accept the speaker's time but establish it themselves'. At 39 Tacitus complains about the subdued clothing of advocates, the small venues in which cases were conducted, and procedural restrictions; see Frier (2010). It is worth pointing out that in the imperial period some trials were held indoors in basilicas or the senate house; this will have affected the atmosphere of trials and the techniques used by advocates; Lintott (2015), 303. But other hearings were conducted amid the distractions of the forum; discussion of judicial arenas in Tuori (2010).

Quintilian, *Institutio Oratoria* 10.3.30

662. Therefore, whether we are in a crowd, on a journey, or even at a party, the mind should make a private place for itself. Otherwise, what will happen when we suddenly are required to deliver a coherent speech in

the middle of the forum, with cases in progress all around us, insults, and even casual shouts intruding, if we cannot recover, except in total solitude, the details which we put in our notes?

For the special ability of the advocate Trachalus to be heard see 12.5.5–6. Quintilian also urges the training of memory to facilitate presentation without excessive notes and achieving the perfect balance with an extempore ability; see also 10.6.2; 10.7.30; 12.9.16.

Seneca, *Controversiae* 9, praef. 4–5

663. In declamations in the schools the opposite happens; everything is softer and more relaxed. In the forum they receive a case, in the school they chose one. In school they are coxed by the judge, in the forum the judge dominates. In the forum your thoughts must be concentrated amid the uproar of the crowd standing round and your voice has to carry to the ears of the judge, in school all eyes are concentrated on the face of the speaker. Therefore, just as the brightness of full daylight blinds those who are emerging from a shady, secluded spot, so everything seeming new and unexpected disturbs those making the transition from the schools to the forum. And they do not gain their strength as an advocate until, putting up with numerous insults, they harden with real work their juvenile mind which has been dulled by the pleasantries of the schools.

For Seneca, see p. 480; for the value of Seneca's *Controversiae*, see p. 350.

Pliny, *Letters* 2.11.10–13

664. The case was adjourned to the next meeting of the senate, and this was a most distinguished sight. The emperor presided, for he was consul, and furthermore in January the city is crowded with large numbers, especially of senators. Furthermore, the importance of the case, the heightened expectation because of the delay and rumours, the natural tendency for men to inquire into big and unusual events, had inspired people to come from all directions. You can guess my nervousness and apprehension since I had to speak on such an important matter in that assembly in the presence of the emperor. It is indeed true that I have frequently spoken in the senate and nowhere am I more kindly received. But now the unaccustomed nature of the case affected me with unusual anxiety. For, in addition to the points I have already mentioned, I noted the difficulties of the case. There stood a man recently of consular rank and a member of the board of

seven for religious banquets, who had now lost his rank. It was particularly difficult to speak for the prosecution against a man who had already been condemned, for although charged with appalling crimes he was protected by sympathy on the grounds that his conviction had already taken place.

For the charge of corruption (*repetundae*) and the trial of Marius Priscus, see p. 312. Even the experienced Pliny could be apprehensive about the tension and excitement of addressing the senate as a court in the presence of the emperor, and the consequences of appearing against such a prominent senator; for the impact and influence of important people in court see pp. 398–400.

CIL 6.9241 = *ILS* 7746

665. To the spirits of the dead. Here lies Helpidius, dead through cruel fate, an outstanding young man, an honourable pleader of cases. He lived for thirty years.

This is an interesting memorial in Rome to a humble young practitioner of the law.

CIL 10.4919 = *ILS* 7750

666. P. Pomponius Philadespotus, freedman of Pomponius, scribe, who wrote wills for twenty-five years without any legal adviser.

Philadespotus probably advised on the legality of the wills he wrote and was presumably less expensive than a lawyer. Of course, a litigant could represent himself in court and some declined any kind of formal legal assistance.

In the Courtroom

Our evidence gives a vivid illustration of how the theory of advocacy was turned into practice in the confrontational atmosphere of the courtroom. Given that most ancient writers came from the educated wealthy classes, we hear a great deal about high-profile cases involving prominent individuals or entire communities wealthy enough to engage in extended lawsuits. However, other evidence particularly from papyri shows the willingness of men and women of humble background to go to law, and the competence and ingenuity of those who represented them, and therefore illustrates the state (represented by magistrates, governors, and officials), either as opponent or facilitator, and citizens in the legal process (nos. 675–88).

CIL 10.7852 = *ILS* 5947 (Esterzili, Sardinia), AD 69

667. In the consulship of Emperor Otho Caesar Augustus on 18 March.

Copied and verified from the notebook equipped with handles of Lucius Helvius Agrippa, proconsul, which Cnaeus Egnatius Fuscus, quaestorian clerk, produced, in which was written that which is written below, tablet five, chapters eight, nine, and ten. On 13 March, Lucius Helvius Agrippa, proconsul, having heard the case, declared:

In the interests of the public good it is proper to abide by a judicial decision, and Marcus Juventius Rixa, most honourable man, procurator of the Emperor, has on several occasions declared in respect of the case of the Patulcenses that the boundaries of the Patulcenses should be kept as they had been settled in the bronze tablet of Marcus Metellus, and declared on the last occasion that he wished to rebuke the Galillenses because they had frequently reopened the dispute and had not obeyed his own decision, but out of respect for the benevolence of the most excellent and greatest Emperor was content to admonish them by edict to desist from causing trouble and abide by the judicial decision, and by the first of October next to withdraw from the land of the Patulcenses and hand over uncontested possession, but that if they persevered in their insolence he would punish severely the instigators of this disobedience. And after this when Caecilius Simplex, most distinguished man, was approached about the same case by the Galillenses claiming that they were going to produce a document pertaining to the matter from the imperial record office, he declared that it was reasonable to approve a postponement and granted a period of three months up to 1 December, by which day, unless the map had been brought, he would follow the one (that is, map) that was in the province.

I also, having been approached by the Galillenses pleading as an excuse that the map had not yet been brought, granted a period until 1 February next, and yet I realize that the delay is welcome to those occupying the land; therefore, the Galillenses are to leave by 1 April next the lands of the Campanian Patulcenses, which they occupied by force. If they do not obey this pronouncement, they must be aware that they will suffer punishment for their long-standing wilful disobedience, which has often been condemned. The following were present in the council … .

This was a land dispute between two local communities mediated by Roman officials before whom their representatives appear; documents and maps formed a significant part of the evidence, but there was a suspicion that the Galillenses, who were in possession of the land, were using the search for documentation as a delaying tactic to achieve further adjournments while they enjoyed the fruits of possession; discussion in Mastino (1993); see also Campbell (2005), especially 323; 328–9. It was often a problem getting people into court and the suit under way.

Fronto, *Ad M. Caes.* 1.6 = Haines (Loeb, vol. 1), p. 159

668. Am I imagining or inventing this? But in this case has this very thing not happened? Where is the defendant who long ago ought to have been here to plead his case? He is on the way. But by what route? He is coming from Asia. And is he still in Asia? It is a long journey, and he is hurrying. Is it by ship or horseback or imperial post that he is making these speedy halts? Meanwhile as soon as the hearing is fixed, the first adjournment is requested from you, Caesar, and granted; when the hearing is fixed again, for a second time an adjournment for two months is requested from you. The two months expired on the last ides, and after that several days have passed by. Is he coming at last? If he has not yet come, is he at least getting close? If he is not yet close, has he at least set out from Asia? If he has not set out, is he at least thinking about setting out? What else does he think about if not keeping control of the goods of someone else, plundering the fruits of this, stripping the fields, and wrecking the whole property? He is not so foolish as to prefer to come before Caesar and lose his case rather than stay in Asia and keep possession.

This is part of a speech Fronto made in a case of a will that had been referred to the emperor (see no. 750) in respect of the opening and verification of the document. Fronto is arguing that it might be in the interests of certain people to delay opening the will while they enjoyed the fruits of the property. He sarcastically notes the eagerness of his opponent for adjournments.

Pliny, *Letters* 10.81–2

669. Pliny to Emperor Trajan. (The context is a legal dispute in Prusa between two leading local citizens. Eumolpus, who represented Flavius Archippus, had insisted that Dio Chrysostom should produce his accounts before a building for which he had been responsible could be transferred to the city. He had also argued that although Dio's wife and son were buried in the building, a statue of Trajan had been erected there.) I agreed to do so at once and to postpone my departure, but Eumolpus asked that I grant a longer time for him to put his case together, and that I should hold the hearing in another community. I replied that I would hear it in Nicaea. But when I had taken my seat to hear the case, Eumolpus again started to seek an adjournment arguing that he was insufficiently prepared, while Dio

demanded that it be heard at once. Many arguments were put on both sides, some of them actually relevant. I thought that I should grant an adjournment so that I could consult you in a matter likely to set a precedent, and I instructed both parties that they should submit written copies of their demands. I wanted you to judge from their very own words what they were setting out. Dio said that he would hand it over. Eumolpus said that he would confine his written submission to what he was seeking on behalf of his community, but that in respect of the burials he was not the accuser, but the representative of Flavius Archippus whose instructions he was following. Archippus, who was assisted by Eumolpus here as at Prusa, said that he would himself present a statement. But neither Eumolpus nor Archippus have up to this point presented a statement although I have waited for several days. Dio has presented his statement, which I have appended to this letter. I have paid a visit to the location at issue, and I also saw your statue in place in the library. However, the place in which the son and wife of Dio are said to be buried is located in an area enclosed by a colonnade. I ask you, sir, to deign to instruct me, especially in this kind of case where there is great expectation, as is inevitable when facts are conceded and defended with precedents.

Trajan to Pliny. My dear Pliny you had no need to hesitate about the matter on which you regarded it essential to consult me. Indeed, you know very well that I do not bring reverence to my name through the fears or concerns of people or through charges of treason. Therefore, you must set aside that issue, which I would not accept even if it were supported with precedents, and ensure that the accounts of the entire public work carried out under the control of Dio are produced, since the well-being of the community demands it, and Dio ought not to refuse and indeed is not refusing.

Since this case involved influential local dignitaries, Pliny was inclined to be cautious. As governor he was exercising *cognitio* and had to decide if Eumolpus' charges had merit; lack of respect to an emperor's statue could constitute treason and presumably had been mentioned to prejudice the case against Dio. But Trajan is having none of it; see Sherwin-White (1966), 675.

Apuleius, *Apologia* 1

670. I was absolutely certain and knew it for the truth, Claudius Maximus, and you who sit in the court, that Sicinius Aemilianus, an old man well-known for his recklessness, and who had begun the case against me before he had properly thought it through, would resort to mere abuse for lack of a real charge. Now,

while an entirely innocent man may be subject to a false accusation, only the true criminal can be convicted. I take special confidence from this observation, and I further congratulate myself because, with you as judge, I have the opportunity and means to clear philosophy of the charges brought by the ignorant, and also to prove myself innocent. Those charges are at first sight serious, and furthermore their unexpectedness makes them difficult to refute.

For you remember that it is only five or six days ago when I was involved in defending a suit on behalf of my wife Pudentilla against the Granius brothers, that his accomplices attacked me maliciously out of the blue and began to make slanderous accusations that I was involved in malevolent magical practices and the death of my stepson, Pontianus. When I understood that these were not so much proper charges for a court but mere insults and abuse, I demanded persistently and aggressively that they proceed with their accusation.

This is Apuleius' opening statement to court at the start of his trial on charges of magic and using magical arts to seduce Pudentilla into marrying him. Apuleius confidently insists that formal charges are produced; on the trial of Apuleius see nos. 24; 596–7.

Suetonius, *Claudius* 15.4

671. It is well established that a Roman *eques* on trial for obscene acts against women, but on a false charge concocted by vicious personal enemies, when he saw that prostitutes were called as witnesses against him and that their words were taken as evidence, threw his pen and notes, which he was holding in his hand, so violently that he seriously cut his (Claudius') cheek, while simultaneously loudly denouncing his stupidity and cruelty.

In this trial over which the emperor himself presided, the *eques*, presumably arraigned under the *lex Aquilia* for *iniuria*, seems to have been defending himself; even the emperor's presence was no guarantee against angry outbursts from the litigants.

CIL 6.266 = *FIRA* 3, no. 165 (AD 226–244)

672. P. Clodius Fortunatus, permanent official of this place, established a shrine to Hercules.

Judgements of Aelius Florianus, Herennius Modestinus, and Faltonius Restitutianus, prefects of the Vigiles, eminent men.
Florianus said: 'In respect of what pertains to the map presented by me, since you are meeting with me, this should be dealt with first. I know that I made a judgement yesterday, namely, that it was the responsibility of the

other litigant to demonstrate that it was based on sacred authority that the payments should not be made; he responded that he could demonstrate by several accounts that this was carried out on sacred authority. And today he says this: "From that time", he claims, "when Augustus began to control the state right up to the present day, these locations never made payments"'.
And below.
Florianus said: 'I saw the place dedicated with sacred images'.
In another chapter:
Modestinus said: 'If any judgement has been delivered it acquires its own authority, if, as I said, a judgement has been delivered; at the moment no evidence is being presented to me to demonstrate that the fullers are legally liable for the payment'.
And in another chapter:
Restitutianus having consulted with his council said: 'It is clear what the eminent men decided; for Florianus fulfilled his responsibility most energetically, since when he came to adjudicate the current issue, he inspected the location, examined all the evidence, and in respect of that location which was most in dispute delivered a judgement which was not appealed'.
And below.
Restitutianus said: 'Modestinus also followed the issue adjudicated by Florianus and forbade the exaction of payments'.
And below.
Restitutianus said: 'That rule will be maintained in respect of the fullers, which they obtained from their several judges, and which they have had up to the present day, and which involves no payment'.
The legal case continued from the consulship of Alexander Augustus for the second time and Marcellus for the second time to the consulship of Peregrinus and Aemilianus.

In this prolonged dispute the payments from which the fullers claimed exemption seem to be a charge on the use of water; the 'sacred authority' referred to may be that of the emperors who had granted the concession; but it is possible that the area was immune from payment because it was sacred to divinities. For Modestinus see Millar (1999), 102. For the jurisdiction of the prefects of the *Vigiles*, see pp. 92–3.

Acts of Scillitan Martyrs (Musurillo (1972), 86–9)

673. When Praesens for the second time and Claudianus were consuls, on 17 July at Carthage, Speratus, Natzalus, Cittinus, Donata, Secunda, and Vestia were brought to trial. Saturninus the proconsul said: 'You can earn the pardon of our lord if you return to your senses'.

Speratus said: 'We have done no wrong, we have committed no iniquity, we have spoken ill of nobody, but when treated badly we have offered thanks. Therefore, we revere our emperor'.

Saturninus the proconsul said: 'We too have religious observances, but our religion is straightforward, and we swear by the spirit of our lord the emperor, and we make offerings for his safety, which you also ought to do'.

Speratus said: 'If you offer a quiet hearing, I shall explain a mystery of simplicity'.

Saturninus the proconsul said: 'I shall not provide a hearing if you begin to insult our rites; instead swear by the spirit of our lord the emperor'.

Speratus said: 'I do not recognize the empire of this world. But instead, I serve that God whom no man has seen nor can see with these eyes. I have not committed a theft; but if I buy anything I pay the tax, because I recognize my lord, king of kings, and emperor of all the peoples'.

Saturninus the proconsul said to the others: 'Give up this persuasion'.

Speratus said: 'It is a bad persuasion to commit murder, to bear false witness'.

Saturninus the proconsul said: 'Do not be part of this madness'.

Cittinus said: 'We have no other whom we should fear except our Lord God, who is in heaven'.

Donata said: 'Honour Caesar as Caesar, but fear God'.

Vestia said: 'I am a Christian'.

Secunda said: 'What I am I want to be'.

Saturninus the proconsul said to Speratus: 'Do you persist in being Christian?'

Speratus said: 'I am a Christian'.

And all agreed with him.

Saturninus the proconsul said: 'Do you want some time to consider?'

Speratus said: 'There is no consideration in a matter as just as this'.

Saturninus the proconsul said: 'What are the things in your bag?'

Speratus said: 'The books and letters of Paul, a just man'.

Saturninus the proconsul said: 'Take a delay of thirty days and think this over'.

Speratus said again: 'I am a Christian'.

And the others agreed with him.

Saturninus the proconsul read out his verdict from a tablet: 'Since Speratus, Natzalus, Cittinus, Donata, Secunda, Vestia, and others have confessed that they live according to Christian rites and have obstinately persevered in this despite having been given the opportunity of returning to Roman practices, I have decided that they should be executed by the sword'.

Speratus said: 'We thank God'.

Natzalus said: 'Today we are martyrs in heaven; thanks be to God'.

Saturninus the proconsul ordered a proclamation to be voiced by the herald: 'I have ordered Speratus, Natzalus, Cittinus, Veturius, Felix, Aquilinus, Lactantius, Januaria, Generosa, Vestia, Donata, and Secunda to be led to execution'.
They all said: 'Thanks be to God'.
And they were immediately beheaded in the name of Christ.

This court appearance occurred in AD 180 when P. Vigellius Saturninus was proconsul of Africa; see Tertullian, *Ad Scapulam* 3.4. Musurillo (1972), xxii–xxiii notes that the text is likely to be close to actual court records of the proceedings; Whittaker (1984), 176–8; see pp. 340–5 for the prosecution of Christians.

Juvenal, *Satires* 16.7–34

674. Let us first consider the benefits all soldiers have, not the least of which is that if a civilian should dare to assault you, even if he is himself thrashed, he will cover it up and will not dare to show the praetor that his teeth have been knocked out and the black marks and swelling bruises all over his face, and his remaining eye about which the doctor is not optimistic. If he wants to seek redress, a judge in heavy boots is granted and hefty jurors sit on the benches, according to ancient military law and the tradition of Camillus, that a soldier may not be sued outside the military camp or far from the standards. But surely the centurion's investigation of a soldier will be entirely fair, and I shall obtain redress if my complaint is justified? But the entire unit is against you and all the men are agreed in making sure that your redress needs a doctor and is worse than the first assault. You would need to be as stupid as the orator Vagellius to cause offence to all those boots and thousands of hobnails while you have two legs. Anyway, who would come so far from the city or be such a loyal friend that he would venture beyond the lofty embankment? It is better to dry your tears at once and do not pester friends who will make excuses. When the judge says 'Bring forward your witness', if any of the people who saw the fight dares to say 'I witnessed it', I will believe that he is worthy to stand with our bearded ancestors. You can more easily find a witness to perjure himself against a civilian than someone to tell the truth against the interests and honour of a soldier.

Juvenal highlights the special problems in bringing a soldier to court. It was necessary to sue in the soldier's forum, which meant the military camp, where military jurisdiction applied, often exercised by a centurion. There may have been bias against a civilian litigant as the army needed to keep soldiers available for duty. See Campbell (1984), 254–63.

FIRA 3, no. 19c

675. Year five of our lord Antoninus (142), third extra day. When Octavius Valens and Cassia Secunda, whose case had been adjourned from yesterday, came into court, Eudaemon (Valerius Eudaemon, prefect of Egypt, 142–3), having consulted with his legal advisers, declared: 'Yesterday, when the memorandum of that splendid man, Heliodoros, was read out, there was a clear reason for an adjournment, namely, in order that judgement should be reached in the case of those who are forbidden (to marry), in the presence of the mother of this boy. Today, having considered the relevant circumstances, I confirm the opinion I gave yesterday. Whether this man served in a legion, a cohort, or a cavalry squadron, the child born to him could not be his legitimate son; moreover, if he is not the legitimate son of his father, who is an Alexandrian citizen, he cannot be an Alexandrian citizen. Therefore, this boy, who was born to Valens while he was serving in a cohort, is his illegitimate son and cannot be admitted to Alexandrian citizenship'. And he added: 'You said yesterday that you had other sons; what ages are they and when were they born?' Octavius Valens replied: 'One recently; the other is older'. Eudaemon said: 'Where were you serving when the older boy was born?' Valens replied: 'In the cohort, and the little one too'. Eudaemon said: 'You must know that they are in the same situation as this one. There are some things that cannot be changed'. Valens said: 'Even now, if it happens that I am away, you yourself could grant permission so that I may obtain my rights through a legal representative. What wrong have the children done?' Eudaemon said: 'I have been foolish in explaining in detail what I could have said in a few words; what you are attempting is impossible, and neither this boy nor your other sons are citizens of Alexandria'.

In this case the soldier represents himself before the prefect of Egypt. The problem for soldiers was that they were prohibited from contracting a legal marriage. Therefore, the children of any liaison with local women would be illegitimate and in the case of intestacy could not inherit their father's property; in this case, not being legitimate, they are unable to obtain Alexandrian citizenship, which brought several privileges and benefits; see Taubenschlag (1955), 574–7; 590–602. The soldier in his final statement perhaps refers to the possibility of renewing his appeal when he is away on military service.

P. Oxy. 40 = *SP* no. 245

676. Copy of a minute of Valerius Eudaemon, the prefect, year ... of Antoninus Caesar the lord, Phamenoth 1 ... claim lodged by Psasnis.

Psasnis came forward and said: 'I am a doctor by profession and have treated these very people who have appointed me to a public liturgy'. Eudaemon said: 'Perhaps you treated them incompetently. If you are a doctor officially carrying out embalming explain the liquid used and you will have immunity'.

This case in which the plaintiff represents himself concerns the claim of a doctor for immunity from an obligation to provide a service for the local community. Eudaemon, Prefect of Egypt 142–3, is brusque and sets him a medical test.

P. Oxy. 237, col. vii, lines 19–29 = *SP* no. 258 (AD 128)

677. From the minutes of Flavius Titianus, previous prefect. Year twelve of the divine Hadrian, Pauni 8, at the court in the marketplace. Antonius, son of Apollonius, came forward and said through his advocate, Isidoros the younger, that Sempronius, his father-in-law, at the urging of his mother had engaged in a quarrel and taken away his daughter against her will. When she became ill because of her grief, Bassus the prefect, being stirred to compassion, pronounced that if they wished to live together, he (Antonius) ought not to be prevented. But this did no good. For Sempronius ignored this decision and approached the prefect with a complaint about violence and had brought back a letter to the effect that the contending parties should be sent for trial. Antonius therefore submitted that, if it was satisfactory to the prefect, he should not be separated from his wife who had feelings of affection for him. Didymos the advocate responded that it was not unreasonable for Sempronius to have taken offence. It was because Antonius had been threatening to bring a charge of incest with his daughter against him that, not submitting to the insult, he had used the power bestowed on him by the laws and had brought accusations … Probatianos, speaking on behalf of Antonius, added that if the marriage had not been annulled the father had no power either over the dowry or over the daughter whom he had given away. Titianus said: 'The crucial point is with whom the married woman wishes to live'. I have read it and signed.

This long papyrus concerns the legal case of one Dionysia who was involved in a long financial dispute with her father, who had also tried to take her from her husband. In her pleadings before the courts, she cited precedents from previous cases relevant to her argument, including the episode cited in this passage. Antonius was arguing that he and his wife wished to live together, but his father-in-law Sempronius had forcibly removed her and ignored a ruling of a previous prefect that she should live with her husband. Sempronius then brought forward a vague charge of violence apparently in response to Antonius' claim that he had committed incest with his daughter. Both men are represented by advocates. Antonius was also eager to prevent Sempronius from reclaiming the dowry. The protagonists are Roman citizens, and the courtroom discussion is arguably conducted in terms of Roman legal practice, the limits of *patria potestas*, and the principle of not disturbing harmonious marriages (*D* 43.30.1.5). Therefore, in this tangled family intrigue, the prefect's humane decision that the wife's wishes should be respected followed Roman legal practice (discussion in Dolganov (2019), 48–55). However, some have argued that the father was pursuing his rights under Egyptian law which gave a father authority over even a married daughter (*P. Oxy.* 237, pp. 148–9).

P. Ryl. 75, lines 1–12 = *SP* no. 259 (AD 150)

678. From the minutes of Munatius. Year thirteen of the divine Aelius Antoninus, Pharmouthi 22. Glykon son of Dionysios and Apollonios son of Glykon were brought in, and during the proceedings Archelaus the advocate said: 'Glykon has no resources and resigns his property'. Munatius said: 'His resources will be investigated; however, there is in existence a principle in accordance with which I have often made judgement, and in my view is equitable in cases of those who resign their property, to the effect that, if they have acted in any way so as to defraud their creditors, the resignation will not be valid.'

The point at issue is whether a debtor could resign his property to his creditor in discharge of the debt in order to avoid a compulsory sale accompanied by public disgrace (*infamia*). See also no. 709 about concerns about ploys to defraud creditors.

P. Oxy. 2131 = *SP* no. 290 (AD 207)

679. Year fifteen of the Emperors and Caesars Lucius Septimius Severus Pius Pertinax Arabicus Adiabenicus Parthicus Maximus and Marcus Aurelius Antoninus Pius, Augusti, and Publius Septimius Geta Caesar Augustus, Phamenoth 29. Totoes, presented as having Senpetsiris as his mother, from the city of Oxyrhynchus, has stated by means of the witnesses set out below that he has taken out and collated from the rolls of collected petitions, which had been presented to his Highness the prefect Subatianus Aquila and put on display at the town of Antinoë, in the temple of Antinoüs, among which was the petition written below, and the subscription beneath; it runs as follows: Number 1009. To Subatianus Aquila, prefect of Egypt, from Totes, presented as having Senpetsiris as his mother,

from the city of Oxyrhynchus. My lord prefect, since you have an inherent sense of justice, which you offer to all mankind, and since I too have suffered injustice, I have come to you requesting that I receive justice. The issue is as follows. In the metropolis I happen to be registered in the Camp quarter and I have always styled myself by the name written above, in accordance with which I was assigned some time ago to guard duty, which I performed without fault, in addition to which throughout the year I have paid my personal taxes, living a peaceful life as a farmer. But I have been designated improperly by Heraklammon, who is the district scribe of the first tribe, as a public mule-driver of this city, which is a very burdensome duty, under another name, Sbichis son of Harmiusis and Taseus, and have been assessed by him as having property to the value of 1,200 drachmae, which I do not possess. Therefore, my lord, since I have been compelled to assume this duty as mule-driver although I entirely lack resources and am not subject to the current district scribe, and since on the contrary our quarter, the Cavalry Camp, must perform public service according to the lot drawn for the districts by his Excellency Gemius Modestus, the *epistrategos*, and since I have been illegally and wildly designated by Heraklammon, I beg you, if it seems appropriate to your most kindly good fortune, to give me a hearing against him, for it lies within your powerful position to act against those who have dared to behave unjustly and unlawfully, so that, receiving justice, I may subsequently in the coming year undertake whatever tasks I may be asked to perform. Farewell … With no prejudice in anything, his Excellency the *epistrategos* will ascertain what (truth is in) the petition. Display. (Signatures of six witnesses.)

Totoes accesses from the records a decision of the prefect relating to his earlier petition; since his complaint had been referred to the court of the *epistrategos* (see p. 120), he presumably was anxious to ensure a speedy response.

P. Oxy. 3094 (c. AD 217–218)

680. Many greetings, Eutychidas. We Serapas and Gaia greet you and offer respect to you and your brother, Herakleides, and your wives and children, before great Serapis. Be aware that after the illegal judgement that Agrippa brought in against Gaia, she approached the then prefect, Datus, requesting that she receive interest from her grant (*donatio*) for maintenance, and he ordered her in a subscription to approach the same Agrippa. And she did approach Agrippa and he accepted the adjudication. Later, after the petition had been published, and the most fortunate prefect, Iulius Basilianus, had most fortunately entered the city, I approached him by means of a

petition, setting out first the order criticized by Agrippa, and other material, and the whole petition submitted to Herakleitos, and the subscript, and the petition to Agrippa criticizing him for pronouncing a judgement contrary to the laws, and criticizing the advocate on the grounds that he did not bring to (the court's) attention rights of mine, and requesting that either the things mentioned in the report, or my own property, should be given to me. He returned the petition and through a subscript ordered me to use the process of the law ('or exercise my legal rights'). And since the subscription was ambiguous, I sent him another petition listing again everything set out previously and asked him if he wished me to follow the subscript of Herakleitos. Once again, he gave a subscript, agreeing to it (that is, the subscript issued by Herakleitos), as it ordered me to follow the process of my legal rights. Therefore, I write to you so that you too … with me … Serapammon sends greetings; we pray that you are well.

This process began with a petition from Gaia to Herakleitos (this prefect was removed from office in 215); his subscription provided the basis of the eventual settlement. Agrippa (of uncertain position and status) then gave a judgement unfavourable to Gaia though it is not clear why. Gaia petitioned the next prefect (Datus) (216), who sent her back to Agrippa. The case was eventually brought with a petition to the subsequent prefect Basilianus (217–18). He apparently told Gaia to pursue her legal rights (that is, presumably proceed on the basis of the response to the original petition), and she, not unreasonably, sought further clarification; *donatio* is a gratuitous gift; see Taubenschlag (1955), 399–401. The plaintiff is notably persistent in pursuing their case in a process that must have seemed slow-moving if not actually obstructionist. Gaia also complains of incompetent legal representation.

Lewis (1989), no. 25 (9 July AD 131)

681. In the presence of the witnesses in attendance who also attached their signatures. Iulia Crispina, daughter of Bernicianus, supervisor of the orphans of Jesus, son of Khthousion, to Babathas, daughter of Simon: 'Since the guardian of the said orphans, Besas son of Jesus, is ill and could not join me in summoning you, I now summon you in accordance with the subscription of his excellency the governor to come with me in person to Petra … to carry out immediately the legal formalities … you occupy by force properties of the said orphans which did not devolve to you, and, equally important, to attend in Hadrianic Petra until we receive a hearing. Otherwise, know that you will be liable regarding this to his excellency the governor'. Babathas, daughter of Simon, replied through her guardian, Maras son of Abdalgos, saying: 'Since you previously summoned me to

Hadrianic Petra before his excellency the governor … for his judgement until we received a hearing on your false allegation against me that I resorted to violence, and I submitted a memorandum against you to his excellency the governor, and he instructed me by his subscription to carry out the legal formalities with you in Petra, therefore I now summon you first before his excellency the governor in Rabbath-Moab in respect of the matter which I have against you, [and?] in accordance with the decision of his excellency the governor I reject the legal formalities [of your summons?]'. Iulia Crispina replied, saying: 'I have carried out the legal formalities relating to the judgement of his excellency the governor in Petra, and if you have any complaint against me, it is possible for you to come to the guardian(?) of the said orphans in the presence of the said Nepos'. Done in Maoza, Zoöra district, in the consulship of Laenas Pontianus and Marcus Antonius Rufinus seven days before the ides of July. Two copies were written.

It was written by Germanos, son of Judah.

In this double document in Greek, the scribe writes Babathas for Babatha used elsewhere. Iulia Crispina summoned Babatha to court on the grounds that allegedly she has occupied without legal right properties of the orphans of Jesus, brother of Babatha's second husband, Judah (see Lewis (1989), nos. 23–4). Babatha has entered a counterclaim. Iulia Crispina is rather mysterious but seems to be a Roman citizen who was able to carry on the legal action without the assistance of a male guardian. Goodman (1991), 172 speculates that she represented the most Romanized of the local aristocracy; see also Czajkowski (2017), chapter 4. For Babatha in court, note nos. 211; 255–7; 338.

P. Oxy. 37 = *FIRA* 3, no. 170 = *SP* no. 257 (AD 49)

682. From the records of Tiberius Claudius Pasion, *strategos*. The ninth year of Emperor Tiberius Claudius Caesar Augustus Germanicus, Pharmouthi 3, at the tribunal. Pesouris against Saraeos. Aristokles, the advocate for Pesouris, said: 'Pesouris for whom I appear, in the seventh year of the lord Tiberius Claudius Caesar, picked up from a dung-heap a male foundling named Heraklas. This he handed over to the defendant, and the agreement for nursing at this point referred to the son of Pesouris. She received her payment for the first year. When the appointed day came round for the second year she again received (payment). Her records, in which she agrees that she received the payments, show that this statement is true. As the foundling was being deprived of sustenance Pesouris took him away. After this, seizing her chance she (the defendant) charged into the

house of my client and made off with the foundling; and she wishes to get possession of the foundling, as her freeborn child. I have here first the written contract for the nursing, and second, I have the receipt for the payments for maintenance. I demand that these be endorsed'.

Saraeos said: 'I weaned my own child, and the foundling of these people was entrusted to me. I received from them in total eight *staters*. Subsequently the foundling died, some *staters* still remaining (that is, she had not earned them). Now they wish to remove my own child'. Theon (her advocate?) said: 'We have documents relating to the foundling'. The *strategos* said: 'Since from its appearance the child seems to be the son of Saraeos, if she and her husband sign a statement that the child entrusted to her by Pesouris has died, I decide that in accordance with the precept of our lord the prefect (of Egypt), if she returns the money that she received she may keep her own child'.

The *strategos* exercises jurisdiction delegated by the prefect, who had given some guidance. The issue of the child's appearance seems arbitrary, but perhaps his physical size fitted the likely age of Saraeos' son.

FIRA 3, no. 171 (AD 63)

683. Copy of the records, tenth year of Emperor Nero Claudius Caesar Augustus Germanicus, on the seventh day of the month of August, in the Great Hall, on the tribunal … on the question of citizenship of discharged soldiers.

Tuscus (prefect of Egypt): 'I have already told you that the status of each of you is neither similar nor identical. For some of you are legionaries, others cavalrymen, others auxiliaries, others sailors, and therefore all do not have the same rights. I shall deal with this matter, and I have written to the *strategoi* in charge of the nomes to ensure that the emperor's beneficence is fully maintained for each of you, in accordance with the rights of each'.

Copy of the complaint.

The legionaries met (him) on the camp road at the temple of Isis. Tuscus the prefect replied to us: 'Do not say anything outrageous. No one is troubling you. Write in a document where each one of you lives, and I will send letters to the *strategoi*, so that no one treats you with contempt'.

On the fourth day of the month of August, we presented documents to him at the camp headquarters, and he said to us: 'Surely each one of you has not presented this individually?' The legionaries replied: 'We have presented it individually'.

On the fifth day of the same month at Rhamnus Paliurus we greeted him and he in turn greeted us. On the seventh day of the same month, we greeted him in the Great Hall when he was seated on the tribunal. Tuscus said to us: 'I have already told you in the camp, and now I repeat the same message. The situation is different for legionaries, auxiliaries, and for sailors. Each of you should return home and not remain here idle'.

This group of veteran soldiers worried about their citizen rights persistently pursued the prefect, first in their military camp, then at the headquarters, when they presented documents, then at another location, and finally before his tribunal where the prefect presided with his council of advisers and announced his decision (7 August). Although he maintains the soldiers' rights, Tuscus clearly loses patience at their persistent pursuit of him.

Mitteis and Wilcken (1912), no. 80 = Crook (1995), p. 70, no. 2 (AD 85)

684. (The case involves a dispute over an alleged failure to repay a loan of wheat.)

Copy from the minutes, year four of Emperor Caesar Domitianus Augustus Germanicus, Mecheir 14 … Kephalo the advocate said: 'I require your goodwill and beg that first and essentially you display mercy since he (the client) has erred in respect of the petition. For he ought to have given you a summary(?), as you wished. We request therefore that he does not receive a flogging. This is his case. The father of his opponent borrowed from the father of my client one hundred *artabae* of wheat. This is properly an inheritance. I think that they (the opponent) should be heirs not just of the money but also pay back what is owed by those whose inheritance they shared'. Aristonikos the advocate said: 'Let him read out the evidence for this debt'. Kephalo read out a receipt of Archios, son of Polydeukes from year eleven of Tiberius Claudius. Aristonikos said: 'People from that area involved in money call him a moneylender of long-standing … my client is a man of property'.

(The prefect is now interrogating the plaintiff.) Phibion said: 'I do not know'. Septimius said: 'If you do not know it neither do we'. Kephalo said: 'This is the receipt of his father. The slave who was his agent has written underneath that he will measure it out, but it was not at all measured out in accordance with the receipt'. The prefect said: 'The first question is: is this the writing of this man's father? The second is: why did you not make this claim before?' … Aristonikos said: 'In this point you ask a good question, but I have a general point for you. The prefects have established a five-year limit for historic cases, and ten years in respect of cases involving debts. Establish therefore in what year his father took action'. Phibion said: 'This man declined the inheritance of his father and I declined that of my own father, since they were corn officials and followed the rule of the emperor'. Aristonikos said: 'If he was owed the debt according to the rule of the emperor, why did he not bring a claim then?' The prefect said: 'Even when there was a famine did you not make a claim for the wheat, if it was owed to you?' Phibion said: 'He called upon me to accept four *minae*'. Aristonikos said: 'If your claim is successful thousands of people will produce receipts of this man's father; and he (my client) is an orphan'. The prefect said to Phibion: 'You deserve to be flogged since you have brought about the arrest of a man of property and his wife. But I will indulge you, low-life as you are, and be generous. You produce a forty-year-old receipt. I grant you half this time. Come back to me after twenty years'. And he ordered that the receipt should be destroyed.

These proceedings before the prefect of Egypt concern the alleged non-repayment of a loan of wheat. The plaintiff (Phibion) has a receipt but has not followed the required procedure in the case; apart from that, the prefect and the defendant's lawyer (Aristonikos) ask why he delayed so long in making the claim; the receipt is dated probably to the reign of Claudius, over thirty years ago. The plaintiff speaks for himself and tries to confuse the issue by alleging that there had been a delay in succeeding to his father's estate, and that the defendant had offered him a small amount in lieu of the debt. The prefect is annoyed that a man of property has been disturbed and rejects the claim, being rude, aggressive, and sarcastic towards the plaintiff, though it is possible that his case was not strong.

BGU 15, col. 1 = Mitteis and Wilcken (1912), no. 393 = *SP* 246 = Crook (1995), p. 89, no. 21 (AD 194)

685. From the minute of proceedings of his Excellency Iulius Quintianus, *epistrategos*, year two of Lucius Septimius Severus Pertinax, Augustus, Mosore 2. Extract: Pekusis, son of Apunchis, was called and appeared. Diadelphos, advocate, said: 'Please call the village scribe of Neilopolis against whom our client makes complaint'. He was called but did not appear. Artemidoros, *strategos*, said: 'Neilopolis does not have a village scribe, but only elders who take it in rotation'. Diadelphos, advocate, said: 'Successive prefects have ordered that people must not be transferred from one village to another but only (perform liturgies) in their village. But because the village scribe is oppressing my client, he has named him, being a collector of money taxes in his own village, to another public service. He

beseeches you, by reading the orders (previous decisions), not to permit him to be dragged from his own village to another'. Quintianus said: 'The *strategos* will decide and will refer to me whatever he finds to be part of my sphere of action'.

Diadelphos had been poorly advised on the issue of the village scribe; furthermore, the rule was that a person already performing a public service could not be required to perform another; Diadelphos carelessly or disingenuously suggests that his client could not be asked to perform liturgies in two different villages, a point not corrected by the judge.

BGU 136 = Mitteis and Wilcken (1912), no. 86 = Crook (1995), p. 77, no. 9 (AD 135)

686. Copy of the records. From the records of Claudius Philoxenos, *archidikastes*. Year nineteen of Emperor Caesar Trajan Hadrian Augustus, Phamenoth 28, in Memphis, at the tribunal. Tapontos acting through a representative, Pasion her husband, against Phanomgeos and(?) ... eos. Berneikianos the advocate said that Petheos, the grandfather of the plaintiff and father of the opponents (in the suit), who had an eldest son of the same name who was the father of the plaintiff, had died; according to the laws he (the eldest son) took a double part of his father's estate and, having provided full details, had arranged for it to pass to his daughter who was still under guardianship. But when he died, the defendants, the girl's uncles, installed themselves in the guardianship, took everything, gave no written account of what had been taken, and left her nothing, not even maintenance. Dionysios and Harpocration, advocates, replied that the father of their opponent was a public mule-driver, and had left many things in a muddle so that they were compelled to take over the affairs, and thought it right to endure loss on this account. If their opponent wishes to enter into her father's estate, she must be responsible for their expenses. Pasion asserted strongly that the plaintiff's father was not a mule-driver. Claudius Philoxenus, official of the great Serapis, and prefect of the first cohort of Damascenes stationed in the Mouseion, priest, and *archidikastes*, said: 'The *strategos* of the nome will investigate this, and if it seems that those with Phanomgeos on these grounds have taken over the plaintiff's family property, he will ensure that it is appropriately restored to her'. I read it.

Petheos seemingly had three sons, the eldest of whom (who was father of the plaintiff, Tapontos) was entitled under Egyptian law to a double share of his father's estate (see Taubenschlag (1955), 184). His daughter Tapontos was under-age and in guardianship when her father died. Acting through her husband Pasion she therefore claimed her father's rightful share of the estate, arguing that his brothers, her uncles, had usurped her inheritance and failed to provide her even with maintenance. Her uncles counter-argued that her father left his own affairs in such a mess that they had to take over the administration of everything and incurred financial loss. The assertion that Tapontos' father was a mule-driver provoked Pasion to intervene personally, despite the presence of the advocate. The judge was a Roman citizen and former commander of a cohort and he referred the matter to the *strategos* of the nome; here the Roman officials administered local Greek legal practice.

SB, Beiheft 2, no. 3, p. 30 = Crook (1995), p. 75, no. 7 (AD 127)

687. (The *strategos* of the Polemonian district of the Arsinoite nome is appointed judge by the prefect to examine the case of Demetrios, a freedman who is suing Paulinos, an ex-Gymnasiarch, for two thousand drachmas, a loan he alleges he made to Paulinos' brother Geminos. There was a receipt although it was made out in the name of Atrenos, a friend of Demetrios. Paulinos is sued because he is now acting as guardian of the heirs of Geminos. The advocates are Ammonios representing the plaintiff, and Palamedes representing the defendant. Ammonios begins by summarizing his client's written statement and continues:) 'I will describe how Geminos got the money. My client, being a freedman and occasional agent of that man, gave him the two thousand drachmas and arranged for a record of the loan to be written out in the name of a friend of his, one Atrenos'. Palamedes, advocate of Paulinos, said: 'My client could have demolished this charge concerning the two thousand drachmas; for he is not the guardian of his brother's children. However, so that you may appreciate the wrongdoing of our opponent he is prepared to offer a defence against other charges ... '. (He then raises an allegation that the plaintiff had cheated in another transaction irrelevant to the question at issue; but the judge compels the plaintiff to give an answer. Palamedes then continues:) 'It is necessary to say this about the parties in the case, namely that Geminos was very well-off, while our opponent is without means and has no way of demonstrating how he would have been able to obtain the money (to make a loan?). Since it is accepted that he (Demetrios) was the freedman and occasional agent of Geminos, ... in respect of the current charge. As a result of this he is accused of ... and with complete lack of the essentials, it is suspected that, spending time in our house, he stole the receipt, which, when he (Geminos) was still alive and it was possible to show more clearly what had happened, he did not bring forward. But when

he died, he comes in search of the money. In addition to this I add the even more important point which shows the deceitfulness of Demetrios. For I claim that he does not even know the name of this Atrenos who drew up the receipt and cannot tell us who he is or from where … '. Demetrios said: 'It is not Atrenos but Deios, a son of Atrenos and my friend, with whom I arranged the drawing up of the receipt'. Palamedes said: 'But he does not even know who this Deios is or where he is. And the documents of Geminos are not sufficient for you, but also those of this Deios, and you have to produce them … '. Demetrios said: 'Indeed I have his receipt'. The *strategos* said: 'Read out the receipts of Geminos and Deios'. (The receipt of Geminos was then read out.) The *strategos* said to Demetrios: 'Why along with this receipt from Geminos is there not one from Deios confirming the reliability of the document?' Demetrios said: 'While Geminos was alive I trusted that he would return the money, but after his death when my opponents contested it, I had to obtain the receipt of Deios also'. Paulinos said: 'His deceit is confirmed by these receipts' (he argues that the dates are inconsistent with the date of Geminos' death). 'Let him say where this Deios is'. Demetrios said: 'My friend is away on business, in the Herakleopolis nome'. Paulinos said: 'He should come here'. The *strategos* said to Demetrios: 'How many days will it take you to produce Deios?' Demetrios said: 'In fifteen days'. Andromachos the *strategos* said to Demetrios: 'A record will be made of this statement in which you request fifteen days; I give you all of thirty days in which to produce Deios, whom you say has the receipt which you are submitting'.

Here is an example of a poor man suing a man of higher social standing for the recovery of a loan, before a *strategos* appointed to act as judge by the prefect. Crook (1995), 75 detects a hostile attitude towards the humble plaintiff; however, he has an advocate and both he and the defendant can intervene personally in the proceedings. It is notable that the defendant's advocate, Palamedes, is permitted to introduce extraneous material relating to the past conduct of the plaintiff. Then Palamedes cleverly tries to undermine the plaintiff's case by suggesting that Geminos was wealthy and unlikely to borrow, while Demetrios was poor and perhaps likely to perpetrate a fraud; furthermore, he had opportunity, since he worked in Geminos' house, to steal the receipt. The receipt had been written in the name of one Deios, though there had been confusion over this since Atrenos had originally been mentioned. Demetrios' lawyer should have noticed that discrepancy. The judge finally decides that Deios must appear in person to confirm that Geminos did give him a receipt for the alleged loan, and an adjournment of thirty days is granted; for the rhetorical skills of Palamedes, see also Edwards and Reed (2004), 66–70.

***P. Oxy.* 486**

688. Iulius Varianus, *epistrategos* of the Heptanomia and Arsinoite nome, from Dionysia, daughter of Chaeremon, mother Hermione, daughter of Chaeremon, inhabitants of the metropolis of the Oxyrhynchite nome. A dispute took place between me and Serapion, son of Mnesitheos, who, in respect of a vineyard and planted cornfields which I bought from his father as long ago as year eleven of Hadrian Caesar the lord, having paid out to his father, and a certain creditor of his, the agreed price, and having received the appropriate contract of sale, stated that I held this land as security. Claudius Quintianus, the *epistrategos*, heard the case and referred it to his excellency the prefect. Therefore, I attended at the court of the prefect, but my opponent did not take any note of this and did not appear. I gave his excellency the prefect a petition, of which I have appended a copy, setting out a full account of this case; and he sent me on to you, my lord, for adjudication of the case. Since my opponent is even now not present, and the time for sowing is upon us, and the need to repair what has been washed away by the river demands my presence, I request, if it is your will, that you allow me to sail back, and have you decide the case in the locality, so that I may obtain justice. Farewell.

This is a copy of the petition which I presented to his excellency the prefect: To his Excellency Titus Flavius Titianus, the prefect, from Dionysia, daughter of Chaeremon, her mother being Hermione, inhabitants of Oxyrhynchus: One Serapion, son of Mnesitheos, brought a charge of poisoning against my mother before Claudius Quintianus, late *epistrategos* of the Heptanomia, and made up a story that he had been cheated in respect of certain property, property that I, Dionysia, had purchased in accordance with proper contracts, having paid its price to his father when he was alive, and to his father's creditors who held the said land on conditions of *hypotheca*; he asserted that it had been registered as security … The *epistrategos* referred the entire case to your beneficence, and it happened that my mother died before the trial. But I, in accordance with the letter of the *epistrategos*, which ordered me along with Serapion to sail down to here (Alexandria), have presented myself here, whereas Serapion paid no attention to the order to sail down. Since therefore while I have been staying here, news has come to me that all my property, houses, lands, and dykes have been destroyed by the exceptional rising of the most sacred river Nile, I beg you, my lord prefect, since my opponent is not present, permit me to sail back so that I may obtain justice, and that I may not, along with the loss of my property, perish from hunger, and that I may obtain redress. Farewell. Year sixteen of Hadrian Caesar, Phaophi 12 (AD 131). 'If this is true, approach the *epistrategos*, giving him (a copy of this)'.

This case concerns a dispute over whether a legitimate sale of land had taken place or whether the land was held as security for a debt. *Hypotheca* was a pledge not handed over to the creditor. It had been referred to the court of the prefect of Egypt in Alexandria by the then *epistrategos*, but the defendant did not turn up and the matter was referred to a subsequent *epistrategos* with no recommendation. The plaintiff suffered problems by the enforced absence from her property and eventually appealed to the *epistrategos* to allow the case to be heard in her own locality. This shows the difficulties of going to law, getting the defendant into court, and dealing with delays. Serapion had seemingly confused the issue by bringing a poisoning charge against the plaintiff's mother.

CIL 3.411 = *ILS* 338 (AD 139)

689. Because of which, pious and benevolent Emperor, instruct that I am to be given a copy of the records, as your divine father agreed.

Emperor Caesar T. Aelius Hadrianus Antoninus Augustus Pius to Sextilius Acutianus. I permit you to copy the verdict of my divine father, if he said anything as verdict. I have replied. I checked. The nineteenth (section?). Transacted on 8 April, at Rome, in the consulship of Caesar Antoninus for the second time and Praesens for the second time.

(There follows a list in Greek of those who were present at the signing of the response.)

Stasimus, Dapenus, extract the verdict or decision from the document(?).

This inscription from Smyrna copies a rescript of Antoninus Pius in Latin. The opening appeal is in Greek. Acutianus was seeking a copy of a previous imperial decision, presumably to assist with a legal case or dispute. Stasimus and Dapenus probably are officials in the imperial record office and are instructed in the emperor's rescript to obtain the relevant document. The checking will have been done by the official who issued the document, and the nineteenth section(?) possibly refers to the place in the imperial archives.

Fairness of the Legal System

The Romans recognized the need for fairness and good practice in government (see pp. 160–7), and discussed the purpose of legal penalties (see pp. 297–300). But did the legal system work fairly? For the efficient operation of the machinery of justice there are two requirements: an upright judge and a process which is designed to provide the judge with the means to come to a correct decision (Kaser (1967), 143). Roman officials and magistrates did respect the supremacy of the law and the importance of access to it and attempted to curb the exploitation of power and influence (see nos. 690–6). However, several factors militated against equality before the law. Money, time, and influence were all important in taking someone to court. A person who lacked influence might find it hard to persuade a praetor or governor to listen to his suit and grant further action; he might also lack good legal advice to enable him to pursue his case most effectively. The costs of the legal process and the collection of evidence could be beyond the means of poorer citizens. A litigant could experience problems in getting to Rome and finding accommodation, sorting out luggage, and identifying a lawyer, although as Ulpian notes the praetor should take that into account (*D* 4.6.15.3). An inexperienced litigant would need some advice to make sense of the various sources of law, including imperial decisions, rescripts, and the views of jurists (see the valuable comments of Jones on the legal system (1964), 470–5). Delays and adjournments at law seem to have been common, and this would put even more pressure on impecunious litigants (see Crook (1995), 68 for delays; also, Turpin (1991)). Doubtless the better-off could spin things out by appeals and make it difficult for poorer citizens to pursue their case.

Arguably the legal system was influenced by bribery, and by the potential favour and influence (*gratia*) exerted by the wealthy and powerful, which was tacitly accepted as a factor in court cases despite the theoretical impartiality of the law (Kelly (1966), 31–68). The plaintiff side will usually have more wealth and power than the defendant side because a 'weak would-be plaintiff will not waste time in suing a defendant he knows to be stronger than himself, because he knows that, being stronger, the defendant is likely to win' (Kelly (1966), 62). Pliny congratulated his friend Calestrius Tiro (proconsul of Baetica) for the even-handedness of his administration of justice, but nevertheless welcomed his preservation of distinctions of class, since if they were muddled 'it follows that there is no greater inequality than equality' (*Letters* 9.5). Then, in certain contexts there was an ill-defined bias in favour of soldiers. There was also discrimination against women through restrictions on their appearance in court (see Grubbs (2002), 60–71), though Halbwachs (2016), 445–50 argues that juristic writings show that women who were *sui iuris* appeared in court in a large range of cases and pleaded successfully. Furthermore, judges were open to bribery or pressure or were simply incompetent. For the execution of judgements see Robinson (1997), 88; 94–5; Du Plessis (2012a), 117–18; for the importance of the personal prestige of witnesses and advocates see Meyer (2016).

It is also true that the legal system was enmeshed with the political context. The praetor was very important in civil cases, and if ambitious for higher office would need the support of powerful sponsors. This was potentially dangerous especially as there was an inherent sociological bias, in that better-off citizens had an easy avenue of approach to magistrates, who came from the same social class. In the formulary procedure before the praetor a distinction could be made at his discretion in favour of certain litigants (Garnsey (1970), 181–206). Furthermore, the praetor by virtue of his office always had considerable leeway to grant legal remedies as he thought best. If any abuse occurred there was no mechanism for checking the competence of court officials or the consistency of decisions made by the praetors.

Finally, by the time of Hadrian at least, more clear-cut discrimination had emerged that undermined any principle of equality before law (Garnsey (1970), 153–72). The *honestiores* (senators, *equites*, local town councillors) were privileged over the *humiliores* (people of lesser degree), and the dual penalty system established different penalties for these groups. This social privilege for the *honestiores* came to be even more important than possession of Roman citizenship. This is related to the question of appeal to the emperor previously available to Roman citizens against trial on a capital offence by a magistrate, and later against a conviction. The grant of universal citizenship by Caracalla made this more difficult because of the number of potential litigants, and appeal in first instance seems to have been removed for *humiliores* (Jones (1960), 64–5; this volume nos. 711–14). For a survey of social status and legal privilege, see Garnsey (1974), Taylor (2016), and for the importance of status in legal penalties, Bauman (1996), 124–40.

With specific reference to the legal process in Egypt, Kelly (2011, 34–8) has noted that the evidence suggests that a limited number of judgements was successfully enforced. Here too the system was complicated, with many opportunities for delays and abuse; it was subject to corruption and was expensive for the poor; furthermore, state officials perhaps tended to get involved with more significant types of case such as property and business interests. In ideological terms the better-off probably identified more with Rome and her officials, and expected more from them (see Kelly (2011), chapter 4, especially 159 for the social profile of petitioners in Egypt, with a predominance of the better-off). However, arguments between individuals could threaten social order, and in this context the process of petition and litigation might help the informal resolution of disputes by giving to individuals in dispute an example of a peaceful framework for resolution without going to law (see no. 710). Officials would often respond appropriately to this, and indeed they perhaps thought that the administration of justice was a moral action that involved doing what was just (as suggested by Kelly (2011), 114). This plays into the Roman attitude to good government.

Despite the potential problems for a litigant of lower social standing, other factors redressed the balance to some extent. In the provinces the system by which the governor toured his province on an annual judicial circuit visiting the assize centres probably brought some benefits (see Burton (1975)); it helped Roman officials to bring justice throughout the province, although it meant that litigants had to travel potentially large distances to get a hearing. As probably no order of hearing cases was announced the litigants might have to wait (see also no. 688). It is possible that the *cognitio* system was a little more helpful to poorer citizens in that the magistrate was in control of the whole procedure including execution of judgement; for the assize districts in Phrygia, see Kantor (2013), 153–6; opportunities for justice for the local population, Kantor (2013), 158–62.

Social pressure and the unwillingness of the upper classes to be embarrassed might cause them to comply with the law. Naturally the praetor would tend to enforce respect for his own jurisdictional authority. Furthermore, patrons were obliged to extend help and advice to their clients. In cases where documentary evidence was important, time was given to consult the archives and records. The law did take some account of the disabled (see no. 640; Gardner (1993), 155; Gaius, *Institutes* 3.105; *D* 3.1.1.3–4). As already noted, evidence suggests representation in court even for parties of modest means (Crook (1995), 62–9), and people of very limited status vigorously asserted their rights; a *strategos* in Egypt (AD 208–10) notes that 1,804 petitions were submitted to the prefect during the judicial *conventus* at a single town in just over two days (*P. Yale* 1.61). The record of many court cases shows that litigants thought that it was worthwhile putting their case and indeed employing an advocate; presumably they thought that they had a chance of obtaining a favourable response. Now, an advocate did not necessarily have significant legal knowledge, and while the services of a jurist would be expensive, *tabelliones* were available as a cheaper source of advice on legal documents and probably wider courtroom issues. Furthermore, it is worth emphasizing that for the litigant court proceedings were often held in public spaces, relevant documentary evidence was read out, and witnesses were examined orally (Kelly (2011), 171); the transparency of proceedings offered some hope of fairness. However, there was still a great deal of uncertainty about a legal process that continued to leave much to the initiative of the individual. On the position of the litigant in court see in general Bablitz (2007), 71–88; (2011), 321–2.

Finally, it was theoretically open to all citizens to approach the emperor with legal questions. In the main, despite all the brutalities of autocracy, emperors preserved a degree of justice; Trajan famously said in a rescript that no one should be condemned on the basis of suspicions, and it was better to let a guilty man's crime go unpunished than to condemn an innocent man (*D* 48.19.5). For a useful summary of the overall quality of justice see Johnston (1999), 122–32.

Cicero, *Pro Caecina* 70–2

690. Therefore it is essential that you arrive at the opinion that nothing in the state must be more carefully preserved than the law. For if this is removed there is no way by which an individual can discover what is his and what belongs to someone else; there is nothing which can be fair to everyone and invariable for everyone. And so in routine disputes and court cases, when the question is whether something is a fact or not, or whether a claim is true or false, it often comes about that a false witness is suborned, or false documents lodged, and on occasion under the guise of honest and fair dealing, an honest juror is deceived or the opportunity given to a dishonest juror to make it seem that he was persuaded by the witness and the documents, when in fact he deliberately brought in a dishonest verdict. Gentlemen, there is nothing like this in law, no false documents, no dishonest witness; indeed, even excessive influence, which thoroughly pervades public life, only in this area alone has no impact. For it has no way in which it can get at a juror, or even lift a finger. For a man who has more presumption than self-respect can say to a juror: 'Bring in a verdict that this took place, or never took place; believe this witness; accept these documents'. But he cannot say: 'Decide that a will has not been broken by the subsequent birth of a son to the testator; decide that a woman can make a binding promise without the permission of her trustee'. Neither the power nor the influence of any man can change this kind of thing. Furthermore, to demonstrate how lofty and untouchable the law is, a juror in a case of this kind cannot be corrupted even by money.

In this speech defending Caecina on the question of whether he was entitled to receive an inheritance, Cicero distinguished issues of fact (always capable of distortion) from issues of law, which depend on established rules and cannot be overturned by influence. Cicero is here thinking of law in the abstract, theoretically immune to corruption, which is however at risk from the facts to which it must be applied, since they can be subject to manipulation; see Kelly (1966), 32–3.

Suetonius, *Tiberius* 33

691. At first, he (Tiberius) intervened only to prevent any wrongful actions. Therefore, he rescinded some decisions of the senate, and sometimes offered himself to magistrates as an adviser when they were holding judicial hearings, by sitting beside them or opposite them at the other end of the platform. And if there was a rumour that any of the defendants were escaping as a result of influence, he would suddenly appear, either from the floor or the judge's platform, and give the jurors advice about the laws, their oath, and the nature of the offence which they were considering. Furthermore, he undertook to correct public morals if they were being corrupted by laziness or bad practice.

Tiberius understood the potential threat of *gratia* (influence) and was prepared to intervene personally. For Tiberius and the law, see no. 721.

D 48.3.6 (Marcianus, *Public Jurisdiction*, Book 2)

692. The divine Hadrian replied to this effect to Iulius Secundus, and there are other similar responses stating that no general credence should be given to the letters of those who send people to the governor as if they have already been condemned. The same instruction was issued concerning *eirenarchs* because it had been discovered that not all of them had written their reports with honest intentions. There is a section from the imperial instructions, which the divine Pius when he was governor of Asia promulgated through his edict, namely that *eirenarchs*, when they arrested robbers, should interrogate them about their associates and those who harboured them, and should incorporate their interrogations in their letters, seal them, and send them for the legal enquiry of the magistrate. Therefore, those who are sent (to court) with the written report (of their questioning) should be tried anew, even if they have been sent along with the letters or even accompanied by the *eirenarchs*. The divine Pius and other emperors issued rescripts to this effect, that even in respect of those who are recorded as being on the wanted list, they should not be treated as if they had already been condemned but tried again from the beginning, if there is anyone to

bring a case against them. Therefore, when someone conducts an enquiry, he must order the *eirenarch* to come forward and explain what he wrote; he should be congratulated if he has done this diligently and faithfully. But if he has acted carelessly and with insufficiently careful analysis, the judge should merely report that the *eirenarch*'s report was unsatisfactory. But if he discovers that his interrogation was improperly conducted or that he reported as said words that were not said, he should punish him to set an example, so that someone else does not attempt anything similar in the future.

Antoninus Pius had been proconsul of Asia 135–6. *Eirenarchs* were local officials with limited responsibilities for maintaining public order; they could pursue bandits and outlaws and conduct investigations and interrogations; the government at least tried to prevent them from exceeding their authority (see Magie (1950), 647 and n. 46). For civil police forces in the eastern provinces see Furhmann (2012), 66–75; in Egypt 75–82.

Smallwood (1967), no. 391, col. ii, Chapter 8

693. In general I order that whenever a prefect has already decided to dismiss a case brought before him, it is not to be brought again for assessment at audit. And if two prefects have been of the same mind, a state accountant who brings up the same matters for audit is also to be punished, seeing that he does nothing else than reserve for himself and the other civil officials a pretext for enrichment. Many persons, in fact, have decided rather to abandon their private possessions, because they have expended more than their value through the same matters being brought to judgement at each audit.

This edict of Tiberius Iulius Alexander, prefect of Egypt in AD 68, attempts to prevent minor government officials from harassing citizens and creating unnecessary delays; the accountants mentioned here were responsible for assessing and collecting the tax of a nome; taxpayers would find it easier to pay up or even cede their property rather than to face the legal costs of contesting a tax demand, with adjournments and reopening of cases.

D 2.11.1 (Gaius, *Provincial Edict*, Book 1)

694. (In respect of appearance in court) The praetor instructs that one day is to be allowed for every twenty miles (the litigant has to travel), and counts also the day on which the promise to appear was made, and the day on which he is obliged to appear in court. For certainly this calculation of journey time is not burdensome for either litigant.

For the requirement to appear in court, see nos. 617–23.

D 5.1.79.1 (Ulpian, *Duties of a Proconsul*, Book 5)

695. Governors normally may state their views when judges are in doubt about the law but should not offer advice if the judges consult them about the facts of the case; instead, they should instruct them to announce their verdict in line with their oath. For these circumstances sometimes cause suspicion and provide opportunity for partiality and bribery.

Suetonius, *Augustus* 32.2

696. He (Augustus) deleted the names of those who had been defendants for a long period and from whose embarrassment nothing was to be gained except the delight of their enemies, laying down that if anyone wished to renew the accusation, he would be liable for the same penalty.

Augustus strikes off the records pending cases where delay was used to humiliate an opponent who would be formally declared a *reus* (defendant); if the charge was renewed and failed the accuser would suffer the same penalty as the defendant would have faced.

Cost

There is little evidence for the cost of lawyers' fees apart from anecdotal evidence about certain individuals or famous incidents (see nos. 642–6). But Haensch (2015), especially 265–71, has argued that there were legal fees of various kinds in the first three centuries of the empire. Small-time lawyers in the provinces will have charged much less than the great men in Rome, and possibly a poor man could have afforded some kind of representation; evidence from papyri shows that lawyers were often employed in routine local disputes. There will have been additional costs for documents and the copying of court records; see also Segni, Patrich and Holum (2003). In the late third century Diocletian's Edict of Maximum Prices placed a limit of one thousand denarii on an advocate's fee for pleading a case.

P. Oxy. 1654 (c. AD 150?)

697. Account of outgoings: Mesore 3, to notaries for writing two memoranda, sixteen obols, papyrus for these, four obols. The fourth, for another papyrus, purchased for cutting up, four drachmae, to an official of the prefect's library, ten obols. The fifth, to notaries of the marketplace,

referred to as …, for examining the memoranda of the *archidikastes*, four obols. The sixth, one notary, four memoranda of Munatius Felix …, and for an extract … .

In this record of expenditure, it is not clear if the notaries involved served in a public or private capacity. Munatius Felix was prefect of Egypt in AD 150–1, which may give a date for the papyrus.

Influence, Bribery, and Sharp Practice

Fronto, *Ad Amicos* 1.1 = Haines (Loeb), vol. 1, p. 282

698. The custom of commending an individual is said to have originated in goodwill, when someone wished to show a friend to another friend and have him welcomed. Gradually from there this custom developed so that it did not seem improper, even in respect of those who were involved in a public or private court case, to give recommendations to judges themselves or to those who advised the court, unless the case should be clearly outrageous, not, in my view, with the object of undermining the fairness of the judge or obstructing an honest verdict. But in court cases the practice was established over a long period that, when the case was completed, a character witness should be brought forward, who could give his opinion of the defendant and set out his own view in good faith. These letters of commendation seem to perform the role of the speech in praise of a man's character.

Why do I have this introduction going back so far into the past? It is so that you do not think that I have given too little consideration to your standing and authority by commending my good friend Cornelianus Sulpicius, who very soon will be speaking before you. But, as I said, on the precedent of long-accepted practice I have taken the liberty of praising my friend to you. (There follows a list of Sulpicius' qualities.) Therefore, to the limits of my ability I ask that you support my friend as he pleads his case.

In this letter to Claudius Severus, Fronto speaks for his friend Sulpicius Cornelianus who was soon to plead a case before Severus. Even though Fronto expresses himself very circumspectly, it suggests that influence is being brought to bear to give Sulpicius a favourable hearing; see Kelly (1966), 58–61, who refers to 'solicitation of judicial favour'; Champlin (1980), 29–30; for Fronto the lawyer see Champlin (1980), 60–78. Garnsey (1970), 207–18 assesses the position of a judge in the face of *potentia* (power), leading to *gratia* (influence) and excessive favour.

Petronius, *Satyricon* 13–14

699. But what shall we do? By what legal process shall we lay claim to our property?

... I was against any underhand methods but thought that we should contest it openly under the civil law, so that if they refused to return the property of another to the rightful owner, they should be faced with an interdict.

But Ascyltus was afraid of the law: 'No one knows us in this place', he said, 'or who will believe what we say? I should certainly prefer to buy the thing although it is ours, as we are well aware, and recover our treasure at small expense, rather than get involved in a perilous lawsuit'.

'Of what use are laws where money alone is in control and where poverty can never triumph? The very people who mock the times by carrying the Cynic's begging pouch have sometimes even sold the truth for money. Therefore, a lawsuit is nothing unless a public auction, and the equestrian who sits on the jury in the case, is giving his approval to something that has been bought'.

Petronius in his novel portrays Encolpius and Ascyltus facing the problem of obtaining justice for the theft of property in an unfamiliar town where they cannot be certain of a fair hearing; there will of course be a degree of satirical exaggeration, but Petronius must be relating what was credible to his audience. Apuleius in his novel (*Metamorphoses* or *Golden Ass*) written in the second century describes the same kind of problem in obtaining redress against a socially much more powerful adversary (no. 700). This fiction can help illustrate well-known problems of law enforcement; see Summers (1970).

Apuleius, *Metamorphoses* 9.35–6

700. For he (the owner of a farm) had three adult sons who had been educated in literature and endowed with good manners, and of whom he was extremely proud. These young men had a long-standing friendship with a poor man who owned a small cottage. But a powerful neighbour, who was both rich and young, owned extensive and prosperous lands bordering on the cottage. He put to ill-use the reputation of his ancestors, became powerful through gangs, and easily got what he wanted in the state. He attacked the poor farm of his humble neighbour like an enemy, killing the sheep, driving away the cattle, tearing up the crops that were not yet ripe. When he had robbed him of the fruits of his careful labours, he longed to remove him from the very land, and starting a false argument about

boundaries, he claimed all the land for himself. Then the farmer, who was usually diffident, but had now been robbed through the greed of a rich man, in trepidation called together many of his friends to mark out the boundaries in order to preserve enough of his ancestral land at least for his own tomb. Among this group were the three brothers who brought as much limited assistance as they could for the misfortunes of their friend. However, that madman was not in the least intimidated or even deterred by the presence of so many citizens into stopping his violent aggression, though he did moderate his language. When they approached him gently and smoothed over his aggressive habits with kind words, suddenly making a most sacred oath and swearing on his own life and that of his family, he asserted that the presence of so many people as mediators had no weight with him, and that he would have his slaves grab the neighbour by the ears and immediately throw him out of his cottage and cart him off far away. This utterance caused great anger among all those who heard it. Then one of the three brothers replied without hesitation and rather boldly that it was pointless to have such confidence in his wealth and to make threats with overbearing arrogance, since moreover the poor had the generous defence of the law and could make their claim in defiance of the aggression of the rich. Like oil on flames or sulphur on a fire, or the whip of a Fury, these words acted as a spur to this man's ferocity. Out of his mind and now completely insane he shouted that they should go and hang themselves along with all their laws and ordered that the huge wild dogs used on his estates by the shepherds, and which often fed on abandoned carcases in the fields and had been reared to take bites out of passing travellers, should be let loose and urged to attack and kill them.

For Apuleius, see also nos. 24; 596–7 for his escapades in court. The *Metamorphoses* or *The Golden Ass* is a novel in which Lucius, changed into an ass by witchcraft, undergoes numerous adventures; many stories with some relation to contemporary life appear in the text.

Ovid, *Amores* 1.10.37–40

701. It is not right for witnesses to be bribed to sell perjured testimony, and it is not right for judges chosen from the panel to take bribes; it is outrageous that the lawyer representing the unfortunate defendants has been bribed, and that a disgraceful court should make a large profit.

For Ovid, see p. 479. The *Amores* are elegiac poems about the problems of lovers, written probably after 16 BC. Perhaps this is another exaggerated criticism of corrupt judges and lawyers, but Ovid himself had been a judge (no. 633); for the importance of wealth and standing see *Amores* 3.8.55–6.

Pliny, *Letters* 1.18

702. I had undertaken the case of Junius Pastor, when there came to me in a dream my mother-in-law who on her knees begged me not to take the case. Indeed, I was a very young man, and I was about to plead the case before the Centumviral Court against men who were politically very powerful, and indeed some were friends of the emperor. Any one of these considerations could have undermined my determination after such a sad dream.

Pliny illustrates the problem of pleading against the interests of the powerful. He is here responding to a letter from Suetonius asking him to seek an adjournment in a case they were conducting since he had had an alarming dream; their opponent may not have thought that this was a compelling reason for delay.

Lucian, *The False Prophet* 57

703. From then on it was total war between us, and I strained every nerve to get my revenge. I had not liked him much even before he tried to murder me, for he always struck me as a most unpleasant character, but now I really set about exposing him. I had plenty of support, especially from scientists of the school of Timocrates. But Avitus, who was then the governor of Bithynia and Pontus, practically implored me to call it off. He said that his friendship with Rutilianus would make it impossible for him to punish Alexander, even if his guilt were manifest. This put an end to the venture, and I gave it up. It was obviously not the moment to stick my neck out when I had to contend with so much prejudice on the bench.

Lucian (see p. 479) had attempted to expose Alexander who had established a fake oracle at Abonoteichos. The governor of Bithynia and Pontus was Lucius Lollianus Avitus (163–5), and the influential person likely to stop him taking any action was Mummius Sisenna Rutilianus (consul 146) who was Alexander's father-in-law.

Martial, *Epigrams* 2.32

704. I have a suit with Balbus, but you do not want to offend Balbus, Ponticus. I also have a suit with Licinus, and he also is a great man. My neighbour Patrobas is often intruding on my little field, but you are afraid to appear against a freedman of the emperor. Laronia keeps my slave and denies it; you reply: 'she is a childless, rich, old widow'. Believe me it is pointless to expect service from a man who is in service; the man who wants to be my master must be free.

In Martial's satirical view the influence of the powerful could also affect more humble legal cases; lawyers subject to many influences were like slaves under obligation to others, which was likely to undermine their presentation of a case.

Seneca, *Controversiae* 10.1.2; 7

705. When are we not contaminated by this wealth? He says: 'Bring an accusation'. Am I, a poor man, to accuse a rich man, or while in mourning accuse a candidate for office? I am not permitted to walk according to my own judgement. He summons me to court: 'Pursue me as defendant; deliver your speech'. Who would dare to accuse the man saying this? He says: 'Why do you pursue me?' It is as if the poor follow one road, the rich another. (7) He came with a crowd of clients and hangers-on, and against my poverty deployed his entire lordly court. 'Why do you not accuse me and prosecute me?' He just about prevented himself from saying: 'What would I not dare to do to you as my accuser, I who arranged for the killing of the man who was merely involved in litigation with me?'

Seneca suggests the influence of the rich in court in this case where a poor man tries to find justice for his murdered father; the son, dressed in mourning, had followed the alleged perpetrator through Rome; Kelly (1966), 49–50 emphasizes that the *Controversiae* contain some ideas that were taken for granted by the audience. In this case, as presented by Seneca, the poor man convinces people that the powerful man is a murderer.

D 4.3.11.1 (Ulpian, *Edict*, Book 11)

706. An action for deceit (*dolus*) should not be granted to certain people, such as children or freedmen against their parents or patrons, since it is defamatory. And it will not be granted to a person of low degree against a man of superior status, for example, to a plebeian against a man of consular rank of established prestige, or to decadent spendthrift against a man of moderate lifestyle. This is also the view of Labeo.

There is a clear prejudice here against people of low degree or allegedly disreputable morals when they appear in court against someone of higher social status. For the formal division of the populace into those of higher and lower standing, see p. 40, and nos. 711–14.

Juvenal, *Satires* 16.35–50

707. Let us now consider still more benefits of military service. If some dishonest neighbour occupies a valley or meadow of my ancestral estate,

and digs up the boundary stone marking the midpoint of the boundary, where I made offerings annually with a cake and a bowl of pulses, or if a debtor refuses to return the money I lent him, claiming that with a forged signature the receipt is useless, I will have to wait since my suit will be assigned the session crowded with the whole population. And even then, I must endure a thousand annoyances and a thousand delays. It often happens that the courtroom is ready, one lawyer is taking off his cloak, and the other has gone out to urinate, and then there is an adjournment. Legal battles are fought out slowly. But the man with weapons and a military uniform will be granted a hearing for his case when it suits him, and their property is not worn away by the blockages of an endless legal process.

This is an interesting evocation of some typical courtroom delays which a soldier and probably people of means could avoid; for the privileged position of soldiers in court, see Campbell (1984), 253–64.

Martial, *Epigrams* 7.65

708. Gargilianus, one lawsuit is wearing you down through the cold of twenty winters in three courts. Poor demented man! Who would go to law for twenty years in a case he might lose?

P. Oxy. 237, col. viii, 7–18 (AD 186)

709. The twenty-second year of the divine Hadrian, Mecheir 20. Copy of a decree. Proclamation of Valerius Eudaemon, prefect of Egypt. In accordance with a most distinguished precedent, the decision of his Excellency Mamertinus, and having myself observed that many debtors when payment is demanded refuse to honour the just demands of the creditors, but by threatening to bring more serious charges attempt either to avoid paying at all, or to postpone payment. Some expect to terrify their creditors, who, worried about the risk, will therefore settle for less, while others think that through the threat of legal action the creditors will renounce their claims. I proclaim that they must desist from such outrageous behaviour and pay what they owe or employ negotiation with those who have just demands. If any person when an action for recovery of debt is lodged against him, does not immediately deny that there is a debt, that is, does not immediately declare that the documents are forged, and write that he will bring an accusation, but at a later date attempts to bring a charge on the basis of forged documents, or false testimony or fraud, he will receive no advantage

from a ploy of this kind, but will be compelled to pay immediately what he owes. Otherwise, he must put the money in a deposit so that what he owes may be recovered, and then, when the suit for the money has been completed, if he is confident in the proof of his accusation, he can enter on the more serious legal case. And even then, he will not be free of his obligations, but is liable to the legal penalties.

This is part of a longer papyrus concerning a petition (in AD 186) of one Dionysia against her father in a long-running financial dispute, and an attempt by her father to force her separation from her husband (see no. 677). In support she cites precedents and decisions by prefects, including in this extract a decision of the prefect Valerius Eudaemon to prevent the evasion of a legal judgement on the payment of money by bringing fresh charges. This illustrates one example of the problems and sharp practice that might face litigants even if they thought that they had a watertight case.

P. Oxy. 2996 with H.C. Youtie *ZPE* 6 (1970), 106–8

710. Anthestianos to Psois the potter, greetings. Recently I sent Sarapammon to you again so that you would finally sort out your records, which previously on several occasions you have failed to do, and pay back what you owe for the remaining price of the chaff and for the hire of animals and for the transportation of this chaff and also of earth, for the current sum of seven hundred drachmas, also … *artabas* of wheat, which you received from Horion the potter … the first year … and another … drachmas of wine … four *chous*. Then, blocking the work again, you departed and paid no attention to Sarapammon, but said to him: 'Work with me now since I have come from abroad with my pitch', (from which) you will have the proof (of my knowledge of what you are up to). Therefore, I had to ask my friend Dionysios to demand from you what you owe, or for you to give it to him in jars. I also wrote to Sarapammon to go to you again in order that you do not persist in this insolent aggression, ignoring my demand and making excuses. But you should comply in every respect, lest I take other steps against you and summon you through the guardian of the law.

Anthestianus is reluctant to go to law except as a last resource to enforce his legal rights for the repayment of a debt, but nevertheless was influenced by perceived judicial practice and due process in how he attempted to settle his dispute; see Kelly (2011), 260. On Youtie's interpretation, Anthestianus quotes the comments of Psois to Sarapammon to show that he is following matters closely and will not be deceived by evasions.

Social Status and Penalties

D 47.14.1.3 (Ulpian, *Duties of a Proconsul*, Book 8)

711. Although Hadrian had laid down the penalty of being sent to the mines, or public works, or execution by the sword, however those who have higher status (*honestiores*) should not suffer these penalties but should be exiled or lose their rank.

See also *D* 48.8.3.5: 'People of lower rank are normally thrown to the beasts, but those of higher station are deported to an island'.

Pauli Sententiae 5.23.1

712. The Cornelian law established the penalty of deportation for the person who killed a man and for that purpose and for committing theft had been armed with a weapon, and established the death penalty for the person who possessed, sold, or prepared poison for the purpose of murdering someone, or provided false testimony in order to bring about someone's death. It was laid down that for all these crimes the death penalty should apply to those of higher rank (*honestiores*), while members of the lower orders (*humiliores*) should be crucified or thrown to the beasts.

For the *lex Cornelia* see pp. 292; 302; no. 549.

D 48.19.9.11–12 (Ulpian, *On the Duties of a Proconsul*, Book 10)

713. These are the penalties that are normally inflicted. But it must be recognized that there are distinctions in the penalties, and the same penalties cannot be inflicted on everyone. For in the first place decurions cannot be condemned to the mines, or to any mining work, or to the gallows, or to be burned alive. But if it has come about that they have incurred a sentence of this kind, they will have to be set free. But that cannot be done by the person who pronounced the sentence; instead, he must refer the matter to the emperor so that by his authority the penalty may be altered, or the man set free. (12) The parents and children of decurions are in the same situation.

Hadrian had established that decurions should not suffer capital punishment unless they had murdered a parent, *D* 48.19.15 (Venuleius Saturninus, *Duties of a Proconsul*, book 1).

CJ 9.41.11 (AD 290)

714. Diocletian and Maximianus Augusti to Boethus. The divine Marcus Aurelius decided that the descendants of the most eminent and distinguished men down to the degree of great-grandchildren should not be subjected to the punishments or torture inflicted on the lower orders, provided that there is no stain on the honour of children of a closer degree through whom that privilege has been transmitted to their descendants. That very learned man, Domitius Ulpianus, in his books dealing with public law states for the information of future generations that this rule should also be applied to decurions and their children.

This confirms the privileged status of the *honestiores* down to the third generation and that this included decurions; interestingly the emperors appeal to the authority of Ulpian.

CHAPTER 8

The Emperor and the Law

Introduction

The triumvirs Antony, Lepidus, and Octavian had received appropriately voted legal powers for a limited period, though of course no one was in a position to challenge their authority. Once secure in power, Augustus did not want to rule merely as victor in a civil war and commander of a now irresistible army. He brought the gift of peace, and with that the idea of stability and the importance of the rule of law. Therefore in 28 BC he permitted his colleague as consul (Marcus Agrippa) to share the *fasces* and swore the traditional oath that during his year of office he had preserved the state from harm (Dio 53.1). Dio's evidence is supported by the minting of a coin in 28 which proclaimed the restoration of laws and rights (*leges et iura*) to the Roman people (Rich and Williams (1999)). Thereafter Augustus arranged his political control along lines suitable to him but also acceptable to the upper classes, who were still concerned with appearances. He adopted offices and powers that could be represented as being within the confines of traditional office-holding, though transformed for his own benefit. He was consul each year from 31 BC to 23 BC, and in 27 the senate and people voted him the administration of a large *provincia*, which contained several territorial provinces, and the command of the army in them; then in 23 BC he received proconsular *imperium* (declared to be *maius*, that is, greater than of any other provincial governor), and the power of a tribune. In his government he was careful to work with the senate and to enhance its prestige while curtailing its political power. The government loyalist Velleius Paterculus describes an ideal community in which the rule of law was prevalent under the protection of a benevolent first citizen who brought majesty to the senate while the courts and magistrates operated as usual; you might indeed say that the traditional framework of the state (*res publica*) had been restored (2.89). In this context it was entirely in character for Augustus, before presenting himself for election as *pontifex maximus*, to wait for the death in 12 BC of the present incumbent, his disgraced former ally Lepidus (*Res Gestae* 10.2). He then celebrated the huge influx of loyal citizens who came into Rome to vote for him.

The legal process of the jury courts (*iudicia publica* or *quaestiones*) continued for serious criminal cases. The praetor continued to be the hinge round which civil case procedure revolved, while other magistrates like the consuls potentially had a role in jurisdiction. Augustus inserted himself into this framework. It is difficult to say to what extent he took the initiative and how far development occurred because individuals asked him to undertake certain actions or posed questions on legal issues to which he felt obliged to make a response. Because of his influence (*auctoritas*) his view would generally be accepted. He began to hear both civil and capital cases brought to his attention, and then other appeals. Furthermore, Augustus was notable as a lawmaker, sponsoring or introducing statutes named after him (*leges Iuliae*).

Once Augustus had gone down this route, his successor Tiberius could hardly avoid following. In any case he regarded most of Augustus' policies as precepts. Indeed, Tiberius emphasized the importance of the law as a counterpoint to the executive and imperial authority (no. 721), and in this respect even won the grudging respect of the hostile Tacitus. Thereafter most emperors at least professed the importance of the law and their willingness to abide by it. This might seem unconvincing, but it at least provided a framework where the conduct of administrators could be guided by equitable assessment and legality. Emperors often worked assiduously to facilitate the operation of the law by hearing cases or providing a response to legal questions. Hadrian, assisted by a council of jurists, was conscientious in adjudication, arranged for the codification of the praetor's edict, appointed four men of consular rank to administer justice, and redefined the emperor's relation with jurists; see Tuori (2016), 234 and this volume, p. 419. Dio describes Septimius Severus' typical daily routine in time of peace as follows: 'He usually was engaged on something before dawn, and then went for a walk while speaking and hearing about the affairs of the empire. Then he held court if there was no substantial festival, and his practice in this was very good in that he allowed sufficient time to the litigants and extended full freedom of speech to those of us who advised him. He used to hear cases until noon and after that he rode, in so far as he was able, and after that he took some kind of gymnastic exercise and had a bath' (76.17); for the imperial administration of justice in the Severan period, see Daalder (2019), especially 62–6.

Against this background, in which emperors held traditional powers and were often enmeshed in legal procedures, we must set the emperor in his role as one who held office by a statute formally voted by senate and people. This idea certainly goes back to the manoeuvres of Augustus, who sought senatorial approval in 27 BC for his formal administrative responsibilities, and remained significant despite the importance in political terms of acceptance by the praetorian guard and the rest of the army. In the chaotic accession of Claudius after the murder of Caligula, although he had the crucial support of the praetorians, he negotiated with the senate for his formal acceptance (Suetonius, *Claudius* 10–11; Levick (1990), 29–39). Nero too had the rapid endorsement of the praetorians but also the senate's support (Tacitus, *Annals* 12.69). Even in the aftermath of civil war the conventions were preserved, as we see from the careful drafting of the law concerning Vespasian's power (no. 719). This was a combination of lawful rights and prerogatives as far as possible based on respectable precedents from previous emperors going back to Augustus (but excluding the disgraced Caligula and Nero). However, it came to be accepted that the emperor was also free from the restriction of the laws (*legibus solutus* – nos. 722–3). This went beyond the caution of Augustus, who had been exempt only from certain laws, but emperors continued to voice respect for the law and in many ways seemed to abide by this principle (for example, no. 721).

The emperor, receiving his power by statute, could himself make law or change administrative procedures. An imperial decision of this nature was a *constitutio*, but the emperor's decisions could take different forms: an edict (*edictum*), which was a direct intervention and a statement usually (though not always) of general relevance to the entire empire; a formal letter (*epistula*) was usually addressed to a specific imperial official, or a group of officials, or a community, which often inscribed it because it was of direct benefit to them. These formal letters were organized by the emperor's correspondence secretary (*ab epistulis*). An emperor could also intervene by making a speech expressing a wish for action, which could pave the way for legal regulations, or by using informal pressure or influence in order to persuade officials responsible for jurisdiction, notably the praetors, to follow a certain course of action, as seems to have happened under Augustus in the case of the development of *fideicommissa* (no. 740); for a valuable collection of imperial constitutions in Greek, see Oliver (1989); Anastasiades and Souris (2000). The fundamental collection of imperial legislation remains that of Gualandi (1963).

In general, emperors were more often passive and waited for legal issues to be brought to them, either in the first instance or on appeal, and then decided whether they wished to respond. The emperor gave judgement in public in an auditorium or location of his own choosing; on these occasions he sometimes heard embassies from cities seeking help or confirmation of privileges; he might have to settle disputes between communities, which would mean hearing the various contending parties. But he would also encounter legal cases involving individuals who had acquired an avenue of approach. He could of course consult whomever he wished, but he was not obliged to do so. The verdict or decision was announced verbally by the emperor as a *decretum.* In these hearings before the emperor, it is sometimes difficult to distinguish between the emperor as benevolent helper of distressed communities, and as judge. See Bablitz (2007), 34–9 for the location of the emperor's court; for a good summary of the emperor's legal role, see Honoré (1981), 1–23.

Apart from hearings in the first instance, throughout the imperial period appeals came from courts of provincial governors or magistrates in Rome to the emperor and his advisers. The right to appeal for Roman citizens was contained in the provisions of the *lex Iulia de vi publica* which laid down a capital charge against a governor who punished or tortured a citizen in contravention of their right of appeal (*provocatio*). This appeal had formerly been to the people, but now became *appellatio ad Caesarem* (*Pauli Sententiae* 5.26.1). The basis for this may have been the grant to Augustus in 30 BC of the powers of a tribune for life, enabling him to bring assistance to Roman citizens in Rome, to judge on appeal, and cast the vote of Athena in all trials (Dio 51.19.6). Augustus was apparently empowered to hear appeals and to exercise a prerogative of mercy (or not) when a jury had condemned on a capital charge. The *lex Iulia de vi publica* suggests that Augustus' ability to hear appeals extended throughout the empire, and this aspect may have been established when Augustus' tenure of the powers of a tribune was confirmed or strengthened in 23 BC (Dio 53.32.5). See Jones (1960), 86–98; Lintott (1993), 116–18; (2015), 314–17 for the Augustan reform of the courts. By the late second century the emergence of the distinction between *honestiores* (senators, *equites*, and local councillors) and *humiliores* (the lower orders) tended to restrict the availability of appeal for lower classes (see p. 398).

A very common practice was the submission of petitions (*libelli*) in writing by private individuals on legal issues; the emperor wrote a response at the end and signed it (*subscriptio*) for return with the petition; this was also known as a rescript. The petitioner had to hand over the *libellus* or have a family relation do it; a town or village might send an embassy to deliver it (see no. 274). Sirks (2001, 129) thinks that the rescript system developed out of the morning salutation (*salutatio*) of clients at which requests could be presented to their patron. The emperor's response would be displayed in public for a time so that the petitioner could read it and make his own copy, but from the second century it is possible that the petitioner received an attested copy while the original remained in the imperial archives (Sirks (2001), 125–8).

The range of queries that came to the emperor is important for the light they shed on social and legal issues, and the relationship between the state (as represented by the emperor) and subjects. It was an important part of imperial ideology that an emperor should be accessible to his subjects and seek to redress grievances, and rescripts were part of this ideal; see Ando (2000), 362–6; 378–9; and n. 184. We also need to bear in mind the context and organization of the various imperial responses, which required record-keeping, the management and supply of information, and numerous officials. Emperors were generally not lawyers, and the range of legal material with which they had to deal was such that they cannot possibly have dealt with all or most of it personally. But what was the contribution of the emperor himself and how far did he rely on his legal advisers? There is a continuing debate about the authorship of rescripts and responsibility for the interpretation of the law. Indeed Honoré (1981, 24–53) attempted by detailed analysis of language to identify the imperial legal secretaries responsible for groups of rescripts under the direction of the secretary for petitions (*a libellis*). Williams (1976) tried to identify personal interventions in responses by Hadrian, Antoninus Pius, and Marcus Aurelius. It is also possible that a diligent and interested emperor could generate more legal activity. Overall, it is reasonable to suppose that officials probably did most of the legal research and reported back to the emperor, perhaps especially bringing to his attention to any potentially sensitive issues of public concern. In some cases, however, the personality of the emperor comes through pretty clearly, and he was not obliged to follow legal opinion (see nos. 752–3). It is important to point out that the rescripts preserved by legal writers represent only a small part of those originally issued. Williams (1986) and Hauken (1998) have useful surveys of petitions based on the evidence of epigraphy. See Corcoran (2014) for letters as part of the mechanism of government communication in the empire.

Rescripts, as documents bearing the emperor's name, were authoritative in the application of the law because he was properly exercising his imperium. As Aelius Aristides pointed out, a convicted defendant or a prosecutor who has lost his case can decline to accept the verdict since another great judge awaits, whom no aspect of justice ever eludes (*To Rome*, 37–8). Rescripts were binding but could not change a court verdict (*CJ* 7.57.3), though they might be the grounds for appeal, and were themselves subject to appeal (see no. 759). However, rescripts posed a problem in that the petitioner gave only his side of the case. Hence the response often began: 'If the facts are as you state …', and many contained little substantive legal argument, making only a basic response (Turpin (1991), 101–2).

These issues lead to questions about the overall function of the rescript system. Rescripts can hardly have been part of significant imperial policy objectives or centralization of judicial control since they mainly deal with private law, and their limited publication will have restricted their influence, even among jurists. They did provide free legal advice, but only to those who could find an avenue of approach to deliver a petition and note the response. Nevertheless, the emperor was a figure of authority and a response with his signature would have weight with any judge. Tuori (2016, 298–418) provides a useful collection of evidence relating to imperial adjudication from Julius Caesar to Severus Alexander, and analyses the gradual development of imperial intervention in legal issues, based on the simple fact of the emperor's ability to sort out problems. From this emerged a shared consensus for the legality and value of the emperor's actions.

Naturally, not all emperors were interested in or capable of conducting legal business. Furthermore, political events, rebellions, and military operations that increasingly occupied emperors in the second century will have made the routine of adjudication more difficult to fulfil. However, an emperor could always delegate legal issues to anyone he thought competent to deal with them. In practice in Rome and Italy the prefect of the city and the praetorian prefect came to exercise significant jurisdiction. Hadrian's prefect, Marcius Turbo, was so busy that he had his own late-night court sessions (Dio 69.18). It is no surprise that in the Severan dynasty several praetorian prefects were distinguished lawyers, such as Papinian and Ulpian; see Bauman (1996), 106–14; no. 147.

Some jurists, especially those operating in Rome and in proximity to the emperor, became very influential and highly regarded. Certain individuals had the *ius publice respondendi*, which could be the right either to give a public response to the people, or a response relating to state business and matters of public concern. According to Pomponius in a problematic text, Augustus was the first to decide that 'in order that the law should have greater authority jurists should give a response on his authority', which amounted to a kind of official regulation. The right may have been mainly honorary, adding to the prestige of lawyers who were already influential, but did not necessarily mean that every pronouncement they made had the force of law. Hadrian attempted to clarify matters in a rescript stating that if the opinions of those legal experts permitted to develop the law agreed, this had the force of law, but if not, a judge could form his own opinion (Gaius, *Institutes* 1.7). This arrangement did not stop other lawyers from offering opinions when asked, and it seems that Gaius did not have the *ius respondendi*. Subsequently, Hadrian when approached by men of praetorian rank seeking permission to give legal opinions, replied that customarily this came about not by petition but was granted on the basis of obvious suitability, and that he would be delighted if anyone who had the self-confidence were to prepare himself for issuing responses to the people; this confirms the importance of merit in the right to give responses and that the initiative for granting the right would come from the emperor (*D* 1.2.2.49–50); brief discussion in Robinson (1997), 10–13; Ibbetson (2005), 185–6; Tuori (2004); du Plessis (2012a), 22–3.

Emperors, when they needed help in foreign policy, administration, or legal matters, could consult their advisory council, the *consilium principis*. Legal experts were doubtless summoned from time to time. Augustus, in judging a case concerning the forgery of a will, 'handed to those who were judging with him not only two tablets for condemnation or acquittal, but a third by which a pardon could be granted to anyone who could be demonstrated to have been induced to sign by fraud or misunderstanding' (Suetonius, *Aug.* 33.2). It is not clear from this if the emperor's fellow-judges were lawyers. In the second century Pliny was certainly present in his capacity as a legal expert at a series of hearings held by Trajan, after which the emperor asked everyone's opinion individually before announcing the council's decision. But the emperor was not obliged to listen to advice or go with the majority opinion (Millar (1977), 238–9; nos. 752–3). By the time of Marcus Aurelius, if not earlier, the legal aspects of the *consilium principis* had become so important and formalized that a lawyer of equestrian rank is found serving on the *consilium* with the title of *consiliarius* and a salary of sixty thousand sesterces. Since the post was at a junior level, he was probably not there to advise the emperor but to act as a kind of legal secretary. Nevertheless, this shows the increasingly formal position of lawyers in imperial deliberations. In the early third century Licinius Rufinus, a legal expert from the Greek east, served as *consiliarius* of the emperor and subsequently *a libellis* (Millar (1999)). Indeed, under the Severan emperors jurists who served on the imperial council were clearly marked out for special honour: 'Our splendid and illustrious emperors (Septimius Severus and Caracalla) decided that those who are learned in the law and have begun to serve as guardians should be exempted if they have been co-opted into the imperial advisory council, since they were active at their side and the honour conferred did not have a set limit of time or place' (*D* 27.1.30pr).

The emperor and his advisers had access to archive material to assist their deliberations. From the first century records of trials and decisions (*commentarii*) had been kept, and these records were intended to be as comprehensive as possible, as can be seen from the letter of Marcus Aurelius and Commodus to the procurator of Mauretania asking him to find out the ages of the children of a chief of the Zegrenses who were to receive Roman citizenship, so that the information could be included in the *commentarii*: 'Faggura, wife of Iulianus, head of the tribe Zegrenses, aged twenty-two, Iuliana aged eight, Maxima aged four, Iulianus aged three, Diogenia aged two, children of Iulianus mentioned above' (Sherwin-White (1973b); Williams (1975), 56–70; no. 29). Siculus Flaccus, writing about land survey probably in the second century AD, notes that maps and registers of land division and allocations to individuals, which often came under dispute, were kept in the emperor's record office (*sanctuarium*), to which it was normal for surveyors to refer (Campbell (2000), p. 121.35; no. 441).

To sum up, emperors were a very frequent presence in the juridical history of empire, using edicts, letters, and speeches to shape policy in areas they felt important; furthermore, policy was also directed, perhaps more effectively than through legislation, by instructions and advice given to magistrates and governors. Emperors could encourage equity and the maintenance of proper procedures by participating in a legal dialogue, by hearing appeals and examining questions initiated by someone else, and by giving consistent responses. When the emperor became a source of law often in response to approaches from below, city magistrates in Rome, provincial governors, procurators, secretaries, legal advisers, and the leaders of local communities, what issues stirred him into action, and what can this reveal about policy and the nature of imperial intervention? Emperors were concerned with effective and responsible government of the provinces, control of the military, supervision of local government and law, management of the upper classes and the preservation of status distinctions, jurisdiction, the nature of citizenship, the management of Rome and Italy, the maintenance of property rights and the effective use of land and water, which were important for the economy, support for courts and magistrates as preservers of order and due process, in which the emperor offered his own court and a source of redress, and of course the maintenance of imperial security. Finally with the day-to-day problems of people of lower degree to whom emperors sent rescripts, by being alert to problems and taking an interest, emperors could influence their officials and bring a distinct style and effectiveness to imperial government at all levels.

The following passages illustrate the emperor's constitutional position (nos. 715–20), his role as a source of law with particular emphasis on aspects of public policy (nos. 724–43), his role in original jurisdiction in criminal and civil cases (nos. 744–56), appeals (nos. 757–63), and his response to individual petitions (nos. 764–825). Naturally the broad range of imperial intervention appears throughout the material cited in this book and can be found in the general index under each emperor.

The Constitutional Position and Legislative Powers of the Emperor

D 1.2.12 (Pomponius, *Manual*, Only Book)

715. Therefore in our state the conduct of affairs is dictated by law, that is statute; or there is our civil law, which is unwritten but is based on the interpretation alone of learned jurists. Or there are actions in law which govern the nature of legal process; or there is the law of plebiscites, which is established without the consent of the senate; or there is the magisterial edict, from which arises law sponsored by magistrates; or there is a decree of the senate, which is promulgated without the authority of statute entirely by vote of the senate; or there is an enactment (*constitutio*) of the emperor, which means that whatever the emperor himself has decided is maintained as having the authority of statute.

Gaius, *Institutes* 1.5

716. An imperial constitution (*constitutio*) is what the emperor has decided by decree, or edict, or letter; it has never been in doubt that this has the force of statute, since the emperor himself receives his power by means of a statute.

D 1.4.1 (Ulpian, *Institutes*, Book 1)

717. Whatever the emperor has decided has the force of statute, since by the royal ordinance, which was passed concerning his power, on him and in

him the people confers all its own power and authority. Therefore, whatever the emperor has decided either through letter, or signature (*subscriptio*), or decreed in judicial hearing, or enunciated publicly, or instructed by edict, it is agreed that this is law. These are what we commonly call constitutions (*constitutiones*).

Brunt (1977), 113 argued that in the statements of Gaius and Ulpian power (*imperium*) was not to be taken in its technical sense of the limited power of a magistrate, but as conveying the totality of imperial power, or sovereignty.

D 1.3.9 (Ulpian, *Edict*, Book 16)

718. It is not in dispute that the senate is able to make law.

It has been suggested that lawyers under the direction of Septimius Severus produced a more authoritarian legal basis of the emperor's position. Passage no. 717 can be interpreted to mean that the senate and people conferred all their own power on the emperor and so deprived themselves of any law-making capabilities. But Ulpian here indicates that the senate was still able to make law, and we must interpret the first passage to mean that the senate and people conferred on the emperor power that was the equivalent of their own.

Lex de Imperio Vespasiani Crawford (1996), 549

719. And that it should be lawful for him to make a treaty with whomever he wishes, just as it was lawful for the divine Augustus, Tiberius Iulius Caesar Augustus, and Tiberius Claudius Caesar Augustus Germanicus.

And that it should be lawful for him to convene the senate, propose a motion, refer business to it, and to pass decrees of the senate by motion and division, just as it was lawful for the divine Augustus, Tiberius Iulius Caesar Augustus, and Tiberius Claudius Caesar Augustus Germanicus.

And that when the senate shall have been convened in accordance with his wish or authority, by his order or instruction, or in his presence, the authority in all issues should be upheld and observed, just as if the senate had been called and convened according to statute..

And that whomever of those seeking a magistracy, power, rightful authority (*imperium*), or responsibility for anything, he shall have commended to the senate and people of Rome, or to whomever he shall have given or promised his support in canvassing, in any elections they are to be treated outside electoral procedure.

And that it should be lawful for him to extend and move forward the sacred boundary of the city (*pomerium*) when he considers it to be in the interests of the state, just as it was lawful for Tiberius Claudius Caesar Augustus Germanicus.

And that whatever he considers to be according to the interests of the state and the majesty of matters divine and human, public and private, he is to have the right and power to carry on and undertake, just as had the divine Augustus, Tiberius Iulius Caesar Augustus, and Tiberius Claudius Caesar Augustus Germanicus.

And that by whatever statutes or plebiscites it was written that the divine Augustus, or Tiberius Iulius Caesar Augustus, or Tiberius Claudius Caesar Augustus Germanicus should not be bound, the Emperor Caesar Vespasian should be free from those statutes and plebiscites; and that whatever it was proper for the divine Augustus, or Tiberius Iulius Caesar Augustus, or Tiberius Claudius Caesar Augustus Germanicus to do in accordance with any statute or proposed statute, it should be lawful for the Emperor Caesar Vespasian Augustus to do all those things.

And that whatever before the proposal of this statute has been done, carried out, decreed, or ordered by Emperor Caesar Vespasian Augustus, or by anyone acting under his order or instruction, they should be lawful and valid, just as if they had been done by order of the people or plebs.

Sanction:

If anyone in executing this statute has done or shall have done anything in contravention of statutes, proposals for statutes, plebiscites, or decrees of the senate, or if in execution of this statute he shall not have done what it shall have been proper for him to do in accordance with a statute, proposal for a statute, plebiscite, or decree of the senate, that must not be a liability to him, nor is he to be required to pay anything to the people because of that matter, nor is anyone to have an action of judicial proceeding concerning that matter, nor is anyone to permit an action to take place before him concerning that matter.

See Brunt (1977). This text contains a *rogatio* or proposal of a statute to the people in a popular assembly. Its purpose was to grant to Vespasian, either in December AD 69 or later in AD 70, powers thought to be inherent in the emperor's position. The sixth clause is particularly important since it seems to give the emperor the formal legal right to do whatever he thinks in the interests of the state. Augustus is cited as a precedent and some think that it is unlikely that he can have had such a power voted to him, given his efforts to cloak his autocratic position. Also, such a sweeping clause would mean that the other clauses were redundant. One answer is that the clause refers only to emergency situations. But this is unlikely since the clause refers not just to public business but also to private matters. Of course, it may be that the precedent referring to Augustus is not accurate. Furthermore, it is possible that the draughtsman, observing the range of Augustus' action in the public domain, assumed that he must have had absolute legal power. This may have been formally stated in AD 37 at the accession of Gaius: 'power and control of all things were granted to him' (Suetonius, *Gaius* 14.1). However, in respect of the crucial phrase 'ex usu rei publicae' translated (p. 423) as 'whatever he shall consider to be according to the interests of the state', Crawford (1996), 550 has suggested another interpretation: 'according to the custom of the *res publica*'; therefore, the emperor is given the power to act in a way that was customary in Roman practice.

Eck et al. (1996); see also Griffin (1997)

720. Cnaeus Piso, although he ought to have borne in mind that he had been assigned as assistant to Germanicus Caesar, who had been sent by our *princeps* with the authority of this order (the senate) to settle overseas matters, which indeed called for the presence of Tiberius Caesar Augustus himself or one of his two sons, taking no account of the majesty of the house of Augustus, and taking no account even of public law, in so far as, when he had been assigned to a proconsul, and in fact to a proconsul concerning whom a statute had been passed by the people, so that in whatever province he entered he should have greater power (*imperium*) than the person who was governing that province as proconsul, with the provision that in every way Tiberius Caesar Augustus should have greater *imperium* than Germanicus Caesar, conducted himself when he was in Syria as if everything ought to be subject to his decision and authority (lines 29–36).

This decree of the senate relating to the trial of Piso for treason shows that Germanicus received his *maius imperium* through a statute voted by the people; this gave him greater legal authority than that of any governor whose province he entered. But the inscription also illuminates the nature of the emperor's position with its specific emphasis that Germanicus' authority took second place to the overriding *imperium* of Tiberius. For other aspects of the trial of Piso, see p. 361.

Tacitus, *Annals* 3.69

721. The emperor cannot possibly know about everything, and it is not right for him to be drawn into the schemes of others. Laws are established to deal with what has been done, precisely because future deeds are

uncertain. Therefore, our ancestors decided that if crimes came first punishment should follow. This was a wise policy, has always found favour, and should not be overturned. Emperors have enough burdens, and indeed enough power. Every time power is increased the law is diminished. When it is possible to act through the laws power should not be used.

The context is the prosecution of a corrupt provincial governor and the disinclination of Tiberius to get himself involved in the monitoring of the activities of senators before they were appointed to office.

Justinian, *Institutes* 2.17.8

722. In accordance with this view, divine Severus and Antoninus constantly stated in rescripts: 'Although we are exempt from the operation of the law we nevertheless live by the law'.

CJ 6.23.3 (AD 232)

723. Emperor Alexander to Antigonus. It has often been established that the emperor cannot claim the inheritance from an invalid will. For although the statute conferring imperial power frees the emperor from the obligations of the law, it is particularly appropriate in the exercise of power to abide by the laws.

These passages show importance attached to rule of law by the imperial administration. Although they were *legibus solutus* many emperors chose to abide by law, at least when it suited their political interests. For example, Severus Alexander and his advisers were keen to present a contrast between his regime and that of his predecessor, Elagabalus, who had been hated by the senators; see Dio 53.18.1; Brunt (1977), 108–9.

The Emperor as a Source of Law

Edictum

In issuing edicts emperors took the initiative, but that might be in response to problems presented to them. Some edicts related to one province or person (see no. 725), while others had wider relevance; Augustus in 4 BC issued an edict to the entire empire affirming his concern for the welfare of his subjects and appended to it a decree of the senate establishing a new procedure for seeking redress from corrupt governors (no. 259).

D 48.18.8pr (Paul, *On Adultery*, Book 2)

724. An edict of divine Augustus which he propagated in the consulship of Vibius Habitus and Lucius Apronianus is extant in the following form: 'I think that examinations by torture are not always desirable in every case and for every person. But, when capital charges and outrageous crimes cannot be examined and investigated in any other way than through the torture of slaves, I think that those examinations are very effective for extracting the truth and should be employed'.

Augustus was establishing rules for the use of evidence in the judicial process; see no. 731 for the relative importance of various types of evidence; on use of torture see no. 728.

FIRA 1, no. 68, II

725. Emperor Caesar Augustus, chief priest, holding the tribunician power for the seventeenth time, declares: It should not be a matter of criticism and abuse of Publius Sextius Scaeva that he took care to send to me in chains from the province of Cyrenaica Aulus Stlaccius Maximus, son of Lucius, and Lucius Stlaccius Macedo, son of Lucius, and Publius Lacutanius Phileros, freedman of Publius, since these men said that they themselves had and wished to reveal information pertaining to my security and to the state. For in this Sextius acted properly and vigilantly. Furthermore, since they know nothing of matters pertaining to me and to the state, and made it clear to me that what they had said in the province was a deceitful fabrication, I have released them and discharged them from custody. However, in respect of Aulus Stlaccius Maximus, whom ambassadors of the Cyrenaicans charge with removing statues from public locations, including one on which the city had engraved my name, until I have investigated this matter, I prohibit him from leaving without my permission.

This is an example of an edict referring specifically to one person and one incident, and it shows Augustus exercising original criminal jurisdiction and announcing his decision. It is unclear who had criticized the governor or referred the matter to the emperor. Other edicts of Augustus affected only the situation in Cyrene (no. 248); see also Tuori (2016), 82–4.

P. Giessen 40, col. 1

726. Emperor Caesar Marcus Aurelius Severus Antoninus Augustus declares: Since there are none for whom we should sooner attribute the

causes and reasons, it is the immortal gods that I should rightly thank that on the occasion of such a (?) they have preserved me safe from harm. Therefore, I think that I can, on a magnificent scale and with piety, do what is commensurate with their divine majesty, if I should bring with me as Romans to the shrines of the gods as many tens of thousands as make up the number of my people. Therefore, I grant Roman citizenship to all who inhabit the civilized world (without impediment to … ?) …, except the *dediticii*. For it is proper that the multitude should not only share all the burdens but should now also be included in the victory.

Caracalla in 212 or 214 took the major step of granting Roman citizenship to everyone in the empire except slaves who had been punished for a serious offence and could not obtain full freedom (*dediticii*). The emperor is celebrating either the successful murder of his brother Geta (212) or his escape from drowning while crossing the Hellespont (214). The crucial word is missing in the papyrus. Caracalla was given to effusive gestures, for example, granting an amnesty to all prisoners in 212. See Imrie (2018) for detailed analysis. The grant of citizenship probably did not include exemption from local obligations. The impact of the grant was limited by the decline in the value of citizenship as the social distinctions between *honestiores* and *humiliores* became of greater significance; see p. 398.

FIRA 1, no. 69 = Smallwood (1967), no. 377

727. Edict of the emperor. It is my decision that graves or tombs which were made to reverence ancestors, or children, or members of the family, should remain undisturbed for all time. If anyone should accuse someone of having destroyed them, or in any other way to have thrown out those who have been buried, or to have moved them to another location by deceitful wickedness, in an offence against the dead, or to have moved tombstones or gravestones, I command that he is tried on the same basis in respect of acts of reverence for men as for the gods. For it is to be of maximum importance to honour those who have been buried. Therefore no one at all must be allowed to disturb them. If anyone does this, it is my wish that he should suffer a capital penalty for tomb desecration.

The author of this imperial edict is uncertain; some have attributed it to Augustus, others to Claudius. For protection of tombs and grave sites, see nos. 580; 586.

Epistula

FIRA 3, no. 185 = Sherk (1969), no. 67 (6 BC)

728. When Kairogenes, son of Leukatheos, was demiorgos.

Emperor Caesar, son of a god, Augustus, chief priest, designated consul for the twelfth time, in the eighteenth year of his tribunician power, to the magistrates, council, and people of Knidos, greetings. Your ambassadors, Dionysios and Dionysios II, sons of Dionysios, met me in Rome and, handing over your decree, accused Euboulos, son of Anaxandridas, now deceased, and Tryphera his wife, who was present, in respect of the death of Euboulos, son of Chrysippos. I ordered my friend, Asinius Gallus, to examine under torture those of the household slaves who were involved in the accusation, and I learned that Phileinos, son of Chrysippos, for three nights in a row had violently attacked the house of Euboulos and Tryphera, virtually putting it under siege; and that on the third night he brought his brother Euboulos along with him, and that the owners of the house, Euboulos and Tryphera, were unable to achieve safety in their own house either by negotiating with Phileinos or by taking defensive measures against his attacks, and that they gave orders to one of their slaves not to kill them, as one might have been driven to do out of justifiable rage, but to ward them off by throwing their (the household's) excrement over them; however, the slave along with the contents let drop the pot, either deliberately or accidentally – he maintained a vigorous denial – and Euboulos fell down under it; it would have been more just if he had been saved rather than his brother. I have also sent to you the actual reports of the interrogations. I would have been astonished at how much the defendants in the case feared the examination of their slaves by you, if you have not appeared extremely hostile to them and to have inappropriately distorted your hatred of wrongdoing, since at those who should have suffered every kind of punishment after they came by night on three occasions to attack another household with insults and violence, and were undermining the common peace of all of you, at those you did not become irate but rather at those who had suffered misfortune even when they were defending themselves and had done nothing wrong at all. However, now you would seem to me to act appropriately if in this affair if you took note of my decision and made the records in the public archives agree with it. Farewell.

This is a letter announcing to Knidos a legal decision of Augustus, though the context is not entirely clear. Either Euboulos and Tryphera had been convicted of murder in Knidos and fled to Rome to ask Augustus to hear the case on appeal, or, fearing hostility against them and suspecting that they would not get a fair trial, they fled to Rome pursued by ambassadors from Knidos in the hope that Augustus would hear their case. Again, he effectively exercises capital jurisdiction; all those involved are not Roman citizens; see also Tuori (2016), 84–9.

Smallwood (1967), no. 370 (AD 41) = Johnson, Coleman-Norton, Bourne (1961), 167

729. Lucius Aemilius Rectus declares: 'Since not all the city's population because of its size was able to be present for the reading of the sacred and most beneficent letter to the city, I considered it essential to publish the letter so that each one of you individually might read it and wonder at the greatness of our god the emperor and feel gratitude for his goodwill towards the city'. Year two of the Emperor Tiberius Claudius Caesar Augustus Germanicus, fourteenth of the month of the New Augustus.

The Emperor Tiberius Claudius Caesar Augustus Germanicus, chief priest, holder of tribunician power, designated as consul, to the city of Alexandria, greetings. (After listing the Alexandrian ambassadors Claudius reviews and accepts the various honours and statues voted to him by the city and confirms existing honours.)

(Line 67) In respect of the city council, I cannot say what your practice was in the time of the ancient kings, but you know very well that you did not have a council in the time of the emperors preceding me. Since this is the promotion of a new idea, and it is unclear if it will benefit the city or my interests, I have written to Aemilius Rectus to investigate and tell me whether this body should be set up, and if it is appropriate to summon one, how this might be brought about.

In respect of which group was responsible for the uproar and strife involving the Jews, or indeed the war if I had to the speak the truth, although your ambassadors, and especially Dionysios son of Theon, argued your case vehemently, I was reluctant to make a detailed investigation, though keeping within me invincible anger against those who renewed the conflict. I tell you finally that unless you desist from this ruinous and obstinate hostility to one another, I shall be forced to show what a benevolent ruler is like when roused to righteous indignation. Therefore, I tell you even now that the Alexandrians should behave gently and considerately towards the Jews, who have lived in the same city for many years, and do not in any way pollute their traditional religious observances in honour of their God, but permit them to maintain the same customs as in the time of the divine Augustus, which I also, having heard both sides, have confirmed. And I specifically order the Jews not to cause trouble in pursuit of more rights than they held before, and not to send separate embassies, as if they were living in two separate cities, an absolutely unprecedented occurrence, and not to force admittance to the games of the gymnasiarchs or *kosmetae*, while they enjoy their own privileges and have a great wealth of good things in a city that is not their own, and not to bring in Jews who sail down from Syria or Egypt, an action which would compel me to form greater suspicions. Otherwise, I shall take action against them in every way as being the instigators of a plague throughout the world. If you both cease this behaviour and are willing to live showing gentleness and considerateness to each other, I myself shall show great concern for the city, which has come to me as if passed on from our ancestors. I publicly mention that my friend Barbillus has always displayed concern for you in my presence, and on this occasion too with great energy he has maintained the struggle on your behalf. I make the same point about my friend Tiberius Claudius Archibius. Farewell.

The Jews in Alexandria formed a coherent group with their own Ethnarch and council of elders but were not recognized as citizens of Alexandria. Under Gaius there had been many attacks on the Jews and their synagogues. Philo the Jewish philosopher and influential leader of the Jews in Alexandria led a deputation to the emperor on the question of Jewish rights. Meanwhile the Jews tried to bring into Alexandria more of their co-religionists and launched counterattacks against the Greeks. The ephebes were young men who had the right to be educated in the Greek gymnasium, from which Jews were excluded. After the murder of Gaius, it fell to Claudius to resolve all the issues. Julius Caesar and Augustus had generally attempted to respect Jewish customs and religious traditions (see pp. 336–8).

Pliny, *Letters* 10.115

730. Trajan to Pliny. My dear Pliny you were right to hesitate about what reply you ought to make to the censors who asked you whether senators who are citizens of other cities in the same province should continue to sit in the senate. For the authority of the law, and long-standing practice against the law, could push you in different directions. My opinion is that we should take a middle course, in that we make no changes in respect of what has arisen from past actions, and that citizens of any community may remain as senators even though they were elected in contravention of the law, but in future Pompey's law must be enforced. But if we attempt to enforce its remit retrospectively, we will inevitably cause enormous confusion.

For Pliny's position in Bithynia see no. 16. The letters to and from Trajan, collected in book 10 of his correspondence, offer an excellent example of imperial letters in answer to a senior governor; several are cited in this chapter and elsewhere as examples relating to the theme of this book. In a previous letter (10.114) Pliny had explained that in Bithynia every city had admitted people to its senate who were citizens of another city even though in Pompey's settlement of the east this had been prohibited. However, this law was out of step with frequent Greek practice of extending equal citizen rights to individuals in another community or even to an entire community (*isopoliteia*). For the nature of internal communications, the gathering of information, and imperial correspondence in response to problems highlighted by provincial governors and others, see Millar (2000).

D 22.5.3.3 (Callistratus, *Judicial Enquiries*, Book 4)

731. Similarly the divine Hadrian replied to Junius Rufinus, proconsul of Macedonia, that he would put faith in witnesses, not written statements. The words of the letter relating to this issue are as follows: 'Alexander brought criminal charges against Aper before me, but because he was unable to prove them or produce witnesses, wished to use written statements, which have no weight with me as I usually interrogate the witnesses themselves. I sent him back to the provincial governor so that he could enquire into the reliability of the witnesses, and unless he (Alexander) could complete what he had started, he should be relegated'.

For rescripts of Hadrian dealing with the treatment of witnesses, see nos. 776–7. For the obtaining of testimony by torture see nos. 18 and 724.

FIRA 1, no. 78 = Smallwood (1966), no. 333 (AD 119)

732. Copy of a letter of [the emperor] translated [into Greek, which] ... [year] three of Trajan Hadrian Augustus when Publius Aelius [for the third time] and Rusticus were consuls, in the winter-quarters of III Cyrenaica legion and XXII Deiotariana legion, 4 August, which is Mesore 11, in the headquarters.

I know, my dear Rammius, that children recognized as theirs by their parents during military service have been prevented from succeeding to their father's property. This did not seem to be harsh since they had acted against military regulations. But I am delighted to begin the process of interpreting more benevolently the rather tough rule of my predecessors. Therefore, since children recognized during military service are not the legitimate heirs of their fathers, I have decided that even they be admitted to a claim on the property in accordance with that part of the edict that allows a claim to relatives by birth. It will be your duty to make this benefaction of mine known to the soldiers and veterans, not so that I may appear to take credit for it in their eyes, but in order that they may make use of it if they do not know about it.

The letter is addressed to Quintus Rammius Martialis, prefect of Egypt 117–19. Soldiers could not contract a legally valid marriage, but many soldiers formed liaisons with local women who were not Roman citizens; consequently, any children would not be citizens and also illegitimate. In cases where the father did not make a will, illegitimate children could not inherit their father's property. Hadrian's concession was limited in so far as the claims of illegitimate children would take second place to those of legitimate children and those descended through the male line, such as the soldier's brothers. But his letter was intended to benefit all soldiers in the empire.

Reynolds (1982), no. 15

733. Emperor Caesar Trajan Hadrian Augustus … sends greetings to the magistrates, council, and people of the Aphrodisians.

I confirmed previously your freedom, autonomy, and other (privileges), which were granted to you by the senate and the emperors who have preceded me.

I have received a petition from an embassy concerning the use of iron and the tax on nails. Although the matter is subject to dispute, since this is not the first occasion on which the tax-collectors have tried to collect from you, nevertheless knowing that in other respects the city is worthy of honour and separate from the schedule of the province (*forma provinciae*), I exempt it from the payment, and I have written to Claudius Agrippinus, my procurator, to order the contractor of the tax in Asia to keep away from your city.

The privileges of Aphrodisias go back to decisions of the triumvirs in 39 BC; it is possible that the nail-tax may have been a tax levied on iron nails about to be imported into the province of Asia and collected at a customs post at the boundary of the territory of Aphrodisias. The *formula provinciae* at the formation of a province defined its territory and established the communities therein and their tribute and obligations.

FIRA 1.79 = Smallwood (1966), no. 442 = Oliver (1989), no. 73 (AD 121)

734. Emperor Caesar Trajan Hadrian Augustus to Popillius Theotimus: I permit wills to be made in Greek concerning those matters that pertain to the succession at the school of Epicurus. But since a successor can more easily be elected if he has the facility of selecting someone from non-Romans as his successor, I grant this also and to the others who will have

the succession; it will be permitted for this right to be transferred to a non-Roman or a Roman citizen.

The headship of the school of Epicurean philosophy in Athens was conveyed through the testamentary provision of the head. The normal practice was that only Roman citizens could be head, and the current incumbent Popillius wanted to choose a non-citizen and to write his will in Greek (normally Latin was required). Hadrian agreed to both requests. The petition had been conveyed to the emperor by Plotina, wife of his predecessor, Trajan. She had an interest in the school of Epicurean philosophy and wrote herself to Popillius asking him to make sure he chose the best man (Oliver (1989), p. 177).

Smallwood (1966), no. 454; with Laffi (1971)

735. I, Emperor Caesar Trajan Hadrian Augustus, father of the fatherland, consul for the third time, in my thirteenth year of tribunician power, restored to Jupiter [... ?] and the community of the Aezani the land given by kings Attalus and Prusias, under the care of Septimius Saturninus, chief centurion, just as King Prusias had aimed.

Avidius Quietus (proconsul of Asia 125/6) to the magistrates, council, and people of Aezani, greetings.

The dispute concerning the sacred land that was from long ago dedicated to Zeus, which has dragged on for many years, has been resolved by the foresight of the greatest emperor. For when I wrote to him explaining the entire affair and asked him what I should do in respect of the two matters that in particular exacerbated the differences between you, and made the affair difficult to examine and resolve, by combining benevolence and justice in accordance with his interest concerning legal cases, he brought to an end your long-standing hostility to and suspicion of one another, as you will learn from the letter that he sent to me, a copy of which I have sent to you. Furthermore, I wrote to Hesperus, procurator of the emperor, asking that he should choose suitable surveyors and make use of them to measure the area so that from this process a good outcome will be available to you. And, in accordance with the revered letter of the emperor, I have made clear what you must pay for each lot according to the judgement of the emperor, from the time when you got the letter, in accordance with the existing portion of sacred land. This is to ensure that some, by returning again to the dispute about the payment, do not become responsible for delaying the city's reception of the benefit of the revenue it is owed. For it is sufficient for them to have enjoyed the fruits up until now.

I have also sent a copy of the letter addressed to Hesperus, and of the letter that Hesperus wrote to me. I pray that you are well.

Copy of the letter written by the emperor to Quietus. If it is not clear how big are the parcels of land, which they call *kleroi*, into which the land, dedicated to Jupiter of Aezani by the kings, was divided, it is best, as you also think, to take as a guide the area of *kleroi* in neighbouring communities, avoiding the biggest and the smallest. Furthermore, if, when Mettius Modestus established that a rent was due for them, he established what lands were divided in *kleroi*, it is reasonable that the rent should be payable from that time. But if he did not establish this, the rent must be paid now from this time, unless some delay has supervened causing them to pay late.

This extract comes from a dossier of documents relating to plots of land dedicated to Zeus of Aezani by two Hellenistic kings, Attalus and Prusias. It contains a letter of Avidius Quietus, proconsul of Asia in 125/6, to the magistrates, council, and people of Aezani, Hadrian's reply to the governor, and several other documents. Quietus had written to the emperor for advice; the problem concerned land consecrated to Zeus which had been rented to tenants; some had ceased paying rents; others had added extra land without paying increased rent. The behaviour of the tenants was probably causing financial loss to the city. Hadrian suggested an approach common in land survey, that if the issue was unclear the practice of neighbouring properties should be observed as a model for Aezani; hence the need for surveyors; see Campbell (2005), 327, 331; Burton (2004), 333–4. Modestus had been proconsul of Asia c. 117–18.

FIRA 1.80 = Smallwood (1966), no. 453 = Oliver (1989), no. 79 (AD 127)

736. Emperor Caesar Trajan Hadrian Augustus, son of the divine Trajan Parthicus, grandson of the divine Nerva, chief priest, in the eleventh year of his tribunician power, consul for the third time, to the archons, council, and people of Hadrianopolis Stratonikea, greetings.

I think that you are asking for things that are appropriate and necessary for a newly established city. I grant you the taxes from the countryside, and in respect of the house of Tiberius Claudius Socrates, which is in the city, either Socrates must repair it or sell it to one of the local people, so that it does not collapse from age and neglect. I have also sent this instruction to the distinguished proconsul, Stertinius Quartus, and to my procurator, Pompeius Severus. Claudius Candidus acted as ambassador. Let the travel allowance be paid to him unless he promised to serve at his own expense. Farewell. First of March, from Rome.

I, Claudius Candidus, delivered the letter to Lollius Rusticus, archon, 14 May, in the assembly.

Hadrian re-founded this city in AD 123. The concession here allows the city to collect a tax from the rural inhabitants, which previously must have gone to the imperial treasury. Claudius Socrates was an absentee landlord. This is one of three letters from Hadrian to the city in response to embassies. For the levying of new taxes, see Burton (2004), 323–4.

Smallwood (1966), no. 452 = Oliver (1989), no. 71 (AD 120)

737. Emperor Caesar Trajan Hadrian Augustus, son of the divine Trajan Parthicus, grandson of the divine Nerva, chief priest, in the fourth year of his tribunician power, consul for the third time, to the *gerousia* of the Ephesians, greetings.

[Mettius] Modestus, distinguished man, did the right thing in granting your rights to [you] at the trial. Since you made clear that many people were stealing your money, holding the property of those who had borrowed from you, and refusing to admit that they were heirs and claiming that the same persons were actually in debt to them, I have sent a copy of your decree to Cornelius Priscus, the distinguished proconsul, so that, if such an issue arises, he can select someone who will judge the dispute and collect everything that is owed to the *gerousia*. The ambassador was Cascellius Ponticus. Let the travel allowance be paid to him unless he promised to serve at his own expense. Farewell. Twenty-seventh of September. Publius Rutilius Bassus [was secretary].

It seems that people who had inherited estates tried to avoid the debts associated with them by denying that they were the heirs. Ephesus was losing out because the debts included money that had apparently been borrowed from the city probably through the temple of Artemis. The *gerousia* at Ephesus consisted of older citizens and had a particular responsibility for the worship and sanctuary of Artemis. Hadrian treats it like a public body by communicating by *epistula*; see also Burton (2004), 319. Cornelius Priscus was proconsul of Asia in 120/1; Modestus was his predecessor.

CIL 3.781 = *ILS* 423 (AD 201)

738. Copy of letter to Heraclitus

Although the community of the Tyrani does not make clear the origin of the privilege which was granted, and privileges which have been appropriated mistakenly or corruptly are not lightly confirmed by the passage of time, nevertheless, since we take account of the letters of the divine Antoninus, our parent, and also of the imperial brothers, and also of

Antonius Hiberus, an eminent governor, in respect of what relates to the Tyrani themselves and those who were adopted into the number of citizens by them in accordance with their laws, we do not want to change anything from previous practice. Therefore, they may keep the basis of their privilege in whatever way it was acquired or taken, and in their business dealings, in respect of which, however, they should remember that on the basis of previous practice they should publish a declaration distinguishing those goods with duty attaching to them. But since it is right that the Illyrian revenues are not reduced by improper influence, they must recognize that those who are admitted as citizens after this will enjoy the benefits of immunity only if our friend, the governor, distinguished man, shall have pronounced by decree that they were worthy of the right of citizenship. We believe that these people will think that sufficient and appropriate consideration for their interests has been taken if they are grateful that, without enquiring into the origin of the privilege, we have directed that they are held to be citizens worthy of the honour.

Ovinius Tertullus to the magistrates, council, and people of Tyrana, greetings. I have attached to this my letter a copy of the godlike letter sent to me by our lords, the invincible and most fortunate emperors, so that you, appreciating their godlike generosity to you, may rejoice in their great good fortune. I pray that you will be well and enjoy good fortune for many years.

Posted on 17 February, eighth day of Leneon in the consulship of Mucianus and Fabianus, in the year 145 of Tyras, in the magistracy of Publius Aelius Calpurnius.

The community of Tyras on the coast of the Black Sea had some taxation privileges and had granted its citizenship to many attracted by this. The government was concerned about the loss to imperial revenues, and after an enquiry the emperors, Septimius Severus and Caracalla, informed Ovinius Tertullus the governor of Moesia Inferior, and Heraclitus the procurator, of the outcome. The concession probably relates to exemption from certain *portoria* revenues collected in the Danubian provinces and was restricted to goods for local use; if goods were put on sale, they had to be identified to explain price differentials in the goods of other merchants who did pay the duty.

P. Oxy. 3106 = Oliver (1989), no. 276[a]; *D* 49.1.25 (AD 222)

739. Emperor Caesar [grandson] of divine Severus Pius, son of divine Antoninus Pius Maximus, M. Aurelius Severus Alexander, chief priest, holding the tribunician power, consul, father of the fatherland, to the council of the Greeks in Bithynia, greetings:

I do not see how anyone could be prevented by [judges] from making an appeal, when it is possible to achieve the same end by the other route and get to me even more quickly. I forbid my [procurators] and provincial governors to employ [abuse] and violence against those who are making an appeal or to place a guard of soldiers round them, or in brief, to block the road to me for them. And they will obey this order of mine, knowing that I have as much concern for the freedom of my subjects as for their goodwill and obedience. However, in respect of those who have been punished on a capital charge and then released, the judge does not accept [...] and cannot authenticate [...] he is to be sent to me.

Severus Alexander's letter addressed to the 'Council of the Greeks in Bithynia' dealt with complaints that imperial officials had even physically prevented persons who had lodged an appeal from travelling to the emperor. The 'other route' may mean a letter sent directly to the emperor.

Other Imperial Pronouncements

Justinian, *Institutes* 2.23.1

740. Trusts (*fideicommissa*) got their name from the fact that they are defined not by any legal rule but only by the honour of those who were asked to fulfil them. Later, divine Augustus, time and time again motivated through goodwill for individuals, or because someone was said to have been asked to fulfil the trust by the safety of the emperor, or because of some egregious act of bad faith on the part of some people, was the first to order the consuls to interpose their authority. Because that seemed just and popular it was gradually converted into regular legal process.

A *fideicommissum* was originally an informal trust by which a testator requested someone, usually his heir, to take some action or make a payment to a third person. This could, for example, get round restrictions on the people to whom legacies could be left. It depended on the honour and goodwill of the heir and could not be enforced at law. Partly through Augustus' informal intervention these trusts became a regular institution for leaving property, and a praetor was designated to deal with it.

BGU 611 = *FIRA* 1, no. 44 = Smallwood (1967), no. 367

741. (col ii) In order that these tricks do not benefit those who plead cases in an underhand way, let us decide, senators, if you agree, that even if there has been an adjournment, those judges who have not brought to

completion within the assigned space of time suits that have been begun, should be compelled to reach a verdict. Of course, I am aware that there will be many deceitful practices by those pleading cases in an outrageous way, against which I hope we have devised remedies. Meanwhile it is enough to have blocked this very common practice among those who bring vexatious suits. For in no way can I tolerate the tyranny of prosecutors who have made their enemies defendants before a diligent court and then leave them hanging on the notice board while they travel abroad as if they had done nothing. For the natural order even more than the law should keep the accuser just as confined and restricted as the defendant.

(col iii) Indeed let us remove from accusers this unfettered tyranny by granting to the praetor the power to bring the accuser to book when the time allotted for the trial has passed, and if he does not appear and produces no excuse, he (the praetor) will pronounce that he apparently has embarked on the case deceitfully for the sake of calumny.

This is part of a speech of Claudius to the senate and gives a strong direction to the praetor for the treatment of the cases brought before him. It shows a concern for fair treatment of those involved in litigation; the accuser must present his case in a timely fashion and not undermine his opponent's reputation by prolonging his status as defendant. For Claudius' judicial activities and his occasionally eccentric intervention in the legal process, see Levick (1990), 115–26. For the imperial speech as a source of law, see Robinson (1997), 126; for experiences in the courtroom, see pp. 375–95.

D 29.1.1pr (Ulpian, *Edict*, Book 45)

742. The divine Caesar was the first to grant to soldiers the right to make a will free from legal requirements. However, that concession was for a limited period only. The divine Titus was the first after this to extend the right, and then Domitian. Subsequently the divine Nerva granted the most extensive indulgence to the troops. Trajan followed this, and from that time onwards the following section began to be inserted in the instructions (*mandata*) to governors; section from the instructions: 'It has been brought to my attention that wills made by my fellow soldiers are frequently being produced which would be the subject of dispute if the full rigour of the law were to be strictly applied to them'.

See no. 79. Soldiers enjoyed unique privileges in making a will; this instruction and the language used emphasize the special relationship cultivated between emperor and soldiers; many other citizens will have been equally ignorant and unable to seek professional help in making a will; see Campbell (1984), 210–29. However, Trajan's vague generosity led to problems of interpretation; see no. 811.

CIL 6.1016a = *ILS* 375 (AD 177–180) (Rome)

743. Emperor Caesar M. Aurelius Antoninus Augustus Germanicus Sarmaticus and Emperor Caesar L. Aurelius Commodus Augustus Germanicus Sarmaticus ordered these stones to be set up, because of the disputes which had arisen between the traders and the retailers, to mark the boundary for the exaction of the tax, no more than once, on goods brought into the forum and produce for sale, in accordance with the established law relating to goods sold on an open market.

The emperors aimed to establish a clear physical line demarcated by stones to assist in the collection of the tax. Locality seems to be important, and the intent may be that the tax (*vectigal*) should be levied only once, on traders or retailers, depending on their position in relation to the line, that is, where they did their deals or had their stalls.

Emperors, Judicial Hearings, and Appeals

Judicial Hearings

Suetonius, *Augustus* 33

744. He himself (Augustus) administered justice assiduously and sometimes up to nightfall, and, if he was unwell, on a litter placed on the tribunal, or even lying in bed. He administered justice not just conscientiously but also leniently; for example, in the case of a man obviously guilty of parricide, to avoid his being sewn up in a sack, which was the penalty only for those who confessed, he interrogated him as follows: 'You surely did not kill your father, did you?'

If a formal verdict was delivered in an imperial judicial hearing it was issued as a *decretum*. Augustus is here exercising original criminal jurisdiction. The traditional penalty for a person convicted of killing a near relative was drowning in a leather sack. For the emperor as judge of first instance in criminal cases, see Millar (1977), 516–27; for the evidence relating to civil cases, Millar (1977), 528–37.

Valerius Maximus 7.7.4

745. Septicia, mother of the Tracali from Ariminum, being angry with her sons, and, since she was no longer able to give birth, to spite them married Publicius an old man and passed over both of her sons in her will. The divine Augustus was approached by them and condemned the woman's marriage and her final wishes; he instructed that the sons should have their mother's estate, and he prohibited the husband from keeping the dowry

since he had not contracted the marriage for the purpose of conceiving children. If Equity herself had examined this case, could she have delivered a more just or impressive verdict?

Augustus' response and assumption that the sons' version of their mother's motivation was correct relates to his marriage legislation and his aim of encouraging the upper classes to have children. It is not clear if Augustus' decision was the result of a formal hearing.

Valerius Maximus 9.15, ext. 1

746. Before the same protector of the state (Augustus) the audacity of a woman from Milan practising a similar deception was overcome. Masquerading as one Rubria, who was falsely believed to have died in a fire, she installed herself in property that did not belong to her, and although not lacking distinguished witnesses from that area, or the support of Caesar's entourage, because of the invincible resoluteness of Augustus she went away defeated in her nefarious enterprise.

This may be the outcome of a formal hearing before the emperor; see Millar (1977), 530.

Suetonius, *Nero* 15.1

747. In the administration of justice he (Nero) was reluctant to give a response to those who presented cases, except on the following day and in a written statement. He followed a procedure for judging cases in which instead of continuous legal pleading he had each litigant in turn present each point separately. Furthermore, whenever he withdrew for consultation, he did not discuss any issue openly with all his advisers, but quietly and in private read their individual written opinions; he then delivered a verdict in accordance with his own opinion, which he represented as the majority view.

Nero's practice is exemplary; to postpone a response for a day would give time for reflection; the presentation by each litigant separately would prevent long, possibly irrelevant speeches by advocates; his decision followed examination of the written opinions of his advisers.

Pliny, *Letters* 6.31.1–2

748. I was delighted to be summoned to attend the advisory council of our emperor at Centum Cellae … There were different types of case that put to the test his judicial skills in several ways. Claudius Ariston, the leading

citizen of Ephesus, a generous man who was popular without being politically threatening, pleaded his own case. But he had been the victim of envy, and an informer was launched against him by people of entirely different character. Consequently, the charge was rejected, and he was acquitted.

Other cases in which Pliny advised the emperor at this meeting included a charge of adultery involving the wife of a military tribune (see no. 574), and a forged will; see also 4.22; 6.22; 7.10; Sherwin-White (1966), 391–6.

Aulus Gellius, *Noctes Atticae* 3.16.12

749. Furthermore, in respect of human birth, despite what I have read in books I discovered that the following actually happened in Rome, namely that a woman of good and respectable character and whose chastity was not in dispute, gave birth in the eleventh month after the death of her husband. The issue arose because of the calculation of the time, with the implication that she had conceived after the death of her husband, since the board of ten (*Decemviri*) had laid down that a child could be born in ten months but not in the eleventh. But divine Hadrian, having heard the case, decreed that a birth could also take place in the eleventh month. I have read the very decree relating to this. In this decree Hadrian stated that he had made the decision after seeking out the views of ancient philosophers and doctors.

This decision of the emperor seems to have followed a judicial hearing. The *Decemviri Stlitibus Iudicandis* were originally junior magistrates in judicial affairs, but later operated within the Centumviral Court which dealt with cases of inheritance and property of high value. The question at issue was: could the child be a legitimate heir?

Fronto, *Ad M. Caesarem* 1.6 = Loeb vol. 1, p. 157

750. In all those matters and cases that are judged by private judges, there is no danger because their verdicts are valid only within the confines of those cases. By contrast, emperor, through your decrees precedents are publicly sanctioned which will be valid for all time … Therefore, if you approve this decision of the proconsul, you will have established a rule for all the governors of all the provinces as to what decision they will reach in similar cases. What will be the consequence of this? Naturally that all wills from distant and overseas provinces will be sent to Rome for a legal hearing before you.

The proconsul of Asia had apparently forwarded to Antoninus Pius a case involving the validation of a will. Fronto, who was pleading in the case, then imagines the inevitable delays that would occur if on the precedent of the emperor's decision in this case all issues involving the validity of wills were brought to Rome for a formal hearing before the emperor. For part of Fronto's speech, see no. 668, where he complains about his opponent's requests for adjournments.

Philostratus, *Lives of the Sophists* 622

751. When Philiscus appeared in court he caused offence by the way he walked, he caused offence by the way he stood, his clothing seems unseemly, his voice effeminate, and his diction was dull, wayward, and not to the point. For these reasons the emperor (Caracalla) was annoyed with Philiscus and interrupted him throughout his speech by making comments in his allotted space and by asking questions. And since Philiscus made replies that did not answer the questions, Caracalla said: 'The hairstyle shows what kind of man he is, his voice what kind of orator'. And after frequently cutting him off like this he sided with the Eordaeans. But when Philiscus said 'You granted me exemption from public obligations when you appointed me to the chair at Athens', the emperor shouted: 'Neither you nor any other teacher is exempt. For I would never for the sake of a few miserable and feeble speeches deprive the cities of men who can undertake public obligations'.

The people of Eordaea in Macedonia had attempted to recruit Philiscus to perform public service in their community (his mother came from there), but he refused, and the case came to the courts and thence to the emperor. This is a good illustration of how important was the emperor's personal response to the litigants. Philostratus had attended the court of Caracalla and should be a reasonable authority.

D 28.5.93 (Paul, *Imperial Decisions Issued in Judicial Proceedings*, Book 1 of 6, or *Decrees*, Book 2)

752. Androsthenes had instituted Pactumeia Magna, daughter of Pactumeius Magnus, as heir to his entire estate and appointed her father as substitute to her. But after Pactumeius Magnus had been killed and there was a rumour that his daughter too was dead, he changed his will and instituted Novius Rufus as heir with this preamble: 'Because it has come about that I cannot have the heirs I wanted, let Novius Rufus be my heir'. Pactumeia Magna petitioned our emperors, who heard the case, and although there was a limitation placed on the institution (of another

heir), as it was a mistaken limitation it could not normally stand as an obstacle (to the institution). However, the emperor decided that she should receive assistance, as that was in accordance with the wishes of the testator. Therefore, he pronounced that the inheritance should go to Pactumeia Magna, but that she was required to pay the legacies bequeathed in the second will, as if she had been declared heir in that second will.

The testator had instituted Rufus as heir with the limitation that this was because his chosen heirs were dead; that was inaccurate and therefore normally would not prevent the institution of a new heir (Rufus). But the emperor decided to help the intended heir in the original will, with the compromise that she should honour all legacies in the second will. Pactumeius Magnus was consul in 183 and was subsequently executed by Commodus.

D 28.4.3 (Marcellus, *Digests*, Book 29)

753. Vibius Zeno said: 'I request, emperor, that you listen to me patiently. What will you decide about the legacies?' Antoninus Caesar replied: 'Do you think that the person who erased the names of the heirs wanted the will to be valid?' Cornelius Priscianus, advocate of Leo, said: 'He erased only the names of the heirs'. Calpurnius Longinus, advocate of the imperial treasury, said: 'No will can be valid if it does not have an heir'. Priscianus said: 'He manumitted several slaves and bequeathed legacies'. Antoninus Caesar had all the parties retire and when he had deliberated and instructed that they be re-admitted, said: 'I think that the current case permits a more humane interpretation; consequently, I take the view that Nepos wanted only what he erased to be annulled'. In fact, he had erased the name of a slave whom he had ordered to be free. Antoninus stated in a rescript that he should nevertheless be set free; he took this decision in order to show favour to freedom.

The context is a legal hearing before Marcus Aurelius about a mutilated will in which the names of the heirs had been erased; if a will was declared invalid the estate could be confiscated to the treasury, to the disadvantage of the legatees. The crucial question was: if the testator (Valerius Nepos in this case) had erased the name of his heirs in the will but not the legatees, did that mean that the entire will should be set aside? The emperor takes a generous view, although there was conflicting legal opinion on the issue.

D 36.1.76(74).1 (Paul, *Decrees*, Book 2)

754. Fabius Antoninus left a son, Antoninus, who had not reached puberty, and a daughter, Honorata. He disinherited them and instituted as heir

their mother, Junia Valeriana, entrusting her with a legacy of three hundred *aurei* and some items for his daughter, and then stated his wish that all the remainder of the inheritance should be restored to his son, Antoninus, when he had reached the twentieth year of his life. But if his son were to die before reaching his twentieth year, he provided that the inheritance should be restored to Honorata. The mother died intestate leaving both her children as her legal heirs. Subsequently, the son, having completed his nineteenth year and entered his twentieth, died before completing that year, leaving a daughter, Fabia Valeriana, as his heir. Her aunt (Honorata) brought suit against her claiming the trust and part of the inheritance in accordance with the will of her (Honorata's) father. And she was successful in a hearing before the governor of the province. The tutors of Valeriana, daughter of Antoninus, pleaded her poverty and cited a decision of the divine Hadrian in which he had instructed that in respect of local obligations the year of life that anyone had entered should be regarded as completed. Our emperor, moved by a concern for justice and the words of the will, 'if to the twentieth year of life', found against the plaintiff, although he admitted that he knew that the divine Marcus had not exempted from a tutor's duties a man who had entered his seventieth year, and although we cited arguments from the *lex Aelia Sentia* and other points.

In this judicial hearing the governor's original decision may have been appealed to the emperor, Septimius Severus. Fabius instituted his wife as heir and among its provisions established a *fideicommissum* that the bulk of his remaining estate should go to his son if he reached his twentieth year. But the mother died intestate before the trust could be fulfilled. The son, who had a young daughter (Valeriana), then died before completing his twentieth year, which prompted her aunt (Honorata) to argue that the trust could not be fulfilled and to claim most of the estate. The case hinged on the exact interpretation of twenty years old. Valeriana's lawyers cleverly produced a precedent from a judgement of Hadrian that the current year of a man's age should be held completed. Although the emperor had access to another judgement of Marcus Aurelius who held the opposite view, he nevertheless found for Valeriana. It seems that he also ignored the advice he received from his lawyers.

SEG 17.759 (AD 216)

755. In the consulship of Sabinus and Aulinus, 27 May, at Antioch, when the Emperor Caesar Marcus Aurelius Antoninus Pius Felix Augustus Parthicus Maximus, Germanicus Maximus, had been saluted by the praetorian prefects, most eminent men, and also by the friends and the heads of the secretariats, and had been seated in the audience chamber, he ordered that Aurelius Carzaeus, son of Sergius, defender of the Goharieni, acting against Avidius Hadrianus, public contractor – a case which our lord

deigned to hear – along with his advocate Egnatius Lollianus, and Avidius Hadrianus, public contractor, along with his advocate Iulianus Aristaenetus, should be admitted. Of these Aristaenetus said: 'I challenge the competence of the court to hear this case'.

Lollianus said: 'You (Caracalla) commanded that the hearing be arranged'.

Aristaenetus said: 'Cases of appeal are submitted in accordance with a legal procedure. Either the governor approves the appeal and places it before your tribunal, or, if the governor does not accept it, in what way can the suit be introduced (into court)? After many hearings and decisions, a request has been put to you on this matter among the petitions of the Goharieni. Although he is neither their accredited representative nor their ambassador, but merely a private person, he (Carzaeus) has introduced the petition so as to have you as the judge instead of the governor; [indeed you have said to him,] 'If you wish me to hear you, I shall do so'. Previously these people did not even raise objections, but now, when we were beginning proceedings in accordance with the legal process of the tribunal, [they petitioned you. But it must be stated] that neither are they making an appeal, nor could they bring one to [your tribunal]'.

Lollianus said: 'Peasants who moved you with other requests have also brought to you this petition. Cassius did not accept the objection to the court's competence [when] the Goharieni came back to him with complaints. He put it among the petitions to go before your imperial tribunal in order that you [might be] the judge'.

Antoninus Augustus said: 'You claim, then, that he has not made an appeal?'

Aristaenetus said: 'They are not making an appeal because they did not have the right to make one'.

Antoninus Augustus said: 'See, then, that I too may say something of my own view in this issue. He has neither made an appeal nor presented a complaint, nor has this matter been pleaded before the governor: "It is before the emperor that I accuse you", he says. Do you not want me to hear the case?'

Aristaenetus said: 'I do'.

Antoninus Augustus said: 'If I were in a hurry to leave this session your objection has a proper time (for a hearing). So, (if I am not in a hurry), what objection is there to my hearing you here and now?'

Lollianus said: 'I shall speak for less than half an hour', and he went on: ' The dispute concerns a matter of piety. For to the peasants, as to you yourself, nothing is more demanding of respect than piety. And so, for this reason they are encouraged in the current circumstances since they are bringing their case before the most pious of rulers and judges. There is in their midst a famous shrine of Zeus. Naturally, it is visited by all the people in the vicinity; they make their way to it and hold processions. The first crime of our opponent is this ... he has immunity from liturgies and, wearing a gold crown ... and has taken a sceptre in his hand and proclaimed himself to be priest of Zeus. Let him demonstrate how he has been considered worthy of this privilege; for in his presence I shall read (a document) that not even his father ... '.

Aristaenetus argues that the case should not come before this court because the correct preliminary requirements had not been fulfilled, in that an appeal from the proceedings in the governor's court required the governor's permission. Caracalla accepts that the plaintiff has not complied with all these requirements, and that Aristaenetus' objection is valid; but those rules existed to ensure that the emperor and his officials were not overburdened with cases. On this occasion Caracalla is willing to hear the case and Aristaenetus immediately agrees. Lollianus with great confidence begins his opening address. The case concerns the complaint of the inhabitants of the village of Goharia that a Roman contractor, Avidius Hadrianus, had improperly elevated himself to the priesthood of Zeus; see Oliver (1974); Tuori (2016), 248–52. For the role of the governor in the appeals process, see no. 656.

SEG 48.1583 (c. AD 160–260) Cibyra in Lycia

756. It escaped our attention what you have endured, in respect of which it was right that they should already have been brought to justice. We wished to write to the governor to punish some of them as an example, because of the illegal exactions which they unnecessarily placed on the local people, and because of the abuse and the assaults which they inflicted on them. We put off judgement about them until we can ascertain more precisely what happened. For we have instructed others to tell us every detail about them, whether they are doing this (as alleged), and how they live. Make sure to pay attention to this and bring them to order, so that they behave with restraint, and in the future after your decision, do not appear to be taking such action. This was published five days before the kalends of November (28 October).

This instruction addressed to an imperial official was intended to bring some relief to local people who had been oppressed; however, the (unknown) emperors are also assembling evidence for a future judicial investigation.

Appeals

D 49.1.21pr-1 (Papirius Justus, *Decisions*, Book 1)

757. Emperors Antoninus and Verus stated in a rescript that appeals which were made directly to the emperor, omitting those people of lower rank to

whom they ought to have been made, should be sent back to the governor. They also stated in a rescript that an appeal from a judge whom someone had accepted from the governor of the province should not correctly be made to the emperor but ought to be sent back to the governor.

Rules existed to control the number of appeals made to emperors (see nos. 636; 754); in the case of an appointed judge, appeal should be made to the person who appointed him. Eventually, in practice the right of appeal for *humiliores* was greatly restricted; see p. 398.

Oliver (1989), no. 184; with Oliver (1970); Jones (1971) (AD 174/5)

758. (Lines 23–7) Athenodorus, son of Agrippa, appealed from Papius Rufus, the previous archon of the Panhellenes, in the last four-year term, against the managers of the property of the splendid Claudius Herodes, but since he provided neither the minutes of the Panhellenes nor the decision that was announced, he is to plead his case before my Quintilii, so that after such a long time he may not be compelled to wait for the occasions when I shall be able, in the midst of military operations, to deal with matters that require judgement.

(Lines 87–94) I think that I have made clear by my pronouncement that I have taken care of every issue, not on the basis of my power, but rather by consideration that in the future Herodes can remain in Athens and with goodwill participate in divine and human affairs, and also pursue his famous passion for culture, and so that the Athenians, mindful of the previous generosity of the splendid Herodes towards them, may confidently take up again their previous goodwill towards each other, as a result of which they do not need even me to reconcile them. For what could still lurk in anyone's mind after the memory of those accusations has been expunged? Now that a solution has been effected in all respects, it should perhaps be possible for the Athenians to love my and their Herodes, since there is no other significant impediment to goodwill.

This is part of an inscription which includes a section of a letter of Marcus Aurelius dealing with 'appealed cases' relating to the internal administration of Athens, priesthoods, the rules governing membership of the Areopagus council, property disputes involving several Athenian citizens, and the city's troubled relationship with its famous citizen, Herodes Atticus. In format the letter has some of the characteristics of an imperial edict (Oliver (1970), 35–7). The Quintilii referred to are probably the consuls of 151, Sextus Quintilius Condianus and Sextus Quintilius Valerius Maximus, who are described by Philostratus (*Lives of the Sophists* 559) as 'ruling Greece' at this time; their formal position remains unclear. It is interesting that Marcus, in the midst of a tough military campaign, as he points out, was still available to hear legal cases, though several were delegated to the Quintilii. Although many of the issues brought to the emperor's attention concerned matters of purely local relevance, he dealt with them in the main according to the usual Roman procedures for delivering justice; see Oliver (1989), pp. 379–88.

D 49.1.1pr-1 (Ulpian, *Appeals*, Book 1)

759. Everyone is aware that the process of making an appeal is both frequent and necessary since it corrects the partiality or ignorance of judges. Nevertheless, it can alter for the worse a sound judgement, for it is not always true that the last person to make a judgement judges better. The question was asked if it is possible to appeal against an imperial rescript, if by chance a provincial governor or someone else consults him (the emperor) and a rescript was issued in response to the consultation. For the question is: does there remain a right of appeal? For what if in consulting the emperor the person had made a mendacious claim? Concerning this issue there is a rescript of the divine Pius addressed to the community of the Thracians which demonstrates that it should be possible to appeal. The text of the rescript is as follows: 'If anyone writes to us and we write anything to him in reply, it is permitted for him, if he wishes, to appeal against our decision. If he can demonstrate that the information supplied to us was mendacious or insufficiently accurate, then it will not be held that we have prejudged anything, since our reply was predicated on inaccurate information'.

For appeals in general see Robinson (1997), 96–9; Millar (1977), 507–16; for the authority of imperial rescripts, see p. 417.

CJ 7.62.2

760. Emperor Alexander Augustus to Plarianus. What you request is not novel and although the authority of a rescript issued by me has intervened (in the case), nevertheless the opportunity to appeal will not be denied to you.

AE 1962.288 (AD 79)

761. Emperor Titus Caesar Vespasianus Augustus, chief priest, in his ninth year of tribunician power, imperator for the fourteenth time, consul for the seventh time, father of the fatherland, sends greetings to the magistrates and town councillors of Munigua. Since you have appealed in order to

avoid paying the money that you owe to Servilius Pollio in accordance with the verdict of Sempronius Fuscus (proconsul of Baetica), it was correct to extract from you the penalty for a vexatious appeal, but I preferred to respond to my goodwill rather than your audacity, and I have remitted the sum of fifty thousand sesterces in respect of the shortage of public funds which you put forward as an excuse. I have written to Gallicanus, my friend and proconsul, that you should pay the money, which was granted to Pollio by the judgement, but that he should free you from any calculation of interest from the day on which the verdict was delivered. Also, it is reasonable that the income from (the collection of) your taxes, which you indicate Pollio has leased out, should come into the calculation lest the community should be deprived of anything for this reason. Goodbye.

Given on 7 September (AD 79).

Servilius Pollio had a contract with Munigua to collect its revenues, but the city had reneged on his payment. Although Titus rejected the community's appeal, he made three concessions reducing the amount that they owed. This was why the city inscribed the emperor's letter. The inscription also provides evidence for the penalty imposed on vexatious appeals (see Tacitus, *Annals* 14.28). Gallicanus had succeeded Fuscus as proconsul.

FIRA 1, no. 91

762. Among the many commendable actions and decisions of my divine parent, I think that it is appropriate to advise that in respect of cases that have been referred on appeal or remitted for the emperor's attention, he recognized that it was necessary that by imposing a requirement they had to be brought to an end, lest honest men might be distressed by lengthy delays, while shrewd men might seek to derive some benefit from a protracted case. Since he observed that this had been going on for many years, he issued a beneficial edict defining the time within which, when people had come from the provinces to litigate, both parties should not leave before they had been brought in to contest the case, otherwise they should recognize that the verdict would be entered when the other party had been heard, or pronounced in favour of the person who was present. But if neither litigant were present, then the case would be removed from the list of judicial investigations of our court ... (The emperor mentions a limit of six months for cases from Italy and a year for those coming from beyond the Alps.) However, seeing that capital cases can permit a little help through delay, nine months will be granted to accusers and defendants in

Italy, and eighteen months to those beyond the Alps and overseas ... (The emperor continues with a reference to appeals in civil cases.)

This papyrus text contains an edict of an unnamed emperor (probably the late second or early third century). The edict is important because in general terms it suggests that cases were coming regularly to the emperor on appeal from the provinces; the emperor's approach though equitable was likely to lead to significant delays for all those involved. See Millar (1977), 512–13.

Theophilus, *Ad Autolycum* 1.11

763. You will say to me, 'Why do you not worship the emperor?' Because he was created not to be worshipped but to be honoured with appropriate honour. He is not God, but a man placed in position by God, not to be worshipped but to judge justly.

See Millar (1977), 507. The comment of Theophilus, Bishop of Antioch in the time of Commodus, suggests that by this time the emperor's role in jurisdiction of all kinds was well established in Christian conceptions of the Roman world.

Individual Access to the Emperor

The emperor and his legal advisers provided responses to *libelli* submitted on many aspects of law, often far removed from matters of high imperial policy, including property issues, legal procedure, rights and exemptions, definition of crimes, legal status, administrative matters at various levels, the role of governors and other officials, abuse by imperial officials, marriage and dowry, wills, and military business. Among miscellaneous personal matters some petitioners sought legal advice, some merely information; for the working of the system see p. 418. Normally, a petitioner was expected to hand in the petition personally, and this requirement will have made it difficult for poorer people to use this approach unless the emperor was visiting their province. It is instructive that when Septimius Severus visited Egypt in 199 he delivered thirteen responses to petitions over three days, as recorded in one papyrus (Oliver (1989), nos. 226–38; and see nos. 792; 797). Furthermore, when the imperial entourage was on the move it might be that the reply was published in a different place from where it was originally delivered. Nevertheless, the replies illustrate issues that concerned citizens across a wide social range about whom we would not normally be well-informed because of the bias of upper-class writers. It was part of the emperor's public persona to respond, or at least give his signature to the response. This is the dramatic interface of state and citizen.

In what follows, imperial replies are grouped in categories although there is some overlap. For an excellent examination of the late third century collection of rescripts in the *Codex Hermogenianus*, and analysis of the system of petition and response at that time, see Connolly (2010), especially chapter 1, for the method of making a petition.

Property

CJ 7.73.1

764. Emperor Antoninus Augustus to Eutropia. If the property of your husband has been confiscated by the treasury (*fiscus*) because of debts relating to his administration as chief centurion, anything which you can clearly prove to be yours will be separated from the rest and restored to you.

Presumably the centurion had been charged with misappropriation of public funds.

CJ 3.34.1 (AD 211)

765. Emperor Antoninus Augustus to Calpurnia. If you believe that legal action is open to you against the man who has constructed a building in a different way from the original plan with the result that it obstructs your light, you will not be prevented from pursuing this in the usual way. The man who is appointed as judge will be aware that customary practice observed over a long time has the status of a servitude, provided that the plaintiff does not possess by force, clandestinely, or by grant (*precario*).

For urban servitudes see p. 241. The point at issue was that the plaintiff argued for an entitlement to light for her property.

CJ 8.1.1 (AD 224)

766. Emperor Alexander Augustus to Aper, *evocatus*. Since you claim that the roots of the trees located in the neighbouring property of Agathangelus are growing and becoming a threat to the foundations of your house, the governor will restore the situation as justice requires, following the interdicts which are posted by the praetor: 'If a tree projects over the house of another'; also 'If a tree projects over the land of another', by which it is made clear that no injury should be caused to a neighbour through the presence of a tree.

See pp. 254–9 on the management of relations between property owners and protection against the activities of a neighbour. *Evocatus* was a time-served soldier retained in the ranks as a veteran.

D 8.3.17 (Papirius Justus, *Decisions*, Book 1)

767. Emperors Antoninus Augustus and Verus Augustus stated in a rescript that it was right for water from a public river to be divided in proportion to the size of the holdings for the irrigation of the fields, unless someone can demonstrate that more was given to him through a private legal agreement. They also stated that it was permitted that water be channelled, provided that it was done without injury to another party.

Fair access to water was a principle preserved by Roman land surveyors; a servitude might provide additional personal rights; for water management see Campbell (2012), 228; 241–4; in general, Bannon (2017); for a private scheme at Lamasba, no. 230.

D 47.21.2 (Callistratus, *Judicial Enquiries*, Book 3)

768. Divine Hadrian stated the following in a rescript: 'Granted that those who move stones placed to mark boundaries have carried out a disgraceful deed, however there is no doubt that in respect of punishment a rule can be established in accordance with the status of the person and his motive in doing the deed. For if the persons convicted are of high rank, then without doubt they did it in order to occupy someone else's land, and they can be banished for a time, as the age of each one allows, that is, a younger man for a longer time, an older man for a shorter time. But if the guilty parties carried out the deed working for someone else and performing a service (for them), they can be punished by being sent to hard labour for two years. And if they appropriated the stones through ignorance or by accident, it will be enough to beat them'.

For *honestiores* and *humiliores* see p. 40. Severus Alexander speaks of severe punishment for those digging up boundary stones – *CJ* 9.2.1 (222); for boundary marking see Campbell (2000), 468–71; importance of boundaries, nos. 89; 157; 160; 163; 173; 217; 300; 631.

BGU 267 = *SP* no. 214 (AD 199)

769. Emperor Caesar Lucius Septimius Severus Pertinax Augustus Arabicus Adiabenicus Parthicus Maximus and Emperor Caesar Marcus

Aurelius Antoninus Augustus to Iuliana, daughter of Sosthenianus, acting through Sosthenes her husband. A plea of long possession lodged by those who have just cause and who have retained possession without any dispute, is established against those (claimants) who dwell in another city by the passage of twenty years, and by ten years against those who dwell in the same city. It was displayed in Alexandria on Tubi 3 of year eight.

For possession as opposed to ownership, see p. 234; for *praescriptio longi temporis* in provincial land, see p. 245 and *SP* 261.

D 1.8.4 (Marcianus, *Institutions*, Book 3)

770. Therefore no one is prohibited from going to the seashore in order to fish, provided that they keep off houses, buildings, and tombs, because they are not subject to the law of nations (*ius gentium*) as the sea is; divine Pius stated this in a rescript to the fishermen of Formiae and Capenae. But virtually all rivers and harbours are public property.

The sea was open to common use; rivers were public property and could be exploited but not to the detriment of other people, for example, by reducing the flow; landholders owned the riverbank. It is interesting that the fisherman had grouped together and got the ear of the emperor.

CJ 4.44.1 (AD 222)

771. Emperor Alexander Augustus to Aurelius Maro, soldier. If your father sold his house under compulsion, the sale will not be considered valid, because it was not executed in good faith and a sale carried out in bad faith is void. If the governor of the province is approached in your name he will exercise his authority, especially since you claim that you are ready to refund to the purchaser what was paid as the price.

Several conditions had to be fulfilled before a sale could be considered valid; the use or threat of force amounted to duress (*metus*); see p. 295.

D 26.5.12.2 (Ulpian, *Duties of a Proconsul*, Book 3)

772. The divine Pius accepted in the following terms the complaint of a mother about her spendthrift sons and her request that a curator be appointed: 'It is not a novelty that some people, even if they seem to be perfectly sensible on the basis of their conversation, nevertheless treat property belonging to them in such a way that, if no one comes to their

aid, they will be reduced to poverty. Therefore, someone should be chosen who can guide them with advice. For it is right for us to look out for those who, so far as applies to their property, produce a disastrous outcome'.

One object of the legal process was to ensure stable management of property to ensure the continuity of the family. For the importance of maintenance of property rights against various threats, see p. 247.

Oliver (1989), no. 224

773. Emperor Caesar Lucius Septimius Severus Pius Pertinax Augustus, Arabicus, Adiabenicus, Parthicus Maximus, and Emperor Caesar Marcus Aurelius Antoninus Pius Augustus to [...]:

[Since] you surrender your property under [our] protection, after your surrender you will suffer no [penalties] at all. [For it seems advantageous to us] to lay down a rule that those who make a surrender should not in the future be made liable for either public or private [debts and not] put under pressure for any other payment but be liberated [so as to be safe from abuse] in respect of the payment of money, and to be free from [liturgies]. Therefore since [many people have already] been reduced to extreme difficulty, we have decided that those who made the surrender of their property have been [unjustly] deprived of their rights. Year eight, Pharmouthi [... .]

This may be an *apokima* or rescript and refers to the surrender of property (*cessio bonorum*) to creditors to satisfy debts; this would avoid the compulsory sale of the debtor's property and consequent *infamia*, which was important for maintenance of status; see p. 59. The translation follows the text of Oliver, who interprets the phrase 'en epitermou chora' as the 'end of the road' or 'extreme difficulty'.

Legal Procedure and Penalties

D 48.19.5pr (Ulpian, *Duties of a Proconsul*, Book 7)

774. The divine Trajan wrote in a rescript to Iulius Fronto that in criminal cases a man should not be condemned in absence. The divine Trajan also wrote in a rescript to Asidius Severus that furthermore no one should be condemned on the basis of suspicions. For it was better that the offence of a guilty man should go unpunished than that an innocent man should be condemned.

For discussion of the nature, function, and value of punishment in legal judgements, see pp. 297–300.

Mosaicarum et Romanarum Legum Collatio 1.11.2

775. The words of the consultation and rescript are as follows: 'Most excellent Emperor, I have given judgement in the case involving Claudius and Euaristus, in respect of the fact that Claudius, the son of Lupus, while being tossed in a cloak during a banquet was so incompetently caught through the fault of Marius Euaristus that after five days he died. Furthermore, it was clear that there was no enmity between him and Euaristus. However, I decided that the fault of immoderate behaviour should be repressed, so that other young men of the same age should be corrected. Therefore, I have banished Marius Euaristus from the city of Rome, Italy, and the province of Baetica for five years, and have decreed that as a form of compensation Euaristus should pay two thousand to his (Claudius') father, as his poverty was manifest'.

The words of the rescript: 'Taurinus, you have correctly reduced the punishment of Marius Euaristus to suit the level of his fault, for it is relevant even in more serious offences whether something was done deliberately or by accident'.

See also *D* 48.8.4.1. Egnatius Taurinus, proconsul of Baetica, was asking Hadrian to review and approve his lenient sentence of relegation for five years; discussion in Millar (2016), 76–7, who notes that this illustrates a minor detail of provincial life which gave rise to a question of general principle requiring the emperor's approval; for issues of legal responsibility, see pp. 281–5.

D 22.5.3.1–2 (Callistratus, *Judicial Enquiries,* Book 4)

776. Therefore the divine Hadrian stated in a rescript to Vibius Varus, governor of the province of Cilicia, that the person who judges a case is in the best position to know how much trust to place in witnesses. The words of the letter are as follows: 'You are in the best position to work out how much trust to place in witnesses, who they are, what their status is, what their reputation is, whether they speak sincerely, whether they have brought one prepared and agreed statement, and whether without hesitating they respond plausibly to the questions you ask them'. There is a rescript of the same emperor to Valerius Verus about assessing the reliability of witnesses. The text is as follows: 'It is not possible to set out adequately and definitively the type and quantity of proof required for each case. The truth of something can often, though not always, be discovered without consulting public records. Sometimes the number of witnesses, sometimes their status and authority, sometimes widespread

opinion confirms the truth of the matter in dispute. To sum up, all I can say to you in my rescript is that an adjudication (*cognitio*) should not immediately tie itself to one type of proof. But you should judge in accordance with your own opinion what you believe or what you think has been insufficiently proved'.

For juristic scrutiny and assessment of witnesses, see no. 630. For Hadrian's policy on the value of testimony as against written statements, see no. 731; for the importance of status, see pp. 397–8.

D 22.5.3.6 (Callistratus, *Judicial Enquiries*, Book 4)

777. Witnesses should not be lightly summoned if they have to travel a long distance, and much less should soldiers be summoned away from the standards and their duties in order to give evidence, as divine Hadrian stated in a rescript. Furthermore, the divine brothers stated in a rescript as follows: 'In respect of summoning witnesses, it is up to the conscientious judge to discover what the practice is in the province in which he is giving judgement'.

This attitude to soldiers may have made it difficult to proceed against them in some cases; for Juvenal's view of getting soldiers into court, see nos. 674; 707.

D 48.2.7.2 (Ulpian, *Duties of a Proconsul*, Book 7)

778. The governor of the province ought not to permit the same man to be accused under the same charges of which he has been acquitted, and the divine Pius stated this in a rescript to Salvius Valens. But it is necessary to consider if he cannot be charged by the same accuser, or not by any other person.

Roman law had the principle of *non bis in idem*, meaning that once a legal issue had been decided it could not be raised again; see Buckland (1975), 696–9; its application is debatable since in Rome private individuals brought accusations; Ulpian held that a new accuser could be accepted if he had no connection to or knowledge of the previous case.

CJ 7.52.2 (AD 215)

779. Emperor Antoninus Augustus to Pacatianus. If cases that have been decided are to be opened up again under the pretext of a new calculation, there will be no end of litigation.

CJ 7.59.1 (AD 211)

780. Emperor Antoninus Augustus to Iulianus. It is agreed that confessions made in court stand as judgements. Therefore, you have no grounds for your wish to renege on your confession and you will be compelled to make payment.

D 50.13.4 (Paul, *Plautius*, Book 4)

781. The divine Pius stated in a rescript that those who were learned in the law who demanded their fees could force payment.

See no. 651 for the debate over the payment of advocates.

D 5.1.36pr (Callistratus, *Judicial Enquiries*, Book 1)

782. From time to time legal proceedings can be adjourned for legitimate reasons and for specific persons, for example if documents relating to the suit are in the possession of those who are away on public business. The divine brothers stated this in a rescript in the following terms: 'It is humane to accept an adjournment in the case of unexpected events, such as when a father involved in litigation loses his son or daughter, or a wife loses her husband, or a son loses a parent, and in similar circumstances the suit can be adjourned until a future time'.

But frequent adjournments also caused problems especially for poorer litigants, e. g., nos. 688; 741; 762 (on the need for adjournments in certain circumstances).

D 1.18.14 (Macer, *Jury Courts*, Book 2)

783. Divine Marcus and Commodus issued a rescript in the following terms to Scapula Tertullus: If it has been clearly proved to your satisfaction that Aelius Priscus is in such a state of insanity that through continuous mental dislocation he lacks all comprehension, and there lurks no suspicion that he murdered his mother while pretending to be mad, you may disregard the type of his punishment since he is being sufficiently punished by his insanity. But he must be very carefully guarded, and, if you think it advisable, even kept in chains, since this will be relevant not so much to his punishment as to his own protection and the safety of those nearby. If, however, as often happens, he has intervals of sanity you should diligently enquire if he committed the crime during one of these intervals, and if no

concession should be made to his illness. If you discover this to be the case, you should consult us so that we can work out if he should be severely punished in relation to the enormity of the crime, if he committed it when it appears that he knew what he was doing.

The emperors also noted that Priscus was in the care of his own family when the murder occurred and suggest that the governor should inquire into why he was so negligently guarded. For crimes of violence, and mitigation, see pp. 285–6; 297.

CJ 9.18.1

784. Emperor Antoninus Augustus. It is a more significant crime to end a man's life by poison than to kill him with a sword.

The use of poison suggests premeditation and therefore deliberate murder, whereas killing with a sword might involve self-defence or another exculpatory motive.

CJ 7.65.1 (AD 213)

785. Emperor Antoninus Augustus to Sabinus. In the case of someone who is absent because of contemptuous obstinacy when he has been summoned to plead his suit, his appeal cannot be received if the matter has previously been summarily examined.

For summons to trial and failure to appear, see pp. 347–8; see no. 762 for imperial efforts to ensure that litigants stayed for their hearing.

CJ 7.49.1 (AD 212)

786. Emperor Antoninus Augustus to Gaudius. It has been decided that in any case, either private, or public, or relating to the treasury, whoever gives money either to a judge or an opponent, lacking confidence in the justness of his case and placing his hope of success in corrupt use of money, loses that suit.

For judicial malfeasance and the *lex Iulia*, see pp. 311–12.

CJ 4.1.2 (AD 223)

787. Emperor Alexander Augustus to Felix. When the sacred tie of an oath is held in contempt it has god as a satisfactory avenger. It has been decided according to the decisions of my divine parents not to inflict corporal

punishment or bring the charge of treason, even though in a moment of excitement someone committed perjury through swearing in the emperor's name.

The charge of treason could sometimes be brought on trivial grounds, which could be exploited by a prosecutor against a personal enemy; see further p. 308; nos. 559–61.

Privileges, Exemptions, and Rights

Reynolds (1982), no. 13

788. Emperor Caesar Augustus, son of divine Julius, wrote to the Samians underneath their petition. It is possible for you yourselves to see that I have given the gift of freedom to no people other than the Aphrodisians, who in the war followed my side and were captured by force because of their loyalty to me. It is not just for the greatest gift of all to be granted randomly and without reason. I have friendly feeling for you, and I would like to indulge my wife who is enthusiastic on your behalf, but not so as to contravene my usual practice. I am not concerned about the money which you contribute towards the tribute, but I do not wish the most prestigious gifts to be given to anyone without a good reason.

Reynolds (1982), 105 dates this response to 38 BC, arguing that the name Augustus was inserted later. The wife to whom he refers must be Livia, who had connections with Samos. Although Livia had been active in support of Samos, Augustus emphasizes the importance of the status of Roman citizenship as a plausible reason for declining their petition. Aphrodisias was specially favoured. For the citizenship, see pp. 26–34.

Reynolds (1982), no. 14 = Oliver (1989), no. 48

789. Emperor Caesar Trajan to the Smyrneans:

I do not wish anyone from the free cities to be forced to undertake a liturgy for you, and especially not from Aphrodisias, since the city has been removed from the schedule of the province, so that it is not liable for the common liturgies of the province of Asia or for others. I free Tiberius Iulianus Attalus from service in the temple at Smyrna, a man who has excellent references from his own community. I have written about these matters to my friend Iulius Balbus, the proconsul.

This is likely to be a subscript to a petition. The Smyrneans had tried to compel Attalus, a citizen of Aphrodisias apparently residing in Smyrna, to undertake a liturgy in their temple. Trajan upholds the rights of free cities and the special status of Aphrodisias; he also notes that Attalus had performed services in his own city, and by implication therefore could not be considered a shirker of public duties. Balbus was proconsul of Asia in 100.

CJ 4.62.1

790. Emperors Severus and Antoninus Augusti to Gavius Victorinus. The exaction of new taxes is not lightly granted. But if your community is so badly off that it requires assistance with extraordinary aid, inform the governor of the province of the material which you put in your petition. He will carefully investigate matters, take account of the common good, and write to us about what he has discovered. We will then consider whether and how far to take account of your request.

Victorinus was seeking on behalf of his community the right to impose some new local taxes; the emperors were concerned to preserve a viable city government capable of collecting taxes due to the Roman state; see also no. 736.

D 49.14.3.6

791. The divine Hadrian expressed himself in a rescript in the following terms: 'That practice is entirely inhumane by which those who lease public revenues and lands are held to remain liable if they cannot be leased out again at a similar figure. Indeed, those who lease will be more easily found if they know that, should they wish to give up the lease when their time has expired, they will not be retained'.

Pressure to maintain public services in local communities meant that certain obligations crucial for city finances had become very onerous, and in some cases almost compulsory in defiance of legal right. We have seen how in Egypt a man taking a lease on unproductive land inserted a clause that he would not be compelled to renew it after it expired (no. 459).

Oliver (1989), 234

792. In Alexandria. Copies of the decisions posted in the stoa of the Gymnasium, year eight, Phamenoth 18. Emperor Caesar Lucius Septimius Severus Pius Pertinax Arabicus Adiabenicus Parthicus Maximus Augustus and Emperor Caesar Marcus Aurelius Antoninus Augustus.

(Lines 35–9) To Kronios, son of Heraklides. Transient sicknesses do not afford relief from municipal liturgies. Those who are chronically ill in body are subject to liturgical services if they are mentally capable of conducting their household affairs.

This papyrus contains thirteen responses made by Septimius Severus and Caracalla in Alexandria during their visit in AD 200. They were published over three successive days and deal with a variety of issues brought to the attention of the emperors, including local rights and abusive officials; for other responses see no. 797; also, Williams (1974).

CJ 10.53(52).1

793. Emperor Antoninus Augustus to Numisius. Since you claim that you are the doctor of the legion II Adiutrix, you will not be compelled to undertake civic obligations while you are absent on public service. However, when you have ceased to be absent, after the end of your exemption under that rule, if you belong to the group of those who share the benefits granted to doctors, you can make use of that immunity.

Those absent from their community on public service were temporarily exempt from local obligations; doctors also enjoyed certain exemptions (see no. 239).

CJ 10.40(39).2

794. Alexander Augustus to Crispus. Those people who spend some time in a locality to pursue their studies are not considered, according to a letter of Hadrian, to reside there, unless they have established their home in that place for ten years, and the same applies to a father who frequently travels to visit his student son. But if you are proved to have established your home in the splendid community of Laodicea for other reasons, your deceit to avoid meeting local obligations will not benefit you.

If the father had for some reason taken up residence in Laodicea, he would be liable for local obligations and services. This is a good indication of eagerness to avoid this kind of burden.

D 25.4.1pr (Ulpian, *Edict*, Book 24)

795. In the time of the divine brothers when it came about that a husband claimed that his wife was pregnant but she denied it, and the emperors were consulted on the matter, they stated the following in a rescript to Valerius Priscianus, the urban praetor: 'Rutilius Severus apparently requests something new, namely the appointment of someone to keep watch on his wife, who is divorced from him and claims that she is not pregnant, and so no

one will be surprised if we too propose a new approach and solution. Therefore, if he persists in his demand, it is most appropriate to choose the home of a very respectable lady to which Domitia may go, and there three midwives of proven skill and honesty, who will have been selected by you, should examine her. If all of them or two of them declare that she seems to be pregnant, then the woman must be prevailed upon to accept an observer, just as if she herself had wanted this. But if she does not give birth, the husband must recognize that his honour and reputation are at stake, in case it will entirely reasonably seem that he has done this in order to injure his wife. But if all or the majority of the midwives declare that she is not pregnant, there will no reason for having an observer'.

The husband, presumably believing that the child had been conceived while his wife was still married to him, wanted to assert his right to have any child born within the control of his *patria potestas*.

D 16.1.2.3 (Ulpian, *Edict*, Book 29)

796. (A senatorial decree brings help to women on account of the weakness of their sex.) But it brings relief to them only if they have not practised any deceit. For divine Pius and Severus stated this in rescripts. For relief is given to those who have been deceived, not to those who deceive. And there is a rescript of Severus in Greek in the following terms: 'The decree of the senate does not offer assistance to women engaged in fraud'; for it is the vulnerability of women not their cunning that merits assistance.

For the supposed weakness of women and Roman law see Gardner (1986), 261–5; Grubbs (2002), 60–71; no. 525.

P. Oxy. 1020 = Oliver (1989), no. 221 (AD 199/200)

797. Emperor Caesar Lucius Septimius Severus Pius Pertinax Augustus, Arabicus, Adiabenicus, Parthicus Maximus, and Emperor Caesar Marcus Aurelius Antoninus Pius Augustus, to Varus son of Damasaeos. If you are entitled to help because of your age, the provincial governor will make a judgement on the suit for release. Published at Alexandria.

The same emperors to Procunda, daughter of Hermaeos, by way of Epagathus, freedman. If you are entitled to help because of your age, the provincial governor will make a judgement on the suit for fraud. Published at Alexandria.

These are probably *apokrimata* (AD 199/200) responses to legal issues raised by petitioners. A person under twenty-five who was not under paternal power was considered unable to manage his own business because of juvenile infirmity of mind; they received special consideration and curators of minors were appointed; see *D* 4.4.

CJ 4.20.2 (AD 223)

798. Emperor Alexander Augustus to Carpus. If you are involved in a dispute about your free birth, defend your suit with evidence and arguments which you think appropriate. For witnesses alone are insufficient to prove free birth.

Hadrian (see no. 731) had emphasized the value of witnesses, but documentary evidence might be necessary in cases of birth status. Note the court case involving the status of Iusta (no. 45) conducted by means of witnesses and documentation.

CJ 12.1.1

799. Emperor Alexander Augustus to Severiana. If, as you claim, you have both a grandfather of consular rank and a father of praetorian rank, and you have married men not of routine rank but of distinction, you will retain your distinguished family heritage.

People of senatorial rank were marked out by free birth, citizenship, and three generations of family status; see pp. 42–4; for the rank and title of women, see no. 65.

Marriage

D 23.2.58 (Marcianus, *Rules*, Book 4)

800. A rescript was issued by the divine Pius stating that if a freedwoman deceived a senator into thinking she was freeborn and married him, on the precedent of the praetor's edict an action should be granted against her, because she can derive no benefit from her dowry which is void.

Augustus' marriage legislation of 18 BC and AD 9 had prohibited marriage between men of senatorial family and freedwomen; see Treggiari (1991), 60–5; a dowry consisted of the property and resources a woman brought to a marriage and part of which she could normally recover after divorce.

CJ 5.18.3 (AD 215)

801. Emperor Antoninus Augustus to Hostilia. If in ignorance of the status of Eros you married him thinking that he was a freeborn man and gave him a dowry, but later it was concluded that he was a slave, you will receive the dowry back from his *peculium* and additionally anything else he clearly owes you. However, your sons, since they were born to a freeborn woman and a man of uncertain status, are reckoned to be illegitimate freeborn children.

There was no legal capacity for marriage with a slave; the children were freeborn since they followed the woman's status; see Treggiari (1991), 52–4.

CJ 5.12.5 (AD 226)

802. Emperor Alexander Augustus to Statia. Whenever the property given for a dowry is appraised, the husband acquires ownership of it but in a way becomes debtor for its monetary value. If therefore there is no agreement that on the dissolution of the marriage the property should be returned, and if it has been properly appraised, he may retain it, as long as he offers you the monetary value.

A dowry could be valued, in which case the husband became liable for the cash amount if the dowry had to be restored. It was problematic if specific items in the dowry were valued, since over time they might depreciate, but the husband would be responsible for the original value.

CJ 2.18(19).13 (AD 230)

803. Emperor Alexander Augustus to Aquila. You cannot recover from your father-in-law money that you spent because of your wife's illness, but ought to put that expense down to the love you have for her. If you expended money on her funeral expenses on the understanding of recovering it, you can legally sue her father to whom the dowry has reverted.

When the husband returned the dowry to his wife's family, he was permitted to deduct certain expenses, which were classified as necessary (such as the repair of a house which might otherwise collapse), useful (such as the creation of a vineyard which would increase profits), or for pleasure (such as the purchase of paintings); *Tituli Ulpiani* 6.14–17. For a survey of the dowry in Roman marriage, see Treggiari (1991), 323–64.

D 23.2.57a (Marcian, *Note on Papinian's Work on Adultery*, Book 2)

804. The emperors the divine Marcus and Lucius to Flavia Tertulla, acting through a freedman, a surveyor, replied as follows: 'We are influenced by the length of time during which in ignorance of the law you were married to your uncle, and by the fact that your marriage was arranged by your grandmother, and also by the number of your children. Therefore, taking account of all these factors, we confirm the status of your children born in that marriage, which was contracted over forty years ago, just as if they had been born as legitimate offspring'.

Although Claudius in AD 49 had introduced legislation permitting a man to follow his example (in marrying Agrippina) and marry his brother's daughter, the practice seems not to have been perpetuated after that time (see Treggiari (1991), 37–8); a marriage deemed as incestuous was void and any offspring illegitimate.

Wills

D 34.1.13.1 (Scaevola, *Responses*, Book 4)

805. The Emperor Antoninus Pius to the freedmen of Sextia Basilia: 'Although the words of the will were phrased to the effect that as long as you remained with Claudius Justus food and clothing were bequeathed to you, nevertheless I interpret that the dead woman's thinking was that after the death of Justus she wanted you to be provided with the same'. He (Scaevola) pronounced that a will written in this way should be accepted as meaning that upkeep should be provided in perpetuity.

In the interpretation of Roman wills great importance was attached to the testator's real intentions; see also no. 806.

***CJ* 6.42.1 (AD 212)**

806. Emperor Antoninus Augustus to Demetrius. If you can prove that Demetrius asked his mother and heir to provide you with a monthly allowance and annual sum for clothes, and that she, following the wishes of her son provided these for a long time, that is, in this kind of case no fewer than three years, you will gain your request that these should be provided in the future, and that the sum owing in so far as they were not provided in the past should be paid.

CJ 3.28.1 (193)

807. Emperors Severus and Antoninus Augusti to Victorinus: When a son wishes to contest the will of his mother on the grounds that it is undutiful, it is not unfair for him to bring a suit against the person who holds the estate on the basis of a trust (*fideicommissum*), since as holder of the trust he is just as much liable as if he held the estate as heir or possessor.

A *querella testamenti inofficiosi* contested a will on the grounds that the testator's nearest relatives had been improperly treated and that he/she had ignored his natural obligations to them; if the complaint was upheld the will was voided and the rules of intestate succession applied; for *fideicommissum* see p. 437.

D 29.2.97 (Paul, *Decrees*, Book 3)

808. Clodius Clodianus having made a first will subsequently instituted the same heir in another will, which was so formulated as to be legally void. The appointed heir, thinking that the later will was valid, wished to accept the inheritance in that will, but subsequently it was discovered to be invalid. Papinian held the view that he had rejected the inheritance under the first will and could not enter into the inheritance under the second will. I expressed the opinion that his belief that the second will was valid did not constitute a rejection of the inheritance (in the first will). He (the emperor) pronounced the verdict that Clodianus had died intestate.

The emperor faced with conflicting advice from his lawyers forms his own opinion but inclines more to that of Papinian; he presumably held that the testator's wishes were unclear since he apparently changed his mind about the first (valid) will.

CJ 6.29.1 (AD 213)

809. Emperor Antoninus Augustus to Brittianus. If after making a will in which the testator made no mention of any posthumous children, he then produced a daughter, he died intestate, since the will is broken by the birth of a posthumous child whom he did not mention. It is well-established law that from the terms of a broken will nothing is due or can be demanded.

A testator who wished to exclude from his will his own children had to do so expressly, otherwise the will was invalid. Therefore, a child born after the testator's death (*postumus*) would also cause the will to be void.

D 37.14.17 (Ulpian, *Lex Iulia et Papia*, Book 11)

810. The divine brothers issued a response in the following terms: 'We have discovered from those skilled in the law that sometimes it has been questioned whether a grandson can seek possession of the estate (*bonorum possessio*) against the will of the testator in respect of the property of the freedman of his grandfather, if the father of the grandson when he was twenty-five years old had brought a capital charge against that freedman, and that Proculus, clearly no slight authority on legal matters, was of the opinion that possession of the estate should not be granted to the grandson in a case of this kind. We also followed this opinion when we responded to the petition of Caesidia Longina. Furthermore, our friend Volusius Maecianus, as well as having a long-standing and well-founded expertise in the law, and also being meticulously careful, was influenced by respect for our rescript to affirm in our presence that he did not think that any other reply should be given. But when we discussed the issue more fully with Maecianus himself and other friends of ours who are legal experts and who had been summoned to a meeting, the preferable view seemed to be that the grandson should not be excluded from the property of the freedman of his grandfather, either by the words or spirit of the law, or of the praetor's edict, as a result of the character of his father or any stain on it; and that this was the opinion of several legal experts and particularly of that distinguished man, our friend Salvius Iulianus'.

This shows how imperial decisions could be based on juristic advice, with the emperors (Marcus Aurelius and Lucius Verus) conscientiously taking detailed, if conflicting, legal opinion in issuing their rescripts. The argument was presumably that the claimant's father had brought a vexatious capital charge deliberately against the freedman in order to get control of his estate. In this case *bonorum possessio* (possession of the estate) is apparently contrary to the will of the testator. Volusius Maecianus had been the tutor of Marcus Aurelius; he was of equestrian rank and had served as prefect of Egypt before being promoted to the rank of senator, after which he held the position of prefect of the public treasury before becoming consul. The emperors refer to a previous rescript issued on the basis of an opinion of Proculus. Since he lived in the first century, they must have had access to his writings; they had also checked the rescript, which must have been available in the imperial archives; discussion in Sirks (2001), 123–5.

Military Business

D 29.1.24 (Florentinus, *Institutions*, Book 10)

811. Divine Trajan wrote in a rescript to Statilius Taurus in the following terms: 'That privilege granted to soldiers by which their wills are regarded as valid howsoever they are made, should be understood in the following way, namely that, first it should be established that a will was made, which can be done without writing it down and by non-soldiers. Therefore if the soldier, concerning whose property there is a case before you, called together his comrades for the purpose of declaring his wishes, and spoke in such terms that he made clear whom he wanted to be his heir and to whom he wanted to grant freedom, it can be agreed that he made a will in this way without writing it down, and his wishes should be ratified. But if, as often happens in casual conversation, he said to someone "I make you my heir" or "I leave my property to you", this should not be taken as a will. It is in no one's interest more than those to whom this privilege was granted for examples of this kind not to be accepted. For it would not be difficult after the death of a soldier for witnesses to appear claiming that they had heard him say that he was leaving his property to someone whom they wished to benefit, and in this way true judgement would be subverted'.

The general direction of policy was to allow soldiers to make a will unencumbered by the usual legal regulations, and Trajan had laid down that soldiers could make wills in whatever way they wished (see Campbell (1984), 210–29, and no. 742). This rescript is a response to some of the problems that emerged from this generous privilege.

D 29.1.15.2 (Ulpian, *Edict*, Book 45)

812. A will made by a soldier before the start of military service should be valid according to military law if he should die during service, 'if the wishes of the soldier do not go against this', as divine Pius stated in a rescript.

The military will retained its validity during military service, but within a year of his discharge a veteran was required to draw up a will in accordance with normal regulations.

CJ 6.21.1 (AD 212)

813. Emperor Antoninus Augustus to Florus, soldier. If your brother while in military service made you heir specifically for his goods at home, you are

not able to claim the goods which he left in the camp, even if the person who was instituted heir of these is unwilling to accept the estate. But those entitled inherit from him as intestate, provided that no substitute was appointed (for the heir), and it is clearly proved that your brother did not wish his camp property to go to you. For the wishes of a soldier engaged on a military expedition are taken as law.

Soldiers even if still in *patria potestas* were permitted to retain in their possession all money and goods obtained through military service and to dispose of them in a will separately from other property; what constituted 'acquired through military service' was open to some debate. See Campbell (1984), 229–36. Once again, we see the importance of a soldier's final wishes.

CJ 2.12(13).9

814. Emperor Antoninus Augustus to Aufidius. Serving soldiers can deal with their own affairs without infringing military discipline. Nor can it be claimed that the man who for an honourable and proper reason has been carrying out business mandated to him is engaging in the business of another. For when in good faith he has accepted the right of action from another, it is not in dispute that he is managing his own affairs. It is absurd and indeed unjust for my soldiers to be prohibited from doing this.

Soldiers were considered in some respects to have a special influence in legal proceedings. Therefore, rules were in place to prevent them from deliberately undertaking the business affairs of another simply to gain an advantage in court. Caracalla on this occasion takes a generous view of the soldier's action; see also nos. 815–16.

CJ 4.61.3

815. Emperors Severus and Antoninus Augusti to Ingenuus, soldier. We have taken thought for the welfare of all our soldiers to make sure that they do not face a penalty for committing an offence because they omitted to make a declaration. Therefore, set aside this fear, and if it seems that you owe some *portoria* tax, pay it.

The *portoria* tax required travellers to make at a customs station a declaration of goods carried across circumscription boundaries; these boundaries might encompass one province or a group of provinces; soldiers had exemption only for personal items carried across.

CJ 5.16.2 (AD 213)

816. Emperor Antoninus Augustus to Marcus, soldier. If you have proved to the governor of the province that the slave girl was bought with your money, and an instrument of sale was written in the name of your mistress for a gift, he will order her to be given back to you. For even though in the absence of a legal marriage a gift could be made, I do not wish my soldiers to be swindled by their mistresses in this way by fictitious displays of affection.

Caracalla is granting a concession to this soldier. In a legal marriage, gifts between husband and wife were not permitted; in this case the soldier was not married and so the gift given to his mistress, complete with her name on the deed of sale, should have been legally valid. The emperor, who liked to present himself as a benevolent fellow-soldier to the army, ignores strict legal rules. The emotive language suggests Caracalla's personal interest in the case.

CJ 12.33(34).1

817. Emperors Severus and Antoninus Augusti, greetings to Antonius. If you wish to put your name forward for military service, present yourselves to those who have the right to check recruits. However, you are not unaware that those who seek to join the army because they are involved in a lawsuit are normally discharged from military service at the request of their opponent.

This suggests that soldiers in court might have a privileged position, for example in getting the case heard more quickly or making their opponent deal with them in the military camp; see nos. 674; 707. Antonius seems to represent a group of potential recruits.

CJ 10.55(54).1

818. Emperor Antoninus Augustus to Verinus. Those who have been dishonourably discharged from military service must avoid public office, but they are not excused from civic obligations.

For military law, dishonourable discharge, and punishments for desertion, see Campbell (1984), 300–14. But there was provision for the granting of discharge benefits pro rata to soldiers who suffered illness or wounds.

D 49.16.3pr (Modestinus, *Penalties*, Book 4)

819. When he has heard his case the governor should send a deserter to his own commander with a report, unless the deserter has committed a more

serious offence in the province where he was found. For he should suffer punishment in the place where he committed the crime, as the divine Severus and Antoninus stated in a rescript.

An *emansor* was a soldier who had been absent from camp for a time and returned voluntarily. A deserter was defined as a soldier who had been absent for an extended time and brought back. His rank, pay, and the post he had deserted were taken into consideration, and whether he had deserted alone or in a group. Soldiers could be reduced in rank or transferred or suffer capital punishment. A soldier who committed another offence during a period of desertion was more heavily punished; for example, a theft was held to be tantamount to a second act of desertion (*D* 49.16.5.2).

D 49.16.13.6 (Macer, *Military Affairs*, Book 2)

820. The divine Pius stated in a rescript that a deserter who had been given up by his father should be demoted to a lesser arm of military service in case, as he said, it should appear that his father had presented his son for execution. Similarly, the divine Severus and Antoninus ordered that a man who surrendered himself after five years as a deserter should be deported, a precedent which we ought to follow in other cases, as Menander wrote.

Execution was a possible punishment for deserters, especially those who were found in Rome. This decision by Pius was perhaps intended to encourage parents to surrender their children who had fled home. Menander described the punishment of deporting to an island a deserter who surrendered himself an act of 'imperial generosity' (*D* 49.16.5.4).

CJ 12.35(36).6

821. The same emperor (Gordian III) to Brutus, soldier. Once soldiers have been discharged for medical reasons, it is not usual to grant reinstatement on the grounds that they have recovered good health, since soldiers are not lightly discharged and only after doctors have declared that they have contracted an infirmity, and this has been rigorously investigated by a suitable judge.

See Campbell (1984), 312–14. Those soldiers medically discharged (*causarii*) were entitled to the privileges of veterans on a scale depending on how long they had served; for example, *causarii* of twenty years' service 'keep a clear record and are eligible for the general privileges granted to veterans' (*CJ* 5.65.1 (Caracalla)).

D 48.3.12pr (Callistratus, *Judicial Enquiries,* Book 5)

822. If soldiers lose a prisoner, they themselves incur risk. For divine Hadrian stated in a rescript to the governor Statilius Secundus that whenever a prisoner escapes from soldiers, he should inquire whether he escaped because the soldiers had been very negligent, or by accident, and whether one escaped out of a larger number, or many escaped at the same time; only at this point should the soldiers from whom the prisoners escaped be executed, if they were significantly negligent. Otherwise, they should be treated in proportion to their negligence. The same emperor stated in a rescript to Salvius the governor of Aquitania that punishment should be inflicted on a soldier who set a prisoner free, or who deliberately guarded him in such a way that he was able to escape. However, if the escape occurred because he was drunk or lazy, he should be beaten and demoted to lower rank. If, however, he lost the prisoner accidentally he should not be punished.

D 49.16.6.7 (Arrius Menander, *Military Affairs,* Book 3)

823. Emperor Hadrian stated in a rescript in respect of a soldier who stabbed himself or tried to commit suicide in another way that the case should be investigated, so that if he chose to die because of inability to withstand pain, or weariness of life, or illness, or insanity, or shame, he should not be executed but dishonourably discharged. If he did not put forward any such reason, he should be executed.

D 49.18.4 (Ulpian, *Duties of a Proconsul,* Book 4)

824. It was stated in a rescript to Iulius Sossianus, veteran, that veterans did not have immunity from the cost of paving a road, since it is clear that veterans are not exempt from the tax on property. Furthermore, that their ships can be subject to requisition was stated in a rescript to Aelius Firmus and Antoninus Clarus, veterans.

For the status and privileges of veterans see Campbell (1984), 282–3; 439–45; (1994), 193–210; Sänger (2011), especially 15–37 (a very useful discussion of the papyrus archive of two veteran soldiers in Egypt, Aelius Sarapammon and Aelius Syrion, including petitions, appeals, and letters; see pp. 340–4 for a collection of legal appeals from veterans in Egypt). Soldiers were exempt from some local obligations (such as holding office) in their community, but not from taxes on property.

CJ 10.44(43).1

825. Emperor Alexander Augustus to Felicianus. Veterans, who, although they can protect themselves with the immunity that has been granted to them, prefer to become decurions in their own community, cannot resume the immunity that they abandoned, unless by a definite arrangement and agreement for preserving their immunity, or if they have accepted part of the burden (of office).

Ulpian (*D* 49.18.2) argued that a veteran's immunity was not undermined if he voluntarily undertook a public office or duty; this rescript suggests that the veteran needed to negotiate a specific agreement if he wished to become a decurion.

List of Jurists and Principal Authors

All dates are AD unless otherwise indicated

Jurists

Africanus, Sextus Caecilius – second century; possibly pupil of Iulianus.

Alfenus Varus – late republic; wrote the *Digesta*.

Aquila, Iulius – contemporary of Ulpian.

Aristo, Titius – member of the *consilium* of Trajan.

Arrius Menander – member of the *consilium* of Septimius Severus and Caracalla; expert on military law.

Callistratus – probably of Greek origin, wrote in the time of Septimius Severus and Caracalla.

Celsus, Publius Iuventius – early second century; held consulship and was a member of the *consilium* of Hadrian; led the Proculian group of lawyers.

Charisius, Aurelius Arcasius – late third, early fourth century; analysed jurisdiction of praetorian prefect.

Florentinus – second century; wrote twelve books of *Institutiones*.

Furius Anthianus – early third century; wrote a commentary on the praetorian edict.

Gaius – mid second century; wrote a legal textbook, the *Institutiones* (*Institutes*) and commentaries on the Twelve Tables, the praetorian edict and provincial edict; Justinian thought highly of him, basing his *Institutes* on Gaius' work.

Hermogenianus – late third century; produced a collection of legal excerpts.

Iavolenus, Octavius Tidius Tossianus L. Iavolenus Priscus – late first and early second century; consul 86; was head of the Sabinian school and teacher of Iulianus; he served on Trajan's *consilium* and held many public offices.

Iulianus, Salvius (Julian) – second century; consul 148; a member of Hadrian's *consilium* and the last known head of the Sabinian group; held many public offices and notably revised the praetorian edict; outstanding jurist frequently quoted by other lawyers.

Labeo, Marcus Antistius – a contemporary of Augustus; teacher and author whose works amounted to 400 books; founded the legal group named Proculian after one of his followers.

Licinnius Rufinus – third century, a pupil of Paul.

Macer, Aemilius – early third century; his works included studies of military law and provincial governorship.

Maecianus, Volusius – mid second century; taught law to Marcus Aurelius and was a member of the emperor's *consilium*; served as secretary of petitions (*libelli*) under Antoninus Pius, and was prefect of Egypt.

Marcellus, Ulpius – second century; served on the *consilium* of Antoninus Pius and Marcus Aurelius.

Marcianus, Aelius – early–mid third century; his sixteen books of *Institutes* are much quoted in the *Digest.*

Mauricianus, Iunius – second century; notable for a commentary on the *lex Iulia et Papia Poppaea.*

Modestinus, Herennius – third century; a pupil of Ulpian, he possibly served as Severus Alexander's secretary for petitions; was also prefect of the *Vigiles.*

Neratius Priscus, L. – second century; was a member of the *consilium* of Trajan and Hadrian; consul in 97 and also governed Lower Germany and Pannonia; last known head of the Proculian group.

Papinianus, Aemilius (Papinian) – late second, early third century; friend of Septimius Severus; served as secretary for petitions; was praetorian prefect from 205 to 211; executed in 212 by Caracalla; highly thought of by Constantine and later lawyers.

Papirius Iustus – second century; collected imperial constitutions.

Paulus, Iulius (Paul) – third century; served in the *consilium* of Septimius Severus and Caracalla and then Severus Alexander; wrote over 300 books and was a major source for the compilers of the *Digest.*

Pedius, Sextus – late first, early second century; his work is known from the comments of other jurists.

Pomponius, Sextus – mid second century, teacher, and author of over 300 books, much quoted in the *Digest.*

Proculus, Sempronius (?) – mid first century; a teacher of law, he was the head of the Proculian group of jurists.

Sabinus, Masurius – first century; taught law and was head of the Sabinian group of jurists; Tiberius permitted him to state his legal opinions on the emperor's authority.

Scaevola, Quintus Cervidius – second century; was prefect of the *Vigiles* and became legal adviser to Marcus Aurelius, and teacher of Paul; much quoted in the *Digest.*

Terentius Clemens – second century; wrote a commentary on *lex Iulia et Papia.*

Tertullianus – possibly early third century; produced the *Quaestiones* and a treatise on *castrense peculium*; unlikely that he is identical with the Christian apologist Tertullian.

Trebatius, Gaius Testa – first century BC; a friend of Cicero who wrote works on civil and divine law; he tutored Labeo.

Tryphonius, Claudius – early third century; he was a member of the *consilium* of Septimius Severus and a pupil of Cervidius Scaevola, on whose work he collected notes.

Ulpianus, Domitius (Ulpian) – third century; from Tyre in Syria Phoenice; from 205 was secretary of petitions for Septimius Severus; in 222 he was prefect of the corn supply, and later that year was appointed prefect of the praetorian guard by Severus Alexander; by 224 he had been murdered by the guardsmen; an outstanding lawyer, his works on the duties of imperial office-holders, statutes, and public law, and commentaries on the praetor's edict and the civil law, were widely quoted in the *Digest.*

Venuleius Saturninus – later second century; his works included treatises on interdicts and *stipulationes.*

Vivianus – first century AD; wrote commentaries on the edicts of the praetor and aediles.

Principal Authors

Agennius Urbicus (possibly late fourth/early fifth century) wrote a treatise for the guidance of practitioners in the principal aspects of land survey; this included a long discussion of land disputes.

Apuleius (born c. AD 125) in Madaurus in the province of Africa Proconsularis was a public speaker and scholar; his works included a Latin novel, the *Metamorphoses*, and the *Apologia*, in which he defended himself against charges of using magic.

Augustus (63 BC–AD 14) became the first emperor of Rome after a long period of civil war; his brief autobiographical memoir, the *Res Gestae*, offers his assessment of his achievements.

Aulus Gellius (c. 125–190?) wrote the *Noctes Atticae* ('Attic Nights'), a collection based on his reading of miscellaneous observations on a wide variety of topics.

Cato (the Elder), Marcus Porcius Cato (234–149 BC) was an important figure in the Roman republic, holding both the consulship and censorship. His *De Agricultura* was a guide to owners of slave-based estates, producing wine and olive oil for sale. He also wrote the first substantial history in Latin.

Cicero, Marcus Tullius Cicero (106–43 BC) was a senator active in politics in the last generation of the Roman republic. He was an outstanding orator; among his literary works, treatises on oratory and philosophy are particularly important, and there is a large body of his private correspondence; he was murdered in 43 in the aftermath of the assassination of Caesar.

Columella, Lucius Iunius Moderatus Columella from Gades in Spain flourished c. 50. He wrote a manual on the management of slave-based farms and a book on orchards.

Dio, Cassius Dio (c. 165–c. 229) was a Greek senator from Nicaea in Bithynia; he served twice as consul and held several provincial governorships; he wrote an annalistic history of the Roman world in eighty books from its foundation down to his own day. Much of the work is not extant, and we rely on excerpts from the text made in Byzantine times.

Eusebius (c. 260–339), bishop of Caesarea, wrote biblical commentaries and sought to defend Christianity, especially in his ten-book *Ecclesiastical History*.

Florus, Publius(?) Annaeus Florus (c. 100–150) wrote an outline of Roman history with special reference to warfare from the start of the republic to the time of Augustus.

Frontinus (c. 30–104), Sextus Iulius Frontinus was an important senator who held three consulships, several governorships, and the post of Superintendent of the Aqueducts; he wrote a treatise on their management, and on military stratagems, and probably a work on land survey.

Fronto, Marcus Cornelius Fronto (c. 95–c. 166), distinguished senator and advocate, tutor to future emperors Marcus Aurelius and Lucius Verus, with whom he remained friendly; known largely through his letters.

Historia Augusta – a collection of biographies of emperors from 117 to 284 allegedly by six different authors; there are many inaccuracies in the biographies, and it is thought to be the work of a single author at the end of the fourth century.

Horace, Quintus Horatius Flaccus (65–8 BC), son of a freedman, fought on the side of Brutus and Cassius at the battle of Philippi in the civil war; his poetry brought him to the attention of Augustus' friend Maecenas who became his patron; Augustus offered him a post on his personal staff, but Horace declined.

Hyginus wrote c. 100 on categories of land, the establishment of boundaries, and land disputes.

Hyginus Gromaticus wrote no later than the second or early third century, offering guidance to land surveyors in the establishment of boundaries, the dimensions of blocks of allocated land, and the consistent designation of the land division system.

Josephus, Flavius Josephus (37/38–?), a Jewish priest of aristocratic background, was politically prominent in Jerusalem before the Jewish rebellion of 66 whose leaders placed him in charge of Galilee; he was captured at the siege of Jotapata, but after allegedly prophesying the accession of Vespasian he became friends with his son, Titus, and eventually came to Rome; his works included a history of the Jewish rebellion and a study of Jewish history.

Juvenal, Decimus Iunius Iuvenalis (second century) wrote satires, the context of which is social and political life in Rome.

Lactantius, Lucius Caelius Firmianus, also called Lactantius (c. 240–c. 320), teacher of rhetoric who became a Christian apologist; the *De Mortibus Persecutorum* aims to show that persecutors always come to a bad end.

Lucian, born c. AD 120, was a Greek sophist who toured Greece and Italy delivering declamations. He wrote essays and dialogues often of a satirical nature.

Macrobius, Ambrosius Theodosius Macrobius (fifth century), scholar and philosopher; his *Saturnalia* is set as a discussion among distinguished Romans on the festival of the Saturnalia (16 December); it contains a wide range of miscellaneous issues and draws heavily on earlier writers.

Martial, Marcus Valerius Martialis (c. 40–c. 104) was a native of Bilbilis in Spain; he came to Rome in 64 and earned favour as a poet at the highest level, addressing some poems to Domitian; his *Epigrams* are short poems, many of which depict characters and activities in contemporary Rome.

Menander Rhetor (c. late third century): among writings under the name of Menander is a treatise on formal, set speeches, for example, in praise of individual cities.

Ovid, Publius Ovidius Naso (43 BC–AD 18), from a family of equestrian rank, studied rhetoric and held some judicial posts before devoting himself to poetry, becoming one of Rome's foremost poets; in AD 8 he offended Augustus in a way which is still obscure and was exiled to Tomi on the Black Sea.

Petronius (died 66) is possibly identical with the senator of consular rank and eminent member of Nero's entourage who was compelled to commit suicide; his *Satyrica*, only part of which survives, is a novel combining prose and verse describing a series of adventures which befell the narrator, Encolpius, and other characters.

Philostratus, Lucius Flavius Philostratus (second to third century), a friend of Iulia Domna, wife of Septimius Severus, was encouraged by her to write a biography of the philosopher Apollonius of Tyana; he also produced *Lives of the Sophists*, an account of orators and rhetoricians down to the author's own day.

Pliny (the Elder), Gaius Plinius Secundus (23/4–79), was a friend of Vespasian and held numerous equestrian offices; as prefect of the fleet at Misenum, sailing to observe the eruption of Vesuvius and bring aid to survivors, he died from inhaling fumes; he wrote the *Natural History*, a voluminous collection of information about art, science, geography, and many aspects of Roman life.

Pliny (the Younger), Gaius Plinius Caecilius Secundus (c. 61–c. 112), nephew of Pliny the Elder, advocate and senior senator, consul in 100 and also prefect of the treasury and curator of the bed and banks of the Tiber; sent by Trajan as governor of Bithynia-Pontus with responsibility for reforming the administration; from the collection of Pliny's correspondence, book ten contains exchanges of letters between Pliny as governor and Trajan, and are a crucial source for the understanding of Roman administration.

Plutarch, Mestrius Plutarchus (c. 40s–120s) was a member of the local aristocracy in Chaeronea in Greece; a philosopher, he lectured and taught in Rome, and was the friend of senior senators; of his numerous works the most well-known are the *Parallel Lives*, in which he compares a famous Greek personality with his equivalent in the Roman world.

Quintilian, Marcus Fabius Quintilianus (c. 35–90s), from Calagurris in Spain; had a school of rhetoric in Rome, numbered Pliny the Younger among his pupils, and became tutor to Domitian's great-nephews and heirs; he wrote the *Institutio Oratoria*, which was published probably before 96, and analyses the training of an orator.

Seneca (the Elder), Lucius Annaeus Seneca (c. 50 BC–c. AD 40), from Corduba in Spain, came from an equestrian family; he was a student of rhetoric and produced a collection of *Controversiae* and *Suasoriae*, training exercises for the oratory of the law courts, dealing with imaginary problems and issues.

Seneca (the Younger), Lucius Annaeus Seneca (c. 4 BC–AD 65), son of Seneca the Elder, was educated in rhetoric and philosophy in Rome; he became a senator and was prominent under Claudius before being sent into exile in 41; recalled in 49 he was appointed tutor to Nero; when Nero became emperor in 54 Seneca along with Burrus, the praetorian prefect, acted as senior adviser; after the latter's death he lost influence and retired from court; after the conspiracy of Piso in 65 he was forced to commit suicide. He wrote a series of dialogues on anger (*De Ira*) and other themes, moral treatises, for example, *De Clementia*, *Naturales Quaestiones* on natural phenomena from a Stoic point of view, and nine tragedies largely based on Greek models. Seneca's *Letters* are not genuine epistles but wide-ranging essays on moral principles.

Siculus Flaccus (possibly second century) wrote a treatise to guide land surveyors, describing the history and practice of surveying, the categories of land and settlements, and boundary marking and related disputes.

Strabo (c. 64 BC–c. AD 21), from Amaseia in Pontus, spent time in Rome and enjoyed patronage from the elite; he produced a geography in seventeen books of the world as the Romans saw it in the age of Augustus.

Suetonius, Gaius Suetonius Tranquillus (c. 70–c. 130) was of equestrian rank; a scholar, advocate, and friend of Pliny (the Younger), he held under Trajan and Hadrian several important secretaryships, including that of correspondence secretary. For historians his most important work is the *Lives of the Caesars*, a set of twelve biographies of rulers of Rome, from Julius Caesar to Domitian.

Tacitus, Publius Cornelius Tacitus (c. 56–c. 118), from Narbonese or Cisalpine Gaul, was a distinguished senator, holding the consulship and several administrative posts; he was an advocate and friend of Pliny (the Younger); Tacitus is most notable for his two histories of Rome, the *Annales* (Annals) covering the period 14–68, and the *Historiae* (Histories) covering events from 69 to 96. His shorter works included a biography of his father-in-law, Cnaeus Iulius Agricola, who had been governor of Britain in AD 77, and a treatise on oratory.

Terentius Varro, Marcus (116–27 BC) held office in Rome and served under Pompey in the civil war; pardoned by Caesar, he was subsequently proscribed by Mark Antony after Caesar's assassination, but managed to escape into retirement. An outstanding scholar, he wrote on a wide range of subjects, including the Latin language, and a treatise of farming (*De Re Rustica*).

Tertullian, Quintus Septimius Florens Tertullianus (c. 160–c. 240) from Carthage was a Christian apologist who wrote a variety of treatises defending Christianity against charges of atheism, sedition, and unwholesome practices; he advocated rigorous rules for the Christian life.

Valerius Maximus (early first century) wrote a handbook, dedicated to the emperor Tiberius, comprising a miscellaneous collection of examples of 'memorable deeds and sayings'. It is a work of uneven quality which nevertheless preserves useful information.

Velleius, Velleius Paterculus (20 or 19 BC–AD 30s) was of equestrian rank, but after distinguished service as military tribune and prefect of cavalry serving under the future emperor Tiberius, he entered the senate and was marked out by Augustus in AD 14 for the praetorship of 15. His general history of Rome ends in AD 29 and the history of his own time gives a valuable view of someone who had benefitted from Augustus' regime and supported it.

Vitruvius Pollio (c. 50 BC–?) served Augustus as prefect of engineers, and addressed to the emperor his treatise on architecture (*De Architectura*) which covered construction, decoration, water supply, and the environment in which people had to live.

Glossary of Legal Terms

Accusatio – the bringing of a criminal charge

Actio – the move by a plaintiff to sue in a legal action

Actio in factum – an action granted by the praetor on the basis of the alleged facts, where no action in civil law was normally available

Addictio in diem – an agreement between vendor and purchaser that allowed the vendor to set aside the sale if he received a better price within a set time

Advocatus – advocate/lawyer

Aedilis (Aedile) – a Roman magistrate elected annually, responsible among other things for buildings and the management of relations between the inhabitants of Rome in the built environment; the aediles also issued an edict dealing with the sale of goods in the city

Aestimatio – a valuation in money of property, or of damage and loss suffered by the actions of a third party

Ager publicus – land owned by the state; it could be sold or leased to individuals

Alieni iuris esse – a Roman citizen legally dependent on the power of another person

Alluvio – the movement of land by river action

Apokrima – a rescript

Bona fides – good faith; honesty

Bonae fidei iudicium – an action in which the judge had the power to decide the matter taking into account the principle of good faith in respect of the sum to be paid to the plaintiff by the defendant

Bona vacantia – an estate with no heir appointed in a will, or through intestacy

Bonorum venditio – the sale of the entire property of an insolvent debtor

Calumnia – deception in legal proceedings, such as a vexatious suit in civil law; in criminal cases the prosecution of someone whom the accuser knew to be innocent

Capitalis – a criminal case involving a penalty of death, loss of liberty, or loss of citizenship

Capitis deminutio – the loss of civil rights

Castrense peculium – property acquired by a soldier during military service over which he had full ownership and the right to leave by will

Causidicus – advocate/lawyer

Cautio – an obligation assumed to guarantee the execution of an existing agreement or duty not covered by the law; also, a written document to provide evidence of a contract or debt

Centuria – a unit of land division, often containing 200 *iugera*

Cessio bonorum – a procedure by which a debtor voluntarily surrendered his property to his creditors, so as to avoid compulsory sale and *infamia*

Cippus – a boundary-marking stone

Cognitio – a legal procedure in which the entire case was heard by a magistrate or delegated official, who then delivered a verdict

Collegium – an association of people often in the same occupation or profession

Colonia – a group of Roman citizens established by Rome in locations throughout the empire; each colony was governed by a charter (*lex coloniae*)

Commercium – for a Roman citizen the right to buy and sell, and conclude legally valid transactions

Conductio – see *locatio*

Conductor – lessee

Consilium principis – the emperor's advisory council

Constitutio principis – a decision or enactment of the emperor deriving from any of his legal powers

Controversia – a dispute, often involving land

Contumacia – refusal to obey the order of a magistrate or a judicial official; non-appearance in court

Conubium – the right of a Roman citizen to conclude a legal marriage

Crimen – an action punishable by a public penalty after an appropriate trial; see *delictum*

Crimina publica – crimes against the interests of the state and social order; traditionally tried in the public jury courts (*quaestiones*)

Culpa – fault or negligence occasioning harm to property or individuals

Damnum infectum – damage that has not yet taken place, but which potentially threatened a neighbour's property

Decretum – a decision of the emperor at a judicial hearing in civil or criminal cases

Decuriae iudicum – panels of jurors

Dediticii – a category of slaves who had committed an offence and could not achieve citizenship even when set free

Delator – an accuser in a criminal trial

Delictum – a wrongful action pursued by private prosecution by the injured person

Denuntiatio litis – the summons issued by a magistrate to a defendant to attend a *cognitio* hearing

Deportatio – permanent banishment involving loss of citizenship, confinement to a particular location, and confiscation of property

Depositum – a deposit given to someone involving the obligation to safeguard and return it on demand

Dolo malo – with malicious and fraudulent intention

Dolus – cunning, deceit, or means used to defraud or cheat another

Dominium – full legal ownership of a thing and the right to dispose of it
Dominus – the owner of a thing; master of a slave
Donatio – a gift; forbidden between man and wife
Dos – a dowry
Edictum – a pronouncement of the emperor establishing a rule or legal practice; the edict of the praetor set out the legal norms he intended to apply during his year of office
Emancipatio – the voluntary release of a child from paternal power by the father
Emptio venditio – purchase and sale in which an object was exchanged for money
Epistula – a letter sent by the emperor often to a senior imperial official or community
Exceptio – a defence put forward by a litigant to undermine a plaintiff's claim
Excusatio a muneribus – exemption from compulsory public services
Exilium – exile, sometimes entered voluntarily by those about to face a criminal trial; as a punishment it involved loss of citizenship and property; see *deportatio*; *relegatio*
Extra ordinem – in private law refers to the *cognitio* procedure (q.v.); criminal cases heard outside the jurisdiction of the public jury courts
Falsum – forgery or counterfeiting
Fenus nauticum – a loan for the purpose of transporting goods by ship
Fideicommissum – a request by a testator to his heir, imposing a moral (not legal) obligation to perform certain actions for a third person
Fides – honesty or integrity relating to the performance of obligations set out in an agreement
Filius familias – a son under the legal power of his father
Fines – boundaries of land
Fiscus – the treasury for monies specifically controlled by the emperor; the *aerarium Saturni* was the public treasury
Formula – in the formulary procedure this was the statement of the relevant legal issues given by a magistrate to a judge, with authorization to reach a decision in relation to the facts
Fraus – fraud, malicious deception
Fructus – the fruits or profits from a property
Furtum – a theft
Hereditas – the estate of a deceased person; the legal position assumed by his heir (*heres*)
Heres – the heir to the estate of the deceased including debts and assets, responsible for paying legacies
Honestiores – a social group defined as senators, *equites*, and decurions (local town councillors); they were not subject to certain types of punishment
Humiliores – a social group defined as all below the *honestiores*
Hypotheca – a form of pledge from debtor to creditor, not involving the handing over of the object or transfer of ownership
Immunitas – exemption from compulsory public services and local obligations

Imperium – the right to give commands and exercise summary jurisdiction inherent in the position of senior magistrates such as praetors and consuls; the sovereignty of the Roman people; in respect of the emperor, his power to make decisions on behalf of the state

Infamia – a state of disgrace resulting from improper conduct or conviction for certain crimes; it involved legal disabilities

Ingenuus – freeborn

Iniuria – a wrongful action; injustice; outrage; offence against the person of an individual or his good name

In ius vocatio – the summons issued by a plaintiff to the defendant to appear before a magistrate

Institor – a manager or agent appointed by another to act on his behalf

Interdictum – a legal instrument issued by the praetor at the request of a plaintiff, imposing on another person a requirement to carry out or refrain from carrying out a certain action; further legal proceedings could follow depending on the response to the interdict

Iudex – a judge appointed for a specific trial by a magistrate from the list of those eligible

Iurisconsultus – a jurist, who, among other things, gave replies to questions on legal issues

Iuris peritus – a jurist; person learned in the law

Iurisprudens – a jurist; person learned in the law

Ius civile – the civil law based on statutes, plebiscites, senatorial decrees, and decisions of emperors, and applicable to all Roman citizens

Ius commune – general law common to all peoples or Roman citizens

Ius divinum – the law dealing with the relationship between people and the gods

Ius gentium – the law applied by all peoples and acceptable in principle to Rome; it could assist in the development of commercial dealings of Romans with non-citizens

Ius honorarium – the law introduced by magistrates through the issue of edicts supporting or modifying existing law

Ius militare – military law applied specifically to soldiers

Ius naturale – sometimes conveys the sense of what is always just and right; otherwise equated with *ius gentium*, or vaguely the natural order of everyday things

Ius privatum – the law relating to the interests of private individuals

Ius publicum – the law as it related to the organization, interests, and legal functioning of the state

Ius respondendi – the right granted by emperors to certain jurists to give authoritative responses on legal issues

Latini – originally inhabitants of Latin colonies with certain rights and privileges; magistrates in these communities could achieve Roman citizenship

Legis actio – an early form of Roman civil procedure using set oral formulae before a magistrate

Lex – a statute passed by popular assemblies in the republic; in the imperial period *lex* came to describe any legislation sponsored by the emperor, sometimes through the senate
Libellus – a petition addressed to an emperor or senior official
Libertus/liberta – freedman/woman
Lis – a legal suit
Litis contestatio – the final stage of legal proceedings when the issues in contention were confirmed and put before the *iudex* for consideration
Locator – the leaser
Locatio conductio – a lease and hire contract by mutual consent
Maiestas – the crime of treason and sedition against the Roman people and the *res publica*; in the imperial period any deeds or words construed to be against the security of the emperor and his family
Mancipatio – a method of conveyance of ownership using a fixed formula; see *res mancipi*
Mandatum – a voluntary contract between friends by which a person agreed to perform a service gratuitously
Manumissio – the freeing of a slave by his master during his lifetime or in his will
Matrimonium – a legally contracted marriage
Merces – a money payment for services rendered; payment of rent
Metus – fear; duress and threats used to force someone to do something
Missio in possessionem (*in bona*) – an action authorized by the praetor permitting a plaintiff to take possession of all or part of a defendant's property to ensure that a trial went ahead, or to preserve a debtor's property for his creditors
Munera – public services which citizens were obliged to perform for their local community
Municipium – in the imperial period a community in Italy or the provinces with a charter including various rights of local self-government and jurisdiction
Mutuum – a loan
Neglegentia – negligence or carelessness; see *culpa*
Occupatio – acquisition of ownership through taking possession of a thing not owned by another
Operae – labour of all kinds
Operarius – one who offers labour
Oratio principis – a speech delivered in the senate by an emperor which could lead to a senatorial decree and in effect make law
Orator – one who spoke on behalf of a litigant before a magistrate or judge, or on behalf of the defendant in a criminal trial
Ordo iudiciorum publicorum – the system of criminal jury courts; see also *quaestiones perpetuae*
Pactum – an agreement between two or more persons about the same object
Pascuum publicum – common pastureland
Pater familias – the head of a household; he was the oldest male ascendant with considerable legal and economic power over other family members

Patria potestas – the power of the *pater familias* over family members dependent on him
Pauperies – damage done by a domestic four-footed animal, though without the fault of its owner
Peculium – a sum of money, property, or business granted by a father to his son in his power, or by a master to his slave
Peregrinus – a non-Roman
Pignus – a pledge of real security given by a debtor to his creditor; any property pledged passed into the possession but not ownership of the creditor
Plebiscitum – a decree or legislation passed by the assembly of the plebeians (*concilium plebis*)
Portorium – a tax paid on the movement of goods
Possessio – physical control of an entity, distinct from ownership
Postliminium – the return of a Roman citizen from captivity among an enemy people and the regaining of his rights
Postulare – to request a magistrate to grant a civil legal action; to bring an accusation in a criminal case
Postumus – a child born after his father's death
Praedium – an estate including land and any buildings thereon
Praedium rusticum – landed property in a rural environment, used for agriculture
Praedium urbanum – a building, even if situated in the countryside
Praescriptio longi temporis – a legal provision applying to land in the provinces, protecting the rights of those who had been in possession for ten years (if both parties lived in the same locality), or twenty years (if they lived in different localities)
Praetor – a senior magistrate with *imperium* responsible for civil jurisdiction; they numbered twelve in the imperial period; the *praetor urbanus* dealt with issues involving Roman citizens, the *praetor peregrinus* with non-Romans; the praetor issued an edict detailing how he would deal with legal actions in his year of office; a praetor usually chaired each of the public jury courts
Probatio – proof or evidence
Procurator – an imperial official; in private law, someone who acted as the authorized agent of another in managing their affairs
Prorogare – to postpone or adjourn
Publicanus – a contractor for the collection of public revenues
Quaestiones perpetuae – permanent public jury courts for criminal trials; a specific offence had its own court
Redhibitio – the return to the vendor of something purchased, because of defects
Relegatio – a form of exile, either for life or a fixed duration, or exclusion from a specified area; it did not necessarily involve loss of citizenship or confiscation of property
Remissio mercedis – a reduction or remission of rent
Repetundae – extortion of money or property by Roman officials, including magistrates and provincial governors
Res communis – things owned in common by two or more people

Res corporales – things that can be touched
Rescriptum – written reply from the emperor and his legal secretaries to petitions and questions sent by private individuals or officials
Res immobiles – things that cannot be moved, such as land and buildings
Res mancipi – things the ownership of which can be conveyed only by *mancipatio* (q.v.)
Res mobiles – movable things
Responsum – answer given by a jurist when consulted about a legal case
Restitutio in integrum – an extraordinary remedy by the praetor annulling a transaction and reinstating the previous legal position for someone who had suffered an unfair loss
Reus – a defendant in a civil trial
Rogatio legis – a proposal for a new statute put before the people
Sanctio – a clause attached to a statute to enhance its impact by establishing penalties for its violation, and to clarify its relation to previous and subsequent legislation
Senatus consultum – a decree passed by the senate; in the imperial period it had the force of law
Sententia – the judge's decision in a civil trial, or the decision of an arbitrator
Sententiam dicere – to pronounce judgement
Servitus – an easement attached to an immovable property giving the beneficiary certain rights in another's land, such as a right of way
Societas – a partnership between two or more people to share profits and losses as defined by a contract
Socius – a partner in a *societas*
Sponsio – the verbal expression of an obligation in early Roman law; an undertaking of a surety to cover what another had promised to pay
Sponsor – one who undertook to stand as surety
Stipulatio – an oral contract in the form of a question and answer between the two parties
Stuprum – illicit sexual intercourse with an unmarried woman or widow of high social class
Subscriptio – the emperor's reply written at the bottom of a petition
Sui iuris – a person who was legally independent of parental power
Superficies – everything that came from the soil or was built upon it belonged to the owner of the land, even if seeds and building materials belonged to another; also defined the right by agreement to use anything on the surface of another's land
Supplicium – a capital penalty, including death
Teneri – to be liable at law
Terminus – a boundary stone
Testamentum – a formal will appointing an heir
Traditio – conveyance of ownership over a thing that was not *res mancipi*
Tributum capitis – the poll tax in the provinces
Tributum soli – the land tax in the provinces

Tutela – guardianship over people who were below the age of puberty (for boys some thought the actual arrival of puberty, others the age of fourteen; for girls twelve)

Tutor – a guardian

Usucapio – obtaining ownership of something by possession of it for a period of time established by law

Ususfructus – the right to make use of the property of another and take certain fruits and profits without damage to its substance

Vacatio – exemption from public services or duties

Vadimonium – an undertaking made by a defendant to appear in court; a requirement by a magistrate or judge to compel litigants to reappear at a fixed time if there was an adjournment

Venditio – see *emptio*

Vicesima manumissionum – a 5 per cent tax of the value of a slave on his manumission; it was paid by the master of the freed slave, or by the slave if he used his own resources to redeem his freedom

Vindicatio – an action asserting your right to property

Vis – violence; the use of force of any kind could induce fear (see *metus*) and impinge on a legal transaction; *vis privata* was violence against a private individual and usually treated as a delict, whereas *vis publica* impinged on the interests of the state and often involved a violent crime or assault, prosecuted in a criminal trial under statute

Voluntas – a wish or intention expressed orally or in writing either in a will or a contract

Bibliography

Abbott, F. F. and Johnson, A. C. (1926) *Municipal Administration in the Roman Empire* (reprt. 1968). Princeton

Adams, C. E. P. (2007) *Land Transport in Roman Egypt. A Study of Economics and Administration in a Roman Province.* Oxford

Aldrete, G. S. (2007) *Floods of the Tiber in Ancient Rome.* Baltimore

Alföldy, A. (1995) 'Eine Bauinschrift aus dem Colosseum', *ZPE* 109: 195–226

Alonso Rodríguez, J. L. (2016) 'Juristic papyrology and Roman law', in du Plessis, Ando, and Tuori : 56–69

Anastasiades, V. I. and Souris, G. A. (2000) *An Index to Roman Imperial Constitutions from Greek Inscriptions and Papyri: 27 BC–AD 284.* Berlin and New York

Ando, C. (2000) *Imperial Ideology and Provincial Loyalty in the Roman Empire.* Berkeley

(2011) *Law, Language and Empire in the Roman Tradition.* Philadelphia

(2019) 'Substantive justice in provincial and Roman legal argument', in Hekster and Verboven : 138–56

Ando, C. and Rüpke, J. (eds.) (2006) *Religion and Law in Classical and Christian Rome.* Stuttgart

Andreau, J. (1987) *La Vie Financière dans le Monde Romain. Les Métiers de Manieurs d'Argent (IVe siècle av. J.-C. – IIIe siècle ap. J.-C.).* Rome

(1999) *Banking and Business in the Roman World* (translated by J. Lloyd). Cambridge

Angelis, F. de (ed.) (2010) *Spaces of Justice in the Roman World.* Leiden

Arangio-Ruiz, V. and Pugliese Carratelli, G. (1954) '*Tabulae Herculanenses* IV', *La Parola del Passato* 9: 54–74

(1955) '*Tabulae Herculanenses* V', *La Parola del Passato* 10: 448–77

Ascough, R. S., Harland, P. A., and Kloppenborg, J. S. (eds.) (2012) *Associations in the Greco-Roman World: a Sourcebook.* Waco

Aubert, J.-J. (1994) *Business Managers in Ancient Rome. A Social and Economic Study of Institores, 200 BC – AD 250.* Leiden

(1999) 'La gestion des *collegia*: aspects juridiques, économiques et sociaux', *Cahiers du Centre Gustave-Glotz* 10: 49–69

(2015) 'Commerce', in Johnston : 213–45

Austin, M., Harries, J., and Smith, C. (1998) *Modus Operandi. Essays in Honour of Geoffrey Rickman. Bulletin of the Institute of Classical Studies*, Supplement 71. London

Bablitz, L. (2007) *Actors and Audience in the Roman Courtroom*. London and New York

(2011) 'Roman society in the courtroom', in Peachin : 317–34

Bagnall, R. (ed.) (2009) *Oxford Handbook of Papyrology*. Oxford and New York

Bagnall, R. and Frier, B. W. (1994) *The Demography of Roman Egypt*. Cambridge

Bang, P. F., Bayly, C. A., and Scheidel, W. (eds.) (2021) *The Oxford World History of Empire. Vol. 2: The Imperial Experience*. Oxford

Bannon, C. J. (2009) *Gardens and Neighbours. Private Water Rights in Roman Italy*. Ann Arbor

(2017) 'Fresh water in Roman law: rights and policy', *JRS* 107: 60–89

Barnes, T. D. (1986) 'The significance of Tacitus' *Dialogus de Oratoribus*', *HSCP* 90: 225–44

Baudy, D. (2006) 'Prohibitions of religion in antiquity: setting the course of Europe's religious history', in Ando and Rüpke : 100–14

Bauman, R. (1989) *Lawyers and Politics in the Early Roman Empire: a Study of Relations between the Roman Jurists and the Emperors from Augustus to Hadrian*. Munich

(1996) *Crime and Punishment in Ancient Rome*. London and New York

Beard, M., North, J., and Price, S. (1998) *Religions of Rome*. Vol. I: *A History*; vol. II: *A Sourcebook*. Cambridge

Beggio, T. (2016) 'Epigraphy', in du Plessis, Ando, and Tuori : 43–55

Behrends, O. et al. (1998) *Frontin, L'Oeuvre Gromatique. Corpus Agrimensorum Romanorum* IV. *Iulius Frontinus*. Luxembourg

Beltrán Lloris, F. (2006) 'An irrigation decree from Roman Spain: the *lex Rivi Hiberiensis*', *JRS* 96: 147–97

Bendlin, A. (2011) 'Associations, funerals, sociality, and Roman law: the collegium of Diana and Antinous in Lanuvium (*CIL*142112) reconsidered', in Öhler : 207–96

Berger, A. (1953) *Encyclopedic Dictionary of Roman Law. Transactions of the American Philosophical Society*, n.s. vol. 43(2). Philadelphia

Berthelot, K. and Price, J. J. (2019) *In the Crucible of Empire: the Impact of Roman Citizenship upon Greeks, Jews and Christians. Interdisciplinary Studies in Ancient Culture and Religion*, vol. 21. Leuven

Birks, P. (ed.) (1989) *New Perspectives in the Roman Law of Property: Essays for Barry Nicolas*. Oxford

Birks, P. and McLeod, G. (1987) *Justinian's Institutes. Translation and Edition*. London

Birley, A. R. (1966) *Marcus Aurelius*. London

(1971) *Septimius Severus. The African Emperor*. London

(1997) *Hadrian. The Restless Emperor*. London and New York

(2005) *The Roman Government of Britain*. Oxford

Bispham, E. (2007) *From Asculum to Actium. The Municipalization of Italy from the Social War to Augustus*. Oxford
Blois, L. de (ed.) (2001) *Administration, Prosopography and Appointment Policies in the Roman Empire: Proceedings of the First Workshop of the International Network Impact of Empire (Roman Empire, 27* BC – AD *406), Leiden, 28 June – 1 July 2000*. Amsterdam
Blume, F., Lachmann, K., and Rudorff, A. (1848–52); 2 vols, *Die Schriften der römischen Feldmesser*. Berlin
Borkowski, A. (2010) *A Textbook on Roman Law*; 4th ed.; 5th ed. (2015) (P. du Plessis). London
Bowersock, G. W. (1969) *Greek Sophists in the Roman Empire*. Oxford
Bowman, A. (1986) *Egypt after the Pharaohs, 332* BC – AD *642*. London
Bowman, A. and Rathbone, D. (1992) 'Cities and administration in Roman Egypt', *JRS* 82: 107–27
Bowman, A., Garnsey, P., and Cameron, A. (eds.) (2005) *The Cambridge Ancient History*, vol. xii (2nd ed.) *The Crisis of Empire,* AD *193–337*. Cambridge
Bradley, K. R. (1984) *Slaves and Masters in the Roman Empire: a Study in Social Control*. Brussels.
(1997) 'Law, magic and culture in the *Apologia* of Apuleius', *Phoenix* 51: 203–23
(2000) 'Prostitution, the law of Rome and social policy', *JRA* 13: 468–75, review of T. McGinn (1998)
Brand, P. and Getzler, J. (eds.) (2012) *Judges and Judging in the History of the Common Law and Civil Law from Antiquity to Modern Times*. Cambridge
Braund, D. (1985) *Augustus to Nero. A Sourcebook on Roman History 31* BC – AD *68*. London and New York
Brunt, P. A. (1961) 'Charges of provincial maladministration under the early principate', *Historia* 10: 189–227 = *Roman Imperial Themes* (1990), 53–95
(1966) 'Procuratorial jurisdiction', *Latomus* 25: 461–89 = *Roman Imperial Themes* (1990): 163–87
(1974) 'The Roman mob', in M. Finley (ed.): 74–102
(1975) 'The administrators of Roman Egypt', *JRS* 65: 124–47
(1977) '*Lex de imperio Vespasiani*', *JRS* 67: 95–116
(1980) 'Labour and public works in Rome', *JRS* 70: 81–100
(1981) 'The revenues of Rome', *JRS* 71: 161–72 = *Roman Imperial Themes* (1990), 324–46
(1990) *Roman Imperial Themes*. Oxford
Bruun, C. and Edmondson, J. C. (eds.) (2015) *The Oxford Handbook of Roman Epigraphy*. Oxford and New York
Bryen, A. Z. (2008) 'Visibility and violence in petitions from Roman Egypt', *GRBS* 48: 181–200
(2013) *Violence in Roman Egypt: a Study in Legal Interpretation*. Philadelphia
(2016) 'Crimes against the individual: violence and sexual crimes', in du Plessis, Ando, and Tuori : 322–32.
Buckland, W. W. (1908) *The Roman Law of Slavery*. Cambridge

(1975) *A Textbook of Roman Law from Augustus to Justinian* (3rd ed., revised by P. Stein). Cambridge

Burton, G. (1975) 'Proconsuls, assizes and the administration of justice under the empire', *JRS* 65: 92–106

(1976) 'The issuing of *mandata* to proconsuls and a new inscription from Cos', *ZPE* 21: 63–8

(1996) 'The *lex Irnitana*, ch. 84, the promise of *vadimonium* and the jurisdiction of the proconsuls', *CQ* 46: 217–21

(2001) 'The imperial state and its impact on the role and status of local magistrates and councillors in the provinces of the empire', in de Blois : 202–14

(2004) 'The Roman imperial state, provincial governors, and the public finances of provincial cities, 27 BC – AD 235', *Historia* 53: 311–42

Cairns, J. W. and du Plessis, P. (eds.) (2007) *Beyond Dogmatics. Law and Society in the Roman World*. Edinburgh

Camodeca, G. (ed.) (1992) *L'Archivio Puteolano dei Sulpicii*. Naples

(ed.) (1999) *Tabulae Pompeianae Sulpiciorum (TPSulp). Edizione critica dell'archivio puteolano dei Sulpicii* (Vetera 12). Rome

Campbell, B. (1984) *The Emperor and the Roman Army, 31 BC – AD 235*. Oxford

(1994) *The Roman Army 31 BC – AD 337. A Sourcebook*. London and New York

(1996) 'Shaping the rural environment: surveyors in ancient Rome', *JRS* 86: 74–99

(2000) *The Writings of the Roman Land Surveyors. Introduction, Translation and Commentary*. London

(2005) '"Setting up true boundaries": land disputes in the Roman empire', *Mediterraneo Antico* 8.1: 307–43

(2012) *Rivers and the Power of Ancient Rome*. Chapel Hill

Capogrossi Colognesi, L. (1998) 'Dominium e possessio', in Cortese (ed.): 141–82

(2018) *Law and Power in the Making of the Roman Commonwealth* (translated by L. Kopp). Cambridge

Carter, M. (2003) 'Gladiatorial ranking and the SC *de Pretiis Gladiatorum Minuendis* (*CIL* 11.6278 = *ILS* 5163)', *Phoenix* 57: 83–114

Champlin, E. (1980) *Fronto and Antonine Rome*. Cambridge, Mass. and London

(1991) *Final Judgements: Duty and Emotion in Roman Wills, 250 BC–AD 250*. Berkeley

Chevallier, R. (1989) *Roman Roads* (revised ed.). London

Chisholm, K. and Ferguson, J. (1981) *Rome. The Augustan Age. A Source Book*. Oxford

Chiusi, T. (2005) 'Babatha vs. the guardians of her son: a struggle for guardianship – legal and practical aspects of P. Yadin 12–15, 27', in Katzoff and Schaps : 105–32

Clavel-Lévêque, M. et al. (1996) *Corpus Agrimensorum Romanorum* IV. *Hygin L'Arpenteur, L'Établissement des Limites*. Luxembourg and Naples

Cloud, J. D. (1988) '*Lex Julia de vi* – I', *Athenaeum* 66: 579–95

(1989) '*Lex Julia de vi* – II', *Athenaeum* 67: 427–65

Connolly, S. (2010) *Lives behind the Laws: the World of the Codex Hermogenianus.* Bloomington, In.
Corcoran, S. (2014) 'State correspondence in the Roman empire: imperial correspondence from Augustus to Justinian', in Radner : 172–209
Corke-Webster, J. (2017) 'Trouble in Pontus: the Pliny–Trajan correspondence on the Christians reconsidered', *TAPA* 147(2): 371–411
Cortés-Copete, J. M. (2019) 'Koinoi Nomoi: Hadrian and the harmonization of local laws', in Hekster and Verboven : 105–21
Cortese, E. (ed.) (1988) *La Proprietà e le Proprietà. Atti del Convegno (Pontignano, 30 settembre – 3 ottobre, 1985).* Milan
Cotton, H. (1993) 'The guardianship of Jesus, son of Babatha: Roman and local law in the province of Arabia', *JRS* 83: 94–108
(1994) 'Loan with hypothec. Another papyrus from the cave of letters', *ZPE* 101: 53–9
Cotton, H., Cockle, W. E. H., and Millar, F. G. B. (1995) 'The papyrology of the Roman near east: a survey', *JRS* 85: 214–35
Cotton, H. and Rodgers, G. M. (2004) *Rome, the Greek World, and the East. Volume 2. Government, Society, and Culture in the Roman Empire. Fergus Millar.* Chapel Hill and London
Cotton, H. and Eck, W. (2005) 'Roman officials in Judaea and Arabia and civil jurisdiction', in Katzoff and Schaps : 23–44
Coulston, J. and Dodge, H. (eds.) (2000) *Ancient Rome. The Archaeology of the Eternal City.* Oxford
Courtney, E. (1980) *A Commentary on the Satires of Juvenal.* London
Cowan, E. (2016) 'Contesting *clementia*: the rhetoric of *severitas* in Tiberian Rome before and after the trial of Clutorius Priscus', *JRS* 106: 77–101
Crawford, M. H. (1995) 'Roman towns and their charters: legislation and experience', in Cunliffe and Keay : 421–30
(ed.) (1996) *Roman Statutes* (2 vols). London
(1998) 'How to create a municipium: Rome and Italy after the Social War', in Austin, Harries and Smith : 31–46
Creed, J. L. (1984) *Lactantius De Mortibus Persecutorum. Edited and Translated.* Oxford
Crook, J. A. (1967) *Law and Life of Rome.* London
(1983) Review of Frier (1980), *JRS* 73: 213–14
(1994a) Review of Camodeca (1992), *JRS* 84: 260–1
(1994b) 'The development of Roman private law', in Crook et al.: 531–63
(1994c) Crook, J. A. et al. (eds.), *Cambridge Ancient History* vol. ix (2nd ed.). Cambridge
(1995) *Legal Advocacy in the Roman World.* London
Cunliffe, B. and Keay, S. (eds.) (1995) *Social Complexity and the Development of Towns in Iberia: from the Copper Age to the Second Century* AD. *Proceedings of the British Academy* 86. Oxford
Cuomo, S. (2011) 'A Roman engineer's tales', *JRS* 101: 143–65

Cursi, M. F. (2012) 'Roman delicts and the construction of fault', in McGinn : 296–319

Czajkowski, K. (2017) *Localized Law: the Babatha and Salome Komaise Archives*. Oxford

Czajkowski, K., Eckhardt, B., and Strothmann, M. (eds.) (2020) *Law in the Roman Provinces*. Oxford

Daalder, E. (2019) 'The Decreta and Imperiales Sententiae of Julius Paulus: law and justice in the judicial decisions of Septimius Severus', in Hekster and Verboven : 49–67

Davenport, C. (2019) *A History of the Roman Equestrian Order*. Cambridge.

Davis, R. (1989) *The Book of the Pontiffs (Liber Pontificalis). The Ancient Biographies of the First Ninety Roman Bishops to* AD *175. Translated with an Introduction*. Liverpool

Delia, D. (1991) *Alexandrian Citizenship during the Roman Principate*. Atlanta

Dench, E. (2018) *Empire and Political Cultures in the Roman World*. Cambridge

Dickey, E. (2012–15) *The Colloquia of the Hermeneumata Pseudodositheana*. 2 vols. Cambridge

(2017) *Stories of Daily Life from the Roman World. Extracts from the Ancient Colloquia*. Cambridge.

Dilke, O. A. W. (1971) *The Roman Land Surveyors*. Newton Abbot

Dixon, S. (1988) *The Roman Mother*. London and Sydney

Dodge, H. (2000) '"Greater than the Pyramids": the water supply of ancient Rome', in Coulston and Dodge : 166–209

Dolganov, A. (2019) 'Reichsrecht and Volksrecht in Theory and Practice: Roman Justice in the province of Egypt (*P. Oxy*. II 237, *P. Oxy*. IV 706, *SB* XII 10929)', *Tyche* 34: 27–60

Duff, P. W. (1938) *Personality in Roman Private Law*. Cambridge

Duncan-Jones, R. P. (1964) 'The purpose and organization of the *alimenta*', *Papers of the British School at Rome* 32: 123–46

(1974) *The Economy of the Roman Empire. Quantitative Studies*. Cambridge

(1994) *Money and Government in the Roman Empire*. Cambridge

Eck, W., Caballos, A., and Ferndández, F. (eds.) (1996) *Das Senatus Consultum de Cn. Pisone Patre* (*Vestigia* 48). Munich

Edwards, M. and Reid, C. (2004) *Oratory in Action*. Manchester

Effenterre, H. van (ed.) (1979) *Points de vue sûr la fiscalité antique*. Centre G. Glotz. Paris

Ehrenberg, V. and Jones, A. H. M. (1976) *Documents illustrating the Reigns of Augustus and Tiberius* (2nd ed., by Stockton, D. L.). Oxford

Erdkamp, P. (2005) *The Grain Market in the Roman Empire. A Social, Political and Economic Study*. Cambridge

Farrar, L. (1998) *Ancient Roman Gardens*. Thrupp

Favro, D. (1996) *The Urban Image of Augustan Rome*. Cambridge

Feissel, D. and Gascou, J. (1989) 'Documents d'archive romain inédits du moyen Euphrate (IIIe siècle après J.-C.)', *CRAI* 133: 535–61

(1995) 'Documents d'archive romain inédits du moyen Euphrate (IIIe siècle après J.-C.), *Les petitions* (T. Euphr. 1 à 5)', *Journal des Savants* 1: 65–119
Finley, M. (ed.) (1974) *Studies in Ancient Society*. London and Boston
(ed.) (1976) *Studies in Roman Property*. Cambridge
Flohr, M. (2013) *The World of the Fullo. Work, Economy, and Society in Roman Italy*. Oxford
Fowden, G. (1988) 'Between pagans and Christians', review of Lane Fox (1986), *JRS* 78: 173–82
Foxhall, L. (1990) 'The dependent tenant: land leasing and labour in Italy and Greece', *JRS* 80: 97–114
Foxhall, L. and Salmon, J. (eds) (1998) *When Men were Men: Masculinity, Power and Identity in Classical Antiquity*. London
Frend, W. H. C. (1956) 'A third-century inscription relating to *angareia* in Phrygia', *JRS* 46: 46–56
Frier, B. (1980) *Landlords and Tenants in Imperial Rome*. Princeton
(1985) *The Rise of the Roman Jurists: Studies in Cicero's 'Pro Caecina'*. Princeton
(1989) *A Casebook on the Roman Law of Delict*. Atlanta
(1989–90) 'Law, economics and disasters down on the farm: *remissio mercedis* revisited', *BIDR* 31–2: 237–70
(2000) 'Roman law's descent into history' (Review of Robinson (1997), and Johnston (1999)), *JRA* 13: 446–8
(2010) 'Finding a place for law in the high empire: Tacitus, Dialogus 39.1–4', in de Angelis : 67–87
(2016) (ed.) *The Codex of Justinian* (3 vols). Cambridge
Frier, B. and McGinn, T. (2004) *A Casebook on Roman Family Law*. Oxford
Frier, B. and Kehoe, D. (2007) 'Law and economic institutions', in Scheidel : 113–43
Fuhrmann, C. J. (2012) *Policing the Roman Empire. Soldiers, Administration, and Public Order*. Oxford
Futrell, A. (2006) *The Roman Games: a Sourcebook*. Oxford
Galsterer, H. (1988) '*Municipium Flavium Irnitanum*: a Latin town in Spain', *JRS* 78: 78–90
Gamauf, R. (2009) 'Slaves doing business: the role of Roman law in the economy of a Roman household', *European Review of History* 16.3: 331–46
(2016) 'Slavery: social position and legal capacity', in du Plessis, Ando, and Tuori : 386–401
Gardner, J. F. (1986) *Women in Roman Law and Society*. Beckenham
(1993) *Being a Roman Citizen*. London and New York
(1998a) *Family and Familia in Roman Law and Life*. Oxford
(1998b) 'Sexing a Roman: imperfect men in Roman law', in Foxhall and Salmon : 136–52
(2001) 'Making citizens: the operation of the lex Irnitana', in Blois, L. de : 215–29
Gardner, J. F. and Wiedemann, T. (1991) *The Roman Household: A Sourcebook*. London and New York

Garnsey, P. (1968) 'The criminal jurisdiction of governors', *JRS* 58: 51–9
(1970) *Social Status and Legal Privilege in the Roman Empire.* Oxford
(1974) 'Legal privilege in the Roman empire', in Finley : 141–65
(1976) 'Urban property investment', in Finley : 123–36
(1980a) 'Non-slave labour in the Roman world', in Garnsey : 34–47
(1980b) (ed.) *Non-Slave Labour in the Greco-Roman World.* Cambridge
(1988) *Famine and Food Supply in the Graeco-Roman World. Responses to Risk and Crisis.* Cambridge
(1998) *Cities, Peasants, and Food in Classical Antiquity. Essays in Social and Economic History* (edited by Scheidel, W.). Cambridge
(2004) 'Roman citizenship and Roman law in the late empire', in Swain and Edwards : 133–55
Garnsey, P. and Saller, R. (1987) *The Roman Empire. Economy, Society and Culture.* Berkeley and Los Angeles
González, J. (1986) 'The *lex Irnitana*: a new copy of the Flavian municipal law', *JRS* 76: 147–243
(ed. 2000) *Trajano Emperador de Roma. Actas del Congresso Internacional 14–17 septiembre 1998, Siviglia.* Madrid
Goodman, M. (1987) *The Ruling Class of Judaea. The Origins of the Jewish Revolt against Rome* AD *66–70.* Cambridge
(1991) 'Babatha's story' (review of Yadin (1989), *JRS* 81: 169–75)
Gordon, W. M. and Robinson, O. F. (1988) *The Institutes of Gaius.* Ithaca, N.Y.
Griffin, M. (1976) *Seneca: a Philosopher in Politics.* Oxford
Griffin, M. (1997) 'The senate's story', review of Eck, Caballos, and Fernández (1996), *JRS* 87: 249–63
Grubbs, J. Evans (2002) *Women and the Law in the Roman Empire: a Sourcebook on Marriage, Divorce and Widowhood.* London and New York
Gualandi, G. (1963) *Legislazione imperiale e giurisprudenza* (2 vols). Milan
Guillaumin, J.-Y. (2010) *Les Arpenteurs romains; Hygin, Siculus Flaccus* (vol. 2). Paris
(2014) *Les Arpenteurs romains; Commentaire Anonyme sur Frontin* (vol. 3). Paris
Haensch, R. (ed.) (2009) *Selbstdarstellung und Kommunikation: die Veröffentlichung staatlicher Urkunden auf Stein und Bronze in der römischen Welt.* Munich
(2015) 'From free to fee? Judicial fees and other litigation costs during the high empire and late antiquity', in Kehoe, Ratzan, and Yiftach : 253–72
Halbwachs, V. (2016) 'Women as legal actors', in du Plessis, Ando, and Tuori : 443–55
Hands, A. R. (1968) *Charities and Social Aid in Greece and Rome.* London
Hanson, A. E. (2005) 'The widow Babatha and the poor orphan boy', in Katzoff and Schaps : 85–103
Harries, J. (2007) *Law and Crime in the Roman World.* Cambridge
(2016) 'Legal education and training of lawyers', in du Plessis, Ando, and Tuori : 151–63
Harris, W. V. (2006) 'A revisionist view of Roman money', *JRS* 96: 1–24

Hauken, T. (1998) *Petition and Response: an Epigraphic Study of Petitions to Roman Emperors, 181–249*. Norwegian Institute at Athens. Bergen.
Hauken, T. and Malay, H. (2009) 'A new edict of Hadrian from the province of Asia setting regulations for requisitioned transport', in Haensch : 327–48
Hausmaninger, H. and Gamauf, R. (2012) *A Casebook on Roman Property Law* (translated by G. A. Sheets). New York and Oxford
Hekster, O. and Verboven, K. (eds.) (2019) *The Impact of Justice on the Roman Empire. Proceedings of the 13th Workshop of the International Network Impact of Empire (Gent, June 21–24, 2017)*. Leiden
Hodge, A. T. (2002) *Roman Aqueducts and Water Supply* (2nd ed.). London
Holford-Strevens, L. (2003) *Aulus Gellius: An Antonine Scholar and his Achievement* (2nd ed.). Oxford
Holleran, C. (2012) *Shopping in the Ancient World. The Retail Trade in the Late Republic and the Principate*. Oxford
Honoré, A. (1962) *Gaius*. Oxford
(1978) *Tribonian*. Ithaca, N.Y.
(1979) 'Imperial rescripts AD 193–305; authorship and authenticity', *JRS* 69: 51–64
(1981) *Emperors and Lawyers* (2nd ed. 1994). London
Hopkins, K. (1978) *Conquerors and Slaves*. Cambridge
(1983) *Death and Renewal*. Cambridge
Hopwood, K. (1989) 'Bandits, elites and rural order', in Wallace-Hadrill : 171–87
Humfress, C. (2014) 'Laws' empire: Roman universalism and legal practice', in Rapp and Drake : 81–108
(2021) 'Law, bureaucracy and the practice of government and rule', in Bang, Bayly, and Scheidel, vol. 1: 266–87
Humphries, M. (2006) *Early Christianity*. London and New York
Ibbetson, D. (2005) 'High classical law', in Bowman, Garnsey, and Cameron : 184–99
(2015) 'Sources of law from the republic to the dominate', in Johnston : 25–44
Imrie, A. (2018) *The Antonine Constitution: an Edict for the Caracallan Empire*. Leiden
Isaac, B. (1992) *The Limits of Empire. The Roman Army in the East* (revised edition). Oxford
Jacobs, A. J. (2006) 'Papinian commands one thing, our Paul another: Romans, Christians and Jewish law in the Collatio legum Mosaicorum et Romanorum', in Ando and Rüpke : 85–99
Johnson, A. C., Coleman-Norton, P. R., and Bourne, F. C. (eds.) (1961) *Ancient Roman Statutes*. Austin
Johnston, D. (1985) 'Munificence and *Municipia*: bequests to towns in classical Roman law', *JRS* 75: 105–25
(1987) 'Three thoughts on Roman private law and the *lex Irnitana*', *JRS* 77: 62–77
(1988) *The Roman Law of Trusts*. Oxford

(1998) 'Law and commercial life in Rome', *Proceedings of the Cambridge Philological Society* 43: 53–65
(1999) *Roman Law in Context*. Cambridge
(2002) 'Peculiar questions', in McKechnie : 5–13
(2005) 'Epiclassical law', in Bowman, Garnsey, and Cameron : 200–7
(ed.) (2015) *Cambridge Companion to Roman Law*. Cambridge
Jolowicz, H. F. and Nicholas, B. (1972) *Historical Introduction to the Study of Roman Law* (3rd ed., revised by B. Nicholas). Cambridge
Jones, A. H. M. (1960) *Studies in Roman Government and Law*. Oxford
(1964) *The Later Roman Empire 284–602* (2 vols). Oxford
(1972) *The Criminal Courts of the Roman Republic and Principate*. Oxford
Jones, C. P. (1971) 'A new letter of Marcus Aurelius to the Athenians', *ZPE* 8: 161–83
Jones, D. (2006) *The Bankers of Puteoli: Finance, Trade and Industry in the Roman World*. Stroud
Joshel, S. R. (1992) *Work, Identity, and Legal Status at Rome: a Study of the Occupational Inscriptions*. Norman, Okla.
Kacprzak, A. (2016) 'Rhetoric and Roman law', in du Plessis, Ando, and Tuori : 200–13
Kalinowski, A. (2002) 'The Vedii Antonini: aspects of patronage and benefaction in second century Ephesos', *Phoenix* 56.1: 109–49
Kantor, G. (2013) 'Law in Roman Phrygia: rules and jurisdictions', in Thonemann : 143–67
Kaser, M. (1967) 'The changing face of Roman jurisdiction', *Irish Jurist* (n.s.) 2: 129–43
(1996) *Das römische Zivilprozessrecht* (2nd ed. by K. Hackl). Munich
Katzoff, R. and Schaps, D. M. (2005) *Law in the Documents of the Judaean Desert*. Leiden
Kay, P. (2014) *Rome's Economic Revolution*. Oxford
Keenan, J. G., Manning, G., and Yiftach-Firanko, U. (eds.) (2014) *Law and Legal Practice in Egypt from Alexander to the Arab Conquest*. Cambridge
Kehoe, D. (1988) 'Allocation of risk and investment on the estates of Pliny the Younger', *Chiron* 18: 15–42
(1997) *Investment, Profit and Tenancy: the Jurists and the Roman Agrarian Economy*. Ann Arbor
(2007) *Land and Rural Economy in the Roman Empire*. Ann Arbor
(2011) 'Law and social formation in the Roman empire', in Peachin : 144–63
(2012a) 'Roman economic policy and the law of contracts', in McGinn : 189–214
(2012b) 'Contract labor', in Scheidel : 114–30
(2015) 'Contracts, agency, and transaction costs in the Roman economy', in Kehoe, Ratzan, and Yiftach : 231–52
(2016) 'Tenure of land and agricultural regulation', in du Plessis, Ando, and Tuori : 646–59
Kehoe, D., Ratzan, D., and Yiftach, U. (eds.) (2015) *Law and Transaction Costs in the Ancient Economy*. Ann Arbor

Kehoe, D. and McGinn, T. A. J. (2017) *Ancient Law, Ancient Society*. Ann Arbor
Kelly, B. (2011) *Petitions, Litigation, and Social Control in Roman Egypt. Oxford Studies in Ancient Documents*. Oxford
Kelly, J. M. (1957) Princeps Iudex. *Eine Untersuchung zur Entwicklung und zu den Grundlagen der kaiserlichen Gerichtsbarkeit*. Weimar
(1966) *Roman Litigation*. Oxford
Keppie, L. (1983) *Colonisation and Veteran Settlement in Italy 47–14 BC*. Rome
Kessler, D. and Temin, T. (2007) 'The organisation of the grain trade in the early Roman Empire', *EHR* 60.2: 313–32
Kirschenbaum, A. (1987) *Sons, Slaves, and Freedmen in Roman Commerce*. Washington
Kokkinia, C. (2003) 'Letters of Roman authorities on local dignitaries: the case of Vedius Antoninus', *ZPE* 142: 197–213
Kolb, A. (2000) *Transport und Nachrichtentransfer im römischen Reich*. Berlin
Kolbert, C. F. (1979) *Justinian. The Digest of Roman Law: Theft, Rapine, Damage and Insult*. Harmondsworth.
Kunkel, W. (1966) *An Introduction to Roman Legal and Constitutional History* (2nd ed., translated by J. M. Kelly). Oxford
(1967) *Herkunft und soziale Stellung der römischen Juristen* (2nd ed.). Graz, Vienna
Laffi, U. (1971) '*I terreni del tempio di Zeus ad Aizanoi. Le iscrizioni sulla parete interna dell'anta destra del pronaos*', *Athenaeum* 49: 3–53
Lane Fox, R. (1986) *Pagans and Christians*. Harmondsworth
Laurence, R. (1999) *The Roads of Roman Italy. Mobility and Cultural Change*. London and New York
Lavan, M. (2019) 'The spread of Roman citizenship from the fourth century BCE to the third century CE', in Berthelot and Price : 21–54
Lebek, W. D. (1990) '*Standeswürde und Berufsverbot unter Tiberius: das SC der Tabula Larinas*', *ZPE* 81: 37–96
Lendon, J. (1997) *Empire of Honour*. Oxford
Lenel, O. (1899) *Palingenesia Iuris Civilis* (2 vols, reprt. 1960). Graz
(1927). *Das Edictum Perpetuum* (3rd ed. reprt. 1956). Leipzig
Levick, B. (1979) 'Poena legis maiestatis', *Historia* 28: 358–79
(1983) 'The *senatus consultum* from Larinum', *JRS* 73: 97–115
(1990) *Claudius*. London
(2000) *The Government of the Roman Empire. A Sourcebook* (2nd ed.). London and New York
Lewis, A. (2015) 'Slavery, family, and status', in Johnston : 151–74
Lewis, N. (1989) *The Documents from the Bar Kokhba Period in the Cave of Letters. Greek Papyri*. Jerusalem
Lewis, N. and Reinhold, M. (1990) *Roman Civilization. Selected Readings* (2 vols., 3rd ed.). New York and Oxford
Lindermann, J.-O., Knobloch, E., and Möller, C. (2018) *Hyginus, Das Feldmesserbuch. Ein Meisterwerk der spätantiken Buchkunst*. Darmstadt
Lintott, A. (1968) *Violence in Republican Rome*. Oxford

(1990) 'Electoral bribery in the Roman republic', *JRS* 80: 1–16
(1993) *Imperium Romanum. Politics and Administration*. London and New York
(1999) *The Constitution of the Roman Republic*. Oxford
(2015) 'Crime and punishment', in Johnston : 301–31
Lott, B. (2004) *The Neighbourhoods of Augustan Rome*. Cambridge
MacMullen, R. (1966) *Enemies of the Roman Order*. Cambridge, Mass.
(1974) *Roman Social Relations*. New Haven and London
Magie, D. (1950) *Roman Rule in Asia Minor to the End of the First Century after Christ* (2 vols.). Princeton
Malloch, S. J. V. (2020) *The Tabula Lugdunensis: a Critical Edition with Translation and Commentary*. Cambridge
Martin, S. D. (1989) *The Roman Jurists and the Organization of Private Building in the Late Republic and Early Empire* (*Collection Latomus* 34). Brussels
Mastino, A. (ed.) (1993) *La Tavola di Esterzili. Il Conflitto tra pastori e contadini nella Barbaria Sarda: Convegno di Studi, Esterlizi, 13 Giugno 1992*. Sassari
Matthews, J. (2006) 'Roman law and Roman history', in Potter : 477–91
Mattingly, D. and Aldrete, S. (2000) 'The feeding of imperial Rome: the mechanics of the food supply system', in Coulston and Dodge : 142–65
Mayer, R. (ed.) (2001) *Tacitus. Dialogus de Oratoribus*. Cambridge
McCrum, M. and Woodhead, A. G. (1961) *Select Documents of the Principates of the Flavian Emperors A.D. 68–9*. Cambridge
McGinn, T. A. J. (1998) *Prostitution, Sexuality, and the Law in Ancient Rome*. Oxford
(ed.) (2012) *Obligations in Roman Law. Past, Present, and Future (Papers and Monographs of the American Academy in Rome*, vol. 33). Ann Arbor
McKechnie, P. (ed.) (2002) *Thinking like a Lawyer. Essays on Legal History and General History for John Crook on his Eightieth Birthday*. Leiden, Boston
Meiggs, R. (1960) *Roman Ostia*. Oxford
Metzger, E. (1997) *A New Outline of the Roman Civil Trial*. Oxford
(ed.) (1998) *A Companion to Justinian's Institutes*. London
(2005) *Litigation in Roman Law*. Oxford
(2007) 'Lawsuits in context', in Cairns and du Plessis : 187–205
(2012a) 'Remedy of prohibition against Roman judges in civil trials', in Brand and Getzler : 177–91
(2012b) 'Obligations in classical procedure', in McGinn : 158–73
(2015) 'Litigation', in Johnston : 272–98
Meyer, E. A. (2004) *Legitimacy and Law in the Roman World.* Tabulae *in Roman Belief and Practice*. Cambridge
(2007) 'Diplomatics, law and Romanisation in documents from the Judaean desert', in Cairns and du Plessis : 53–82
(2016) 'Evidence and Argument. The truth of prestige and its performance', in du Plessis, Ando, and Tuori : 270–82
Millar, F. (1964) *A Study of Cassius Dio*. Oxford
(1977) *The Emperor in the Roman World*. London
(1981) 'The world of the *Golden Ass*', *JRS* 71: 63–75

(1983) 'Empire and city, Augustus to Julian: obligations, excuses and status', *JRS* 73: 76–96
(1986) 'A new approach to the Roman jurists', *JRS* 76: 272–80
(1993) *The Roman Near East 31* BC – AD *337*. Cambridge, Mass. and London
(1999) 'The Greek east and Roman law: the dossier of M. Cn. Licinius Rufinus', *JRS* 89: 90–108
(2000) 'Trajan: government by correspondence', in González (ed.): 363–88 (reprinted in Cotton and Rodgers (2004): 23–46).
(2016) 'Imperial letters in Latin: Pliny and Trajan, Egnatius Taurinus and Hadrian', *Scripta Classica Israelica* 35: 65–83
Millar, F. and Segal, E. (eds.) (1984) *Caesar Augustus, Seven Aspects*. Oxford
Milnor, K. (2005) *Gender, Domesticity, and the Age of Augustus: Inventing Private Life*. Oxford
Minns, D. P. (2007) 'The rescript of Hadrian', in Parvis and Foster: 38–49
Mitchell, S. (1976) 'Requisitioned transport in the Roman empire: a new inscription from Pisidia', *JRS* 66: 106–31
(1993) *Anatolia: Land, Rulers and Gods in Asia Minor* (2 vols). Oxford
Mitteis, L. and Wilcken, U. (1912) *Grundzüge und Chrestomathie der Papyruskunde, vol. 2, Juristischer Teil*. Leipzig
Moatti, C. (1993) *Archives et Partage de la Terre dans le Monde Romain (IIe siècle avant – Ier siècle après J.-C.)*. Rome
Moore, D. W. (2012) 'A note on *CIL* VI.1585A–B and the role of Adrastus, procurator of the column of Marcus Aurelius', *ZPE* 181: 221–9
Mouritsen, H. (2011) *The Freedman in the Roman World*. Cambridge
(2016) 'Manumission', in du Plessis, Ando, and Tuori : 402–15
Musurillo, H. (1972) *The Acts of the Christian Martyrs*. Oxford
Nicholas, B. (1962) *Introduction to Roman Law* (revised ed. 2008). Oxford
Nicolet, C. (1979) 'Deux remarques sur l'organisation des sociétés de publicains à la fin de la république romaine', in Effenterre : 69–95
(1984) 'Augustus, government, and the propertied classes', in Millar and Segal : 89–128
Nielsen, I. (1990; 2nd ed. 1993) *Thermae et Balnea: the Architecture and Cultural History of Roman Public Baths* (2 vols). Aarhus
Nippel, W. (1984) 'Policing Rome', *JRS* 74: 20–9
(1995) *Public Order in Ancient Rome*. Cambridge
Öhler, M. (ed.) (2011) *Aposteldekret und antikes Vereinswesen: Gemeinshaft und ihre Ordnung*. Tübingen
Oliver, J. H. (1970) *Hesperia (Supplement* XIII*): Marcus Aurelius. Aspects of Civic and Cultural Policy in the East*. Princeton
(1974) 'Minutes of a trial conducted by Caracalla at Antioch in AD 216', in *Mélanges Helléniques offerts à Georges Daux*: 289–94. Paris
(1979) 'Greek applications for Roman trials', *AJP* 100.4: 543–58
(1989) *Greek Constitutions of Early Roman Emperors from Inscriptions and Papyri*. *Memoirs of the American Philosophical Society* 178. Philadelphia

Oliver, J. H. and Palmer, R. E. A. (1955) 'Minutes of an act of the Roman senate', *Hesperia* 24.4: 320–49

Parkin, T. G. and Pomeroy, A. J. (2007) *Roman Social History. A Sourcebook.* London and New York

Parvis, S. and Foster, P. (eds.) (2007) *Justin Martyr and his Worlds.* Minneapolis

Patterson, J. R. (2006) *Landscape and Cities. Rural Settlement and Civic Transformation in Early Imperial Italy.* Oxford

Peachin, M. (1996) *Iudex vice Caesaris: Deputy Emperors and the Administration of Justice during the Principate.* Stuttgart

(2011) (ed.) *The Oxford Handbook of Social Relations in the Roman World.* Oxford

Perry, J. S. (2011) 'Organized societies: collegia', in Peachin : 499–515

Perry, M. J. (2016) 'Defining gender', in Du Plessis, Ando, and Tuori : 432–42

Petsas, Ph. M. et al. (2000) *Inscriptions du Sanctuaire le la Mère des Dieux Autochtone de Leukopétra (Macédonie).* Athens

Pflaum, H.-G. (1960–1961) *Les Carrières Procuratoriennes Équestres sous le Haut-Empire Romain.* Paris

Plessis, P. du (2012a) *Studying Roman Law.* London and New York

(2012b) 'Theory and practice in the Roman law of contracts', in McGinn : 131–57

(2016) 'Urban landlords and tenants', in du Plessis, Ando, and Tuori : 635–45

Plessis, P. du, Ando, C., and Tuori, K. (eds.) (2016) *The Oxford Handbook of Roman Law and Society.* Oxford

Poel, Van der, Edwards, M., and Murphy, J. J. (eds.) (2021) *The Oxford Handbook of Quintilian.* Oxford

Potter, D. S. (ed.) (2006) *A Companion to the Roman Empire.* Oxford

Preisigke, F. (et al. eds.) (1915–) *Sammelbuch griechischer Urkunden aus Ägypten.* Strassburg

Pugliese Carratelli, G. (1948) '*Tabulae Herculanenses* II', *La Parola del Passato* 3: 165–84

Radner, K. (ed.) (2014) *State Correspondence in the Ancient World; from New Kingdom Egypt to the Roman Empire.* Oxford and New York

Rapp, C. and Drake, H. A. (eds.) (2014) *The City in the Classical and Post-Classical World: Changing Contexts of Power and Identity.* Cambridge

Rawson, E. (1987) '*Discrimina ordinum*: the *lex Julia Theatralis*', *PBSR* 55: 83–114

Rea, J. (1977) 'A new version of *P. Yale* Inv. 299', *ZPE* 27: 151–6

Reden, Sitta von (2012) 'Money and finance', in Scheidel : 266–86

Reynolds, J. (1982) Aphrodisias and Rome. *Journal of Roman Studies Monographs*, 1. London

Riccobono, S. et al. (eds.) (1940–3) *Fontes Iuris Romani Anteiustiniani* (3 vols., 2nd ed. of vol. 1). Florence

Rich, J. H. and Williams, J. H. C. (1999) '*Leges et iura P.R. Restituit*: a new aureus of Octavian and the settlement of 28–27 B.C.', *Numismatic Chronicle* 159: 169–213

Richardson, J. S. (1983) 'The *Tabula Contrebiensis*: Roman law in Spain in the early first century BC', *JRS* 73: 33–41
(1991) '*Imperium Romanum*: empire and the language of power', *JRS* 81: 1–9
(1997) 'The senate, the courts and the *SC de Pisone patre*', *CQ* 47: 510–18
(2015) 'Roman law in the provinces', in Johnston : 45–58
(2016) 'Provincial administration', in du Plessis, Ando, and Tuori : 111–23
Rickman, G. (1980) *The Corn Supply of Ancient Rome*. Oxford
Riess, W. (2011) 'The Roman bandit (*latro*) as criminal and outsider', in Peachin : 693–714
Riggsby, A. M. (2010) *Roman Law and the Legal World of the Romans*. Cambridge
Rio, A. (ed.) (2011) *Law, Custom, and Justice in Late Antiquity and the Early Middle Ages: Proceedings of the 2008 Byzantine Colloquium*. Centre for Hellenic Studies. Occasional Publications 2. London
Rives, J. B. (1999) 'The decree of Decius and the religion of empire', *JRS* 89: 135–54
(2003) 'Magic in Roman law: the reconstruction of a crime', *CA* 22.2: 313–39
(2006) 'Magic, religion, and law: the case of the *lex Cornelia de sicariis et veneficiis*', in Ando and Rüpke : 47–67
(2011) 'Magicians and astrologers', in Peachin : 679–92
Robinson, O. F. (1990–2) 'The repression of Christians in the pre-Decian period: a legal problem still', *Irish Jurist* 25–7: 269–92
(1992) *Ancient Rome: City Planning and Administration*. London and New York
(1995) *The Criminal Law of Ancient Rome*. London
(1996) 'The role of the senate in Roman criminal law during the principate', *JLH* 17.2: 130–43
(1997) *The Sources of Roman Law*. London and New York
(2003) 'Quintilian (Book iii) and his use of Roman law', in Tellegen-Couperus : 59–66
(2007) *Penal Practice and Penal Policy in Ancient Rome*. London and New York
Rodger, A. (1972) *Owners and Neighbours in Roman Law*. Oxford
(1990) 'The jurisdiction of local magistrates and chapter 84 of the *lex Irnitana*', *ZPE* 84: 147–61
(1991) 'The *lex Irnitana* and procedure in the civil courts', *JRS* 81: 74–90
Rostovtzeff, M. (1957) *The Social and Economic History of the Roman Empire* (2 vols; 2nd ed., revised by P. M. Fraser). Oxford
Rüfner, T. (2016) 'Imperial cognitio process', in du Plessis, Ando, and Tuori : 257–69
Rüpke, J. (2006) 'Religion in the *lex Ursonensis*', in Ando and Rüpke : 34–46
Russell, D. A. and Wilson, N. G. (1981) *Menander Rhetor: Edited with Translation and Commentary*. Oxford
Rutledge, S. H. (2001) *Imperial Inquisitions: Prosecutors and Informants from Tiberius to Domitian*. London and New York
Saller, R. (1994) *Patriarchy, Property and Death in the Roman Family*. Cambridge
Sänger, P. (2011) *Veteranen unter den Severern und frühen Soldatenkaisern. Die Dokumentensammlungen der Veteranen Aelius Sarapammon und Aelius Syrion*. Stuttgart

Scheidel, W. (ed.) (2012) *The Cambridge Companion to the Roman Economy.* Cambridge

Scheidel, W., Morris, I., and Saller, R. P. (eds.) (2007) *The Cambridge Economic History of the Greco-Roman World.* Cambridge.

Schulz, F. (1951) *Classical Roman Law.* Oxford

Segni, L. di, Patrich, J., and Holum, K. G. (2003) 'A schedule of fees (*sportulae*) for official services from Caesarea Maritima, Israel', *ZPE* 145: 273–98

Shaw, B. D. (1982) 'Lamasba: an ancient irrigation community', *Antiquités Africaines* 18 (1982), 61–103

(1995) *Environment and Society in Roman North Africa: Studies in History and Archaeology.* Aldershot

(2013) *Bringing in the Sheaves: Economy and Metaphor in the Roman World.* Toronto

(2015) 'The myth of the Neronian persecution', *JRS* 105: 73–100

Sherk, R. K. (1969) *Roman Documents from the Greek East. Senatus Consulta and Epistulae to the Age of Augustus.* Baltimore

(1970) *The Municipal Decrees of the Roman West.* Buffalo

(1984) *Rome and the Greek East to the Death of Augustus. Translated Documents of Greece and Rome* 4. Cambridge

(1988) *The Roman Empire: Augustus to Hadrian. Translated Documents of Greece and Rome* 6. Cambridge

Sherwin-White, A. N. (1966) *The Letters of Pliny. A Historical and Social Commentary.* Oxford

(1973a) *The Roman Citizenship* (2nd ed.). Oxford

(1973b) 'The Tabula of Banasa and the *Constitutio Antoniniana*', *JRS* 63: 86–98

Sirks, A. J. B. (2001) 'Making a request to the emperor: rescripts in the Roman Empire', in de Blois : 121–35

(2015a) 'Delicts', in Johnston : 246–71

(2015b) 'Public law', in Johnston : 332–52

Smallwood, E. M. (1966) *Documents Illustrating the Principates of Nerva Trajan and Hadrian.* Cambridge

(1967) *Documents Illustrating the Principates of Gaius Claudius and Nero.* Cambridge

Stark, R. (1996) *The Rise of Christianity: a Sociologist Reconsiders History.* Princeton

Stevenson, J. (1987) *A New Eusebius. Documents Illustrating the History of the Church to* AD *337* (2nd ed., revised by W. H. C. Frend). London

Stolte, B. H. (2001) 'The impact of Roman law in Egypt and the near east in the third century A.D.: the documentary evidence. Some considerations in the margin of the Euphrates papyri (P. Euphr.)', in de Blois : 167–79

Summers, R. G. (1970) 'Roman justice and Apuleius' Metamorphoses', *TAPA* 101: 511–31

Swain, S. and Edwards, M. (eds.) (2004) *Approaching Late Antiquity: the Transformation from Early to Late Empire.* Oxford

Swarney, P. R. (1970) *The Ptolemaic and Roman Idios Logos.* Toronto

Talbert, R. (1984) *The Senate of Imperial Rome.* Princeton.

Taubenschlag, R. (1955) *The Law of Greco-Roman Egypt in the Light of the Papyri 332 BC–640 AD* (2nd ed.). Warsaw

Taylor, R. (2000) *Public Needs and Private Pleasures: Water Distribution, the Tiber River and the Urban Development of Ancient Rome. Studia Archaeologica* 109. Rome

Taylor, T. S. (2016) 'Social status, legal status, and legal privilege', in du Plessis, Ando, and Tuori : 349–61

Tellegen-Couperus, O. (ed.) (2003) *Quintilian and the Law: The Art of Persuasion in Law and Politics*. Leuven

(2021) 'Quintilian and the law', in van der Poel : 259–77

Temin, P. (2013) *The Roman Market Economy*. Princeton

Thomas, J. A. C. (1976) *Textbook of Roman Law*. Amsterdam

Thonemann, P. (ed.) (2013) *Roman Phrygia: Culture and Society*. Cambridge

Thulin, C. (1913) *Corpus Agrimensorum Romanorum* (reprt. 1971). Stuttgart

Toynbee, J. (1971) *Death and Burial in the Roman World*. London

Treggiari, S. (1969) *Roman Freedmen during the Late Republic*. Oxford

(1980) 'Urban labour in Rome: Mercennarii and Tabernarii', in Garnsey : 48–64

(1991) *Roman Marriage.* Iusti Coniuges *from the Time of Cicero to the Time of Ulpian*. Oxford

Tuori, K. (2004) 'The *ius respondendi* and the freedom of Roman jurisprudence', *Revue Internationale des Droits de l'Antiquité* 51: 295–337

(2010) 'A place for jurists in the spaces of justice?' in de Angelis : 43–65

(2016) *The Emperor of Law, The Emergence of Roman Imperial Adjudication*. Oxford

Turpin, W. (1991) 'Imperial subscriptions and the administration of justice', *JRS* 81: 101–18

(1999) '*Formula, cognitio,* and proceedings *extra ordinem*', *Revue Internationale des Droits de l'Antiquité* 46: 499–574

Verboven, K. (2017) 'Guilds and the organization of urban populations during the principate', in Verboven and Laes : 173–202.

Verboven, K. and Laes, C. (eds.) (2017) *Work, Labour, and Professions in the Roman World. Impact of Empire 23*. Leiden

Waldstein, W. (1986) *Operae Libertorum: Untersuchungen zur Dienstpflicht freigelassenen Sklaven*. Stuttgart

Walker, S. (2000) 'The moral museum: Augustus and the city of Rome', in Coulston and Dodge : 61–75

Wallace-Hadrill, A. (ed.) (1989) *Patronage in Ancient Society*. London and New York

Watson, A. (1987) *Roman Slave Law*. Baltimore

(1991) *Roman Law and Comparative Law*. Athens, Ga.

(1992) *The State, Law and Religion: Pagan Rome*. Athens, Ga.

(1994) '*Prolegomena* to establishing pre-Justinianic texts', *Tijdschrift voor Rechtsgeschiedenis* 62: 113–25

(1995) *The Spirit of Roman Law*. Athens, Ga.

(ed.) (1998) *The Digest of Justinian* (4 vols.). Philadelphia

(2007) 'Law and society', in Cairns and du Plessis : 9–36
Whittaker, M. (1984) *Jews and Christians: Graeco-Roman Views*. Cambridge
Wiedemann, T. (1981) *Greek and Roman Slavery*. London
(1989) *Adults and Children in the Roman Empire*. London
(1992) *Emperors and Gladiators*. London and New York
Williams, W. (1974) 'The *libellus* procedure and the Severan papyri', *JRS* 64: 86–103
(1975) 'Formal and historical aspects of two new documents of Marcus Aurelius', *ZPE* 17: 37–78
(1976) 'Individuality in the imperial constitutions', *JRS* 66: 67–83
(1986) 'Epigraphic texts of imperial subscripts: a survey', *ZPE* 66: 181–207
Williamson, C. (2016) 'Crimes against the state', in du Plessis, Ando, and Tuori : 333–44
Wiseman, T. P. (1970) 'The definition of "Eques Romanus" in the late republic and early empire', *Historia* 19: 67–83
Woolf, G. (1990) 'Food, poverty and patronage. The significance of the epigraphy of the Roman alimentary schemes in early imperial Italy', *PBSR* 58: 197–228
Yiftach-Firanko, U. (2009) 'Law in Graeco-Roman Egypt: Hellenization, fusion, Romanization', in Bagnall : 541–60
Youni, M. S. (2010) 'Transforming Greek practice into Roman law: manumissions in Roman Macedonia', *Tijdschrift voor Rechtsgeschiedenis* 78: 311–40
Zimmermann, R. (1996) *The Law of Obligations: Roman Foundations of the Civilian Tradition* (reprt.). Oxford
Zulueta, F. de (ed.) (1945; reprt. 1966) *The Roman Law of Sale: Introduction and Select Texts*. Oxford
(1946; 1953) *The Institutes of Gaius (Parts* I *and* II*)*. Oxford

Index of Passages Cited

Papyri and Writing Tablets

COINS

Index of Names and Subjects

References to cited passages are in bold type.

For EU product safety concerns, contact us at Calle de José Abascal, 56–1°, 28003 Madrid, Spain or eugpsr@cambridge.org.

www.ingramcontent.com/pod-product-compliance
Lightning Source LLC
Chambersburg PA
CBHW070719070126
37842CB00004B/49

9781107163164